Best Wishes.

Hope you enjoy.

Thanks.

INTO THE SUN

A Memoir

NEIL VOLZ

authorHOUSE®

AuthorHouse™
1663 Liberty Drive
Bloomington, IN 47403
www.authorhouse.com
Phone: 1-800-839-8640

First published by AuthorHouse 11/18/2011

ISBN: 978-1-4678-6814-3 (e)
ISBN: 978-1-4678-6815-0 (sc)

Library of Congress Control Number: 2011919832

Printed in the United States of America

For my parents,

Buzz and Gay Volz

Acknowledgments

Writing *Into the Sun* has been a collective effort. To everyone who helped, I thank you from the bottom of my heart. I am grateful for the love and support. I would like to especially thank Rose Kent Solomon, my former high school English teacher, for her unyielding dedication to this project.

Foreword

For years, my professional accomplishments brought pride to our Midwestern middle class family. Boasting far and wide, my relatives relayed stories of "what Neil is doing in Washington." Not anymore. My misdeeds hung over my grandmother's funeral ceremony like an embarrassing black cloud. Tarnishing such a sacred ritual, for Gram of all people, felt overwhelming. I fought hard to keep the pain inside.

Our celebration of Gram's life took place between two dramatic bookends in my legal story. Days before, I ended months of Justice Department, Congressional and media investigations into my involvement in the Abramoff scandal by pleading guilty to felony conspiracy charges - charges related to what some historians were calling "the biggest Washington corruption scandal since Watergate."

As part of my plea deal, I agreed to assist law enforcement with their ongoing investigation into graft on Capitol Hill and throughout the government. Before the scandal was over, I would end up testifying as a witness for the Department of Justice in four federal corruption trials. That being the case, I had an early flight back to Washington the next day to prepare with federal prosecutors and FBI agents for my upcoming testimony in a case against a senior White House official.

To the public, it was a dramatic makeover. Suddenly I was helping those who had been stalking me weeks and months earlier. Not only did I go from criminal target to government co-operator, but I was what the press kept referring to as the Justice Department's "star witness" in the case.

Of course, the word "star" was a terribly inaccurate way to describe me as far as I was concerned. Depending on the day, fool, greedy has-been, or rat would have been far better terms to use. Nothing propped up that sentiment more than the booking process I went through three days before Gram's service. Getting finger-printed, answering questions and having a few mug shots taken was followed by some quality time in a District of Columbia jail cell.

While the door slammed behind me, I eased down on a steel bunk bed surrounded by nothing but dried up vomit, a non-descript sink, a roughed-up urinal, and an immense feeling of shame. With real jail time in my future a distinct possibility, I stared through the small opening in the door and nervously contemplated life as a prisoner.

Slowly, after what seemed like an eternity, I drifted off to sleep. My bad dream was halted by the loud scream of a prison guard yelling down our long row of cells.

"Volz!" he barked as I jumped to my feet. Opening the door, the older looking grey-haired man gave me the once over before saying, "Don't come back here, you look like a nice guy."

"Thanks," I replied meekly.

72 hours later, seeing so many loved ones at Gram's service gave me a boost only family can provide. Then again, to say the timing was unfortunate would be a major understatement.

Gram had been a giant not only in my life, but in many others', as well. A former librarian, she instilled in nearly everyone she met a great love of literature. Few were as influential, life-affirming or compassionate. Yet, every time a cousin or other family member gave me an extra hug or a pat on the back that day, I felt like I was taking love and positive energy away from her.

Therefore, as the cold lake air whipped through the Cleveland cemetery, I made a promise to Gram. I would write the book she had wanted me to write when I left for Washington years before.

Ever since I was a kid, I've wanted to be an author. Stories of mythical pirate ships and dragon's lairs filled my grade school notebooks. In high school, heroic adventures of space travel and sports stars came to life all around me.

As I became more aware of the world, the focus of my writing changed. Whether I was working for a newspaper, fighting for public opinion during a political campaign or advancing the cause of my law firm's clients, much of those efforts consisted of connecting with what was to me a new and ever-changing world.

Rarely did a day pass during those many years when the dream of being an author wasn't at least rummaging through my subconscious. However, it wasn't until I moved from small town Ohio to Washington that the idea of writing a book about my own experience was born. Initially, the thought was nothing more than a few seeds sowed by Gram when she heard I was going to work in a Congressman's office.

"Neil, you should keep a journal while you are in Washington," she said proudly before adding, "Maybe you could write a book when you are all done." Her heartfelt expression of hope that my experience in Washington would be something worth memorializing fully planted the thought of writing a memoir in my head. From there it never really left.

Over time, roots sprouted here and there while I continued to gnaw on the idea. For someone like me, though, whose livelihood depended on keeping in good graces with Members of Congress and White House officials, getting my hands around the idea of a public diary was a pretty heavy lift. First off, I was too busy having a great time to stop the party. More significantly, I gained influence and power in Washington, initially as a Congressional staffer on Capitol Hill, and later on K Street as a lobbyist.

While this allowed me to play politics at the highest level and make a lot of money, it also put me in a position where spilling the beans by writing a book would have been a disastrous career move. Yet the thought didn't perish. Occasionally it even picked up momentum. Ultimately, however, I decided the need to protect my paycheck, as well as my own and my family's privacy, were more important than my dream to write a memoir.

Then the Jack Abramoff lobbying scandal hit. It changed everything. Named "Staffer B" in the court documents laying out the criminal case against Abramoff, I saw my lucrative lobbying career abruptly end. My new identity was splashed across newspapers and television screens throughout the country. I faced jail time. Worst of all, I knew it was my own bad choices that had helped to shatter my image, upend age-old relationships and destroy far too many dreams to count. They also left me broke and in the age of Google, Twitter and Facebook, unable to run away from past mistakes. Suddenly, the book idea was back on the table. This time for different reasons.

What seems like a lifetime ago I had once hoped to write a book regaling readers with my exploits in Washington, discussing policies I had helped implement, and campaigns I had helped win. Now, I am writing because I believe - I need to believe - that in some small way writing this can help heal what I have harmed. Of course, settling scores, making money and clearing my name have also motivated me to write this book. To say otherwise would be a lie.

But those pursuits alone are not enough. What inspires me more than anything is the thought that this story might teach a young person or aspiring leader to avoid flying into the sun by reading how I had burned myself years before. Likewise, if I can shed some light on the Byzantine business of Washington lobbying and its impact on our nation, so much the better.

Beyond those lofty-sounding goals, my hope is this book will at times entertain you or provoke a thought about how you interact with the government. After all, it is our government. A flesh and blood government made up "of the people."

Decisions about what to include and what to leave out were not easy. Having lost many friends along the way, I was not eager to upset even more by writing about what some would surely prefer be kept quiet. In certain cases, that desire alone led me to avoid specific topics and stories. I chose the opposite approach in other cases. The Abramoff scandal was a public matter involving public officials, and people have a right to know how their government operates. Whatever happens, the chips will fall where they may, and again I'll live with my decisions.

Throughout this endeavor, my objective has been to complete this project in the most honorable manner possible. I don't pretend to have all the answers to the problems people see in our government, but at a minimum, I want to feel proud of my public service again. Please know every word written here comes from the heart.

Understanding in theory that writing about my corrupt past would be therapeutic for me, in practice it didn't always seem that way. There were moments when forward movement appeared downright unachievable. Instead of arriving at personal accountability and growth, I found myself cornered by denial and never-ending rationalizations. Season followed season. Steps were made both forward and backward. But like anything, with a lot of care, a decent amount of patience and some well-timed luck, my grandmother's seeds began to grow.

With them, a book was born. More importantly, so was a new life. Just like Gram knew it would.

Prologue

In CONTRAST TO THE YEARS of deliberations concerning whether to write a book or not, my decision to move to Washington wasn't a choice at all. Looking back, moving to Capitol Hill after the historic elections of 1994 was something I had to do, a flight I needed to make. "The first day of the rest of my life," friends and family would say when they heard the news.

Years later, Congressman Bob Ney and I would joke incessantly to anyone who would listen about the process of how I got to Washington. One week I was signing up for classes, ready to begin my senior year at The Ohio State University. The next I was speeding toward the Capital Beltway in a rental car with a firm grip on the lifetime lottery ticket it appeared I had just won. "Falling upstairs" was how I described my good fortune.

Little did either of us know back then, when Bob offered me a job in his Congressional office, of what was to come. Over time, I would be named the Congressman's Chief of Staff and assume the role of both roommate and confidante. From there, I joined others in helping Bob earn a powerful Committee Chairman position and watch as he became a major player on Capitol Hill. After leaving his office, I continued to be one of his most important political allies, as well as one of his largest campaign contributors. In the process, I became a major player too. It was a Washington life.

My time in what many of us called "Ney World" ended when I decided to help the Department of Justice put the Congressman in jail for his role in the Abramoff lobbying scandal. Having also played a role in the scandal, I knew the corruption far too well. To those of us closest to the flame, the stories have lost some of their humor and light-heartedness along the way. Nonetheless, there is much to learn from this cautionary tale.

Bob called me on a Thursday afternoon in late December to offer me the job of press secretary in his office. It felt like I was dreaming. He said they needed an answer by the end of business the following Monday. I had one hundred hours to decide. During that time, I faced two very different futures. On the one hand was the known. Staying the course. It consisted of family, friends and a potentially promising new career as a statehouse staffer for the Ohio Senate President.

On the other hand was the unknown. The only thing I really knew about Washington before 1995 was what I remembered from my junior high school government trip, and what I had read or seen in movies. Since all I could recall from our visit was a scant memory of boys in parachute pants trying to impress girls wearing "Madonna-style" dance clothes as we paraded from museum to museum, there wasn't a whole lot to go on.

I knew even less about some of the people I would end up working with at the time. Though I volunteered vigorously on the campaign, had been an intern in Bob's Columbus-based State Senate office and wrote several press releases during the election, numerous members of the Congressman-elect's incoming senior staff worked in parts of the operation with which I was not familiar. Many I had never met. Therefore, it was a bit nerve-wracking to hear the job offer included living with the Congressman, his chief of staff and several other staffers.

Our house would be just up the street from the Capitol Building. There was a lot of opportunity tied into such an offer. *"But what if I don't like my colleagues or the dynamic of living with the boss?"* I asked myself. *"Washington is a long way away."*

Additionally, the deal consisted of a $15,000 yearly salary, which was less than what I was making at my two part-time jobs as a college student. Combined with the fact I had just signed a one-year rental agreement I couldn't get out of for the next year, I remember thinking the money picture looked pretty bleak.

Finally, the offer to take a slot in Bob's Washington office required me, at least initially, to drop out of college. In a family of teachers and people committed to higher education, this was yet another serious obstacle. On its face the deal included several gaping holes. But none of that mattered. Like Icarus naively climbing into his wings or a moth flying uncontrollably in the night, the pulsating lights of history were calling. Moving to Washington to join in the glory of a political revolution was an offer I couldn't refuse.

My mother initially opposed the idea. I couldn't blame her. Here was a woman who years ago, along with my dad, made a commitment of saving enough money on her high school teacher's salary to pay for both my and my brother's college tuition. Amazingly to those who don't know her, she and my dad met that goal. And now her youngest wanted to run off and play politics without finishing his degree. This was considered heresy in our house. But she could see it in my eyes. Like breathing air or eating food, I needed to go. For the first time, a major decision impacting every aspect of my young life was mine and mine alone.

Before heading East I promised that I would eventually graduate. Almost six years later my degree from Ohio State arrived in the mail. By that point, I was starting my second full year as the Congressman's chief of staff. After attending night and weekend courses with three different universities, it was finally done. Taking more than a decade to graduate was not a normal flight plan. But then again, no one has ever accused me of taking the path most traveled.

I'm not the first to make such a trek to our nation's capital riding an election-year wave of promise, purpose and aspiration. Far from it. It happens year after year. Just as many more are building on what we did during our tenure, I was merely following in the footsteps of the countless others who came before me.

At the time, though, to me, it was big. Really big. My family is the farthest thing in the world from political royalty, and working on Capitol Hill seemed exquisitely extravagant. I mean, I was just some regular kid from Cincinnati who had lived my entire life in Ohio. And then suddenly I found myself part of something larger than anything I lived through before. Playing a role in the first transfer of power in the United States House of Representatives since before my parents could vote was an awakening of sorts for me. We were going to change things. Make lives better. It was even bigger than really big.

Despite the gravity of how the elections would impact our country, not to mention how idealistically I attached myself to their political meaning, I still look back on those one hundred hours more as a time of personal growth and priority making than some sort of career advancement or ego boost. Future internal struggles about ambition, power, greed, loyalty and survival were nowhere to be found. Important late-night negotiations over life-impacting legislation remained but a dream. Since the right choice was never in question, what took up most of my focus, and quite frankly scared me more than anything, was trying to figure out whether I really had what it took to swing for the fences and chase my dreams.

Looking back on that fateful choice to join Bob's Congressional office, I am always stunned by my unyielding focus and willingness to think through every aspect of the decision. During the years ahead, I would meet Presidents, CEOs and world leaders, while engaging in decision making that to some would make my little 1994 decision pale in comparison. Yet, for those one hundred hours, I thought of almost nothing else.

After I got off the phone with Bob, visions of a new life danced in my head. The opportunities seemed endless. Part of me was troubled, though, by the instant urge to join the Congressman's Washington team sight unseen. Those impulsive thoughts represented the sort of childlike flight of fancy which had failed me in the past. *"Neil, it is time to grow up,"* I said. *"People in the real world don't get to run off with Don Quixote to chase windmills or join the Knights of the Roundtable in their quest for the Holy Grail."*

On the other hand, I knew the side of me where fear lived always argued against any yearning I had for meaning and adventure. Luckily, at the time, I also knew not to listen to that part of me for too long.

"How will I look myself in the mirror years down the road knowing you chose to just sit back and pay the mortgage when you had a shot at the big time?" I would ask, re-balancing my internal debate. *"I mean seriously, what would your pals from the old neighborhood think if you chickened out now?"* I continued. In the end, this was more than just my ticket to join the action on the ultimate stage. It was about taking part in something larger than myself.

Every road led to the same destination. Get in the ring. Even if I would never be more than a bit player, I knew there was no other choice.

Life sure was simple back then. Such a statement sounds like it should be coming from a person in line for the blue plate special instead of someone much younger like me, I know. But it is true.

As I told friends and family members of my plans to move to Capitol Hill, there were no lawyers or federal prosecutors to check in with. Packing everything I owned into a two-door sedan, there was no worrying about the media rummaging through my trash, the FBI recording my conversations or dealing with an identity in crisis. And as I hit the road, instead of being tormented by thoughts of jail, divorce and bankruptcy, my mind was filled with optimism, a commitment to our cause and dreams galore. More than a decade later, I was forced to pack up many of those same dreams no longer meant for me, and watch a political revolution I identified so strongly with sputter to an unknown conclusion. Yet, I couldn't help but constantly reflect on that brief snap shot in time.

Even the directions given to me before leaving Ohio were simple. I met my new boss in Columbus. He told me the address of our Capitol Hill group house. While I wrote it down, he then said simply, "Drive to DC, from there, if you are facing the Capitol Building, the street is on the right hand side of the building." With that, he was done and I was ready. Several days later, embracing the quintessential American concept of chasing a dream, I took off. Nothing would ever be the same.

Judgement Day

MY LONG AWAITED SENTENCING DATE had finally arrived. Not a day passed during the previous few years when I hadn't contemplated the possibilities. *"Would the Judge put me in jail like she did the Congressman? Or would my punishment be something else? Time in a half way house? A hefty fine?"* I would find out soon enough. Though prepared to go to prison, I desperately hoped for a lesser sentence.

Because of my decision to cooperate with the Department of Justice's public corruption investigation, the prosecutors managing my case went to bat for me. In paperwork filed with the court, they requested a punishment of home detention. It was the best possible sentence the department could legally request from the Judge. Recognizing that I would likely have been facing multiple years in prison without their assistance, I was comforted by their proposal.

But the government's input would only go so far. As Judge Ellen Segal Huvelle had shown months before when she sentenced Congressman Ney to three months more time in jail than what the prosecutors had requested, their suggestions were not binding in her courtroom. Combined with the fact that the high-profile Abramoff lobbying scandal remained very much in the public eye, anything seemed possible.

Whatever the outcome, it was a relief to know the uncertainty of my future would soon be over. Yearning to move forward, I viewed my sentencing like a lighthouse during a dreary, fog-filled storm.

For almost four years, life as I knew it was turned upside down by the far-reaching tentacles of Washington scandal. Bit by bit, the slow grind of the Justice Department's inquisition had taken over my life. I became a professional pariah to avoid at all costs. Relationships were lost. Lawyers, prosecutors and FBI agents slowly replaced clients, consultants and constituents as constants in my day. Opportunities disappeared. Not a day passed when I didn't think I was going to jail. Fear permeated my every move. And with the media's relentless focus on the worst side of me, in many ways, even my identity stopped being my own.

Deep down, though, I knew that facing Judge Huvelle would at last give me a chance to break through that stuck-in-the-mud feeling of the previous few years. *"No matter what she decides, there will at least be certainty,"* I told myself. *"Solid ground under my feet."* Still, I was scared to death.

Months earlier in the same courtroom, my two former bosses, lobbyist Jack Abramoff and Congressman Bob Ney, had also faced Judge Huvelle. And both were sent to prison. Now it was my turn to accept the consequences for my involvement in our criminal conspiracy.

Pundits called our crimes a lobbying scandal - and debated its significance and root cause. For those of us involved, however, it was much more personal. Our greed and unchecked ambition represented individual failings that went above and beyond the admittedly serious crimes of trading political favors for extravagant trips, high-priced sports tickets and free meals. They symbolized a spiritual corrosion. Failures that needed fixing. Something I was finally aware of as I walked into the Judge's chambers.

Reporters and law enforcement sat on the left side of the room, family and friends on the right. Having been through numerous gut-wrenchingly raw conversations in private with my attorneys during the scandal, our small talk at the witness table seemed somewhat superficial. I nervously went through the motions. It was just another day in the fishbowl. People were watching my every move.

Nonetheless, I remained a very lucky man. In the pews behind me sat my loving family - many of whom had flown in from all over the country to provide their support. Friends in the District took the day off work to attend the hearing. Others had written letters to the Judge on my behalf. Anxiously awaiting the verdict, they had seen it all, the rise as well as the fall.

Slumping over in a courtroom chair more than a decade after idealistically flying off to Capitol Hill in an effort to fix a broken government, I sat at the bottom of an incredibly slippery slope. Originally intent on changing the corrupt ways of Washington, I instead had allowed myself to become a poster child of the very corruption I had pledged to help change. It was obvious to all that I had lost my way. Looking around the assembled crowd, I felt extremely ashamed.

Wanting to run, I incessantly stared down at my watch. Time sped up, then slowed down. As if I were trapped in a Salvador Dali painting with melting clocks and faces on the walls, minutes suddenly seemed like hours. And vice versa.

"*Why are you here? How did this happen?*" I asked myself for what seemed like the millionth time. "*What has become of your life?*"

Such questions haunted me daily. Deeply. Like an archeologist inspecting the dig of a lifetime, I sifted through the rubble. Despite the non-stop introspection, I still couldn't fully grasp why I had participated in such corrupt activities.

"*I mean, when exactly did that young purposeful kid who moved to Washington morph into the criminal who is on trial today?*" I asked as my demeaning and harsh inner dialog continued. It remained tough to know for sure.

What was clear, however, was that much had changed. I was different. Washington was different. When the Abramoff scandal became public in early 2004, Republicans dominated every aspect of the federal government. It was a high-water mark of our political revolution, the Republican Revolution.

By the time a series of *Washington Post* stories surrounding our lobbying team's work captured the attention of official Washington in late 2004, however, the narrative had already begun to change. Outsiders no more, we Republicans had become the establishment. And we were behaving like it. With corruption in the air, investigations into Team Abramoff, the name for the lobbying team I was a part of, started in Congress, the Department of Justice and the U.S Attorney's office in South Florida. The glare of the media followed.

During the fall of 2004, just days after I helped President Bush win re-election, the growing scandal turned even more personal for me when I was officially contacted by Senator John McCain's staff to discuss my relationship with Jack and Bob. McCain's committee staff specifically wanted to talk about my efforts to attach a provision to a piece of legislation that Bob was in charge of managing for the House of Representatives. The provision would have opened a casino on tribal land for one of Jack's American Indian clients. McCain's staff also wanted to know how Jack's all-expense paid golf trip to Scotland had impacted Bob's decision making.

Within days, the vice of scandal gripped me tighter. A skyrocketing career became unglued. Finally, after more than a year of leaked news stories and legal innuendo, my lobbying career came to an abrupt end when I was publicly named a target of the investigation in Jack's high profile plea agreement.

At the same time, in the political arena, the Democratic Party was successfully rallying public opinion against what they called a Republican "culture of corruption" on Capitol Hill. Because of mistakes occurring on our watch, the Democrats were ultimately able to win back control of Congress for the first time in twelve years. By convincing voters it was time for a change, they helped put a stake through the heart of the very political movement that brought me to Washington in the first place. And now I was in a federal courtroom, steps from the Capitol Building, facing prison.

Having spent much of the previous evening reading through my statement to the Judge and answering potential questions, I thought I was ready for what was to come. Then Judge Huvelle walked into the courtroom. Her swift entrance created an emotional tsunami that shook me to my core. I quickly assumed the worst.

"*She is going to throw me in jail,*" I thought as adrenaline surged through my veins. Panicking, I thought, "*Not only is she going to throw me in jail, she is going to throw me in jail today.*"

Huvelle's presence quickly and irrevocably changed the dynamic in the room. There was no doubt who was in charge. She was. Her long black robe, lofty perch and domineering demeanor made me feel like I was, well, being judged. At which point, the proceeding began.

"Criminal case 06-119, United States of America versus Neil G. Volz," the courtroom clerk announced in a squawky monotone manner. Having merely whispered those horrible "United States versus Neil Volz" syllables quietly to myself before hearing them officially read aloud, I felt like a traitor. It was horrible.

Judge Huvelle jumped into the fray, and began talking to my attorney and the Department of Justice prosecutors. "The government has filed for the reduction," she said, referring to the prosecutor's request to put me in a lower sentencing guideline range. Since judges generally follow the guidelines when issuing an offender's punishment, her view on whether to grant the request for a reduction would be telling. My future hung in the balance.

"That will be granted," she said. I sighed with relief.

Because I was a co-operator, such a reduction was assumed. Part of the deal. Of course, I never completely believed it would really happen. Until it did.

Her decision didn't give me a get-out-of-jail free card, but it did immediately lessen my fear of spending a year or more in prison. For that I was grateful, even jubilant. Worries of a disastrous sentence began yielding to the hope of a lenient one. *"Maybe I will be walking out of the courtroom with a punishment of probation or a few months of home detention after all,"* I quietly thought, as the importance of her decision began to sink in.

"It appears from what you have told me that you view Mr. Volz in a slightly less culpable category than Mr. Heaton, whom I have already sentenced," Huvelle continued in her conversation with the prosecutors.

Her comments struck a nerve. Will Heaton, the man she mentioned, had succeeded me as Congressman Ney's chief of staff after I left to become a lobbyist. Like me, Heaton pleaded guilty to criminal conspiracy charges in the Abramoff scandal. Also like me, he had cooperated with the Justice Department's investigation. His assistance included wearing a wire and taping conversations for the FBI, conversations he and Bob had had about the relationship between Abramoff, the Congressman and myself.

Unlike me, however, Heaton was never a lobbyist or a member of Jack's lobbying team. Therefore, since I was involved in both sides of the conspiracy, namely giving as well as receiving things of value in return for official Congressional actions, Judge Huvelle couldn't really think I was less culpable than Heaton could she? Likewise, I had violated the one-year ban, a law that requires certain government employees who become lobbyists from lobbying their former employers for at least a year. Her statement made me very nervous.

Kendall Day, a prosecutor for the Justice Department, stepped to the podium to respond. "Your Honor, I would phrase it just a little differently. We view him as someone who has given more substantial assistance and therefore is worthy of a greater 5K departure than Mr. Heaton," he said using the legal term for how law enforcement bargains on behalf of people who cooperate in their investigations.

It was the best answer he could have given, I thought. By emphasizing my cooperation instead of my culpability, Prosecutor Day was playing to my strengths. Since I knew more about the inner workings of the Abramoff and Ney relationship than Heaton did, due to the fact I worked for both men, the prosecution's emphasis on that side of the equation had to be helpful, I assumed. Or hoped.

Since I was already intently focused on every angle of the proceeding, the comparison of my situation to Heaton's had me watching even closer. I was convinced that every raised eyebrow by the Judge or muscle twitch by the prosecution meant something. Nothing was unimportant.

After all, in July, Heaton had received a sentence from Judge Huvelle of probation, community service and a fine for his role in the conspiracy.

For him, it was the perfect outcome. For me, it was the perfect marker. A ray of hope. No jail time, no halfway house and no home detention. Instead of increasing Heaton's sentence from what the government was requesting like she had done for Bob, Judge Huvelle had actually reduced it. For the preceding two months, I had considered it a positive reminder of what was possible.

Whether she reduced Heaton's punishment because he was a smaller player in the conspiracy, had cooperated in the investigation or because she found him to be a good guy caught up in something bad, I didn't know. But my mind raced trying to figure it out.

"All right," Judge Huvelle replied noncommittally while continuing to outline my assistance in the case. "You've set forth his cooperation. He has provided substantial assistance and will get a lot of credit for that obviously," she continued. "You also seem to imply that his activities, while he violated the one-year ban as well as gave and received things of value, is somewhat less egregious than some of the cases we've seen before. Is that fair?"

"That is fair, Your Honor," Day replied. "I guess the one thing I would emphasize that we've already touched upon is that, in our view, we could have successfully prosecuted Congressman Ney with the assistance of Mr. Volz, but without his assistance we could not have brought a successful prosecution," he continued, going back once again to my cooperation in their case against my former boss. "That is different than the assistance Mr. Heaton gave," he said. "His assistance alone wouldn't have allowed a successful prosecution."

"Okay," Judge Huvelle replied .

Staring blankly ahead, I beamed internally with joy. Day and the team of prosecutors were going to bat for me.

"From your point of view," she asked him, "if one of my goals as a judge is to have a certain equity or parity among those in similar situations, if I take into consideration the sentence I gave Mr. Heaton, is there any reason in your view to deviate in any substantial way?"

"*Did she really just say that?*" I asked myself incredulously. "*Is there any reason to deviate in any substantial way?*"

Knowing the dream outcome was to get the same sentence Heaton had received, I let her words fuel my growing excitement. Everything seemed to be falling into place. All I needed now was for my colleagues over at the prosecutor's table to tell the Judge there was no reason to deviate from Heaton's sentence.

Unfortunately, my secret celebration didn't last long. Instead of just saying no, Day went into a thorough dissection of Heaton's punishment in comparison to what they were requesting for me. As a substitute to my previous impulse of wanting to high-five my Justice Department teammates, Day's statements served as a harsh reminder that the folks with the badges weren't there to help me get a good sentence. They were there to administer justice, as they envisioned it.

"We do feel that it's important that there be some deprivation of liberty," Prosecutor Day said, regarding my impending punishment. "Given the crimes to which Mr. Volz pled guilty and in which he participated, some restriction on his personal liberty is necessary."

Watching the words "deprivation of liberty" spill from Day's mouth, in his slow Kansas drawl, was like getting kicked in the chest by a mule. Wanting to feel betrayed, I knew better. He was doing his job. And his words were now out there.

Like earlier, Judge Huvelle's reaction to her give and take with the prosecutors was muted. Whether any of their comments would make a difference or not, I would just have to wait and see.

From there, it was my attorney's turn to address the Judge. Right on cue, Tim Broas rose from the chair next to me. His movement provided a much-needed break in the action. A collective sigh rose from the room. Reporters' pens scribbled. The team of prosecutors and FBI agents, sitting to my right, quietly but knowingly spoke to one another through their subtle facial expressions and body language. Everyone else's attention was focused on my attorney. Everyone but the Judge. The intense glare of Judge Huvelle bore down on me like she was inspecting my very soul. Her eyes never wavered.

Tim began to speak. "One cannot grasp the circumstances of the offense without understanding the history and character of Neil Volz," he said, commanding the attention of not only the audience, but finally, Huvelle as well. "Mr. Volz grew up in a small town in Ohio - Finneytown, Ohio, living in an apartment."

"Both parents were school teachers, and his older brother, who is here with us today along with his parents and other members of his family and his wife's family, is a teacher at that school now," he continued.

The mention of my family immediately triggered within me the ever-present demons of shame and embarrassment that came to life whenever I thought about my family having to live with my well-known criminal status back in our hometown. In Finneytown, the dialog had changed. Gone was the source of family pride who bounded into his old classrooms to regale

7

students with stories of political intrigue and hard work on behalf of the people of Ohio. In his place was a corrupt former Congressional staffer, greedy lobbyist and convicted felon. My heart broke for them.

I felt as if I were watching my own funeral. Tears welled up in my eyes. Looking back at my wife, my brother, my parents and the support system I was lucky to have, I wished from the bottom of my heart that none of their support was needed. It infuriated me knowing that they were being buried by my past few years of baggage, baggage that was continuing to pile up. I wanted it all to end.

"In many ways his story is a classic American story," Tim said plainly. "A small-town boy goes to a big state university, gets an internship with a rising political star, and before you know it, they are on their way to Washington. Very, very heady stuff for a young man who is still in college. But for Mr. Volz, this was a dream come true."

"And despite the doubts and fears of his family and friends in Ohio, they all supported him and wished him well," he continued. "Mr. Volz worked hard and rose to be Mr. Ney's chief of staff, and then staff director of the House Administration Committee. As the Republican Revolution unfolded, Neil and his boss were among the rising stars."

Judge Huvelle's watchful gaze followed my every move. Since she undoubtedly had read the reams of paperwork on the case already, I presumed that she wanted to get a better feel for who I was with her own eyes.

Included in the judge's pre-sentencing documents were 61 letters written on my behalf by family members, friends, neighbors and colleagues. Assuming she had read through each one of the letters, Tim directed much of the opening part of his presentation to them.

"The letters describe a wholesome upbringing in a supportive and loving family, imparting values to their children," he said. "These letters provide the context, the history, the blood lines, if you will, to understand how Neil Volz came to commit these offenses, accept responsibility, and seek to atone for them through his cooperation with the Justice Department and his enduring character and generosity of spirit and commitment to serving the public good," he continued.

On a roll, Tim said, "He is a good man who committed a serious error in judgment. Neil found himself in a sort of moral vertigo," he went on, outlining the pull I felt between loyalty to my bosses and doing the right thing.

"He trusted the integrity and judgment of two highly respected and powerful men who, unbeknownst to him, were corrupting themselves, stealing from clients, and cheating the American public of honest services."

"Naïve? Yes. Excuses? No. Mr. Volz has accepted responsibility, and in the face of ridicule, loss of employment, public humiliation, financial despair, and shame among those near and dear, he boldly stepped forward and chose to admit his errors and to pay his debt to society by helping the Department of Justice conduct this investigation and bring other wrongdoers to justice."

Despite the fact that his words were coming from a person getting paid hundreds of dollars an hour to say them, they were still nice to hear.

"Unlike many others, Mr. Volz did not publicly protest. He did not enter a joint defense agreement. He did not choose to be a victim. He came forward in April 2005, before anyone else had pleaded guilty, and began cooperating with the Department of Justice. And in the process, he led the Department of Justice to three major convictions, not including his own."

The more Tim spoke the more I began to feel like my entire life itself was on trial. "Mr. Volz is a young man with potential to recover, and has a bright future," he continued. "He has suffered immeasurably already. He is a convicted felon. He cannot find employment. His reputation is forever soiled and tarnished. His good name will always be associated with this scandal."

Looking back at my family, I saw that they were now the ones fighting back tears. "His cooperation has been so valuable that the convictions he has helped DOJ obtain will undoubtedly deter public officials and lobbyists from committing similar crimes in the future," he said, subtly making the argument that a lenient sentence for me could encourage other potential cooperators in the case to come forward.

"Can anyone doubt these convictions - and no doubt there are more to come - have put all of official Washington on notice?" my attorney asked. "Putting Mr. Volz in jail will not advance the course of deterrence, Your Honor, nor would it advance the respect for the law. In fact, it would have just the opposite effect."

Judge Huvelle sat expressionless, listening to my defense with her arms crossed.

"Last and quickly, Your Honor, with respect to Mr. Volz's cooperation, he testified as the government's main witness in the Safavian trial. He was the first and only cooperator in this investigation to testify. He described Mr. Ney and Mr. Heaton and Mr. Safavian's conduct on the infamous Scotland golf trip, complete with photographs and bar receipts, all provided by Mr. Volz."

"People took notice immediately," my lawyer continued. "Mr. Heaton

9

began cooperating shortly thereafter, in June 2006, and ultimately pleaded guilty to a felony. Mr. Ney began discussions with the Department of Justice, and he ultimately pleaded guilty and is now serving a 30-month sentence in jail. And it's not over. Your Honor, Mr. Volz has promised to continue to cooperate, and is doing so literally as we speak."

As planned, my attorney's presentation was short. His was just the beginning of the conversation. Like Tim had told me days before, "I am not the one the Judge wants to hear from. It is your story that she wants to hear."

****

The Revolution

THE FRENZIED CROWD IN THE main ballroom of Undo's Restaurant, in the Appalachian region of Ohio, leapt to their feet at the first appearance of State Senator Ney. The screaming lasted for several minutes as Bob slowly headed toward the podium. He shook hands while he walked. Flash bulbs lit up the room.

Interrupting the Senator's victory speech with loud non-stop chants of "All the way with Bob Ney," our passion filled the hall. I stood right behind him, amazed. Bob could have been a rock star on stage or a professional athlete who just won a big game, the crowd noise was so earsplitting. The adoration was palpable. For the future Congressman, his constituents, his staff and his country, it was an historic moment. Change was coming to Washington.

For 40 years, the Democrats had run the House of Representatives. With an iron fist, they monopolized the legislative branch of government, the branch responsible for managing the nation's checkbook. On their watch, from 1954 to 1994, Washington transformed from a sleepy federal city along the Potomac River to the bustling capital of the world.

All that influence came at a price. Wielding unchecked power for so long, many became corrupt. A bank scandal crippled Capitol Hill. The Speaker of the House resigned, and elected officials were sent to jail. Also, the Democratic Congress, along with Republican Presidents, were responsible for creating a massive national debt with huge annual deficits. The nation's budget had not been balanced since the 1960s. Still, for more than a generation, imagining a Congress run by anyone but Democrats was like imagining a New Year's Eve party without Dick Clark. It just didn't seem possible.

Then along came the 1994 congressional elections. Pitchforks in hand, "We the people" rambunctiously stormed the castle. It was like a tea party on steroids. Seeing the impact motivated people could have on our government was empowering. Decades of entrenched, one-party rule melted away with each election night announcement, swinging the proverbial pendulum of history in the process. Bob joined a rapidly growing band of Republican candidates who were winning seats that had been held by Democrats for decades. Hope pumped through our veins.

The party went late into the evening. Many of us couldn't help but pinch ourselves - and drink celebratory whiskey shots - while we talked about the ongoing turnover. "Since before my parents could vote the Democrats had been in charge of Congress," I remarked to some fellow staffers. Naming the Presidents who resided in the White House during the Democrat's one-party reign resulted in yet another round of drinks, high-fives and hugs. We ticked off the names, Eisenhower, Kennedy, Johnson, Nixon, Ford, Carter, Reagan, Bush, and Clinton. It had been a long time.

Celebrations like ours were not just taking place in the foothills of Appalachia. From the banks of the Hudson River, the beaches of the Pacific, and especially in the bastions of the old Confederacy, Republican candidates for Congress were sweeping into office all over the country. Real power was changing hands and a new direction was being set. Dethroning such an institutional behemoth seemed to verify our self-described revolution. We called it the Republican Revolution. To us, it was nothing less than American renewal. A changing of the guard.

For me personally, the 1994 elections were also a milestone. After volunteering on Governor Bill Clinton's 1992 presidential campaign, I soaked up political principles and economic ideas of every stripe for the next two years. During that time, I turned into a true-blue American conservative. I spent hours reading. Ayn Rand. George Will. Adam Smith. Additionally, I devoured biographies of our movement's icons. Goldwater. Buckley. Reagan.

If radio commentator Rush Limbaugh wasn't blaring through the car speakers on my way to work at the Capitol building in downtown Columbus, then certainly some other conservative commentator was outlining our plan for a political uprising. In thought and action, I was a radical. An early 90's college revolutionary. And I wasn't alone.

Those of us riding the wave of ballot-box driven euphoria in the fall of 1994 were the missionaries of our movement. Purity of purpose permeated the election night air. Our mission was clear. We were going to create a better country by restraining the spending and runaway encroachment of Washington's influence in the lives of everyday Americans.

We intended to balance the federal budget "for the first time since Neil Armstrong walked on the moon," cut taxes "for families and small businesses," and replace "a broken welfare system with an opportunity society." A new Republican Congress was going to decrease the size of the federal government and return political power to individuals, communities and states.

Implementing such age-old conservative goals, however, meant more than just changing public policy. It also meant changing the way Washington worked. Fundamentally, that had to start with ending the ongoing corruption which seemed to be strangling the Democratic majority on Capitol Hill.

Hijacked by lobbyists and special interests, Congress was broken. At least that is the way it seemed from the heartland. From my vantage point, Washington had become nothing more than a scene out of George Orwell's *Animal Farm.* Instead of conducting the people's business, public servants filled cozy high-priced restaurants, dining at the trough of big money. All the while the rest of us, looking in from the outside, seemed to work harder for less.

I thought the corruption I saw resulted from the liberal ideology held by so many members of the majority party in Congress. "Their power comes from giving people and groups money," I told friends. "Not from letting them be left alone." It seemed pretty straightforward. "Since they get money back from the same people they give tax dollars to, it is no wonder the Democrats have become corrupt. Their arrogance is everywhere."

The Congress had recently exempted themselves from their own laws. Bills were being written by lobbyists in the dark of night. Answers to the problems facing our country seemed to come from Washington to the people, instead of the other way around. It was as if many of those in power actually believed the perks and privileges of life on the Hill were theirs by divine right, and not merely on loan from the voters. I was angry.

I was also young and idealistic. As I wrote in an early 1994 Ohio State student newspaper editorial, "Lifetime Beltway leaders of the modern-day political class have become the enemy of everyday Americans. Even the well-intentioned ruling elite in Washington who think they can effectively micro-manage the economies and social lives of Americans need to be shown the error in their ways."

With words that would drip with irony years later, I implored others to hear my call.

"Since the federal government started taxing the incomes of the

American electorate just 81 years ago, it has grown into a bloated and corruptive system run by lobbyists, lawyers and the political elite. Usually, at the start of a new year people make a resolution in an effort to improve themselves, but in my opinion it's time people begin thinking about making a new-year revolution in an effort to save our country. A revolution by middle-class Americans of every type, who are sick and tired of paying enormous amounts of taxes to a government that doesn't work."

My like-minded friends and colleagues promised to make things better. On election night, throwing tea in the Boston harbor would probably have been more representative of our political convictions than what we did - dance the night away to the music of Garth Brooks and Billy Ray Cyrus. Nonetheless, having won, we were going to keep our promise to change Washington. No one believed that more than I did.

Waking up the next day, I couldn't wipe the smile off my face. All that work had paid off. The late nights stuffing envelopes. The long days knocking on doors. As our rag tag group of true believers geared up for the impending march to Washington, idealism gushed from my pores. Though my journey was just getting started, I already felt a long way from home.

Politics wasn't a part of my Cincinnati youth. When political discussions arose, they were usually eloquent stories told by my grandparents about the glories of Franklin Roosevelt and John Kennedy, or animated arguments about Vietnam and America's place in the world. We were just a regular middle class family with typical middle class discussions.

I was born in 1970. My early years revolved around going to school, playing sports and attending Sunday Mass. Before the word *Congress* even entered my vocabulary, I longed to play professional baseball with Pete Rose, Joe Morgan, Tony Perez and the exalted Cincinnati Reds. The Big Red Machine. Living in an apartment on a street full of apartments, with lots of other children, I carried a baseball glove with me wherever I went, so getting a game started was rarely a problem.

My older brother and I were lucky to have great parents. They taught us the basics. Work hard and laugh often. Play by the rules and take care of each other. Most significantly, they taught us the power of unconditional love, the value of following your dreams, and the importance of God.

Like all families, my parents, my brother and I weathered storms and enjoyed good times. I remember the feeling of terror that overtook me when my dad lost his job. The worry of having nowhere to go stayed with me for years. At the same time, I learned early on how fortunate I was to have both my mom and my dad together in one home.

Politically, the Volz clan was a mixed bag. Many in my family were what would soon be known as Reagan Democrats: blue collar workers and Catholics alarmed by the counter-culture and stagnant economy of the 1970s. As a group, we lacked any real political leaning. Get-togethers were sure to contain a healthy smattering of Republicans, Democrats and Independents discussing the day's events. It was fun. The banter was energetic, and I learned a lot. The discussions helped connect me to the world. As I got older, few topics garnered such passion or seemed so real.

Still, understanding how my little life could possibly be affected by politics took a while to grasp. And I was busy. As you would expect from a kid voted "Best All Around" by his high school classmates, my voyage took many twists and turns. I tried everything. Skipping school to party was balanced out with volunteer work. I was a jock, but also participated in theatrical productions.

Stubborn to a fault, I abhorred labels and questioned authority at every turn. Granted, I did it with my own version of Irish wit and German sense of duty. Being irreverent and a risk taker, I enjoyed seeing what I could get away with. Talking and joking my way through school seemed normal. I was a Bart Simpson Boy Scout, and a natural born politician.

Two high school teachers, Dave Bean and Steve Elliott, helped me begin my political exploration. Each of them guided that expedition in a different way.

Mr. Bean was my soccer and wrestling coach. He also taught me history and current events. His lessons were more personal than anything. Two stick out above the rest. One, he told me that the only real fairness in life is that you get out of something what you put into it. That was true in sports and in the real world, he would continue. This lesson put the responsibility of learning squarely on my shoulders. Second, he taught me the importance of listening to all sides of a debate. This helped teach me how to think. To this day, I have no idea what Mr. Bean's political leanings were at the time. But I know he valued the pursuit of one's political opinions as much as the outcome.

In contrast, Mr. Elliott was the bearded bleeding-heart history teacher we should all be so lucky to have. More than anything, he helped to shape me by laying down the prism through which I would view the world of politics, history in the making. At its core, he said, American politics was an ongoing struggle between the views championed by our first Secretary of State, Thomas Jefferson, and those of our first Secretary of the Treasury, Alexander Hamilton. To scholars it is simply known as The Jefferson vs. Hamilton debate.

In one corner, the spirit of Hamilton argues for a strong central government. In the other, Jefferson suggests the states take the primary role in social and economic decision making. Digging into the debate heartily, I listened to all sides. Still do. Both make good points, and different times seem to call for one over the other. Yet the prism doesn't change.

In college, I was interested in everything. Everything but being in class. Despite testing into the Honors Program, I decided against such an unwavering focus on the classroom. Not sure what to major in, I wandered. Religious Studies was followed by History. Philosophy led to Photography. Finally I settled on Journalism and Political Science.

Throughout my time at Ohio State, I vigorously dug into a changing world. The Internet age was beginning and the AIDS virus was spreading. Passionate vigils discussing Kant, Nietzsche and Marx were joined by fall football games, chasing girls and going to parties. The wall fell in Berlin. Kuwait was freed. Russian tanks rolled through the Kremlin. And Los Angeles burned.

Having opened my mind to every viewpoint possible over the years, I found that by late 1993, my own beliefs were also taking shape. It was Jefferson vs. Hamilton all over again. This time the man providing most of the answers to the many questions reverberating in my head was Newt Gingrich, the firebrand visionary leader of a budding conservative revolt in the House of Representatives.

I approached one of my political science professors to ask him for assistance in finding a volunteer position at the Ohio Statehouse. It was time for me to make a choice. Getting in the ring meant choosing sides.

"Do you want to work for a Republican, a Democrat or does it matter?" my professor asked.

"Republican," I said, surprising myself somewhat in the vigor of my own response. Although I never liked labels, I embraced this one. My professor then told me about a job opening in a young State Senator's office. "Senator Ney is running for Congress," he said. "And Ney might just win. Who knows, you could end up in Washington."

Bob Ney was an even more unlikely revolutionary than I. Elected to the Statehouse when he was 24, Bob had been in office for more than a decade. He was a career politician. Comfortable in the pay-to-play world of Ohio statehouse politics, he had former staffers throughout Columbus making six-figure salaries as lobbyists. He also had a history of voting for tax increases, and cutting deals with Democrats to increase state spending. Nonetheless, Bob fervently made the case for change.

Because of his understanding of the political process, Senator Ney knew better than most that the budget situation in Washington was bankrupting the country's future. He also knew there wasn't a single other Republican in the state who could win Ohio's 18th Congressional district. In a region where fewer than 15% of the voters were registered Republicans, Bob was the movement's only hope. And he knew it.

I began as an unpaid intern in his State Senate office. Bob was the powerful Finance Committee Chairman, responsible for putting together the annual state budget. His well groomed offices adjoined the Senate floor and provided a direct entrance to the chamber where the voting took place. Aside from the Senate President, Ney was the most powerful member of the Senate. Not bad for a guy who wasn't even 40 yet.

Since he was actively campaigning for Congress, Bob spent most of his time hours away in his Southeastern Ohio district with the voters. Therefore, despite working in the Senator's office for weeks, I knew all about his impressive biography but hadn't actually met him. My expectations were unrealistic. I anticipated seeing the air fly out the doors when this powerful man entered the office. But that wasn't his way. In fact, my immediate impression of Bob was just the opposite.

His lukewarm handshake was non-threatening, almost weak. "*This man in front of me can't possibly be the same guy who boldly moved to Iran in the late 1970s after college, without a cent to his name,*" I thought. "*Or the person who spent more than a year hustling his way through Saudi Arabia. Hell, there isn't even a hint of the gregarious wheeler and dealer who has already delivered more state money for his Senate district than most elected officials accomplish in a lifetime.*" I felt confused. The man who had just brought thousands of jobs to the district through his control of the state budget, didn't seem to match up with the guy I was meeting. I expected Elvis. Instead, I got a regular guy.

As it turned out, such a low-key demeanor was an integral part of the Bob Ney brilliance. After establishing himself as a so-called "Joe six-pack," Ney slowly proceeded to turn on the charm and take control of the situation. More often than not, his sales pitch worked perfectly. This day was no different.

"You know, Neil," he said quietly after catching up with some of the gathered staff, "You have the most important job in this office." While trying to comprehend what seemed to me a most ludicrous comment, I noticed the other staffers listening to our conversation. In fact, by the time Bob pulled up the chair next to me and sat down, the entire focus of the room had swung my way. I loved the attention. At that moment, my impression of the future Congressman began to change. Bob may have acted like he was just a normal guy off the street, but it didn't take long to see with my own eyes that this was a man who had serious power.

Even more than that, Senator Ney was no longer a caricature to catalyze my political education, or a far off boss to wonder about. Instead, he was an influential regular guy taking time out of his busy day to chat with me - as if there was no one else in the room. "If you don't answer that phone or clip those news articles, I won't know what is going on," he continued. "And if I don't know what is going on, I can't serve my constituents. You know what I mean?" Bob asked. Awed, I nodded along like a bobble-headed version of myself. Within just a few minutes, I could see that the Senator was every bit the hard charging good ol' boy everyone talked about. He came across as undeniably genuine.

Bob then feverishly began outlining the importance of communication during a campaign. He encouraged me to call with any news I thought was important. Stressing the point, the Senator not only gave me his home phone number but the number to a plug-in box phone he had in his car. His field staff all had pagers, he added, saying they could usually get to a pay phone in the district to respond within half an hour. This was 1994, and their use of new technology was astounding.

"If I can't serve my constituents, I will lose this race," Bob continued in what was by that point a monologue. Then without irony, he said, "And if I lose this race, we may not be able to change the Congress."

Picking up the pace and raising the volume word by word, Bob again rhetorically asked, "You know what I'm saying?" Without waiting for a response he continued. "That means they will keep spending our kids' money and bankrupt this country."

With those words, I was hooked. Ney's reference to the Democrat Congress and the ballooning federal deficit occurring on its watch turned a young intern into putty in his hands. Not only did he tap into my conservative idealism, he made me feel like a very important member of the team. Bob was bringing me along for a ride, a ride that could lead to something much bigger than either of us. Like a scene out of Roald Dahl's children's classic, the future Congressman was giving me a dream ticket. Charlie may have had his Chocolate Factory, but thanks to Bob Ney I had passage to something greater, something that would change the nation.

Joining the Republican Revolution was more magical than anything Willy Wonka could have created. No longer would I just be someone arguing politics over beers or a political scientist wonk crunching numbers on a chalkboard. From that point on, I wasn't a poser. I was in the game.

I rewarded Bob by giving the job everything I had. In the history of unpaid interns, few have ever answered phones or clipped newspapers like I did during those early months in Ney World. Despite holding down several jobs and going to school, winning the election soon became my highest priority.

Throughout the campaign my admiration for Bob grew. I could relate to him. We both came from humble beginnings, liked to laugh and were excited about the future. We both also knew this was no ordinary election. Some campaigns seem like a formulaic TV movie with a predictable ending. As the year chugged along, we could tell that wasn't the case. The stars were aligning for something special. The polls showed it, and we could feel it on the street.

As election day drew nearer, I spent more and more time in the district. Campaigning in Appalachia was refreshing, eye-opening and educational. Since I had lived in the city and the suburbs all my life, it took me a while to grasp the hard-scrabble lifestyle of rural eastern Ohio. Learning first hand about the small town culture of the region was a highlight of our door-to-door campaigning. It also showed me the expansive reach our movement was having. Not only was the revolution against big government about taxes, health care, and spending, it was about also very much about our values. Our identity.

I learned that in an unexpected way. During a day of door-to-door work, I found myself walking up a long winding dirt road toward a dilapidated house. As I got closer, the owner appeared wearing nothing but greasy blue work pants. His bare feet and jiggling belly grabbed my attention, but not as much as the shotgun he pointed at me.

Already well on his property by then, I knew he was none too pleased to see me. With scenes from the movie *Deliverance* running through my head, I wasn't sure what to do. So I stuck with the script. "I'm here to drop off some campaign literature for Bob Ney," I said, trying to hide my nervousness.

"Who?" he demanded, verifying his unhappiness with my presence.

"Bob Ney," I said more forcefully.

"Where is he on guns?" the man asked.

"He is the endorsed candidate of the National Rifle Association," I told him as confidently as I could. With our Democrat opponent running around the same neighborhoods outlining his support for gun rights, it was a line we all had been taught. The NRA endorsement mattered. Gun owners trust them to protect their rights. And as in much of rural America, guns were not a partisan issue in Appalachia.

A big smile suddenly splashed across the guy's face. "He's got my vote," he said before grabbing several leaflets out of my hand. Promising to pass our campaign literature out to family and friends, the man told me he was a lifelong Democrat who would be voting Republican in November for the first time in his life. With the Democratic Congress getting ready to pass a bill banning guns, he said he had no other choice. "Something needs to change out there," he said, no doubt referring to Washington.

"I couldn't agree more," I replied, trying to conceal both my relief at not being shot and my joy at lining up a vote.

Six weeks before the election, Bob briefly left the campaign trail to join his fellow Republican candidates in Washington for an unveiling of the "Contract with America." The contract was a series of campaign promises summarizing a potential Republican majority's national priorities. Each promise reflected a conservative governing philosophy. It also included a specific list of government reforms meant to rid Washington of corruption and make the House of Representatives run more openly. A technology geek, my favorite was the commitment to put all committee and congressional business on the Internet. We promised to implement many of the changes on the first day of a Republican Congress.

If elected, we specifically promised to vote on a constitutional amendment requiring a balanced federal budget, implement a series of pro-growth and pro-family tax cuts and call for an end to welfare as a federal entitlement. Additionally, we promised to expand the North Atlantic Treaty Organization to include numerous former Soviet allies as well as a "Loser Pays" law to reduce frivolous lawsuits.

Led by Newt Gingrich, our national reform proposals were geared to draw a contrast with the Democrats and the status quo over who was best positioned to usher the country into the post-Cold War world. Some components of the contract worked better in certain communities than others. Where my parents lived, in the Cincinnati suburbs, the emphasis on tax cuts was especially popular. In part, this was true because of the Democrats' recently enacted tax increases. On campus in Columbus, with so many students gazing ahead and seeing a generation of massive government debt, the balanced budget amendment struck a nerve. Meanwhile, in Bob's overwhelmingly poor Congressional district, where many voters witnessed first-hand what they viewed as an overly generous safety net, welfare reform was top of mind.

The Contract united Republican candidates from all over the country. It helped to nationalize the 1994 elections as a referendum on the unpopular

Clinton Administration and its allies on the Hill. In some parts of the country, fewer than four in ten voters said they supported the president. After Democrats passed the largest tax increase in history, tried to pass a government-run health care plan, and engulfed Washington in scandal, we could tell that we had our political opponents on the run.

Honing the skills that would later lead many of his colleagues to describe him as "the best retail politician in Congress," Bob stoked his constituents' desire for change. At a whistle-stop event near an old train station in Eastern Ohio, the depth of the public's desire for Bob's message was on full display.

Hundreds of denim-clad voters patiently waited for "Senator Ney" to address the crowd. Bales of hay surrounded the podium. The race was in high gear. At his late-October best, the future Congressman connected with his constituents in the moment. Instead of immediately jumping up before the assembled crowd, Bob took the time to personally work the crowd and talk with every voter interested in a conversation. Giving the big campaign contributors a little unnoticed extra attention, the economic development folks a special thanks for their work, and the political types some inside scoop on the campaign, he met with them all. In the meantime, staffers like me stood at the ready, in our green "Ney" T-shirts, diligently parking cars, cooking food and taking photos.

It was classic small town politicking. The scene could have been confused with a Norman Rockwell painting or a county fair from the 1950s. Then Bob got up to speak. Like Bob Dylan years before, the Ney concert performance went from acoustic to electric. The entire dynamic changed. All of a sudden everybody's favorite low-key neighbor transformed into a vibrant hilltop version of Huey Long. At one point, he was screaming so loud for change I thought people in the crowd were going to think the Senator had gone strait-jacket crazy. I couldn't have been more wrong. They loved it.

"This election is about the wallet," Bob screamed into the microphone. His face reddened in anger. "The money working people put into their wallets and the money the government takes out," he continued. The crowd erupted. It seemed as if a riot was about to ensue.

From there, the Senator added fuel to the fire. He talked about the recently enacted gun control legislation and the decades of environmental regulations that had shuttered local coal and steel towns throughout the region. Cheers turned to boos. Bob was on a roll. His mutinous song struck a chord. Picking up the tune, the hard-working, predominantly Democratic voters of Ohio's 18ᵗʰ Congressional district joined the chorus. They wanted change, too.

Election Day approached, and the impossible began to feel possible. With the crescendo building, my enthusiasm grew. Voters were saying very clearly that 40 years of centralizing power in Washington was long enough. In the never-ending battle between Jefferson and Hamilton, the man from Monticello was in line for a big win. Feeling like I was one of the good guys, ready to ride into to town and clean up Washington, I desperately hoped that the voters would give us the keys to the city.

"Tomorrow is election day," I wrote in Ohio State's student newspaper. "It's a time for us to reflect on where our country is and decide where we think it should go. I encourage anyone reading this article to be a part of it."

"Every individual in this country has felt the gradual loss of freedom being imposed on us by Congress. Well, it's time to fight back. Taxation without hesitation is not fair. Continue the Reagan Revolution. Vote Republican."

Outlining how we were prepared to "place trust in the people to reshape America," while the Democrats wanted to "place their trust in the government to shape the people," I made a last-minute plea to young voters. *"If we didn't end the march to big government now, would we ever?"* I thought. The political fates were watching. History was calling. It was me at my dramatic best.

"That is what this election is all about," I wrote. "Of course, this isn't a new idea," I continued. "It is the fundamental premise this country was founded on. It's up to us to create our future. No matter who you vote for this year, just do it. But when you go to the polls tomorrow remember the immortal words of Thomas Jefferson: "Were we directed from Washington when to sow and when to reap, we should soon want for bread.'"

And the revolution began.

January 4, 1995
Washington, DC

Freshman Year

I walked past the Capitol Building. My eyes were transfixed by the sun-like sparkle reflecting off the glass of the dome. It was a dream-come-true to be in Washington. The excitement of my first day working for Bob's Congressional office beat back the brisk winter breeze. Our new office was a few blocks away from the row house we had moved into over the weekend.

A bus full of Ney supporters had arrived from Ohio the night before. By the time I got to the office, many of them were already squeezed into our sixth floor Longworth House Office Building space. No one wanted to miss Bob's swearing-in. It wasn't even 9:00 AM yet, but the pandemonium was already beginning. Everything from coats, boots and purses, to trays of food and red plastic cups lined our sparsely decorated workplace. Within moments of my arrival, the soon-to-be Congressman motioned me into his office.

"We need to write a press release," Bob said, with a sense of urgency.

"Sounds good," I replied, eager to begin my work as his press secretary.

"Make sure to outline all the changes we are doing today," he continued. "And give out our office numbers. And our addresses. Then show it to me before it goes out."

Bob was moving a mile a minute. Just as soon as he finished with me, someone else arrived to take his attention. Already halfway out of his office, he yelled in my direction.

"Make sure to contact the local media who are in town covering the story. If they want to interview me, set it up," he said now somewhat off in the distance.

"You got it," I replied.

I had no idea what to do next. In my corner office space, there were no chairs and no desks. We had no letterhead, no functioning computers and a fax machine inherited from Bob's predecessor, which looked like a relic from a bad science fiction movie. I was a lost ball in high weed. We all were. Only the feeling of togetherness made things seem doable.

Hoping to move things along, two of my fellow staffers and I bounded out the office's front door. We hurriedly shuffled down our busy freshmen hallway. The sixth floor was filled with new Members of Congress and staff from all over the country. As if our job was to feverishly sift through a flea market of furniture, the three of us meandered through different floors and different buildings in search of chairs, desks and other much needed office wares.

Over the last few days, unwanted office items had been placed in the hallways by those staffers leaving the Hill. With such a large turnover, nearly every floor contained a smorgasbord of ancient wooden artifacts. The procurement process worked on the honor system. If there was no sign claiming an item, it was fair game to take to your office, we were told. The three of us reveled in the moment. In our minds, nothing said the end of 40 years of Democratic rule of Congress like former staffers' furnishings strewn all over the place.

"Is that how they did things in 1954?" we yelled to each other with a laugh while trying out chairs and desks. Like character actors, each of us took on new personas as we auditioned new pieces of equipment. Before that morning, the three of us had never met. Yet, within fifteen minutes of scouring the Halls of Congress for beat-up office furnishings, my fellow staffers and I felt like kindred spirits. Freshmen navigating our new school.

Since the chairs had wheels, we brought them back to the office first. Next came the lamps. Then it was time for the desks. With sweat pouring through our dress shirts and down our foreheads, our little gang pushed and prodded our new desks across the floor. From there, we precariously leaned them up several escalators before pushing with all our might to squeeze them into the elevators that would take us to our office. The elevators were generally packed with visitors from across the country, which made our activity somewhat awkward.

Within an hour, the three of us had successfully placed our new furniture into the tight, open-air back office area we would call home for the next two years. Family, friends and supporters of the Congressman looked on with glee.

By this point, several House information technology professionals had joined the circus in Bob's office. The 18-year Member of Congress Bob replaced did not have computers for most of his staff. Therefore, the IT professionals diligently worked to get my new system up and running. Thinking I was smarter than I was, I told anyone who would listen how outrageous it was that the office we were replacing still had typewriters. Pacing back and forth, I impatiently stared at my watch. I didn't want to miss my first official press secretary deadline, nor did I want anyone to think I wasn't doing everything I could to get the job done.

Live C-Span coverage of the House of Representatives floor lit up the television screens set up throughout the office. Our crowd erupted whenever the slightest visual of soon-to-be Speaker Newt Gingrich appeared. To us, Gingrich was more than a political figure. He was our teacher, as well as the leader of the Republican Revolution. More than anything else, Gingrich's articulation of what we stood for helped to identify our movement. A Balanced Budget Amendment to the Constitution. Term limits. Welfare reform.

"We are not going to replace left-wing social engineering with right-wing social engineering," Gingrich said. For a social libertarian like me, his words were music to my ears. They were ideas the soon-to-be Speaker had been sharing with our growing legions for years. Newt disseminated his ideas in many ways, including through a reading list.

"How cool is that," I liked to say. "Name the last politician with a book list." His list was like an extended book club for us true believers. It included a wide array of literary work, ranging from historian Myamoto Musashi to management expert Peter Drucker. My two new desk-pushing colleagues turned out to be members of the club. One of them said that he was reading Alvin Tofler's *Third Wave*. Outlining the enormous potential of the Information Age, Newt quoted Tofler all the time. "Great book," I said. "I read that last year." Our camaraderie was growing by the moment.

"I'm reading Gordon Wood's, *The Radicalism of the American Revolution*," said my other colleague. It, too, was a book on Gingrich's list. I couldn't believe it. At Ohio State, it was hard to find anyone who read the same books I did. And yet now I was surrounded by fellow revolutionaries.

As he readied himself to join Newt and the rest of the caucus on the House floor, Bob walked into our back office suite. After shaking some hands, the Congressman fixed his tie while he leaned against the corner of one of our newly acquired desks and told us how it had been Gingrich who convinced him to run for Congress.

"Newt was the one," Bob said. "For years, party leaders had been trying to get me to run for Congress. They all said the same thing." he continued. "Each of them told me how Congress was a step up from the state legislature. How it was more prominent," Bob said in an almost mocking tone. "To which I told them, I am the Appropriations Committee Chairman in Columbus. We run things. I built a jail and a school in my district. How is becoming a freshman Congressman who will be stuck in the minority forever a step up from that? You guys have been in Washington too long." His line got a big laugh from us. So he picked up the pace.

"Then they said I would have more staff and be able to travel all over the world. I already do that, I told them. So I said no." By this point, more people were gathering around Bob. We all knew that in a few short moments, he was going to be sworn in as a part of the 73-person freshman class of the 104th Congress. His story was helping us connect with that journey.

"Then Newt comes along," Bob said, getting visibly more excited. "He talked to me in a completely different way. He told me we needed to change the Congress or they were going to bankrupt the country. And our children and grandchildren would have to pay the bills. 'Your country needs you,' he said. 'You are the only one who can win Ohio's 18th district,'" the soon-to-be Congressman recounted. "'And if you don't do it, that means I have to find someone in some other part of the country to put us over the top.'"

"So despite saying no for years, I told him I would run on the spot," Bob concluded, with a big smile on his face. It was a great story. I related to it right away. Coming to Washington didn't seem to be a choice for Bob either. His tale made my first day on the Hill even more meaningful.

Like the other Members of Congress, Bob's first official vote was for Speaker of the House. The race for Speaker was between Gingrich and Missouri Congressman Dick Gephardt. Gephardt was the leader of the House Democrats. The outcome was a forgone conclusion. But the process was important. The vote verified the recent elections.

With Gingrich's victory came a barrage of foot-stomping, yelling, back-slapping and applause The noise reverberated throughout the House floor. Back at Ney headquarters, we joined in the celebration. For us young staffers, it was like watching the previous year's graduation on your first day at school.

Gephardt spoke first. He was well aware of the gravity of the moment. It was the end of four decades of one-party rule in the House of Representatives.

"As you might imagine, this is not a moment I had been waiting for," the Congressman said. Gingrich stood by his side.

"I speak from the bottom of my heart when I say that I wish you the best in these coming two years," he continued, looking at the soon-to-be Speaker. "For when this gavel passes into your hands, so do the futures and fortunes of millions of Americans."

Listening intently with Bob's supporters, I could have heard a pin drop. Like others, I began to focus on that not so symbolic gavel the Congressman from Missouri continued to hold in his hands. That gavel represented real power. Within its authority, the Speaker's gavel had the power to tax, the power to regulate and power to declare war. And yet very soon, in front of our eyes, it was going to change hands.

"So, with partnership, but with purpose, I pass this great gavel of our government," Gephardt said, handing the gavel to Gingrich. "With resignation but with resolve, I hereby end 40 years of Democratic rule of this House."

Another celebration ensued, greater than the one that had followed the vote for Speaker. At Ney Headquarters, people screamed and hugged. The tears flowed.

Like a conquering hero, Newt began to speak.

"We're starting the 104th Congress," the Speaker said. "I don't know if you've ever thought about the concept, but for 208 years, we gather together, the most diverse country in the history of the world. We send all sorts of people. Each of us could find at least one Member we thought was weird. And I'll tell you, if you went around the room the person chosen to be weird would be different for virtually every one of us. Because we do allow and insist upon the right of a free people to send an extraordinary diversity of people here."

Slipping into teacher mode, the former college professor turned Speaker continued.

"Brian Lamb of C-SPAN read to me Friday a phrase from de Tocqueville that was so central to the House," he said. "I've been reading Remini's biography of Henry Clay. And Henry Clay always preferred the House. He was the first strong Speaker. And he preferred the House to the Senate, although he served in both. Well he said the House is more vital, more active, more dynamic, more common.

And this is what de Tocqueville wrote. 'Often there is not a distinguished man in the whole number. Its members are almost all obscure individuals whose names bring no associations to mind. They are mostly village lawyers, men in trade, or even persons belonging to the lower classes of society.'

"Now, if you put women in with men, I don't know that we'd change much," continued Gingrich. "But the word *vulgar* in de Tocqueville's time had a very particular meaning. And it's a meaning the world would do well to study in this room. You see, de Tocqueville was an aristocrat. He lived in a world of kings and princes. And the folks who come here, come here by the one single act - that their citizens freely chose them."

Captive to Gingrich's words, those of us in Ney World took it all in. Bob's supporters represented the Speaker's words. Some had been friends with Ney since they were kids. Some were family. Others barely knew him at all, yet shared his political beliefs. Most had knocked on doors or stuffed envelopes during the campaign. To them, Bob was both a person and a cause. A guy they knew, and a representative of their people. Very simply, he was their Member of Congress.

"Every one of the 435 people here have equal standing because their citizens freely sent them," Speaker Gingrich continued. "And their voice should be heard, and they should have a right to participate. And it is the most marvelous act of a complex, giant country trying to argue and talk. And, as Dick Gephardt said, to have a great debate, to reach great decisions, not through a civil war, not by bombing one of our regional capitals, not by killing a half million people, not by having snipers."

I had expected an intellectual tour-de-force by Gingrich. Instead I felt a genuine emotional pull from the Speaker's words.

"The Congress is where freedom has to be fought out," he continued. His words made me shiver.

"Here we are as commoners together, to some extent Democrats and Republicans, to some extent liberals and conservatives, but Americans all."

I couldn't help but feel that the Speaker was talking to me, and about me. I was a commoner, working for another commoner. I was also a freshman. And now, I was a "House guy," working for the people. I liked how that made me feel. It made me want to roll up my sleeves and get to work. My Washington identity was taking shape.

A Washington Education

My first year in Washington was an adventure. I loved learning about the city, meeting new people and working. Late in that year, sitting in the ornate House Ways and Means committee hearing room, I waited for Speaker Gingrich to arrive. He was scheduled to talk with our assembled group of Republican press secretaries about the ongoing shutdown of the federal government. The shutdown was a hot topic of conversation among my fellow press secretaries, the reporters we dealt with on a regular basis, and the voters, who were paying close attention to the budget negotiations between the Congress and President Clinton.

For months, the Hill and the White House had tried to negotiate a deal on the nation's budget. But the differences between us and the Clinton Administration were stark. A deal both sides could accept was unachievable. The talks ended, and the government was shut down, due to lack of funds.

Each of our offices received an outline of what to do. Throughout the government, employees were categorized as either "non-essential" or "essential." Those classified as non-essential were put on leave. No work. No pay. Despite knowing that key government operations would go unmet because of the shutdown, the whole thing was refreshingly radical to me and my conservative colleagues. "If they are non-essential, why are they needed anyway?" I would ask during most conversations on the topic.

Not everyone saw the budget negotiations in such simple terms. President Clinton argued that balancing the budget in seven years, as we demanded, was too radical. He said that such a quick reduction in spending would harm the economy and devastate key programs like Social Security, Medicare and education. We revolutionaries couldn't have disagreed more. Balancing the budget was one of the main reasons we were sent to Washington. Therefore, if the President wouldn't agree to a balanced budget, Speaker Gingrich and the Congressional leadership decided it was best to shut the government down. They assumed the shutdown would be bad politically for President Clinton, and he would quickly accede to our demands. Ney World rallied behind our leadership.

Key to the ongoing drama over the budget were "The Freshmen," the 73 new members of the 104th Congress who, like Bob, had promised their constituents dramatic change. Unlike the Congressman, a large number of his classmates had never served in office before. Still, in many ways, Bob's situation was a microcosm of what his freshmen colleagues were experiencing. On the one hand, he ran and won his seat on a promise to balance the budget. On the other hand, he knew that shutting down the federal government was wrought with political danger. Sending government workers home, closing national parks and jeopardizing key programs meant angering his constituents - his voters. But like the rest of his freshmen colleagues, Bob knew that balancing the budget was the right thing to do.

Representing one in seven members of the House of Representatives, Speaker Gingrich used the freshmen as a foil in his negotiations with the President. He suggested that we could not be controlled, that we were radical non-politicians who would not accept anything less than an actual balanced budget. At the same time, Gingrich never really knew if he could reign his freshmen in for something that our increasingly tight-knit community considered a bad deal. The Speaker was playing a dangerous game. The more he fed into the extremism of Bob and his classmates, the more we believed it.

The media began to label the freshmen as zealots and uncompromising fire-breathers. We wore their insults like badges of honor. Such a shutdown may have been an unprecedented move, we would say, but it was our duty. Cutting off the flow of taxpayer money to an out-of-control government was a necessary prerogative of the Congress. "If the voters don't approve, they can vote us out," I told numerous reporters. Like snarling dogs, we young Capitol Hill staffers dug in for the fight.

While my fellow freshmen and I felt like the black sheep of Washington, my life on Capitol Hill was awesome. I quickly made lots of friends. My days were spent working, and my nights were spent hanging out at the numerous large gatherings that occurred on a regular basis. One night the National Pork Producers hosted a get-together. The next night it was the National Beer Wholesalers Association. Because the parties were what people called, "widely attended events," our drinks and food were free. The thought behind that policy was that buying a couple dollars worth of drinks and food for hundreds of people was less corrupting than buying hundreds of dollars worth of drinks and food for one or two people. It seemed to make sense.

The group of young staffers I ran around with, none of whom were paid much, quickly learned to share notes about where these parties were occurring. We then finagled our way in to at least one free meal a day when the Congress was in session. The process was pretty simple. While eating finger food with professionals from the transportation industry, we talked about roads, airports and trains. At events with the financial services industry, we discussed housing, real estate and banking. The people I met wanted to know my opinion, what I thought. Working for a Congressman made me feel influential. I liked that.

Before long, my new lifestyle started to feel normal, as if I were exactly where I wanted to be. And not just because I was having a good time.

Politics was more than just a job to me. It was my passion. My life. Most of my Washington friends felt similarly. We were in our early twenties, from all over the country, and unquestionably dedicated to our bosses - both the people and the causes they represented. Our group of Capitol Hill newcomers even had a nickname - we called ourselves "The Hill Rats."

Like the freshmen we were, my group of friends were all activists and explorers who did everything together. We partied. We laughed. We talked. Whether at work, on the softball fields, or in the bars, we debated current events and political philosophy. "Why are there more employees in the Department of Agriculture than there are farmers?" one of us would ask. "What exactly does the federal education department do to help a classroom full of students and teachers?" another would say. Then there were my favorites, which I stole from opinion editorial writer George Will. "Why does the federal government run a railroad? Did art exist in this country before the creation of the National Endowment for the Arts? What exactly would it be like if there was no Energy Department?" Our debates were always good theater and reminded me of similar conversations I had had in school.

Looking around, it was hard not to see my new life through the prism of high school - an incredibly ambitious high school. Our little group of fresh-faced Washingtonians knew full well that there were big-picture cliques and rivalries at play throughout Capitol Hill. But most of us weren't that interested in them. We were more focused on the challenge of figuring out how to fit into our new school. All of us wanted to stay pure in our revolutionary fervor and committed to the purpose that brought each of us to Washington. But we weren't sure what we were doing. At the same time, our bosses, their constituents and nearly everyone else had different opinions about how we were supposed to do our jobs. The opinions swirling around us changed by the day. Identifying our role in the process became a constant debate. In that respect, the Hill was more like prison than high school. Declaring our allegiance to the cause, the party and the Congressman was a several times a day occurrence. Constituents I spoke with wanted to know that the Congressman and I could identify with them. Colleagues wanted to know that we were on the same team. And Bob wanted to know that I was looking out for his interests first.

It quickly became apparent to me that ongoing identity debates were just a part of the political process. Therefore, it was important to know the buzz words associated with these kind of discussions. Such knowledge helped to cut through the day-to-day clutter.

"I'm a social conservative," one colleague would say. Labeling himself as a social conservative was a quick way of letting people know that he was Pro-Life, and part of what was known as the family values wing of our party.

"I'm a Western libertarian Republican," another colleague would say. Labeling herself that way was like saying that say she was part of the Republican team, but less comfortable with the idea of such a values-driven agenda. There were more labels than you could imagine. I had friends who were "pro-business Democrats," and "Pro-environment Republicans." The identity debates never stopped. Our hopes and beliefs, as well as what politicians we liked and didn't like were all discussed through these ongoing debates over identity. Comments like, "He is a tax-raiser," or, "She is too close to the unions," said as much about us as it did the elected officials we were describing.

Like our Congressional bosses, we staffers were learning to deal with the fact that our profession involved being both a person and a cause. Having an identity on Capitol Hill was more than a personal statement or individual label. It wasn't just an expression of one's tastes or styles. Our professional identities also served to advance the causes my colleagues and I believed in, like balancing the budget. When I talked with a reporter, for instance, I was representing the cause of Bob Ney. The same was true when I worked with other offices to push a specific budget provision or piece of legislation on behalf of the Congressman's constituents. But when I was out partying with friends, I was just a person being me. Unless the Congressman was there. Or someone else whom I wanted to impress. Then it got complicated.

For both me and my Washington friends, proclaiming a belief in our conservative revolution was like waving a flag or wearing a school jersey. My friends and I even had our own language geared around these efforts. Independence Avenue, for instance, became, "Dependence Avenue." Because of the large number of federal buildings lining the street, including the department in charge of administering the federal food stamp program, we decided it needed a name change. Likewise, when someone or someone's boss strayed too far from conservative orthodoxy, refused to take a tough vote, or appeared to be veering from the purity of our revolutionary goals, we labeled him or her, "a Squish." Being a squish was like being a moderate, something that was frowned upon in our conservative-dominated Hill culture.

In addition to the stances we took on the issues, the jobs we held also helped us in our efforts to find our way through Washington during the early stages of the revolution. Within each Congressional office, there are numerous positions: a chief of staff who runs the office, a Legislative Director who coordinates the legislative staff, a Scheduler, some interns, and people who handle correspondence and answer phones. In the district, there are case managers who help constituents with problems like disability claims and Social Security questions, as well as office professionals who work with local, county and state officials to advance the Congressman's interests.

My job was Ney's Press Secretary. I loved it. My primary responsibility revolved around working through the media to communicate with the Congressman's constituents. That meant everything from writing weekly columns for our local newspapers to alerting the press when Bob was available for an interview or in town for an event. Being a press secretary also included being actively engaged in the energetic give and take of public debate. Whether that included spinning what was happening on the Hill through interviews, newsletters or press releases, I loved the daily battle of ideas. So did all the folks who had been sitting around with me, waiting for Speaker Gingrich to arrive.

Like a exultant conquistador, Gingrich strolled into the ornate committee chambers. Whispers of his arrival preceded our leaders appearance. The crowd erupted into a standing ovation at the first sight of the Speaker's familiar white mane. The fight over the government shutdown had turned into a massive public relations debate with the White House, so Gingrich called us press secretaries together for a talk. His goal was to define the debate. The Speaker wanted to remind us of our revolutionary cause. Newt's confident demeanor soothed any anxiety I was feeling about the ongoing conflict over the budget. More pep rally than policy critique, Gingrich quickly began to fire up the troops. He reminded us that what we were doing was bigger than just balancing the budget. "This is about the future of the country," he said.

"If the public views this as a small parochial matter about their favorite government programs, we will lose this debate," he said. "But if they see it as a big fight about the future of our country, we will win," the Speaker continued. "That is where you press secretaries come into play. You are the front lines." Staffers to the left and right of me scribbled madly. Likewise, I frantically wrote down as many notes as possible.

"We can't force President Clinton to see things the way we see them," he told our group. "But the public can. Only once since World War II has the government reduced annual spending from the year before," the Speaker said several times. "It was the year after Ronald Reagan's election," he said. "Why? Because the public demanded it - and they are doing it again."

With the crescendo of an Italian opera, Gingrich worked the room into a frenzy.

"What we are doing here is nothing less than an extension of the fight which created the Magna Carta," the Speaker said. His words hit me like a brick. I shuddered at the thought of what he was saying. *"Did he just say that?"* I asked myself. Looking around, I could tell that I wasn't the only one stunned by the Magna Carta reference the Speaker had just made.

The Magna Carta is one of democracy's founding documents. A copy of it sits in the National Archives, a few blocks from the Capitol Building. Originally written in Latin, the Magna Carta is a predecessor to the United States Constitution. Written in the year 1215, the agreement between King John and the land barons of Runnymeade bound the English monarchy to the rule of the people for the first time in history. While it did not create a full-on democracy in the Kingdom, its limited democratic concessions, like legal guarantees such as *habeas corpus* and the right to appeal unlawful imprisonment, led to the establishment of common law, constitutional law and, ultimately, the creation of America's system of governance.

Speaker Gingrich's words fired me up. Saving the country and saving freedom were big causes. I felt honored to be a part of them. Yet, for the first time, I began to worry about whether the voters saw our actions through the same historic lens as our leaders. It was a debate that would take years to conclude, but one that began as our revolution was still at its zenith.

On the other side of town, in the office of lobbyist Jack Abramoff, another debate about the federal budget was also underway. Like the rest of

34

official Washington, Jack was focused on the negotiations over the multi-trillion dollar federal budget. In that respect, he was no different than the 15,000 other registered lobbyists in Washington.

Jack was primarily concerned about how the government's spending decisions would impact his lobbying clients. But like conservatives throughout the country, he, too, was concerned about what the budget battle meant to the revolution and the identity of the conservative movement.

Jack already knew how Washington worked. He was a player. A professional lobbyist paid to protect the interests of his clients. In terms of the federal budget, his main specific worry revolved around his tribal client, the Mississippi Band of Choctaw Indians. Because of Congressional efforts to balance the budget, the Hill was looking at taxing tribal casinos, like those run by the Choctaw. Since the multibillion dollar tribal casino industry was big business, and not generally taxed by the federal government, those tribes who would potentially be affected by such a change were looking at the prospect of hundreds of millions of dollars in lost revenue. Such an impact sent a shock wave through Indian Country.

With many of the tribe's legislative champions on the Hill now in the Democratic minority and unable to help, tribes like the Choctaw looked elsewhere for assistance in navigating the new Congress. That was where Jack came into the picture.

Abramoff had been a leader in the conservative movement for years, and had a wide array of contacts throughout the new Republican-led House and Senate. When Jack outlined his credentials, the Mississippi tribe liked what they heard. They also like Jack personally. It was hard not to like Jack. But more pressing was the fact that they needed him. At the time, in early 1995, Abramoff was one of only a handful of pioneering Republican lobbyists in the new Washington. Uniquely positioned, Jack quickly joined forces with the Choctaw.

Part of Jack's pitch to his new clients was his belief that the new Congress required them to fundamentally change the way they lobbied. It wasn't just about getting the right contacts, Jack argued. The tribe also needed the right philosophy. They needed to embrace conservative principles to better advance their cause, he said. For Jack, the new approach was a win-win. His clients would advance their own interests by supporting the conservative causes and elected officials Jack supported. In return, his clients would help him become an even bigger player in Washington. It was lobbying 101, and the Choctaw got it right away.

The tribe's fight was a prime example of this theory put into practice.

In an effort to pass a budget which was balanced in seven years, the House Ways and Means Committee included a provision to the bill which raised revenue from Indian casinos by taxing their profits. This effort was led by two members of Congress who felt the tribes had an unfair tax advantage over their local competitors, since those competitors had to tax the gas, cigarettes and food they sold - while the tribes did not. Likewise, while most tribal gaming operations shared their revenue with the states they operated in, few provided any money directly to the federal government. Those being the facts, many members of the new majority on Capitol Hill concluded that taxing tribal casinos was a fair way to raise needed revenue for our budget balancing efforts.

Jack saw the debate differently. Instead of arguing over the fairness or worthiness of the revenue in question, like he and his client might have done under the previous majority, he suggested that his clients see the debate from the perspective of a conservative. Jack told the tribe that their lobbying campaign should be centered around the mission of convincing conservatives that this move was anti-business, that it was nothing more than a tax on employers. After all, Jack argued, taxing business was as anathema to what the revolution was all about as unbalanced budgets.

This new outlook was the merging of three causes: the cause of the Choctaw, who needed the money for their community; the cause of strengthening Jack's political identity, namely bringing more people and money into the conservative fold; and the cause of Jack the lobbyist, who wanted to get paid.

The Choctaw and Jack jumped into the fray. As opposed to saying they needed the money for important programs that benefited the tribe, Jack and his client's campaign was geared around engaging in the same identity debate we were having on the Hill. "What does it mean to be a conservative? How can we best stay pure in our revolutionary mission?"

Jack and the tribe injected their own questions into the debate. "Is it conservative to raise taxes? Were conservatives sent to Washington to be anti-business?" It was an interesting juxtaposition. By labeling any business tax or regulation an abandonment of conservative principle, Abramoff and his allies were creating their own cottage industry. The strategy worked perfectly. Jack's was not only a compelling argument, but a winning argument. Arizona's Republican Senator John McCain helped beat back the tax increase in the Senate. In the House, Jack aligned himself with the powerful House Majority Whip, Tom DeLay, from Texas. DeLay, the only member of the elected House leadership who was not a part of Newt's hand-picked slate of candidates, would soon become good friends with Jack. Both men knew the negotiations over the budget would help define the upcoming elections, the make up of the next Congress and the ongoing debate over the identity of the conservative movement. And both wanted that identity to include an iron-clad commitment against any sort of tax increase, including for tribes. It was a quintessential Jack move, smart, aggressive, and based on conservative rhetoric. Jack's stock was on the rise. He had come a long way.

Abramoff was born in Atlantic City. In 1968, when he was nine years old, Jack and his family moved to California. He attended Beverly Hills High School. When he was a young man, Jack played sports and was active in student politics. He also had a transformative religious experience, becoming a *Baal Teshuva*, otherwise known as an Orthodox Jew. He began to observe the Sabbath and other tenets of his Orthodox faith.

In the late 1970s, Jack attended Brandeis University, where he served as Chairman of the Massachusetts Alliance of College Republicans. During his tenure, the College Republicans worked to generate student volunteers for the 1980 presidential campaign of fellow California conservative, Ronald Reagan. Like the 1994 congressional campaigns did for me, Reagan's 1980 presidential campaign galvanized Abramoff's idealism and ideology. His conservative faith meshed perfectly with his conservative politics. And another true believer was born.

After he graduated from Brandeis in 1981, Jack ran for and won the National Chairmanship of the College Republicans. The post was a big deal. As Jack had promised during his campaign, he changed the direction and culture of the College Republicans. Under Jack's leadership, they became more traditionally conservative and ideologically pure. Very simply, they became a movement. It is safe to say that the College Republicans of the Abramoff-era were no longer a place for students to go who just wanted to party and socialize.

As Chairman, Jack developed relationships with College Republican leaders across the country. In 1984, he used those contacts and others to start the USA Foundation. Though technically non-partisan, Jack's foundation rallied young anti-communist conservatives on campus during President Reagan's re-election. .

In 1985, Jack then led an organization called Citizens for America. Unabashedly pro-Reagan, the group worked to build support for anti-Communist causes throughout the world. Their cause included efforts to support everyone from the Contras in Nicaragua to the Mujahedeen in Afghanistan.

The next year Jack was appointed to the United States Holocaust Memorial Council by President Reagan.

In the late-1980s, Jack moved back to California, where he wrote and produced movies. His most famous work was 1989's *Red Scorpion*, an anti-communist action film starring the actor Dolph Lundgren. Lundgren, best known for his role as a Russian boxer opposite Sylvester Stallone in the movie *Rocky III*, played a Soviet assassin who decides to switch sides mid-movie and become an anti-Communist freedom fighter in Africa. It was Jack at his right-wing best.

By 1994, Abramoff was back in Washington. With the Republican takeover of Congress, he found himself in the luxurious position of being courted by law firms and lobby shops who were looking for people with street credibility among the new GOP power brokers on Capitol Hill. A month before the new Congress began, Jack started working with the law and lobbying firm Preston Gates LLP.

He quickly swung into action. Within his first six months at the firm, Jack brought on several clients. In addition to the Mississippi Band of Choctaw Indians, he signed up the United States Commonwealth of the Northern Mariana Islands, a group of islands in the Pacific, west of Hawaii. These two clients provided the foundation for Jack's rapidly growing lobbying practice.

On Capitol Hill, Bob Ney was also laying the foundation for his political career in Washington. Days before the government shutdown, he broke with his Republican colleagues for the first time on a major vote. Bob's move was eye-opening for me. The provision he supported involved the collective bargaining rights of union workers. The Congressman was one of only a handful of Republican House members who balked at the goal of eliminating union worker protections through the federal funding process. For both political and personal reasons, Bob opposed the measure.

His Ohio Congressional district contained hundreds of thousands of union members. Voting against collective bargaining would have been an unpopular move. At the same time, Bob had grown up in the district, and he told our assembled staff that he thought the measure wasn't good for "his people." We sent a press release out to the union-leaning part of the district. Our hope was to get word of Bob's defense of union workers into the steel mills and coal mines along the river, without upsetting our more agricultural and pro-business portion of the district in the West. .

During the vote, Bob said several of his fellow freshmen got in his face and yelled at him. So did members of the House leadership.

"They called me a union squish," he said, after returning to the office.

"What did you tell them?" I asked.

"I told them they just weren't getting my vote on this one." His answer was pretty straightforward. "Some of those guys have a God complex," he said.

"What is that?"

"Since the voters put them in office one time, they think the voters will continue to support whatever they are doing," he answered. "It doesn't work that way. You see that kind of shit overseas. Some general gets elected president and then never has another election. It is scary to think like that. The fact is voters change their minds, and you have to keep in contact with them. My voters weren't thinking about collective bargaining when they put me in office, but they could be next time," he continued. "And as I told them," Bob went on, "We can't balance the budget if we aren't in office."

It was a prescient point. Or several of them. Bob's actions showed me that if he had to choose between the purity of our conservative revolution and the interests of his constituents, he would choose the cause of his constituents. That was a telling moment for me. And yet, at the same time, he was showing me that our revolution was important, but that it was only possible if we had the power to implement it. And that meant winning elections.

NOVEMBER 5, 1996
ST. CLAIRSVILLE, OH

Election Day

BOB AND I WERE WORRIED about the election.

"I'm sure your going to win Jim," Ney said. "But I'm not sure about me." The Congressman was talking on the phone to his successor in the Ohio Legislature, State Senator Jim Carnes. The two of us were driving toward Undo's Restaurant for Bob's election party. As we weaved our way through Southeastern Ohio's hilly, picturesque, autumn roads, I could see the concern on my boss's face.

Hour later, Bob was barely re-elected.

Elections provide the rhythm for our representative government. The decisions made by the public every other November determine what laws and regulations are implemented. These decisions also create the environment in which staffers, lobbyists and all of official Washington operate.

Ney and I were joined by several other staffers in a hotel conference room to wait for the results. It was excruciating to sit there without being able to do anything to impact the outcome. Bob nervously made phone calls, and paced back and forth while we waited. The process bound the Congressman to his constituents in a way that was both emotional and intellectual. If he lost, we would all be out looking for work. But he won. With just over 50% of the vote, Bob narrowly defeated his opponent, Democratic State Senator Rob Burch. His margin of victory was about 7,000 votes.

I drove to Ohio for the last few weeks of the election. We campaigned on our efforts to balance the budget, touted the welfare reform bill President Clinton signed into law, and championed an improving economy. Our opponent focused on Bob's votes to cut the budget. He said the Congressman had supported cuts in Medicare and was nothing more than a "Newt Gingrich" clone. It was an effective attack since Gingrich's poll numbers had plummeted after the government shutdown. According to our polls, less than 40% of the people in Bob's district held a favorable view of the Speaker.

There was also a major steelworker's strike during the campaign. A few months before the election, thousands of steelworkers walked off the job to protest their wages and benefits. It was a crucial issue in the district, and one our opponent used to his advantage. Some of the steelworkers joined a protest that took place in front of Bob's local office. The Congressman was attacked for taking a $500 check from the company's CEO. Crucial to Bob's political survival, and our outreach with the steelworkers, was the Congressman's vote a year earlier to protect the collective bargaining rights of workers. We argued that the vote showed how Bob prioritized the people of his district over the politics of Washington. It was an important part of our re-election efforts.

Several of Bob's fellow freshmen lost their races and the margin in the Congress narrowed, but we kept our majority. In the Senate, Republicans picked up two seats, remaining in power with a margin of 53-47. President Clinton was also re-elected, defeating the Republican nominee, Senator Bob Dole. In Ohio, the President carried Bob's district by about 23,000 votes. The basic makeup of the government did not change. Clinton remained in the White House and the Republicans ran the Congress.

Election Day

I ONCE AGAIN SAT IN THE hotel conference room next to Undo's Restaurant and awaited the election results. This time the Congressman his Campaign Manager and I casually reached out to supporters and friends as we waited. All of us knew Bob was going to win. His Campaign Manager and I had spent the previous night blanketing the hometown of our opponent with yard signs. There wasn't a street without a handful of green "Bob Ney" signs. Our late-night exploits represented an exclamation point of our successful two-year campaign to keep Bob in office.

The 1998 campaign practically began the day after the previous election. Because of Bob's near defeat in 1996, we focused like a laser on the race. Instead of running as revolutionaries, the Congressman decided it was best to run a local campaign. We de-emphasized big Washington policy debates in favor of district-oriented debates over local water rates, economic development, highway projects, and jobs.

We also ran a negative campaign against Bob's opponent. From day one, we worked to label him a big government liberal. Since we had the same opponent from the previous cycle, the last name "Burch" was rarely mentioned without the new first name we gave him, "Liberal." The negative campaigning worked. So did our ability to secure nearly $30 million in road projects for the district in the federal highway bill. Our campaign's local focus, combined with an improving economy, resulted in a 10% upswing in the Congressman's re-election numbers. Instead of winning with 50% of the vote, Bob won with 60%.

The election results weren't so positive for Republicans across the country. Despite Speaker Gingrich's prediction that we would pick up nearly 40 new members, House Republicans lost seats. Our margin in the House of

Representatives slipped from 228-207, to 223-212, a six-seat majority. Such a reality meant any six Republican members of Congress could derail a piece of legislation. It was a major step backward for the revolution. Three days after the election, Speaker Gingrich resigned.

Republicans continued to hold on to a narrow majority in the Senate.

JANUARY 20, 1999
WASHINGTON, DC

A New Focus on Washington

O UR AIR HORNS AND WHISTLES could be heard inside the Capitol. There were thousands of us rallying along the West front of the building. After Bob's impressive election victory, Ney World was ready to focus on the next campaign: increasing our influence in Washington.

The Capitol Hill Police requested that the gathered protesters quiet down. Their request resulted in a prolonged chorus of boos and whistles. Raising my arm skyward, I defiantly joined the moment by hitting the button on my air horn, over and over again. "The debate over the impeachment of President Clinton is occurring on the Senate floor," one of the officers said. "The Senators can hear you inside."

The officer's request for serenity fell on deaf ears. Few of the 4,000 steelworkers at our Stand Up for Steel rally cared much for the decorum preferences of the United States Senate. After all, the stated goal of the crowd was to try to get the attention of their government. Now that they had it, the last thing they wanted to do was be quiet. "The Capitol Hill police didn't tell Martin Luther King to be quiet!" yelled Wheeling-Pittsburgh Steel Chairman Paul Bucha, a Medal of Honor recipient for his heroism during the Vietnam War. "They didn't tell the Vietnam Veterans who gathered here to be quiet. The steelworkers aren't going to be quiet either!" he continued from behind his Capitol-front podium. "This is *our* house!" Passion in steel country had been riding high for months.

Late the previous evening, thousands of steelworkers, their families and their neighbors loaded into 75 buses to travel from the Ohio Valley to Washington. Bob and I were there to help them. He was due to speak soon. As we scrambled out of the office toward the rally, the two of us contemplated how best to get Bob arrested. After the steelworkers marched down

44

Pennsylvania Avenue, the Congressman wanted to show his support for the cause by being detained outside the White House. "Getting arrested would draw attention to the steel issue," he said. With the media glare squarely on the sexually-charged impeachment debate, few people were aware of the growing controversy involving foreign steel imports and the impact they were having on communities throughout the United States. Communities like those in Bob's district.

The situation was pretty simple. Because countries like China, Russia and Japan were subsidizing their domestic steel production, the U.S. market was being flooded with cheap steel imports. In some cases, this imported steel was selling for less than it cost to produce. A debate arose. Some suggested the subsidies were illegal. Others disagreed. Either way, such an unfair advantage was significantly altering the domestic steel industry. And the people paying the price for those changes were America's steelworkers and their families, tens of thousands of whom had already lost their jobs. Many of those were Bob's constituents.

Unlike our earlier Capitol Hill battles, which were nationally focused and ideologically-driven, the fight for the steel industry and its workers was about the Congressman's district. His people. His heart.

The goal of our rally was to pressure the Clinton White House to stop the flood of what we believed to be illegally subsidized imports. Since Congress granted the President the necessary tools to intervene in these kind of cases in the early 1970s, we were hoping the President would do for steel what President Reagan had done for motorcycles in the mid-1980s. When motorcycle manufacturers in Japan were dumping subsidized bikes into the United States as a way to gain market share, Reagan imposed specific tariffs on certain products in order to protect Harley Davidson and the other U.S. motorcycle manufacturers. Reagan's decision saved an industry, an American icon and tens of thousands of jobs from unfair competition.

After the rally at the Capitol, the plan was to march two and a half miles through Washington, with the steelworkers, and then rally again at the White House in the afternoon. The Congressman called President Clinton's protocol office before we left to let them know of his plans to get arrested as a part of the protest. Bob and I knew the Secret Service would have a perimeter built around the grounds of the White House. Therefore, we figured that crossing the security perimeter would be the best way to get taken into custody. While we discussed our options, the Congressman suggested locking himself to the front gate instead of breaking through the police barrier.

"The press would love it," he said. "If only we had some handcuffs. We really should have been thinking ahead," he continued. At that point, one the Congressman's staffers told us she had a set of handcuffs in her desk drawer.

"I'm not even asking," I said, while she swung the cuffs around her index and middle fingers, before giving them to Bob. We all laughed. Ney put the cuffs and keys in the beat up leather jacket he wore for the event. "Cuffing yourself to the gate will be a lot better," I told him, as we finally walked out the door. Both of us loved the political theater. The game. Of course, we both also knew the importance of the issues we were addressing.

Scattered throughout Bob's district were small towns built around steel mills and coal mines. Steel and coal represented the heart and soul of those communities. In some cases, nearly half of a town's tax base was dependent on the production of either coal or steel. This revenue helped to fund schools, firehouses and hospitals. It wasn't political hyperbole to say that if a mill or mine was forced to shut down, an adjoining town could be shuttered along with it.

Because of the massive influx of steel imports, many towns in the greater-Ohio Valley region were beginning to envision such a future. They were towns like Steubenville, Ohio, and Weirton, West Virginia. In many respects, Weirton was the lifeblood of the Stand Up for Steel movement. In the previous few months, Weirton Steel had been forced to lay off nearly one thousand local steelworkers.

Weirton was also where President Clinton had visited in 1992 when he was campaigning for the presidency. During his stop, the future President promised to protect the domestic steel market from countries and competitors who illegally dumped their steel. Both the city of Weirton and the state of West Virginia had applauded his commitment and voted overwhelmingly for him.

Having watched family members, friends and neighbors lose jobs without any substantive response from the White House, however, Weirton was no longer Clinton country. The local steelworkers union went so far as to hold a press conference to take President Clinton's picture off their union hall wall. Many believed the President was putting global financial interests ahead of the local steel industry. To an extent, that was true. And it made for a complicated debate.

On the one hand, Clinton knew that strong capital markets were crucial to the American economy. With countries like Russia teetering on the edge of collapse due to the Asian currency crisis, blocking their steel imports, and the hard currency it produced, could have had a domino affect that negatively impacted other domestic industries. Similarly, in parts of the country where steel is used to build cars and ships, the newly inexpensive steel was viewed somewhat favorably. As such, with Wall Street, automakers and shipbuilders all benefiting from the situation, President Clinton found himself in a box. Do you help Ohio and West Virginia at the expense of Michigan, New York and the state of Washington? Not that it was so cut and dry. Nor that the complexities of the situation were much concern to the people feeling the brunt of the economic pain. As in the impeachment debate, President Clinton's honesty became a galvanizing issue.

"I think it is fair to say he lied to the Ohio Valley," said Independent Steelworkers Union President Mark Glyptis, during his speech at the Capitol-front rally. "President Clinton was not elected to be president of the world. He was elected to represent the American people." Glyptis spoke from the heart, and his sentiment symbolized the opinion of the thousands who gathered in Washington.

From Bob's perspective, Glyptis was the spirit of the steel movement. He was the spoke in the cause's wheel. As the two led the march down Pennsylvania Avenue together, they carried a large banner that read, "Stand Up for Steel." Bob exuded determination and resolve. He and Glyptis had become good friends, bonding over the issue. The Republican congressman and the union leader. The two may not have agreed on everything, but they agreed on steel.

I walked a few feet behind the two men. The view was unbelievable. For as far as the eye could see, there were signs and people parading down a major Washington thoroughfare. Bare trees and streetlights framed the passion in the road. Our next stop was the White House.

A lot had changed in the last four years. President Clinton's re-election in 1996 forced us to dampen our revolutionary fervor. After being outmaneuvered by the president during the government shutdown, a détente between the White House and Congress had been reached. Daily conflict turned to bipartisan compromise at the end of every fiscal year. The budget picture improved. For the first time in a generation, yearly surpluses replaced deficits.

The politics of the House of Representatives also changed. Following the 1998 elections, Speaker Gingrich was forced from office. Many members of the House Republican team were convinced that the Speaker's management style posed a threat to the long-term viability of our majority. Of our cause. It was horrible to watch. But a good lesson. Advancing our goals meant keeping the majority. Without the votes, there was no way to keep the flame of our revolution alive, even if it meant getting rid of the man who had helped build the movement.

In Bob's personal office, the 1998 elections also represented a season of transition. No longer freshmen, we found ourselves transitioning from an office singularly focused on getting re-elected to an office focused more on gaining power in Washington. This new outlook was the result of Bob's re-election success.

In Washington political circles, Members of Congress who win less than 55% of the vote tend to be considered vulnerable for the next election cycle. When Bob barely won 50% of the vote in 1996, that meant the organizations and individuals who coordinate campaigns for the Democratic coalition continued to target him for the next two years. By winning 60% of the vote in 1998, however, we took Bob off the target list. Having secured home base, it was time to expand our efforts in Washington. As the steel rally showed, increasing our presence in Washington was not some sort of abandonment of Bob's district. It was just the opposite. From our perspective, the more power Bob got in Congress, the more he could do for the folks back home.

No longer strangers in a strange land, Ney World began to make a name for itself in the nation's capital. Known for our hard-charging work ethic, we were also known for our late-night revelry. There were offices that worked as hard as we did. And there were offices that partied as hard as we did. But there were few offices that both worked and partied the way we did.

This attribute was a cultural reflection of the Congressman. A Ney rule. He didn't care if you were out until 3:00 AM as long as you were bright-eyed, bushy-tailed and on time to meet the group of school kids touring the Capitol the next day at 6:30 AM. "If the Congressman can do it, we all can do it," I would say. Meetings took place early in the morning over coffee in our House Office Building cafeteria, and late at night in the bar rooms of The Hawk and Dove, Heads and The Capitol Lounge. Burning the candle at both ends was simply part of our overall identity. Bob and I loved it. The lifestyle was practically policy. And if you had a problem with the policy, you didn't last long.

In large part because of our growing bond, the Congressman named me his chief of staff after our 1998 election success. Bob's old chief of staff had moved on to become a lobbyist a few months before the campaign ended.

My new perch ushered me into a different world. Now that I was managing staff, overseeing legislative work, and coordinating the Congressman's fundraising operation, my decisions directly affected people's lives. At first, the additional responsibility was a bit overwhelming. My mistakes negatively impacted others, which made me feel guilty, until their mistakes made me look bad. We all adjusted to my new role in Ney World. Since I didn't want to give up my press portfolio, I also remained Bob's press secretary.

Making my initial transition easier was the fact that the Congressman was a micro-manager. Nothing substantive happened in Bob's Washington office or his district office without him knowing about it. This was in part because of his personality. It also had to do with his history.

A specific incident involving his staff occurred during Bob's 1982 re-election bid that changed the way he ran his office. The event took place at the end of the only election he ever lost. As Election Day neared, Bob had let his staff put together two of the final mail pieces of the campaign. One of the mailers was geared toward those people who supported public education. The other was for people who supported private education, like parochial schools. Bob's message was a little different for each group, something that became a much bigger deal when the mailer for the public school supporters was sent to the private school supporters, and vice versa.

On election night, Bob lost by a little more than a hundred votes. From that day forward, he vowed to never worry about micromanaging or hurting his staff's feelings again. Worrying about how to deal with his hands-on approach was now my job.

My new job represented a move up the Capitol Hill ladder of power. I liked it. People I didn't know suddenly knew all about me. They went out of there way to meet with me and influence my decisions. It was heady stuff. My phone calls all started getting returned, and I even began to get noticed around the Hill as an up-and-comer. Someone to watch. In a town of winners and losers, being a chief of staff meant that I was a winner. All I had to do was read my own press clippings to see that was the case.

My job duties weren't the only change in my professional life. My perspective was changing, too. Bit by bit, I slowly changed from someone who believed a principled insurrection against the way Washington works was the best way to advance our cause, to a person who believed that winning the Washington game was actually the best way to achieve our goals. "You either have a majority to make something happen or you don't," I said. "There are no moral victories in a system based on the vote. You either win, or you lose."

My evolving views reflected the, "outcome-based approach that is the foundation of our political system," I would continue. "It is winner take all. Winning is what matters. If you want to advance a cause or help a town in the district, you either accomplish the goal or fail. There is no in-between."

Such a mentality helped to clarify my ever-present battle over issues of political identity. Conversations I used to see as fun freshmen fodder, I now saw as crucial to mine and Bob's success. With who "we" are so crucial to advancing "our" common goals, defining "us" and "them" became a relentless win-or-lose, poll-driven battle. In the case of the steelworkers, the "us" were those people who wanted the government to block the flood of imported steel. For most political fights, however, the "we" was the Republican majority; "them," were the Democrats. In the same way we worked to define President Clinton and his Democratic Congressional allies, they worked to define us. It was a nonstop public relations battle. A sales pitch without end.

In Ney World, my sales pitch became a twenty-four-hour-a-day job. By the time I became chief of staff, there were no professional boundaries. Whether I was out having a beer with a friend or attending a neighborhood picnic, the "we" I focused on was Bob, his office and our shared professional interests. If I was at an event with a conservative audience or person, my sales pitch meant emphasizing our conservative credentials. If I was working with a Democrat office, I emphasized our willingness to work in a bipartisan way.

Such a change in my code of conduct occurred slowly, a step at a time. Initially, I viewed it as a byproduct of being Bob's press secretary. Like with any other communications job, my responsibility was to advance Bob's views, not my views. But because politics can be such a personal thing, I struggled the first few times that I needed to advance one of those issues where Bob and I disagreed. It touched a nerve. But then I got used to it.

The same rationalization process played out when I started skirting some of the campaign regulations I was supposed to follow as one of Bob's staffers. Technically, for instance, a paid Congressional staffer is not supposed to conduct campaign work while on the clock. If a staffer wants to go door-to-door passing out the Congressman's campaign literature, or make fundraising phone calls, he can do it, but on *his own time*. Since none of Bob's employees worked for an hourly rate, *their own time* was pretty broadly defined - and was more and more broadly defined the closer we got to Election Day.

The rules were even more vague when it came to my responsibilities as a press secretary. Technically, I was not allowed to actively engage in the campaign during work hours or from my Congressional office. However, I was allowed to walk across the street to Republican headquarters and use their phones, computers and fax machines in order to promote Bob's campaign. Again, I just needed to do so *on my time*, which became another way of saying whenever I wanted. On numerous occasions, I would walk over to headquarters and fax out a press release attacking the Congressman's opponent. At that point, I would typically call reporters covering the campaign to let them know something had been sent over and that they could reach me at party headquarters.

None of the reporters called back there. They preferred to call me at Bob's congressional office. The reporters knew the rules, too. They knew I could not actively engage them on campaign news, meaning call them to specifically attack Bob's opponent. But if they engaged me, I could reply. Even in the office. From a practical perspective, that meant all I had to do was wait for a reporter to mention the Congressman's opponent and I could talk about him in whatever way I wanted. Since reporters were usually under deadline, and time was tight, most just quickly asked me about Bob's opponent so they could get a comment. Before long, I didn't even think about the process. It was all part of our renewed focus on playing the Washington game.

With loud chants of "Dump Rubin, not Steel," our rally passed the Treasury Building. We were almost to the White House. Robert Rubin was President Clinton's Secretary of the Treasury. To the steelworkers, he was responsible for the Clinton Administration's inaction on the steel import issue. Marching into Lafayette Park, Bob and I turned around to look at the crowd. With the White House on our right, I watched the protestors fill the tree-lined square.

In a sign of the times, impeachment talk was everywhere. Men in wigs were dressed as former White House intern Monica Lewinsky, whose affair with the President was at the heart of the impeachment debate. A woman who looked like a steelworker held up a large sign reading, "Mr. President, would a blow job save my job?"

Bob looked over at me with wide white eyes. We couldn't help but laugh.

"These are Democrats," he said excitedly. "Union Democrats, can you believe it?"

The Congressman then turned his attention to Independent

51

Steelworker's Union President Mark Glyptis. At nearly every turn in the steel debate, Bob liked to touch base with Glyptic - not because he felt like he needed to get his approval, but because Bob's approach to politics was very personal. For most major projects or causes, the Congressman assigned them a face. A person. When he heard steel dumping, for instance, he thought Mark Glyptis. As I was learning, this kind of approach helped Bob to quickly navigate complex situations. Since he worked that way, I began to work that way, too.

Finally, the moment of truth arrived. It was time for Bob to get arrested. After a rip roaring speech, he looked over to a group of us staffers as if to say, "Well, here goes." When he started walking toward the White House, I had no idea what to expect. The cameras followed Bob as he approached the gate.

"He is a stud," I told one of my colleagues, who quickly agreed. "I could never do that." It was great drama. From afar, none of us could really tell what was going on. In his torn-up jeans and leather jacket, Bob appeared to just be standing there at the front gate. We were too far away to hear what was being said.

"I'm here representing those people," Bob said, according to media reports and his own re-telling of the story. He pointed to the large crowd of protestors as he spoke. The folks at the White House knew full well who he was talking about. "All those Democrats," he continued. "And I want to be let in."

It was a classic Ney move. On the spot, he changed his mind about getting arrested. Instead of being a headline, he chose to became a champion for the steelworkers with the White House. The administration had no choice but to open their doors. The Congressman walked across the side lawn with a throng of screaming steelworkers behind him. Unfortunately, the President was out of town, so Bob spoke with several of the White House's top Congressional lobbyists. They told him they understood the steelworkers' concerns and wanted to help, but were not able to block the imports.

Bob was infuriated by their response. Nonetheless, he returned to a hero's welcome. The Congressman filled in the crowd and the news media on his meeting. He then reached out to Glyptis. Even during stressful and high-impact moments, Bob was able to keep things on a personal level. It was like his meeting in the White House was just another conversation to report to his union friend.

Bob's personal touch worked more often than not. But the approach had its downside. Speaker Gingrich's resignation was a prime example. For four years, the Congressman built a personal relationship with the Speaker. No one was a bigger fan of Gingrich than Bob. The decision to orient his professional ambitions around the Speaker was based on both Bob's personal affinity for Newt and the fact that Gingrich was the House's leader.

A similar approach had worked well for the Congressman in the past. By ingratiating himself with the House Speaker and Senate President when he was in the Ohio Legislature, Bob quickly leaped past others to acquire powerful positions. Bob's goal was to do the same with Gingrich. His efforts were both professional and personal. If there was a vote the Speaker needed, Ney made sure Gingrich knew of his actions. Bob also worked to ensure that the Speaker liked him personally. Sometimes, he went to outlandish lengths to succeed in his charm offensive.

One day, for instance, the Congressman was meeting with Gingrich in the Speaker's Capitol office. There were a handful of other Members there. Midway through the meeting, Gingrich told the assembled officials that his staff would be bringing in lunch for him. Seeing an opportunity, Bob quietly stood up and left the room as if he had an important phone call. He then slipped into the kitchen downstairs where the Speaker's meals were made. Bob then took out one of his business cards and wrote on the backside, "Don't you think Ney would make a great House Administration Chairman?"

Seeing one of the ladies preparing the Speaker's meal, Bob politely asked if he could put the note under the silver top that was used to cover the plate, and keep the food warm. That way, Ney figured, when the top was removed, the Speaker would see the note. The Congressman's plan worked perfectly. Midway through what Bob said was a contentious meeting, the Speaker's food arrived. As Gingrich removed the silver cover, Bob watched the Speaker read his note. He burst out in laughter.

"Ney, you are crazy," said the Speaker. "And we'll see about that chairmanship."

A few months later, Speaker Gingrich told Bob that he might be willing to support Ney's efforts for a chairmanship. We were pumped up by the news. With all of our eggs in the Gingrich basket, the future looked bright. Until the Speaker resigned. And we had to start all over again.

LATE 1999
WASHINGTON, DC

Mike and Jack

With the departure of Speaker Gingrich, House Majority Whip Tom DeLay became the most influential member of the Republican-led House of Representatives. Mike Scanlon was DeLay's Communications Director, and his closeness to the new House leader was on full display in Bob's back office. We focused on our next move.

It was mid-July and word had begun to spread that a member of the powerful Appropriations Committee was stepping down. Bob quickly mobilized a team to try to get himself put on the committee known around the Hill simply as, "Approps." The opening on the prominent check-writing panel provided the Congressman and me an early opportunity to increase our influence in Washington. And Scanlon was a crucial member of our team. He told us what House leadership was saying about the opening. He told us who else was running for the post, and shared with us his insight on how the final decision would be made. Bob was appreciative of the insight and advice.

"It is good to have a DeLay guy helping our cause," Ney said. We both knew that getting on Approps would be a big deal. It would dramatically increase Bob's ability to return money back to his district and stay in office.

Since every member interested in getting on the Appropriations Committee would talk with Scanlon's boss, we knew actually getting Congressman DeLay to openly support Bob was not going to happen. It wasn't in his interest to choose one member over another. But Bob worked him anyway. Because Bob was a Deputy Whip, one of those members charged with helping DeLay count votes and marshal bills through the House, Ney had a strong working relationship with the House leader.

From Texas, DeLay was known as, "The Hammer." His influence was derived from his hard-charging demeanor, his discipline and his political intelligence. If Gingrich was the visionary, DeLay was the implementer. He was a disciplinarian. He made the trains run on time. While DeLay's title was House Republican Whip, his responsibility was enforcing order in a closely aligned Congress. The Whip's success resulted from his innate ability to remain in tune with the elected officials he was charged with leading. Over time, DeLay's members learned to trust him implicitly. During his tenure as the Whip, the Republican leadership would never lose a meaningful vote on the floor of the House.

In keeping with his efforts to establish order, DeLay strongly believed in using the appropriations committee as a tool to get bills passed, and Members elected. "Need an extra vote for a bill?" DeLay would ask. "Put some money in an undecided members district. Got a Republican Congressman with bad poll numbers? Give them an appropriation to build a hospital or airport in their hometown." It was the DeLay way. Not that it was new. Buying votes is as old as the Congress. But some thought the Whip's use of the appropriations process was controversial. Others accused him of being hypocritical about his conservative beliefs. Not me.

DeLay believed in keeping the budget as small as possible, and then using the power of the purse to strengthen the majority. It was a different kind of politics than what I expected when I moved to Washington in 1995. But it was a style of politics that Bob and others had shown me was necessary if we wanted to keep the majority.

"Using the budget was how we kept the majority in the Statehouse when I was chairman," Bob said, said in reference to his leadership in the Ohio Legislature. "We had a one vote margin, so we funded projects all over the state that were mainly geared toward helping our Senators get re-elected."

Because of Bob's relationship with DeLay, Ney wasn't looking for Scanlon to help us convince his boss that the Congressman would be a good fit on the committee. DeLay already knew that. Instead, Bob wanted someone in the Whip's inner circle on the team to help us with the intangibles.

"We need to know what is really going on," Bob said. "We've got to have real-time information, and to have a friend in the room when DeLay is finally ready to make a move." Scanlon was our friend in the room.

He fit in with the culture of Ney World. Scanlon was gregarious, hard working and liked to party. He first met Bob and Bob's Deputy Chief of Staff during a Congressional retreat. When they got back to Washington, the two raved about "DeLay's press guy," and told me how Scanlon had won several thousand dollars playing cards and rolling dice at the get-together. Weeks later, at a Whip meeting, Bob introduced me to Scanlon, and we also became friends. Before long, we were playing cards together several times a month, usually in either Bob's office or in DeLay's Capitol office.

Because Scanlon ran the press operation for the most important member in the House of Representatives, he was a big-time player. And he knew it. All you had to do was ask him. That said, I admired the way Scanlon handled the press. He aggressively worked every angle to advance the interests of his boss, a man who was not very well liked by Washington's mainstream media.

The more we talked in Bob's office about the Appropriations Committee opening, the more Scanlon seemed willing to help. His access to information was crucial. And like DeLay, Scanlon believed in being proactive. When Bob suggested calling every Member in the conference to outline why he should be on the committee, Scanlon said he thought it was a good idea.

"Can't hurt," he said. "Since the final determination for the slot is technically a decision of many Members of the Republican team, talking to everyone we could would help cover our bases."

He also bluntly told us about the challenges he thought Bob faced moving up the ladder. Based on what he was hearing from other members and leadership staff, Scanlon said people knew Bob was a good politician, but they were worried about how close he was to the unions. In terms of the Approps slot specifically, Scanlon also said he had heard from a lot of other offices that the Midwest was already over-represented on the committee. "With all the Southern conservatives in leadership, putting me on Approps would provide us some regional balance," Bob joked in reply.

"What people don't understand is that if I don't vote with the unions sometimes, we'll have a five-vote majority instead of a six-vote majority," the Congressman said, referencing the increasingly narrow margin of votes between the majority and minority coalitions in the House. The fact six defections could bring down a bill was a daily reality for those of us involved in the legislative process.

"Because of my tough district, I know better than most how to keep this majority," Bob continued. His words would become the message we decided to lead with in our quest for the seat, along with the Congressman's experience as appropriations chairman in the Ohio Statehouse. Before long, Bob officially reached out to DeLay and the rest of the elected leadership. He also sent a letter to the Appropriations Chairman outlining his interest in being on the committee.

"I am writing this letter concerning a request to seek a position on the House Appropriations Committee," Bob's letter started. "I would like to take a minute to explain to you how I would be helpful for our caucus. As the former Chairman of the Finance and Appropriations Committee in the Ohio Senate, I know first-hand how finance and appropriation bills move through committee, the full legislature and are eventually signed into law," he continued. "As a member of the Appropriations Committee, I will work together with the leadership of the House and the leadership of the committee to keep our majority in Congress."

After sending the letter to the Chairman, our staff worked furiously to get Bob in personal contact with every Republican Member of the House Republican team. If Bob talked with a member, whether on the phone, at a bar or on the House floor, I marked it down. We then instantly sent them a copy of our letter. After four years of non-stop campaigning in the district, we didn't want there to be any confusion. Ney World was ready to play ball in Washington.

Bob and I waited for word on the committee. But none came. Over the next few months, our appropriations mission lingered. But it was never too far from my mind. The importance of the appropriations committee even came up during a visit to my old high school, when I was talking to a group of history students.

"What is the appropriations committee, and how does it work?" I asked. "Lets look back at World War II," I told the kids. "It starts with President Franklin Roosevelt. Midway through the war, the President sent word to the Congress requesting that the Chairman of the Senate Appropriations committee visit him in the White House. The appropriation chairman's name was Kenneth McKellar. He was from Tennessee," I continued. "When the chairman arrived, President Roosevelt told the Senator about the recent advances in science by people like Albert Einstein, and of our country's need to build an atomic bomb. It will be expensive, the president said. But we need to move quickly and quietly. We can't let our enemies find out about the project."

I loved telling the Atomic Bomb meets the Appropriations Committee story. Whether the kids liked it or not, I'm not sure. But I continued on.

"The project Roosevelt was talking abut was the Manhattan Project. It was one of the largest science projects in history," I continued.

"'How much money are we talking about?' McKellar asked Roosevelt. '$2 billion,' was the President's reply," I told the kids with a smile. "So then Senator McKellar tells President Roosevelt that he had both an answer for him, and a question." I pause.

"What do you want first Mr. President?' the Appropriations Chairman asked. What is the answer? Roosevelt replied. We can definitely do it," said the Senator. That is good, and what is your question?" the President then asked. Where exactly in Tennessee do you want to spend this $2 billion?"

I laughed out loud at my own story. I always did. At that point, I told the kids how that kind of, "You scratch my back and I'll scratch yours deal helped to win a war."

Such a deal was exciting to think about. Both Bob and I yearned for him to get on the Appropriations Committee. For months, we waited to hear what was going on. Finally, in early January, the open appropriations seat was given to a Democrat Member of Congress who agreed to switch parties and organize with the Republicans in the House. Scanlon, among others, gave us the heads up. DeLay had helped to coordinate the switch. In doing so, leadership took an offer from a member giving them something Bob could not match, another vote for the majority. We moved on.

With the loss of the Appropriations position, our efforts returned to Bob's previous goal, securing the Chairmanship of the House Administration Committee. It was the Chairmanship that Gingrich had promised to help Ney secure. But he was gone. Again, DeLay would be crucial to our efforts. So would Scanlon, who was also leaving.

Scanlon told me he was leaving the Hill to go make some money as a public relations professional at a large firm. In that context, he also offered to take me on a trip to the Commonwealth of Northern Mariana Islands. "Going on the trip would help me with one of my clients," he said. I told him I would have to ask Bob, but assumed it would be fine.

It was a timely offer. The Congressman was a big believer in trips. "They are a good way to learn, meet people and have fun," he said. Nonetheless, Bob had instituted a policy banning all staff travel during his first four years in office. He did not want a nasty story about some exotic trip to ruin his re-election chances. After his big 1998 election victory, however, the trip policy was abolished.

"Scanlon wants to take me to some islands in the Pacific," I told Bob. Without either of us knowing the specifics, the Congressman told me to go. Bob thought it was a good opportunity for the office to have me spend some quality time with Scanlon. In fact, he was so adamant about the point, he told me he would send somebody else if I didn't want to go. Without blinking, I told the Congressman I wanted to go on the trip. Island-hopping with Scanlon sounded more like a free vacation than work, except for the fact that I was getting paid to travel.

Before we left, Scanlon and I met with a senior DeLay staffer who was also accompanying us on the trip. The three of us talked in the Whip's Capitol office conference room. Scanlon said the official reason for the trip was to learn about the CNMI. The 4 small islands that made up the commonwealth had big transportation and labor issues, he said. "Having a Ney staffer who works for a guy on the Transportation Committee and is familiar with union issues makes perfect sense," Scanlon said.

"I'm sure it also helps you with your new job," I retorted. To which we all agreed.

It wasn't that Bob or I really cared what the official reason was for the trip. As long as there was some sort of official tie-in for the excursion, we were both happy to help Scanlon. Why wouldn't we? He was a friend who was helping us with DeLay. And taking me on a free trip.

Up until the minute before we took off, Scanlon was on his mobile phone. While we walked through the airport, he boisterously leaked pieces of news to a variety of reporters. Most of the information involved news from the elected leadership meeting earlier in the day. Scanlon's access to House decision-makers made it seem like he hadn't even left DeLay's office yet. His arrogance was fun to watch.

"Who takes care of you baby?" Scanlon asked one reporter. "Who is the man?" he asked another. Mike didn't stop talking until seconds before takeoff.

"*So this is how the other half lives,*" I thought, as we got situated in our first-class seats. The two of us practically had our own corner of the plane. The extra room was nice since we were looking at a long flight. Getting to the Marianas from DC required one layover in Texas and another one in Hawaii, before finally arriving in the islands.

Scanlon and I kicked back with a couple of bottles of red wine. We watched *Jerry McGuire*, a film in which the actor Tom Cruise plays a sports agent who has a client that likes yelling, "Show me the money!" The two of us quickly rallied around the line. High-fiving back and forth in our front row seats, we rowdily mimicked the phrase over and over. "Show me the money!"

As we drove toward our hotel, Scanlon's personality suddenly changed. He became a dreary, dispassionate version of himself. When our cabbie asked him what he did, Scanlon replied, "I'm a golf course developer." He then shot me a quick look as if to say, "No worries, it's cool." After we got out, he told me there was an election going on. "Jack is pretty controversial," Scanlon said. "And everyone is related somehow around here," he continued. "So you have to be careful."

"I get elections," I told him, still somewhat confused. *"This is Scanlon,"* I thought to myself. *"He is capable of saying anything."*

At the same time, his actions reminded me of how I would have been in Bob's district during an election. As I told Scanlon, "If someone from outside Eastern Ohio was coming in to visit during the campaign, I would want to control who knew about it too. I mean, it's a small island," I continued. "What, are there 70,000 people on the four islands?"

In the moment, what stuck out to me about our conversation was not Scanlon's politicking. It was the way he said the word, "Jack." His inflection suggested that this person Jack was pretty special. I made a mental note to follow up.

We pulled into our hotel in Saipan. The Hyatt Regency's resort-style rooms lined the silky white beaches of the Pacific. It was awesome. I stared out my room's window. The water seemed to be almost two-toned. There was a little bit of light blue water that directly surrounded the island. This was encircled by the larger swath of darker blue water which stretched as far as the eye could see.

"Jack can't meet with us today," Scanlon said. *"There was that inflection again,"* I noted. "He doesn't work on the Sabbath. But we will see him tomorrow," he continued. That is when it hit me. The Jack he was talking about was Jack Abramoff.

"I've heard of Abramoff," I told Scanlon. I was pretty sure I had met him during a DeLay function in the Capitol, but didn't feel confident enough to say that for sure.

"Jack is very close to Tom," Scanlon said, in reference to Abramoff's relationship with DeLay.

I was impressed. Enough to quickly boost my confidence.

"Yea, I think I met him in your office one time," I said.

"Probably," he replied.

"This is too good to be true," I told myself. Scanlon was touting how close this guy Abramoff was to DeLay, like the two were best friends. *"What a coup for us."* Connecting with another member of DeLay's inner circle was just what Ney World needed.

Scanlon and I walked to the beach from the hotel. The two of us talked and drank island cocktails for the next few hours. Despite all our card-playing and hanging out, we had never hung out together, just the two of us. Sitting under some palm trees and hand-made Tiki Huts, the former DeLay aide told how me had played tennis against Andre Agassi as a kid, and continued working as a lifeguard, despite his busy political life. He also told me that he was hearing a lot of talk about Bob's future in the House. "It is bright," Scanlon said. The words were good to hear. I followed up the compliment by telling Scanlon how conservative the Congressman was, and how much he admired DeLay and his entire staff. I don't know who was trying to impress whom more, but both Scanlon and I seemed intent on telling the other person what he wanted to hear.

The next morning, Scanlon, DeLay's staffer and I toured the islands. They were beautiful, and contained some amazing history. We saw where the Enola Gay took off before dropping the first atomic bomb on Hiroshima at the end of World War II. We saw the Spanish architecture that remained from the days of Spain's rule over the region. So close to Asia, the commonwealth gave me a whole new perspective on the west coast and the Pacific island regions of our country.

At each stop, I was introduced as Bob Ney's Chief of Staff who sits on the Transportation Committee. Since we were touring ports and airport runways, Scanlon's sales pitch made sense. In many ways, it even reminded me of previous visits to Ney's home district for meetings with local economic development officials. But the more Scanlon paraded me around like a prize poodle, the more scripted everything felt. Being a pawn for my friend, instead of working for our constituents, made me feel uneasy. It was what I would later call a red flag moment.

The moment didn't last too long. Within a few hours, my feelings changed. After numerous introductions, I asked myself, *"Why should I care if I feel like a pawn? I'm using Mike too. Not to mention, helping Bob gain power is the same thing as helping his constituents."* It was a complete 180 degree turn in mindset. *"If they want to look good, great. I'll help. We're all on the same side. The Republican side. The side of Ney and DeLay. Don't worry about it."*

From then on out I stopped worrying about being Scanlon's showpiece. In fact, I learned to like it. The more important he made me sound, the more the local officials I met sucked up to me. It was like we were a team. "Mike is great," I would say. "He is a killer. I am happy to help." And on and on.

The next day I golfed with Jack. Abramoff loved to golf. The first thing he told me was how excited he was to get on the course.

With the Pacific Ocean waters crashing into the deep rock walls framing the Kingfisher Golf Course, Jack and I got to know each other. It started with some small talk about the course. He told me how Japanese businessmen flew to the CNMI to avoid the high Tokyo-area prices.

"So it is cheaper to fly back and forth to the Marianas than it is to play golf in Japan?" I asked incredulously.

"Either that or they are really stupid over there," Jack replied.

His response made me laugh.

The more time I spent with him the more Jack's wit reminded me of the comedian Jerry Seinfeld. He seemed to be able to talk about anything. And nothing.

"Bob is great," Jack said as if he knew the Congressman. "We were in the College Republicans together," he continued.

"Cool," I replied, thinking the trip was going to be even better for us than we initially presumed. I couldn't remember if Bob ever mentioned anything to me about Abramoff. But since the Congressman had been in the College Republicans, I went with it. Why not?

When Scanlon and Abramoff were together, Jack's humor transformed from that of a stand-up comedian to the main player in a comedy duo. The two poked fun at each other constantly. As Scanlon and Jack harassed each other on the course, we played a game called Wolf, a game built around stalking the other players. It led to even more sarcastic banter. I loved the camaraderie.

With us on the course was a representative from the garment manufacturing industry. Nearly everyone I talked with while I was on the islands said the textile business was the CNMI's most important sector of the economy. My pre-trip research showed the same thing. The foundation of the local garment manufacturer's business model was an exemption in the law governing immigration policy for the CNMI. The loophole allowed island businesses to ship in workers from throughout Asia without being required to pay them the minimum wage. Several multi-national corporations took advantage of the regionally based quirk in the law to set up textile operations in the CNMI. Outside of tourism, these companies became one of the few large-scale job producers in the area.

The golf course was the perfect environment for Jack to pitch me on the island's importance to the Republican Congress. His promotion was built around the idea that the same "us vs. them" battle that was occurring on Capitol Hill, was also occurring in the CNMI. "It is a microcosm of the battle between liberals and conservatives," Jack said. I listened intently.

"We're the good guys," he said, lumping me in with he and his CNMI colleagues. "We are on the side of free markets and capitalism. They are on the side of big government and economic decline. If liberals in Washington were able to successfully take over this far-away island's economy, then the prospering garment manufacturing industry would fall apart," Jack said. "By making local businesses pay a minimum wage vastly higher than any of their neighbors, people would be hurt," he continued.

Telling me he would work for the islands for free if he could, Jack's clarion call against any changes to the CNMI's immigration status made sense to me. Not that I was in the mood to argue, or really cared that much. In my mind, as long as the CNMI wasn't dumping steel, we were going to be just fine. After all, I wasn't on the trip to crusade for anything but Bob Ney's interests.

Jack picked up on my indifference.

"These guys just don't get it," he said in reference to the island officials I met during my stay. "They want to book you on tour after tour," Jack said. "Obviously, we have to do some of that. But what better way is there to build relationships than on a golf course? We fly hundreds of staffers here. It is always like this. They want staff to do a bunch of official stuff. But I tell them no." I liked Jack, and his comments made me like him even more. They were real.

"Do you guys want to have friends on the Hill who can help you?" he said he told the island officials. "Or do you want to make enemies by boring them to death with your official presentations and tours?"

I laughed, and couldn't have agreed more. From my perspective, his advice seemed imminently practical. Time with Abramoff and Scanlon was more valuable to mine and Bob's and my interests than any meeting we could have attended. Getting to know those two meant building two more champions for Bob in Majority Whip DeLay's inner circle. Cultivating those relationships was crucial. Of course, I wasn't the only one doing the cultivating. Scanlon and Jack were cultivating me, too.

The Congressional Record

For the last few years, my colleagues and I in Ney World advanced several important goals. We fought for those steel communities being battered by unfair trade practices, for a stalled conservative revolution, and to personally gain influence in Washington. Helping Mike Scanlon was a part of that effort. In a unique twist of fate, these goals merged and reached a crescendo as the 2000 election approached.

With Bob's victory assured, our team's campaign efforts focused on races outside of the Congressman's district. Our hope for everything from a Ney chairmanship to a transformed federal government depended on keeping the House Republican majority. During the last two years, Bob had traveled to help candidates in their districts, made himself available to offices in need of campaign assistance and met his fundraising quota for the party. As the election neared, we redoubled those efforts. That meant raising even more money and helping even more candidates. We cut last-minute checks from Bob's political account, and team members of Ney World were dispatched to work on campaigns throughout the country.

Our efforts to keep the House majority were intertwined with our efforts to get Texas Governor George W. Bush elected president. Bob and I knew that a strong Republican presidential candidate on the top of the ticket would help Republicans running for the House. Increasing our influence in Congress was dependent on a GOP majority. But there was more at work than just gaining power. As the election neared, we also began to see that a potential political deal was possible between the steel communities of the Ohio Valley and the Bush campaign. It was a time of action, a time to use that power.

The 2000 campaign was the last election during the Clinton

administration. For me, this represented a big change. I was thirty years old, and Bill Clinton had been the only president in my Washington life. Picturing a new person in the White House wasn't easy. It was especially hard to imagine that person being Vice President Al Gore, who was running to replace President Clinton. Still, as close as the race was, anything seemed possible. Heading into the final week of the campaign, there were still a handful of states that could go for either Governor Bush or Vice President Gore. These tossup races would determine the presidency. Key congressional elections also hung in the balance.

Weeks earlier in Ohio, the Vice President's campaign pulled their television advertisements from most of the state's media markets. The move was a major concession. It was not a concession that Gore's campaign was giving up completely on the Buckeye State. Polling clearly had the Vice President within striking distance. But it was a concession that the Gore campaign was low on money, and other states, like West Virginia and Florida, were higher priorities.

For those of us in Ney World, Gore's decision to de-emphasize Ohio meant focusing on motivating voters for Governor Bush across the Ohio river in West Virginia. The race between Gore and Bush was even closer there. The transition was seamless. Bob and our staff were very familiar with the Mountaineer State. The Congressman shared a media market with the Wheeling area, knew steel and coal leaders throughout the region, and had a cultural connection with much of the state. Additionally, the Ney team had been working for months to help a Republican Congressional challenger in West Virginia, a woman named Shelly-Moore Capito. Moore-Capito was a skilled politician who was on the verge of adding another seat to the House Republican majority.

Since Bob was one of the few Congressional Republicans with any ties to the region, our willingness to help was immediately appreciated by the Bush team. My phone rang off the hook. Emails rolled in. As much as anything, the campaign wanted to talk about what was going on in steel country. With the Clinton administration continuing to oppose any move that involved closing the domestic steel market to imports, the steel crisis in the Ohio Valley had worsened over time. And the Gore campaign was paying the political price for those decisions.

The rules governing my interaction with the Bush campaign again impacted how I conducted myself during the election. As long as my conversations with the Bush campaign were about things like scheduling and public policy, communicating on my government email was generally appropriate.

In contrast, I was advised that I could talk with them about any aspect of the campaign via my private email account. Over time, therefore, all my conversations with the campaign moved to my private email. Why wouldn't they?

In large part because of the steel crisis, Governor Bush was running neck and neck with Vice President Gore in West Virginia, a state where no non-incumbent Republican presidential candidate had won since before Franklin Roosevelt in 1932. The Bush campaign scoured through our records for material. With a full press and paid media push, they amplified Bob's local attacks on Gore. In addition to steel, the Congressman blasted the Vice President's support for gun control and anti-coal environmental regulations. Gore's policies might have been popular elsewhere, but in rural coal country they added weight to the steel anchor already pulling him down. As close as the presidential election was across the country, we all knew a swing in West Virginia's five electoral votes could very well make the difference between a Bush and Gore presidency. Likewise, picking up an additional Congressional seat in West Virginia would undoubtedly bolster our efforts at keeping our House majority - and securing a Ney chairmanship.

Because of the fluid political situation, talk of a steel deal began to reverberate through the Bush campaign. It was what Bob had been pushing for weeks. For months. "You want their votes, give them what they want," he said. "Stop the dumping." Such discussions were not unusual. Campaigns have them all the time. Expand your coalition of supporters through your public policy decisions. Or as Bob said, "We'll protect your jobs, you give us your votes." It was a simple deal, an acceptable and perfectly legal bribe.

"Who in the steel community should we contact?" I was asked by one of the Bush campaign's regional directors. "Do you think it is a good idea for Secretary Cheney to visit Weirton to talk steel?" asked another operative. "If so, what should we include in his speech?"

For nearly three years, the steel crisis had been a job debilitating slow-grind. Weirton, the epicenter of the crisis, remained a devastated town. According to some reports, nearly a third of Weirton's steelworkers were now without work. And yet suddenly, during a high-stakes political campaign, hope for a better future appeared in the form of Vice Presidential candidate Dick Cheney.

The former Secretary of Defense spoke to several hundred steelworkers in front of a massive American flag. It was a typical campaign event. The enormous flag hung from the outstretched arm of a large, local crane. A truck entrance to a local steel plant provided the rest of the backdrop for the gathered crowd. Listening intently, many of the steelworkers kept their hard hats on through the speech. Cheney started by saying he wasn't there to tell the people of West Virginia that everything would be fine. Or that they would agree fundamentally with the free-trade policies of a potential Bush administration. But he did talk about how important steel was for national security, and how vital a strong industrial base was for the manufacture of ships, planes and guns.

He then touched upon President Clinton's 1992 visit to Weirton, and the promise to look out for steelworkers. Everyone in attendance was aware of the history. The removal of the president's picture from the union hall. The rally in Washington. With typical Cheney calmness, he told them, "We can't always tell you what you want to hear, but we will never lie to you." The crowd applauded wildly. "If our trading partners violate trade laws, we will respond swiftly and firmly," Cheney continued. "We will enforce our trade laws," he promised. "There will be no more looking the other way." The speech was a political home run. It also locked the Bush-Cheney team in to a high-profile promise that much of Ohio, Pennsylvania and West Virginia would be watching for years to come.

While Cheney was in West Virginia for his speech, I was in Washington working on a myriad of other projects. One involved working with the party to put out a press release attacking Gore for his stance on coal. It contained some hard-hitting quotes by Bob. Another project was one we were working on for Mike Scanlon. This one involved submitting a statement on Scanlon's behalf into the *Congressional Record*.

The *Congressional Record* is the official record of the United States Congress. The record is printed every day and includes a transcript of the day's floor debates, committee activity and what are called, "Extension of Remarks." These remarks are found in the back of the record, after the day's summary of speeches and debate. Extension of Remarks include everything from local congratulatory tributes to random political statements that Members of Congress want to submit for whatever reason.

Since as far back as his days in the state legislature, Bob used such remarks in the record to congratulate local 4H students, area churches and winning football teams. He also used them to express his personal views on certain topics.

The topic of Scanlon's submission request was a set of boat-based casinos in Florida called SunCruz Casinos. It was his second Suncruz-related *Congressional Record* request. Six months earlier, Bob and I placed a similar statement into the *Record* on behalf of Congressman DeLay's former spokesman. As such, when Scanlon approached me to see if Ney would be willing to submit another statement on SunCruz into the *Congressional Record*, the concept and topic wasn't new. But time was tight.

In March, when we received Scanlon's first request, Bob and I knew he was asking for us to help one of his gambling-related clients. Which one, I didn't know. Nor did I really care. After Bob said he was cool with helping Scanlon, the specifics of why our friend was asking didn't matter to me nearly as much as what was in the statement. From my perspective, the statement needed to make sense from Bob's point of view. And from the point of view of a potential inquiring reporter or political opponent. *It was like a powerful constituent asking us to submit a statement celebrating his daughter's science project award*, I told myself. *As long as the science project wasn't an analysis of how to end coal production, we would just do it.*

Therefore, I told Scanlon to write something up so the Congressman could see it. "Whatever you give me needs to include what you want in the submission," I told Mike. "It also needs to include a reference to Bob's district and Bob's agnostic view on gaming. We need something to hang our hat on, just in case a reporter asks us why Bob submitted the statement," I continued.

Scanlon got to work and gave me his proposal a couple of days later. The gist of his request was for Bob to question the actions of the owner and operator of SunCruz Casinos, a man named Gus Boulis. To bolster his case, Scanlon brought over some articles from Florida newspapers outlining how and why the Florida Attorney General was investigating the cruise line.

I looked it over, and then passed it on to Bob and our Deputy Chief of Staff in the district. They also looked through the material. From my point of view, I was content, knowing that the submission included Bob's view on gaming, a mention of his home state and some sort of verifiable information. Ultimately, only one opinion mattered in Ney World, and that was Bob's. His only concern was specifically mentioning Boulis by name.

"Ask Scanlon if he really wants that," Bob told me. So I did.

"I will take whatever you give us," Mike said, before telling me he very much was hoping that the Congressman could keep the name Gus Boulis in the document.

Bob agreed to do so. "It's Scanlon," we both said.

In the back of that day's *Congressional Record*, the Congressman ripped into our friend's target. "Mr. Speaker, how SunCruz Casinos and Gus Boulis conduct themselves with regard to Florida laws is very unnerving.

Florida authorities have repeatedly reprimanded SunCruz Casinos and its owner Gus Boulis for taking illegal bets, not paying their customers properly and had to take steps to prevent SunCruz from conducting operations altogether."

Boulis called the office the next day. Bob said he wasn't surprised. When Boulis asked for the Congressman, Ney told me to call the casino owner back. I did. The casino owner was appalled and confused as to why an Ohio Congressman would be so interested in his cruise line. Boulis was nervous, and said he was working on improving their operation. He also asked me where we had heard about Suncruz. I told him we read about it in the paper, and pulled out the newspapers Scanlon had dropped off at the office. Telling somebody I didn't know that we were really just helping a lobbyist friend wasn't something I was going to say. That kind of comment would make Bob look horrible in the papers and get me in trouble with my boss.

The first Boulis *Congressional Record* statement ran in March. Seven months later, Scanlon was back for more. This time he was hoping we would submit a statement in the *Congressional Record* praising the new owner of Suncruz Casinos, a man named Adam Kidan. No one in Ney World knew Kidan from a hole in the wall, though by that point he had attended a fundraiser for Bob in one of Jack Abramoff's sports suites. The Congressman and I undoubtedly met and talked with Kidan at the event. But we did a lot of events and made small talk with a lot of people. As far as Bob and I were concerned, Kidan was just a part of "Scanlon's event." That isn't to diminish Kidan, nor suggest that I should have remembered him. Who he was didn't even register. Scanlon was the face of the project. And by that point a good friend.

After the Marianas' trip, Scanlon and I had continued to hang out. We played golf, went to sporting events and partied. And like similar lobbyist relationships I had at the time, he paid for it all. Still, because of his prominence in the DeLay operation and his fun-loving demeanor, Scanlon remained special. My pre-wedding Washington bachelor party exemplified this. Ney, Scanlon and the rest of the guys took me downtown for an evening of revelry. This led to us getting kicked out of several of DC's best strip clubs. Instead of calling it a night, we took the party back to Mike's $17,000 a month Ritz Carlton loft. It was a great time. But it also represented a life on the edge. I was changing. I was pushing the margins in my life to the side, and getting comfortable looking past the rules, regulations and morality that I had been raised to follow. For staffers like me, there was a ban on gifts that cost more than fifty dollars, and public reporting requirements that I was supposed to follow. I rarely did. And my impression was that a lot of other staffers behaved in a similar manner.

Nothing brought the regular crowd of Scanlon and Volz colleagues together like playing cards. Making up our late-night clique of card players were Republican staffers, Republican lobbyists and Capitol Hill reporters. Whether we were gathering information or developing relationships, all of us benefited from the games. In that way, the card playing was work. More than anything, though, it was fun.

A venomous combination of male competitiveness, professional ambition and personal vanity fueled our games. On many occasions, the pot for our games grew beyond a thousand dollars. Several times it surpassed five thousand dollars. For the congressional staffers and reporters especially, that was a lot of money. But we liked playing with an edge. IOUs were written on the backs of business cards in lieu of paying with cash or writing a check. We staffers used to wonder where the reporters got their money to play, and we assumed that they were skeptical of us as well. But the payment system always seemed to operate above board.

Bob joined in the card playing whenever he could. Since our group generally got together when Congress wasn't in session, however, he was usually in Ohio when we played. Also, when Bob joined the festivities, the crowd tended to stay on their best behavior. The Congressman hated that. Not that he ever said anything. He didn't have to. Being his chief of staff for two years had taught me to read him pretty well. I watched everything. I listened. He was the sun in my professional solar system. I took special pride in realizing where the Congressman was going to end up on an issue before he did.

I learned about my new job responsibilities as quickly as possible. Some areas I already knew. Others were new to me, such as fundraising. Like the nuanced conversations between reporters and press secretaries during campaign season, there was a code associated with making fundraising calls for the Congressman. For example, I was not allowed to proactively solicit contributions from the office for Bob. But I could walk across the street to the phone booth section of party headquarters and call anyone I wanted. Unlike the similar reporter situation, if someone called me back at the office, I still could not ask for money. However, I could talk about a fundraising event the Congressman was having, since that pertained to his schedule. Therefore, if a lobbyist or some other supporter called to RSVP for Bob's event, we knew we were talking about a donation to the Congressman - without actually talking about a donation. Saying, "I'll be at the event," instead of, "I have money for Bob," was a pretty easy distinction to learn.

Engaging in such nuanced fundraising conversations required both the donor and the recipient to learn the code. This new code covered for the fact that neither a contributor nor recipient was supposed to directly associate a political contribution with an official government act, yet allowed most fundraising calls to include conversations about money and legislative activity at the same time. To dance around the restrictions, fundraising conversations were usually couched in terms of relationship building, district-based issues and the achievement of political goals - in contrast to specific legislative goals.

The discussions also tended to revolve around the needs of the employees of the company or union making the donation rather than the result of any contribution. Words like, "I've got ten local banks in Ohio interested in this bill," or, "We have 750 employees in your district concerned about what is happening," were a far more appropriate way to discuss a specific piece of legislation than to say, "I am paying $2,000 to come talk with the Congressman at his fundraiser." Yet the action associated with the contribution symbolized the same fact: paying for access is a totally legal activity.

For me, such nuances were frustrating. The lines seemed to be everywhere, and then nowhere. For instance, many of my chief of staff colleagues carried two separate mobile phones with them. One was for fundraising and one was for their government work. This meant one phone was paid by campaign monies and the other by the taxpayer. "Call me on the other phone," became a common refrain for those staffers. Bob and I scoffed at such practices. "Why is that the hoop to jump through?" we would ask. In an environment where it is entirely appropriate for a constituent to send $50 or $150 in cash to the Congressman with a note thanking him for voting one way or another, clearly all fundraising was not the same. So we searched out our own lines. Was there really a line between the Congressman, the person, and the Congressman, the cause? If so, where was that line? And did the situation matter? As I was learning, engaging in the energetic give and take of public debate meant sometimes living in the grey zone. Or in my case, the edge of the grey zone.

Some of the change I was dealing with was more personal in nature. At the beginning of my tenure as the top staffer in Ney World, Bob's retiring chief of staff pulled me aside. He told me my relationship with Bob and the office was about to change. And that the change would be dramatic. "There is another side to Bob," he said. "He has an angry perfectionism and controlling impulse you have to watch. When Bob is drinking it can be a real problem." His words surprised me. I drank with the Congressman three or four times a week and had barely seen hints of a temper. "Just be ready for it," he said.

The new dynamic shocked me. Despite living with Bob for three years before I became chief of staff, I soon learned that our old chief of staff was right. Behind the Congressman's jovial and intelligent public persona was a controlling and melodramatic political shark. Bob kept an internal catalog of personal and professional failures on every staffer in Ney World. Few days went by when he did not peruse the catalog and want to fire one or more of our employees. I didn't know how to deal with this compartmentalized rage. That side of Bob usually came out late in the evening after lots of drinking. Perfectly enjoyable dinners with constituents or lobbyists would turn into a seething spew of anger after our guests and the rest of the staff left. We would re-live that anger in the morning, until Bob ate breakfast, at which point, the fun-loving, fair and self-deprecating Congressman returned. The cycle quickly became part of my new routine.

Like always, I learned to adapt. Certain decisions and people were blocked out from what those of us in the know called, "the hot zone." Staff meetings were scheduled for right after breakfast. But mostly I learned to adapt by putting myself in Bob's shoes. Like me, he, too, was living his dream, and keeping that dream going meant living with a lot of pressure. I commiserated with him about the pressure and rallied around our shared dreams. His anxiety about a lack of control over events impacting our office was an anxiety I carried with me too. Like Bob, my need for control was balanced out by my enjoyment of the drama. The same could be said about our professional perfectionism. Neither of us wanted someone else's mistakes to get in the way of our ambitions. Mostly, though, we shared a fear of failure. In a town of winners and losers, our ultimate fear was becoming a loser.

Bob saw my fear-driven ambition during the competition for his chief of staff position. The internal battle for the top staff spot in Ney World came down to a campaign between two of my colleagues and me. Competing against me were our Legislative Director and Campaign Manager. I wanted the job so badly, sometimes it seemed like that was all I thought about. My desire to become Chief of Staff fueled my daily ambition. The win. The title. The power. I wanted it all. Similar to Bob's desire for the chairmanship, my drive for the Chief of Staff position was relentless and passionate.

One night, the Congressman hinted that I might get the job. "But I'm not sure," he said. "It is going to be a tough decision," Bob continued, telling me what he probably told the other two as well. As the decision approached, the Congressman revealed to me that he was starting to lean against one of the other two candidates. Because this staffer and his wife had decided to attend a couple of weddings that year, Bob said he began questioning his commitment to the office. It was an election year after all.

I took his comments as a test - a test of my commitment to him, our office, and our shared ambition. Since I had a wedding in Chicago to attend days before the election, which the Congressman knew about, it was hard to take Bob's comments any other way. The wedding was important to me. Two good friends were getting married. Also, my fiancée, Alison, was in the wedding party. The event was important to us as a couple. Nonetheless, I cancelled at the last minute. "The Congressman needs me in the district," I said. Days later, Bob told me I had the job. The new post was a fulfillment of my desire, hard work and ambition. It was also just the beginning.

If Election Day went well, Bob and I planned to transition into a full-scale campaign for the chairmanship of the House Administration Committee. Bob had a good shot at securing the post. Since the current chairman was term limited, a new chairman would be named after the election. DeLay's office and the Speaker's office would be key. So would being able to show that we had done everything necessary to protect the majority. One way of showing that was by meeting our fundraising targets for the Republican party. Members of the House Republican team who were in a position to help were encouraged to raise money for their colleagues in close races, and to help win new seats. Everyone benefited by working together.

Scanlon knew that process as well as anyone. He also knew how hard we were working for the chairmanship. Therefore, when Scanlon asked me if a $10,000 check for the Republican Party would be helpful to meeting our fundraising goals, while also asking me if Bob would submit another statement in the *Congressional Record*, I told him yes, a check would definitely be helpful to our chairmanship goals. Even though Bob had already met his quota, adding $10,000 to the Ney ledger over at the party would improve the overall number we would be pointing to while making our case for the chairmanship in a few weeks. Of course, the dollar figure paled in comparison to the million dollar event Bob was co-hosting for the party in Columbus the next day.

The last-minute contribution to the party was also good for Scanlon. Being a good operator, Scanlon knew it was in his best interest to also take credit for the check over at party headquarters. Members of Congress weren't the only ones who needed to continually show their party loyalty. Republican lobbyists and consultants needed to, as well.

The problem with my conversation with Scanlon was the directness in which we discussed his contribution as it related to our second *Congressional Record* submission, the one mentioning the new owner of SunCruise Casinos. Instead of going back and forth on potential drafts, like we did on the first *Congressional Record* statement, I quickly put Scanlon and me on the phone with Bob to talk through the matter. We talked about the statement, we talked about the campaign and we talked about the contribution. The conversation was short and sweet. There was no time to waste. Nor was there some direct "do this for that" linkage of the statement to the contribution - not in words at least.

Nonetheless, Bob told Scanlon he would submit the statement. When the Congressman and I talked moments later, however, Bob seemed nervous. It was just the two of us on the phone, for probably our tenth or fifteenth call of the day. We were two weeks away from an election.

I read Bob the statement again. "Do you really think we should do this?" he asked me when I finished. His response was a surprise. Bob rarely second-guessed a decision.

"Why wouldn't we?" I asked. "We did the first one." He gave his final go-ahead.

Bob's unease was definitely a red flag moment. Talking about the money for the party and the *Congressional Record* statement in the same moment was awkward. We shouldn't have done it. Professional fundraising conversations are normally geared toward avoiding such direct connections between money and official activity, even when a direct connection exists. Combined with the fact that we went from slamming one owner to praising another, neither of whom we knew, I couldn't help but feel like I was crossing into new territory. Instead of saying something, though, I remained quiet.

It was only a couple of sentences, a slight sliver of the day, but by failing to cultivate the apprehension Bob was feeling, I let both of us down. He deserved better from me. I should have asked him why he was nervous. Who knows what would have happened if we had just slowed down and talked further. Bob may have made a different decision. But we didn't, and the Congressman gave the order.

Convincing myself that we were somehow adhering to a higher calling than the simplicity of doing the right thing in the moment, the allure of Bob becoming a chairman had become all-consuming. I knew that getting the chairmanship would mean that Bob could better help his constituents. It also meant more power for me and the Congressman. The chairmanship, therefore, became the ultimate rationalization. It was almost like anything was acceptable if it had to do with the worthy goal of getting the chairmanship.

Engrossed in my own ambition and loyalty to Bob, winning the new post was everything, no matter what. In an effort to separate myself and the cause of Bob Ney from the rest of the competition, I pushed my life further and further to the edge. Whether it was partying and cards or my professional aspirations, the relentless rush from failure chipped away at any sense of margin I had in my life.

If my day-to-day existence were a formatted document on a computer, the admittedly nuanced rules of life and the regulations of politics would have existed along the paper's margins, margins meant to keep me comfortably in compliance with my own sense of right and wrong, as well as with the law. Under that theory, a step over the line, or outside the margins, could put me out of compliance, but not so far out of compliance that I couldn't get back in good standing. Life on the edge, however, didn't provide that much margin for error. Whether my decision to help Scanlon with his *Congressional Record* submission was my last step before the edge, or my first step off the edge, I'm not sure. But something had changed. I was becoming corrupt.

Election Day

NEY WORLD CELEBRATED ANOTHER ELECTION victory at Undo's Restaurant. Bob's race was not even close. In contrast, the race for the presidency was as close as any presidential race in history. I went to bed election night thinking Governor George W. Bush had been elected President of the United States, but wasn't sure. Only a couple thousand votes separated the two candidates in the state of Florida.

Nationally, as it stood on the night of the election, Bush was ahead of Vice President Gore 271-266 in the Electoral College. His victory in West Virginia appeared to have been crucial. Of course, a protracted battle in the Sunshine State loomed.

In the House, we lost a total of one seat. The narrowest House margin in decades got even narrower, going from a margin of 223-211, to 222-212. Five votes now separated us from the minority. Again, the race in West Virginia had been crucial. Congresswoman-elect Capito's victory helped to save us from a four-seat majority.

In the Senate, the GOP margin dropped to 50-50. That meant incoming Vice President Cheney's vote to break ties in the upper chamber represented the margin between a Republican and a Democratic majority.

Because of the closeness of the presidential race, pundits declared the United States a red nation and a blue nation, "a country divided." Yet, in Washington, Republicans were poised to run a unified Congress and White House.

January 19, 2001
Washington, DC

Chairman Ney

AFTER THE 2000 ELECTIONS, BOB was named chairman of the House Administration Committee. Once again, my flight pattern was taking a major turn. Our hard work had paid off. Ney was getting a gavel.

While most of Washington was focused on George W. Bush's upcoming presidential inauguration, the Chairman and I focused on putting our new team together. There was a lot of work ahead of me. I needed to hire new staffers, move into new office space and learn a new role. It was a major move for Bob to have a gavel, and both of us were ecstatic.

In the House of Representatives, there were 19 full committees. Only 19 of the 435 Members had committee gavels. As the first member of his class to join such elite company, Bob's ascent was impressive. Again, he decided to bring me along for the ride by naming me the committee's top staffer. In doing so, he made me the youngest Staff Director on Capitol Hill. Both of our stars' were on the rise.

As the title would suggest, the House Administration is the committee responsible for administering the internal operations of the House of Representatives. This included everything from the House cafeterias and parking garages to the Library of Congress and the Smithsonian. Our oversight responsibilities stretched from the House computer systems and building maintenance to Capitol Hill security. We were also responsible for administering the office budgets of each individual member of Congress, in addition to those of the other congressional committees. That meant if an office had a question about whether they could spend money on a particular service or product, they needed to call us for approval. It was the ultimate insider's committee. Because of that, people quickly started referring to Bob as, "The mayor of Capitol Hill."

House Administration also had a public policy portfolio. Since we oversaw the Federal Election Commission, any legislation that involved the financing of political campaigns or the administration of federal elections fell under my committee's jurisdiction. Since Bob had served on the committee for the last six years, we both knew that the committee was not normally a busy legislative committee. We also knew that this cycle looked to be different.

With the controversy surrounding the 2000 presidential campaign, the Speaker told Bob and me that passing a bill to fix some of the vote-counting problems which had come to light during the protracted election debate in Florida needed to be one of the committee's top priorities. Many people in the country were questioning the legitimacy of President Bush's election. "Not responding to the contentious voting dispute in Florida would be a mistake," Speaker Hastert said, in one of our first meeting with the Speaker. "The direction you take is up to you," he continued. "But something needs to be done to alleviate the ill-will in the House, and the country."

Bob told the Speaker, "We are already on it," which we were. Both of us had reached out to numerous election professionals to get their advice in preceding days. But now, with the Speaker giving us our orders, it was the real thing. The Chairman and I bounded out of Hastert's Capitol office and down the main hallway that runs out to Statuary Hall and the Rotunda.

The two of us darted down the spiral staircase that took us to the ground floor of the Capitol. I felt incredibly blessed to think that these new Capitol walkways would soon become a regular part of my day.

Having been a committee chairman in the Ohio Senate, Bob knew as well as anyone that committees were the lifeblood of the Congress. They are where the work of passing laws is done. The process is pretty simple. In the House, when a bill is introduced by a Member of Congress, it is then given to the committee with jurisdiction over that specific issue. From there, the chairman of the committee decides what to do next. Before a bill is voted on by the full House, it is either debated, formulated, voted out of committee, or the chairman can decide to do nothing with the bill. In many respects, therefore, committees are like a mini-Congress within the Congress, with the Chairman playing the role of Speaker.

A lot of work and luck had gone into Bob's successful effort to get the chairmanship. What had started as a promise from Speaker Gingrich had turned into a multiple-year courtship of Majority Whip DeLay. Getting DeLay's approval then put us through to the final test, Speaker Hastert. Whether Bob would ultimately get the job or not had been up to the

Speaker and his senior staff. This led to several intense weeks of work after the election.

Before the Speaker's staff made their decision, the Congressman and I had visited the Hastert's office several times to discuss the committee with his top lieutenants. Half the time the conversations felt like a job interview. The other half felt like a theoretical chalkboard exercise on how the committee should run. Our meetings were like a crash course on the insular world of Capitol operations - a world that included more that 10,000 employees. We discussed the role of the Government Printing Office and its several thousand employees. We talked about how much input the average member of Congress should have on decisions involving the Capitol Building, the Library of Congress and the security of the entire complex. We also tiptoed around the drama surrounding the ongoing animosity between the current House Administration chairman and the Speaker's staff.

Having been a committee member and his staffer for six years, Bob and I were well aware of the anger between the current Chairman's staff and the Speaker's staff. The Committee staff pre-dated the Speaker's staff, and much of the unease involved the simple fact that Speaker Hastert's team wanted to be more involved in the internal operations of the House than Speaker Gingrich's staff had been. It was a classic turf battle. Many of the senior staffers on both sides didn't speak to each other. At the same time, they all maintained that they were there to serve the institutional interests of the House of Representatives.

For those reasons and more, the discussions Bob and I had with the Speaker's staff were a balancing act. On one hand, with DeLay and most of the leadership supportive of Bob's efforts, the environment around the Speaker gave him every incentive to give Ney the gavel. On the other hand, we knew if we gave the Speaker's staff a reason to choose someone else, they probably could convince the Speaker to follow their advice. The foul relationship between the Speaker's staff and the previous chairman convinced us that it was important to show Hastert's office that we were team players.

The Congressman turned on the charm. For several weeks, he focused like a laser on keeping the Speaker's staff laughing, informed and enjoying their time with the down-to-earth guy who asked to simply be called, "Bob." Compared to the dysfunctional communication they were dealing with at the time, it must have seemed almost heavenly. Bob's plan was working.

"It is like being a substitute teacher in reverse," he said to me about the meetings. "In the classroom, you can go from tough to nice, but not the other way around. Here, we have to start with nice." Which is exactly what we did.

Several times, Bob was asked if he would support certain changes. Not surprisingly, most of the proposed changes would take power away from the committee and give it to the Speaker's staff. He agreed with some minor changes and disagreed with others. The one major issue we kept dancing around involved the committee's authority for pre-approval of certain expenditures and new-hires within the House-side of the Capitol complex. Controlling the flow of money and people was a huge source of power for the committee.

Instead of telling the Speaker's guys he was opposed to changing that policy, Bob said he thought the idea sounded interesting. He even went so far as to say he was open to the concept if it meant the House would run more smoothly. Basically, the Congressman got as close to saying yes as he could without actually saying the word. It was a virtuoso performance.

"There is no way we are giving up that power," Bob said, after the meeting ended. "I'm fine with giving up a little to get a lot, but I'm not fine with giving a lot to get a little."

Before long, we started to finally see the finish line. Even the Speaker's staff began to act like Bob was going to be the next Chairman of the House Administration Committee. We had cleared all their hurdles, or at least thought so. But as Bob was being told the job was his, an additional hurdle presented itself.

Sitting across from Bob and me in his ornate Capitol office was one of the Speaker's senior staffers. This staffer told us the Speaker would soon officially be telling Bob that he had the job. "Barring something I am not aware of, the chairmanship is yours," the staffer told Bob. His words were like music to my ears. Then the Speaker's staffer asked us for a favor. He asked that Bob fire his most ardent rival, an important House Administration Committee staffer. Bob and I found ourselves in an interesting predicament. On the one hand, Bob had been told he had the job. Yet the way the Speaker's staff had set it up, we didn't really have it yet. Therefore, the Speaker's staff wasn't making our decision about firing a staffer contingent on Bob becoming chairman, at least not technically. But it sure felt that way.

Technically or not, with the leverage he had, the Speaker's point person wanted us to get rid of a man who had been the heartbeat of the House Administration committee staff for years. He was a true public servant who had retired from the United States military before continuing his service to the country by honorably working for the House of Representatives. Bob and I had seen this particular staff member's commitment to the Congress on display at the committee over the years. In many ways, he was the protector of the committee's prerogatives, the committee's turf. His bully to bully battles with the Speaker's staff were legendary. Even seasoned professionals, those with hundreds or thousands of employees, quaked in their boots at the prospect of getting in between the two offices.

Bob and I respected and liked the man the Speaker's office asked us to fire. We had talked about keeping him. But we weren't sure. His institutional knowledge and infighting ability would be helpful, Bob and I both knew. Yet we also wanted to bring in our own people. So we thought about the decision. The Speaker's staff was really playing hardball. Was this really a fight we wanted to pick? At the end of the day, Bob and I agreed that it was best to let the committee staffer go. It was a Faustian Deal. But we cut it. And it fell to me to do the dirty work.

"How did it go?" Bob asked me, after I told the longtime committee-staffer the news.

"I just fired a really good man," I replied.

"Yes, I know," said the new Chairman. "But sometimes you just have to cut the deal."

"I understand," I said. "I know we had to do it. I'm just not happy that it looks like we caved. But I guess that is all part of the learning process."

Despite my years of work geared toward getting the chairmanship, it didn't take long for me to feel in over my head as the committee's Staff Director. Each meeting I attended reminded me of how much I didn't know. And how much I needed to learn. Ultimately, though, my insecurities were overwhelmed by the sheer rush of power associated with my new job. Even if I didn't know certain matters, I made decisions about them. And others followed. It was like an adrenaline shot to the vein, day after day after day.

Becoming Chief of Staff had been a gradual ascension. Most of the people I ended up supervising had known me as the Congressman's Press Secretary. Becoming Staff Director was different. Within hours of the public announcement, Bob and I were touring our new committee digs, and talking to our new staff, all of whom wanted to impress us. With nearly fifty total staffers on the House Administration Committee, the ranks of Ney World continued to grow. Bob and I moved quickly. We started by interviewing the staff to decide who we wanted to keep. Sitting down with each staffer to hear what he or she did was a continuation of my crash course on Washington's inside game.

"The Speaker's office is your enemy," one staffer told me.

"Priority number one is to protect the Speaker's interests," said another.

To each, I replied, "What about the Chairman's interests?" With so many competing interests in the Capitol, I didn't want anyone to be confused about where the loyalty of our committee's staff would be - it would be to Bob.

"That is what I meant to say," they both answered.

It was empowering to design a new component of Ney World. I made it clear to all of our new staffers that protecting Ney's interests was our top priority. "He gets to decide if the Speaker's interests are more important than his interests," I said.

The more I learned, the more excited I got about the prospect of using our new tools to continue building the chairman's political base. "This is going to be fun," I told Bob. Parking spots, office furniture and computer upgrades may not seem like a big deal, but those members of Congress who wanted them surely thought they were. The push for special parking spots and office space got so great that the committee actually had "yes" lawyers and "no" lawyers. If you were a friend of Bob's, we would send you to the yes lawyers so they could figure out how to get you what you wanted. If you were an enemy of Bob's, we would send you to the "no" lawyers so they could figure out a reason to tell you no. And if an office was agnostic on the chairman, our staff was taught to initially say no to the request, before telling that Member to find the Chairman and ask him for the help in person. That way we could intentionally build effective relationships with different offices.

The committee's broad reach kept things interesting. One day, we'd handle an issue involving the Library of Congress. The next day's issue involved the House Gym, or the Smithsonian. We had influence in practically every quarter of the Congress. This also meant dealing with lobbyists and outside consultants who wanted our help. One of the first people to walk in for a meeting in my new office at the committee was a representative from a company called Foxcom Wireless. They were a client of Jack Abarmoff's.

"Foxcom wants to install wireless infrastructure in the House of Representatives to improve phone and email service throughout the complex," the representative told me.

Another company was competing with them for the work. "Improving wireless communications is a cool idea." I replied. "Give me a few weeks to look into the project, and then get back in touch with me."

During our next conversation, the company's representative mentioned to me that leadership of his organization was friendly with Jack. "Jack said he knows you and Ney, and promised that you guys would give us a fair hearing," he said. I sang Jack's praises like I always did. Before long, we were setting up a meeting for the Chairman, Jack, our committee staff and the company's representative to discuss the House project. I would be present, as well.

Bob and I weren't the only ones who had made a move. Jack had also moved to a new location. He and his team of lobbyists were now at a law firm named Greenberg Traurig. Team Abramoff had taken its multi-million dollar practice from one firm to another. News of the move was all over Capitol Hill, in part because of the newest addition to Jack's team, former Tom DeLay Deputy Chief of Staff, Tony Rudy. Rudy was a big-time player. He had been one of the most powerful staffers on Capitol Hill before moving to Jack's shop. Rudy was one of the few leadership staffers who primarily dealt with the members of Congress themselves. I looked up to him.

But things changed. Rudy started lobbying with Jack, and I became one of the most powerful staffers on Capitol Hill. The two of us got closer. In fact, Rudy began to replace Scanlon as my main contact with Team Abramoff. With my sphere of influence and network of friends growing exponentially, my ego lapped up the attention and expanded accordingly. Once again, my opportunities seemed endless. I loved that lines formed in front of my office and that meetings began when I walked in a room. Word spread when I was in a bad mood, and people I didn't know would go out of their way to introduce themselves to me.

If I had any worries, they revolved around my time away from home. My new wife and I had begun occasionally talking about my need to leave Ney World. It was one thing to work 16-hour days and put Bob at the top of my priority list before my wedding. But things were supposed to get better after we got married. I promised Alison that the hard work would eventually create more time at home and give us a chance to build a life together.

But that all changed when Bob became chairman. I was now a Staff Director, I told my wife. "With everything going on, it would be stupid for me to get out now," I said. "Sure, the hours are long. And I am never home. But going down this path is in both our best interests," I assured her.

For a while, we both did our best to believe that was the case. But it was more complicated than that. The adrenaline-like shots of power I received daily had quickly become an addiction. They boosted my ego and provided me such a unique life experience that my addiction to power grew by the day. And like most addicts, I probably would have told her anything to keep getting my fix.

AUGUST 8, 2001
ISTANBUL, TURKEY

Embracing a New Identity

THE BUS SLOWLY APPROACHED A red light near the Bosporus Bridge, with a full group of business leaders, foreign policy professionals and congressional staff on board. Having witnessed a beautiful post-dinner sunset with Turkish officials on one of Istanbul's famed Seven Hills, we were on our way back to the hotel. The golden light reflecting off the unique terrain of mosques, spires, hotels and ships was like a scene out of a modern day *1001 Arabian Nights.*

I only had a split second to keep the party going. Jumping out of my seat, I smacked my hand on the side of the bus and asked our driver to open the door. Pointing to a night club throbbing with disco beats along the water next to us, I yelled "Who's in?" Several younger staffers joined me in rushing off the bus to follow the pulsating rhythm near the river.

It had taken less than a day for Istanbul to become one of my favorite places on earth. I was mesmerized by the culture and energy of such a Muslim metropolis. In addition to its immaculate architecture, Turkey's largest municipality is the only city in the world that can lay claim to being the capital at one time or another of the Roman, Byzantine and Ottoman Empires. Ten bicentennials of greatness. Also, it is a city of two continents, with the Bosporus River not only separating the New-York-City-sized region, but Europe and Asia as well.

Our group of congressional staffers were staying on the European side. It was our last night "in the west." Like many who come through town to travel the Silk Road or the Orient Express, the former Constantinople was our embarkation point for two weeks of official business in Asia. The travel itinerary included Turkey, China, two former Soviet Republics, and Thailand. That night, however, the Laila Disco was our final stop. While drinking and people watching, our small group of staffers took in the fever-ish music of Tarkan, a hot local pop sensation.

Then, despite the embassy's advice to keep a low profile, I rallied our little group to the boat slips behind the bar. There was a lot of activity - mainly by local fishermen. Pulling out a wad of American dollars, I asked a boater if he would take us on a joy ride up and down the Bosporus. Without blinking, he said yes. With the Turkish currency in freefall, I knew the prospect of some stable U.S. dollars would be hard for him to turn down. Laughing and taking in the sights for half an hour, we had a blast on our ad hoc river adventure.

To me, our driver wasn't any different than the good ol' boys along the Ohio River who gave my buddies and me boat rides for cash when I was younger. Our group's senior Turkish handlers, however, didn't view it that way. Their faces turned a deep red the next day when they heard about our excursion. "You should be careful," I was told. "There are Islamic terrorists and people in need of money who would like to get their hands on some Capitol Hill staffers."

I knew if Bob had been with me at the time he would have joined the celebration in the boat, alongside the rest of us. That meant I wasn't too worried about upsetting anybody. If Bob was fine, I was fine. Nonetheless, I was very respectful of our hosts. They had worked hard to teach us about their country. And had many reasons to be proud. From meeting with busi-ness leaders at their stock exchange to representatives in their government, I learned more in my day-and-a-half stay in Turkey than I could have in a myriad of college courses.

Traveling to Kyrgyzstan the next day, I quickly began to better under-stand our Turkish friend's concerns. A former Soviet republic, Kyrgyzstan is a desolate and poor country. It is surrounded by hotbeds of Islamic fundamentalism like Afghanistan, Pakistan, Uzbekistan and Tajikistan. Spending time there opened my eyes to the challenges of the region. During dinner with the Kyrgyzstan President, for example, a member of his entou-rage started talking about recent activity in the area by a man named Osama Bin Laden. Like most of my Capitol Hill colleagues enjoying a fine meal along the beautiful scenery of Lake Issyk-kul, I knew a little bit about bin Laden, but not much more than the basics. He was some sort of terrorist. Nodding along as the man told our group about rumors he heard regarding bin Laden visiting Kyrgyzstan, I acted like I knew more than I actually did. Appearances were important, and so was my pride. The insecurity I carried around because of my new job was never too far from the surface.

The next day, during our group's long drive to Kazakhstan, I finally asked the foreign policy staffer for a senior Senator about the man's comments. He gave me an in-depth tutorial on bin Laden and his group, Al Queda. "Bin Laden is the largest financial backer of international terrorism in the world," my fellow traveler said. "He funded the attack on the World Trade Center in 1993 and on our embassies in Africa." I was spellbound.

"Thanks for the lesson," I said. "My title suggests that I know more than I really do."

Life in Central Asia was much different from in Washington. Nowhere was that more true than the in-your-face importance oil played in the daily lives of the people we met throughout the region. In many respects, American decision making about issues like the placement and protection of oil pipelines had a bigger impact on the local citizenry than the decisions of their own governments. It was a responsibility many of us staffers' didn't want to accept, and a narrative people like bin Laden played into, I was told.

In Kyrgyzstan, for instance, there is almost no oil. And no pipeline. Combined with the devastating economic impact of the Soviet Union's collapse, this lack of natural resources resulted in the country being one of the poorest in the region, and in the world. Their best hotel, where we stayed, would not have even come close to meeting U.S. health and safety standards, let alone be a place where an American family would want to vacation. Goopy brown water dripped from the spigots in my room, and the bathroom floors were made of rotting wood. The food situation was similar. The rotten meat looked raw and the vegetables barely grown. I tried not to offend anyone. But my stomach threw a fit while I was in Kyrgyzstan. The only thing I ended up eating during our twenty-four hours there were the handful of Power Bars I had stuffed in my backpack.

Arriving in Kazakhstan, on the other hand, was more like landing on another planet than crossing a border. Sitting along the oil-rich Caspian Sea, Kazakhstan is one of the 15 largest providers of oil in the world. It was no wonder, then, that Russia's interest in this former republic remained higher than in some of the others. That being the case, many of our conversations with business and government officials took on the eerie feel of Cold War diplomacy. Russian was the language of choice and vodka the drink of preference - even in the morning.

Whether we were visiting a former nuclear weapons facility or touring a community festival, nearly every stop included some sort of discussion on the placement and protection of oil pipelines.

As one of our more intellectual guides on the trip said, "You can't truly understand the history of the 20ᵗʰ century without studying the history of oil. Likewise," he continued, "knowledge of the modern oil business is required to truly comprehend the dysfunction of our region."

As in many of our talks, I felt way in over my head. My insecurity was only heightened by the fact that I was now a Staff Director. The new title meant I was expected to converse intelligently during our meetings with other high-level government officials. In some cases, this was fine. When we were meeting with folks from the Istanbul Stock Exchange or talking about American politics, there were no problems. I knew the basics. Discussing the history of American involvement in the creation of a single European currency, or the impact of the World Trade Organization on agriculture policy in Central Asia, however, was something else entirely.

Nonetheless, I learned to fake it. As one of the senior staffers on our trip, I also was treated with more respect than I probably deserved. People assumed I knew things I didn't. They gave me the benefit of the doubt. While I should have appreciated the additional respect, it ultimately had the unintended consequence of feeding my ego and feeling of self-importance. The dichotomy between my insecurity and arrogance led to some embarrassing moments.

One such moment was our first official meal in Kazakhstan. Without realizing just how hungry I was after 24 hours of Power Bar sustenance and a couple of mid-day vodka shots, I stumbled into our meeting like I was on a drunken binge. With the smell of lamb emanating from the kitchen, stacks of cured meat irresistibly stared at me from the middle of our shared table. Not taking the time to introduce myself fully to the government officials on each side of me, I leapt into the devouringly gorgeous deli-like set up. Right away, I felt better. "As far as I am concerned, pepperoni and salami are the true nectar of the gods," I said, like some cartoon character or member of a college fraternity. As it turned out, that wasn't what I was eating.

"Funny, normally the Americans don't like horse," the well groomed older lady sitting next to me said, as I continued to chow down on yet another handful of cured meat. My large white eyes and raised eyebrows gave away my surprise. And alarm.

"Horse, huh,' I said, slowing my eat-a-thon down dramatically. Looking around, I realized I was on center stage. And embarrassed by my own naiveté. People were watching my every move. "You can't bring me anywhere," I said with a laugh.

Like in the Mariana Islands trip with Scanlon and Jack, the trip to Asia was a lot of fun. But this was no Abramoff excursion. We spent twelve-to-fourteen-hour days dissecting current military, economic and social events with foreign leaders at the highest level. We talked with Buddhist monks in China two days after a heated discussion about America's obligation to Taiwan with the Chinese Foreign Minister. Every discussion broadened my understanding of the world. In many respects, the two week trip was like an abbreviated Master's seminar on Asia foreign policy and business.

It felt completely different than my trip to the Marianas. When I traveled with Jack and Scanlon, I felt like they were cultivating me personally. In contrast, my trip to Asia was focused more on cultivating me as a public official, as a representative of my country. I still had fun, and I met people who became friends. But it was different.

The foundation coordinating our activities, for instance, seemed much more interested in connecting the group with our colleagues in other governments to have an intellectual exchange, rather than in pushing any specific private agenda. In fact, the only agenda being pushed or debated during our stay was our country's agenda. The debates pumped me up and played into my growing ambition. After a few days in China, I started feeling like I was finally becoming a leader on the trip. My personal pendulum began to swing back from feelings of insecurity toward those of confidence.

Back in Washington, Team Abramoff was also on the march. Jack's lobbying team was growing exponentially. His new firm brought in client after client. One reason for it's growth was President Bush's election victory. Because of the change in power, a revolving door of senior Republican officials changed jobs. Lobbyists, lawyers and consultants who had been out of government returned to public service. Likewise, people in government decided to join the private sector. Jack's team exemplified this change. Some of his lobbyists decided to return to government. He filled the void created by their departure by hiring staffers like Tony Rudy. This expanded the reach of Jack's conservative-leaning lobbying team even more. By the time of my trip to Asia, the press had already begun calling him a super-lobbyist.

There were many reasons for Jack's ongoing growth. One reason for the growth was the addition of Rudy. Rudy was proving to be an even better lobbyist than he had been a staffer. Few had the connections, insight or moxie to pull the levers of government the way Majority Whip DeLay's former Deputy Chief of Staff did. He slowly replaced Scanlon as our main point of contact in the office. Not a week passed when Rudy wasn't offering me or someone in Bob's office hockey, basketball, football or concert tickets. Other members of Jack's team also took us out for meals and drinks.

Because of Bob's ascension to chairman and my corresponding climb to Staff Director, Abramoff's lobbying team, like other lobbyists, began to treat us differently. We did the same to them. Though Bob and I continued to want to stay close to those who were close to DeLay, we also began to view Jack and his team as people whose positions of influence could help us beyond just the Majority Whip's office. With Bob and I now in regular contact with the Speaker's office and the leadership of the House, our relationship with lobbyists like Jack had more to do with our priorities and next steps. It was also about having fun and improving our quality of life.

Rudy came into Bob's office, for instance, to ask if he would co-sponsor legislation with a Democratic Member of Congress to protect the Mariana Islands' garment industry. The Chairman said yes right away. The main purpose of the bill was to allow CNMI-produced clothing to be labeled, "Made in the USA," despite the fact that much of the workforce was shipped in from elsewhere and paid less than the minimum wage.

The Congressman's decision to help Rudy and Jack was a result of this new post-DeLay-oriented relationship with Team Abramoff. They gave us campaign contributions, tickets and free meals. They also promoted Bob throughout Washington, and fed us much-needed information. Our lifestyles and professional standing were improved by their largesse. In exchange, we gave them easy access to the office. Extra influence. That isn't to say that Bob and I would have taken actions for Jack's team that conflicted with the direct interests of his district. We wouldn't have. And Jack and Rudy knew that fact. So they wouldn't have asked. Still, it was a relationship that, bit by bit, was growing corrupt.

The connection between our offices was what people on Jack's lobbying team called, "The joke." Their help for the cause of Ney World resulted in our help for their clients. And vice versa. Like many activities in Washington that generated their own idioms, to lobbyists, staffers and elected officials, "You scratch my back, and I'll scratch yours," was replaced by the phrase, "Getting the joke."

Of course, the whole relationship almost fell apart weeks before I left for Asia. Causing such a potential shift were the statements we placed in the *Congressional Record* for Scanlon. The excitement started in early February. Gus Boulis, the original owner of SunCruz casinos, and the man Bob and I attacked in the *Congressional Record*, was found dead in his car on the streets of South Florida. The police said it was murder. Bob alerted me to the situation weeks later.

Though he was privately perturbed by the news, the Congressman initially wasn't too alarmed by the situation. After all, the news of the dead casino owner seemed to verify the bad things we said about him. In a weird way, Bob learned to wear the news as a badge of honor to Jack and Scanlon. "It takes a lot more than a Mafia hit to make me nervous," Bob would joke. At the same time, Ney didn't want anyone on our congressional staff to know about the murder, or for those of us who did to talk about it beyond our walls. "Gossip leads to news stories. In politics, if you've told your secretary something, you have told one too many people," he warned. I didn't tell anybody, not my wife, a close friend or a family member. For the next five months, there was radio silence.

Then, two weeks before I left for Asia, I got a call from a reporter who worked for the *Florida Sun-Sentinel*. He wanted to ask Bob about the Boulis murder, and his comments in the *Congressional Record* regarding SunCruz. The Congressman told me to handle the call.

Before I returned the reporters' call, I reached out to Scanlon. He tried to fill in the blanks. Kidan, whom our second *Congressional Record* statement praised, was a business partner of Jack's, Scanlon said. "The two bought SunCruz," he said. "But then the deal fell apart and it was all Kidan's fault."

I told him that Bob was upset. "He probably would have still helped," I continued. "But he needs to know what is going on when he helps. We deserved better, Mike," I told Scanlon, just the way Bob wanted me to.

"I am deeply sorry to you and the Congressman," he said.

When I finally got on the phone with the *Sun-Sentinel*, the reporter told me that Boulis was allegedly part of the Mafia and that his gangland style murder looked like a mob hit. Listening intently, I said nothing. He then told me that Bob's statement had been used as a part of the negotiations between Adam Kidan and his team's effort to buy SunCruz from Boulis.

"The statement was used to pressure Boulis to make a deal," the reporter told me.

I replied that we did not know all that when we agreed to officially submit the statements. off the Record, meaning not for print, I told him we did it as a favor to Scanlon, someone we had known for a while. On the record, I told him that Bob's campaign was returning the $1,000 check Kidan had donated the year before, and that if Bob knew everything then that he knows now things would have been different. But I kept it vague. Bob had said he didn't want me to offend Jack but didn't care what I said about Scanlon.

Knowing that his relationship with Bob and our office was in jeopardy,

Scanlon openly apologized to the Congressman in the story and blamed the whole matter on Adam Kidan, the same guy our *Congressional Record* submission had praised months earlier. The circus atmosphere was too much for Bob to take. After the article was published, he remained furious with Scanlon and told me to let Jack know we didn't want to work with DeLay's former staffer anymore.

Jack took the news well, and in typical Abramoff fashion, he spun it to his advantage. The first thing Jack did was to quickly throw Scanlon under the bus. "Mike goes way over the line sometimes," he said. "Even though I had nothing to do with it, please apologize to Bob for me. Bob is such a good guy, and Scanlon should have told him what was going on."

Then he distanced himself even further from Scanlon. "I rarely know everything that Mike is doing," the super-lobbyist continued. "We don't work together as much as we used to. I mean we do some work together, but, you know, he is a little crazy. It's Scanlon," Jack said with a laugh. I chuckled along.

At that point, Jack pulled out the victim card, and played it perfectly. He apologized again to Bob and asked me to personally send the Congressman his deepest apologies. "I should have called him myself," Jack said. "But my mind was elsewhere. If you can believe it, as bad as all this is for Bob, it is a thousand times worse for me," he continued. "I knew Kidan from when we were in the College Republicans together. I trusted him, and he lied to me. He got me involved in all this stuff. Sure, I probably lost a couple million dollars and that is going to hurt, but what hurts worse is that I lost a friend. And I'm worried about losing you guys as friends. I sure hope this isn't going get in the way of my relationship with you and Bob," Jack concluded.

"Of course not," I replied. "That sounds horrible. What a crazy story. I'm sorry you have to deal with that." I filled Bob in about my conversation with Jack. He immediately felt as bad for Abramoff as I did. The fact is we both wanted to believe Jack's story, so we did. In that way, the death of Gus Boulis actually brought us closer to the Abramoff lobbying team. Bob and I figured that Jack had probably come to the same conclusion about Scanlon that we did, and distanced himself as well. "After all, Scanlon isn't a part of Jack's lobbying team anymore," I said. "He is doing his own thing, with some public relations company. And Jack's got Rudy now," I concluded.

Bob and I decided to put Scanlon in the rear view mirror and continue working with Jack. It was an important relationship, even more important now that Rudy was Jack's right hand man. Or so we thought.

SEPTEMBER 11, 2001
WASHINGTON, DC

Terror in Washington

STARING OUT THE WINDOW, I waited for a plane to crash into the Capitol Building. Only a few of us knew the fourth hijacked airliner was on its way. Visions of Washington without the dome rushed through my head. Until a few hours earlier, such a scenario would have been considered ludicrous. Yet there I stood, on the seventh floor of Capitol Police Headquarters, watching in horror, unable to do a damn thing to stop it.

Smoke billowed from the Pentagon. Television scenes of a collapsed World Trade Center served as a reminder of what surely was to come. Helplessly, I waited for the inevitable. More people dead. Another explosion. This time in the holy midpoint of our capital city. The noble home of our representative bazaar. My motionless thousand yard stare is seared into my brain forever.

As time passed, I began to think something was wrong. Or, more accurately, that something was right. Maybe a plane wasn't going to come into view after all.

Not sure what to think, I tapped my feet nervously on the Capitol Police Chief's office floor. Like anxious family members at a hospital, Senate Majority Leader Tom Daschle, Senate Majority Whip Harry Reid and Senate Minority Leader Trent Lott paced back and forth in the hallway. Similarly, in deep thought, House Majority Whip Tom DeLay meandered from room to room. A morbid silence surrounded us all.

Normally, when senior Congressional officials gather together in Washington, you can smell the ambition in the room. The quest for power and control underpins nearly every major conversation. Every major decision. But not that morning. On September 11th, no one was in control. And the only thing you could smell was fear.

Minutes earlier, Secret Service had landed a helicopter on the east lawn of the Capitol grounds. Rushing past security to the floor of the House of Representatives, they whisked Speaker Hastert off to safety. Being third in line to the presidency meant such contingency plans for the Speaker were theoretically always on the table. Still, it was an unprecedented move.

For rank and file senators and members of Congress, the evacuation wasn't so easy. They were forced to deal with the pandemonium like anyone else: on their own. No longer masters of the political universe, everyday congressmen found themselves running alongside the tens of thousands of people flooding the streets and subway stations of Washington in a panic-induced exodus from Capitol Hill.

In contrast, the congressional leadership ended up at Capitol Police headquarters that morning. Since each of them had law enforcement detail, when word of the Pentagon attack spread, they were instantly rushed to the Hill's main police station.

My journey to police headquarters was a little different. Unlike our leaders, I chose to get involved. However, none of us at police headquarters had ever expected that a potential scalping of our political system was possible when we arrived at work earlier in the day.

When I walked into my Capitol Hill office a little before 6:00 A.M. on Tuesday, everything was quiet. All indications were that it was going to be just another ordinary, hot summer day. I had just spent two weeks in France and Spain on my honeymoon, and had a lot of catching up to do. Some early morning "alone time" was the best way to make headway into the backlog, I figured.

I began by downing a few large cups of coffee and rummaging through the nearly three-foot high inbox of paper which had built up while I was gone. The first thing I grabbed was the post-Congressional recess special edition of *Roll Call*. Every half-year or so the newspaper compiled a list of the fifty most powerful staffers on Capitol Hill. I wanted to make sure I was still on it.

From there, I moved on to my schedule. Compared to the luxury of the last few weeks, it looked brutal. It always did. Both the Chairman and I had non-stop meetings throughout the day, most of which revolved around the committee's legislative priorities, namely campaign finance reform and election reform. Since they were hot-button topics, there wasn't a second to spare.

At that point, I noticed I was double-booked for the evening. My scheduler had me attending both a barbecue picnic at the White House with

President George W. Bush and a baseball game in Baltimore with Jack. Knowing I couldn't do both, I quickly shot off an email to a friend of mine who worked on the Hill, to see if he was interested in going to the game. After all, as I told him, seeing one of legendary baseball player Cal Ripken's last home games from within the cozy confines of Abramoff's stadium suite would be a lot of fun. Also, I didn't want Jack's tickets to go to waste.

Life sure seemed good. For four of the last six weeks, I had been overseas. Additionally, my work was exhilarating. I loved it. On most days, I wasn't bothered one bit by the fact that when I was working, my job consumed nearly every waking hour of my life. After all, because of the opportunities and experiences Ney World provided, I was living a life I never could have dreamed of years before. But such a life was taking its toll. Nothing exemplified that more than the trouble I was having in my young marriage. Alison rightfully felt neglected by my constant broken promises to be home at a reasonable hour.

Because we were married during an election year, we had postponed our honeymoon. At first, the postponement didn't seem like a big deal. It was only a year and a month. We emphasized the positive, a cool trip in the near future. But our time away was illuminating. In addition to experiencing the passion of Parisian life along the Champs-Elysees and taking in the bullfights of Seville, Alison and I decided it was time for me to leave Ney World.

The time away had allowed me to realize first-hand how my priorities were falling out of line. Due to my unyielding drive to please the Congressman, as well as my never-ending internal desire for more power and prestige, everything else was being pushed aside. My family. My friends. My faith. Everything.

Even worse, I had developed a dangerous process of rationalization which at times allowed me to truly believe that by putting work above everything else, I was actually on a long-term path toward a life of proper priorities. *"If I just miss one more family function or tell my wife I'll be home late just one more time, everything will work out,"* I thought to myself.

It wasn't like I was one of the millions of hard-working parents and spouses in America who get up, work hard at a job simply to support their family, and fall in bed exhausted. Mine wasn't a struggle for survival. In fact, deciding to stay at a bar with the Congressman until 2:00 A.M. night after night because that is when the real decisions occurred wasn't a struggle at all. It was a choice. A selfish choice.

Since I had helped to build Ney World, the decision to leave wasn't easy.

Bob's career was skyrocketing. Mine was, too. At 31, I was still the youngest staff director on Capitol Hill, in charge of my own committee. The fun, the office camaraderie and the appeal of public service were very real. *"All of that is a lot to give up,"* I said, during my internal debate.

Yet, by the end of the trip, I could see how the time constraints, unhealthy partying lifestyle and chains of secrecy surrounding my life as Bob's chief of staff were hurting more than they were helping. Additionally, with people like Jack suggesting I could remain in politics and have a better quality of life off the Hill as a lobbyist on Team Abramoff, any downside to a change seemed to be outweighed by such terrific opportunities. It was a win-win. What I needed to do, therefore, seemed pretty clear. Until we returned to U.S. soil.

After I had been in my office for only a few hours, the clarity of my overseas decision became murky. All of a sudden, I wasn't so sure about leaving. *"Do I really want to give all this up?"* I asked, while looking over at the historic painting of the Capitol that hung on my office wall. *"That is from the official House collection. You picked it out yourself. Where else can you do that?"*

Pandora's box re-opened, and along with it the ironclad promise I had made to my wife about getting things right. Knowing there would be a price to pay for any decision, I decided to let the dust settle a little bit before locking in any plans. Several hours later, out of the blue, my communications director called with news of a plane crashing into the World Trade Center. Flipping on the television, I immediately emailed a colleague, "Holy shit – turn on CNN."

Getting up, I left my office to grab a few of the guys from the committee and marched into our conference room. News had spread. We put *The Today Show* on the big screen television and awaited the Chairman's arrival. Minutes later, the second tower was hit. Instantly, we all assumed the worst. Terrorists were attacking. As an NBC reporter suggested the buildings may have been accidentally struck because of air traffic controller problems, Bob entered the room. He pretty much summed up all of our sentiment by saying to no one in particular, "You can see a fucking building."

After the Congressman dismissed the suggestion that the pilots of two large planes could have somehow accidentally flown into large city buildings, a free flowing conversation began about who could have been behind the attacks. Bob blurted out that he just, "knew Ariel Sharon was going to cause World War III."

The Congressman wasn't saying he thought the attacks were conducted by Israel. He was saying that he thought the attacks were part of the Second

Intifada, a murderous uprising occurring at the time between the Israelis and Palestinians. Along with many others, Bob believed Prime Minister Sharon's visit to the Temple Mount had started the murderous uprising, which would end up killing nearly 7,000 Israelis and Palestinians, and was initially what the Congressman thought to be the impetus behind the attack on New York..

Having lived in both Iran and Saudi Arabia, the Congressman was well-versed in foreign affairs. Nonetheless, the suggestion that Israel's policies were somehow responsible for attacks on the United States seemed outlandish. Unnerving. But then again, so did the mere idea of people flying huge planes into buildings. My view was that the perpetrators were either Iranian-funded Hezbollah or bin Laden's group. Either those, or home grown terrorists like those we had seen in Oklahoma City years earlier.

None of us had much time to really ponder the possibilities. Within a few minutes, a junior staff assistant for the committee ran into the conference room with word that one of our legal counsels had just witnessed an American Airlines plane flying into the side of the Pentagon. "He was on I-395 returning from a dentist appointment," she said. "The explosion rattled his car." The situation was growing more intense by the moment.

Almost instantaneously, the Deputy Sergeant of Arms for the House of Representatives called the Chairman. The Sergeant of Arms is responsible for working with the Capitol Hill Police and others to coordinate security around Capitol Hill. Since we oversaw their office, they were responsible for reporting to our committee. Especially in emergencies.

News of the attack on the Pentagon ran rampant. We all agreed it represented a threat to the entire Capitol complex. As Bob hung up the phone, he looked over in my direction and declared, "Well, that's enough for me. Let's get everyone out of here."

With all hell breaking loose, the Chairman was decisive. At a minimum, his efforts helped to provide a catalyst for what would become an imperfect evacuation of the House-side of the Capitol complex. Unfortunately, many people never got the word to leave. At the same time, many were evacuated safely.

Running through our front office, I caught a picture of one of the World Trade Center towers out of the corner of my eye. It was on the television screen in the front office, a screen usually used to monitor the House floor. Like others, I'm sure, that gut wrenching moment when the first tower collapsed still provokes a raw emotional response within me. Seeing the tower fall stopped me dead in my tracks. For nearly a minute, my eyes remained fully transfixed by the images on the television hanging over the committee's main entrance doorway. "Those poor people," I told myself over and over. "Drinking their coffee. Taking care of their business."

I called my wife to tell her I would be leaving soon. I also received calls from my dad and a cousin. I told them I was leaving, and would make sure to be safe. But as the Chairman and his Executive Assistant, a young man named Will Heaton, joined most of our staff in the pressure-filled evacuation of the Longworth Building, something just didn't seem right. I returned to my office.

Seconds later, two colleagues appeared at my office door. Channing Nuss, the committee's Deputy Staff Director and Reynold Schweichart, the committee's Technology Director, were also hesitant to leave. "We might have a role to play in this," Channing said, before suggesting flat-out that we shouldn't evacuate. Deep down, I knew he was right. Since we were responsible for overseeing much of the internal operations of the Capitol complex, there really shouldn't have been any question about staying put. But, like almost everyone, I was scared.

"Should we go?" Channing asked, clearly wanting my buy-in. Though I was desperate for some time to think, we didn't have that option. I went with my gut. "Let's stay," I said. And with that, we began to move.

I called the Chairman and told him the three of us were not leaving. "We are going to the Capitol to help deal with the day," I said, before asking Bob whether he wanted to join us. He declined. Bob said he thought we should evacuate along with everyone else, but that he wasn't going to force us to. We thanked him and hung up.

By the time the three of us exited onto Independence Avenue, signs of panic were everywhere. Tributaries of people running toward their cars, their homes and the metro merged into a river of human departure. Abject terror was taking hold of Capitol Hill. The three of us ran across the street as some cops set up a security perimeter around the Capitol. While the police turned away a Washington correspondent for CNN, we flashed our House Administration badges and entered the complex. Instead of walking into the Capitol as planned, we joined several staff members from the Sergeant at Arms Office and the Capitol Hill police who were meeting just outside the building. Underneath a large tree, our group huddled to share notes and discuss the current state of play. Two F-16s flew overhead. The sonic boom shook us like an earthquake.

Within minutes, the police activity around us escalated dramatically. Radios shrieked. Guns were drawn. Something new was happening. A group of uniformed police officers ran purposefully in our direction. Before reaching us, one of them yelled, "ATF is reporting there is another hijacked plane twenty minutes to the north coming directly toward Washington. Get the fuck out of here!" He was screaming at the top of his lungs.

Doing our best Olympic athlete impersonations, we each sprinted across the Capitol lawn, moving as fast as we could in our tailored business suits. I felt like we were in a surreal run for our lives. Approaching the Capitol Police headquarters a few blocks away, our small group began to slow down. My pulse was racing. Chest heaving, I tried to call Alison again. This time I finally got through. Regrettably, the machine picked up.

Blurting out random thoughts in the moment, my exact words on the message were: "Hey it's me. My phone's not working. It took me about 15 times to get through to you. Another plane has been hijacked 20 minutes north of DC. The entire complex is being shut down. We were just sprinting through the Capitol. We're going over to Police headquarters. I'll be there soon. I'll call you. See you. Love you. Bye."

I made my way to the building's top floor. We began to wait. And then wait some more. Slowly putting it all together, I started to realize that the air cover overhead meant the fourth plane probably wasn't coming. "Had it been shot down?" I wondered. Television news was reporting a downed plane in the fields of Pennsylvania.

With the initial panic starting to subside, it quickly became clear to Channing, Reynold, the rest of the staff present, and me, that we had work to do. Offices had been abandoned, and the simple logistics of communicating with what were normally well-connected public officials were going to be a challenge. But communicating with them was something that we clearly needed to do. Figuring out what to say was also going to be a hurdle.

The discussion between House Majority Whip DeLay and Senate Majority Leader Daschle over next steps was a classic exercise in contrasts. Their conversation not only highlighted the personal differences between the two men, but the institutions they were representing as well.

DeLay, in typical House leadership fashion, wanted to tell Members of Congress to report to police headquarters at a specific time. That was how the House worked. If you have 218 votes, you are in charge and get to tell people what to do. Daschle, on the other hand, suggested that we reach out to each of the Senators and Members and let them know we would be following up. That way we could pass pertinent information along if needed. His preference was not to tell them to report for duty. This approach was typical for a Senate leader. Because Senate rules grant each individual

Senator enormous influence over the legislative process, telling your Senate colleagues what to do is rarely an effective practice for Senate leaders who want to accomplish anything.

In the grand Washington tradition of negotiations between the House and the Senate, DeLay and Daschle reached a compromise. Most of the leaders at police headquarters would join the Speaker at his undisclosed location, they said. We staff would then reach out to those members of Congress who had scattered throughout the region and suggest that they take part in one of two meetings at police headquarters. Elected officials who didn't want to return to Capitol Hill could take part in the meetings over the phone.

The first meeting was set for early in the afternoon. The second would be held later in the afternoon. In the meantime, we would provide all the offices the number at police headquarters to call if they wanted updated news or needed anything else.

It all seemed like pretty simple stuff. What made it difficult, however, was the environment in which we found ourselves working. At any given point, representatives from the FBI or CIA would show up to give us tense classified briefings concerning additional planes still in the sky or to discuss what was going on in New York, and at the Pentagon. Our ad hoc group of staff and professional administrators remained in a heightened level of stress throughout the day.

The first decision we made was to transfer the Washington office phone lines of every member of Congress over to their district office lines. Due to the evacuation of Capitol Hill, constituents and family members calling their Member of Congress in Washington were getting either an answering machine or nothing at all. "Why not make sure frightened constituents, friends and family members get through to a human being?" most of us figured. We were being especially mindful of the New York and Northern Virginia delegations, places in which the attacks had actually occurred. "Their phones just had to be ringing off the hook," one of my fellow staffers said.

From there our little group began assembling ideas about how best to communicate the leader's plans to the hundreds of elected officials holed up all over the city. With sporadic mobile phone communication and empty Washington offices, Members' district offices quickly became a key component of our communication strategy. Home numbers were another option. So was Blackberry email service, which was working but not widely available. Only a handful of offices had the technology. Amazingly, most

Members of Congress were still being alerted to votes and official business through the use of early 1990's-style pagers. Glorified beepers. Technology was not on our side. But we had a plan.

Our next step was to actually come up with a message. I worked on that with DeLay and his office. When we were done, I called Chairman Ney to get his sign-off on the final script. It took me at least ten calls before I got through to Bob. Our first effort at communicating was bare bones. The message simply told the Members of Congress to check their DC-area homes and district offices for further information. It also suggested that they call Capitol Police Headquarters. Initially, we didn't use the pager system.

Because of the lack of response to our first attempt at communication, a discussion started about the pagers. Using the devices the Members were used to carrying would be helpful, we all agreed. But to send out a message via the pagers, someone needed to physically get into the Capitol Building. And the police maintained that option was too dangerous.

"The Capitol remains a target," both the House and Senate Sergeant at Arms said. A debate ensued. Ultimately, any question about whether we should or should not use the pagers ended when a team from the Clerk of the House returned to the Capitol and sent out our message. As far as I was concerned, that was a heroic mission. It was also a successful one. The phones at police headquarters began to ring. We were making progress.

Needing a break, Channing and I stepped outside for a few minutes. The two of us decided to visit with some of the reporters who were gathering in the front of the building. We looked for a specific Capitol Hill reporter friend of ours. The two of us knew he would have some cigarettes.

Our reporter friend filled us in on the latest information from New York. It was tragic. News reports were suggesting as many as 30,000 people could end up dead. From the New York area, our friend was shaken up. But still working. He asked us where the Speaker had been taken. Channing and I both refused to give him that information, despite his promise not to report it right away. What we did say was that we wanted some cigarettes. As expected, he had some. In fact, he had three packs. In a brief moment of levity, our reporter friend joked about how he had run to the money machine and the store for cigarettes the minute the second plane hit the World Trade Center tower.

"If the world was coming to an end, I was going to have cigarettes," he said with a sheepish grin. The two of us stayed outside for a while commiserating with various reporters about the horrid activities of the day, all the while enjoying arguably the best tasting pack of Marlboro Reds in the history of filtered cigarettes.

The first Congressional briefing at headquarters took place on the fourth floor. Bob showed up at that time. Tensions were high. Several of the elected officials were rabidly questioning the House and Senate Sergeants of Arms about the current state of security. The elected officials were concerned about whether it was safe to go back into the Capitol Building. Both Sergeants said the building was still a target, but the Senate Sergeant suggested the building was safe now that F-16s were flying air cover over Washington. I shuddered again at the thought of us needing air cover.

Many of the same issues were addressed during the bipartisan conference call later in the day. More than three hundred Members took part. Our message was really getting out. For the call, Bob and our ranking Democrat on the House Administration Committee, Steny Hoyer, as well as some of his staff, listened together in a conference room at headquarters. Hoyer was calm throughout. In between calls, we negotiated our bipartisan Election Reform bill, the legislation we were writing in response to the disputed 2000 Presidential Election.

Like they had earlier, a group of elected officials began to demand that Congress reconvene. "If we don't conduct session in the Capitol tonight, the public will think the terrorists have won this day," one of them said. The comment angered Congressman Hoyer. He hit the mute button on our speaker phone, and said, "They already won today." He then went on to make an entirely appropriate crack about the self-importance with which some Members of Congress view themselves. "Is someone sitting at home going to suddenly view this as a victorious day because they see us on C-Span?" Hoyer asked sarcastically. He had a point. We had bigger issues to deal with. Nonetheless, the movement to take some sort of action in the Capitol Building was growing.

A few hours later, Hoyer played an important role in a very emotional and eventful 5:00 P.M. briefing about how exactly the Congress was going to react to the events of the day. In front of a packed house, the meeting started with Speaker Hastert and House Minority Leader Gephardt talking to the group via speakerphone. Their voices echoed from a phone that sat on a lonely table in front of the gathered Members.

The leaders told all of us we would not be going into session that night. Instead, they said the bipartisan and bicameral leadership would be having a press conference in front of the Capitol building. What that meant was a group of six or eight Members of Congress speaking from a podium. Right away, it was clear to me they had no idea what their own membership was thinking. It wasn't that a bipartisan press conference was a bad idea, but dropping it out there like that was the only solution fanned the growing flames of mutiny, a movement to open the Congress and conduct session.

"The shit is going to hit the fan," I told the staffer for Tom DeLay, who was standing next to me. With calls for going into session suddenly growing louder by the moment, the same DeLay staffer replied by asking me if Bob would stand up to help stop the brewing rebellion. Ney rose to the challenge. He vociferously backed up the Speaker's decision. For his courage, Bob was skewered by many of his colleagues. And the budding insurgency continued to grow.

At that point, Congressman Hoyer stepped into the debate. On the spot, he suggested that all the Members present walk to the Capitol steps and stand behind the leaders during their press conference. Because law enforcement was strongly advising against actually going into the building en masse, that would not be done, he said sternly.

Instead, he continued with even more passion, the Congress itself, namely the members, would stand on the steps of the Capitol behind the leadership. "This would have the same impact as going into session," Hoyer said. "It would also show bipartisan unity." Showing just how much had changed, even in a harshly divided town, Hoyer's bipartisan sentiment was instantly well received.

For a moment or two there was silence. Through the phone in the front of the room, Speaker Hastert signed off on Hoyer's plan. "We should all do this together," the Speaker said, connecting with the vibe in the room. Others joined in support. Hope and resolve replaced rebellion and anger. The quick thinking of a few good men had averted a potential disaster.

Feeling relief in the air, the House chaplain led the gathering in prayer. Hand in hand we prayed. When we were done, the whole room broke out in a heartfelt rendition of, "God Bless America". People who barely knew each other hugged at length. Many were crying. It was a precursor to the famous image of our elected leaders singing that night on the steps of the Capitol Building. With pride. In unity. Under God.

Sometimes I regret skipping out on the press conference on the Capitol steps, but I needed to get home. Family and friends were waiting. Without a car or access to a cab, the first step toward getting to my Woodley Park neighborhood meant traveling to Chairman Ney's boat on the Potomac. Bob's floating home had served as a gathering point for our staff throughout the day.

When I arrived, the fresh air circulating off the river prompted me to think of when I was a kid and my brother and I would play along the banks of the Ohio River. I don't know why that came to my mind. Sitting down and opening a can of beer, I experienced the first sense of calm I had felt in hours.

Hanging over every thought, however, was a queasy feeling that nothing was ever going to be the same. The last ten hours had changed everything. I mean it had been years since I told my mom and my dad that I loved them, but that was the first thing I uttered when they answered after I called them from the boat. From the top of Bob's boat we watched Air Force One return to Washington. It was a reminder of our new collective reality. Our small group intently stared off in the sky as the only plane anywhere for miles slowly passed by overhead, now knowing it could fall out of the sky at any moment. The President was coming back to a whole new world, we all agreed.

Hitching a ride home with my friend and fellow Congressional staffer Chet Khalis, I couldn't help but comment on how quiet the roads were. For miles, we didn't see another car. Even cabs were nonexistent. The metro had shut down. A "haunted house atmosphere," was how Chet described it.

During the drive, Chet and I discussed the changes occurring right in front of our eyes. My colleague was upset.

"You know the Pentagon is shuffling the chairs in the Middle East as we speak," I said plainly to Chet, trying to connect.

"That is what has me worried," he replied.

Twenty years older than me and a lifelong blue collar Democrat, Chet had experienced Vietnam from the vantage point of the working class streets of Appalachia. He had family, friends and neighbors who had been either drafted or died in service.

"How you respond to a traumatic incident is sometimes more important than the incident itself," he said.

Though his comments didn't seem to meet the same moment I was experiencing, I again tried to connect.

"It can also crystallize your thinking," I said.

"Both can be true at the same time," he replied, to which I agreed.

Neither of us knew for sure who had attacked us or what to expect going forward. But we were both pretty sure the dysfunction of the modern Middle East was partly to blame for the attacks. We also agreed that change in the region was needed for the safety of the United States. Change that appeared to be coming. According to my journal entry from the next day, "We woke up to prepare the Capitol and the country for war."

October 17, 2001
Washington, DC

Anthrax

GETTING TESTED FOR ANTHRAX EXPOSURE is not exactly what Webster would define as an enjoyable experience. Yet, there I sat in the House Physicians' picturesque office along the ground floor of the Capitol Building. The large cotton swab on a 6-inch stick menacingly taunted me from the doctor's hand as he outlined the situation.

"Swabbing for anthrax spores is an imprecise science," the doctor said. "Since people's noses begin to filter the fungus out of their system, it is crucial to dig deep for the best results," he continued. The suddenly stern, white-coated professional then shoved the swab up my nose like he was gutting a fish. I mean he shoved that poor cotton swab into the deepest possible regions of what felt like my brain.

At the time, hundreds, possibly thousands, of congressional staffers and elected officials were lining up to get tested for exposure to what the medical community was calling *bacillus anthracis*. For Bob and me, it was yet another episode of Capitol Hill pandemonium. This one was the result of a bioterror attack on the Senate Majority Leader's office two days earlier, when an envelope containing anthrax had been opened in his office. Days and weeks before the attack on the Capitol, tabloid publisher American Media Inc. in Florida, Tom Brokaw and *NBC Nightly News* in New York, and a Microsoft office near Reno, Nevada, all had been hit by anthrax. Therefore, when the same white powdery substance reached into the Senator's office, it wasn't a complete surprise.

Instantly, our House team of security and administrative professionals shut down the mail service for the entire Capitol complex. After that, our team began implementing additional security screening measures, such as blocking couriers and messengers from delivering packages directly to individual Member offices; making screening mandatory for UPS, FedEx and DHL packages; and requesting that individual offices decline any mail items from "walk in" visitors.

Having learned first hand during 9/11 about the need for constant communication during a crisis, our committee quickly sent out an announcement to Congressional staff about a meeting the next day to discuss security procedures and the proper handling of mail and suspicious packages. Ultimately, because of increased demand, we held three meetings, instead of just one, with Capitol Police threat assessment professionals and Inspectors from the United States Post Office.

In between those somewhat public meetings with Congressional staff, I joined the House security team for summaries of the private sessions with biologists and terror specialists from the Environmental Protection Agency and the Centers for Disease Control. Their findings were eye-opening. We were told that the Congress was dealing with a specific type of airborne anthrax which could easily navigate through the Capitol buildings' ventilation system, and potentially end up on the House floor. Such news was a complete contradiction of the basic facts we had been working with up to that point. That fact alone increased the tension in the room. And since we weren't sure whether or not there were already anthrax-laden letters in our shut-down mailrooms, the increased danger level heightened our tension even more.

Since Bob and I were in the Capitol around the time the first letter was opened, we called to set up an appointment for the test. At the time of our anthrax tests, 31 Capitol Hill staffers had already tested positive and been prescribed ciprofloxacin. That would be our future, we assumed, if any exposure to the deadly spore was detected. As fate would have it, the Chairman's future and mine were going to be a lot more complicated than a prescription. We learned that minutes later when Speaker Hastert made public his decision to shut down the House side of the Capitol Building, due to possible anthrax exposure.

Implementing the Speaker's orders meant our committee would be part of the team shutting down the entire House side of the Capitol, and the myriad of House office buildings, for the next week. Specifically, the Speaker's plan was for the Congress to finish up an abbreviated week of legislative work immediately, adjourn, and re-open the House of Representatives the following Tuesday. If we could.

Hastert's decision was fraught with logistical challenges. It was our team's responsibility to fill in the blanks. Do you test all 435 offices for anthrax? If so, how can possibly do so in a week? How do we end the testing process, let alone begin it? These and many other challenges presented themselves immediately. At the direction of the Speaker's staff, we broke down the issues of responsibility for the next week into several general areas: the closure of the House side of the Capitol complex, the environmental assessment itself, coordination and creation of off-site Congressional work space, and communication of all of the above to the elected officials, their staff, and the public when pertinent.

But first we used the new All-House emergency communication procedures born out of our experience at Capitol Police headquarters on 9/11. Within hours of the Speaker's decision, the first message was sent out. It was entitled, "Urgent House Personnel Advisory." Sad as the reason for the message was, watching this new communications tool swing into motion represented a step forward toward better emergency communications.

The communiqué hit six major points: it announced the House would conclude its legislative business later that afternoon; made clear an environmental assessment would take place and that no one would be allowed in the buildings or parking garages from that evening at 8:00 P.M. until 5:00 A.M. Tuesday morning; outlined such procedures as the transfer of DC phone lines to district offices; gave an emergency number to call with questions; re-stated the stoppage of all Congressional mail; and suggested that each office back-up its individual computer systems. The whole thing sounded very elementary, but since even changing a light bulb on Capitol Hill can stir controversy, we decided to err on the side of simplicity and directness.

During the next week, the entire Capitol complex was transformed from a bustling temple of democracy into an eerie, closed off house of ghouls. Bio-hazard teams and hazmat professionals milled around like ghosts in their white, hooded, air-tight space suits, balloon-like gloves and goggled gas masks.

Since the Speaker laid down an unbreakable promise that the Congress would be back in session Tuesday, setting up a secure, new and fully functioning floor of the House of Representatives elsewhere became priority number one. If the environmental assessments came back with positive anthrax results, returning to the actual Capitol Building would be impossible. Therefore, we had to be ready. Like setting up the alternative House floor, we also knew that we had to set up temporary office space for individual Members of Congress to conduct their work, if their offices could not be re-opened. The dome may have still been intact, but the nightmare possibility of losing a working Congress to terrorism was becoming more of a reality by the minute.

Our mission to create an emergency House of Representatives took us to Fort McNair, the third oldest Army post in the United States. In 1791, when Pierre C. L'Enfant designed the layout for Washington, he placed the post strategically on the point of land where the "Federal City's" two rivers merge. Explosions during the War of 1812 and the hanging of those who took part in President Lincoln's assassination all occurred in the area of what is now called Fort McNair. The fort was named after Lesley J. McNair, the commander of Army Ground forces during World War II, and is the home of the National Defense University. Of course, movie fans may know the base more for its starring role in the Jack Nicholson, Tom Cruise and Demi Moore film, *A Few Good Men.* Speaker Hastert's decision to close the House meant we would be adding to Fort McNair's legacy by constructing emergency Congressional chambers its auditorium.

While we worked day and night at the base, the Capitol Building was completely shuttered. Members of Congress were forced to relocate their working offices for the first time since the Civil War. The rapid changes resulting from the anthrax attack represented just another piece of the never-ending challenges of post-9/11 Washington, even while the anthrax scare was terrifying all on its own. A lot had changed in five weeks.

We were now at war. Following 9/11, the Congress passed Public Law 107-40 authorizing the use of military force "against those responsible" for the attacks. President Bush then commenced Operation Enduring Freedom to remove the Taliban from power for their refusal to shut down terror bases in Afghanistan and turn over Osama bin Laden.

It was a whole new world. On September 12th, for the first time ever, the NATO alliance declared Article Five outlining an attack on one as an attack on all. Most of the world united behind the United States. The *Star Spangled Banner* rang out in front of Big Ben and the Brandenburg Gate as millions across the globe showed their support. Long term international battle lines shifted abruptly. Pakistan, the only majority Muslim country with a nuclear arsenal, went from foe to friend almost overnight. In contrast, Pakistan severed their diplomatic ties to their Taliban neighbors. Just as quickly, the United States changed a half century of Cold War-based foreign policy by announcing official support for a Palestinian state along Israel's border.

Here at home, healing became the priority. Political campaigns, angry talk radio and trash television were put on hold as the country's citizenry united. The creation of relief funds to help those most impacted by the terror replaced massive search and rescue operations around Ground Zero, the Pentagon, and Shanksville, PA, the town where passengers brought down the fourth hijacked plane on 9/11. Congress passed a $40 billion emergency spending bill, and, because air traffic had been grounded and new security needed, a $20 billion airline bailout.

Healing also meant seeking justice. Instituting the single largest investigation of its kind, codenamed PENTTBOM, the FBI probed all angles of the 9/11 massacre. This included tapping phones and questioning thousands of Muslim and Arab Americans, as well as detaining nearly five thousand foreign nationals.

In our little corner of Capitol Hill, the House Administration Committee's focus was security and preparations for a possible attack. Working with others, we closed streets and placed snipers around the Capitol. We added mandatory ID checks and full automobile searches in the parking garages. To reduce glass breakage, we approved a Mylar protective coating for all the windows. We signed off on new rules mandating full use of the metal detectors, and we instituted interim evacuation plans. Also, we commenced a full safety review and focused like a laser on improving emergency communications, starting with the purchase of mobile email devices for every office.

For me personally, the trauma of the attacks had me yearning for solace and peace. The nostalgia I felt for a better time reminded me that I had not been to Church in years. There was a hole in my life. I felt it during President Bush's speech to the Congress days after the attacks. As I sat in the House chamber, the President said, "Justice and cruelty have always been at war, and God is not neutral between them." His words sent shivers up my spine. It was enough of a jolt to get me back to Church for a few weeks. But, like I had for years, my busy schedule became a reason to stay away. Not that a change in spirit couldn't be felt all around me.

In a short period of time, the mindset on the Hill changed dramatically. Bipartisanship replaced Partisanship. Capitol Hill began to feel like a unified community. Grief counseling programs and support groups sprang up. Our deliberations even took on a new tone. All of a sudden, patriotism and respect for the other side reigned supreme. It was a breath of fresh air from the nasty partisan rancor of the last decade, and this was the environment in which we labored at Fort McNair.

Hour after hour we met, discussed and worked toward creating a space in which official Congressional business could be conducted. We installed podiums and record keeping measures. Security, press credentialing and research had to be addressed. All the while I laughed to myself, thinking that I wanted to tell Bob that constructing a whole new House of Representatives in a few day's time was not a responsibility I expected when he offered me the staff director position.

Our moment of truth occurred when Congressman Hoyer visited the facility to check on our work. His inspection would be a big test of our efforts. Opening up the large room's doors for the Congressman was spine chilling. With a big smile on his face, Steny did the politician thing. And I mean that in a good way. Shaking hands and saying thanks, he followed with a few solemn words. "The room is perfect; it almost looks like the House floor," Steny said. He was impressed. Walking with him through the chambers, I realized the House *would* be in session Tuesday, whether the Capitol's doors opened or not. It was a proud moment.

What I wasn't so proud about, however, was my lack of follow-through on the two month-old promise I had made to Alison about leaving Ney World. "There is just too much going on right now," I told her. She said she understood. After all, there really was a lot happening at the time. Then again, there was always a lot going on.

Our House-transition team, led by Jay Eagen, the House of Representative's Chief Administrative Officer; Jeff Trandahl, the Clerk of the House; and Bill Livingood, the House Sergeant at Arms; had passed the test. The alternate site was ready.

Just hours before Hoyer's successful visit, I had signed off on the nearly two million dollars in emergency expenditures needed to create the chamber at Ft. McNair. My signature, on Bob's behalf, granted the team the authority to not only create a new House chamber, but also the emergency congressional office space being arranged simultaneously in a federal building downtown. We were really rolling. All we had to do now was await the results. Rarely had I ever seen all of us work so well together. Common purpose will do that. In fact, by the time Congressman Hoyer left, we all had an extra bounce in our step.

If only the entire week had run so smoothly. Days earlier, a troubling and dysfunctional personnel matter almost derailed our collective government. I received an urgent email from CAO Eagan asking for a "face-to-face chat."

"*This can't be good,*" I told myself. Of all of us insiders, Eagan played the fewest political games. A boy scout, power plays were not Eagan's thing. He was a quintessential manager, someone who took his trade seriously. Efficiency, accountability and camaraderie challenged him to be at his best. Even more than that, he was and is one of the single most honorable people I have ever met in my life. But our committee was responsible for overseeing his operation. And his operation was responsible for administering the small city of people who made sure everything from the House cafeterias to the credit unions functioned properly. Therefore, when I got his email I knew we wouldn't be discussing something petty.

Walking off to a nondescript room in the administrative offices of Ft. McNair headquarters to talk about his concerns, I could tell Eagan was frustrated. Like me, he had been working 18-hour days since the attacks of 9/11, and even longer days in the last week. Jay said one of my staffers was mucking up the works by demanding to be involved in and sign off on every minor, mid-level and major decision he and the rest of the managers were trying to make. "It is more than just slowing the process down," he continued.

Since that is how the Chairman and I demanded our staff operate, his comments did not surprise me. At first, I didn't reply. Exhausted, Eagan said he knew we were all in a unique situation. "But we need to do our job," he said. Basically, Eagan wanted me to call off the dogs. I couldn't blame him. Our time-sensitive project posed special challenges. If I were in his shoes, I would have said the same thing. But I wasn't in his shoes. I was in mine. Therefore, even though I instantly knew he was right, I also knew what he wanted wasn't so simple.

Immediately, I reviewed the fundamentals, even though Eagan knew them better than I did. "My boss, the chairman of the Committee on House Administration, is appointed by the Speaker to be the elected point-person responsible for overseeing the internal operations of the House," I said. "Like the Speaker, he is accountable to the elected Members of Congress. Our 435 elected bosses run the show," I continued. "Because Bob is being overwhelmed by his colleagues innumerable questions about their offices, my staffers are under immense pressure from the Chairman to stay on top of your work. Answering those questions is crucial to keeping the political consensus necessary for quick decision making," I told Eagan. "I mean, if the Speaker and the Chairman have to start pulling arrows out of their backs because elected officials were out of the loop, we will have screwed up big time," I continued.

Eagan knew where I was coming from. He told me that moving quickly did require political consensus and understood how our committee staff helped in that process. "This is a unique situation," he said. "Get rid of me if I do a bad job, but let me do my job." At that time, the seriousness of the situation reestablished itself in my heart and mind. *"I am getting in his way,"* I thought. Then I agreed to cut a deal with him. "I wholeheartedly understand how your team needs the freedom to get things done. This is important. I will loosen our grip, if you make sure we are always fully and completely informed on what is happening. No surprises."

"You got it," Eagan replied. "But there is one more thing," he said. "I don't want any future retribution by your staff because I asked for this favor. So I am asking you not to tell them about our conversation."

"No problem," I said, as we shook hands. Then I laughed nervously. "I won't say anything Jay, but that promise is only true for me," I replied. "If the Chairman says something in the next few weeks, I can't control that." Eagan stared at me. "I gotta tell Bob," I said. Begrudgingly, the House's Chief Administrative Officer accepted the deal. He had no other choice. With that behind us, the full team was once again able to focus our efforts on going forward.

Hours after my meeting with Eagan, new anthrax-testing results arrived. There was an additional positive anthrax reading in one of the House Office Buildings, specifically, the Ford House Office Building mailroom. Things once again looked gloomy. We sent an emergency communication out to the Members and their staff as quickly as possible. We wanted to make sure our people heard the news from us instead of from CNN or FOX.

The message read: "A positive anthrax sample test has been found in the Ford House Office Building mailroom. One mail bundling machine located in the Ford Building used for Longworth House Office Building mail is the machine that tested positive. All other bundling machine tests are negative. Because of the suspension of mail delivery, it is not known whether any affected mail was delivered. The House Child Care Center has been tested and found to be clean. At this time, the Centers for Disease Control and Prevention does not recommend additional individual testing."

Tension was at peak levels. Tuesday morning loomed around the corner. A positive test like that inevitably required additional testing, and time was running out. The screenings, which included actual wiping samples, called "sock pickups," as well as air samples in each strategic area, required a 24-hour turnaround. That meant it was becoming increasingly likely the Congressional House Office Buildings, where the Members worked, were going to be closed beyond our initial deadline.

This reality meant three things. One, we had to start focusing more on setting up the alternative office space. Two, we needed to set up another Members-only conference call because the angst level among staff and the Congress was rising by the minute as the news media fanned the flames of fear. Three, it was time to pray. I hadn't prayed in years. But we needed all the help we could get. Unfortunately, help was nowhere to be found. Around that same time, a machine at the P Street Off-Site Mail Delivery Center also tested positive. With bad news, however, came good news. The Page Dorm Facility had tested clean. Also, the initial feedback on the House floor was good. Certainty would be required, though, before anyone stepped foot on those marble floors.

Finally, on Monday the Capitol Building was cleared for use. Despite numerous jokes about how disappointing it was not to use the off-site location, the news was an immense relief. But we didn't celebrate for long. After all, the very real challenge of relocating every Congressional office in the House of Representatives to another federal building was hanging over our heads like a wide noose on a big tree.

Similar to the chamber relocation project, the office relocation project began with a general brainstorming session to outline all the possible needs and concerns associated with the operation. This included coordinating shuttle services to our new home at the General Accounting Office, and setting up phones, computers and public document rooms with printers, office supplies, stationery and copiers. In addition, we needed to handle logistics concerning security, communications and allocation of office space.

As expected, no one wanted to touch the office space issue. After all, dealing with the political headache of assigning office space was something Eagan and the rest of the house officers were looking to avoid. I couldn't blame them. Self-important politicians, especially powerful politicians, were not real keen on being told what to do or where to go. Herding Members was our territory.

The committee worked to relocate the other committees and offices. They, in turn, had their own work to do. It wasn't like the Congress could take a break. Much of the Patriot Act, for instance, was written by the House Judiciary Committee while Members where shuttling between their temporary offices at the GAO. Seeing Congressional business take place invigorated me and filled me with a sense of purpose. It also made me feel powerful. Whether I liked the purpose or the power better, I'm not sure, but I definitely liked the rush of activity.

Luckily, by the end of the second day away from the Hill, full environmental assessments had been completed on all of the targeted House offices. The good news was we could re-open all but two of the House Office Buildings. The bad news was the people who worked in the Longworth and Ford House Office Buildings would be closed out of their offices for days if not weeks longer. An email exchange between Eagan and me on Wednesday evening at 11:14 PM expressed our mixed feeling about the news;

"Jay, you and your team are really working your tails off, just wanted to let you know of the Chairman's press statement expressing his appreciation of your work," I said while forwarding a press release we had put together concerning the building openings.

WASHINGTON-The following are Chairman Bob Ney's (R-OH) comments on the opening of the Cannon, O'Neill and Rayburn HOB which will open at 9:00 a.m. Thursday, October 25th.

"The people's House will not be silenced," said Chairman Ney. "The American people can be proud our House office buildings will be open for business tomorrow and proud of Speaker Hastert's leadership during this ordeal. In addition, I would like to thank all the people working so diligently to keep the Congress operating. They have been patriots through this entire process."

Eagan replied simply;

"Thanks Neil. Running out of steam, I have to confess!!!"

We all were. It had been a long, dramatic month-and-a-half.

Looking the Other Way

Watching the House of Representatives pass Election Reform was an awesome experience. Few events compare with the thrill of witnessing legislation you helped to write get debated and passed. After nearly a year of long hours and tedious work, House passage of the Help America Vote Act meant the Congress was taking a big step toward bringing our nation's election system into the 21st century. Pride rushed through my veins as I took in the debate.

On the floor, it was the Bob and Steny show. Despite their partisan differences, Chairman Ney and Ranking Member Hoyer were able to put together a bill which received the vast support of both political parties. It was a testament to the two men, our teams, and the unique moment in which the debate occurred. The last ninety days had ushered in a true feeling of bipartisanship on Capitol Hill. Such sentiment was verified by the fact that a bill born of the partisan rancor of the 2000 presidential election passed the House of Representatives with overwhelming bipartisan support.

Bob kicked off the debate.

"Mr. Speaker, I rise today in support of H.R. 3295, the Help America Vote Act of 2001. This legislation is a culmination of a long series of hearings, discussions, and negotiations. In crafting this bipartisan election reform bill, we heard from and consulted with groups from across the United States that represent the interests of voters, election officials, state and local governments, and others who care about this issue."

Bob summed up the process. This was not a small bill. Steny summed up the politics.

"One year ago tonight, in Bush v. Gore, the United States Supreme Court effectively determined the outcome of our last Presidential election,"

Congressman Hoyer said with passion. "But today this House has an historic opportunity to let this day be remembered not for one of the most controversial decisions in the Court's history, but for congressional action to protect our most cherished democratic right: the right to vote and the right to have that vote counted."

Steny was right. The Supreme Court had based its unprecedented decision in part on the election-counting mismanagement in the state of Florida. Therefore, the court's ruling not only decided a presidency, but also made a compelling case for election reform. That case was strengthened the more the committee looked into the issue.

"One hundred million Americans went to the polls on November 7, 2000," Hoyer pointed out. "But an estimated six million, according to the CalTech-MIT study, failed to have their votes counted," he continued with a righteous indignation we all felt. "Thus, today, on this one-year anniversary of Bush v. Gore, I am pleased to join our colleague, the gentleman from Ohio, the chairman of our committee, and Members from both sides of the aisle in strongly supporting H.R. 3295 , the Help America Vote Act of 2001."

I sat next to Bob as Steny spoke. The two of us took in the moment. "A year ago, this vote would have seemed inconceivable," the chairman said, and I agreed. Yet there we were. Because of the controversy surrounding President Bush's election, many in the country and the Congress still could not accept the former Texas Governor as a legitimately elected president. This had led to an equally strong defense by those who supported the Bush presidency. With such a growing divide, the chips initially seemed stacked against any progress on election reform. But slowly the facts began to change the political dynamics of the debate.

Even before the 2000 presidential election polls closed in Florida, an impending tragedy was apparent. Several of the television networks decided to call the election in the state for Vice President Al Gore, despite the fact that counties in what is known as Florida's panhandle region were still voting. The media based their decisions on exit polls. Those are polls conducted as voters leave the voting booth. Thanks to the network's announcements, a Gore presidency loomed on the horizon. Then Florida began counting votes. Within a few hours, those same media outlets were forced to retract their projections. Before long, in fact, they decided the vote tallies they were seeing actually projected that Governor Bush would win the contest. And with that, he was soon perceived as the next President of the United States.

The next day, however, the margin between Bush and Gore remained incredibly slim, at only a few thousand votes. In a state of nearly twenty million people, that represented less than one half of one percent of Florida's total votes. The situation put Gore in a tough spot. Most of the country already presumed that Bush was the next president. In addition, a protracted legal battle for the presidency was unprecedented. It had never happened before. Still, as the Vice President's public supporters pointed out, he had received a half a million more votes than Governor Bush nationwide. But because of a couple of thousand votes in Florida, he was looking at electoral defeat. The results looked bleak for the Vice President and his tens of millions of supporters. Gore was then told of numerous instances of voter irregularities throughout the state. He decided to challenge the results through a recount. Several Democratic-leaning counties quickly began that process.

For the next month, partisan county officials on both sides argued over votes their aging punch card machines were not able to accurately count. The media beamed discomforting images of election workers across the world. In some cases, the workers were staring wildly at pieces of paper through large magnifying glasses. It was embarrassing. We looked like a third-world country. The pictures of old voting equipment obscuring our presidential election were a horrible contrast to the image of technology innovator and champion of democracy that our country would prefer to have seen beaming throughout the globe.

There were a lot of reasons for the voting problems in Florida, and our Committee dug into them immediately. Many of the errors in voting occurred because voters were confused by a ballot design, the butterfly ballot, used in certain precincts. More than anything though, the problems in Florida stemmed from the use of decades-old, paper-based punch card voting machines.

For months, the committee met with experts and analyzed data. Any piece of information we needed, we got. Ultimately, our information gathering all led to the same depressing reality. In communities with shoddy old equipment, the percentage of votes that were not counted was dramatically higher than in communities with new electronic equipment. This dichotomy generally broke down along economic lines, with wealthier suburbs having higher counts than poor rural communities or city neighborhoods. The inefficient election equipment and process had created a huge disparity in how Florida's votes were counted, and the numbers showed this was happening all across the country.

Such a reality was described to me in one meeting the following way:

"Imagine 100 people waiting in line to vote," the gentleman making the presentation said. "Then imagine that same number of people in another part of town or another part of the state," he continued. "When the first group votes on a touch-screen or electronic device, 100 out of 100 votes are counted. In the second group, only 98 or 99 votes are counted." The man's comments took my breath away. I was appalled thinking about the situation he described. "Now multiply that by a thousand," he continued. It was a powerful presentation, and a harsh reminder that we were walking on sacred ground - ground involving the fundamental premise of democracy: one person, one vote.

With the stakes so high, Bob, Steny and our committee moved expeditiously to construct the building blocks of the Help America Vote Act. They included three basic provisions. One, the federal government would pay for states and local governments to replace punch card ballots with better, electronic machines. Two, the bill would create an Elections Assistance Commission to administer federal elections. And three, Congress would create a set of minimum election administration standards to ensure proper election management throughout the country.

Day after day and week after week, the negotiations with our Democratic counterparts in the House, state officials and interested parties picked up steam. Not that there weren't bumps in the road. One week, our team of negotiators hammered through several key pieces of legislation. The next week the whole process bogged down in a battle over whether to use the word *and* or the word *or*. The debates were rarely personal. They were professional. And time consuming. In the debate of *and* versus *or*, for instance, both sides needed to reach out to lobbyists working on the issue, to see what they could support.

On our side, we worked with organizations representing local and state governments, voting machine companies, party officials, anti-voter fraud activists, veterans groups, the disabled community, and others. The Democrats worked with the civil rights community, the Hispanic community, party officials, voter access activists, voting machine companies and others. Many groups and lobbyists worked with both sides. Over time, we learned to build common ground and work out our differences.

Like Bob said on the floor of the House, "The staffs of the Committee on House Administration on both sides of the aisle all came together to make these ideas gel. Republicans and Democrats nationwide and here in this Congress agree on the necessity of ensuring that all citizens who wish to vote can, and that their votes will be counted accurately." Bob then went off script, which is when he was usually at his best.

"I hope, Mr. Speaker, that one day the way we will see punch card machines in the United States is to go to the Smithsonian in order to view them. This bill authorizes funds to make that happen," he continued before bringing the last ninety days of national turbulence together. "As we look around at what has happened to this country, as we look around at those who have tried to attack our very foundation, we realize that the election of individuals from all levels is important, because we do have the greatest democracy in the world." Steny picked up where Bob left off.

"This is an extraordinarily good bill," Hoyer said. "It is not a perfect bill, but it goes much further than anybody would have thought at the beginning of this session," he continued. "In fact, in a recent op-ed column in the *Washington Post*, former Presidents Ford and Carter observed: 'With the exception of the civil rights laws of the 1960s, this bill,' that is on the floor today, 'could provide the most important improvements in our democratic election system in our lifetimes.'"

Despite the intensity of Bob and Steny's political rhetoric, by the time the debate ended many hours later, my mind was elsewhere. I was thinking about my recent conversations with Jack. In recent weeks, I had begun negotiating with him to join his firm and the lobbyists of Team Abramoff. Ever since Bob's ascension to the chairmanship, Jack had made sure to let me know he had a position for me as a member of his lobbying team if I ever wanted to leave the Hill. Other lobbyists had told me the same thing. But Jack wasn't just any other lobbyist. He was special. All you had to do was read the newspaper to know that was the case.

In article after article, Jack was crowned the king of the lobbying industry. Such rhetoric was backed up by the rapid growth in lobbying revenues at Jack's new firm, Greenberg Traurig. In the first-year of Abramoff's time at Greenberg, the firm had moved from a mid-level lobbying operation to a top-five firm. As *The Hill* newspaper said, Jack's addition to the firm had Greenberg rapidly closing in on the top position, the lobbying firm with the most revenue.

My first substantive conversation about a job with Jack took place in the fall of 2001. He was hosting a food-tasting at his home showcasing the chef of his soon-to-be-opened downtown DC restaurant. With menus and food scattered throughout his posh Silver Spring, Maryland, home, Jack told those of us in attendance that his restaurant would have a political theme, and probably be named *Archives*. "The walls will be lined with historic pictures and items," he continued. "Each of will be signed and up for sale."

Jack's house was immaculate. While the group tried several different culinary offerings in his white-walled living room, Abramoff captivated Senator Hutchison with stories from his days as a political activist and movie producer. He told the Senator, who had an extremely conservative voting record, how he had left the Reagan team when "the Bushies" took over midway through President Reagan's second term. It was Jack's way of saying he was a true conservative, unlike the more moderate President George H.W. Bush. Jack then went on to court Senator Hutchison with a tale of how he and his director fought constantly over the director's decision to use profanity in Jack's film, *Red Scorpion*. Starring the actor Dolph Lundgren, *Red Scorpion* was an anti-communist action film, something he made sure to point out to the Senator.

"Jack's always on message," I laughed to myself. *"But, hey, he walks the walk. I mean here he is, talking to a conservative Senator about his time working for Reagan and his work producing an anti-communist film. Hell, he even had been a battle over family values and cursing in the movie."* I found Abramoff's authenticity and ideological commitment incredibly appealing. The fact that he made no bones about wanting to make money only added to his appeal. *"What is wrong with making money?"* I asked myself. *"We are all capitalists, aren't we?"*

Before long, Jack had the Senator and others laughing about how his movie had outperformed Sylvester Stallone's *Rambo* films in several Asian countries. While they continued to talk, I slipped downstairs to try out the new video golfing game Abramoff told me he just had installed in his basement. The screen took up an entire wall. A projector sat about twelve feet away and displayed the video of whatever golf course you were "playing" on the screen. From there, players stepped up and played just like regular golf - line up the ball and swing. The computer took care of the rest. It was too cool. And since it had cost $50,000, according to the guys I met downstairs while playing, it should have been.

Before walking upstairs, I continued to script myself for the upcoming conversation. In the days leading up to the event at Jack's house, Alison and I had talked about what I should say. We were enthusiastic about the opportunity of me to work for Jack. His professional trajectory suggested that such a decision would be good for me both economically and politically, and also allow me to get back into public service if I didn't like lobbying. Also, on numerous occasions, Jack had mentioned to me that he was proud of the work environment he created for his team It was one that allowed Team Abramoff to prioritize their families and their free time, he said. That was also a big selling point for us.

After Senator Hutchison left, I pulled Jack aside to talk. I told him I was interested in taking him up on his offer to join the team. He was excited. "Neil, that is wonderful," Jack said. "Lets get moving on that right away."

His words were just what I wanted to hear. "That is awesome," I said, while eagerly envisioning my new future. But I had not yet breathed a word of this potential employment change to Bob. Some of his former staffers, whom I did consult, thought Bob would be happy with my choice to leave but relieved that I'd be working for Jack, whom he admired. Still, I was concerned about Bob's reaction and told Jack so, along with the fact that Bob hated lengthy transitions.

"I love Bob," Jack said. "But if you're going to join the team, let's make sure it works for you first." His words startled me. Instead of embracing Jack's declaration of my independence, I felt scared by it. For the last seven years, my world was built around a simple premise: by always putting Bob's interests first, I also advanced my own interests. It was a classic co-dependent relationship. I may have enabled many of Bob's worst habits, but I was always there to pick up the pieces. And now Jack was telling me to stop looking at the world that way.

"Call my assistant and set up some time to talk about the job," Jack said. "Lets do it over golf, or a game."

"You got it," I replied.

Looking around at Jack's spacious house, I thought back to his stories about working for President Reagan. *"He has done what I want to do,"* I said to myself. *"Put in your public service time and then move on."* The spoils of political success surrounding me were beyond anything I had ever hoped to own. *"If Jack could do it, why shouldn't I?"* I asked. *"It is now or never. Next year will be an election year, and leaving Bob at that point won't be an option."*

At the end of the evening, Jack saw me off, but not without a final question.

"I forgot to ask earlier," he said. "But how are we progressing on the Foxcom thing?" Foxcom was the company competing for the wireless infrastructure contract in the House of Representatives. Jack had visited the committee to talk with Bob and me about at the committee about the project. "They are such good guys, and they're not even my clients," he said about the company. "My clients pay hundreds of thousands of dollars a month. This is personal."

The last words he used were nearly the exact words he used after Bob and I met with him and the company earlier in the year, before the September 11th attacks. Like most of the committee's projects, "the Foxcom thing" was an ongoing process. Initially, it slowed to a halt after the anthrax attacks and the changes around the Capitol associated with our new security footing. But now that an increased emphasis was being put on wireless communications, the Foxcom project was starting to pick up steam.

Of course, from the company's perspective, the project was moving far too slowly. They were used to operating on business-time, not Capitol-operations time. Also, Foxcom was not alone. There were two companies that hoped to install the high-end wireless infrastructure throughout the House side of the Capitol complex. The lobbyist representing Foxcom's competition had successfully positioned his client, not Foxcom, as the front-runner for the project during the tenure of the previous chairman. But then Bob and I took over, and weighed-in on behalf of Jack's company.

Part of the pitch against Foxcom was the fact that they were an Israeli-based company. People within and outside the government thought it was dangerous to hire a foreign company for such a sensitive project. After all, information flow within the Capitol-complex is a sensitive matter. This angered Jack greatly. He was a huge proponent of Israel, and brought it up during every conversation. "That is why this is personal for me," Jack said. It was a comment that reflected the changing nature of our relationship.

By the time Jack fully engaged Bob and me on the Foxcom project, we were only a few months into the Ney chairmanship. Foxcom wasn't our only Abramoff venture. We were also working with Jack and his team on several other projects. Our relationship was getting closer, and more corrupt. The closer relationship meant an influx of tickets, meals and campaign contributions from Team Abramoff. It also meant our view of Jack was expanding beyond his relationship with DeLay. We saw that Jack's increased influence could help us in other areas as well. The Chairman's increased power meant that there were more ways for Bob to help jack, too. Foxcom was a prime example.

Jack personally visited the committee along with a company representative. Bob and I, as well as a couple of committee staffers, joined them around a large wood conference table. We talked about the merits of the wireless project, and then discussed the company's plans and their history of working on these kind of projects. After the meeting wrapped up, and the company representatives and our staff dispersed, Bob and I spoke with Jack. Right away, I could tell that Bob wanted to go with Jack on the project.

Like me, Bob was learning to personally enjoy spending time with Jack. And vice versa. Jack took advantage of the budding friendship and went in for the sale.

He told the Chairman how much he appreciated Bob's even-handedness with the company. Jack said Congressman Hoyer supported Foxcom's bid, and so did the Israeli embassy. "We are all angry at how the other side is playing this," Abramoff said, in reference to his lobbying competition. "Therefore, the project is being watched by much of the DC-area Jewish community. This is personal."

Jack then promised to fully engage the company and what he called the company's "friends." They would support Bob if the Committee went with Foxcom, Jack said. He was suggesting that Bob could help a community, as much as a company, and get that community's political support, including campaign contributions. His words were nuanced, but Jack's intention was clear. If we gave him what his clients wanted, he'd see to it that the favor was repaid in contributions. Both parties would benefit.

Before committing, Bob told Jack we needed to get our ducks in a row. Jack understood where the Chairman was coming from. "If the National Security Agency or the House security professionals have a problem with Foxcom, it won't go anywhere," Abramoff said. "We all get that." Then he left.

After Jack walked out, Bob had me call Foxcom's competitors to hear their side of the argument They, too, were nuanced. But in a different way. Their approach revolved around trying to torpedo Foxcom for being an Israeli company, without saying that was the problem. I gave Bob the rundown. If there was any question about where we were going, my conversation with the lobbyist for Foxcom's competitors ended it. As long as everything checked out, Foxcom was going to get the work.

Of course, that was just the first step. Rarely did non-emergencies move quickly in the House. The project began and then stopped. It inched forward, then stood still. The events of September 11th didn't help. But the fundamental decision about the project had been made. Foxcom was in the drivers' seat.

After my conversation at Jack's house about employment, we met again to talk further at a hockey game. Sitting a few rows off the glass, Jack asked me what kind of salary I thought I deserved. Having asked some friends and colleagues their advice, I figured a salary of about $250,000 was a good starting point. But then, while I was at the game, I decided I didn't want Jack to think I was greedy, so I told him somewhere around $195,000 would be good.

"Wow, that is high," he said immediately. It was something he probably would have said whether I told him $50 or $500,000. "Since you're not joining the team with an existing book of lobbying clients, bringing you on is a risk," he said. "Not every good staffer turns into a good lobbyist. But I'll see what I can do."

Within seconds, we were talking about Foxcom again. Jack said he had been told that progress on their project slowed up again.

"Any chance we can push that along?" he asked.

His words made me shudder. Within two minutes, we had gone from discussing my potential salary as a lobbyist to my helping him as a staffer. I suddenly felt uncomfortable. *"If I don't help Jack, will he torpedo my job offer?"* I wondered. *"Or if I do, will he raise my salary?"*

Looking around, I was surrounded by thousands of screaming fans. And a big red flag staring me right in the face. I knew the merging of our two conversations was wrong. But I chose to walk right on by that fact. *"Bob would want me to move this project forward,"* I rationalized. *"I mean, the Chairman is fine with Foxcom and the general outcome of the project,"* I continued to myself. *"Speeding it along only helps all involved. I mean, what am I supposed to do?"* I grasped for an appropriate reason to do what my gut was telling me was inappropriate. So I pushed the project along.

Jack's hiring process was the opposite of what Bob's had been, namely taking a job and moving to Washington on about a weeks' notice. The first thing Jack asked me for was a list of all the contacts I had on the Hill and at the White House. He was tediously thorough. "Rate them all between 1 and 3," he said. "One meaning you know someone pretty well and three meaning you know them very well. "We want a good feel for what kind of access you will bring to the team." I gave him a list of hundreds of contacts. I also gave Jack a list of five references, with phone numbers for him to call. It was important that my potential new boss see how my relationships could benefit his team.

One of my references was the Chairman of the House Education and the Workforce Committee, John Boehner. He was from Ohio, and I wanted Jack to know I was close to the influential Ohio delegation. Another reference of mine was Congressman Tom Reynolds from New York. He was the chairman of the National Republican Congressional Committee. Adding him to my reference list was meant to show the firm that I understood the campaign aspect of the legislative and regulatory process, and could use that experience to create leverage for our clients. The Chief of Staff for the White House Office of Strategic Initiatives was also on my list. I included him so my potential employer knew that I was plugged in at the highest level to President Bush's operation.

Jack liked what he saw. He then told me to put together a business plan of the potential clients I could bring in during my first year or two at the firm.

From there, "You have to meet with several of the partners at the firm to get their buy-in for the move," Jack said. "Don't worry about all that too much," he continued. "But make sure they like you." As my progression from one job to the other progressed, I began mentioning to a few business contacts that I would be reaching out to them about becoming their lobbyist after I left Bob's office. Team Abramoff member and former DeLay staffer Tony Rudy suggested that I take a much more aggressive approach.

"Try to snag some clients before officially leaving Ney's office," he said. "You could park them here with me," he continued. "When you officially join the firm, you can then take them over," he said.

I told Rudy that was too much for me. "I could get caught doing that for sure," I said. Using my official office to line up paying clients for a future lobbying job was definitely something to stay away from. It was wrought with conflicts of interest, and, as I told Rudy, it could hurt Bob on the campaign trail.

"Bob would not approve," I continued in my conversation with Rudy. "And he is being a superstar about all this."

The chairman was very helpful in my move. When I first told him about my conversation with Jack, however, he was very sad. "I'm going to miss seeing you every day," he said, as we lit up a couple of cigarettes. But he also told me he understood. "It is good to move on sometimes," Bob continued. I sat back as the Chairman responded to my news. The two of us were sitting out on a park bench, watching the Independence Avenue traffic whisk by. Without a moment's hesitation, Bob told me he would help however he could. The Chairman saw the up side of the move for me professionally. He also saw that my joining Abramoff's team had an upside for his own career. But, mostly, Bob wanted to help me out because we were friends.

In the next couple of weeks, Ney and I put together a potential client list that I used as a part of my ongoing salary negotiations with Jack. It included several entities we thought would hire me immediately after I left Bob's office. The more the Chairman and I talked, the more clear it became that what Bob and I were talking about was a mutually beneficial agreement. Getting clients would mean more money for me and Jack. It would also mean more political allies for the Congressman. And since neither of us were remotely interested in winning any ethics in government awards, mapping out such a plan seemed relatively harmless.

I grew more and more excited about the move. But I also grew frustrated by the slow pace of the process. I went back and forth with Jack for weeks, then months. Many of our conversations took place via email. The most nerve-racking moments occurred when Jack would send several emails at once, including an email to my official government account asking me to check my private email account. Usually, that meant he was asking me about some sort of official project on my government account and then talking with me about the hiring process on the other. It was almost like he was paying me for official actions.

The first time it happened, I felt a tug in my gut that was similar to what I had felt during the hockey game. But, again, I chose to walk right on by my own conscience. Very simply, I looked the other way. *"This is just part of the process,"* I told myself. *"Everything will be better once my transition from staffer to lobbyist is done."*

FEBRUARY 12, 2002
WASHINGTON, DC

Leaving the Hill

SITTING SEVERAL CHAIRS AWAY FROM Bob, I took in the increasingly rancorous debate. It was my last day as a Capitol Hill staffer. The Chairman's new Staff Director sat next to him. My negotiations with Jack over the new job had taken months. But the change was finally here.

Once again, I was on the floor of the House of Representatives. This time I was there to watch the House pass Campaign Finance Reform. Unlike Election Reform, where the legislation involved voters actually voting, Campaign Finance Reform involved the process associated with influencing voters. Like Election Reform, the debate over how campaigns are financed in this country had consumed much of my time at the Committee. Meant to reduce the influence of big money in politics, campaign finance reform represented the most sweeping set of changes to political fundraising since Watergate. The anti-corruption legislation was a few hours away from passing. And after blocking the bill for nearly a year, we could no longer stop it.

Not yet gone from Congress, nor officially a lobbyist, I watched the legislative proceedings from a position of professional purgatory. On one hand, I listened to the debate from the perspective of the Capitol Hill staffer I had been for the last seven years. On the other, I viewed the proceedings from the perspective of the lobbyist I would soon become. Or already was. More than anything, however, I took in the action from the position of a newly christened member of Washington's political class. Moving on meant I was part of the club. One of the cool kids. Whatever the analogy, my transition from Ney World to Team Abramoff had me feeling every bit of what author Tom Wolfe called, "A Master of the Universe."

With an impressive salary all set, an office picked out and the Chairman

126

up to speed on the needs of my future clients, I might as well have already been a lobbyist. As I watched Congressman after Congressman step to the podium to discuss the topic of political corruption and big money in politics, my future clients, my future law firm and my future paychecks were never far from my mind.

Days earlier, a local Hill newspaper had broken the news that I was leaving Bob's office. Because of the growing intensity surrounding the campaign finance fight, neither Bob nor I had wanted that word to get out. We both knew it would look bad for the top staffer for the chairman leading the charge against reform to be seen cashing out as the Congress debated the role of big money in politics. But someone leaked word to the press, so there was nothing we could do but embrace the news.

"Neil Volz, majority staff director for the House Administration committee, is leaving the Hill after eight years as an aide to Rep. Bob Ney. (R-Ohio)," the article read.

"In recent months, Volz has found himself at the center of the Congressional response to anthrax attacks, including helping set up temporary office space for displaced lawmakers, as well as helping his boss play a key role in the campaign finance reform fight."

Bob was nice enough to go on record with a comment. There were always questions when someone left an office on Capitol Hill. In a sign to those who may have thought such a departure represented a souring of my relationship with the Chairman, Ney said in the article; "Neil is a great friend who I have enjoyed working with the last eight years. I was proud of his work as a member of my office and know his skills will take him far as he joins the K Street crowd down the street."

With the news suddenly out in the open, I scrambled to blast out an email to my many contacts on the Hill and throughout town. I had hoped to wait until after the campaign finance fight to alert everyone of my move. But, again, all I could do was embrace the news. "After nearly eight great years of working for Team Ney, I am leaving this wonderful job and entering another," my email message started. "I have accepted a position with the law and lobbying firm Greenberg Traurig. This is a great opportunity, and I am looking forward to the many new challenges it will bring."

"It is not easy leaving here," my message continued. "Bob is such a great friend and has been a fantastic boss. Whether it was working as an unpaid intern in the State Senate what feels like decades ago, or managing our operation as Staff Director and Chief of Staff right now, I have enjoyed every minute of it. My last day in the office will be next Wednesday. Paul

Vinovich will be the new Staff Director for the committee, while Will Heaton will be both the Chief of Staff for the personal office and remain the Chairman's Executive Assistant at the committee. Clearly, Team Ney is in extremely capable hands and ready for whatever the future throws our way. I look forward to saying goodbye and/or explaining my new responsibilities further to people on an individual basis. I'll let you know my new numbers and address as soon as I get them. Please take care."

The responses started flying in from all over Washington. Friends on the Hill sent messages of congratulations and good luck. At the White House, one of the lobbyists for President Bush wrote, "Neil, congrats! I am very happy for you. Obviously, we are sorry to see a friend leave the Hill, but know you will do very well in your new role. Don't hesitate to call if I can be of any help."

My media colleagues weighed in as well. "Spin me baby," said the bureau chief for one newspaper. "Bummer man," stated a reporter for an Ohio daily, before adding "We'll miss you, but I'm sure you'll rake in the big bucks and that's a very Republican thing to do. . . ."

Several people mentioned my new lobbying team. A few also specifically mentioned my new lobbying partner, Tony Rudy. "Ah, the firm with the hockey tickets," said one fellow Staff Director. "Congrats. Is this a sign that the Ney amendment on CFR doesn't have the votes?" Another colleague said, "It is good to see that Tony Rudy will have some competition." While still another said, "Congratulations, you will have to get over there and show up Rudy."

My new comrades in the lobbying business didn't miss a chance to make sure they covered themselves, too. "Do I know Will Heaton? Where did he come from?" one lobbyist said before asking me to make sure he got an introduction to the new top staffers in Bob's shop before I left.

"Thanks for all your patient help this past year," said another lobbyist before telling me to stay in touch. I liked that last part. It suggested a potential business opportunity. The revolving door was revolving.

Many of the professionals with whom I worked at the House of Representatives also replied. From one of the men in charge of the Capitol Hill police, I was told, "Congrats on the new job. It was a pleasure to work with you, particularly through the challenges that faced our great institution in the aftermath of the 9/11 tragedy. You served the House of Reps in an exemplary fashion. Keep in touch." From a different police officer I was told, "I am sorry to see you go. It has been a pleasure working with you on some pretty important and difficult issues." Still another colleague told me, "In a crisis and under normal operation you remain calm, cool and focused with a poker face most people would pay to be able to create." I liked the compliments, and believed them. But I tried to appear humble in my replies.

Around the same time I received an email from a public affairs professional at the Government Printing Office. The GPO was one of the numerous entities in which Bob's committee had oversight. "If there is anything we can do for you, please don't hesitate to let me know," he said. I forwarded that note along to Rudy with a comment that we needed to go after some of the multi-billion dollar printing business conducted by the GPO. Though filled with pride about some of my past work as a staffer, my heart and hopes for the future were clearly now with Team Abramoff.

As the Campaign Finance Reform debate droned on, my mind wandered. Last minute office packing was going to keep me late into the night. That meant I would be exhausted the next day as I left for Prague on a Valentine's Day trip with my wife. Unfortunately, I didn't worry too much about that. *"Alison is used to it,"* I told myself. Not to mention, she was happy that I was finally getting away from Bob's undue influence over our lives. Or so we thought. Either way, I was graduating, and happy to be moving on.

Joining the many lawyers, lobbyists, journalists, businessmen and political professionals of the permanent DC establishment, I felt like part of the Washington machine. Gone was the punishing reality of working for a fickle electorate. No longer reporting directly to the voters but to paid interests looking for special influence, I found myself being ushered into an insular new world. Even debates like campaign finance reform took on a new dynamic. I suddenly started seeing myself as above it all. My hard-earned professional network now provided me the safety of knowing I would be economically secure no matter what happened to the campaign finance bill. Or any other bill.

After all, there wasn't a major decision in the world that didn't have to come through Washington. No matter who was in power, big money was always at stake, working both sides of the aisle. That meant there was plenty of money to go around for insiders like me. Getting my piece of the pie, therefore, meant simply looking out for the best interests of the machine. You look out for me, I'll look out for you - that was the perspective of the Washington machine I was now joining.

Sitting on the House floor with my new perspective, I pondered the fundraising changes about to be implemented. Even though I opposed them, few knew them better than I did. That knowledge alone would be good at the next level. New rules meant new loopholes. New ways to do business. Why shouldn't I profit from the changes? Somebody was going to. Why shouldn't that somebody be me?

Unlike Election Reform, in which the Congress worked on a bipartisan basis to proactively change the nation's election system, the battle over campaign finance reform was a partisan food fight, an ideological struggle between those who wanted to further regulate the political market and those who did not. That was my view, at least. With few exceptions, liberal Members of Congress who wanted more government control over how money was spent in campaigns sat on the left side. Conservatives, who had more of a *laissez-faire* attitude about how political campaigns were funded, sat on the right.

Helping to create an even more fevered pitch was the fact that, by the time the campaign finance reform battle made its way to the House floor, the debate had moved beyond being just a contentious ideological fight. This dynamic happens in legislative fights all the time. In an effort to buy off enough votes for passage, the legislators had also waged a battle over the specific rules of the fundraising game. It was picking winners and losers. To secure specific votes, certain campaign money, such as that spent or generated by media corporations, was allowed to be included in the political debate in an unregulated manner. For those elected officials who were not so willing to change their vote, it was not. Spoils of the new system followed the support of specific Members of Congress. We might as well have been voting on a budget bill.

The legislation didn't start out that way. Born out of the fundraising abuses of the Clinton Administration during the mid-1990s, the debate over political fundraising had taken many turns over the years. It began when President Clinton's campaign team pried open a loophole in the law which allowed people and organizations to contribute unlimited amounts of money to state parties for long-term capital expenditures like new buildings. Instead of using these six-and seven-figure contributions for actual capital expenditures, however, the Clinton team used them to pay for television advertisements attacking Republicans.

In political-speak, unlimited money raised this way was known as "soft money." It was money which did not have to adhere to the spending restrictions of the regulated money normally used for campaigning. Television advertisements purchased with this type of soft money were known as "issue advertisements," or "issue ads."

Because the ads didn't use the phrase "vote for" or "vote against," under the law they weren't technically considered campaign advertisements. Not that they weren't meant to influence the political debate. There isn't a person alive who couldn't see how spending tens of millions of dollars in soft money television ads calling Speaker Gingrich a pompous, hate-filled, evil blowhard could impact public opinion. That's exactly why the Democrats ran them in the first place. We Republicans did the same thing.

At first glance, therefore, the basic building blocks of the problem seemed simple enough. So did the solution. Close the soft money loophole. A movement began. On one side of the debate was a bipartisan group of reformers. These true believers' core mission was to rid the political system of corruption through government regulation. Their perspective was that big money was corrupt, and so was soft money. The group was led by Arizona's Republican Senator John McCain, or as Bob called him, "Saint John." The Congressman thought McCain had a sanctimonious attitude. I did too.

Our offices didn't like each other. It was common knowledge that our debate with Senator McCain over legislation had turned personal. The press had reported on the dynamic. When our committee had field hearings in McCain's home state of Arizona, *Roll Call* outlined the dynamic in an article titled, "Targeting McCain?"

"House Republican are always coming up with creative ways to tweak Sen. John McCain (R-Ariz.), the article read. House Administration Chairman Bob Ney (R-Ohio), a foe of the McCain-Feingold campaign reform bill, is launching field hearings on the issue across the country just as the Senate prepares to start debating the matter next week. First stop? McCain's home state of Arizona, with a visit to the Phoenix City Council chambers March 17, during which the panel plans to raise constitutional questions about the reform legislation."

The piece was a typical inside-Washington soap opera. Bob acted like we weren't targeting McCain, and McCain's staff acted like they didn't care what we did. Of course, none of us were telling the truth. Respected journalist Robert Novak also began chronicling the tension between our offices. "Ney irritates McCain" was the headline of his first story about the hearing. Novak outlined how Bob's decision was being "cheered by fellow Republicans as payback against Senator John McCain." The reporting was accurate. Many conservatives were upset with the Senator's decision to visit vulnerable Republicans and campaign against them, because of their views on Campaign Finance Reform. Granted, conservatives weren't the only people who were upset. Senator McCain was as well. According to Novak, "McCain's aides made it clear they did not appreciate Ney's visit.

The congressman's staff ran into trouble pinning down the Phoenix City Hall for the hearings, and previously scheduled Arizona witnesses suddenly dropped out."

Two months later, when the Senator refused to join other supporters of his legislation in testifying before our committee, Novak's piece stated that McCain had been spotted casually hanging out with his Democratic allies - despite telling us he had official scheduling conflict. "Ney and McCain have been at odds ever since the congressman held a town meeting in Arizona, the senator's home state, that featured criticism of his bill," the article read. It was good political theater. And there were real differences between the two sides.

When introducing their bill in the Senate, McCain laid out the reformers' view:

"The many sponsors of this legislation have but one purpose: to enact fair, bipartisan campaign finance reform that seeks no special advantage for one party or another, but that helps change the public's widespread belief that politicians have no greater purpose than our own re-election."

His opening salvo rang hollow to me. The suggestion that elected politicians should operate outside of their own electoral interests seemed wildly unrealistic. To me, nothing was more cynical than a call for an end to political cynicism. Sincere or not, McCain's view contradicted the view we took over at the Committee. After a year of hearings and investigations about the issue, we concluded that McCain's approach to reducing corruption infringed on people's First Amendment rights to engage their government. It infringed on the marketplace of ideas. The give and take of public debate being what it is, we believed the issue was more complicated than what the Senator was suggesting. After all, other groups ran issue ads, too. It wasn't just the political parties who did so. Citizen groups, unions and corporations also raised unregulated soft money for their issue ads. Bob and I had seen this first hand.

During Ney's 1996 narrow election victory, the National Education Association, a union comprised of millions of teachers, ran television advertisements attacking Bob in his district. They spent hundreds of thousands of dollars on the effort. The union's barrage slammed Ney's voting record in the weeks leading up to the election.

One ad contained a grainy, nasty picture of Bob, some scary background music and a visual of him driving a bus full of schoolchildren off a cliff. The union's ads were effective. Bob's poll numbers dropped. But since the ads never mentioned the key phrases "vote for" or "vote against," the union's expenditures did not have to adhere to the $5,000 spending limit, which was the amount they could technically have spent "campaigning" directly for or against Bob in the general election. From the union's perspective, the ads weren't officially campaign advertisements. They were issue ads - ads that were educational in nature, meant to inform the voters of the issues, they said. From our perspective, of course, that was all bullshit. Aside from the obvious fact that we were frustrated and angry because we didn't have the money to respond ourselves, and there were no groups coming to our defense that late in the campaign, what were we going to do? Pass a law to shut down the voices of millions of teachers upset with Bob's voting record? That didn't seem like the right solution.

Leading our side of the debate was House Majority Whip Tom DeLay, "the Hammer." It was a clash of the Titans. McCain the moderate vs. DeLay the conservative. Their contrasts were stark, their approaches different.

"This bill strips citizens of their political rights and unconstitutionally attempts to regulate political speech," DeLay said, sounding the themes of a classic conservative argument. "The primary protection of our first amendment is the right of average citizens to get together and to freely and fully criticize their government," he continued. "Political speech is the key to political freedom, and this bill would radically weaken our first amendment right by inappropriately and unwisely constraining the right to political speech. It denies American citizens their fundamental right to criticize politicians."

Unlike McCain, who focused on the big money, DeLay focused on the individual citizen. He viewed money in the form of campaign contributions to candidates and causes as speech, something to be protected. I saw it that way, too. I was a purist. "How people spend their money engaging in the constitutionally protected give and take of public debate is not the government's business," I said. "Donations to a candidate or cause may be worthy of government oversight," I said at the time. "But I surely don't think they should be a crime."

McCain fired back against those type of sentiments. His view was that they were an overly simplistic interpretation of the Constitution. "Some will argue that the First Amendment of the Constitution renders unlawful any restrictions on the right of anyone to raise unlimited amounts of money for political campaigns," McCain fiercely declared. "Mr. President, which drafter of the Constitution believed or anticipated that the First Amendment would be exercised in political campaigns by the relatively few at the expense of the many?" he asked.

"Any voter with a healthy understanding of the flaws of human nature and who notices the vast amounts of money solicited and received by politicians cannot help but believe we are unduly influenced by our benefactor's generosity," the Senator continued. "Why can't we all agree to this very simple, very obvious truth: that campaign contributions from a single source that run into the hundreds of thousands or millions of dollars are not healthy to a democracy?" he asked. "Is that not self-evident?"

The more the debate progressed the more it became clear that we were not just looking at two different opinions on a piece of legislation. We were looking at two different world views.

DeLay stayed on the offensive. His goal? Raise questions about the McCain bill's ban on issue ads. The bill's ban would stop millions of citizens from expressing their point of view, the House Majority Whip thought. Like the advertisements run against Bob by the teachers, groups as varied as the National Rifle Association, the Sierra Club, the National Right to Life and Planned Parenthood all ran ads in the months preceding an election. DeLay knew that if the McCain bill passed, all those voices would be silenced. "Now, we all know that the last days before an election are a very crucial period of political dialogue," the Whip said. "That is when voters are really paying attention, and that is the precise reason that the incumbent protection scheme that is in the bill will suppress political speech sixty days before Election Day."

"This is a sham, DeLay said. "It shuts down the system. It shuts down political speech. It shuts down the opportunity to participate in elections. In a country the size of the United States, an individual citizen has very little chance of joining the political debate without banding together with others, so by blocking citizens' groups from participating in days leading up to an election, the bill removes a very vital tool that citizens can use to hold elected officials accountable."

Behind closed doors, it was hard to find someone who didn't believe DeLay had a point. Few people truly engaged in the issue thought McCain's provision banning citizen groups from running political ads was constitutional. "The courts will throw that provision out like they have similar past provisions," one legal scholars told me. Of course, those of us discussing the bill behind closed doors also knew the bill was good politics. McCain's argument about cleaning up government struck a nerve with the public. It always does. People inherently support reducing the influence of big money in their government.

What we were facing was a classic inside vs. outside debate, meaning the public discussion over campaign finance reform was different from the private debate. Since elected officials never want to appear to be influenced by money, discussing the issues openly is next to impossible. After all, it is far easier and more effective to demagogue an elected official who honestly admits that campaign contributions impact his work, than try to become more educated on the American system of government.

The idea of buying access to politicians is a prime example. In our system, the practice of citizens pooling resources to buy access to elected officials is a linchpin of the political process. With few exceptions, a couple of thousand dollars can buy nearly anyone a meeting with a Member of Congress or local official. This has good aspects and bad aspects. Either way, it smells dirty, enough to cause politicians to lose elections. Therefore, people whose names are on the ballot are justifiably hesitant to speak so plainly about the role that buying access plays in American politics. Yet it remains a key component of the process.

In a suit I had seen him wear a hundred times, Bob shuffled through the towering stack of papers situated on the podium in front of him. Watching the Congressman organize his thoughts, I began to have second thoughts about leaving his office. Like I was abandoning him or something, I found myself considering how big a role Bob had played in my life. Few people had meant more over the years. My professional success would not have been possible without his decision to give me a shot at the big time.

"Maybe I shouldn't go," I thought. *"Now is a bad time."* The whispers about Bob becoming a future leader, even Speaker, had gone from the backroom to the newsroom. *"It's possible he needs me now more than ever."* The buyers' remorse had begun. People told me it would.

"You can't replicate life on the Hill," said one of my buddies who had returned to the Congress after lobbying for a few years. Overcome by emotion, I got up and walked off the floor of the House.

"What an amazing eight years," I told myself as I sauntered, one more time, through the Capitol Building. I knew that once I turned in my badge, I would no longer be allowed to walk unaccompanied through these hallowed halls. Whether my feelings revolved around my fear of giving up the power, the fact the Committee remained as busy as ever, or were merely what people go through when they leave a long-term employer, I wasn't sure. But the remorse felt real. Still, I knew it was time go. It hadn't even been 18 months since our wedding, and my wife and I were already in counseling. Also, the allure of Team Abramoff was calling. I had been offered other jobs by other lobbyists, but Team Abramoff is where I wanted to be. Working

for Jack symbolized the next wrung up of Washington's ladder of influence. The move would let me fly higher and faster.

As I returned to the House floor for the last time as a Hill staffer, Jack was nearly two thousand miles away. Unbeknownst to me, he and Scanlon were meeting with a potential new client, the Tigua Indian tribe of El Paso, Texas. The tribe's casino had recently been shut down by the Lone Star state. They were in dire straits. Desperate for help, the Tigua's schools, medical facilities and job base all depended on their recently shuttered casino. In part because of Jack and Scanlon's work on behalf of another client, the tribe's gaming operation was now closed. The Tigua had not been the target of their efforts, but the tribe had still paid the price. Now Jack and Scanlon wanted the Tigua to pay them $5 million to get the Congress to re-open their casino. After that, the duo wanted the tribe to agree to hire Team Abramoff as their lobbyists in Washington. The two weren't talking about buying access. Jack and Scanlon were talking about buying results.

The basics of their plan were outlined in a memo the two gave the tribe's Texas consultant a few days earlier, when they set up the meeting with the Tigua's elected leadership.

Jack emailed Scanlon. "Fire up the jet baby, we're going to El Paso!!"

"I want all their MONEY," Scanlon replied before the two sent off the following proposal:

"Attached please find Mike Scanlon's Operation Open Doors plan. I appreciate your conveying this to the Governor and Tribal Council.

As we discussed, until we are able to achieve the federal legislative fix, we at Greenberg Traurig will not be engaged by the tribe for services officially. All our work will be done on a pro bono basis. Once the legislation is signed by the President, we would anticipate the tribe engaging us to represent it at the federal level and assist with the effort to obtain a Class III compact. Our normal rate in our tribal government practice is between $125, 000 to $175,000 per month for our clients.

I know the prospect of a lobbying firm working for free until the major victory has been achieved is unusual, but, with the success rate we have had over the past decade, we are sufficiently confident in our abilities that we can afford to take this risk. Our motivations for this representation are manifold, including the critical importance of not allowing tribal sovereignty to be eroded by the actions of the State of Texas. While we are Republicans, and normally want all Republicans to prevail in electoral challenges, this ill advised decision on the part of the Republican leadership in Texas must not stand, and we intend to right this using, in part, Republican leaders from Washington.

Of course, it would be insincere of me to not note that our other motivations include the hope and expectation that, if we succeed, we can expect to have a long term relationship with the tribe by representing their interests on the federal level.

The proposal Mike Scanlon has prepared is, in our view, the best chance the tribe has to overcome the gross indignity perpetrated by the Texas State authorities. Indeed, as I mentioned on the phone, the several day delay getting this to you was the consequence of our wanting to ensure that we have a path to get this done, and a couple Senators willing to ram this through initially. I am pleased to note that both are in place.

Coupled with this plan, we anticipate that the tribe will have to make approximately $300,000 in federal political contributions. We are currently preparing a target list of those contributions and hope to have them to you shortly. Perhaps in the interim, the tribal council could approve the gross amount, with details to follow.

Mike and I are both free to answer any questions you might have on this proposal and we look forward to getting moving rapidly."

While Jack and Scanlon sat in El Paso meeting with the Tigua, they knew the tribe desperately needed their help. That need meant they were about to land a new client. What they didn't know, though, was that they were also testing the limits of the very corruption issue being debated on the House floor. And likewise, what I didn't know at the time was that I was about to become part of something more corrupt than anything I had seen in my time on Capitol Hill.

Joining Team Abramoff

It was a brisk but beautiful winter morning. I eagerly made my way downtown. My first day as a lobbyist had finally arrived. Before moving to Washington, I wasn't a hundred percent sure what a lobbyist really did. I saw them in Columbus while working as a statehouse intern for Bob, but didn't have much interaction with them. They seemed more like friends of then-Senator Ney, than anything else. As far as I could tell, lobbyists were like political agents. Instead of representing athletes or actors, they represented organizations, such as corporations or unions. Lobbyists held the door open and smiled. Or, at least that is what I thought. Over time, I learned that lobbying wasn't so simple. Not that the caricature wasn't accurate, just that the business of lobbying has more to it than I initially thought.

Most lobbyists view themselves as problem solvers. Fixers. People who manipulate the levers of government on behalf of a client, an employer or a cause. According to Capital lore, it was President Ulysses S. Grant who first coined the term, *lobbyist*. Grant, a well known drinker and smoker, was a regular at Washington's Willard Hotel. It was there that he described the wheelers and dealers who spent time in the hotel's lobby trying to influence him as *lobbyists*. And a label was born.

Much has changed since the late 1800s. No longer a cottage industry run by a few hotel hangers-on, there are now tens of thousands of paid lobbyists in Washington. Like journalists, who are protected by the First Amendment, lobbyists also find shelter in the Constitution. Because of the "right to petition" clause, citizens and organized groups have the right to fully engage their government. Even if voters wanted to ban special interest lobbying, as they have tried, Congress cannot deny people the right to fully access the political process. As such, allowing for a full "redress of grievances" has become quite a lucrative practice. Residing at the intersection of government and commerce, lobbyists influence every major issue addressed in this country. If the federal government impacts an activity, the lobbying industry impacts that activity. In fact, over time, the industry has become what some people call the fourth branch of government. The money branch. And I was ready to get my piece of the pie.

For me, becoming a lobbyist meant simply hanging up my Capitol Hill jersey to join Team Abramoff at the law firm of Greenberg Traurig. Based in Miami, Greenberg is one of the largest law firms in the world. Its D.C. office, a mountain of marble, glass and concrete, stands on the corner of the proverbial K Street corridor of downtown Washington. Across one street is the White House. Across another is the national headquarters of the Chamber of Commerce.

In many respects, walking into Greenberg's office represented exactly the kind of fresh start I needed, and things certainly seemed different. No longer driving to work, I instead took the metro. No longer working on the Hill, I made my professional home in DC's business district. Opening the gold framed glass door at the front of Greenberg's headquarters was nothing like entering the Capitol Building. Instead of armed police officers, magnetometers and the pandemonium of the tourist trade, I was met by the serene smile of a lone security guard. Dressed in a well-tailored suit, the guard sat behind a desk midway down a marble-laden hallway. He motioned me toward to the elevator. As the steel doors closed behind me, I hit the button for the fifth floor.

When I've been asked to answer the question, "When was your first day as a member of Team Abramoff?" riding the elevator is the moment that pops in my head. Standing alone in that elevator, however, the transition wasn't so clear cut. In fact, my transition to Team Abramoff stood in stark contrast to the simple process of stepping into that elevator. Unlike the elevator, where the doors opened, I got in, and then immediately changed from being on the outside standing still to being on the inside and moving, becoming a lobbyist was more of an incremental transformation.

Even though I had not moved into my new office yet, I felt like I was already a member of the lobbying team. After all, many of the people I would be working with at Greenberg were folks I had already been working with in Bob's office. Similarly, many of the issues I would be working on as a lobbyist for Team Abramoff were ones I worked on at the Committee. The issues and the people were the same. It was the relationship between the people and the issues that changed.

In part, the overlap of work explains why I felt so relieved to finally become an official member of Jack's team. After months of awkward back and forth negotiations, during which I was assisting Jack's clients while also discussing my future job with him, finally getting there represented an end to my own shadowy behavior. Because of the conflict of interest associated with helping Jack while negotiating for my future salary, I should have told my future boss that I couldn't help his clients' matters while we were negotiating. But now that it was all over, I stopped worrying.

"That kind of thing is just part of the process, right?" I asked myself. *"I mean, nearly half of the Members of Congress who retired in the last ten years went in to the lobbying business. Surely they had similar problems navigating the conflicts associated with disentangling themselves from one job in order to get to another,"* I rationalized. Ultimately, I didn't know for sure whether other people had gone through similar situations or not. Nor did I really care. Looking in the mirror for some introspection wasn't my business. My business was to get paid. And to join the ranks of the well-to-do professionals who lived in the upscale neighborhoods of the District and its sprawling suburbs.

Becoming a lobbyist seemed like a natural next step for me. It was like I was taking part in a natural exodus of senior Republican staffers who were becoming lobbyists. Many of my fellow chiefs of staff and I used to receive regular email updates from DeLay's office, and others, with lists of open, high-paying lobbying jobs. It was an acknowledged fact that lobbying firms and companies were looking to hire Republicans like me who were in charge of the machinery of government. The collusion of big business and big government was on cruise control. Like certain Democrats had done for decades, many of us Republicans were merely following the Washington money trail, a trail that inevitably leads to the lobbying industry. It was like going from high school to college. As much as possible, I tried to sell myself on the idea that walking through the revolving door from public servant to paid political operative was a natural progression of our aging political revolution. "More of an evolution of sorts," I would say. The free market at work. But deep down, I had my doubts.

When the elevator doors opened, I was met by a beautiful young receptionist who asked me to take a seat. Straight ahead was a large, glass-enclosed conference room overlooking the Washington Monument and the White House. On both sides of the room hung large flat-screen televisions with loud news talk emanating from them.

Pointing at the scenic terrace overlooking Pennsylvania Avenue, I instinctively commented on the security challenges our office surely posed to the White House in the new post-9/11 environment. "Yeah, we have to call Secret Service every time we have a party out there," she replied. Though I still wasn't exactly sure what I was getting into, sitting on a black leather chair talking about White House security in Greenberg's plush lobby had me suddenly feeling very comfortable. Any nervousness about the job, about Jack, about leaving Bob, started to subside.

The first person I met with was the firm's Office Manager. She had me fill out some paperwork and showed me to my new office. It was spacious and, in contrast to my Hill office, full of modern furniture. It also had a balcony which overlooked the White House. Tony Rudy's office was next door. He was next to Jack. In simple terms, the Southeastern corner of Greenberg's fifth floor was a key part of Team Abramoff's real estate.

Next, I met with the Managing Partner of the Washington office, Joe Reeder. Reeder, a proud Texas Democrat, was a hard working rainmaker for the firm. A rainmaker is someone who brings in lots of clients and corresponding revenue. Before his work as a DC lawyer, Reeder had been Undersecretary of the United States Army for the Clinton Administration. Even in a GOP-led town, he was a big deal. It wasn't the first time we had met. At the end of my several month-long hiring process at Greenberg, the two of us spoke briefly. By that point I had already been hired. Nonetheless, the head of the firm's government affairs department in Florida told me I needed to speak with Reeder, "As a courtesy." Reeder was, after all, the Managing Partner of the Washington office. But the meeting was just a formality. As it turned out, that was a good thing. Quizzing me about my contacts, my business plan and how well I knew Jack, Reeder was clearly irked that I was coming on board without his pre-approval. Or, at least, that is what I thought had him irate. Whatever it was, our meeting was contentious. He questioned everything I said. I couldn't blame him. Who would? He was supposed to be the boss, yet he was meeting with some guy who had already been hired without his input. The longer I sat there, the more I felt for him.

Our second meeting went better. Reeder was generally gracious, but there was some conflict. After a few minutes of "Welcome to Greenberg" small talk, Joe told me to make sure I received appropriate ethics training from the firm. He stressed the point several times and kept referring to me as, "One of Jack's guys." I didn't like the label. I wanted him to like me, and I could tell the label was one of derision. Additionally, I wasn't sure why Reeder thought all the badgering was necessary. Before I left, my new

Managing Partner told me that if I had any problems with the firm's ethics training, or received any blowback or resistance to his instructions to let him know. I told him I would.

As quickly as I could, I took Reeder's advice into Jack's office. "Fuck Joe," Abramoff said plainly. "Don't even listen to him. Joe is the old regime. We are taking over this firm." Jack labeled Reeder an "old-school Democrat," while stoking the fire of what was called The K Street Project. Or as we generally called it, "The cause." To Jack and me, the cause was nothing more than our ongoing efforts to expand the reach of the Republican Revolution beyond just the institutions of government. Jack's words fired me up. We both knew that getting conservatives placed into organizations that influenced American public policy would help advance the goals of limited government and free markets. If that meant getting paid really well to infiltrate traditionally liberal institutions like the media, higher education, think tanks and law firms, "So be it," Jack said, as we laughed.

While Jack and I went back and forth, I watched my new boss quickly morph from the guy raging against Reeder to the humble, sarcastic and irreverent jokester who was so captivating. Several golf clubs leaned against the back wall of his office. Swinging them back and forth, Jack changed the subject to the big opening night party for Signatures, his downtown restaurant. "Is Bob going to be there?" Jack asked.

""I'll call him now," I replied, taking out my mobile phone. My action was meant to show Jack what kind of access I still had with Bob. Before I could call, Jack asked me how Bob was taking my transition. "Some Members of Congress don't take it well," he commented. I told him everything was fine. "Everyone says things are good," he continued. "Seriously, is Bob taking it well?" he asked again with a heightened sense of purpose.

Again, I told him Bob was taking it well. "I think he misses me on a day to day basis, but we continue to talk all the time," I said. "I am helping him to train his new chief of staff and committee staff director, and he is giving me ideas on clients and how best to make my new life here at the firm work," I continued. Jack smiled. He seemed happy. That made me happy.

One thing we didn't discuss was what Reeder was worried about, namely my ethics training. Like many former top Hill staffers, I was supposed to adhere to a one-year lobbying ban that was passed into law as a way to slow down the revolving door used by former public officials, like me, who went on to become lobbyists. The one-year ban was designed to reduce corruption by creating a cooling off period between the two jobs. During that cooling off period, former staffers and legislators are not supposed to influence their former staff or bosses and colleagues on public policy matters. That meant I couldn't lobby the Congressman, his staff or any of the members of the House Administration Committee.

For the most part, Jack left conversations about ethics to others. My new colleagues helped to fill in the blanks. In one conversations I had with a member of Jack's team, we discussed how the rules governing my one-year ban were too nebulous to even worry about. "Define lobbying," my colleague told me. "You can't. Who says you can't have beers or talk politics with Bob or his staff? You guys are friends. It isn't lobbying."

"That kind of thing is unenforceable," he continued. "Just be careful." Though I was nervous about how I was supposed to interact with Bob's office, his words made sense. In fact, on a certain level, they were exactly what I wanted to hear. I didn't want the one year ban to restrict my job too much. But then I didn't yearn to break the ban either.

Since it was my first day, I decided to take a quick walk across the street to check out the new neighborhood. From Greenberg's front door, it was 227 steps to the front gate at the White House. To get there, I had to walk through Lafayette Square. The square and the gate reminded me of the Stand Up for Steel Rally and Bob's exploits at the event. Years later, President Bush ended up implementing the trade sanctions on foreign steel like his campaign had promised the steelworkers. *"A lot happens here,"* I thought to myself, familiarizing myself with my new surroundings. Despite living in DC for more than seven years, the area around the White House remained somewhat new territory for me.

As I took everything in, I started to miss the Capitol Building. It suddenly felt like I would never be there again. The thought made me laugh. *"Jack won't pay my salary for too long if I don't go to Capitol Hill,"* I chuckled. In the middle of Lafayette Square is a large equestrian statue of President Andrew Jackson, the seventh President of the United States. Jackson, our first and arguably only true populist Commander in Chief, was one of the founders of the Democrat Party. His battles with the banks would have been popular in Bob's district. *"The blue collar farmers of Appalachia would have eaten up his attacks on the elite and the rich."* I thought. *My new lobbying clients will have a different point of view. Not because they are rich and powerful, but because they are American Indian tribes."*

Before becoming President and ushering in what continues to be known as "Jacksonian Democracy," Andrew Jackson had been a war hero. As the military governor of Florida, his battles with the Seminole Indians were legendary. It was during this time that the future president began to build support for the removal of American Indians from the Southeastern region of the United States. Two of our tribal clients, the Choctaw and the Coushatta, were impacted by those policies, policies which became known as the Trail of Tears.

For thousands of years, the Choctaw Indians had resided in what is now the American Southeast. They helped the 13 colonies in the Revolutionary War. Decades later, they sided with the United States in the War of 1812 against Britain and Tecumsah's Shawnee tribe. With Jackson's election in 1828, however, things started to change. Tribes like the Choctaw and Coushatta were told to move west. There were reservations for them there. But they refused to leave. Isolation and poverty followed.

Already an advocate for my clients, I felt the tinge of an oppressive history as I circled Jackson's statue. Looking back at our office, I couldn't help but also feel an ironic sense of justice as I thought about how several of the tribes he had tried to remove were now paying for our lobbying team's high-end Washington DC office space. The fact that our team had just secured a $16 million check from the Department of Justice for construction of a jail on the Choctaw reservation only made me smile more. Jackson was probably turning in his grave.

Becoming a member of the team meant learning about the politics of Indian Country. And how tribes operate. In our system, American Indian tribes are unique entities. They can be taxed and regulated like either a business or a government entity, depending on the situation. My new lobbying team were experts at exploiting such a unique status. It was a skill I would quickly learn. Were the tribes a government? A business? Or both? It depended on what was most advantageous. If we found ourselves in as situation where the client could qualify for a grant as a government entity, then they were a government. If the client could be exempt from certain taxes because they were a business, well, then they were a business. Everything was relative. The rules depended on the situation.

It was no wonder that Reeder insisted on me getting ethics training. Nor was it a surprise that I didn't do it. The situation was a microcosm of the firm's relationship with Jack. From their perspective, Team Abramoff represented a volatile mix of risk and reward. Jack's multimillion dollar book of business was a big attraction. But the win-at-all-costs attitude of the team also created a *laissez faire* approach toward the rules. All the rules. This included the rules that defined a tribal entity as well as the rules governing what gifts Members of Congress and their staffs could take from lobbyists. With Jack opening his own restaurant and people like me ready to use it, the possibility of public servants getting free drinks, meals and events had to be a concern to the firm.

But how do you control Team Abramoff? Having been assembled at another firm, the team was just entering its second year at our new firm when I arrived. And since part of our goal was to take over the firm, most of the team couldn't care less about ingratiating ourselves with the firm as a whole. We were "renting space," as one of my colleagues put it. The tension was apparent to me from day one. It grew even more so as days passed.

Sometime during my first few weeks at Greenberg, this struggle manifested itself during a meeting of the Washington office's full lobbying team. Though Team Abramoff was by far the largest lobbying group in the firm, the DC office's full lobbying team was also comprised of numerous smaller lobbying groups. With the Florida leadership in town for the get-together, the firm announced new ethics guidelines and accounting procedures for the lobbyists in the Washington office. Under the new guidelines, the names of every elected official or staffer who received a gift of any kind had to be accounted for in writing before a lobbyist could be reimbursed for that expense. This included meals, drinks, tickets, trips and anything else that could be defined as a gift.

An argument ensued. Actually two arguments ensued, one was in public and one behind the scenes. My new lobbying colleague, Kevin Ring, led the public charge against the firm's move on behalf of Team Abramoff. Kevin was worried about how our contacts on the Hill, and at the White House, would feel about the new rules. After all, our contacts were supposed to adhere to certain gift and meal limits on what they could and could not take from lobbyists. "Recording their names would make them uncomfortable," he said. "And that would then make them less likely to help our clients."

"If no one is doing anything wrong, then we don't have anything to worry about," said the firm's Florida leadership in response. It was a tough statement to dispute. But it also didn't reflect the reality of Washington lobbying. When I worked on Capitol Hill, I broke the $50 gift limit for meals and events several times a week, with different lobbyists. Though I didn't know it with certainty, my impression was that more staffers in my position than not conducted themselves in a similar manner. It was pretty straightforward. A staffer goes to lunch, dinner or drinks with a lobbyist to network and talk. The lobbyist pays the cost of the get-together, and the specifics of the transaction are barely discussed. Neither party wants to get into the details. The lobbyists in the room at our full-office meeting were all familiar with the process. Each operated differently, but knew that what Kevin was saying had merit. That fact necessitated the second, more private argument about the new rules.

"I will never fucking turn over a single name of a person I am spending money on," my colleague Todd Boulanger said in Jack's office after the meeting. Several members of Jack's team were there. Many of the guys felt defensive about the new policies. "They are singling us out," one of them said, before going on his own tirade about the meeting. He told Jack the firm was trying to hamstring the team's success. "They want to control us," he said.

Jack shook his head. He knew better. "No one wants a public fight," Abramoff said. "And no one wants to do anything that would hurt the clients." He was right. The clients pay the bills. "If we didn't give them names, what will they do?" Jack asked, as the room slowly quieted down. "Nothing? Come up with something we can live with?"

Not having any answers, I just listened. The debate was fascinating. Unlike Ney World, where there was a single line of authority and we were all on the same team, I could see that my law firm worked differently. There were several centers of influence in the Washington office, let alone the firm as a whole. Knowing who buttered my bread, I lined up squarely and unequivocally behind Jack. The contours of the next few years were already taking shape.

MARCH 18, 2002
WASHINGTON, DC

"We're f'ing gold!!!!"

"Jack and I need to go see the man," Rudy emailed me. The "man" Rudy was talking about was Bob. Word among the team was that Jack was working on a project. A big tribal project, one that entailed attaching a provision to a moving piece of legislation. That being the case, from his perch as the House Chairman responsible for negotiating Election Reform with the Senate, Bob was indeed the man to see. If anyone had the power to affix an amendment to a bill, it was Chairman Ney.

Rudy was the first one to mention the Tigua tribe to me. When he said Jack was looking at reeling in another big Indian client, right away I wanted in. I didn't even ask any questions. Still the new guy in the office, I figured that watching Jack manage a client from beginning to end was something that had to be good for me. After Rudy mentioned that this new mystery client needed to get an amendment quietly attached to a bill without its home state Senators knowing about it, our conversation inevitably drifted toward Election Reform.

Getting a provision attached to a bill can be hard. Getting a provision attached to a bill without the hometown Senator's knowing about it is very hard. It required a powerful champion who was willing to not only move the provision but be quiet about it. Jack, Rudy and I all knew Bob would be willing to cut that kind of deal. He had proven his toughness with the Gus Boulis *Congressional Record* statement. From there, the three of us debated whether Election Reform was the right bill for us to target. We needed to make sure that any bill we targeted would become law. Attaching a provision to a bill that wasn't going to pass would have been a stupid move.

Because of the politics of Election Reform, namely that it stemmed from the high-profile 2000 presidential election in Florida, action on the

Hill had to happen. "Both sides need it politically," I said. "Trust me, I know this shit," I told Rudy. "It is a "must-pass" bill for sure."

Rudy didn't doubt that I knew what I was talking about; nonetheless, he suggested that some of the conservatives in the House didn't think the GOP needed to actually pass an Election Reform bill. "They are saying it is too expensive," Rudy told me. "We need to check it out. We also need to find out what the Democrats who run the Senate are thinking," he continued. "This is too big of a deal for us to pick the wrong legislative vehicle." His thoroughness made sense to me.

Days later, Rudy and I picked up the conversation with several of our Democrat colleagues, including those who were close to Senate Majority Whip Harry Reid. A few of my new colleagues lobbied the Reid office. And one, a former staffer for the Majority Whip's office, had just joined Team Abramoff in the last few weeks. Even though he was a Democrat and I was a Republican, we shared notes. We learned about the team and about being lobbyists together. It was nice to have someone else going through the process of joining the team, despite our party differences. It was also nice to have the kind of access to senior Democrat offices that my lobbying colleagues had. With the Democrats running the Senate, their insight on the prospects for the Election Reform bill was invaluable.

After numerous calls and conversations with our various Hill contacts, Rudy and my Democrat colleagues concluded that both sides of the aisle were, in fact, feeling enough political pressure to view Election Reform as a "must-pass" bill, namely something that needed to be done before the upcoming midterm elections. The more we looked the more we realized that Election Reform was a good target. It was one of the few legislative trains in town that seemed destined for the President's signature. Our clients appeared to have a vehicle.

Rudy requested that I help set up a meeting between Jack and Bob. I sprang into action. Despite only being at Greenberg for a month, I knew full well that Jack rarely visited the Hill. If he was going, it was a big deal. Right away, I called Heaton. With similar instincts, Bob's new chief of staff sprang into action. He pulled up the schedule on his computer as we talked on the phone. It felt like I was still Bob's top staffer. Heaton, who months earlier had been the Chairman's 22-year-old Executive Assistant and driver, worked with me to quickly lock in a time. After thanking Bob's new chief of staff for the quick turnaround, I filled Rudy in on the specifics.

"So, what is this about?" I asked. Having already set up the meeting for Jack and Bob, I figured Rudy would start filling me in on the details. He said the project had to do with some tribe. "Of course it has to do with some tribe," I told him. I already knew that. "Most of our practice revolves around tribes. Come on, man. What are we talking about?" Rudy said it had to do with a tribe in Texas but that he didn't really know all the specifics. He said I should talk to Jack. It was a classic stiff-arm.

Rudy's run-around made me angry. "*He knows better,*" I thought to myself. "*If it deals with Bob, it is my business.*" If my colleague was protecting his professional territory by keeping me away from some contact or another that I didn't know, or wasn't Bob, I could understand. But he was too smart to mess with my old office, I assumed. His gamesmanship had to be something else. "*Maybe he is worried about my one-year ban,*" I continued thinking. Could be. But that also seemed like an unlikely reason. "*We both know I'm not going to the meeting because of my ban; is he really scared to even talk about what was going on when it is just the two of us in his office? I mean, I just set the meeting up. That isn't Rudy. It has to be something else.*"

We all knew I had one-year ban issues. And with Jack asking Bob to attach a provision to Election Reform, it was obvious to all of us that I was not going to be included in the meeting. Knowing I would not be taking part in "the ask" had me concerned. Nonetheless, I was determined not to let the lobbying ban force me to give up any territorial rights over my valuable Ney turf. I convinced myself that while attending the meeting was inappropriate, setting it up and prepping all sides for the summit was somehow acceptable under the one-year ban. In that way, I made sure to remain fully involved in the process. If Rudy thought he was going to use the ban to block me out of my friendship with Bob in any way, he had another thing coming. Not that I was a hundred percent sure that Rudy was encroaching on my relationships. It didn't make sense for him to operate that way. But I wanted to make sure.

After all, making sure my relationship with Bob remained healthy was in all of our interests. Mine. Jack's. Rudy's. And Bob's. It was something no one disputed. As Jack said, he had brought me on board in part because of my relationship with the Chairman. When I talked with Bob a few hours later, he told me Heaton had informed him of the meeting. "I won't be there," I said. "But Jack will. He rarely goes to the Hill," I continued. "This is a big deal."

"Speaking of that, what is the deal?" Bob wanted to know.

"I'm not sure," I said. "It has something to do with Indians and Election Reform," I continued suddenly sounding like Rudy. That didn't cut it for Bob. Like I was still working for him, he chastised me about not having all the information. "I wish I knew more. Talk to Jack," I said.

Since I left Bob's office, having to clamor for information was nothing new. The team had more than thirty clients, and was always talking about bringing on new business. I tried to keep up. But it was more than just the clients that I needed to learn about. There was also the team. My new colleagues came from all over Washington. Their experiences impacted what the team could do for our clients, so I needed to know about them. And yet, at the same time, I needed to focus on managing my own transition from staffer to lobbyist. That meant bringing my contacts and friends up to speed with my new clients and Team Abramoff. It was a cycle that kept me feeling behind. In fact, much of my time felt like a crash course on lobbying, and another crash course on Team Abramoff. And there wasn't a syllabus anywhere to be found.

"For the first six months, your main job is to turn your Rolodex over to the team," said my new colleague Kevin Ring. "Over time, you'll learn how to bring in clients, manage the process and make money," he continued. "Until then, let us know who your contacts are so we can use them." In lobbying parlance, Kevin was describing my short-term role as that of an "access lobbyist." The responsibility of an access lobbyist is to open doors, to provide access. That meant placing an emphasis on relationship building and keeping fresh contacts in the government. Or, in the case of a new guy, letting the team know what kind of access I had.

Kevin was the unofficial Chief Operating Officer of Team Abramoff. He was also the main intermediary between Jack's team and the rest of the firm. Not personally close to Abramoff, Kevin nonetheless had a reputation for being the hardest working member of the team. I wanted him to like me. More importantly, I wanted him to know that I could help him make money. His words seemed pretty straightforward, I told Kevin. "I get it," I said. "Our clients have complex needs, some of which need to be learned on the job. Through osmosis so to speak. That said, you're welcome to my contacts," I continued. "But there is one problem. There is no way I'm going to wait six months to become fully integrated into the team." Peppering Kevin with questions, I told him I wanted to know about the firm. Who made things work. Who didn't. I wanted to know about Jack. What made him tick. Things like that. Kevin just smiled. Weeks later, Kevin asked me to help him manage a new small business client he had brought into the firm. I liked how the team worked. You scratch my back, I'll scratch yours.

In addition to a handful of personal clients, Kevin was the client-manager for the Choctaw Indian representation. That meant he was responsible for the day-to-day management of Team Abramoff's most important client.

Since 1995, the Choctaw had been the linchpin of Jack's lobbying team and lobbying success. In large part, that was because of Chief Phillip Martin. In Indian Country, Chief Martin was a legend. During his three decades as the Choctaws' Chief, Martin had helped transform the poverty-stricken tribe of several thousand into one of the largest employers in the state of Mississippi. Operating more like a corporate CEO than a local politician, the Chief had successfully turned the Choctaws' initial small-scale gaming operation into a global manufacturing, services and entertainment empire. This increase in revenue meant the tribe now had well-run schools, a plethora of housing, a hospital and the financial resources to allow the tribe to prosper.

Jack used the Chief's cachet during his pitch to other tribes. "I can make you the next Chief Martin," he would say. To the tribal leaders looking for representation in Washington, it was a powerful message.

Adding to that message was Kevin and the team's recent success at securing $16 million in federal money to build a jail on the Choctaw reservation. Few issues resonated to clients like actual money in the pocket. "You give us one dollar," Jack would say. "And we will give you twenty dollars." The jail was a prime example. The team had worked with friends on the Hill and in the White House to secure the $16 million, over the objections of numerous career civil servants at the Department of Justice. The jail was a cause for celebration. It was also a feather in the cap for our hard-charging team, the result of a legitimate need amplified by sheer political leverage.

Kevin's former boss, Congressman John Doolittle, knew all about that process. In addition to being on the appropriations committee, he was also a champion in the cause of Team Abramoff. "He gets the joke," Kevin would say, meaning that Doolittle understood the give and take of the lobbying process. Doolittle was a member of my old committee, so I knew him personally. And liked him. He was a proud conservative. It didn't take much to see why he and Jack had hit it off. But there was more to their relationship than mere ideological symmetry or public policy agreement. As Kevin said, "Doolittle is a champion for our clients." That meant he helped in whatever way he could. In turn, Kevin was a champion for the Congressman within our team, amongst our clients and throughout the lobbying community. I would soon be working with and on Bob's behalf in a similar manner.

Kevin made sure to let his clients and Jack know how much Doolittle was doing to help. Everything mattered. Even little things like nuggets of news passed along by the office, staff meeting requests that were accommodated, and questions asked at hearings were all communicated to the clients and the team. "They are the kind of things that make it easier to justify campaign contributions, concert tickets and other expenditures," one of my colleagues said. I took it all in. The team operated in a pretty straightforward way. The more someone helped, the more money he received.

It was more direct than when I had been on the other side, making fundraising calls as a public official, and explaining to lobbyists what a good friend Bob had been to their cause. From that perspective, fundraising seemed like business as usual, a combination of selling access and funding a cause. The dynamic of lobbyists taking credit for government activity, however, represented a contrast to how things worked on the Hill. After all, no Member of Congress likes his or her actions to be publicly associated with lobbyists or any sort of lobbying endeavor, even though they all know lobbyists are invaluable to the legislative process. Nonetheless, I learned quickly that it was important to promote the assistance Bob or others gave to our clients.

Within this new environment, one of lobbyists taking credit for the actions of public officials, I wanted to maximize Jack's meeting with Bob. Their relationship was continuing to grow. Therefore, to help both the Chairman and myself, I tried to champion Bob internally with the team. This would help in terms of future fundraisers, leadership races and in other ways.

Bob did the same. His time with Jack represented an opportunity to showcase himself to a key member of the ever-important lobbying community. Assisting Jack's tribe would also assist the Congressman in reaching out to the lucrative tribal gaming industry. Knowing of Jack's influence with DeLay's office and throughout the conservative movement, Bob additionally figured this project could help to showcase himself as a player on policy issues, not just on internal congressional administration. Because Bob's rapidly growing professional relationship with my new boss was a byproduct of their budding personal friendship, this meeting was also simply about Jack.

Hours before the meeting, I met with Jack and Rudy in Abramoff's office. "Bob is a wheeler-dealer, as you guys know," I told them. "But as a policy guy he likes to know everything. That gives him maximum flexibility. It lets him know where he can maneuver. Therefore, please make sure to tell him everything. He isn't afraid to take one on the chin for a friend," I continued. "He just doesn't like to be taken off guard."

The two nodded. A little more information about the tribe leaked out. But even as they thanked me for prepping them on the meeting with Bob, both men continued to share very little about the specifics of the project.

I interpreted that as a one year ban issue, and kept my mouth shut. "We'll fill him in," Jack said, while telling me that the goal was to slip something into a bill to open a tribal casino without the two Texas senators noticing. "This would be a huge win," he continued. "But it is something we need to be absolutely quiet about."

Used to controlling the flow of information in and out of Bob's office, I found it hard to watch Jack and Rudy prepare for their Hill meeting from the sidelines. I still didn't know much. That frustrated me. Even more frustrating was the fact I wanted to hear what was said, and how both sides replied. One of my best skills is the ability to read a room. Hearing about it later just wasn't the same. But ultimately I accepted the reality that I could no longer know everything, see everything, or stick my head in whatever meeting I wanted. It was the price to pay for the one-year ban. A price to pay for moving on. But that didn't mean I liked it. So I waited, all the while doing my best to continue learning about the team, and our clients.

Based in Kinder, Louisiana, the Coushatta tribe was another one of the team's large tribal clients. Like the Choctaw, the tribe was an anchor client. There were many lobbyists, lawyers and administrative staff who fed off its six-figure a month retainer. Unlike the Choctaw, for whom we had successfully secured direct appropriations from the federal government, we were fighting to block the government from taking action that would allow another tribe in the area to open a casino. That tribe was known as the Jena band. Blocking their efforts to open a casino near our Coushatta client's reservation was what the team called, "The Jena Fight."

Scattered throughout rural central Louisiana, the Jena had cut a deal in January with the state's governor to build a casino off-reservation near the Texas border. With much of the Coushatta's business coming from East Texas, this deal clearly represented a major threat to our client's $300 million a year casino operation. It was a battle over market share. But this battle used the instruments of government to benefit one company at the expense of another. Team Abramoff went to work. Using every tool in the lobbying toolbox, our job was to manipulate every possible lever of the federal government to block the Jena's casino deal with the state. Specifically, that meant focusing on the Department of Interior's approval process. Whether it meant walking in the department's front door, enlisting the help of our friends on the Hill with influence over at Interior, or paying outside groups to manipulate public opinion, we were on it. Fresh off our Choctaw victory, we reveled in the fight.

Coordinated by the Coushatta's client manager, a former staffer for Louisiana's Democrat Senator, it was all-hands-on-deck. Sitting in Greenberg's large conference room, the team met to discuss the current state of play on the Jena Fight and what needed to be done. I found the process fascinating, especially as I watched the breadth and depth of our teams' relationships in action. Team Abramoff was a mosaic. We were full of both Republicans and Democrats; old and young; men and women; gay and straight. Between our personal contacts and the money of our clients, there were few offices or organizations we couldn't access quickly.

Most of our lobbying efforts, however, were built around what we called our champions. Champions were those staffers and Members of Congress who were close to the team. They were our eyes and ears in meetings we could not attend. They advocated for our clients in letters and on the phone. Most importantly, they made our fights their fights. After all, when it comes to the legislative process, it is often better to have one committed supporter than the passive support of everyone in the room, if you actually want something pushed into fruition.

Over time, in part because we were constantly assigning credit for official actions to our friends and contacts, the team's champions became clear to one and all. My colleagues would say, "Congressman Ney is a champion for Neil, Congressman Doolittle is a champion for Kevin." And on and on. Sometimes we had upwards of twenty lobbyists in our team meetings, each with their own champions.

In addition to our champions, there were usually some natural constituencies we could activate for our fights. Sometimes we used a local politician to achieve a shared goal, or they used us for the same. Sometimes an issue-based organization helped us out. In the case of tribal gaming, for example, we played whatever angle was needed. If someone hated gambling, for instance, on the issue we would join forces with them to block our competition. Basically, we would engage that person in whatever way was necessary to make sure he or she helped our cause.

For an emergency effort like the Coushatta's, every possible connection to the Interior Department was discussed. We dissected them all. If the team knew someone on the committee funding the department, we called them. If we had a contact on the committee responsible for regulations administered by the department, we called him too. If we knew a reporter working with Interior or another lobbyist who did the same, we reached out. Any potential pressure that could be applied was analyzed and then used if it passed muster. The stakes, and our nearly two million dollar a year retainer, were too high for us not to go all out.

Going all out also meant buying our way into offices, if that was our only ticket in the door. It was always better to work with someone with whom the team already had an existing relationship. But that wasn't always possible. Meeting new people and attending fundraisers was part of the job. Therefore, like other lobbying groups, we planned on throwing money to those offices who were either willing to help the cause or were thinking about helping the cause. Money helped open doors and make common cause. Having hundreds of thousands of dollars in potential donations can open a lot of doors and grease a lot of deals.

The guy who coordinated Jack's tribal fundraising operation was Todd Boulanger. A former skater punk from New Hampshire, Todd had an edge about him. He was also very direct. "No one gets any money from Jack's tribes unless it comes through me," he said when I asked him how the Team Abramoff fundraising process worked. "Republicans get two-thirds of the money, and Democrats get one-third of the money," Todd elaborated. Since the Republicans ran the White House and the Congress, such a breakdown made sense. "We focus on appropriators, House leadership and Senate Democrats. If there is no justification for the money, they don't get a check," he continued. "We take care of our friends, but only if they get the joke."

From there Boulanger told me to put a list together of between $15,000 and $20,000 in contribution requests, and send the list to Jack, with a copy for Todd. "The Coushatta will be cutting more checks soon," he said. While I was a bit shocked by how direct Todd was in connecting contributions to political favors, I could tell right away that Team Abramoff was every bit the well-oiled machine I thought we were. I was already putting the list together in my head as we talked. Every few months the team would put together a similar list of hundreds of thousands of dollars in contribution requests. Jack managed the tribes in such a way as to ensure a constant flow of contributions to his team members. One month it would be the Choctaw. Another the Coushatta. Then the Saginaw Chippewa. The Agua Caliente. And others.

With checks aplenty, the team then hit the streets. The fundraising circuit in Washington is non-stop. Having the money to access the never-ending event-based cycle was crucial. As in the Coushatta fight, when action was needed we were armed and ready for battle. Our team could get in to see anybody we wanted. Not everyone agreed to help. But we were a mini-army of lobbyists who got results.

By early March, several key players on Capitol Hill had weighed in against the Jena tribe's casino pact with the state. Elected officials like

Senator Harry Reid of Nevada wrote letters opposing the Jena expansion. Reid, the Senate Majority Whip, was the perfect target for Team Abramoff's appeal. He sat on the Appropriations Committee and was an influential Democrat. The Senator also had home-state casino interests who were opposed to more gaming. Additionally, several of my new colleagues worked closely with his office. Reid's fellow Nevada Senator, John Ensign, also wrote a letter. Ensign was a Republican. Like most big battles, the Jena Fight was a bipartisan effort.

Weeks later, the Interior Department opposed the Jena's compact. It was a huge victory for the team. Combined with the big Choctaw win, it also meant we were on a roll.

With the victory came the gloating. In our lobbying meetings, the team always spent time scrambling to assign credit for those official actions which were beneficial to our clients. Of course, since there are usually many reasons behind an elected official's decision, you never really knew who to believe. But I quickly learned to join the fray. The dichotomy between this and how things worked on the Hill remained eye-opening to me. "Few elected officials ever admit that their actions are influenced by lobbyists," I joked to one of my colleagues. "It is like two different worlds." Yet the two worlds coexisted on a daily basis.

When Bob's office phone number popped up on my mobile phone, I knew the Tigua meeting with Jack and Tony was over. I picked up. It was Heaton, Bob's new chief of staff. He said the meeting went well. "Jack and Bob really hit it off," Will said. I was pumped. Minutes later, when I saw Jack walk by my office, I jumped up to check in with him. He was ecstatic.

"You're going to be a great lobbyist," Jack told me.

That was all I needed to hear. I didn't ask anything else. After walking out of Abramoff's office, I poked my head into Rudy's workspace. He would give me the details. But Rudy wasn't there, so I returned to my office. There was a big smile on my face. If the Tigua meeting was my first college-style exam, I had just aced it.

A little while later, Rudy shot over an email asking me for the address and name of Bob's various fundraising and campaign entities. That fired me up even more. Making sure both Bob and Jack were happy was crucially important to my well being. In fact, it was my top concern.

In the meantime, Jack was shooting off an email to Scanlon, and showing his own excitement. "Just met with Ney!!! We're f'ing gold!!!!" Jack wrote. "He's going to do Tigua."

APRIL 10, 2002
WASHINGTON, DC

The Deal

Bob's fundraising dinner could not have been going better. It was my first fundraiser as a lobbyist, and Signatures, Jack's restaurant, was packed. We were surrounded by throngs of people, and many of the twenty-plus folks who were sharing our private dining room for the event had paid as much as $1,000 to be there. We were on our way to raising nearly $45,000 in campaign contributions, $35,000 more than the industry's per-event standard.

"Thanks for all of this," Bob said, shaking my hand. It felt weird to be doing business this way with my former boss, but I appreciated his gesture, since it expressed a different kind of gratitude than what I saw from him when I was his Chief of Staff. And while it was true that this fundraiser was meant to help him, he was also helping Team Abramoff by working with Jack on the Texas tribe and other projects. That was part of the give-and-take of the lobbying effort.

I looked confidently around the restaurant that had quickly become part of my new professional home. I waved at lobbyist friends having dinner in the main dining room and nodded to White House contacts sitting across the bar. And I soaked in the adulation of the moment. One of the most powerful members of the United States Congress had just thanked me for a dinner I was hosting at my new and powerful boss's restaurant. I felt incredibly cool.

The fundraiser had started off in high gear, but Jack's appearance took it to the next level. Abramoff walked into the room just as the waiters and waitresses were bringing in the food. Bob jumped up to shake Jack's hand, grinning and joking, "Hey, who'd you pay to get that New York Times article?" Acting like long-time friends, Jack and Bob reminded the group

157

that they had been in the College Republicans together. Jack followed that by noting to the party attendees that Bob was a rising star and a good conservative. He then thanked everyone for coming to Signatures for the event. Bob responded by saying that it was weird to have his former staffer host a fundraiser for him. The one-year ban didn't prevent me from doing that, even though it did make it illegal for me to make official requests of the Congressman; after all, even for lobbyists, no law can infringe on the First Amendment right to engage in the political process.

Our party was reminiscent of Bob's younger days in the Ohio legislature, during which time he had cut deals over free drinks and meals at downtown Columbus restaurants and bars. There had been no gift ban in Ohio like there was in Washington, and Bob had enjoyed the perks that came his way.

Ney made another joke about the New York Times profile on Abramoff, calling it a "puff piece." It had run on the first page the week before and was titled, "At $500 an Hour, Lobbyist's Influence Rises with the G.O.P." It captured the essence of the man I would later describe as a person who could sweet-talk a dog off a meat truck.

> *WASHINGTON, April 2— In the last six months of 2001, the Coushatta Indians, a tribe with 800 members and a large casino in southwest Louisiana, paid $1.76 million to the law firm of Jack Abramoff, a Republican lobbyist here.*
>
> *Last month, the Bush administration handed the tribe a big victory by blocking construction of a casino by a rival tribe that would have drained off much of the Coushattas' business. William Worfel, vice chairman of the Coushattas, views the administration's decision as a direct benefit of the eye-popping lobbying fees his tribe paid Mr. Abramoff, more money than many giant corporations like AOL Time Warner and American Airlines paid lobbyists in the same period.*
>
> *"I call Jack Abramoff, and I get results," Mr. Worfel said. "You get everything you pay for."*
>
> *In the seven years since Republicans gained control of the House of Representatives, Mr. Abramoff, 43, has used his close ties to Representative Tom DeLay of Texas, the Republican whip,*

and other conservatives in the House to become one of the most influential -- and, at $500 an hour, best compensated -- lobbyists in Washington. He is also an important Republican fund-raiser. Mr. Abramoff's recent success and importance in Republican circles is a reminder that even as much of official Washington has been focused on the war in Afghanistan, efforts to beef up national security after Sept. 11 and the crisis in the Middle East, the business of lobbying has been humming along quite nicely, more out of the spotlight than usual but more profitable than ever for those with the right connections.

Unlike many lobbyists who take almost any client who is willing to pay their fee, Mr. Abramoff says he represents only those who stand for conservative principles. They include three Indian tribes with big casinos and, until recently, the Northern Mariana Islands.

"All of my political work," he said, "is driven by philosophical interests, not by a desire to gain wealth."

Mr. Abramoff argues that Indian reservations and the island territory, which is exempt from United States labor laws, are "just what conservatives have always wanted, which is enterprise zones -- tax-free, regulation-free zones where with the right motivation, great industry could take place and spill out into the general communities."

His success in making this case to Republicans in the House has paid off handsomely. At the beginning of last year, Mr. Abramoff left Preston Gates Ellis & Rouvelas Meeds, the law firm where he had worked since he became a lobbyist in 1995, and joined the Washington office of Greenberg Traurig, a firm based in Miami. Mostly as a consequence, Greenberg Traurig, which received only $1.7 million in lobbying fees during the first half of 2000, had $8.7 million in the first half of 2001, fifth most of any firm in Washington, according to rankings by National Journal. Preston Gates, which had been ranked fifth, saw its lobbying fees cut in half and fell out of the magazine's top 10.

159

As is often true of the work of lobbyists, it is hard to tell how much influence Mr. Abramoff really has over government decisions, and his recent victory for the Coushattas is a case in point. Indian reservations are not covered by state laws regulating gambling. The Bureau of Indian Affairs in the Interior Department has the final say on whether casinos can be built on reservations, and the decisions have not always been free from political influence. Mr. Abramoff did not even directly approach the Interior Department himself, but instead organized a group of lawmakers and other Indian tribes with gambling interests to express to the department their opposition to the new casino.

For lobbyists, perception of influence can often be as valuable as actual influence. Mr. Worfel, the vice chairman of the Coushattas, said he was delighted with Mr. Abramoff's representation and happy to pay his firm's retainer of nearly $300,000 a month. Mr. Abramoff's fee of $500 an hour is matched by few if any other lobbyists in Washington.

Mr. Abramoff's background and personality hardly fit the mold of the typical Washington lobbyist. He is an Orthodox Jew who says that even more than politics, his religion is a central element of his life. He is a teetotaler with a soft voice and a gentle manner who once held a high school weight-lifting record in California. He spent several years in Hollywood producing movies -- "Red Scorpion," an anticommunist thriller, was the most successful -- before becoming a lobbyist.

Most unusual, he is, by his own description, a committed ideologue. In the early 1980's, Mr. Abramoff was chairman of the College Republican National Committee, where he made important contacts. Among those on his staff were Grover Norquist, now a leading conservative strategist here and president of Americans for Tax Reform, and Ralph Reed, the former director of the Christian Coalition, who is a prominent Republican political consultant.

Mr. Abramoff tries hard to persuade his fellow Washington lobbyists to give more generously to the Republican Party, its *candidates and conservative organizations. He expects to raise as much as $5 million this year, he said, and plans to donate as much as $250,000 personally. Mr. Abramoff's rising influence is also illustrative of another trend in lobbying: success can be built on a strong relationship between a lobbyist and a single, powerful lawmaker. His interest in raising money for Republicans and conservative causes is the foundation of Mr. Abramoff's relationship with Mr. DeLay, who is determined to meld the lobbyists on K Street here into the Republican Party's political, legislative and fund-raising operations.*

Mr. Abramoff described the bond this way: "We are the same politically and philosophically. Tom's goal is specific -- to keep Republicans in power and advance the conservative movement. I have Tom's goal precisely."

Mr. Norquist, who is friendly with both men, said of Mr. Abramoff, "He walks in to see DeLay and DeLay knows that he is representing clients whose views are in sync with DeLay's views." It is difficult to gauge the importance of this relationship to Mr. Abramoff's success. Some of his clients said in interviews that Mr. Abramoff did not mention the relationship when he was seeking their business and that it was not the reason they retained him.

"Everybody is important in Congress, not just DeLay," said Philip Martin, chief of the Mississippi Band of Choctaw Indians. The tribe, which runs a large casino and resort, was one of Mr. Abramoff's first clients and is still one of the most lucrative. The Mississippi Choctaws paid Greenberg Traurig more than $1 million in the last half of 2001. "Definitely we get our money's worth, or we wouldn't be doing it," Mr. Martin said.

Mr. DeLay did help put Mr. Abramoff on the lobbying map, assisting his clients on two sensitive matters in 1995, the first year Mr. DeLay was whip and Mr. Abramoff's first year as a lobbyist. But it is not clear that the whip was any more active on these measures than he was on other bills before the House that year. One of Mr. Abramoff's issues was his opposition to a federal tax on Indian gambling revenues. The tax was included in the nonbinding budget resolution the House approved.

But on behalf of the Mississippi Choctaws, Mr. Abramoff said he went to Mr. DeLay and other Republican leaders and explained, "Regardless of what you feel about gaming, what you are creating here is a tax on these people, and conservatives should never be in favor of new taxes." The proposed tax was killed, Mr. Abramoff said, "once they discerned a conservative principle."

The other big issue for Mr. Abramoff in 1995 that promoted his career was a bill passed by the Senate that would have stripped the Northern Mariana Islands of their exemption from the United States minimum wage and immigration laws. The main industry in the Marianas is textiles. Inexpensive clothes are made there, mostly by immigrant Chinese women who work for low wages in substandard conditions, and the garments are shipped duty-free to the United States with a "Made in the U.S.A." label.

With Mr. DeLay's help, Mr. Abramoff managed to get the legislation defeated in the House, using the argument that the Marianas represented low taxes and free enterprise and should be left alone. Representative George Miller, a California Democrat who sponsored the legislation in the House, is still furious about Mr. Abramoff's action. In a recent interview, Mr. Miller said, "He spent a lot of time, effort and money to protect a system that was a growth industry for sex shops, prostitution, abuse of women, slavery, illegal immigration, worker exploitation and narcotics, and he did it all in the name of freedom."

Asked about this, Mr. Abramoff replied: "Congressman Miller has an agenda, and he wants the facts to fit his thesis. No lobbyist could have convinced Congress to support the system he describes."

After the bill was defeated, Mr. Abramoff took 150 lawmakers and staff members to the Northern Marianas, 200 *miles north of Guam, and Mr. DeLay came back enthralled. Unfortunately for Mr. Abramoff, turning the islands' economy into an ideological cause has come back to haunt him. In last November's election for governor, he supported the candidate of the garment industry, Benigno Fitial, against the Republican candidate, Juan Babauta. Mr. Babauta won and soon after he took office in January, he canceled the government's $100,000 per month contract with Mr. Abramoff.*

"The U.S. territories have traditionally been handled in Washington in a bipartisan manner," an associate of the new governor said. "Abramoff marked an end to that approach. So in a change of government, it was only natural that he be dropped."

Setting up this fundraiser for Bob was one of the first things I did after joining Team Abramoff. Hosting or merely taking part in another event before this one would have been a bad idea. First of all, it would have angered Ney. Secondly, some within the echo chamber of the Washington lobbying community would have used such a slight to suggest that Bob and I weren't on good terms. "Maybe Volz wasn't as close to Ney as we all thought," my new lobbying competitors would suggest.

"Was there a falling-out after Neil decided to leave?" others might ask. Those who knew Ney World the best would watch the most closely. Not every former staffer who worked for Bob and then moved on to become a lobbyist had stayed in the Chairman's good graces. Some just left, leaving a void. And power voids are filled quickly in Washington. If a staff departure led to a hole in an important office, successful lobbyists knew how to get someone they knew into the open spot.

Such nuances of the power game were what lobbyists like me were paid to notice and influence. Playing the nuance right could be the difference between winning and losing influence. Months from now, for instance, I knew it was entirely possible that some of those same lobbyists dining with Bob and me could soon be referring clients my way, since they saw that the Chairman and I remained close. Perception was important.

Few knew how to play the perception game better than Jack. It wasn't an accident that the media labeled him a super-lobbyist. Unlike most of his colleagues who preferred to stay behind the scenes, Jack embraced the concept of a high-profile lifestyle. Being seen as a super-lobbyist by Washington's opinion leaders helped him land the kind of clients he liked – those with big checkbooks.

Jack was also able to seamlessly intertwine the rest of his life with the needs of his job. Living that way started by wrapping his client's paid interests into his right-wing ideological world view. This helped in several ways. His fellow conservative activists, who saw him advancing conservative causes, held him in high esteem as a true believer in the conservative movement. His clients saw his efforts to portray their needs as conservative principles as a way for him to be an even stronger advocate for their shared economic interests. As he had done in the New York Times interview, Jack painted himself as someone who wasn't representing his clients for material gain, but rather to advance the cause of conservatism. Tribal casinos turned into tax-free enterprise zones. Online gaming became an issue of individual liberties, and the Mariana Islands morphed into a laboratory of capitalism. Setting up his lobbying practice that way wove Jack's work into his personal life, meaning his work and his political views were publicly intertwined 24 hours a day.

Adding his second-to-none salesmanship skills to his lobbying lifestyle made it even easier to see why Jack was so successful. By the time I joined Team Abramoff, his influence was growing by the day, and the public merger of Jack's personal and political life immediately became a model I wanted to follow. Like a chemical reaction that generates cyclical waves of energy, the Abramoff process of gaining influence was built around using the team's current sphere of influence to gain still more influence. "If we aren't growing, we are shrinking. That is why I need you to succeed. We all benefit by working as a team," he often reminded us. And the team worked like a fine-tuned machine.

Team Abramoff had every tool in the lobbyist's tool box. We had well-connected lobbyists who competed with each other to generate positive results for our clients and get paid. We also had access to large campaign contributions and expense accounts, neither of which we were afraid to use. In fact, our super-lobbyist boss encouraged us to shower our elected officials with all of his influence. "Become their best friend," Jack told us. In the process, members of the team gained their own influence, which made Jack even more powerful. It was a self-generating cycle.

For Washington's Republican establishment, Jack's restaurant quickly became one of the places in which to be seen. Named for the signatures on historic documents whose replicas lined the walls, Signatures was lavish to the extreme. It was situated directly across from the National Archives and was loaded with political memorabilia. A $500,000 rocking chair used by President Kennedy sat near a President Ford-signed replica of Richard Nixon's pardon. In many ways, Signatures was the perfect venue of operations for our team. It was like our diner. We hosted all kinds of events there: fundraisers, new-client pitches, and various other kinds of business meetings. Days before Bob's party, Signatures had hosted an event for Majority Whip DeLay.

Events like those for DeLay and Bob worked to increase our lobbying team's credibility within the K Street community. Having Signatures as part of our team's extended office made impressing potential clients and government officials easier. On most days, I had at least one meal at "Sigs," and sometimes, when Congress was in session, I was there for all three. Key staffers and political figures usually joined me. The waiters, waitresses, and bartenders all played a role on the team – to make me and all of Team Abramoff members look like rock stars. It was "Mr. Volz" here and "Mr. Volz" there. This made for good theater. And the clients paid for everything.

By the night of Bob's party, I had been a lobbyist for less than two months, yet I was already mesmerized by the business. My current boss had just been profiled by *The New York Times*, and my former boss was standing next to him, laughing it up as if they were good chums. Once again, I felt like I was falling upstairs.

This feeling was in stark contrast to the feelings I had recently experienced when I returned briefly to Ohio for my grandfather's funeral. There, the differences between my Washington life and my upbringing started to gnaw at me. I could see that I was living in a different world from the rest of my family members. They were teachers, salesmen, landscapers; they worked in retail, in construction, in manufacturing. Despite the fact that many of them were smarter than I was and exhibited a stronger work ethic, they were just ordinary people living ordinary lives. On the other hand, I was living an extraordinary, almost fantasy life as a high-priced lobbyist. The differences quickly became apparent.

At family functions, even those before and after the funeral, I constantly checked my email and name-dropped, knowing that I looked and sounded impressive. It was who I was, I told those close to me; I needed to bring my job with me wherever I went. I was becoming a member of the Washington elite, the ultimate clique. We spoke the same language and read the same articles. We were high achievers who weren't in Washington just to be near the federal government; we were there to do something. We were there for the acquisition of power necessary to fuel our efforts.

Nowhere was that more true that with the growing connection I had with my fellow members of Team Abramoff. The guys who made up the core of our lobbying team quickly joined Bob and his key lieutenants in my growing wolf pack of close friends in Washington. As did the members of Ney World, the members of Team Abramoff lived by the mantra of working hard and playing harder. We looked out for each other's interests and wanted to win, no matter the cost. And victory for me was being more and more defined by my place in the Washington power structure.

I liked the power associated with my new job. It was different from the power I had had on Capitol Hill. I didn't have to hide my swagger. Being powerful was now always a good thing. Clients paid money for my perceived power. Colleagues wanted tickets and campaign donations. I was asked to sit on boards and be references for people looking to move up their own ladders of success. The power was exhilarating. There's a high associated with such influence, and I couldn't get enough. Neither could Bob.

"It's time to start thinking bigger," he told me that night at Signatures. "Getting the Chairmanship was just the beginning."

I didn't need to contemplate about what he said. I was already thinking the same thing. Why not go for more? Why not feed my need for more money, glory and power? It didn't seem like there was anything wrong with the urge to fly higher. My hunger for success in the influence game overpowered everything else. Therefore, instead of getting out of Ney World, as I had promised my wife, here I was, jumping right back in.

Being a member in good standing with Ney World was vital to my success with Team Abramoff, even if that meant continuing to work almost non-stop. "My influence as a lobbyist derives from my relationships on the Hill," I explained to Alison. "It will just be for a little while."

So it seemed that the Congressman and I would be working together awhile longer. We both saw Jack as a shared avenue for success. And Jack saw us in a similar way. As their personal closeness grew, Bob's ascension became a priority for Jack, who let Signatures become Ney's playground. Jack opened his sports suites and concert ticket supplies to the Congressman and his staff. He even began talking with Bob about traveling to Scotland together. In return, Team Abramoff's clients became big priorities for Ney World. It was exactly the type of corrupt relationship my one-year ban was designed to prevent.

The ban hovered over much of the conversation I had with Bob in the hours between his fundraiser's ending and his departure from Signatures' bar. Although I knew I wasn't supposed to ask Bob directly for any favors,

I rationalized that I could still obtain information from him to give to Jack. Jack was especially interested in what Bob could do to help his Tigua casino project. "So this is how it will work," Bob said, during one of our several trips to the bar. "Jack's project will be attached at the end. After the Election Reform negotiations are done. Attaching the provision at the end will keep it out of the negotiations," Bob explained.

That made sense to me. Bob's election reform counterpart in the Senate would definitely use the provision as leverage to get Bob to give in on something else if he thought the Congressman was "asking" for the Tigua provision. "Since Jack said he could get Dodd on board," Bob continued, "it is best to just add the thing after the bill is done." Senator Dodd was the Chairman's Senate counterpart for the election reform negotiations.

Bob's words fired me up. Shortly after our conversation, I tracked Jack down and shared the information with him. Any worries Jack may have had about whether Bob was fully on board with the Tigua effort dissipated in front of me. "Great job," he said to me, smiling broadly. I basked in his approval. Later he added that I should let Bob know that "there will be a lot more where that came from if this Election Reform thing goes through, if you know what I mean."

A red flag of alarm went up before my eyes. To carry that message was not only a direct violation of my one-year ban, but also the kind of potential gratuity or quid pro that could get me in trouble. Bob knew it, too, and stammered around for a bit while debating how to reply. Finally, he told me simply to tell Jack thanks, "without saying thanks. You know what I am saying."

That nuanced conversation was a big step forward in Bob and Jack's relationship, and their relationship with me. It wasn't simply a dollars and cents discussion. It was a merger of professional ambition and personal interests and lifestyles. All three of us benefited from the deal. Jack's willingness to provide Bob free food and drink at Signatures, concert and sports tickets, access to his Rolodex of political contacts and campaign contributions fit perfectly into the Chairman's vision for his own political advancement. Likewise, Bob's willingness to hang out at Signatures, introduce Jack to key political players and use his office to advance the team's interests helped Jack to further his financial goals. All the while, I stood in the middle, reaping the twin rewards of more political influence and more money.

Of course, we didn't talk about our relationships that way. Bob and I agreed to tell Jack that the Chairman remained very interested in reaching out to the Native American community and that he enjoyed working with

Abramoff to try to sway the tribes to become more Republican. "You know," he said again before we left, "tell him thanks without telling him thanks."

"Got it," I said. Of course, I didn't feel so good about "getting it." This was a major red flag moment for me, one of the biggest I would face. My conscience screamed out that having this conversation and continuing it with Jack was wrong. I knew that it was wrong. But, ultimately, I didn't care. *Who's going to find out?* I asked myself. *"If it isn't Jack, Bob and me, someone else will gladly slide in here and take this business. Life is short."* So I told Jack that Bob and I understood what he was saying, and that Bob "was looking forward to working on the tribal matter."

JULY 25, 2002
WASHINGTON, DC

─────────────────

The Deal Unravels

JACK, BOB AND I MET in the back room of Signatures with the door closed. It was just the three of us. Rudy's absence loomed large. Aside from periodic nights like the one Bob and I had during his fundraiser at Signatures, Rudy had been the main "official" intermediary between Bob and Jack. During the last five months, he attended meetings and had conversations with the Chairman and his staff about a variety of Election Reform-related projects. But now Rudy was gone. His abrupt decision to leave the firm catapulted me even further into the center of the Tigua storm.

Bob's face was red. His breath was short. He looked visibly shaken. "Your deal on Election Reform isn't going to happen," Bob told Jack. "Dodd doesn't support it." And as we all knew, without the approval of Senator Dodd, Bob's counterpart and lead Senate negotiator for Election Reform, there was no way to attach the tribe's provision to the bill. That meant the Tigua casino would remain closed.

Ney told Abramoff about his conversation with Senator Dodd. "I mentioned your name to him," Bob told Jack, before explaining how he pointed out to the Senator that he understood Dodd to be on board with "the Abramoff's provision." Bob said his fellow Chairman looked at him with a blank stare on his face before saying that he could not support such a legislative rider. "He has Indian issues back home in Connecticut and can't do it," Ney concluded.

I felt devastated. The vision I harbored of immediate success as a lobbyist fell apart in seconds. Getting the Tigua deal done would have been huge. But now the plan was dead. Gone with it were my hopes of helping the tribe, as well as my goal of managing a major client, something that had been on my mind for months. I desperately wanted to become Jack's point man for a big-money client like the Tigua. It would have resulted in a big salary increase. It also would have meant a lot more political clout to throw around town. Campaign contributions. Tickets. Trips. Watching it all melt away was painful.

Because he felt like he had somehow let Jack down, Bob was also personally upset. He wanted to be a champion for Jack's tribes. Making it worse was the fact that we were merely days away from our trip to Scotland. Having this kind of failure hang over our head was going to be brutal. Tigua was big. I didn't even want to think about dealing with Jack now that the deal fell through. "We did get that Infovoter thing included in the bill though," Bob said, trying to soothe Jack's disappointment. My jaw almost hit the ground when those words come out of Bob's mouth. Jack didn't know about Infovoter. As if things couldn't get any worse. I felt like crumpling that last statement up in a ball, throwing it out the window and asking the Chairman to just be quiet. Not that he knew what kind of hornet's nest he had just smacked.

"That is a Tony thing," I told Jack as Bob watched my internal team discussion with Abramoff. Ney had a confused look on his face. Infovoter, an election-related phone services company, had hired Rudy to get a provision benefiting the company included in the Election Reform bill. Jack didn't seem to know about it. Normally, he wouldn't have cared. In Jack's world, such a concern wasn't a big enough money deal to warrant his attention. But now with Rudy leaving, Jack probably viewed the former DeLay staffer's work for the company as some sort of insubordination, like Rudy had used all the free drinks, meals, contributions and trip-offers meant for Jack's projects to help with this other client.

Sweat dripped from my brow. I knew Bob was just trying to appease Jack with the Infovoter news. I understood his thinking. To the Congressman, anything brought to him by Jack's team was an Abramoff project. But since Rudy was no longer a part of the team, the news clearly stung Jack like a knife in the back. His face became stone cold when he heard the news.

"How could Bob not know that was Rudy's project?" I asked myself. I should have done a better job at communicating. Still, I continued, when the Chairman agreed to add several provisions for Team Abramoff onto Election Reform, I personally let him know that Jack's top priority was the Tigua tribe's fix. There were several other projects but the casino re-opening was the one we always called "Jack's project." In part because of my one-year ban, however, I had not filled Bob in like I should have. Since the ban meant I wasn't supposed to lobby the Chairman, during the few times we did talk

about client issues, our conversations were generally over drinks or pretty vague, especially when others were present. "*Not communicating better was stupid,*" I thought to myself. "*We were always so cryptic.*"

Before I could get too worked up, Jack put Bob at ease. He thanked the Congressman profusely for his support, and quickly got us back on track. Jack told Bob that it was his impression that Chairman Dodd had been on board. "The Senator is the issue, not you," Jack said. "And if Rudy got some project done in the bill, great," he continued. "Would you be willing to continue helping the tribe? It would sure mean a lot to me."

"Of course," Bob replied. And at that point the meeting broke. The Chairman said he needed to get back to the Hill, and Jack said he had a meeting. The awkwardness of the meeting had me confused. I knew how happy Bob was, since Election Reform was about to become law, yet it felt like he needed to act sad. Jack was acting in just the opposite manner. He was furious about the Tigua situation, but felt like he needed to act happy. In the meantime, the middleman on the project, Tony Rudy, had just up and left the firm days before the trip to Scotland. All the while, none of us wanted to discuss my one-year ban, a rule I was potentially breaking just by being in the meeting. Or discuss what my lobbying role should be now that Rudy left, or why Jack was so invested in this potential client. With so many dueling interests, the three of us seemed more comfortable telling each other what we wanted to hear than digging into any of those questions. It was all spin all the time, and we weren't just spinning each other - we were spinning ourselves.

The mystery lifted a bit as Jack and I slid into his chauffeured black BMW and headed back to the office. He opened his computer and rattled the keyboard with his fast moving fingers. I didn't know it, but Jack was sending Scanlon, who was now running his own public relations company, an email.

'I just spoke with Ney who met today with Dodd on the bill and raised our provision," Jack's email to Scanlon read. "Dodd looked at him like a deer in headlights and said he never made such a commitment and that, with the problems of new casinos in Connecticut, it is a problem!!! Mike, please call me immediately to tell me how we wired this, or were supposed to wire it. Ney feels we left him out to dry. Please call me!!!"

Jack's phone rang. It was Scanlon. Looking out the car window, I couldn't believe what I heard next. In a profanity-laced tirade, Abramoff exploded on Scanlon. He demanded that Mike explain to him why they did not have Dodd on board. I couldn't hear the other side of the conversation, but to me it sounded like the two had spent a lot of money trying to sway the Senator and his staff on the Tigua matter, apparently to no avail.

I knew he had it in him, but I had never seen Jack like that before. It was my first direct insight into the "other side." The other side didn't mean Jack's anger. After all, we can all get angry. What I was seeing for the first time was a glimpse of the bigger picture. Right away, I could tell there was more going on than just a few lobbyists making a play for a potential future client. What I didn't know was that the Tigua had already paid Scanlon and Jack over four million dollars. Nor did I know that Jack and Rudy had been hitting up the tribe and others for money to pay for our Scotland trip. Like the contents of Abramoff's email to Scanlon, those were facts I wouldn't learn until after the scandal broke.

But I did get a glimpse of Jack and Scanlon at work. And it scared the hell out of me. And not in some hypocritical, "I was being a choir boy" kind of way. What had me scared was hearing how up to speed Scanlon was with all that I had been doing on the Election Reform bill. It was clear he knew about my contacts with Bob and his office. My one-year ban issues were not something I wanted Scanlon to know anything about. Likewise, I didn't want him to know what Bob was doing. It was one thing to let Rudy in on the details. Scanlon was an entirely different situation. After the SunCruz Congressional Record debacle, letting him anywhere near Bob was a bad idea. *"Or was it?"* I wondered. Bob and I both knew that Jack and Scanlon still worked on some projects together, and I had seen Scanlon once or twice after joining the team. *"Maybe Jack has filled Bob in on Scanlon's role in the Tigua project. They are spending lots of time together at Sigs."* Despite stewing about Scanlon, as I sat next to Jack in the car, I decided against saying anything. Interjecting myself in such an unclear situation was something for me to ponder, not act on.

Rudy's departure had changed everything. Without him greasing the machine, it felt like I was in a whole new world. The preparations for our Scotland trip illustrated the point. Not until Rudy left in early July was I even slated for the Scotland trip. It was his departure which opened up a slot for me. Before then, I was on the sidelines, shuttling what information I knew between the various players. Not that I knew much. I occasionally learned about the specifics of the trip through bits and pieces of news from the Abramoff side, and then the Ney side. At the time, Rudy had been my main source of information on the trip.

Initially, Rudy said that he and Jack were trying to put together an appropriations trip, meaning a trip built around appropriations staffers and elected officials. With much of the team's client focus geared toward securing earmarks and direct line-item appropriations, that kind of trip seemed to make sense. This was especially pertinent since every indication I got from Jack was that he wanted to base participation in the Scotland trip on those friends who were helping to deliver for his clients.

After Bob agreed to do the Tigua bill, Rudy told me he was going to ask the Chairman about going to Scotland. I told him I thought it was a great idea. The Congressman said he was interested. After the scandal, some people suggested Bob solicited the trip. That never happened. Similarly, I couldn't imagine Rudy and Jack telling Bob that he was being invited because of his support for the Tigua provision, nor could I see the Chairman directly saying he was willing to go to Scotland as a payoff for his tribal support. But because of timing of the trip, and the corrupt nature of our relationship, Bob's Election Reform efforts were on all of our minds as the Scotland outing developed. There was no elaboration necessary.

As I listened to the back and forth between Ney World and Team Abramoff, I couldn't help but wonder whether this was how most Hill-related trips were put together. The individuals who organized every trip I had been on had some sort of interest related to Capitol Hill. It is hard not to have an interest in the federal government. At the same time, these groups needs were usually a step or two removed from any sort of direct action; more often than not they were members of a foundation or non-lobbying entity. After all, there needed to be a purpose for any privately-funded trip, aside from the ongoing and important work of getting to know people who work on Capitol Hill. Something educational. A fact finding trip. That kind of thing.

It was the purpose of the Scotland trip where there seemed to be the most confusion. Bob told me the trip was set up to raise money for a charity. Jack said it was to meet Scottish Parliamentarians. Without thinking, I just assumed it involved a little bit of both. But mostly, as we all knew, the trip was about golf.

As a late addition, I didn't want to look like I didn't know what was going on. Therefore, I kept my questions to a minimum. Why wouldn't I? Bob was going. Jack was going. What else did I need to know? It wasn't the first time Jack had put together such a trip. "We did this with DeLay," he would say nearly any time a question was raised about Scotland. It was the ultimate rebuttal. Jack talked so much about his "DeLay trip" that the Majority Leader's 2000 venture to Scotland became the model I looked to for guidance. For comfort. In many respects, it was my security blanket.

Granted, I had my own individual concerns that had me worried, namely the one-year ban. More than anything, that was the top concern I had about the trip. Wanting to go, however, it wasn't too hard to convince myself that everything was fine. If I could spend time drinking with Bob at Signatures, then surely I could go on a trip with him, right? It made sense to me.

Weeks before the trip, the situation surrounding Scotland still remained foggy. Only Jack knew what was really going on for sure, and getting information from him was hit or miss. Nor was it easy to deal with the tension between Rudy and Jack. Abramoff initially told me to tell Rudy that he still had his slot on the trip. When I asked Jack if that was really the case, he played coy. I didn't inquire further. Coming from Ney World, I accepted Jack and Rudy's departure-related actions as a testament to the complexities of life in DeLay, Inc. Through that prism, I understood that there was always a lot going on underneath the surface. Just like in Ney World, long-time relationships needed managing, and what seemed like minute decisions to an outsider, might have actually meant a lot. Making it more complicated was the fact that Tony was leaving one baron of DeLay's operation, Jack, to work with another baron, DeLay's former chief of staff, and big-time lobbyist, Ed Buckham. It was important that I watch what I say.

Therefore, when Tony called or emailed to inquire about the trip, I asked Jack how he wanted me to respond. He eventually told me he wasn't sure what to do. "Maybe he'll still go, or maybe not," Jack said. Before long, he suggested that I not talk with Tony about the trip. We both knew that wasn't possible for long. *"Their relationship is too important to blow it up over something like a trip,"* I assumed. Eventually, Jack told me to just tell Rudy his slot had been given out. I could tell there was a lot more going on there, but, I was ultimately just happy to end the drama. From my perspective, it was straightforward. Tony's loss was my gain.

That said, the whole process surrounding the trip continued to frustrate me. My job had always been to get events organized for Bob. Yet, now I didn't have enough control to engage in the way that I would have liked. It got so bad that one of my lobbying colleagues had to pull me aside and tell me to stop sweating about the trip. "Jack has this under control," he said. "If Jack wants someone to else to go, or to add something to the trip, he'll make sure it happens," he continued. I appreciated the advice. Not getting intertwined in what I couldn't control was definitely the way to proceed.

Then Bob's chief of staff, Will Heaton, called me. He wanted my help in nudging Bob into the yes column for the trip. "I thought he already was in the yes column," I told Heaton. "That is what he told Jack," I continued with emphasis.

"He is hedging," Heaton replied.

"Rudy is trying to torpedo the team," I thought, without sharing my fears. Suddenly things weren't so simple. And we were dealing with Ney World. Choosing not to get intertwined was not an option, despite my one-year ban.

"You know, Bob isn't really a golfer," Will continued. "But he does want to get away, and obviously thinks spending time with Jack would be a good idea."

"He told Jack he would go," I replied again. Something didn't smell right. Then it hit me. My conversation with Heaton was an exercise. Bob was molding his young chief of staff. I should have seen it coming. It was a script I knew all too well. Ney had done the same thing to me.

"How do we get this moving?" I asked Heaton, when I realized our conversation was right out of the Ney playbook. It was the chapter on how to train a new chief of staff to deal with the old chief of staff, who was now a lobbyist. I had gone through the same thing.

"How do we get this moving?" Will asked me in return. "Invite me."

"Oh really?" I laughed. It wasn't the specific reply I had expected.

"If I don't go, Bob doesn't go," he said, as if he was literally reading off a piece of paper.

"Nice move," I replied, continuing to chuckle. "Strong."

Will let out a bit of a laugh. I assumed that meant Bob wasn't standing next to him for the conversation, though it wouldn't have surprised me if he was.

"I'm on to what is happening here," I said. Heaton and I both knew what was going on. Since Ney viewed his top staffer as an extension of himself, Bob wanted to make sure Heaton was sufficiently establishing control of our relationship. It was important for the Congressman to know that I was not able to get Heaton to help Jack's clients without Bob's specific instruction. It was his way of staying in charge. Something I understood completely.

"No worries," I told Heaton, and meant it. Heaton's aggressiveness was actually good to see. I had been worried about whether Bob's new chief was up for the job, and the stress associated with the Chairman's different personalities. It felt good to see Heaton learning the new job so quickly. My financial success depended on him being a good chief of staff. And as long as I had direct access to Bob, both Heaton and I knew that he would never really have control of my relationship with the Chairman. But we were a team, and I knew what he was going through. So I played along.

Heaton wasn't the only person undergoing a transition. I was also learning a new job. The request from Bob's office had blown up my previous decision to lay low and let the trip correspondence take care of itself. Therefore, I headed into Jack's office and told him about my conversation with Heaton. The request had me worried. I wasn't sure how Jack would react. But he didn't blink an eye. Right there, on the spot, Abramoff added another person to the trip list. Heaton was in. Walking out of Jack's office, I couldn't help but think that this post-Tony thing might work out better than I expected. Working directly with Abramoff had its benefits.

As it turned out, I couldn't have been more wrong. What Rudy really knew about the trip, I'm not sure. But as my soon-to-be-former colleague was leaving the firm, he made a couple of comments in passing that should have made me re-think my involvement in the trip. "I don't know how Jack can keep all the balls in the air without something falling," Rudy said in what seemed to be a reference to the trip. I initially took his comments as a compliment to Jack. I assumed Rudy meant that Abramoff's ability to keep the many moving parts of his operation away from the press was a good thing. Being a high profile lobbyist was something Jack cultivated, but he didn't go around telling reporters about the trips he set up for elected officials, or the food he gave them for free at his restaurant. What lobbyist would?

Rudy also used our last day of working together to tell me, "You have to decide whether you're on Scanlon's side or not." It seemed like a silly comment for him to make. Of course, I didn't want to work with Scanlon. Rudy knew that. But Mike was one of Jack's vendors, and Jack was my boss. If Jack wanted me to work with Scanlon, I would work with Scanlon. No matter what Rudy suggested. Besides, based on what I had seen during the last year, Abramoff's relationship with Scanlon didn't seem like that big of a deal. And Rudy and Scanlon's hatred for each other was legendary. This fact lessened the weight of Rudy's comments. He knew what I thought about his relationship with Scanlon. When I started working for Team Abramoff, I had to tell Rudy that I wasn't taking sides in their dispute.

"You are both cool with me," I said. "Whatever happened between you and Mike is not my business."

"I don't really talk about it," Rudy replied. "Lets just say it had to do with money."

When I told Jack about my conversation with Rudy, he said he was glad to hear it. "No reason to fight. There is plenty of money to go around for all of us," Jack continued. The whole situation was weird. But I liked the way Jack handled the matter. Granted, I liked the way Jack handled just about anything at that point.

I wasn't alone in my infatuation with Jack and the benefits of being part of the Abramoff family. Bob experienced it too. In fact, in less than a year, the mushrooming relationship between Bob and Jack had transcended into something I had not seen before: Ney in an all-consuming professional relationship with a lobbyist who was not a former staffer. In both Columbus and Washington, he developed incredibly close working relationships with former staffers and colleagues who became lobbyists. But, as far as I had seen, his relationship with Jack was something new. Bob changed his behavior around Jack. He treated Abramoff with a reverence I had only seen the Chairman reserve for his constituents.

Bob also watched his alcohol intake around Jack. Openly religious, my new boss was not a drinker. Similarly, since Jack did not curse in public, Bob restrained his use of public profanity as well. With Abramoff more culturally at home watching opera than laughing with Bob and me about an episode of the *Jerry Springer Show*, it was also fun to watch Bob emphasize his more refined side. I did the same.

Of course, the deal worked both ways. Jack also comported himself in a manner that strengthened his ties with Bob. He loosened up around the Congressman. His drinking jokes changed from having a negative connotation to a positive one whenever Bob was present. He also supported issues important to the Chairman, even those that ran counter to his long-held views. Likewise, he promoted Bob in conservative circles as a trusted future leader of the party and the movement.

Nowhere did their relationship flourish more than at Signatures. Jack gave the Congressman free reign of his restaurant. Anything Bob wanted was his for the taking. It was more than just free food and free drinks. If the Chairman wanted to change the Sushi menu, it was done. If the bartenders ran out of his favorite beer or brand of cigarettes, someone would run to get them.

A few months before our trip, over drinks at Signatures, Heaton and I had discussed the growing rapport between Bob and Jack. He said the Chairman had made it clear to him that Jack was an important linchpin in his political future. It was something Bob had said to me on many occasions as well. "Having the most influential lobbyist in town on your side can only help us move up the ladder from committee chairman to House leader,"

Heaton said. "People are talking about Ney being Speaker," he continued with excitement. I felt the pull of the joke. Stoking the flames of corruption, I not only backed up what Heaton was hearing around the Hill, but reminded him that Bob and Jack's growing influence would also be good for us. Heaton was about as old as I was when I moved to Washington, yet he was a chief of staff already. "That is already an amazing accomplishment," I told him. "Now visualize yourself as the Speaker of the House's chief of staff." His eyes lit up. "You would be more powerful than most members of Congress. And then you could cash out big time," I said. He nodded along, lapping up every word.

At that point, I mentioned the Tigua deal. Jack would have been proud. The tribal fix was something Heaton and the Congressman had been talking about earlier that morning, he said. This was before we knew the provision was dead.

"Sometimes you just have to do a deal like that one," Heaton recounted Bob telling him. Agreeing to insert the tribe's provision into the Election Reform bill was a way to curry favor with Jack, he continued. In return, Jack's influence could help Bob become even more powerful. I agreed. "The joke is pretty simple," I told him. "It is a way to gain power. For all of us. Me as much or more than anyone. It is a win-win." We all saw it.

Jack's predominant desire revolved around getting Bob to help him make money. Bob's goal was for Jack to help him gain political power. My role was to facilitate the relationship, knowing both the money and power were part of the deal for me, too. It was the perfect circle. Heaton and I agreed that Jack was a kingmaker. And our guy had a shot at being king. "If DeLay could do it, so could Bob," he said. The whole thing seemed too good to be true, mainly because it was.

The truth is, the relationship among Bob, Jack and me wasn't some sort of casual business relationship, or a somewhat forced political relationship. It was a corrupt relationship. A relationship that traded private gain for public actions. And sadly, I couldn't live without it. In a short period of time, my political addiction had grown exponentially. Not only did the game of politics mesmerize me, but the joke made me feel like I was a player. I loved all of it. The power. The money. The feeling of being at the center of the world.

That being the case, it isn't that surprising that I decided to personally fill the void created by Rudy's departure from the team. Such a void meant making a fundamental decision. How do I deal with my one-year ban requirements going forward? While I felt like the pressure was on me to fill

Rudy's role, the decision to completely disregard my one-year ban was mine and mine alone. It wasn't like I ever really cared about actually complying with my one-year ban requirements, but maintaining the appearance of compliance was something that had been important to me, especially earlier on in my tenure at the firm. Rudy made that easier for me by serving as the public bridge between Bob and Jack.

Meetings like those in the Chairman's office concerning the Tigua were easy to live with when I knew that Rudy was the one doing the work. It wasn't something we devised or talked about. It was just was what it was. Everyone knew I was still spending plenty of time working and partying with the Ney crew at night. I just wasn't spending time in the office. It gave us all plausible deniability if some reporter were to call and ask if I were lobbying the Congressman's office. Now, things were changing.

On a practical level, I had to figure out whether I would introduce a colleague to the Congressman and his office so he or she could play Rudy's role until my one-year ban was up in six months, or I could just fill the void by working Bob's office myself. After very little thought, I chose the latter. After all, the growing relationship between Jack and Bob was my ticket to more power and a bigger paycheck. The more that I thought about it, the more the idea of turning the Ney office over to one of my colleagues became unacceptable. It was one thing to have Rudy working my old office and gaining insight into the complex workings of Ney World. It would be entirely different to turn my precious turf over to someone else. One-year ban or no one-year ban, I wasn't going to go through that again.

This led to the matter of Scanlon, and his involvement in the Tigua matter. Getting out of Jack's car, I was worried about what I heard, namely of Scanlon's involvement in Bob and Jack's Election Reform deal. I thought about my options. On the one hand, Bob needed to know that Scanlon was involved. On the other hand, telling him about Mike wasn't going to be easy. Things were different now. I worked for Jack, who had his own relationship with Bob. Now that the Chairman was fully ensconced into all-things Team Abramoff, telling him any sort of bad news could get complicated. It cut several ways. One, I assumed Jack had shielded Bob from Scanlon's work on the tribe as much as he had shielded me. But I wasn't sure. Therefore, since I didn't know the full story, being able to tell Bob the full story required that I ask Jack a lot of awkward questions. A move like that could have some negative consequences. My conversation with Rudy about choosing whether I was on Scanlon's side came to mind. That just made me more confused.

Instead of focusing on Jack, I returned my attention to Bob. There were roadblocks in Ney World as well. As irrational as it might sound, part of me assumed that Bob was going to be disappointed in me when I told him of Scanlon's involvement in the Tigua project. After all, not only did Bob have a lot invested in Jack, he liked to put himself in Jack's shoes whenever he judged my career decisions. It is admittedly kind of weird to say, but while the Chairman like being up to speed on pertinent information, I visualized Bob accusing me of being disloyal to Jack by telling him about Scanlon. I saw it that way because, as my former boss, telling him anything private about my current bosses work could be viewed as disloyal. Nonetheless, I bit the bullet and told Bob that Jack had called Scanlon after our Tigua conversation at Signatures. Surprisingly, he said it was no big deal.

"Jack told me he doesn't like Scanlon but still does some work with him because he is good at his job," Bob told me. Based on the inflection in his voice and my years of work with him, I wasn't sure whether Bob was being straight forward with me or not. But I didn't push, deciding it was better to just let it play out. If it was an issue, I knew I would be told to me the next time the Chairman and I were out having drinks.

Scanlon's emergence on the scene shook me up. It made me worry about my one-year-ban and our trip. I called Bob again. I told him I was worried about Scotland, and Jack's involvement with Scanlon. Without discussing it, my one-year ban was an implied issue. We both knew about it, and we were both fine with me breaking it. But that didn't mean we wanted other people to know what was happening.

Bob told me not to worry.

"Jack has it covered. He took DeLay on the same trip. Your good to go. Besides, who is going to find out?" the Chairman asked.

"Yeah, who is going to know?" I replied. "Jack has this thing locked down."

With that, I put my worries to the side. Both my bosses, two of the most powerful men in Washington, were fine with me going on the trip. Why should I worry? It was time to have a good time.

AUGUST 3, 2002
ST. ANDREWS, SCOTLAND

The Trip

THE GULFSTREAM JET THAT JACK chartered for the trip circled the St. Andrews airport for nearly an hour that morning. A Scottish storm was threatening to divert us to Edinburgh. Because of our tight schedule, such a detour would have been disastrous. The weather broke just in time and the airport staff quickly checked our passports before whisking us off the tarmac. Within minutes of leaving the airport, our group approached the Old Course Hotel.

St. Andrews is the oldest golf course in the world. It is a Mecca for people who love the sport. Since the time of Columbus, golfers have made the pilgrimage to the green rolling hills of Eastern Scotland. It is "where the game began," locals would tell us. Nine of us made the trip: Jack; his son; my Team Abramoff lobbying colleague Mike Williams; Jack's business partner and former Executive Director of the Christian Coalition, Ralph Reed; Bob; Heaton; House Administration Committee Staff Director Paul Vinovich; David Safavian, who was a senior Bush Administration official; and me.

Bordering the picturesque 18th hole stood the course's five-star hotel. It would be our home for the next five days. Like a postcard, the coastline merged with the centuries-old set of fairways and greens. We grabbed breakfast as the hotel staff checked us into our rooms. I was battling jet-lag and dehydration. Therefore, with the rest of the group picking their way through the buffet, I quickly ate one of the most fulfilling bowls of fresh fruit in history. Surrounded by the hotel's glass-enclosed dining area, I took in the Old Course's stunning beauty. My growing sense of excitement gained momentum. Looking around, any worries I still had about being on the trip slowly subsided. I could tell this was going to be a journey I would never forget.

Bob and I pointed at the large panes of glass in front of our table. We joked to the group that a lot of these expensive windows were going to be broken when the two of us hit the Old Course. It was our way of reminding the guys we weren't very good at golf. Like that reminder was needed. The group's schedule was tight, so the guide Jack had hired loaded the clubs in our van while we devoured what was left of breakfast. Minutes later, it was go time. Kingsbarns was calling.

In a part of Scotland known as East Fife, Kingsbarns was just outside of St. Andrews. Set against the rugged coastline of the North Sea, the region had a long history of golf. That said, the Kingsbarns course itself was only a few years old. Not as tough as Carnoustie or as majestic as the Old Course, it was a good place for us to start. Unlike in the jet when much of our talk revolved around politics, we mostly talked golf on the way to the course. Our guide told us a bit about Kingbarns and the kind of weather we could expect while we played today, and for the rest of the trip. "The wild temperature swings and swirling wind will impact your play," he said. In between weather reports, Jack discussed some golf highlights from his much-hyped trip to St. Andrews with Majority Leader DeLay.

Bounding out of the van like a group of circus clowns, we hurriedly approached the course. It was finally time to play some golf. With a steep roof and large columns, the Kingsbarns Club House seemed built to withstand the nastiest of winter snowfalls. The large columns escorted us through the front door. In a corner of the Pro Shop, Jack pulled me aside to clarify his rules for the trip. "Whatever the elected officials want to buy, get it for them," he said. "Keep your receipts and we will reimburse you. That goes for food, drinks, shirts, golf expenses or whatever," he continued.

Jack's comments were somewhat alarming. The constant use of the term "elected officials" to describe Bob, Will, David and the rest made everything seem very impersonal, as if the trip was all one big business transaction. On the other hand, his comments were also a relief. The idea that we were getting reimbursed made me feel better. I wasn't sure how all that was going to play out. Reimbursement meant that I didn't have to spend personal money on the trip. Additionally, it also reinforced the idea that some sort of appropriate "official" entity would be paying for the trip. Who that was exactly, I did not know for sure. But I knew Jack had it covered. At least, I hoped he did.

As my boss continued to talk, however, I started feeling nervous. It wasn't any ethical issue that had me feeling that way, but the fact that I had only brought one credit card with me. *"How much am I going to rack up on this thing?"* I asked myself. Luckily, it was my American Express card that

I brought. It didn't have a limit. *"But not everyone takes American Express,"* my worrying continued. *"If only I had known this was how it was going to be. I would have planned to bring other cards. Oh well, whatever. I've got to go buy some golf balls, sweatshirts, t-shirts and hats. It is time to get this trip started."*

Jack included Bob and me in his foursome. In typical Abramoff extravagance, Jack had also paid to have some guy tag along with us to film his play. "The footage will help me study my swing," Jack said. The move was yet another step in my boss's unending effort to improve his golf game. His diligence was impressive. My colleague Mike Williams filled out the group.

Our first round went about as expected. Jack hit like someone who played a couple days a week, while Williams hit like someone who could play on the pro tour. In the meantime, Bob and I played like crap, as usual. Ball after ball went into the rough. Over the green. Or into the woods. And to make things worse, it was all on film. Nonetheless, my wise-cracking group of friends was surrounded by some of the most beautiful rolling hills on the planet. If our group wasn't hitting into the sandy soils, hallows or undulating ridges, then the grassy cambo burn running into the sea was guiding us through the course. It was like walking into the *Lord of the Rings.* "What a great start to the trip," I told the guys. For a travel-nerd like me, the mere experience of walking in such historic footsteps was heavenly. It made me feel alive, bad game and all.

Next up was Carnoustie. Known as "the Beast," Carnoustie is a notoriously rough course, one of the toughest in the world. Over the years, legends of the game with names like Watson, Hogan and Player have battled the course's renowned weather, deep rough and thin fairways to earn victories at the British Open. Again, I played alongside Mike Williams. After playing horribly on day one, I was determined to redeem myself at Carnoustie. As we approached the first hole, I asked one of the caddies for a rundown on the course. In his Gaelic-sounding English, he laid out what to expect. My jaw dropped. Though I didn't grasp every word he muttered, it wasn't hard to understand comments like, "Narrow fairways, no room for error, tight landing areas and they tend to let the rough grow deep."

"That is why they call it Car-nasty," said Williams before hitting his first shot, a screamer down the middle of the fairway. I didn't fare so well. Despite losing a ball on the first hole, in what the course literature called, "unmanicured rough and gorse," I did my best not to succumb to the Carnoustie effect, a term created after the 1999 British Open when several pro players were literally led to tears because of the course's tough conditions.

My caddie did his best to feed off my positive energy. "All you have to do is thread the bunkers and the rough," he said as I prepared to drive from the second tee. His advice touched a nerve. Laughing out loud, I told him, "Dude, I'll be lucky to hit the fairway." It was then that I decided my day was not going to be defined by my score. *"Why ruin such a great experience with unrealistic expectations?"* I told myself. It was the best decision I made on the trip. Even though I continued to lose nearly a ball a hole, I had a great time. Williams played like a pro. Watching him shoot in the seventies was awe-inspiring. Since many elected officials only played with high-end golfers, I was reminded why his play was such an asset to his lobbying practice.

The highlight of my comedy of errors occurred when I lost yet another ball in the rough near the end of the day. Looking up, I yelled to my off-in-the-distance caddie. In golf, you are allowed to pick up your ball when it is in a bad spot and drop it into the low-cut grass of the fairway, if you are willing to take one stroke off your score. "Should I hit it again, or just drop one on the fairway and take a stroke?" I asked.

"That depends on whether you want to lose another ball," my caddie said with classic Scottish sarcasm. His timing was perfect. Our whole four-some laughed until it hurt.

While golf was the main focus of the trip, our group did have other scheduled activities. One of them was a visit to Edinburgh for the Military Tattoo. Aside from a dinner with Scottish Parliamentarians, watching the Tattoo was the closest thing to an official activity on our calendar. In Scotland, the military celebration is a major event. It commemorates the special cultural and political relationship between the United States and the United Kingdom. Exemplifying that point was the fact that Queen Elizabeth was in attendance. Bob and I saw her driving by as we labored up a long winding road toward the show. It was a cool moment. But it was also rather awkward.

Normally, a group like ours, one with a congressional chairman and a senior Bush administration official, would have been a part of the actual commemoration. That is especially true since the event celebrates the relationship between our two countries. Instead, our group all sat in the stands. Not that walking or sitting among the throngs of thousands was bad. In fact, it was great. We lived it up. It just did not match up with what any of my previous official trips suggested would have been appropriate for an official congressionally-related trip. I could tell Bob was thinking the same thing.

The Edinburgh castle lit up in the background as the numerous military bands put on a great show. The cool summer air whipped through the stands. One after another, the many different groups marched in unison and entertained the crowd. At the end of the performance, Bob and Heaton darted off toward a group of troops they saw standing underneath the stands. I scurried over to join them. The event's tear-down was already under way. From where we were, the underbelly of the performance looked more like a high school football game than a multinational salute. Still, Bob talked with anyone he could find. As he said later, "I was hoping was that a couple of them were from Ohio, or that some sort of official connection could be made." Unfortunately, we had no such luck. With the sun setting, our group returned to St. Andrews.

After salivating at its historic fairways and greens from the hotel, I was finally ready to play the Old Course. The walk to the Club House took less than ten minutes. I took in the excitement with some of the guys from the trip, having seen the walk numerous times on television. Like the many other gathered tourists, we enjoyed the view of the 17th green, gawked at the Swilcan Bridge midway through the 18th fairway, and watched as a foursome putted their final shots of their round. Rifling through my pockets as we approached, I made sure I still had a hundred dollars or so in cash for each of our caddies. With Jack playing elsewhere, I was on the clock, responsible for getting our group of four onto the course.

But there was a problem which had me feeling nervous. The rules of St. Andrews state that a golfer has to have less than a 25 handicap to play the Old Course. A person's handicap is a reflection of the quality of their game. Demanding a certain number handicap was a way of making sure people who would tear up the course or slow down play didn't get on the course. Unfortunately, that meant a few of us didn't qualify, myself included. Like everything else, Jack said we would be fine. "I've taken care of it," he said. As our foursome approached the starter, I couldn't help but put together a back-up plan in my head, just in case we were denied access to the course. But as Jack had promised, we were allowed to proceed.

Unlike Carnoustie, the Old Course is filled with wide fairways and large shared greens. For me, that was just about perfect. The Old Course was nestled in between the town and the coast, a perfectly breathtaking location. Nearly every hole provided views of the city's historic stone and brick buildings as well as the surf crashing onto the rocky shore, its thundering roar providing a natural soundtrack. Despite the unpredictable weather - first rainy, then cold and dry, then warm, all within fifteen minutes - I could relax and enjoy the game, thanks largely to the wide fairways and large shared greens.

The wide fairways helped minimize the problems that stemmed from my lack of control off the tee. Likewise, my inability to chip around the hole was masked by the overly large greens. With Jack gone, the beers started flowing on the first hole. Cigars followed. Right away, I could tell this day was going to be different from my frustrating previous days of golf.

On the tenth hole, I nailed my drive. It may have been the best golf shot of my life.

"Now that's a golf shot!" I yelled as the ball rolled on to the green. The phrase was an inside joke. It was the Ney contingent's way of poking fun at Ralph Reed. The soft-spoken Reed was generally pretty quiet on the course, especially when he was playing poorly. But, like all of us, when his game got going he became a different person. Cocky, boastful and tough on the caddies, the former political crusader could yell and scream his way through the course with the best of them. Several times he yelled, "Now that's a golf shot!" The phrase instantly became part of our trip lexicon. Nothing but a gentleman through the entire trip, Reed took the joking well.

The tenth hole was a par four. My first shot had landed on the green. I was fifteen feet from the pin. Two putts later I had a birdie. My game was finally starting to come together. The 11th hole was a par three. I put that tee shot on the green, too. Suddenly I felt the excitement of actually playing real golf. All it took was two good shots. My confidence grew by the moment.

"See that big plane across the water?" one of the caddies asked me a few holes later. "Hit the ball right at it."

"Are you kidding me?" I replied in jest. "That is our plane." And it was. Shining in the summer light sat the plane Jack had chartered for our trip. In a sign of how much things can change in a single day, I nailed the ball, placing it exactly where the caddie told me. "Now that's a golf shot!" one of the guys yelled from off in the distance. Everything seemed to be going right. As we approached the hallowed ground of the 17th hole, I was eleven strokes from breaking one hundred on a legitimate course for the first time in my life. Not that that is something to brag about. Nonetheless, the idea of breaking one hundred on the Old Course had become a big deal to me. And there were only two holes left.

The 17th is shaped somewhat like a letter "C," with the fairway breaking to the right as you approach the green. It is also a hole lined with tourists. Normally, that would be a game-wrecker. I don't have nearly enough confidence in my golf game to handle a bunch of people gawking at me as I play. Not on the seventeenth hole. The gathered crowd only added to the festivities. Standing at the tee, my caddie told me I had two options. One,

I could play it safe and hit the ball softly to the left. That way I would avoid the bunkers along the right side of the fairway and set myself up with a straight shot to the hole, he said.

The second option, my caddie said, was to hit it hard enough to clear the bunkers and land where the fairway was already turning right toward the "C-part" of the fairway, approaching the green. "You would be much closer to the hole for your second shot that way," he explained. "Taking that approach means not only hitting the ball over the bunkers but clearing a set of old railroad sheds as well," he continued. "It is a risk." Unlike hitting it to the left, where a screw up would not be too painful, messing up on the right side of the hole could result in an out-of-bounds shot, and the loss of a stroke. I knew what I was getting into when I set the ball up on the tee. Looking square at the ball, I swung back and let the ball have it. "Oh shit." I said. "Oh shit." As I looked up, my ball was spinning wildly to the right. "I should have gone left," I screamed. But it was too late. The ball was slicing. Quickly. I mean really quickly. "Fore!" I yelled, suddenly realizing that the trajectory of the ball seemed to be coinciding with some poor tourist's head. "Dammit, dammit," I moaned, kicking the ground. The old Neil was back. Along with some sort of double-cursing condition.

Shaking my head, I knew the ball I just hit was going out of bounds. My hopes for breaking a hundred were ruined. An out-of-bounds shot would cost me several strokes. It was a killer. But as I got closer, I noticed two tourists, a man and a woman, sitting on a wooden bench waving their arms. They kept pointing to the building. Then the fairway. The building. The fairway. "It bounced into the fairway!" the woman yelled. "It hit the building and bounced in the fairway!" A deep Dr. Seuss-like Grinchian smile appeared on my face.

"*Are you kidding me?*" I thought to myself. "*The ball careened off the side of the building and into the fairway? Are you kidding me?*" But lo and behold, there it was, my little white friend, sitting on a tuft of grass. "Now that's a golf shot!" we all started shouting as I ran toward my ball, thanking the tourists for their help. It was like the golf-gods had wanted me to break a hundred. There was no going back now. I ended up shooting a ninety-eight.

Our celebration carried into the evening. Up the street from the Old Course was the Dunvegan Lounge Bar. A large square brick building, the Dunvegan helped line one of St. Andrew's picturesque streets. Their tag line was, "Only a nine iron from the Old Course." Golf pictures lined the lively bar's walls. We chowed down on wings, greasy steak sandwiches and some awesome fish n' chips. Even better than the food was the couple hundred dollars worth of old malt whiskey that helped us wash it all down. I doubt very many golfers have celebrated a score of 98 on the Old Course like we did that night.

Unfortunately, not every day was that fun. Midway through the trip, we heard that our group's dinner with the Scottish Parliamentarians had been cancelled. I was confused. The public officials needed that meeting. It was the purpose of the trip. Bob, Heaton, Safavian and Vinovich had to be able to say there was some sort of official work associated with our stay in Scotland. Hell, to stay on Bob's good side, I needed there to be a meeting, too. It was the hook for being able to pay for such a privately-funded junket, I assumed. And now it was gone.

Just like that, our trip, which cost hundreds of thousands of dollars, lost its cover story. Having only a single substantive meeting planned for such a trip exemplified the professional culture I was growing used to operating in, a culture with little margin for error, and one that accepted life on the edge. Because the official dinner was not going to happen, our trip had become one hundred percent leisure time. A meal followed by an evening of drinks with some fellow legislators would not have eliminated any of that leisure time, but it would have given us cover for the trip. Years later, I'm still not sure what happened - whether the parliamentarians cancelled, we cancelled, or some outside forces intervened. Maybe there wasn't even a get-together planned. During their investigation, I was asked by the FBI whether I knew for sure that a dinner with parliamentarians was going to occur. I answered that, sside from seeing it on the trip's schedule before we left, I didn't know for sure. Whatever the cause, the dinner providing the supposed "purpose" for the public officials to be on our trip never took place.

Instead of meeting with the parliamentarians, our whole group got together for dinner in the hotel's restaurant. It was the only time we all met as a group away from the golf course, and, as far as I know, there wasn't a single parliamentarian for miles. After dinner, our core Ney group, along with Williams and Safavian, went upstairs to the hotel's bar for some drinks and cigars. Not a word was said about the cancellation.

Had I been only with Williams or with the Ney Group, we might have discussed the odd turn of events. But to discuss it among the six of us would have been awkward due to our various relationships with Jack. After all, to suggest that jack didn't have everything under control would have suggested some sort of disloyalty to our patron. We maintained our faith in him in public. But there were worries. We just talked about them in private.

"I don't know how Bob is going to justify this trip," Safavian said to me the next day. A former lobbyist with Jack's team who was now a rapidly rising star within the Bush administration, he knew what he was talking about. As the Chief of Staff for the General Services Administration, the federal agency which administered everything from federal government computers to federal government property, Safavian normally knew what he was talking about. An intelligent and hard working operator, Safavian and Jack had been friends for years.

"This is a personal trip for me," Safavian said. "It isn't work." Having not heard him say anything like that before word of the dinner's cancellation, I was alarmed by what I was hearing.

"If Safavian doesn't think the trip was legitimate, how could Bob?" I asked myself.

Instead of taking the position that our Scotland jaunt was an official trip, Safavian told me that he had cut Jack a check for his portion of the venture. "It was a couple thousand dollars," he told me. I quickly connected the dots in my head. *"If there was no official purpose for the trip, then Safavian is suggesting that the best thing to do is to just admit that is the case,"* I thought. *"Makes sense."*

As usual, Safavian was on his game. David was known for his ability to intelligently sidestep political landmines. This was a prime example. The couple thousand dollar figure he quoted me was obviously low if we were talking about actual payment for his share of all the costs. But it sure seemed like a defensible number to me if a reporter were ever to call and ask him about the trip. They wouldn't know how high-end our accommodations had been. On top of that, by paying Jack, Safavaian didn't have to suggest that what we were doing was somehow official business. Problem solved. Or so it seemed.

The biggest hole in that argument was the work Jack's White House friend did in the days and weeks leading up to the trip. Safavian had been working with Jack on two projects. Both involved federal property, and both involved the use of Safavian's official office for the advancement of Jack's private interests. The first revolved around a parcel of land in Maryland where Jack wanted to relocate his school, the Eshkol Academy. Securing a new location would have been a boondoggle for Jack's school.

The Academy, which Abramoff established and had been working on for years, was near and dear to Jack's heart, both as a personal priority and a client of the firm, He personally spent millions of dollars on the small Jewish academy, and he talked about the students and what was going on at the school quite often.

Since the General Services Administration (GSA) administered property for the federal government, Safavian was crucial to the process of trying to secure land for the school. Jack peppered him with requests. The two stayed in constant contact leading up to the trip. They exchanged information and strategic advice on how best to buy or lease GSA buildings. They also set up a secret meeting for Jack's wife with GSA officials just days before we left for Scotland. As he did with the Congressman, Abramoff was tying Safavian's official activities to our trip. We had even discussed putting a provision in the Election Reform bill which would have transferred a specific plot of GSA-controlled land to Jack's school.

The second project, involving the Old Post Office Pavilion on Pennsylvania Avenue, was handled in a similar manner. The government had begun the process of turning the towering downtown structure into a hotel. At Jack's suggestion, one of our tribal clients became interested in the project. We were hoping to rig the contracting requirements to help our client get the post office-to-hotel business. As the point man for Jack on the effort, I interacted with Safavian on a regular basis.

Our goal was to use a small business or minority set-aside program, one set up to provide special preferences for small business or minority contractors, to make sure any project proposal that came out of GSA for the post office project included a contracting advantage for our tribal client - an entity that could be either a small business or a minority contractor. Safavian knew the process better than we lobbyists did and was willing to help. Therefore, while our lobbying team worked Capitol Hill to get letters from Members of Congress encouraging GSA to use such a contracting exemption, Safavian operated as our ace in the hole within the agency. Our inside champion.

As our group flew from St. Andrews to London to begin the final leg of our venture, it was easy to see why I had been so nervous about the trip to begin with. Nothing official had occurred. No work had been done. I tried not to look at it that way. In fact, I tried my best just to rationalize it all as business as usual. *"Every trip has a similar kind of tension,"* I told myself. *"Even the purest of them are funded by organizations who want something from the Hill. Right? I mean, when the Defense Department took me on a submarine trip, they did it so I would support their programs. We all say it is because they want us to learn about military operations, but what they really want is for us to get our bosses to vote for their programs."* Nonetheless, I knew full well that I had never before been on a trip like the one to Scotland.

"When the oil and gas industry flew me out to Colorado for several days of

skiing, it was luxurious." I desperately hoped for an explanation. *"That trip was fun,"* I continued. *"I partied and met people. But it also included several hours a day of presentations, meetings and pipeline seminars. Shit, even my trip with Scanlon to the CNMI included several hours of tours and meetings with public officials."* There was no getting around it. The Scotland trip lacked anything that could be described as an official purpose for us to hang our hats on. We could say whatever we wanted, but a drive-by look at of the Queen at a military tattoo did not qualify as an official activity.

Bob called me the day after we got home. He thanked me for the trip and said he had a great time. I told him the same. He was in Ohio during our call, and recounted his time in London. While I had been visiting friends, he and Heaton had gone to the British Parliament, the Chairman said. "They were out of session," Bob continued, "so we sat down with whomever they could find. I had to do something," he added. "We would have met with an intern if that would have helped." He was frank about the need to have an official meeting of some sort to justify his trip.

"I guess," I replied, laughing at his joke. "Maybe taking the Safavian route is the way to go," I suggested. Bob didn't reply. I knew writing a check was expensive, and I also knew that Ney wouldn't be interested in taking that approach. I wouldn't have taken that route either. Both of us figured it was better to just move on. Maybe, as Bob had said before we left, no one would find out about the trip. Or the lack of official business.

August 12, 2002
Washington, DC

Playing Both Sides

Bob returned from Ohio to meet with the Tigua. The tribe was hoping for an update on our effort to open their casino. Having just spent a week with the Congressman in Scotland, it felt weird not be included in the get-together. But Jack didn't think I should be present. For a client to see me break my one-year ban was not a good idea, he said. So I didn't go.

The Tigua's casino had been shuttered for almost six months. Their people were feeling the pain of a massive loss in revenue. Election Reform represented hope for a reopened casino and a better future. Meeting with Bob made sense. But there was a problem. Bob, Jack and I all knew the Tigua provision wasn't going to be included in the bill no matter what the Chairman did. As we had learned before the trip to Scotland, the tribe's fix was unacceptable to the lead Senate negotiator, Senator Chris Dodd, who represented the Mohegan and Mashantucket Pequot Indian Tribes, two major gaming employers in his state. He wasn't going to do anything on Election Reform that involved Indian Country.

Knowing the tribe's provision wasn't going to be included in the bill, what could we say to the Tigua? "We can't tell them we failed," Jack said. "But we should tell them we are looking at other solutions in case Election Reform doesn't work out," he continued. "Lets start to lay the groundwork for them so it isn't a total shock when their fix doesn't end up in the bill."

Twiddling my thumbs, I awaited word on the meeting. Heaton had promised to call when the tribe and Bob had finished talking. A half-hour passed. Then an hour. I heard nothing. It was the August recess, so things were slow on the Hill. Bob was one of the few members of Congress in town. "If Ney is bored, he is liable to talk with them forever," I joked. My instincts were right. Bob had decided to take the tribe on a tour of the Capitol. He loved giving people tours. As the House Administration Chairman, he also had access to places most of his colleagues did not. The tribe walked away impressed. They also walked away still thinking their provision was included in the bill. But we knew better.

Some of us knew more than others. In my case, I didn't know exactly what had been said in the meeting with the tribe. Nor did I know that Jack had already been paid millions of dollars from the Tigua, or that the tribe had been approached about funding the trip to Scotland. Whether Jack, Rudy and Bob had conversed about those topics while I was not around, I don't know. Nonetheless, like Bob, I knew the Tigua project was Jack's top priority. I also knew that Jack put together our tip to Scotland. Not knowing the full picture doesn't change those two fundamental facts. It also doesn't dilute the fact that the Congressman and I knowingly misled the tribe about the prospects of their provision on Election Reform. Ultimately, we all played a role in defrauding the tribe.

With Jack continuing to manage the Tigua relationship, my attention shifted toward finding another legislative vehicle to attach the tribe's legislative fix. Bob said he would continue to help, but since he couldn't directly place a provision in another Member's bill, like he could on his own Election Reform, everyone involved knew his assistance would be reduced going forward. My perspective on the Tigua project also changed. While I continued to want the tribe to do business with us, I didn't know the Tigua had already become a big-money client of Jack's. So I didn't share his urgency about their needs.

Looking back on it, if Jack hadn't remain so energized, my efforts to help the tribe would have ended when Senator Dodd said the provision wasn't acceptable to him. Going forward, I slowly started to focus more of my attention on those clients whom I knew were actually paying the firm. Of course, with Jack still pushing the Tigua fix, I continued looking for ways to help the tribe, and Bob's office even went so far as to attempt some last-minute efforts to attach the provision to Election Reform. But the effort was futile. Everyone knew the fix wasn't going anywhere. Everyone, that is, but the tribe.

The change in my lobbying practice had actually started before hearing that the Tigua provision would not be included in Election Reform, about a month before we left for Scotland. Rudy was still on the team. He and Jack had just conducted my six-month review for the firm. They sang my praises. Such praise made me feel like I was starting to understand the lobbying process better. Days later, when Rudy announced he was leaving, I quickly focused on the new lobbying opportunities his departure presented for me within Team Abramoff. Because of his move, I was able to take over Rudy's client manager responsibilities for one of Jack's larger clients. The name of the client was Rose Garden.

Team Abramoff had nearly fifty clients. Of those, only a handful were considered anchor clients, those companies, tribes and entities which paid a high enough monthly retainer to keep numerous team members busy on any given day. Rose Garden was one of those clients.

Becoming their client manager opened my eyes further to the business side of lobbying and to how the team really operated. Managing a client meant looking at our lobbying efforts from the perspective of the organization paying to influence the government, in this case Rose Garden, who paid us $50,000 a month for our efforts. The client was named after a group of properties controlled by Willie Tan, a garment manufacturer in the Mariana Islands. Willie was one of Jack's closest professional friends. In many ways, Rose Garden was a place-holder for Team Abramoff's ongoing representation of the Mariana Islands. A new government had been elected in the CNMI a few months before I arrived. Since Jack had supported the other side in the campaign, the team lost the official account of the islands. Both Jack and Willie had been through such a change before.

Since both men wanted the team to regain the official lobbying contract with the CNMI government at some point, Jack and Willie decided to keep Team Abramoff engaged in the islands' issues by creating a client - Rose Garden. It was a win-win agreement. Willie didn't trust the lobbyists hired by the new island government to successfully look out for his garment business in the CNMI, and Jack wanted to continue getting paid to protect Willie's interests.

"Rose Garden is a dumping ground for expenses," Rudy told me days before he left, while handing his old client's paperwork over to me. "They only have a couple issues to monitor," he said. "Jack uses the account as a slush fund for people who need hours and to pay for tickets and stuff." My eyes were opened wide during the conversation. The idea of someone paying us to do nothing didn't seem right. Such worries didn't stem from my desire to be an ethical lobbyist. Far from it. They stemmed from my belief that people capable of paying a group of lobbyists $50,000 a month probably didn't get rich by giving money away to do nothing. So I went to Jack. He didn't disagree with Rudy's assessment completely. "We are being paid more to block something bad from happening than actively making something good happen," he said. Instead, Jack emphasized that we needed to stay on top of the numerous immigration, tax and trade issues that impacted the island. "Willie is a friend," he continued, outlining that the CNMI had new lobbyists. "There may not be a need for us to get involved all the time, but we should stay informed," he continued. "Something could come up."

I promised Jack to cover all the bases, and I appreciated his confidence in me. He could have chosen to give the client to someone else. Others had been interested. My understanding of the Hill and the Executive Branch, as well as my trip to the Marianas, were all useful in terms of being able to quickly grasp the client's legislative and regulatory concerns.

The bigger challenge for me was learning how to be a client manager. Until that point, my work revolved around coordinating my lobbying efforts with the other client managers. Administratively, that simply involved giving my assistant the names of the clients and the hours I had worked during the previous week. She then input that data into the firm's client billing system. It was simple. I knew how much I worked, and for whom. Being a client manager, however, meant monitoring other people's hours and expenses. As an access lobbyist, my primary concern had been managing key public official relationships, in order to keep doors open on Capitol Hill and throughout the government. Being a client manager now required that I focus on the client relationship, that I be the client's eyes and ears in Washington. It involved understanding the substance of their legislative and regulatory concerns. It also involved administering the client's monthly lobbying budget and monitoring the activities of the team working for the client.

I liked being a client manager. Jack's client managers were his top lieutenants. Since he didn't personally manage the day-to-day minutiae of any client, Jack's relationship with those organizations depended on us. This made me feel even more like I was moving up among the ranks of the team's pecking order.

Becoming a client manager also showed me the bipartisan nature of Team Abramoff. If someone just read the news articles about Jack, it would be easy to presume that our team was a Republican-only lobbying operation. We weren't. Discussions with the other client managers showed me how much our team worked with both Democrats and Republicans. Whether it was billing hours, expensing meals or securing campaign contributions, the team's Republicans and Democrats operated in the same way, and as a cohesive unit. We were paid to succeed for our clients, not advance a political agenda. Advancing our individual political goals was secondary to winning for our clients. If achieving success could be accomplished by working with a Democratic office instead of a Republican office, so be it.

Because of Jack's personal ideological views, I didn't grasp the depth of that fact at first. But watching the flow of our clients' money showed me the true nature of our team.

Seeing how our bipartisan team used Jack's four skyboxes showed how we all worked together. The sports suites and concert tickets were invaluable tools for our lobbying efforts. As any citizen who has ever written a letter or made a call to Capitol Hill knows, getting and keeping a staffer's or elected official's attention is not always easy. Giving them tickets to their home team's big game or their favorite artist's concert helped us to get the kind of access we needed to do our jobs. Having spent lots of time as a staffer watching games and concerts in luxurious suites, I knew first hand how effective they were in advancing a client's cause. Going to games and concerts for free was not an unusual occurrence in Washington. Both my Republican and Democrat colleagues gave out tickets.

Jack thought the concert and sports tickets were so valuable that he spent nearly a million dollars a year leasing the skyboxes. Because of our clients' largesse, the team had access to two suites at FedEx Field, where NFL football games took place, one at the MCI Center, where professional basketball and hockey games occurred, and one at Camden Yards, where professional baseball games were played. The members of our team incorporated the use of the suites into our daily and weekly activities. But they were Jack's suites. That is how we viewed them. With pictures of the clients on the walls, and Jack's name on the front doors, it was impossible to come to any other conclusion.

According to the Congressional rules at the time, rules Scanlon said were specifically passed by DeLay's office to benefit lobbyists like Jack, the official cost of skybox tickets was listed as $49.00. That was one dollar less than the $50 gift limitation staffers and elected officials were supposed to follow. For lobbyists and public officials alike, such a loophole led to a free-for-all of ticket-giving and taking. As I had seen Rudy and Scanlon do, within weeks of joining Team Abramoff, I was sending out mass emails to my contacts on the Hill offering them tickets.

"Want to see Jordan play?" I would ask in reference to the legendary basketball player, Michael Jordan, during his two-year stint with the Washington Wizards. Or, "Caps game next week?" I asked my contacts interested in hockey. The tickets were a big hit and great for business. They made for an enjoyable night and a great way to get some valuable uninterrupted time with key government decision-makers. It was all part of the show, part of the joke.

As one of my fellow lobbyists wrote to several members of the team, "I am soliciting your thoughts on how we can maximize the benefits of Jack's suites." He labeled the name of our group the "Suite Improvement Caucus," and wanted to discuss how the team could better use the tickets we had available for our lobbying efforts. His was a typical message. Direct. And to the point. "Now is the time to figure this out - before Congress returns again."

My colleagues and I worked hard to keep the suites full. New elected officials, staffers, or client contacts were quickly brought into the system. Staffers, clients and public officials learned, like I did, to proactively ask for tickets. Bob and his staff were no exception. When more people asked for tickets than we had, Jack was the final arbiter for who got them. He normally based his ticket decisions by gauging who was most helpful to our clients. This meant that different members of the team often argued over the net worth of their contacts.

I saw this competitive, bipartisan dynamic of our team play itself out during one of my first events as a lobbyist. Along with a small group of Hill friends, I attended a concert at the MCI Center. Many of my fellow lobbyists also brought along their public official contacts. One of my Democrat colleagues, for instance, brought the top staffer for a key Appropriations Committee. The committee funded billions of dollars of projects across the country every year. It was a big-time committee, which made our guest a big-time staffer. "This is Harry Reid's top appropriations staffer," my colleague told me during introductions.

Since the top priority of several of our clients was to secure funding for various projects, I quickly saw the connection between the committee and our practice. More specifically, with the Democrats running the Senate, this specific appropriation committee's top staffer was a person who represented a crucial contact for the team. My colleague paraded his contact around the suite. He introduced him to the array of assembled concert-goers. I was impressed. The three of us talked periodically during the show. As lobbyists it didn't matter if someone was a Democrat or a Republican. If that person helped our clients, we viewed them as a part of the team.

We talked about Harry Reid, his boss. As both a member of the Democratic leadership and a senior member of the appropriations committee, Senator Reid was a well-known entity. Neither my colleague nor Reid's staffer needed to remind me of the Senator's importance. But they did any way. I replied with some similar comments about Bob. I then told them I had heard good things about Reid, that he was a tough politician who knew how to get legislation passed. "Reid is our DeLay," my colleague replied. "He gets the joke, and knows how to get things done. The Senator is very committed to reaching out to the lobbying community in the same way DeLay does with the K. Street Project." he continued.

I was intrigued by our conversation. For years, DeLay had been criticized by both the media and Congressional Democrats for his working relationship with lobbyists. Because DeLay viewed the lobbying business as an extension of the ideological battles that took place on the Hill, he was outspoken about wanting more companies to hire Republican lobbyists. I agreed with him. It made sense. Why would a Republican-led Congress want more Democrat lobbyists? Or, why would a company that wants to work with the majority party on Capitol Hill hire people who couldn't work with them? DeLay's efforts caused controversy, but, apparently not to everyone. Here were two influential Democrats outlining how their leadership worked the same way, or wanted to, at least. I liked what I heard.

"The Senator gets working with lobbyists," my colleague continued. "He knows we need to be more like you guys to win the Congress and the Presidency back." Considering DeLay was at the pinnacle of his power, the comment was about as good a compliment as you could get. His words also struck me in a different way. *"Our revolution isn't so unique after all,"* I thought to myself. *"The goals change. But it really is just business as usual, the Washington machine at work."*

Like DeLay, Reid was aggressive. He also seemed to be skilled at maneuvering between being an elected official acting as an individual, and being an elected official acting as the leader of a cause. Whether conservative or liberal, both leaders knew they were allowed to tie campaign contributions or lobbying decisions to their official actions, when they were acting as leaders of their respective causes. Vote for a bill to expand unions because it is a part of your movement and take money from those same unions? No problem. Taking such action becomes a problem when the reason for the official activity involves an elected official acting as an individual who lets money influence his decision making. But if it is for the cause, there shouldn't be a problem. Of course, without knowing why someone makes a decision, it is hard to figure out whether an elected official is acting as an individual or as a cause. As my conversation in Jack's suite showed, this balancing act, in which leaders like Delay and Reid engaged, was not a partisan issue. It was business as usual.

Nowhere was our team's bipartisan commitment to business as usual more on display than in the appropriations process. Getting money for the clients we represented was our bread and butter. It allowed us to keep our clients no matter what else happened. Senator Reid wasn't the only appropriator we worked with to get money for our clients. The team cultivated relationships with appropriators on both sides of the aisle. This was important since the Appropriations Committee is the most bipartisan committee on Capitol Hill. That is why seasoned Washington professionals like to say that there are three parties on Capitol Hill; Republicans, Democrats and Appropriators. Over the years, the appropriations process has developed in a way that ensures successful passage of vital budget bills needed to funded the government. This process allows members of Congress from both parties to fund pet projects in their individual appropriation bills. These projects, known as earmarks, helped grease the wheels for ensuring enactment of legislation.

Think about it. If a Member or Senator has a $10 million project in his district or state, it is more likely they will vote for a bill. It also means those individual members on the appropriations committee, both Republicans and Democrats, have a lot of individual influence over their bills. Our lobbying team used this bipartisan process to help our clients get money. But there were rules about engaging Members of Congress. Jack's rules. I learned about them from him first hand.

One such lesson occurred during my first successful foray into the appropriations process as a lobbyist. I had successfully worked with a Democrat Congressman's office to secure language in a bill for a client. I told Jack about our success. I also told him about my conversation with the Congressman's chief of staff, a professional friend from my days on the Hill. The two of us had worked together on steel issues. While thanking him for the assistance, I told my Chief of Staff friend to make sure and invite me to the Congressman's next fundraiser. I used the right language, the right code, everything. That meant I didn't tell the Congressman's top staffer that I wanted to give them money for helping us. I told him that my client supported the cause of the technology that the Congressman supported. He didn't follow along. The Congressman's chief of staff was much more direct in his reply.

"Don't worry," he told me. "The first one is free." Not sure what to say, I smiled at my friend and once again told him to send me an invite to the Congressman's next fundraiser.

When I told Jack the story, he was not pleased. Not because of the ethics involved, but because of the partisan divide.

"It isn't a good idea for you to donate money to a Democrat," he said forcefully. "You need to be able to tell our guys that you are a Republican first. Get one of our Democrats to give the Congressman money, or we can get client money for him. But don't ruin your identity by donating to Democrats," Jack continued. "Trust me. It will hurt you with Republicans. With conservatives. I can't send you into an office and tell them you are a believer in the cause, if you've given money to Democrats." I was stunned by Jack's vehemence. But right way, I knew he was right. I felt stupid for offering to help one of our ideological opponents. I could see a lot of my conservative friends frowning upon the news that I had operated in that manner. *"Wouldn't I think that way if I were in their shoes?"* I asked myself. Understanding that different constituencies kept different scores was another lobbying nuance that was important for me to learn. I thanked Jack for setting me straight.

The importance of understanding the nuances of the Washington money game was on full display as I took in the concert in Jack's suite with my colleague and Senator Reid's staffer. One such nuance involved stepping in and out of different roles. Senator Reid's outreach to the lobbying community exemplified that point. Over the years, Reid had helped the team with our Mariana Island representation. Why he did that, I didn't know. But it was important for our Rose Garden client to continue to stay in good graces with the Senator. Therefore, after becoming client manager, I asked those who worked Reid's office to keep helping with our client's issues. I also told them I would be keeping tabs on what was being done to help our Rose Garden client. In turn, I knew that offices like Senator Reid's and others would be simultaneously keeping tabs on what our clients were doing to help their various causes, as well. Such an approach wasn't a partisan phenomenon. Again, it was business as usual in Washington.

SEPTEMBER 3, 2002
WASHINGTON, DC

Passing the Smell Test

CONGRESS RETURNED FROM THE AUGUST recess. Their impending elections loomed. With two months to go, the campaign industry was in high gear. Ads were being cut, polls conducted, and speeches written. Pundits and prognosticators predicted what to expect. All the while, we lobbyists closely watched the numbers. While Team Abramoff worked to advance our clients' interests in a bipartisan manner, each individual lobbyist had his or her own partisan affiliation and understood the importance of the election process on our business. After all, every two years, the people we needed to influence could change.

Historically, the President's party loses congressional seats in the midterm elections. But the 2002 election cycle seemed different. Going into the summer, President Bush's job approval ratings continued to hover near 70 percent in the Gallup Organization's polling. This was highest rating of any President in fifty years. With the well-being of my lobbying career tied to the prospects of the narrow Republican majority in the House, that was good news. The President's increased popularity would help keep the majority by creating several political advantages. One, it allowed Republicans to recruit top tier candidates to run for office. Convincing someone to take on an incumbent senator or run for an open House seat is easier to do when the President's political team can promise lots of support, and when the environment is conducive to a political victory. Two, it allowed President Bush to lead a unified effort in defining the upcoming congressional elections as a referendum on his wartime leadership. The issues primarily driving that message home were the impending Congressional vote to authorize the use of force in Iraq, and the President's effort to create a new Department of Homeland Security.

For the first time since Ney's election to Congress, neither Bob nor I had to deal with that manic rush leading up to Election Day. The Congressman's newly re-configured post-census congressional district (congressional lines are drawn every ten years) was more Republican than it had been in the past. When combined with his strong public support locally and impressive fundraising strength in Washington, this meant no Democratic opponent stepped up to run against him. Therefore, Bob spent much of his time trying to help other candidates get elected. Creating more GOP Congressmen was good for Bob personally and good for the cause of conservatism.

I focused squarely on the behind-the-scenes maneuvering that accompanies the election process in Washington. My lobbying responsibilities meant working to navigate the shifting partisan market on behalf of my clients in the short-term, and working to best position them for a post-election Washington in the long-term. Before I could really move forward, however, there remained some unfinished business from Scotland.

Heaton called me early in the morning. He said that he and the Chairman needed to fill out their Travel Disclosure Forms for the Scotland trip. The disclosure form topic was something I had been avoiding. But that was no longer an option. Under the law, elected officials and/or staff who take a trip paid for by someone else have to file a disclosure form within thirty days of their travel. That meant Bob and his staff's forms were due before the end of the day. The disclosure documents were pretty simple. Hundreds get filed after every August recess. There is a line on the form for the dates of the excursion, a line for the costs, the purpose, and the name of the entity who paid for the trip. Unfortunately, about the only line Heaton and Bob could fill out was the one for the dates we were in Scotland. And the clock was ticking.

Days earlier, Bob had begun the process of creating a cover story for the trip by zeroing in on the previous DeLay trip. Even more than before, that trip became a security blanket for Bob, Heaton, me, and all of Ney World. "DeLay took the same trip," became Bob's single-bullet talking point. Such a focus worked much better than the facts, namely that some charity of Jack's, which had to do with kids and sports, had taken us on a golf vacation. Because of that, the Chairman gave Heaton instructions to tailor the disclosure forms as closely as possible to the forms filed by the House Leader and his staff.

That led us to the National Center for Public Policy Research (NCPPR). Named on the disclosure forms as the group funding DeLay's 2000 Scotland trip, the NCPPR was one of numerous organizations which I thought Jack either ran or heavily supported financially. I gave Heaton the director's phone number. Unfortunately, she wasn't returning his calls.

I didn't know what to say. Like Bob, I had been thinking about their travel disclosure form responsibilities as well. Part of me wanted to once again suggest that the Chairman and his team do what Safavian did, pay for a portion of the trip. But the more I dug into that proposal, the more I thought it was a bad idea. The mere suggestion of paying their own way had already gone over like a lead balloon with Bob and his guys. Pushing them further would have only made the situation worse. I envisioned how it would play out. For years, Bob would remind me and others that I cost him and his team several thousand dollars each. "Going on a free trip with Neil only costs a couple thousand dollars," I could hear him saying, both in front of me and behind my back. It was money neither he nor his guys had readily available. Even worse than the verbal assault, Bob would probably punish my lobbying work for a while as well. Calls or meeting requests would go unreturned. He'd limit my access to him. No matter how I war-gamed the conversation about paying for the trip in my head, it always led to the same place - a dead-end.

Complicating the situation was the fact that I didn't know anything about the NCPPR. All I knew was that DeLay's trip had been funded through that group, and that Jack was associated with them. "All roads lead back to Abramoff," I told Will. "When I submitted my receipts for re-imbursement, the organization reimbursing me for the costs of the trip was the Capital Athletic Foundation, not the NCPPR. But that is another one of Jack's groups." Heaton remained quiet on the end of the other line. I knew everything I was saying would be repeated to the Congressman.

On the one hand, Bob wanted us to make sure the forms matched up with the DeLay trip. He wasn't demanding it, or, in some nefarious manner, telling us to make something up. But he did want the comfort associated with being able to say his Scotland venture with Jack was like the Majority Leader's trip. On the other hand, I knew it was the Capital Athletic Foundation who reimbursed my trip costs. *"Wouldn't they be funding the Ney part of the trip, too?"* I asked myself. There was only one thing for me to do.

As the sand filled the bottom of the hour glass, I told Heaton I would call him back, and ran into Jack's office. I sat down in the chair across from his desk and didn't move. Having tried unsuccessfully several times to talk with him in preceding days, I was determined to make him deal with the disclosure form issue immediately. Jack was on the phone. While he talked,

I tried to get my ducks in a row. *"Why isn't the director calling Will back? Didn't she work for Jack or something?"* The longer I sat there the more I wanted to emphasize to Abramoff that he needed to make this right, since I was convinced that he was unaware of just how nervous the Ney team was about the trip. Myself included. When Jack hung up the phone. I quickly asked him who paid for the trip. Throwing his hands up in the air, Jack redirected the conversation.

"What do they want?" he asked. In a flash, I told him that the Congressman was hoping to mirror what DeLay did on his trip as much as possible. But the folks at NCPPR weren't returning their calls. "That is how they want to do it?" Jack said, suggesting he had told Bob something else. "If they want to say that is who the trip is from, then that is who the trip is from," he said calmly. Jack's words stunned me. It wasn't exactly what I wanted to hear. What I wanted to hear was that the NCPPR somehow actually did have something to do with funding the trip. That would at least suggest some sort of substance that we could give to a reporter if asked. As I stood there, Jack told his assistant to connect him with the organization's director. Holding the receiver in his hand, Jack talked at me, periodically shaking the black piece of plastic around for effect. Within a few seconds, he and the director were on the phone together.

Laughing, he told her, "I understand you got a call from Congressman Ney's chief of staff. He is calling about that trip we did with the Congressman. You remember, to Scotland, right?" This was followed by more laughter. "Oh, did I not tell you about that one?" he continued. I tried to follow along. Not hearing the other end of the conversation created some confusion. I could tell they were joking, but things also seemed under control. In ways few people could, Jack's actions simultaneously made me feel both more nervous and more secure. "I should have said something to you about it earlier," he continued before their conversation slipped into other topics.

"Tell them we are fine," Jack said to me when he got off the phone. "Also, talk to the girls," he continued in reference to his two female assistants. "They can get you an estimate on the food, the flight and the lodging for the forms."

"The guys are just worried about the dinner being cancelled and everything," I said to Jack belatedly.

"That is the perfect reason for them to come next year, then," he replied with a laugh. I stood there looking at Jack for a moment. It was a brief moment. My boss leaned back in his chair. Waving his arms again, he looked at me as if to say, "Is there anything else?" I felt an urge to talk further, to address my concerns. If I was going to say anything about the fake conversation I had just witnessed or the contradiction between Jack's levity and Bob's worry, this was the time. But I said nothing. Instead, turning on my heels, I walked out.

When I re-run that moment in my head, my mind always returns to a story I read about a woman who was on the verge of dying. The reporter had asked about her life. She said that she would live most the years of her life the same way if she could do it all over again, but that there were a few minutes she would definitely do differently. Looking back, for me, that time in Jack's office was one of those minutes. I deeply regretted going on the Scotland trip. The regret associated with those few minutes in which I helped Bob and his staff file fraudulent travel disclosure forms makes me wish I would have made different decisions. Instead of stopping and asking some questions, I closed my eyes to the facts in front of me. Instead of listening to that tug in the back of my head, that pull on my conscience, I walked away. It was easier.

Leaving Jack's office, I got right back on the phone with Heaton. "Jack talked to them," I told him. "I'm not sure what to think, but he told me to tell you guys everything is fine." We talked further. To save time, I told Heaton I was working with Jack's assistants to get some estimates for airfare, lodging and the rest. After that was done, I told him I would fill out a draft disclosure form and fax it over to him. "You can then do whatever you want at that point."

We both knew the whole thing was a mess. My stomach ached. What I was doing epitomized the nature of my corrupt relationship with Jack, Bob and our fellow co-conspirators. In certain respects, the corruption wasn't what many people think. There was no whispering in dark corners with secret bags of cash or people screaming out demands. Our corruption was much more subtle, more nuanced. I knew that we were stepping beyond the typical Washington, "You scratch my back, I'll scratch yours," but I tried to convince myself otherwise. The others seemed to agree. It was as if my mentors, my protégés, and I all agreed to say, "If this reality isn't working for us, then let's create a new one, because no one will really know anyway."

Our game plan was set. Hastily, I started filling out the forms. I was now in implementation mode. Nothing else mattered. With pen in hand, my biggest worry as I scribbled away was that some reporter digging through the disclosure forms was going to write a nasty story about Bob going on a trip to Scotland. Every quarter the *Columbus Dispatch* or the *Cleveland Plain Dealer* went through the Ohio forms searching for an official to pillory. They usually followed a similar storyline. In Bob's case, it would read something like, "While the factory shut down, Bob Ney was on a junket to Scotland. Playing golf. Or, as his disclosure form says, visiting with Scottish parliamentarians."

Determined to make sure that story never came to fruition, I scribbled my ideas down on a printed copy of the disclosure form my assistant had downloaded for me. Under purpose of the trip I wrote, "Visit Scottish parliamentarians? Visit English parliament? Attend military tattoo?" Rationalizing away, I remember thinking that the parliamentarians had actually been the purpose of the trip. If a meeting didn't happen, what was the Congressman to do? It isn't like the purpose of the trip had changed. I threw it all out there. *"Bob's office can decide what they want to put on the final copy,"* I figured. *"As long as it passes the smell test of a potential reporter, we will be fine."* It was time to move on.

At no point did I worry about what would eventually happen, namely that the Department of Justice would investigate the legitimacy of that document. Such a perspective was incredibly arrogant. I knew it was against the law for a lobbyist to give such a gift to a Member of Congress or White House official with the intent of trying to influence their decision-making. And deep down I knew that is exactly what Jack had done with the trip. What *we* had done with the trip. No matter what organization we named on the form, no one thought that anyone but Jack had pulled the strings of our trip to Scotland.

Likewise, I knew it was illegal for public officials to accept such a gift from a lobbyist who was intending to influence them. And, again, deep down I knew that was exactly what Bob was doing. Again, what *we* were doing. In a world of fuzzy lines though, sadly, it all seemed acceptable. As long as we jumped through the "right" hoops, everything would be fine.

By getting Jack to call the NCPPR, I had done my part. The rest was Bob's to decide. While figuratively holding my nose, I faxed over my suggestions. I couldn't be responsible for everything. Looking back, I wish I had taken the decision to fill out the Congressman's forms more seriously. But I didn't. A few days later, Bob and I joked about the disclosure forms. He told me again how he and Heaton had run through the Halls of Parliament in London looking for someone to meet with. We howled in laughter as he re-created a picture of those two desperately searching for an intern or security guard to talk with. We figured you could either laugh or cry about our predicament. And as usual, we chose to laugh.

The Congressman said that during the internal discussion in the office there had been talk of not filing any disclosure form at all. He said he scoffed at that notion. "You have to fill out something," he told me he said to the guys in his office. I couldn't disagree. And with that, we moved on.

Our dishonesty seemed like a small deal in the moment. On the day I helped the Congressman and his staff fill out their forms, each of us probably made hundreds of decisions, for our clients, ourselves, our constituents, our colleagues and our families. The decisions over what to file probably book-ended between decisions that seemed much more important. So without asking a single diligent question or gauging the moral aspect of such a choice, we made our decision. And then what seemed so small gradually grew in importance.

Like many others who have sealed their fates with a stupid, reckless or arrogant decision, I was in denial. Hopeful that Jack could somehow turn black into white, I convinced myself that everything was just fine. That we were above all our worries, our little tugs at the conscience. After all, when you make the rules, lying on a Congressional Travel Disclosure Form is nothing more than a public relations exercise. Sure, I could get caught, but we had covered ourselves pretty well. Even worse, the minute after I faxed the information to Bob's office for his disclosure forms, I began rationalizing away my own behavior. When you're a Master of the Universe big-shot lobbyist, you aren't giving tens of thousands of dollars in campaign contributions and flying to Scotland with the intent of convincing Congressman Ney to take official actions on your client's behalf, or thanking him for having done so. No. "*Of course not,*" I told myself. "*I'm just doing my job.*" It was the Yuppie Nuremburg defense.

I very much wanted to believe my own words. But the fact is, instead of looking at things as they were, I was looking at things as I wished them to be. The free drinks, meals, games, trips and campaign donations were just a means to an end. An end where Jack was more wealthy, Bob more powerful - and me both powerful and wealthy. Very simply, I was in a scary place. I had jumped off the edge. And I liked it.

OCTOBER 8, 2002
WASHINGTON, DC

Following the Money

I COULDN'T WAIT FOR THE CONVERSATION to be over. The Tigua soap op-era had turned into a complete debacle. It wasn't until Election Reform actually passed that Jack told the client about Senator Dodd's refusal to include a provision in the bill to re-open their casino. In the meantime, he continued to push me to try and find a solution to the tribe's problem. His expectations were unrealistic. So were the clients'. Getting a provision like the one we wanted included in a bill was not as easy as Jack had told the tribe. They were expecting the impossible. The whole situation was awk-ward. Nonetheless, I searched for other bills to which we could attach their provision, all to no avail. Therefore, while the team's continued success in other areas had me learning to enjoy my life as a lobbyist, the Tigua project remained depressing. I hoped the tribe's phone call with the Chairman would finally end the drama.

"What does Jack want me to say?" Bob asked, before the conference call with Abramoff and the Tigua.

"Tell him it wasn't Jack's fault," I said. "And tell them we are going to find another vehicle for their provision."

"Ok," he replied.

The story was the same, but the situation was now different. Election Reform had passed without the Tigua provision being included in the bill. Jack said the tribe was heartbroken by the news. I was too. Despite a last ditch effort by Bob's staff to get the Senate negotiators to support the mea-sure, we had known for months that the tribe's provision wasn't going to be included in the bill. Now that the news was out, however, Jack was urgently working to soothe the Tigua's concerns. He asked Bob to take part in a con-ference call with the tribe. After telling Jack about my quick conversation with Bob, I asked Jack if there was any need to contact the Chairman again before the conference call with the tribe. Jack said he thought we were fine. He told me that he had talked with Bob about the call the night before at Signatures. "Don't worry about it," he told me.

Like all the meetings that took place between the Chairman, Jack and the tribe, I was on the outside looking in for the actual conversation. My only insight into the discussion came from Jack's periodic email messages. "This is awkward," he told me early on, when Bob was late for the call. Jack then asked me to see if I could track down the Chairman. I called Heaton. "He'll be on the call shortly," Ney's chief of staff told me. I relayed the message to Jack.

Not hearing anything for a while, I assumed everything was going fine. Then Jack emailed me. "Bob is fucking this up," he said venomously. I asked what was going on. "He is off script," Jack replied.

I quickly called Heaton. He didn't pick up. We wouldn't talk until later in the day. Eventually, Heaton said that Bob didn't want to talk with me about the call. "Is he mad?" I asked.

"No, the Chairman is busy," he replied. His comment struck me funny. Bob was rarely too busy to take my calls. I knew something wasn't right.

"Seriously?" I asked Heaton. "I don't believe that. Come on, Will. Tell me straight."

"He was a little upset that he didn't have more information," Heaton said. "But everything is cool."

Before Heaton had gotten back to me, I had walked into Jack's office. "Everything OK?" I asked.

"Bob was fine," he said. "He just talks too much." That was Jack's way of blowing me off. He looked dejected. His comments made me worry about what was going on with Bob. *What happened on that call?* I wondered. *Did Bob tell the tribe what really happened? That we knew we were in trouble months ago?* Whatever happened, Jack clearly didn't want to talk about it.

"We'll get another client," I told him.

"It isn't that easy," Jack replied. "We need to take care of these guys." I could tell there was more to the Tigua story than he was sharing. But I wasn't sure what to do next. *"Do I ask my boss what is wrong? Do I suggest that we stop asking our friends on the Hill to help us with what was surely a doomed project, so we can just move on?"* Looking at Jack, I could tell the answer was obvious. He wanted to keep pushing. And I wanted to make him happy. Therefore, Jack and I talked about other pieces of legislation where we could potentially add the tribe's provision. I went through my whole list. "None of these are very promising," I continued. Jack saw it differently. He grew more invigorated.

He also worked to get me more excited about the project. Since our new potential legislative targets didn't have to do with Bob's office, my one-year ban situation didn't have to be so uncomfortable, we both knew. Touching on the topic, Jack told me it was time for him to introduce me to the tribe. "Lets get this done," he said. "It will be good for you to spend time with the client. And obviously, if you can pull this off, Neil, you'll get a big pay raise." His words were music to my ears. Once again, I started focusing on becoming a client manager for the Tigua tribe. The benefits were right in front of me. All I needed to do was make the client happy, and the money would follow.

NOVEMBER 5, 2002
WASHINGTON, DC

Election Day

IT WAS MY FIRST ELECTION Night in Washington. The lights flashed and the flickering television screens lined the walls as I walked into the *ESPN Sports Zone*, a downtown restaurant. Red mahogany tables and chairs filled the spacious sports-themed bar, game room and dining facility. There were hundreds of lobbyists, Congressional staffers, and other political professionals in attendance. Like an intense sporting event, we watched the election results roll in from across the country. Majority Whip DeLay's office had rented out the *Sports Zone* for the night. It was a great time.

As expected, the Republican majority in the House of Representatives grew by several seats. Going into Election Day, we held a 221 to 212 margin over the Democratic minority. After the votes were counted, the margin for the Republicans in the House grew to 229 members. The number of Democratic members shrank to 204.

There was also good news in the Senate. After more than a year in the minority, the Republicans regained control of the upper legislative chamber. The partisan balance in the Senate had changed midway through President Bush's first year in office, when a GOP Senator from Rhode Island decided to switch parties. But after the votes were counted on Election Day, the Senate flipped from 49 Republicans and 51 Democrats, to 51 Republicans and 49 Democrats. The switch of just two races had returned the chairman's gavels in the Senate, and the machinery of the entire federal government, back in to Republican hands.

The CNMI

THE DECISIONS VOTERS MAKE AT the polls on Election Day impacts Washington's lobbying business. Team Abramoff's work on behalf of the Commonwealth of the Northern Marianas (CNMI) exemplified that point. Two years earlier, after the 2000 elections, Jack's team had lost the official CNMI account. For years the CNMI had been a six-figure-a-month client for the team. But because the island government switched hands, the new CNMI leadership hired a different set of lobbyists to represent the Commonwealth in Washington.

In response to that election-driven decision, Team Abramoff began our representation of Rose Garden, a group of properties owned by one of the CNMI's largest garment manufacturers. After November's election, the voter's decisions once again impacted our CNMI-related work, this time through our work for Rose Garden.

Shortly after the election, President Bush signed the homeland security bill into law. The legislation creating the Department of Homeland Security represented the biggest reorganization of the federal government since the Department of Defense was created in 1947. It merged 22 government agencies, including the Coast Guard, the Border Patrol and the Immigration and Naturalization Service, into one massive department. "Today we are taking historic action to defend the U.S. and protect our citizens against the dangers of a new era," Bush said in prepared remarks at the signing ceremony. The creation of the department was the result of security failures and gaps in intelligence-gathering that had been exposed in the aftermath of the 9/11 attacks. "Creating a new Department of Homeland Security will ensure that our efforts to defend this country are comprehensive and united," the President continued.

The bill was 187 pages long. Our lobbying team's provision protecting the garment manufacturers of the Mariana Islands was on page seven. Since the bill impacted immigration policy throughout the government, the team and I had worked with our friends on the Hill to ensure that any changes included in the legislation did not hurt Rose Garden or the CNMI's garment manufacturing industry. My work on behalf of Jack's client epitomized how lobbying intersected with business and politics. Like any other business, the fundamental goal of my firm, my client and myself was to make money. In the case of individual lobbyists and firms, that means getting paid by organizations and individuals to manipulate the government. In this case, for instance, my job was to protect the immigration loophole used by the Mariana's garment manufacturers. The team and I accomplished that by manipulating the homeland security bill.

Whether a lobbyist is successful or not is generally determined by whether they get a good return on their client's investment. Like the thousands of other lobbyists working on the homeland security bill, our goal was to protect our client's financial interests. In most cases, organizations and individuals pay lobbyists money in order to get more money. Such success usually plays out in one of two ways: a lobbyist helps to block something that would be costly to his client, or helps enact something that would be beneficial. The government action involved is normally a tax, a regulation, or some sort of direct payment.

In the case of our Rose Garden client, we wanted to block proposed regulations that would have been costly to the garment industry. Specifically, that meant beating back efforts by those who wanted to use the reorganization of the federal immigration department to reform how business was done in the Marianas. After President Bush began pushing for the creation of a homeland security department, in mid-2002, momentum for the reorganization efforts grew on Capitol Hill. The bill soon reached a tipping point, and became what most of our contacts thought was a "must pass" piece of legislation. At that point, the many professional political-types who were interested in the potential changes, everyone from career civil servants and lobbyists to paid consultants and corporate executives, began to join in the discussion about how best to reorganize the federal government.

One of my fellow lobbyists got word from a Capitol Hill contact that some public officials within the Executive Branch were looking at making changes to the CNMI's immigration status. Specifically, we were told, there was a move afoot by several officials within the Department of Labor and their allies on the Hill to try to close the loophole in the law granting the

CNMI local control over their immigration administration. No matter how serious their efforts, such a move was a direct threat to our client's business and the CNMI garment industry, in general. We knew our opponents argument. They had been making it for years. Their view was that the CNMI garment manufacturer's use of guest workers from China, Indonesia, the Philippines and elsewhere represented an unfair labor practice. Such practices now represented a risk to homeland security as well, our opponents said. It was a decent argument. "If I was getting paid to lobby for them, that is what I would say, too," I told a colleague.

Alerted to their efforts, our team swung into action. As the client manager for our Rose Garden representation, I was responsible for the overall effort. My first job was to work with the team to gather information about the bill, the potential changes, and who specifically had the power to implement those changes. Since Jack had represented the islands for years, and had organized hundreds of trips to the CNMI for staffers and elected officials, we had contacts throughout the government who were willing to help. My teammates and I let our contacts know what we were hearing. In turn, they reported back any news they heard. It was Lobbying 101. After learning about the danger to our client's interests, we prepared our response and waited for the right time to move.

Reorganizing 22 federal agencies was a gargantuan effort. The new agency's budget was $40 billion, according to the White House. While there were certainly substantial policy and security reasons to make the changes, creating such a department was also an overtly political act. President Bush initially opposed the idea. He didn't think it would work. By early summer, however, the President changed his mind. It was good policy, he said. It was also good politics, so good that by midway through the fall campaign, creating the Department of Homeland Security had become the President's top legislative priority.

Bush was not on the ballot, but a successful midterm election was crucial for him and our center-right governing coalition. The margin in the House remained narrow, and winning the Senate back was within in reach. And the President was uniquely positioned with the public to advance the conservative cause. Normally, off-year elections are bad for sitting presidents. But President Bush remained popular. In part because of his response to the 9/11 attacks, the President's job approval numbers were strong, especially when it came to defending the homeland. Therefore, the White House and conservative leaders decided to use that popularity to bolster the Republican House, and try to win back the Democratic Senate.

More than anything else, those efforts were built around the issue of terror-ism, and protecting the country from future attacks. As a lobbyist, it was important for me to be in tune with the politics of the moment, in case we needed to take action on behalf of our clients. After all, just as the legisla-tive process is intertwined with the political mood of the country, so, too, is the lobbying business.

For months, negotiations over the creation of the new department progressed. Shortly before the election, however, legislative battle lines be-gan to develop between Republicans and Democrats. The biggest dispute concerned the issue of labor rights within the new 170,000-person depart-ment. The President, who believed public employee unions had too much say over the government, believed the new department should be structured in a way that allowed the organization to run more like a business, or like the defense department. That meant being able to hire, fire and shift em-ployees more freely than in other government entities. The unions, and their Democratic allies on Capitol Hill, saw that approach as a threat to the well being of their members, their legislative agenda, and their pocketbooks. Progress on the bill broke down. The two sides then took their case to the final arbiter in American politics - the people. In this case, they went to the people of Georgia.

The 2002 Senate race in Georgia was a contest between incumbent Democrat Senator Max Cleland and Republican Congressman Saxby Chambliss. In the final weeks of the campaign, the dispute over union issues in the new homeland security department took over the public con-versation between the two candidates. Trailing in the polls, Chambliss, the Republican, ran an ad accusing his opponent of being weak on homeland security. The heart of the GOP argument was that the Senator was putting the interests of unions ahead of the nation's safety. "Max Cleland says he has the courage to lead, but the record proves that is just misleading," the announcer in the advertisement said. The piece then accused Cleland of voting 11 times against the creation of the Homeland Security Department, as pictures of Osama bin Laden and Saddam Hussein flashed across the screen. Even though the Democrat Senator had voted for a version of the department that included more union protections, the charge was techni-cally true. If not for the union objections, the Senate would have passed legislation creating the new department before the election. It was a fact the Democratic incumbent, Cleland, could not dispute.

As expected, the pictures of bin Laden and Hussein ignited a con-troversy over the ad. Cleland, a triple-amputee who had been injured in

Vietnam, accused his Republican opponent of questioning his patriotism. His fellow Georgia Democratic Senator, Zell Miller, rushed to his defense. "It's disgraceful for anybody to question Max Cleland's commitment to our national security," Miller said. "Max Cleland is my hero," Senator Miller continued. The problem for Cleland was that Miller, his Georgia counterpart in the Senate, had voted against the unions on the homeland security bill. Such a fact provided my fellow Republicans a great contrast.

In fact, on the Senate floor, while voting for the provision, Senator Miller said; "We must give the President the flexibility to respond to terrorism on a moment's notice. He's got to be able to shift resources, including personnel, at the blink of an eye." The Senator was one of only a few Democrats to defy the unions, but the in-state contrast could not be more clear. Such a difference between the two Democratic Senator's votes allowed the GOP to claim, that on the substance of the legislation, Cleland was the one out Georgia's political mainstream. On Election Day, the Republicans picked up the seat.

This was one of the two seats needed to wrest back control of the Senate. We lobbyists watched the election closely. According to polling at the time, Cleland dropped nearly ten points after the homeland security advertisement. That kind of shift in voter sentiment is noticed quickly in Washington, and by politicians skilled in self preservation. Within days of the election, Senate Democrats gave up their objections to the President's labor demands. They had gotten the voter's message, and an immediate mandate for the new department was created.

With the machinery of the government beginning to move, my lobbying colleagues and I quickly jumped into the fray. Our Mariana Island opponents didn't know what hit them. Because of the voters' mandate, the homeland security legislation was brought before the Congress just a few days after the election. The principal decision-makers for the bill in the House were staffers for the elected leadership, staffers in Majority Whip DeLay's office and others. Since most of the legislation had already been agreed upon, the primary goal for those negotiating the remaining differences between the House and the Senate was to move right away. We knew that meant the bill was moving fast. It also meant our contacts in the House leadership were perfectly positioned to help our client's efforts.

Like us, those people who were working to change the CNMI's immigration policies scrambled to catch up with the rapidly developing negotiations. Despite our various staff contacts' willingness to help, the team remained worried. Our main concern was that there were so many moving pieces in the bill, and time was in short supply. With the Democrats still technically running the Senate, that meant a well connected adversary could slip language into the legislation in a way that was tough to find. Looking at the bill later, it was easy to see why we were worried. Some provisions dealing with the new department were pretty straightforward, like the definition of a local government;

The term "local government" means -

(A) a county, municipality, city, town, township, local public authority, school district, special district, intrastate district, council of governments (regardless of whether the council of governments is incorporated as a nonprofit corporation under State law), regional or interstate government entity, or agency or instrumentality of a local government;

(B) an Indian tribe or authorized tribal organization, or in Alaska a Native village or Alaska Regional Native Corporation; and

(C) a rural community, unincorporated town or village, or other public entity.

Other provisions, however, like the next definition on that same page, the one defining a major disaster, weren't so simple.

The term "major disaster" has the meaning given in section 102(2) of the Robert T. Stafford Disaster Relief and Emergency Assistance Act (42 U.S.C. 5122).

This type of unclear legislative language is what had us worried. While willing to be helpful, our contacts on the Hill didn't have the time to scrub every corner of the bill. Nor could they give us all the text so we could go through each questionable provision ourselves. After all, they were trying to move a massive piece of legislation in about a week. With questionable provisions changing constantly, handing out large portions of the bill to lobbyist friends was not a good idea. Everyone involved understood that fact. Ultimately, we settled on a simple solution to the problem. At the beginning of the bill, in the same definition section where local governments, major disasters and numerous other designations were written, we included language that clearly protected the status quo for the CNMI's immigration policies. Our provision, 16B, immediately followed the definition of the United States, as it pertained to the new homeland security department;

(16)(A) The term "United States", when used in a geographic sense, means any State of the United States, the District of Columbia, the Commonwealth of Puerto Rico, the Virgin Islands, Guam, American Samoa, the Commonwealth of the Northern Mariana Islands, any possession of the United States, and any waters within the jurisdiction of the United States.

(B) Nothing in this paragraph or any other provision of this Act shall be construed to modify the definition of "United States" for the purposes of the Immigration and Nationality Act or any other immigration or nationality law.

I was fired up when I saw the provision in the bill. *"Jack will like to see that,"* I thought to myself. *"And it is going to put some more money in my wallet."* The immigration provision represented another win for the team. When the legislation, including our provision, was agreed upon by both the House and the Senate, on November 13, 2002, I passed the final word along to Jack. He was ecstatic, and thanked me profusely. Pleasing my boss made me feel like an even more valuable part of Team Abramoff. I quickly added the provision to my growing list of accomplishments I was due to present to Jack during our end-of-year negotiations over my salary.

As far as I was concerned, nothing but good could come from delivering for one of the team's bigger clients. Additionally, such success convinced me that I was learning how to be an effective lobbyist. That, too, felt good. This could be seen in my ego-laden email announcing our victory. I sent it to Jack, assuming he would pass it along to the client.

"Jack, we had a huge win today with the Homeland Security bill. After months of pushing, we got our concerns taken care of. Specifically, our concerns about the backdoor takeover in the definition section of the bill has been clarified. Through a lot of hard work from your team, we were able to do the unthinkable - just bulldoze our changes onto the definition section itself (which no one thought was possible) instead of clarifying language at the end of the bill. The language we inserted can be found specifically in Sec 2 - Definitions - Subsection 16(B) which now includes our language to keep the status quo for immigration authority."

"Nothing in this paragraph or any other provision of this Act shall be construed to modify the definition of United States for the purposes of the Immigration and Nationality Act or any other immigration or nationality act."

"Good stuff."

It was good stuff indeed. As my success for Rose Garden showed, working on homeland security issues was proving to be lucrative. The increased funding, throughout Washington, on all things homeland security meant the potential business for those companies and organizations in the domestic security market was increasing. This, in turn, meant more potential homeland security lobbying clients for me and my firm. The equation was pretty simple: the more the government spent on homeland security technology and personnel, the more money there was for lobbyists to try to procure for their clients. After the attacks of 9/11, there was an explosion of homeland security-related spending. Tens of billions of dollars was quickly spent on additional airline security, new computer systems and anti-terrorism employees. Lobbyists all over Washington followed the money. I was no exception.

Few weeks went by in late 2002 when some technology company or scientist with a great idea didn't approach the firm in search of a lobbying team. One day it was a bomb-sniffing-dog business who wanted in with the new Transportation Security Administration, and the next it was a software entrepreneur who felt his remediation technology could improve how government defended itself against cyber-attacks. The firm, the team and I brought in new homeland clients. Including my experiences on Capitol Hill during 9/11, as well as during the anthrax attacks, was helpful in that process. The stories were a good hook. They added to my lobbying pitch.

As usual, delivering for our clients was the best way for the team to create new business and get paid. After all, the lobbying community in Washington watched each other pretty closely. If a multimillion dollar federal decision was being made, you could bet that a lobbyist was behind the scenes trying to influence it. You could also bet on the fact that the lobbyist's competitors were watching to see if he or she was successful. With my client success rate improving, I found myself clamoring for more money, money that was being generated by more government spending. This created a conflict between my ideological commitment to smaller government and my desire for a bigger paycheck.

JANUARY 03, 2003
TEMPE, ARIZONA

Champions

THE DEAFENING ROAR OF THE crowd went quiet. Most of the 77,502 people in attendance were Ohio State fans. We had flown in from all over the country for the game. Sun Devil Stadium was filled to capacity with our scarlet and grey hats, jerseys and clothes. Not since 1968 had my Buckeyes won a national championship in football. Becoming champions, however, was suddenly within our grasp.

For more than four quarters my Ohio brethren had been rocking the house. We screamed at the top of our lungs, and carried on with an impassioned roar that few fan bases can match. Then the fourth quarter ended. The game took a turn for the worse. It was overtime, and fourth down. We were trailing 24-17. If the guys didn't get at least 14 yards on the next play, the University of Miami was going to win the national championship. Dejected, I shook my head from side to side before plopping down in one of our seats along the 30-yard line. "It's over," I said.

"No it isn't," one of my Team Abramoff colleagues replied. "They can do this," he said optimistically. His eyes lit up as he looked over at me. Right away, I jumped to my feet. It was a momentary lapse.

"And you're not even an Ohio State fan," I joked.

"I am tonight," he said, as we gave each other a high-five.

The two of us had reason to celebrate. Not only was it the night of the college football national championship game, it was also a night for our champions. Joining my Team Abramoff colleague and I at the game were two of our lobbying team's most important public official champions, those who helped us out when we needed it most. My guest was Bob, who brought along one of his staffers. My colleague's guest was a senior appropriations staffer for Senator Reid, who also brought a guest.

220

By the time we got to Arizona, I had met Reid's staffer several times. He worked with several of my colleagues, one of whom had been a staffer for the Senator before joining Team Abramoff. Like me, both Bob and Reid's staffer were Ohio State graduates and fans of the team. Offering the Chairman tickets to the big game was a sign of our friendship and a reason to have a good time. But more than that, it was a way to show my appreciation for all he had done to help me and my clients in the last year. As far as I could tell, my lobbying colleague seemed to be doing the same thing for his Hill contact, though, I didn't know that for sure.

Our trip started when my lobbying colleague heard about me buying tickets for Bob. He stopped into my office to talk about the game. "How did you get tickets?" my colleague asked. He then told me that his appropriations contact in Reid's office was an Ohio State graduate and a huge fan. "He would enjoy watching the Buckeyes play," my colleague said of his contact. "So how again did you get tickets?"

"Easy," I replied. "I bought them from an online ticket broker, and am going to charge them to the clients."

"Maybe I should do the same," he said. "Can I put some of it on Rose Garden?" he asked, making reference to the CNMI-related client I managed for Jack. "Of course. Put a couple hundred bucks on there. You can put the rest on the tribes. Do whatever."

The more we talked, the more excited we got. So a plan was hatched. We'd go to the national championship game together. I would work the Ney angle, and he would work the Reid angle. Ultimately, I'm not sure how my colleague and his Reid staffer contact ended up funding their portion of the trip. But we sat together, shared a room together, and had a great time.

As the clock ticked down, Ohio State's quarterback approached the center. I was nervous. If the Buckeyes didn't get a first down, the game would be over. White knuckled, hands clasped in front of my face, I watched the play develop. "First down!" I screamed. It was a completed pass. Our small cadre of fans erupted in cheers, along with the rest of the crowd.

With renewed hope, our bipartisan group of Buckeye fans was having fun again. It was great to hang out with the group. Like the Scotland trip, having such a good time didn't seem to resemble work. But in a way it was. The time spent with Reid's senior staffer, for instance, was definitely helpful for my colleagues' lobbying career. It was also good for me. While I never lobbied this specific staffer, being able to relate to my Democratic colleagues about his importance to the team showed that that I was willing to work both sides of the aisle. Unlike mine and Bob's situation, where, aside from

Jack, I remained the primary point of contact with Ney World, there were several members of Team Abramoff who worked with Harry Reid's office.

Minutes later, it was drama time all over again. With the ball on the five-yard line, the Buckeyes faced another fourth down. Just like before, if they didn't run a successful play, Miami would win the game. Rubbing my hands together like I was trying to start a fire, I anxiously stared ahead. Our guys were wearing their white jerseys. The Buckeye stickers on the side of their helmets glistened in the desert air. "Come on," I screamed. Then it was over.

The ball hit the ground. I was devastated. Miami's fans rushed the field in celebration. Their orange, white and green clothing contrasted sharply with Buckeye Nation, so did the smiles on their faces. It was pandemonium. But then I saw a fellow fan a few rows excitedly over pointing at the field. There was a yellow flag in the back of the end zone. It stopped the Miami fans' on-field party. We again waited nervously, this time to hear what the referees had to say. It was a penalty on the Hurricanes. The game wasn't over after all. "Pass interference baby!" I screamed in Bob's ear. Our fans' exuberance was resurrected. Three plays later, our quarterback ran the ball in to the end zone. His touchdown tied the score and pushed the game into double overtime. The play swung momentum in our direction.

Like Bob's assistance for Jack and me, Senator Reid's help for Team Abramoff increased quite a bit after a former staffer of his office joined the team. Why the Senator chose to engage on behalf of our clients, I am not sure. While I was present at the fundraiser Reid attended at our firm, I didn't sit in any of the official meetings with his office. But the results were clear. In the nine months before the game, Reid's assistance included writing three letters on behalf of Team Abramoff's tribal clients, meeting with the Prime Minister of Malaysia, and making his office available to the team.

In March, for example, Senator Reid sent a letter to the Interior Department opposing the Jena tribe's effort to set up a casino, which was helpful to our client, the Coushatta Tribe. Days after the letter was written, an Abramoff-approved check for $5,000 was given to Reid's political committee, The Searchlight Leadership Fund.

A few months later, the Senator sent another letter to the Interior Department. This time he wrote urging Gale Norton, the Interior Secretary, to reject a proposal by the Cuyapaipe Band of Mission Indians to convert land for a health clinic into a casino in southern California. This letter was a big win for our California tribal client, the Agua Caliente Tribe of Palm Springs. Like the Coushatta Tribe in Louisiana, the Agua Caliente would have been harmed by the potential increase in tribal gaming. A new casino, by a rival tribe, would have directly competed with the gambling establishment run by our client.

Reid additionally took one of our client's legislative fights to the floor of the Senate. Similar to his other efforts, the Senator worked to block a Michigan tribe from setting up a casino near the lucrative gaming market of one of our clients. In this case, Reid opposed one of his own Democratic colleagues, Michigan Senator Debbie Stabenow. Stabenow had hoped to secure Congressional approval for the Bay Mills Indians to set up a casino. But Reid helped to block her efforts. "The legislation is fundamentally flawed," he argued on the Senate floor. Blocking Bay Mills was a huge priority for our Michigan client, the Saginaw Chippewa Tribe. Across the board, Reid's efforts were beneficial to Team Abramoff.

In December, the Senator once again weighed in on behalf of the Saginaw Chippewa. One of the tribe's top legislative priorities was to secure federal money for a school construction project on their reservation. To help further that goal, Reid sent a letter asking President Bush's administration to increase spending for tribal school construction by $30 million. In writing the letter, the Senator was not only helping our client, the Saginaw Chippewa, but also the Mississippi Band of Choctaw Indians, who were our clients, as well. They, too, were looking for school construction funds. Why did Reid's office agree to help on all those projects? Again, I'm not sure. I wasn't in those meetings. No matter what the reason, Reid and his staff were behaving like champions.

Of course, the Reid office's help didn't stop there. His office's work on the Appropriations committee also helped our clients. One client that benefited from the Senator's perch on the Energy and Water Appropriations committee was the Dry Prairie Rural Water Authority. In dire need of money for their rural water project, the Dry Prairie Rural Water Authority in Montana hired our lobbying team to help their cause. Led by my colleague Kevin Ring, it was a straight forward money deal, meaning the water authority spent thousands of local taxpayer dollars a month on a lobbyist to secure millions of taxpayer dollars a year. There was nothing unusual about the arrangement. Thousands of public and private organizations operate in a similar manner. Granted, many of those groups didn't have the lobbying tools or high-level contacts that we had available to advance our client's goals. Nor did they succeed like we did.

In 2002, Dry Prairie spent about $100,000 for their lobbying efforts. Since the water authority was from Montana, that meant working with the state's Congressional delegation. It also meant working with people like the team's staff contacts in Senator Reid's office. Working for a senior Senator on the specific appropriations committee funding Dry Prairie's project meant having an immense amount of influence. The team used to joke that millions of dollars dropped out of the pockets of appropriation staffers every day. Those quips were usually followed up with similar jokes about making sure that money made its way to our clients. And in the case of Dry Prairie, it certainly did.

In the FY 2001 appropriations bill, the Dry Prairie water project received $435,000 in direct appropriations. After they hired the team, it was our responsibility to increase that number. In the FY 2002 bill, their funding jumped to $4.0 million. And finally in FY 2003, it jumped even further to $7.5 million. There was much to celebrate.

If the Buckeyes won, we would celebrate even more. The further the game progressed, the more likely that outcome seemed.

"This has turned into a clash of the titans," I told our assembled group of Buckeye supporters. "If we win, it could be one of the all-time great upsets." Stacked with future NFL stars, Miami was riding a 34 game winning streak. In contrast, our starting running back was a 19-year-old freshman from Youngstown, who helped us to win the game. We reveled in the victory and ran toward the field. The game was over. Of course, the championship celebrations were just beginning.

JUNE 3, 2003
WASHINGTON, DC

The Speaker Event

Speaker Hastert's security team swept through the building before he arrived. The Hastert fundraiser was an important event for Team Abramoff. Spending time with the man who was third in line to the presidency was sure to show our clients and potential clients the kind of influence the team had. We were raising money for the Speaker's Leadership PAC, or political action committee, which was the organization he used to support other Republican candidates and causes. Because the Speaker was in a safe congressional district and did not have to worry about re-election, his Leadership PAC was his most important fundraising entity.

The event was taking place in the large, wood-walled, back room at Signatures. After the Speaker's security detail gave us the green light to proceed, we went right to work. "Everything has to be immaculate," I told the waiters and staff setting up the room. Finishing the preparations didn't help to soothe my nerves. For weeks, I had been working on the Speaker event. Yet, I knew a legislative snafu in the House or some sort of national emergency could pull the Speaker away from our fundraiser and abort our event before it even began.

Because of the contacts I had in Hastert's office and my unyielding will to spearhead the get-together, I successfully beat back attempts by Team Abramoff colleagues for control of the fundraiser. It was a classic turf battle among those of us on the team who worked with the Speaker's staff. I eventually won the skirmish.

Being the man on such a project was important to me. My identity within the team, with my clients, and within the general lobbying community was at stake. There wasn't an issue on the Hill that the Speaker couldn't dramatically influence. All the big debates went through his office.

When one committee wrote a telecommunications bill favoring the cable companies and another wrote one favoring the wireless industry, it was the Speaker and his fellow House leaders who settled the dispute. These kind of disagreements occurred frequently. When the Republican team was split between those who favored the health care industry over the information technology industry, during a dispute over the definition of a trademark, the Speaker's office had to weigh in and pick sides. Being known as "the Speaker's contact" at the firm would undoubtedly increase my value to our clients on a broader variety of issues. And getting more work meant getting more pay.

It was also good to be seen as close to the Speaker's office outside the firm. To the lobbyists and staffers who made up the Capitol Hill community, my closeness to the highest levels of power showed that I had influence. It showed that I was a winner. In the world of hired gun lobbyists, few things mattered more than an influential reputation. The perception of success was a crucial professional barometer. It was what separated those of us who got the big-paying clients from those who did not.

While Team Abramoff's lobbying reputation was ultimately built on real accomplishments for clients, selling ourselves as a successful unit remained vitally important. I learned to enjoy the sale. Being known as a nice guy was great. But it didn't put food on my table. Or give me my swagger. As much as I liked being well-regarded, client-based lobbyists like me didn't get paid to be nice. We got paid to win, to get results. The concept of winning and success was very much a part of the Team Abramoff culture, a culture that, at that time, I was proud to both work in and perpetuate.

If a potential client sat down with me or any one of my colleagues, the theme of success would inevitably follow. It was in our DNA. "You want to block a bill?" the potential client would ask. "No problem. Shape a regulation? You got it. Get a million dollar line-item appropriation for your company? We do that in our sleep. Your organization needs help with Republicans? Democrats? We do it all. We are the best in the business." And we were.

I was instructed that the minimum amount required to host a fundraiser with Speaker Hastert was $50,000. That was $40,000 above the average cost of an event for most members of Congress. "Denny doesn't do a lot of fundraisers in DC," I was told by Hastert's fundraiser. Most of his fundraising took place either near his hometown of Chicago, in another Member's Congressional District or at an industry-specific event, like at a consumer electronics convention or real estate conference. Despite the price tag, I promised Jack that we could get to $50,000 if he could deliver a few $5,000 checks from the tribes. Without even thinking about it, Jack said, "Let's do it." He also said he would donate whatever he needed to personally to get us over the top, and he would encourage the rest of the team to do the same. The goal when we set up the event was to strengthen our relationship with the Speaker by purchasing some of his time. We didn't necessarily have a specific issue we planned to discuss.

As the event got closer, Jack's directions to me were fairly simple. The first thing he said was that the fundraiser had to be at Signatures. That was a no-brainer. Second, as the event neared, he told me to get the Speaker to help us with the Coushatta tribe's ongoing fight with the Jena band and their effort to build a nearby casino. Making no promises, I told him I would make sure the Coushatta were the top priority whenever I had access to the Speaker's office. Beyond those simple directions, the event was mine. I could stage-manage it however I wanted.

The Abramoff team normally liked to keep events within the family. That meant no other lobbyists. Just us and our clients. We didn't have distractions from potential competitors that way. For a $10,000 fundraiser, that wasn't much of a problem. Getting to $50,000 with just our clients, on a few weeks' notice, wasn't as easy. Therefore, I decided to open up the event to other lobbyists. Jack did not like the change at first, but, the closer we got to the Hastert event, he accepted the need to fill the room this way. Like all of us, Jack was excited about the fact that the Speaker of the House was having lunch at his restaurant.

Circling the room with name tags and signs in hand, I used the seating chart I had devised to organize the tables. Jack and one of the tribal chiefs would sit next to Hastert at the main table. I would sit next to the Speaker's top political advisor. Next, I made sure the rest of our clients and all the guys on the team had good seats. Included at the event were several of my new personal clients. They were impressed that my team was putting together an event for the Speaker. When I started at Greenberg, the idea of somebody paying me $25,000 a month to lobby for them would have been preposterous. In contrast, by the time of the Hastert fundraiser, few days passed when I wasn't thinking about how to get my clients to pay me even more.

Most of our clients were attuned to the fundraising process. They knew a sit-down like the Signatures event, with tables full of other lobbyists, wasn't the place to ask for anything in particular from the Speaker. But talking directly to Hastert was a great way for our clients to show their bosses, usually in far-away corporate offices, that they were working to advance their organization's interests in Washington.

I had two main goals for the event. The first was to address the Coushatta's Jena matter with the Speaker's staff. The second was to advocate for Bob with the Speaker. Since Hastert was Bob's boss, and Bob was my main Congressional champion, it made sense for me to promote the Congressman. From Bob's perspective, being mentioned during the fundraiser would give him some credit with the Speaker. In turn, I would gain credit with Bob for making that happen. Knowing I would only have a few minutes to talk with the Speaker and his staff before everyone else got a chance, I told the Speaker at my first opportunity how much Bob enjoyed his work as House Administration Chairman. "Bob made a few calls for the event," I told the Speaker, before reminding Hastert how hard the Chairman was working to keep the majority. When Ney called me days later to tell me how the Speaker enjoyed the event with "your guy," it made the day for both of us.

The spinning didn't stop there. To my clients who weren't in attendance, I sent an update that included a few paragraphs relating to their lobbying priorities, and then tied those priorities into "my conversation with the Speaker." It was a name-dropping masterpiece. If I wanted to keep getting paid, it was important for my clients to think that their interests were always my top priority. I had learned that by watching Jack. He made lobbying look easy.

Abramoff and I spoke for a few minutes before the Speaker's event began. Since Jack was so good on his feet, I didn't need to worry about the actual presentation of the meal, the question and answer session with Hastert, or the flow of the conversation. It went without saying that Jack would simply arrive and begin playing master of ceremonies. My job was to make sure the clients were comfortable, secure a meeting with the Speaker's staff about the Coushatta-Jena matter, and have a good time.

During the fundraiser, I talked with the Speaker's staffer, and a couple other nearby lobbyists about my time working with Bob, Hastert and the House Administration Committee. We discussed the many legislative battles we had been through together. Whether it was trying to block Campaign Finance Reform or pass Election Reform, "It was a lot of fun," I remember saying. As the event wound down, I leaned over to the Speaker's senior aide and asked him if I could come in to talk with him for a few minutes. My hope, I told him, was to generally discuss the issue of tribal gaming, and specifically discuss the issue of the Jena band's efforts to set up a casino in Louisiana. Because of some previous conversations, he was already aware of the situation and told me to call his assistant to get put on his schedule. A few days later we met in his Capitol office.

In the room with the Speaker's staffer and me was another lobbyist promoting the interests of non-tribal casinos throughout the Southeastern United States. Like our clients, the Coushatta and the Choctaw, this casino lobbyist did not want the Jena Band to set up a casino near the Houston border. Such a move threatened their share of the gaming market as well. Though we normally disagreed with other corporate casino interests because they tended to view tribal gaming as a threat, in this case, we were on the same side. And our coalition was growing.

Over thirty members of Congress would ultimately write letters urging the Department of Interior to reject the Jena Band's casino efforts. Letters came from elected officials all over the country. Some sent more than one. Senate Majority Whip Reid, for instance, wrote two letters outlining his opposition to the Louisiana casino. It was Reid's fourth letter on behalf of our clients in a year. Each letter resulted in the Senator receiving a campaign contribution from Team Abramoff or our clients.

According to legal scholars, it is not necessarily improper for an elected official to receive money around the same time that they conduct official acts that are helpful to that specific contributor. Whether something is improper or not goes back to the dichotomy between public officials being both individuals and representative of various causes.

After all, part of Senator Reid's job was to look out for his home state of Nevada's gaming industry. In theory, therefore, tribal gaming anywhere, even two thousand miles away, threatened his state's interests. In those instances when Reid opposed tribal gaming operations that threatened other tribe's businesses, like the Coushatta and Choctaw, the Senator was able to help two industries at the same time. Both industries then donated to his campaign because of the positions he took, which is a presumably a legal practice. After all, they were supporting a shared cause.

As Reid did by letter, our hope was that Speaker Hastert would also agree to weigh in on the issue with the Interior Department. Having letters from both the Democratic Senate leadership and the Republican House leadership would create a high-level, bipartisan umbrella of influence, which we hoped would prompt our allies in the Department of Interior to block the Jena efforts.

During our meeting in the Capitol, my staffer friend told me that Hastert had problems with what was called "Reservation shopping."

Reservation shopping referred to the practice of a tribe and its business partners attempting to establish a legal reservation, which would allow them to gamble, in the most lucrative location possible - instead of where their actual ancestral line placed them. "The Speaker's concerns stem directly from his Congressional District," Hastert's staffer continued. "Denny has tribes at home who are trying to set up a casino in the Chicago market." For years, Hastert had fought reservation shopping in Illinois. When the Ho-Chunk Nation and the Potawatomi tribe worked to establish reservation rights around Chicago, he even co-sponsored legislation to thwart the practice.

Our conversation eventually turned to the specifics of the Jena Band's casino deal. I was told that the Speaker had been contacted by an influential Louisiana Congressman who opposed what the Jena were trying to do. That was good to hear. Our lobbying team had been working with that office as well. Hastert's senior staffer then said he had been contacted by Majority Leader Delay's office. DeLay and the rest of the elected leadership in the House were thinking about writing a joint letter, he said. Again, that had come about from our lobbying work. "That is great," I replied, knowing that several of my lobbying colleagues had recently been in contact with DeLay's office. The meeting could not have gone better. Like Reid, Speaker Hastert had plenty of reasons to pay attention to the issue. One of those reasons was our lobbying team's fundraising support. The access we bought helped us to make our case, and move the process along.

Whether the Speaker would have found the time to get involved in the specific Jena matter without our financial support, I don't know. Nor did I care. It wasn't like I knew Hastert well enough to know how he made decisions. But I did know that I had worked with the Speaker and his staff for years on campaign finance issues, and one of the foundations of our efforts was that in a capitalist system like ours, individuals and organizations should be allowed to buy access to their elected leaders. Team Abramoff did that all the time, and that wasn't what got us into trouble. After all, there is a big difference between buying access and buying results.

I was ecstatic when I received the letter from the Speaker's office a few days later. The correspondence to the Interior Department was signed by Hastert, DeLay, House Majority Whip Roy Blunt and Chief Deputy Whip Eric Cantor. The June 10, 2003, letter hit all of our points.

"*We write to express our concerns over recent attempts of certain Indian tribes to develop off-reservation casino sites,*" it said simply. "*We strongly believe that these attempts run counter to Congressional intent.*"

"When Congress passed the Indian Gaming Regulatory Act (IGRA) in 1988, they did not intend to authorize "reservation shopping" by Indian tribes. However, some Indian tribes are apparently attempting to take advantage of IGRA's provisions and move into lucrative casino markets far from their reservations and lands where they have a historical connection."

This background was important. While Jack and the team wished that the letter would specifically demand that the Department not approve the Jena-pact, the group made its thoughts on the matter known.

"We strongly urge the Department of Interior to enforce IGRA and to carefully scrutinize all efforts to acquire a favorable casino location," the letter continued. "This matter has received a great deal of attention recently because of the ongoing attempt by the Jena Band of Choctaw Indians to take off-reservation land into trust for gaming."

There it was. The mention of the Jena situation by four of the highest ranking members of the House of Representatives was like gold. I felt like a Master of the Universe when I shared the letter with the team.

"That will leave a mark," said my colleague Todd Boulanger, who managed the Jena fight for Jack, the team and our clients. It felt good to know I was helping the cause. It felt even better to know that my work with the Speaker's office would bolster my lobbying reputation. I had delivered. I was a winner, and convinced that no one could take that away from me.

OCTOBER 31, 2003
WASHINGTON, DC

========

Life in Fantasyland

I DRESSED UP AS ELVIS PRESLEY. Wearing an Elvis costume for Halloween involved more of a responsibility than I had expected. Within minutes of squeezing into that sequined jumpsuit, slipping on those speckled sunglasses and snapping that wavy black wig on my head, friends and strangers alike began insisting that I be in character. It was like the King of Rock and Roll had become my identity for the night. And why not get into character? My life had turned into a fantasyland of hundred dollar meals, expensive trips and a lifestyle the kid who grew up in an apartment never could have dreamed of.

While my wife and I walked up Pennsylvania Avenue toward the party, people I didn't even know began yelling at me. "Yo, Elvis," one guy said. "I knew you were alive. Where is your snarl?" I saluted in reply, without saying a word. "Sing me a song," a woman screeched next, while passing us by on the sidewalk near Signatures. "Oh, hey baby," I replied, with a deep southern drawl, a hip swivel, and a karate kick. Alison jokingly smacked me in the arm. She was dressed as Priscilla. Not always a fan of my work-first lifestyle, both Alison and I enjoyed the perks of my professional success. Being the King was fun.

Several hundred staffers, lobbyists and friends bought tickets for the Halloween party, which was a fundraiser for my Dad. Our goal was to raise money for the Cincinnati-area branch of the American Parkinson Disease Association. Dad had started volunteering there after his Parkinson's diagnosis. The group's mission is to promote community awareness about the disease, provide local services for those in need and raise funds for national research. Dad's work there helped him to learn more about his disease, and to help those living with it. Both Alison and I wanted to show our support, to Dad, and Mom, as well.

Bob had initially planned on attending the Halloween party, but couldn't make it because of a scheduling conflict. Instead, he donated $1,000. It was a generous gesture, and one I very much appreciated. Bob's generosity was personal. He and my father had met several times, and they always enjoyed their conversations together.

Unlike Bob, Jack didn't know my Dad. But Jack was also very generous. He let me have the bar-half of the restaurant for the night and agreed to donate all the appetizers and food that circulated during the party. I never saw the bill, but it had to have been pricey. Several thousand dollars for sure. For Jack, the assistance wasn't a personal gesture toward my father as much as it was a commitment to the principle of helping family. It was great working for someone who valued his team that way.

My opinion of Jack had evolved over the eighteen months I had worked for him, growing more favorable in some areas and less so in others. For instance, I truly appreciated his commitment to his family. Throughout our relationship, Abramoff remained an unquestioned family man. Not only would he have taken a bullet for his wife or any of his kids, but Jack very much emphasized how important it was for me to look out for my own family. As an example, he made comments during my salary negotiations that I should make sure my wife and parents would benefit from the higher pay. At first, comments like that seemed intrusive, but over time I learned to see them as positive sentiments coming from a good place.

Nonetheless, by the time of the Halloween party, I wasn't as personally close to Jack as I had been a year earlier. Nor was I as loyal. While I liked Jack, we were business associates more than friends. Additionally, over time I had noticed that he rarely shared the full story with me about projects where we worked together. That led to a certain amount of growing suspicion on my part. It didn't start that way.

When I first joined the team, I constantly worked to help my new boss. I shared whatever I was hearing with him, and put his needs in the moment ahead of my own. The answer to any question he asked was yes. I took the Ney loyalty model and transferred it from Bob to Jack. It wasn't like Jack had put a gun to my head and told me to give my heart and soul to the team, but that is what I chose to do. At least, initially. Bit by bit, the dynamic slowly changed.

I started letting the newer members of the team be the first to reply to Jack's many emails. Like I had once been, they were fired up to please the man who was paying them. As I told some of my more seasoned Team Abramoff colleagues, it was good to be close to Jack, but I had more important things to do than chase down his abundant and sometimes random business ideas, many of which led to nowhere. Therefore, while I still respectfully worked for Jack's clients and utilized their sports suites and campaign contributions, I continued focusing on building my own lobbying practice. With time being limited, having my own practice meant de-emphasizing the work I did for Jack.

The clients I brought into the firm were primarily corporations and technology companies who worked with the government. The work didn't have much overlap with many of our other clients. Instead of focusing on the Interior Department and Resources Committee, I focused more on the Homeland Security Department and technology legislation. The change wasn't detrimental, but it created a different dynamic with Jack than when I first started working for the team.

I wasn't alone in my evolving and enigmatic relationship with Jack. Other senior members of his team operated in a similar way. Like me, they knew that all of Jack's efforts were not equal. "Being the first to reply to his emails isn't always the best practice," one of them told me. Like my colleagues, I began settling into a routine in which I treated Jack as more of a brand than a day-to-day lobbyist. He was the team's salesman, we were the worker bees. For me, that meant selling the Abramoff brand to potential clients, the media and official Washington, while personally working with the rest of the team to focus on my client work. In many respects, it was a win-win scenario.

With Jack continuing to bring in new, high-paying clients, he made sure to provide us with the tools necessary to service them. That meant contributions, tickets and larger and larger expense accounts. These tools allowed us to help our own individual clients, as well as Jack's clients. We just needed to strike the right balance between our many competing interests. Jack understood the desire to branch out on our own, and was generally fine with such an approach. His work with the restaurants and his school kept him busy, too. Therefore, as long as his clients were happy, Jack was happy. And I worked hard to make sure his clients were happy.

From an outside view, my professional life looked pretty appealing. I had a job that paid well and consisted of interesting and intellectually stimulating work. It also included lots of partying, going to concerts and attending sporting events. Underneath that veneer of success, however, cracks were developing. A phone conversation one night with an old friend from college illuminated the point. John was surprised by my call. After catching up for a few minutes, I started complaining about my job.

"I don't know if I can even make it out tonight," I told him, in reference to a fundraiser I was hosting in the evening. It was a Thursday. I had been to fundraisers for the majority of breakfasts, lunches and dinners already that week, in addition to my arduous office-based client responsibilities. "I feel like I have to be somebody else out there," I told him. The comment felt weird to hear coming out of my own mouth. I wasn't even sure what it meant. Yet, at the same time, it felt nice to talk without worrying about the specific meaning of every word I uttered. John didn't care about my appearances. He just wanted me to be happy. After college in Ohio, I moved to Washington while he and his future wife moved out West to be whitewater rafting guides. We had remained good friends. "It is like they are paying for my thoughts and my beliefs," I continued, exhausted and rambling.

John listened and tried to understand what I was saying. Instead of telling me I sounded crazy, like I suddenly felt, he told me that was how a lot of jobs made people feel. "Many people have to do and say things they wouldn't normally," he said.

"*Maybe he is right,*" I thought, before persisting further. "But I don't talk like we did when we were young," I replied. "I don't tell people what I think or believe at these events. I tell them what my clients want them to hear. And I'm good at it."

"Dude, I don't know what to say," he finally said. "If you hate it, get out. But all I know is that when we were in college, if someone said you could get paid to party at cool places every night with cool people, we would have called that a dream job. Fantasyland. It would have sounded too good to be true. Yet, you're doing it man." His words were encouraging. I thanked him for the pep talk. But it didn't answer the questions that were beginning to gnaw at me, questions which had precipitated the call.

Some of those questions revolved around my relationship with Jack. It seemed that the more I got to know him, the more questions I had about what really drove Jack's decision making. On the one hand, he was a dedicated family man and person of genuine faith. On the other, he was a secretive and ruthless businessman. His-win-at-all-costs attitude was similar to the style Bob had mentored me into on the Hill. Therefore, I was comfortable with it for a while. I even liked it.

The dynamic wasn't a new concept. I knew Jack liked making money and was an aggressive lobbyist before I agreed to join the team. His hard charging way of life, in fact, was one of the reasons I joined the team. We played on the edge, even if playing on the edge meant going over the line sometimes. The process of going over the line also led to numerous questions. Looking back, my questions didn't arise from the big picture, or from some personal introspection that should have stopped me in my tracks - like cutting a deal with Bob on the Tigua provision, or going to Scotland. Instead, my questions arose from the day-to-day application of our lobbying business, in the small decisions the team made in the moment - decisions that hinted at bigger problems.

One example involved Congressional legislation banning the practice of Internet gaming, or gambling on the Internet. For years, even before I arrived, Jack's team represented clients involved in the Internet gaming industry. This included everything from online poker and slots, to online state lotteries and sports betting. At any given point, we were usually working for one or two companies that operated Internet-based gaming sites in the United States. Our gaming tribes were also normally interested in the issue. Because of our clients' interests, the team was finely tuned to the efforts of those on Capitol Hill who wanted to ban Internet gaming in the United States. That is why I was so surprised when I started getting calls from staffers and members of Congress in the House about an effort to ban the practice.

"I shouldn't be the first one hearing about this," I thought to myself. Surely one of the client-managers monitoring this issue would have been alerted to what was happening and then would have alerted the team. But I hadn't heard anything. Right away, that concerned me. *"Why aren't we more engaged with what is happening in the House?"* I wondered. It was like Bob said to me when he called about the moving piece of internet gaming legislation, "Aren't you guys working this issue? Should I call Jack?"

"Not that I know of," I told Bob. "But, I'll ask around." I walked downstairs to talk it through with one of our tribe's client managers. I figured he would know the answer.

"We're not doing anything on that right now," he said. His body language told me that he knew more than what he was saying. When I asked for more information, I was rebuffed. "Just let it go," he said. It was an awkward conversation for me to have with someone I had worked with closely on other issues. But I dropped it.

Weeks later, I learned that Jack had been pitching a large client during the House debate on Internet gaming. Like our other gaming clients, this new potential client was concerned about Congress potentially outlawing Internet gaming. To add leverage to his negotiations with this new potential business relationship, Jack pulled our lobbying team from the legislative field. We probably could have killed the bill in the House like we had done numerous times. But Jack knew that if the House passed a bill banning Internet gaming it would make the potential client even more concerned about the legislation, and he would therefore be willing to pay an even higher fee to stop it. In the dark about the negotiations, I watched as the House took action to ban Internet gaming. Shortly thereafter, we had a new client, one who was willing to spend millions of dollars to block the bill in the Senate.

After one of my other colleagues asked me to start helping the new client, I heard the full story. I was upset at the exclusion. Since I had key contacts on the Hill who would be helpful in blocking the bill, the guys working with Jack on the client pitch knew I would be needed for the project. Yet I hadn't been included. As I thought about it further, being excluded from the team pitching the new client didn't bother me as much as not being told about what was happening. From my colleagues' perspective, there were some perfectly reasonable reasons for my exclusion from the initial interaction with the client. One was the simple fact that the more people who were included the pitch, the more people there were to split the client's payments. Also, since the strategy involved the Senate, where I wasn't as well-connected, I could see why they didn't want to include me. Still, I was angry, and somewhat alarmed.

Not only had Jack and the team decided to put the interests of some of our clients behind the interests of making more money with another client, they didn't tell me about it. When I complained, I was told not to worry about how things played out. "Our plan was always to kill it in the Senate," one of my colleagues said. Considering the role the Senate plays in our political system, namely that it is where legislation goes to die, I found it pretty easy to quickly rationalize away any questions I had about the incident. But the situation left a mark and raised questions about what else Jack might be keeping from me.

This became an even bigger issue when my colleague, Kevin Ring, told me that several of the guys involved in the pitch of the new Internet gaming client had actually been paid directly by Jack - instead of through the firm. Kevin was nervous about cashing his check. It was for $25,000. Anxiety was written all over his face. I told him to cash the check. He then said and it wasn't that easy. "That isn't the first check I got from Jack," Kevin continued. "There was another project too," he said. "Scanlon was involved." My eyes lit up at his words. "I feel like giving this check back to Jack, but I'm afraid he will fire me." It was then that I realized there was a lot going on that I didn't know about.

It was more than the just my colleagues talking, however, that had me suddenly asking questions about my lobbying team, and about Jack. Concerns and complaints I heard from colleagues on the Hill also began to raise internal red flags about what I was doing. One such complaint came from a staffer who worked for Congressman John Boehner. It involved Jack's client, Rose Garden, and our work for the garment manufacturing facilities in the Northern Mariana Islands. Congressman Boehner was the Chairman of the Education and the Workforce Committee, the committee with oversight of the Department of Labor. Since Willie Tan, the top garment manufacturer in the CNMI, and point person for our Rose Garden account, was having some problems with the Labor Department, I requested a meeting with the Education and Workforce committee staff. Joining me for the meeting was one of Willie's lawyers. The two of us met with one of the committee's senior staffers.

Boehner's committee staffer contact listened as Willie's lawyer and I outlined our concerns. The two of us told him that we were worried about a Department of Labor investigation into the garment manufacturing company we represented, an investigation concerning worker's wages. Our specific concern involved the people conducting the investigation. It was my client's belief that the investigative team looking into the wage dispute had a personal and political vendetta against Willie and his company. That being the case, we asked my friend if the committee and Chairman Boehner would be willing to weigh in with the Department on our behalf. He was noncommittal, and told us he would have to discuss the request with his colleagues before getting back to me.

The next time we spoke, the committee staffer contact told me that Chairman Boehner and the committee weren't going to help my client. Whether he personally discussed the issue with Boehner, spoke with his fellow staffers about it or made the decision on his own, I don't know. He simply told me that they weren't going to assist us. He then told me not to bring Willie's company in to their office again. "You are welcome to meet with us, Neil, but don't ever bring those guys in here again," he continued.

I was flabbergasted by the harshness of his words. My friend could tell by the bewildered look on my face. "This isn't about you, Neil," he said, as if he was trying to console me. "Like I said, you are always welcome. But we are not helping those guys."

I nervously tried to joke my way through the conflict. "Well, I guess if everybody loved them, they wouldn't need their lobbyists, huh?" I half-heartedly laughed. Chairman Boehner's representative smiled. Seeing his positive reaction soothed my concern about the incident. I didn't want to ruin my relationship with the committee. Having learned that sometimes *no* is the second best answer to *yes*, I thanked my friend for his candor. As I returned to the office, the vehement *no* to our request made me stop and think about who I was fighting for. It was the most pondering I had done about the morality of my work in a long time. My work was fun and made me feel like a person who was having an impact. Therefore, I didn't want to stop and think about the comments for more than a few moments. My initial introspection about that conversation didn't last much longer than a cab ride. Nonetheless, the moment stayed with me - even as I carried on.

Alison coordinated the logistics for our Halloween fundraiser. She interviewed the bands, printed the invitations and worked with Signatures on the food selection. The party was something we enjoyed working on together. It had a work component to it, but it was also something we could do as a couple. My primary responsibility was to deliver people and make sure those who attended had a good time. That meant putting a host committee together for the event which included many of my fellow lobbyists, both members of Team Abramoff, and those who worked around town. Each of the hosts agreed to spend a couple hundred dollars on drinks. In that respect, it was like a typical lobbyist event, with my colleagues and I using the party to access time with our key contacts and government official colleagues. I also invited friends whom I didn't work with, both Democrats and Republicans. While such a move represented a departure from Jack's view about being seen as a true-blue partisan, it did follow his model of synthesizing my personal life with my work life.

Signatures was quite a sight. Instead of individuals in suits and ties, there were people dressed up as pirates, priests and nurses. There were Spider-Man and Matrix costumes, a Michael Jackson impersonator, Cub's fan Steve Bartman, and a couple dressed up as Kid Rock and Pamela Anderson. Being in Washington, we also had a staffer clad as Majority Leader DeLay's Press Secretary. Everyone had a good time, and after paying for the band and the alcohol, my wife and I raised about $6,000 for Dad's Parkinson's organization.

The charity fundraiser even made the papers. It was referred to as a Halloween party put on by "lobbyist Neil Volz." The publicity made me happy. I liked that my work was associated with such an event. Jack had showed me the up-side of promoting my lobbying activities through the media. Even before the press attention, I felt the fundraiser further solidified my identity as a Washington lobbyist. It showed that I was beginning to step out of Jack and Bob's shadow, that I was making a name for myself. My public identity was again changing, and I felt more in charge of defining it than I ever had before.

The activity surrounding the party provided me yet another high during my ongoing fantasyland lifestyle. I didn't know it, but I needed the fix. Being a fun-loving and powerful man in a powerful town meant feeding my own personal power meter on a regular basis. Generating such influence required a mindset geared toward winning, or at least proclaiming victory. Success meant having a good party, getting something in a bill for a client or being associated with someone else who was perceived to be successful. Unfortunately, such a fantasyland mindset had a numbing impact on my perspective. Success no longer revolved around long term pursuits like healthy relationships, sound financial decisions and regular guidance from God. Instead, success came in short-bursts of selfish praise, personal pleasure and greed. As long as I got my regular fix, or high, life in fantasyland churned along.

A few weeks after the party, I picked up my Halloween pictures. I was excited to see them. Lobbying involved putting on a good show, and my day as Elvis had been a hit. Right away, I ripped open the package containing my photos. They weren't remotely what I expected. Going into the night, I knew that I didn't look like the young Elvis, or the crew cut Elvis entering the Army. But I didn't think I looked like the end-of-career fat Elvis either. Yet that is exactly what I saw staring back at me.

I rifled through the pictures again and again. I couldn't believe it. Not only wasn't I skinny Elvis, I wasn't midsize Elvis either. I was actually fat Elvis. It broke my heart. *"Have I not looked in the mirror recently?"* I asked myself. At home that night, I jumped on the scale. The arrow raced up past the numbers two hundred and fifty. Since I had moved to Washington, I had gained over sixty pounds. Clearly, my twenty-four hours a day, seven-days a week, work-first lifestyle was taking its toll on me. Maybe my identity wasn't what I thought after all. That started to scare me even more the pictures.

The Scandal Goes Public

FOR WEEKS, THE TEAM AND I waited for the *Washington Post* article to appear. Rumor circulated around rumor. No one was sure what to expect, but most of us assumed the paper's investigation into Jack and our lobbying team would be anything but flattering. Days earlier, my former colleague Tony Rudy had gone so far as to offer me a job at his new firm. "You know Jack's house of cards is about to fall," he said.

A little before 11:00 P.M., my hand-wringing ended when the much-anticipated piece appeared on the *Post*'s website. Having been tipped off by a reporter friend about the timing of the story, I had incessantly checked the newspaper's site all evening. When it showed up, I forwarded it along to two different groups within our lobbying team. The first was a group called "DCCasino." That was the name of the email distribution list for those of us hard-charging Republican lobbyists who were both professionally and politically close to Jack.

I also sent the article to a smaller group of lobbyists later nicknamed "the Four Horsemen" by our law firm's management team. That group - led by my colleague Kevin Ring - were members of Jack's team who were working behind the scenes to prepare for and survive whatever was about to come. Fundamentally, our smaller bipartisan group of four doubted that Jack could survive the kind of press attention we presumed was coming. This meant preparing to keep as many Team Abramoff lobbyists and clients together as possible after Jack's demise. Our group had developed over the previous few months. Being told that the *Post* had paid investigators looking into Jack and Scanlon scared many members of the team. We started to share our worries. Stories about people taking money from Jack percolated. I was also worried about the scrutiny, but made sure not to share stories that related to Bob. As loyal as I was to my fellow Four Horsemen, my loyalty to the Chairman remained paramount. With the *Post* piece online, my three lobbying colleagues and I planned a covert conference call for the morning. We needed to discuss next steps.

"A Jackpot From Indian Gaming Tribes – Lobbying, PR Firms Paid $45 Million Over 3 Years" screamed the *Post*'s page one headline. The story outlined the complex business relationship among Jack, Scanlon, and many of the tribal clients who worked with our lobbying team. Reporter Susan Schmidt would end up winning a Pulitzer Prize for her work. Like *Post* icons Bob Woodward and Carl Bernstein before her, she built her story by diligently following the money. Tracking what limited expenditures she could, her first story merely suggested collusion between Jack and Scanlon. But for people on the inside like me, who saw the dots of the big picture being publicly connected for the first time, we knew better.

The simple fact that Jack had helped Scanlon make over $30 million in three years from our clients said it all. To me, this alone was huge news, and answered any question I had about whether the two were in business together. Of course they were in business together. I mean, anyone who knew him understood Jack wasn't going to help someone else make that kind of money without taking a cut. After all, the money they were making was quite a bit bigger than the several million dollars our lobbying team made off those same clients. Still, Jack denied that there was a business relationship between the two men. Scanlon was a "vendor," he said in the article. His comments defied common sense. I knew there was no way Jack would help a vendor make that kind of money off our clients without getting his share first.

The cards began toppling instantly. Within days, the public contours of the largest Washington corruption scandal since Watergate would be on full display. Schmidt's article included a witch's brew of scandalous story lines. It touched upon everything. It included how Jack's ownership deal of SunCruz ended when Gus Boulis was killed in a gangland style mafia hit in South Florida. It reported Scanlon's shady election work on behalf of a variety of our tribal clients. Schmidt also established Jack and Scanlon's links to the Bush White House, the Republican leadership in Congress and numerous influential conservative activists.

From there, the *Post* tied the two men, as well as our whole lobbying team, to the rise of Indian gaming as an economic and political force in the United States. Who could blame them? Not only was it true, but it was a good story. Conservative Republicans being paid by the gambling industry reeked of hypocrisy, especially when the group included members of Congress. Working for gaming companies was an awkward dynamic the conservative part of the team had learned to live with over the years. But that was in the shallow shadows of the Washington fundraising circuit. Being front page news changed that dynamic completely. Such attention wasn't good.

In addition, the *Post* foreshadowed articles to come by describing how the FBI had begun interviewing tribe members and analyzing the millions of dollars Jack and Scanlon were running through "obscure groups" with Orwellian names like the American International Center and the Council for Republican Environmental Advocacy. I read and re-read the story. The amount of tribal money infiltrating every component of our operation was staggering. Certain sentences leapt off the page. Major red flags went up. The portion of the article outlining the incredible growth of Scanlon's wealth since leaving the Hill a few years earlier was a prime example. Having played cards with Mike numerous times at his Ritz Carlton apartment in Washington's West End, I knew Scanlon was banking quite a bit of money. Likewise, I also knew he was cherry-picking work from the team. But that didn't stop the article from helping to turn my understanding of Jack's operation on its head. Based on the numbers in the paper, it seemed like the team was cherry-picking off of Jack and Scanlon's work, instead of the other way around.

As the world would eventually find out, the basics usually worked in the following manner. When our lobbying team brought on a new tribal client, Abramoff would try to coerce them into hiring Scanlon for accompanying grassroots services like direct mail and political phone calls. But few calls or mailings were ever made, according to former clients, and as Schmidt's story correctly pointed out, the tens of millions of dollars that Scanlon's grassroots firm received was many times what our law firm was paid in the same period.

According to the article, Scanlon had gone from struggling to pay his college loans to buying tens of millions of dollars in beach-front property in a few years' time. This included a mansion he bought with $4.7 million in cash. The whole thing smelled to high heaven. Assuming anything but the worst at that point would have simply been stupid. Right away, I could see the makings of the Greek tragedy my work with Jack and Scanlon would soon become.

The email I wrote to DCCasino, which included Jack, was titled "FYI-Post Story is Online, Running in the AM...."

The first person to respond was my fellow lobbyist Duane Gibson, a former GOP Hill staffer who had gained a bit of notoriety in 2000 for his role in the so-called Khaki rebellion during the Presidential recount in Florida. "Not all that bad," Duane said. I was stunned. In fact, I remember being utterly amazed by his lack of amazement. I wasn't the only one who felt that way. Duane's nonchalance led to what would be just one of many rabid conversations among the Four Horsemen. Our group conversations reflected the fact that the four of us were all very much living double lives. At any given moment, as a group or individually, we were either working diligently to destroy or to preserve Team Abramoff.

The four of us knew a clean beheading of Jack would mean working like crazy to maintain the team and our sizeable client base without him. For many of our clients, the idea of the team without Jack would be counterintuitive, something that would take time to get used to. But since Jack didn't personally do much lobbying, most of the clients had day-to-day relationships with the team that went far beyond the face of our group. And they knew who was succeeding for them. If push came to shove, we assumed that most of the clients would remain with us if Jack fell. If he were able to professionally survive the *Post* story, however, the team situation would get much more complicated. What would the firm do with Jack? Or our clients? Would the team split up? Until we saw what happened, these questions would remain unanswered.

Therefore, like the politicians we Four Horsemen were, each of us kept our options open. For me, I took my ability to spin a story to new heights, telling disparate tales to different audiences so that each would hear what they wanted to hear. It was a nefarious way of life the idealistic kid from Finneytown never would have accepted. Instead of telling people the truth, I let my environment and the potential outcome of a circumstance determine what I said.

Like a swift kick in the groin, reading about our team in the paper was eye-opening and painful. No one who plays politics in Washington, at one point or another, has not been told the old adage about being careful to avoid doing anything that you wouldn't want to read about on the front page of the *Washington Post*. It was advice I chose not to hear. Wishing the article away, I remember thinking if I were a spy or secretly working on noble pursuits of some kind, my duplicitous behavior might have been appropriate. Even exciting. But, obviously, that wasn't the case. As I looked at the article, there was no running anymore from the fact that I was just some Washington hack worried about my own self-interest. Sure, I was well paid and well respected. But at the end of the day, I was nothing more than a political pirate for sale to the highest bidder.

"*Working eighty or ninety hour weeks for your principles or the people of Ohio is one thing,*" I said to myself, "*but those days are long gone. You're just a political prostitute, Neil. If someone can pay you, you will work for them.*" It was a breakthrough. I was starting to look at myself differently. I also began looking at my team differently. We were a group who prided itself on working for the "black hats." Because the black hats had big problems, we knew they would pay big money. For our clients, we Republican lobbyists would create conservative arguments to convince our contacts to help their bottom line. At the same time, our Democratic colleagues would create liberal arguments to convince their contacts to advance their clients' private interests.

It was all about the money, something that was outlined very clearly in the *Post* piece and something that wasn't going to be easy to hide anymore, or rationalize away. Not that any of my teammates or I had much time for introspection. We Four Horsemen were too busy responding to the news article that would change each of our lives. Our colleague Duane's "not all that bad" response to the article provided the initial fodder.

In Mike William's aggressive fashion, he jumped in first. "Is he tone deaf or is it me? Shouldn't the mention of the FBI alarm a legal eagle like him?"

To which Mike Smith, Smitty, the only Democrat amongst the Four Horsemen, replied, "This is a total embarrassment. My friends all have it on the bberry's and are asking a ton of questions. This goes from here to Roll Call to the Hill and on."

In agreeing with Smitty's assessment that the article raised many questions and was just the beginning of the press coverage, Williams added;

"Same here! But they are R's! What about this statement from the article. In terms of Mike or any other third party, the firm does not have any formal relationship to my knowledge with any third-party vendor used by any of the tribes for some of their activities." Jack's Clintonian denial about his relationship with Scanlon was one we all knew could not withstand the test of time. I added, "I second that – just got a call from a friend who read the article – his quote, "bad news."" The friend I was referring to was Bob. The article had him spooked, too.

Kevin then joined the party. "I just woke up and read it," he said. "Lots of damning facts in there. To be very honest, the Scanlon stuff makes me sick to my stomach – buying up property in cash. I am glad she did not know more about AIC, but the firm does. If people start chiming in with stupid quotes like Duane's, I am going to snap. Talk to you guys in the AM."

The next day our dual lives converged when Jack called a mandatory meeting of the key members of the lobbying team. He wanted to discuss the ramifications of the *Post* piece. About fifteen people were in attendance. I was nervous. Would people rally behind Jack or come to their senses? Or would everyone just keep quiet and whisper to one another? For the Four Horsemen, it was a moment of truth. Over the last few weeks, we had been quietly working together in a collective effort to survive Jack's demise. But now that the story was public, we had a whole different ballgame to play.

While many of the specifics may have been new to me, stories from unhappy clients had been circulating among the team for years. The basic gist of the stories was the same: Scanlon did not do the work he promised the tribes he would do. It got so bad that several of my colleagues began maneuvering quietly behind Jack's back to keep the new tribes we brought in away from Scanlon. This activity was the first real mission of what would become the Four Horsemen. Since I had my own clients to focus on, I was not directly involved in the interaction between the team and the new tribal clients. But I knew about the efforts and supported them however I could.

Our efforts to keep Scanlon away from any new clients was not done out of altruism or because we were good guys, but because Scanlon's low level of work threatened our relationship with our tribal clients - the same clients who paid all of us. Our team-within-the-team was generally successful in keeping Scanlon away from the new tribes. But it required that we operate in the dark and in opposition to Jack's interests. Anyone who spent time with the group could feel the growing tension. Even as our lobbying group delivered for clients upset with Scanlon's work, we all wondered whether Jack would choose Scanlon ahead of our lobbying team if push ever came to shove. The money the *Post* story uncovered showed us why he might.

Instead of riding the metro into town like usual, I decided to take a cab. I needed the solitude. It was the middle of winter, but sweat poured out of me like a faucet. Plopping down on a cushioned seat in a quiet car provided a much-needed reprieve from the non-stop fright show ricocheting around in my head. Eyes closed, I began visualizing my future. The thought that Jack could survive this and still be working weeks or months later unnerved me greatly. With only one night of real introspection, I already yearned to put him and the whole mess in my past. I just wanted to snap my fingers and be done with it all. Lesson learned. At the same time, I knew it was hypocritical of me to blame my actions on Jack and Scanlon - especially since, deep down, what scared me the most were the things I had done. Things that weren't in the papers. At least, not yet.

We slowly gathered in Jack's office. One by one each of us took our seats. There was little eye contact. Because we knew that the many email messages we sent everyday could soon pose a problem, our Blackberrys remained dormant in their holsters. As if we were hermetically sealed in that room, neither the air nor any of us moved as we waited for our embattled boss to arrive.

It was a different Jack Abramoff who walked into the room for our team meeting. He seemed unsure, even fragile. Gone were the quips and Godfather references that normally accompanied our get-togethers. For the first time in my memory, Jack's usually impeccably pressed suits looked disheveled. Even his trademark sarcasm was missing.

Laptop squarely under his arm, Jack entered the room. In previous months, he had spent a lot of time and money successfully losing a great deal of weight, but his stocky build still left him with a short, square stride. His sullen face seemed to carry the frigid winter weather into the office with him. For a few minutes, Jack stared blankly into the monitor as he fiddled to fit his computer into the case behind his desk. We all stared in his direction, awaiting his words. The wind swirled outside. The office's view of the White House suddenly seemed distant - like Jack was now an outsider looking in.

We could have heard a pin drop. Clearly, Jack was worried. His voice cracked when he started speaking. It looked like his nerves were fraying in front of us. I had expected him to act like a bull charging out of a gate. But that wasn't the case. His vulnerability shocked me. So did his approach.

Unfortunately, Jack decided to start spinning the story to the team instead of either apologizing, telling us the truth, or telling us he couldn't discuss certain things because they were private. Even with us, his team, he didn't seem able or willing to step out of his lobbyist role. Did he not comprehend that we were all putting the pieces together? That we had read about the tens of millions of dollars he had been paid by tribes like the Tigua? Since we all knew more bullets were on the way, most of us on the team believed that Jack owed us a real explanation. His decision to spin us instead of to shoot straight was offensive on many levels. In the moment, it felt as bad as the article itself. The feeling of betrayal in the room escalated as Jack ducked question after question. The fact that our leader still believed he could shuck and jive the very people who knew better was insulting.

Those members of the team still drinking the Jack Kool-Aid could feel the tension and tried to help rally the troops. Arguing that Jack and Scanlon were somehow victims, my lobbying colleague Todd Boulanger tried to explain away the story as the cost of being so successful for our clients. That idea flew right in the face of the facts. At least the facts as I knew them, which was a part of the problem. *What are the facts? "I mean, what is the real story on the Tigua? The Coushatta? And the others? Why did Rudy leave? What did he know?"* I asked myself during the meeting. For that matter, I still couldn't help but wonder whether the lobbying team, or as Jack used to call it, "the family," was actually the center of his operation. Or, as it appeared in the paper, was his business relationship with Scanlon the top priority? Based on money alone, most of us in the room had clearly come to the conclusion that his relationship with Scanlon was more important than his relationship with the team. Such a thought permeated every question and comment.

Struggling to connect with a suddenly disconnected team, Jack resorted to tired old phrases like, "If we don't hang together, we will surely hang separately," and "We may not have dotted all the Is and crossed the Ts along the way," and, "We were busy succeeding for our clients." It was too much to take. And he knew it. The more he avoided addressing us squarely, the more he lost the hearts and minds of the team. Jack wasn't used to this type of audience. A loyal pack of wolves, we were his to manipulate. And, normally, we would have wanted to believe his assertions. But not anymore.

Jack could tell his lack of forthrightness was making us mad, so he started trying to mollify the mob with some limited candor. To a degree, that worked. But there were too many holes to fill at once. His relationship with Scanlon was one of them.

Having learned in the article that Scanlon and Jack were splitting millions of dollars from tribes like the Tigua while I worked for nothing was infuriating. I felt ripped off. Because of all the public attention, I also felt vulnerable.

For years, Jack had succeeded in obscuring the full extent of Scanlon's involvement in our operation by playing a classic game of hide the ball. He would sprinkle a little bit of Scanlon over here with one group and a little more over there with another. But he did not fully fill anyone in on everything. Or at least, he didn't fill *me* in on everything. Therefore, when the group as a whole realized that tens of millions of dollars had been given to Scanlon by our tribes, it was a shock. It also meant that Scanlon's absence that afternoon was an elephant in the room. Many of us wondered why he wasn't there to help explain what was happening. Too much had come out in the *Post* for all of us to keep looking the other way.

I was angry, and secretly jealous of the kind of money Jack and Scanlon were making. More than anything, though, I was upset because I knew the sunlight shining on their fraud and greed threatened to expose my own fraud and greed. I had clearly gotten caught up in something much bigger than I had expected.

To a degree, Jack was paying the price for how he played the game. How we played the game. After years of using our aggressive T-Rex style of business to bludgeon clients away from other lobbyists, and play favorites in Indian Country, Jack's enemies had piled up. About the time I joined the team, their anger was growing quickly, and finally it came back to haunt us when several of them went to the *Post* with the general outline of his tribal empire. As his enemies and unanswered questions continued to pile up, Jack started treading water. Then he began to sink.

"Jack, this article looks like something written by lawyers instead of public relations people," I said near the end of the meeting. "That is never good."

Fully aware that four of the firm's attorneys had joined Jack when Susan Schmidt came to the office for her interview, I was merely piling on by that point. But I was angry. Including the lawyers in the conversation surely validated her reporter instincts the moment she walked in, I told my colleague who gave me the news. It was a stupid move. Continuing on, I simply told Jack, "That scares me," before asking, "What else can we expect?"

His reply scared me even more.

"I'm not sure what to expect, Neil, because I don't know what else she has got," he said calmly.

My blood boiled. Until the last few months, I had given Jack my complete loyalty. And even though I was far from perfect, I felt like I deserved the full story. But right then I knew I would never get it from Jack. Telling us that his lawyers demanded he not answer questions would have been so much better. Instead, he was playing possum. There was no speaking in code; no head fake; no "there may be more out there but we'll be fine" with a wink or a nod. Nothing. By the end of the get-together, most of us knew we were in the middle of a tornado. After the meeting, many of the guys I talked to were angry and confused. Some were devastated. My office, still two doors down from Jack's, became ground zero for a second closed-door meeting. This one was led by the Four Horsemen. It was time for action. There were too many unanswered questions. All of us present agreed that if the firm did not cut Jack loose, we were going to leave.

Of course, my fellow lobbyists and I weren't the only people with questions. Within days, the firm hired outside counsel and began an internal investigation into the matter. In addition, the Senate Indian Affairs Committee announced plans to investigate, and the House Chairman responsible for funding the Department of Justice wrote a letter urging the Department to look into the allegations, as well. It was a scary time. Shoes were dropping left and right. News stories multiplied. No one had any idea what to expect.

Days after the *Post* piece ran, Jack flew to our firm's corporate headquarters in Miami to try to save his job. It was quite a transformation. The face of the firm's rapidly growing Washington office was suddenly on thin ice. Of course, he knew more than anyone the extent of his trouble. As Jack told Bob after the *Post* piece, "Can you imagine someone having all your emails?" It was a question that hung out there for all of us. But for Jack, whose emails captured nearly every moment of the day, there was an especially damning paper trail. Years later, the Justice Department would tell me that they viewed our emails as "an electronic wire tap." After all, many members of the team cataloged nearly every movement they made, myself included. There were discussions about trips, tickets and fundraisers, as well as conversations with public officials, and about public officials. Jack clearly understood the situation. Therefore, as the internal office investigation picked up steam, he quickly decided it was his best bet to throw himself at the mercy of the firm.

On his way home that Friday, he was optimistic but guarded. Most of the team didn't know about his trip. But Jack had told a colleague, one of my fellow Four Horsemen, that he was convinced the firm would keep him on board. In the same sentence, I was told, he was also deeply concerned that they could end up terminating him right away. "I'll need some time to maneuver, and I'm not sure they will give it to me if this thing goes south," Jack reportedly said. "I can't be publicly let go," he continued. I found that story unsettling. Like my boss, I was worried about how best to maneuver in these suddenly choppy waters.

Still, I remained hopeful that Jack would be fired. Before long my own past would catch up with me, but in the throes of the moment I rationalized away much of it in the sheer hope of surviving. "I may have broken my one-year ban and could have filled out some paperwork wrong," I would say to those few with whom I shared my worries. "But I didn't take money outside the firm." That became my early public line in the sand. While I deeply feared any revelation about my corrupt relationship with Jack and Bob, for the first few months, I continued to follow the line of thinking that "money outside the firm" was the dividing line between appropriate and inappropriate behavior. Having convinced myself that my infractions were minor, or in the case of my relationship with Bob, undetectable, my desperate hope was to just get away, move forward - and hope things would be fine.

Early the next week, Greenberg Traurig fired Jack. While the news was huge to me, my friends and my firm, much of official Washington was focused elsewhere. It was March 2nd, 2004, the day Massachusetts Senator John Kerry wrapped up the Democratic nomination for President. President Bush had an opponent. And the country was facing a choice. Soon, I would be, as well.

MARCH 18, 2004
ALEXANDRIA, VA

A Changing Identity

"AFTER WE PUT A HUNDRED million dollars of paid media behind that quote, Kerry is done," my old Capitol Hill colleague and current Bush-Cheney presidential campaign press secretary, boldly predicted. "If we do our jobs, this election is over." He and I were sitting at a bar and talking about the upcoming election. It was a nice reprieve to discuss something besides Jack's departure from the firm. For the last few weeks, the team and my firm had been in professional hyper drive. Jack was gone. Our clients were nervous. An internal investigation continued. And rumors of future trouble loomed at every turn. Getting away represented nothing less than a much needed sanity-break .

I was hosting a fundraising event for President Bush's campaign. White House advisor Karl Rove had just fired up the standing-room-only crowd with a guns-a-blazing speech about the President's upcoming re-election effort. The hundreds of people milling around the Birchmere were abuzz about the campaign. Our Washington style political pep rally only added to the festive atmosphere of my friend's good news. Two days earlier, Senator Kerry, the Democratic nominee for president was asked about a vote he took against funding the war effort in Iraq and Afghanistan. Kerry had responded by saying, "I actually voted for the $87 billion before I voted against it."

His flip-flop style comment was the kind of made-for-television campaign gaffe Bush's press secretary and I both knew could be used to advance the cause of a second presidential term. The Senator's remarks succinctly encapsulated several issues the campaign hoped to exploit. Specifically, the Bush team wanted to paint the Massachusetts Senator as indecisive, weak on national security and beholden to liberal special interests. His comment helped on all counts.

For me, it was exciting to sit there and ponder the possibilities of a second Bush term. Nothing epitomized that more than the sheer enjoyment I received from egging my friend on to read and re-read the Senator's quote to anyone we knew who came by the bar for a drink. He got fired up every time he pulled his Blackberry out of the holster to read the quote, and then he'd outline what a devastating impact the miscue would have on the Kerry campaign, and how a Bush victory would positively impact our shared futures.

Throwing myself into the drama of the president's re-election was the perfect tonic for the confusion I was feeling about the developing Abramoff scandal and Jack's departure from the firm. Over the last two years, it was clear to anyone who paid attention that my perspective and role within the political process had changed. I liked the excitement, influence and money that came along with being a lobbyist, and I desperately wanted to keep the team together. But the guilt I felt about the simmering scandal also had me missing the purity of the election process, so much so that I told myself maybe it was time to stop lobbying. *"Helping the Bush campaign could be just what the doctor ordered,"* I thought, while talking with the many conservative activists attending our fundraiser that night. It was a fleeting moment.

By the end of the night, my situation would bring me back to the arduous process of working day and night to keep our lobbying team intact and functioning. There wasn't one specific issue pulling me back. Ultimately, the pressure to pay for my new Chevy Chase house, the loyalty I felt to my lobbying colleagues and clients, and the fear that stepping down would be an acknowledgement of failure all came together to keep me in line. But for a few hours, I allowed myself to dream about a different future, one that returned me to public service via the Bush White House.

Providing a catalyst for my thoughts that night was the group with whom I was hosting the fundraiser, "Young Professionals for George W. Bush." I had grown up on Capitol Hill with many of those "young professionals." Many of us were now lobbyists or still worked on the Hill, while others had become part of the Bush Administration. In some way or another, most of us had softened our revolutionary fervor over the years, but deep down the embers from our younger, more revolutionary days still burned.

We bantered back and forth about the prospects of a second Bush Administration. Because 9/11 had upended the political order during the President's first term, implementing many of our long-held domestic policy goals had not been attempted. If we kept the Congress and the Presidency, however, most of the group agreed we could attempt to pass such far-reaching reforms as privatizing Social Security and transforming the health care system, including implementation of major changes to such mammoth entitlement programs as Medicaid and Medicare. Each of us had his or her own opinion about President Bush and his first term, but none of us doubted that he had the nerve to try to push through the kind of vitally important, yet politically unpopular, reforms we were discussing.

While we had become somewhat jaded, our understanding of the process also gave us hope for such possibilities. We knew that the stars were aligning to create an environment in which 2005 could be for President Bush what 1997 was supposed to have been for President Clinton - a time to push through legacy-building reforms to Social Security, Medicare and Medicaid. "Those kind of moments don't come along often," one of my old Hill pals said. He was right. President Clinton had squandered his moment by involving himself in the Monica Lewinsky sex scandal. Despite offering up a plan to place certain Social Security contributions into the stock market, President Clinton's weakened position blocked any meaningful entitlement reform from being implemented after the scandal. Those of us at the campaign party were determined to do what we could to help President Bush tackle the type of long-term problems his predecessor had failed to address. For a few moments, it felt like 1994 all over again. I liked the sense of purpose I felt when discussing the campaign.

Working to take the Abramoff out of Team Abramoff, on the other hand, didn't make me feel so purposeful. Yet it preoccupied most of my time. At first, the onslaught of negative publicity and shared concern about the future resulted in the team rallying around each other. Together we swam upstream against the torrent of bad press. The team members leaned on each other to protect our shared Hill and White House contacts, while continuing to deliver for our understandably nervous clients.

Our goal was simple. In order to keep the team together, we needed to preserve enough of our paying clients to support our lobbying salaries and administrative costs. We also needed to preserve enough of the team for us to continue to service our client's needs effectively. It was a catch-22. Clients wanted to know whether the team would be staying together, and the team and the firm needed to know if the clients were staying. Our clients were also concerned about just how much the team's effectiveness had been impacted by Jack's departure. All of this meant we had to work even harder than before.

In the meantime, Jack began interviewing with other lobbying firms.

His pitch was straightforward. He told his suitors that Greenberg was nervous about the bad publicity. Jack then told them that his clients and his team were sitting over at the firm waiting for him to land somewhere. When he did, the clients, the team and the big payday would follow, he would say. It was a good proposal. But it wasn't true. Back at Greenberg, a struggle for the future of Team Abramoff was underway.

Several of our co-workers who were also committed to keeping the team together without Jack joined in the efforts of the Four Horseman. Since we trusted neither the firm nor Jack's guys to look out for our group's interests, we met almost nightly outside the office to talk. Normally we met at the bar inside the Hay Adams, a landmark hotel across the park from the White House. *Off the Record* was the bar's name, an amusing irony since our conversations were not supposed to be shared with either Greenberg or Abramoff loyalists. Discussing all our options, we considered splitting the team up, joining another firm, and continuing with the status quo.

The battle lines developed slowly. As in a political campaign, our group built a base of core supporters and then reached out to undecided co-workers. Since Jack kept in daily contact with certain members of the team, we picked our contacts carefully. In order to give us the best chance of persuading the largest number of people to stay together, our growing group decided to avoid the combustion of telling Jack our plans as a group. Nonetheless, it became a battle of the Four Horsemen versus Abramoff. Everyone handled the dynamic differently. I was the first of our core group to tell Jack that I wasn't going with him. Whether it was because I was worried about what I had done in the past or because I was anxious to embrace the future, I wasn't sure, but it felt good to tell Jack my plans.

"Don't close the door, Neil," he replied. "It is important for all of us to keep our options open." He was persuasive, but I told him to plan on moving ahead without me. A few weeks later, Jack's efforts began to make headway with some of the guys. Rumors of job offers by Jack's new firm began to circulate among the team. They included large signing bonuses and big salary increases. After seeing one of the offers a colleague was contemplating, I started to second guess how the drama would ultimately play out. Despite the fact that the firm was embracing our Four Horseman-led efforts to keep the team together, many within the firm wanted to jettison several of those individuals who had been closest to Jack. Not surprisingly, those were the folks getting the offers.

Jack didn't give up easily in his campaign to take me with him to his new firm. "You're the central spoke of the team," Jack said. "If you lead, others will follow." I didn't believe a word I was hearing. Two years ago I would have been putty in his hands. Not this time. I once again told Jack that I was staying at Greenberg. He then told me, "Neil, I love you." I almost dropped the phone. *"He is really desperate,"* I told myself. Still feeling a strong tinge of loyalty to Jack, it hurt to see him like that.

Over drinks at *Off the Record*, I rehashed the awkward exchange between Jack and me with what was now a growing group of former Team Abramoff members. It led to some stress-reducing hilarity. For the next hour or so, we ad-libbed additional irreverent lines to the story, and helped to work through our shared anxiety. "You can either laugh or cry," was a common refrain during our group's meetings. Most nights, like that night, I chose to laugh. Humor helped me get through the day and cope with my fears. Many of my co-workers operated the same way. It was no surprise, then, that most everyone in the group at *Off the Record* that night made sure to tell me, "I love you, Neil," on the way out of the bar. I didn't know whether to laugh or cry.

One thing that did have me smiling at the time was the March 17, 2004 edition of *Influence Magazine*, a publication that followed the lobbying industry. The magazine contained an article about the impact of Jack's departure on our firm. The piece was built around the question of whether there was a mass exodus of clients and lobbyists from Greenberg now that Jack was gone. One of the clients I was lead on, Unisys Corporation, was quoted in the article.

"At least two of Abramoff's other clients said they will stick with the firm, including Unisys Corp., an information technology services company that paid Greenberg $240,000 in the first half of 2003."

"Our contract was with Greenberg Traurig, not with an individual partner, so we are continuing with Greenberg," says David Pingree, the company's vice president for government relations."

David's words and the decision of his company to stay with the firm were like gold to me. Since I helped to coordinate the interview and worked to keep the company as a client, I earned some much needed financial security and professional gravitas. Paying clients like the Pennsylvania information technology company were the lifeblood of my hired gun existence. My professional survival meant securing their support during this uneasy time. Since Jack's departure was such big news, keeping my clients happy remained a daily priority. Unfortunately, keeping them happy sometimes meant keeping them in the dark.

That Jack and Scanlon had made tens of millions of dollars off our clients was now common knowledge in the lobbying community. Client and colleague questions followed that had to be addressed. Did I know about Jack and Scanlon's business arrangement? Were there other members of the team who were being paid by Jack outside of the firm? What about my one-year ban, or my relationship with Bob? I knew I had screwed up, but I wasn't sure how much to share with my clients or colleagues. So I did my best to survive day by day. Sometimes that meant lying about my worries, while at other times I was forthright and open.

When certain clients asked how things were going, I told them, "Everything is fine." If they asked if I had known about Jack and Scanlon, I said no. On the other hand, I continued to open up to some of my lobbying colleagues. "The one year ban isn't that big of a deal," I told a few of them during several moments of unguarded candor. "How can you even enforce that?"

At the same time, I continued to keep to myself anything that related to Bob. This included the changing nature of my relationship with the Chairman. As far as my colleagues and clients knew, there were no problems between us. But the news surrounding Jack's departure had added tension to my relationship with the Chairman. He wasn't sure how to deal with the news surrounding the scandal, or the split between Jack and me. Legal concerns also started to permeate our thinking.

For the previous two years, managing the relationship between Jack and me was relatively easy for Bob. I worked for Jack. In Bob's mind, that meant Abramoff and I were one entity. But that was no longer the case. The Chairman now found himself managing two relationships. Alarmed by the information he had read about Jack in the papers, Bob told me he was disassociating himself with my former boss. But he still remained in contact with Jack. Since I was still talking with my old boss too, the tension Bob and I felt generally remained below the surface and unspoken.

Occasionally, however, there were instances when the simmering conflict bubbled over. In one instance, Bob threatened to stop helping my clients. "What, don't you trust me?" he asked. It was awkward. Even as I had remained a lobbyist and he remained an elected official, the public nature of the scandal was changing our relationship. "Your behaving like Jack and all those other lobbyists who just view me as a vehicle to make themselves rich," he told me one night. "If you didn't want me to help your client, you wouldn't have called." Not all our conversations were so direct. Sometimes jokes spoke volumes about what was really happening under the surface.

"Don't worry, I'm OK to be around," Bob half-jokingly told me one night. "I haven't talked to Jack." His comment stunned me. I didn't know what to say. It wasn't like I was asking Bob not to speak with Jack. But he didn't believe me. Nor did his staff, who made it clear to me that Ney wasn't going to choose between Jack and I. To which I told them again and again, "I'm not asking him to do that for me."

Unsure of what was the best way out of a complex situation, I found myself looking backwards, and then looking forward. My relationship with Bob mirrored the rest of my professional and personal uncertainty. Things got hot, then cold. Over time, I figured it was best to focus my efforts on where I was going instead of on what had happened. It seemed easier. Also, if I wanted to keep my fantasyland life in tact, that had to be my priority.

JULY 21, 2004
WASHINGTON, DC

The President's Dinner

THE PRESIDENT'S DINNER IS THE ultimate Washington fundraiser. It is the pinnacle political event for the party holding the White House, for the establishment. Headlined by President Bush, the annual fundraiser brought in tens of millions of dollars for Republicans running for the House and the Senate. Thousands of lobbyists, activists and public officials filled the main ballroom of the Washington Convention Center. I arrived early. In my tuxedo, I was herded toward the hundreds of pre-set, ten-person tables in the main ballroom. But that wasn't my destination. I was going to see the President.

Since the President's Dinner is very much a "who's who" type of event, lobbyists like me tended to eyeball our competitors to compare who was sitting where and with whom. High-paying donors flew in from all over the country, and party professionals planned their own secondary events around the swarm of well-heeled and well-connected attendees. I told everyone I saw that I was going to the special pre-party get-together with President Bush. It was my way of assuring folks that I was still on top of my game.

Each year, a handful of lobbyists secured seats along the stage of tables set up on each side of the President's podium. They joined the leadership of the House and the Senate, the President and his wife, as well as a variety of other dignitaries. Last year, Jack had been part of that auspicious group at the head table. His seat had cost $100,000. The team reveled in watching Jack cavort with the President and the other VIPs up on the big stage. We joked about turning the tables on our leader, peppering him with email requests, as he often did to us.

"Hey Jack, ask the President about the Jena," one of the guys said. "Talk with the Majority Leader about Internet gaming," said another. The more examples we came up with the more we laughed.

This year was different. Jack was gone. Because of the scandal, most of the team saw the President's Dinner as a major public relations challenge. Our goal was simple. We wanted people to see that we remained influential enough, despite the bad media stories, to keep our clients and our standing within the political community. Most of my colleagues and I could not envision how the scandal would finally play out. After all, we couldn't see that far ahead. Our focus was simply to survive Jack's departure, one day at a time.

I was no different. After withstanding the initial onslaught of bad publicity, my focus returned to work. The single-mindedness paid off. Weeks before the President's Dinner, I was named to *The Hill's* annual list of Top Lobbyists. "Talk about landing on your feet," I said to a colleague after opening up the newspaper and seeing their list of accolades. "This is big," I continued, knowing such high praise would help me generate new clients - and more money.

Day after day, my lobbying colleagues and I started to feel like we were actually beginning to thrive again. The camaraderie of my colleagues and the reduction of fear I was feeling about my future made me question my initial idea of moving on, or joining to the Bush White House at some point. I also began to think that the President might not get re-elected. The war in Iraq was becoming increasingly unpopular. *"Is now really the time to go?"* I asked myself. *"Maybe things aren't so bad after all. I could lobby a little longer. I mean, there is a lot of money to be made."*

My renewed professional success wasn't occurring in a vacuum. As usual, the increasingly high arc of my flight had a lot to do with Bob. He, too, was rising fast, through the professional ranks of the House of Representatives. Bob's role in the President's Dinner exemplified his ascension. As was customary, a representative from either the House or the Senate made a speech along with President Bush. Bob was making this year's speech. That was big. The Capitol Hill media reported on Bob's role in the President's Dinner. Political insiders told the papers that Ney seemed to be on the fast-track to a higher position in the House leadership, possibly Speaker. We were back. Since none of the initial articles about Jack and Scanlon implicated Bob in any way, about the worst thing anyone wrote or said publicly was that the event represented a test for the Chairman, and people would be watching to see if he passed.

For both of us, Bob's decision to headline the event meant spending a lot more time on the phones making fundraising calls. It was a team effort, with lots of major players pitching in to make sure the party exceeded last year's numbers. I did everything I could do to help. At times, I felt like I was working for the Chairman again. I cheer-leaded Bob's efforts all over town and attended the official meetings at party headquarters. The better he did, the better I would do. At the same time, I finally began to feel like I had moved beyond the staffer role. My goal of getting out of Jack and Bob's shadow seemed to be coming to fruition. People saw Bob and me as a team, working as colleagues. Many of my clients donated to the event. Over time, my lobbying colleagues and I raised enough to secure a slot in the pre-event get-together with President Bush. Because of Bob's leadership role, I was selected to represent the group for the meeting with the President.

After saying hello to some of my clients and colleagues, I slipped back to the pre-event get-together. Waiting to see President Bush felt like standing in line at a really exclusive night club. There was a long curtain-lined hallway winding along the back of the convention center. Within the line, there appeared to be a cultural split among the group. The Washington insiders like me waited impatiently to do our job. I had met and talked with President Bush several times, and was very excited to see him. But the impending grip and grin photo with the President was more about work, and showing my clients that I had been with Bush before the event. The people who flew in from outside Washington for the event, however, were wildly excited about the opportunity to meet the President. As I stood there waiting, I labeled the people around me. They were either jaded political professionals like me, or excited rich people who had bought themselves fifteen seconds with the most powerful man on the planet. I quickly grew bored.

Then Bob showed up. He pulled me out of line and took me with him, darting back and forth between big donors and elected officials. Between conversations, Bob sneaked me in for my photo with Bush. People wondered who I was, this guy joking around with a potential future Speaker. I liked the attention, and Bob liked the company. Having someone to talk to saved him from getting bogged down in the small talk that is inevitably a part of events like that one.

Minutes later, I made my way toward our table. Several clients were there with my lobbying colleagues. They wanted to hear about my time with the President. Before sitting down and embellishing my experience for them, I zipped off an email to Bob. "Good luck with your speech," I wrote, feeling incredibly proud of him. We were having a great night.

Bob stood behind the podium, at his zenith, hosting a dinner with the

President of the United States. The fundraising goals for the event had been exceeded. The night was already a success. As Bob joked with me via email about how no one ever listened to Presidents' Dinner speeches, he seemed genuinely excited to just hang out with me. I liked having that feeling again. I beamed with joy. My favorite phrase, *falling upstairs*, came to mind, as I tried to describe how lucky I felt. After all my worries, it was beginning to feel like everything was going to be just fine.

The Campaign

HAPHAZARDLY I SCURRIED AROUND THE house. Getting ready to spend the next month in Ohio helping the Bush campaign had me feeling scatter-brained. I juggled last-minute laundry, car maintenance, work responsibilities and other logistical challenges. Not seeing Alison until after the election would be tough. Then again, our partisan differences always made elections tough, especially in a town of partisan good guys and bad guys.

From a professional perspective, I still wasn't sure why I was going to Ohio. But I knew I wanted to go. Part of me continued to think about getting out of lobbying and going to work for the White House. Taking part in the campaign would be helpful in that endeavor. For the first few months after the *Post* piece, I was almost certain that I would leave the firm after the election. The light shining on Team Abramoff frightened me. My colleagues and I spent too much time worrying about what to expect from the scandal. For me, that meant worrying about my own illegal behavior. I just wanted it all to go away. Moving to the White House would help me get beyond the public scrutiny and give me a chance to reset my professional political career, I figured.

At the same time, part of me wanted to keep sprinting forward with what was an increasingly lucrative lobbying career. *"I survived the initial sting of the scandal,"* I told myself. *"Keep going."* Helping impact the campaign in a key swing state like Ohio would help no matter what path I took.

It would undoubtedly advance a future lobbying career, assuming Bush won. In many respects, the campaign work was like writing a big check. The sweat equity of working for the President's re-election would keep doors open to me within the Bush White House for years.

"I could lobby for the next term and get out," I would say, continuing to shuttle back and forth between wanting to stay and wanting to go. "Lobbying doesn't need to be my career." Despite the fact that I liked the money, selling my services to the highest bidder had become uncomfortable. The longer I lobbied, the more the process made me feel like my own beliefs were being diminished in favor of the paid causes I was supposed to advance. Nonetheless, continuing my work for a little while longer seemed acceptable. *"If I keep saving and investing, I'll be set for the rest of my life by the end of Bush's term,"* I thought, in a continuation of the Faustian agreement I cut with myself years earlier.

It wasn't like I hadn't kept my mouth shut about my own beliefs before; in order to advance the cause of Ney World while working as a staffer, I had suppressed some of my more liberal beliefs. But lobbying was different. At least when I worked for Bob, he knew what I believed. Most of my clients had no idea that their conservative lobbyist supported abortion rights, gay marriage and open borders. It felt shallow.

The firm was fine with me taking a month-long leave of absence. They knew that helping to coordinate voter turnout efforts for the President would serve our shared interests. Their view was that as long as my clients were fine, they were fine. And my clients were fine. Therefore, having packed, gassed up the car and taken care of a few incidental home issues, I was ready for yet another even-year autumn adventure.

The idea of parachuting into Ohio for the final push of the campaign began during a conversation I had with Ken Mehlman months earlier. Mehlman, the chairman of the Republican National Committee, was the special guest at a fundraiser for Speaker Hastert. As a member of the "Coaches' Circle," a name Hastert's office gave to his biggest fundraisers, I was admitted free to the event. "We need a grey hair without an ego for the end," Mehlman told me. "And you are a perfect fit." The two of us had been chiefs of staff on the Hill together. Mehlman's comments were nice to hear. And the more I thought about it, his idea of including me at the end of the campaign seemed to be the perfect way to embrace the next four years of life in Washington, no matter what happened with the Abramoff scandal.

"Heading to Ohio...." was the title of an email I sent to a few senior White House political operatives before leaving the next day.

"I'm finally leaving DC, and am meeting with Bob Paduchik tomorrow at Columbus headquarters to get my marching orders for work in SE Ohio," the email started. Paduchik was the state Campaign Manager for Bush-Cheney 2004. "We have a nice crew heading out for some groundwork over the next few weeks. Let me know if I can do anything to help...take care."

Within minutes, the National Field Director for the Bush-Cheney campaign replied. The two of us had worked together during the 2000 campaign in Ohio and West Virginia. "Giddyup! Go bring it home brother – and thank you!" he said.

The White House's Political Director sent the next reply. "Thanks for doing this, Neil. Do the Lord's work there," he continued.

Finally, I reached out to Bob to remind him I was leaving in the morning. Weeks before, he had offered to let me stay at his house during the campaign. With appreciation, I accepted his offer. The arrangement was good for both of us. I didn't need to pay for my stay, and Bob had a friend at the house providing him another layer of political information during what promised to be a close campaign.

In typical Ney fashion, the Congressman responded to my email by including me on his ongoing email traffic with the Bush campaign. Not surprisingly, it concerned the state of the campaign in Ohio. The subject line of the specific email read "The Wild Card, Republicans and Democrats agree, is southeast Ohio." The Chairman's note included an Associated Press article describing the Appalachian region of the state as the most politically volatile, one that might swing toward one or the other candidate at the last minute. I couldn't quibble with the assessment. It was the closeness of the race that was providing me the professional value in coming home in the first place. The Political Director of the White House wasn't as concerned about the turnout of some small rural counties in a state like Massachusetts, because the race there wasn't so competitive. He cared that I was going to rural southeastern Ohio because those counties were in very-competitive Ohio. After all, my goal was to impact the race.

The sun was setting as I pulled into Bush-Cheney campaign headquarters in Columbus, Ohio. Our meeting started right on time. It was a reflection of the man on the top of the ticket. In a conference room filled with yard signs, empty coffee cups, a myriad of Bush family pictures and boxes of marketing material, I met with Paduchik and two regional field coordinators for the Ohio Bush team. They were the staffers who organized the campaign's efforts in the Appalachian region of the state. Without any semblance of small talk, we jumped right into a discussion about the next few weeks. There was no time to waste. We discussed eleven Southern Ohio counties who needed help, most of them were in Bob's congressional district.

My role was to simply help turn out voters. More than anything, that meant implementing the backbone of the voter turnout effort for the Bush campaign, what was called the "72 hour" program. The 72 hour program was just another way of talking about the campaign's plans for the final three days of the election. While everything is important in a campaign, actually turning out supporters is a paramount concern. It is more important than fundraising, though the efforts are tied together since money used to help get voters to the polls. That being said, much of the campaign's work over the last four years had revolved around developing an accurate list of people who were sure to vote for President Bush's re-election. This neighbor-to-neighbor outreach, monitoring and persuasion then became the foundation for our 72 hour program.

Upon reaching the last three days of the campaign, it would be the responsibility of people like me, and many others, to "flush out" those pre-screened Bush voters. *Flushing* is campaign jargon for getting a specific sides' voters to the polls. We planned to flush our voters by having at least one local volunteer monitoring each of the 88,000 individual voting precincts in the state. It was a big goal. But with the right technology, team and passionate supporters, the vast majority of precincts could be covered.

The process was very basic. On Election Day, volunteers would periodically enter their local precinct, read the updated voting list to see who had voted, and call a volunteer-manned phone bank to pass along the information. From there, the volunteers in the phone bank with the voter lists would personally call the people who had not yet voted and encourage them to get to the polls. It wasn't rocket science, nor was it easy. The process took discipline, hard work and the ability to keep volunteers motivated going into the election.

Because of the harsh realities of money, time management and the practical need to "go where the voters are," the campaign leadership had built their statewide turnout operation around the most populous counties. Unfortunately, that meant in small rural counties like ours in Appalachia, paid operatives were few and far between. That is where I came into play. I was excited about the opportunity of re-engaging in the election process.

I was also excited about the prospect of spending time with Bob. In the last few months, after the initial uncertainty surrounding Jack's departure from the firm, the Chairman and I had started drifting apart. There were good reasons for the new dynamic. With Signatures no longer available for Ney World's high-end parties, that portion of our regular routine stopped occurring. Also, for me, trying to survive day-to-day at the firm was a twenty-four hour job. This reality kept me focused on the numerous challenges associated with managing the Abramoff scandal. Every day, it seemed, a client concern or news story would create a situation that threatened the team's ongoing efforts at keeping our operation together. Such professional choices came at the expense of important relationships, even the one I had with Bob. Granted, my schedule wasn't the only catalyst for the increasing awkwardness in our relationship.

The soap opera nature of Jack's split from the firm worsened the disconnect between Bob and me. Reporters began to inquire about the relationship between the chairman and my former boss. These initial inquiries didn't go too far, not with both men working to deflect the attention. But the questions were worrisome. Bob and I both knew they could lead to trouble. Bit by bit, Ney began to subtly distance himself from me. When I started hearing about lobbying get-togethers, what Bob called his kitchen cabinet meetings, occurring without me, I was hurt. But I told his staff that I understood the need to be prudent. "Washington is a small town," I said. Bob's guys nodded along, without saying a word. They didn't want to talk about it nor admit that it was happening. I assumed that was because the Chairman didn't want them verifying anything to me. Having worked for the man, I understood that, too.

The decision to stay with Bob, while I was in Ohio, opened up my eyes to just how far the schism between us had grown. It wasn't that there was animosity, just a difference in how we were dealing with the growing scandal. After my meeting in Columbus, I contacted Bob during the two-hour drive to his house. The Chairman told me not to talk with anybody, in the office or out of the office, about the Abramoff scandal. He said most people in the district had no idea about the trip to Scotland or his relationship with Jack. His comments alarmed me. In Washington, among my colleagues on Team Abramoff as well as in Ney World, it was hard NOT to talk about the Abramoff scandal. We constantly worried about it, so much so that most of us had already changed our own behavior in response to the public scrutiny.

These changes started right away. When rumors of the *Post* story began to circulate, Bob decided it was best to start paying for his own meals and drinks at Signatures. Likewise, after Jack left the firm, Bob's staffers began picking up the cost for their own drinks, meals and rounds of golf. Even our trips were different. In the summer, a few months before my return to Ohio for the campaign, I joined Bob and some of the guys on his team for a short trip to Montana. It was nothing like our previous trips to Scotland, Arizona, New Orleans, or New York. On the Montana trip, all our costs were evenly split. Almost down to the dollar.

Despite being willing to change our behavior, few members of Ney World discussed the reasons behind the changes. Instead, our conversations tended to revolve around the drama of the scandal. News articles usually provided the catalyst for these discussions, discussions focused squarely on the public relations or political impact of what was being reported. At my firm, the discussions about the scandal were more in-depth. They were also focused more on the legal implications of what was occurring, and what those discussions could mean to us.

My colleagues and I at Greenberg continually shared information with each other about what had happened when we worked with Jack. As the stories spread, the reality of how big the scandal could become unnerved us. We began to address some of our concerns. There were certain administrative requirements, for example, which the team had not handled properly over the years. Therefore, we worked to get our paperwork in line. The conversations concerning our potential vulnerabilities made me better understand the evolving nature of the scandal. While I still wasn't sharing my worst fears with many of my lobbying colleagues, as a whole, we did talk about the scandal. We talked about Jack's work with Scanlon, what we were hearing about investigations on the Hill, and whether the FBI was really investigating our old boss, as was commonly rumored.

That open and introspective approach would change when I arrived in Ohio. Because of Bob's decree, I started to minimize my discussions about all things Abramoff, even as it appeared that the scandal might be getting worse. *"These are Bob's constituents and Ohio staff,"* I told myself, understanding the alarm such conversations could create. Eventually, I disposed of any worries I had about the Chairman's decision. In part, I did so because I quickly realized how nice it was to focus on something aside from all things Abramoff. Forgetting about the burgeoning investigation was possible in Ohio. The same could couldn't be said about Washington.

Days before my departure to the Buckeye State, Senator McCain's Indian Affairs committee had held a hearing on the scandal. They subpoenaed Jack to testify. While most of the media was focused on the daily horse race of the presidential campaign, much of professional Washington took notice. There were two storylines: the legal story and the political story.

Politically speaking, the McCain - Abramoff debate was framed as a subplot to a larger battle between McCain and the conservative wing of the Republican Party, led by Majority Leader Delay. Such a debate had presidential implications, and therefore gained more attention. Many pundits correctly outlined how DeLay's conservative allies had been crucial in stopping Senator McCain's insurgent campaign against Governor Bush in the 2000 presidential race. This was especially true in the key state of South Carolina, where DeLay allies like Jack helped to fund the more conservative Bush campaign. "Was McCain now using Abramoff to position himself to run for president again in 2008?" many of these same pundits and experts asked. It was hard not to agree with that assessment. Behind the scenes of the political debate, however, there were brewing legal concerns. Both presented themselves during the question and answer session.

The committee members pummeled Jack with questions about his work for the tribes. They also discussed his relationship with Majority Leader DeLay. Instead of answering their questions, Jack pleaded the fifth. He just sat there. His decision to claim his Constitutional right against self-incrimination was deafening to everyone following the scandal. In theory, legal scholars say taking the fifth should not be viewed as an admittance of guilt, but anyone who knew Jack knew that he wanted to defend himself. We also knew he could have represented himself very well in front of the Indian Affairs committee. His salesmanship would have helped his cause immensely. With the assistance of his allies in Indian Country, Jack probably could have even generated some sympathetic questions from a few Senators. But it didn't turn out that way. Jack's legal concerns left him defenseless in the political arena. He became a punching bag.

Outside the Indian Affairs committee, in places like my firm, Jack's decision to stay quiet set off alarm bells. It alerted me and my colleagues to the Abramoff legal teams' posture, namely that his professional aspirations were less of a priority than whatever legal issues he was facing. The same issues raised eyebrows among those reporters, lawyers and other interested parties who were following the scandal closely.

"There must have been some real issues there for Jack not to talk," one of my colleagues said.

"Sure looks like it," I replied. "Maybe it will look different after the election." I could only hope.

NOVEMBER 2, 2004
ST. CLAIRSVILLE, OHIO

Election Day

ELECTION DAY, THE RAWEST OF our national rituals. Anguish and anticipation shadow box each other like predators readying for a kill. Last minute should-have and could-have worries start to fade, along with any sense of control over the outcome. And then the snapshot in time is over. I love every minute of it. Therefore, for this brief day, I was able to block everything else out, even the scandal and my deteriorating relationship with Bob.

For me, the ever-escalating Kabuki dance of Election Day is both an emotional symphony and a gut-wrenching punch in the stomach. Our blood, sweat and tears were about to boil down to twelve dizzying hours of activity. It was still dark outside when I woke up. I had slept on the pull-out bed in Bob's busy living room. Despite the room being full of volunteers scampering in and out, I had gotten a great night's sleep. Feeling confident, I quickly shot off a few email messages to the Bush team.

"Don't care what the media says, we WILL win Ohio," I typed quickly. "Having spent several weeks in restaurants, bowling alleys, bars, churches, going door-to-door, etc., these folks will vote to re-elect the President," I continued. "Our volunteers are great, we are organized, and energized. 11 of 12 counties here in SE Ohio are fully implementing the flushing program and I guess it's time to get it done"

"You are the one making it happen – bring home the SE for us!" the campaign's National Field Director responded from the national Bush campaign headquarters.

"Thanks for all your help Neil. We feel DAMN good!!!" Bob Paduchik, the state campaign manager, replied from Columbus. His exuberance was contagious. Game day had arrived. For campaign hacks like me, the uncertainty associated with the final hours of the election inevitably turns into a slow motion mosh-pit of information gathering and rumor mongering. The whole thing represents an unquenchable thirst for news that can't fully be satiated until the polls finally close, and the votes get counted. Talking on the phone all day or sitting in front of a computer debating the unavoidable seemed like a prescription for a major headache. Therefore, days earlier, I decided to spend my time in the field.

Working the field meant joining other volunteers in traveling to a specific region and administering the flushing program. I teamed myself up with a senior congressional staffer from Washington who worked for Bob. He and I were responsible for the precincts in the community of Barnesville, OH. Slowly, we made our way into town. Just off Interstate I-70, Barnesville sits nearly 1,300 feet above sea level in the foothills of the Appalachian Mountains.

Waiting for the voting to begin, we drank coffee and read the paper at a local diner. It was cold outside. Winter was around the corner. More leaves had fallen off the trees lining the street than now hung on the branches. Around 10:00 AM, the two of us plunged into our assigned voting precincts. Introducing each other to the poll workers and familiarizing ourselves with each of the four operations in town, we quickly concluded there were no monitors from Senator Kerry's campaign in Barnesville. That was a good sign. Switching back and forth from precinct to precinct, we both took our time perusing the voter rolls. Checking them against our list of Bush voters, we each then stepped out of the voting area to call the volunteer team monitoring the phone bank. Throughout the day, volunteers at the phone bank would be continually encouraging every possible Bush supporter who had not yet voted throughout the day.

By noon, the persistent buzz of activity at our precincts meant things were proceeding as planned. Jim Van de Hei, a reporter covering the campaign for the *Washington Post*, called to see what was going on in Ohio. "Turnout is looking strong," I told him. "But it is too early to provide any real assessment." We agreed to talk later.

Around that time, news from exit polling began to trickle out. In these exit surveys, professional pollsters use the sample information collected from a small percentage of voters to estimate how a larger group of people are expected to vote. The media use this polling to make their projections. In the field, the polls were like nuggets of gold for those of us desperate to get any sort of big picture insight. Whether it would even be possible for me to leave my lobbying job after the election and join the Bush Administration depended on the voters' impending decision, and the exit polls provided us the best possible insight into what the voters were thinking.

When word of the exit polls reached us, our finely tuned political nervous system went into a heightened state of alert. Phone calls and Blackberry messages increased in number and frequency as we churned away at the meaning of the numbers. One of Bob's staffers passed along the specifics of the exit polls to our in-Ohio network of Ney volunteers. Senator Kerry was up four in Florida, four in Wisconsin, twenty in Pennsylvania, four in Ohio and four in Michigan. "Could be a blowout for Kerry," he said. His words were a dagger to the heart.

Determined not to jump into the fray of speculation, and therefore lose my focus, I initially watched the ongoing debate from afar. The replies came quickly. "The first batches of exit polls in 2000 had similar numbers for Gore. Also, the spreads in some of those states don't match any recent polling numbers – even if Kerry got all the undecideds," said one colleague.

Will Heaton, Ney's chief of staff, chimed in. "Exit polls aren't usually accurate until 6pm," he said.

That was quickly followed by another blast from one of Bob's staffers, with news from the Drudge Report. "Drudge is now saying those first polls were based on a 59-41 women to men ratio......Smoke 'em if you got 'em," he continued, suddenly suggesting Bush was not only in good shape but in a commanding position. His comments were based on the facts that women generally tend to vote more Democratic, and that most presidential elections have a similar percentage of men and women voting, not such a lopsided margin like in the exit polling.

The roller coaster was starting. Within minutes, our little rag tag group saw the poll numbers as good news, not bad, since there was no way the final election numbers could include a 59 percent make up of women voters. Men tend to vote more Republican than women, while women tend to lean more toward the Democrats.

Entering one of the Barnesville precincts after hearing the news, I couldn't help but notice that 11 of the 13 voters were men. *Maybe there is something to that exit polling information,* I thought. Whether they knew it or not, the decisions of voters like those thirteen people were very much going to impact how the hundreds of thousands of lobbyists, consultants, lawyers and other political professionals that make up official Washington conduct their business. That was certainly true for me. The people I would be trying to influence and the causes I would be supporting were dependent, in part, on the choices voters' across the country were making.

About that same time, I got another call from Van de Hei over at the *Post*, who also wanted to discuss the exit polling. Talking to Van de Hei gave me a better feel for what was going on elsewhere. He told me how both campaigns were critiquing the polls, and then added that what his campaign contacts really wanted to know was what was actually going on in places like Ohio. I told him what little I knew. I didn't have statewide information because I was in the field. But I did have insight into what was going on in our counties. "Turnout here continues to be sky high," I said.

"It is that way everywhere in the state," he replied, which worried me. Conventional wisdom held that Republicans tend to vote in greater percentages than Democrats in Ohio. That meant low turnout models worked better for Republicans. "A big turnout could be a problem for us," I told my reporter friend.

The crescendo of chatter and drone of information trading continued to grow. A few minutes after 4:00 PM, my Democrat buddy, fellow Four Horsemen member and former Team Abramoff lobbyist Mike Smith, touched base. Smitty was in a betting mood. Unlike the hand-wringing on our side over the exit polling, Kerry supporters had reason to celebrate. Smitty had run the Midwest region of the country for the Gore campaign in 2000. He knew full well the many dynamics of the race in my home state, as well as the importance of what the exit polls were reporting. All my Republican explaining aside, it is always better to be up in the polls.

"I think we will win Ohio. Do you disagree?" Smitty asked.

"Yes, I disagree. Rural vote will give it to us," I replied.

To which he said, "I will take that bet. What are the stakes?"

"Drinks in DC," I replied. "Double or nothing on Florida?"

"Yep," he said quickly, as the plot thickened.

Smitty and I were friends and on the same lobbying team. But we both knew our personal pocketbooks and political principles were at stake here. If I decided to keep lobbying, four more years of Republican rule meant bigger paychecks and more influence for me. In contrast, Smitty would benefit with big wins by the Democrats. Of course, a bipartisan team like ours would be fine no matter what the outcome.

An hour or so later, additional new exit polling was released. It showed the gap between Bush and Kerry closing to within one point of each other in both Ohio and Florida. I was doubly relieved. Those type of numbers meant partisan voters were holding firm and turning out on both sides. Because of the way Congressional seats are drawn, a large GOP turnout meant that our congressional majority would remain intact no matter what happened to Bush. At a minimum, my lobbying job was safe for two more years, I figured. A Bush victory would only further solidify my standing.

As the end of voting approached on the east coast, the Bush campaign in Washington, like the rest of us, remained focused on the ever-changing exit polls. In 2000, they "looked a good deal bleaker than what we are seeing today," the campaign said in a broadly transmitted analysis. At nearly the same time, however, respected pollster John Zogby publicly called the race for John Kerry. His projections had the Senator winning more than 300 electoral votes. I was shocked. The dichotomy in news had me grabbing our voter lists and suggesting to the guy I was with that we actually drive to the house of every single "Bush voter" in Barnesville who still had not voted. "We could personally remind them to vote," I suggested. "Hell, we could take them to the polls if needed." The lesson of the 2000 voting fiasco in Florida was fresh in my mind; so was the fear of losing. "We still have an hour," I reminded him. Doing the math in my head, I figured we could hit at least fifteen houses if we left right away.

Unfortunately, my car decided not to cooperate. Having traveled thousands of miles in my Ohio-assembled Honda over the past few days and weeks, all of a sudden I couldn't get the engine to turn over. Luckily, I was eventually able to get my car started and make my way to Bob's election party.

Shortly after the polls closed, I joined Bob's campaign manager in a conference room next to Undo's Restaurant, where the Ney victory party was taking place. Despite Bob's absence, it felt like old times. The two of us started calling election boards to gather results. Hanging on the wall was a large white board. While I called the county officials, Bob's campaign manager marked down the numbers. Right away, we could tell Bush was doing well in our counties. He was hitting his marks, and exceeding them in some cases. With each passing call, we gave each other high-fives. However, because of problems with some voting machines, a judge had ordered polls in the Democrat stronghold of Cleveland to remain open. What this meant in terms of results, we didn't know.

"They are trying to steal this thing," one of my lobbying colleagues said. That wasn't inconceivable, I thought to myself. *There are a lot of votes up there.* The worrying began.

The more election boards I called the better I felt, no matter what was happening in Cleveland, or what my lobbying colleagues were saying. It was like I was in a completely different universe than my friends in Washington. Things were falling into place, yet people on the outside were assuming the worst.

"I'm feeling good in Ohio, but friends in DC are in a panic," I wrote to several contacts at the campaign.

"Tell them not to worry – they are looking at exit polling data which is WAY WRONG," wrote my field director contact at the campaign.

In a very different tone, the chief of staff for Karl Rove, President Bush's top political advisor told me, "Too much time gossiping about bad exit poll numbers…they should have been in the field working."

As expected, all eyes slowly began to focus on Ohio and Florida. "Give me some Ohio news," one friend asked.

"Give me some good news," said another.

"Ohio is Bush Country," I kept saying over and over. The trend lines were in our favor, and the positive attention I was getting made me once again feel like I was putting the Abramoff matter behind me. *Elections have a way of sweeping the previous political cycle into the past*, I told myself, hoping that held true for scandals as well.

Van de Hei from the *Post* called again to get my take on the Ohio numbers. I told him what counties were expected to perform or under-perform, while he filled me in on what was going on outside of our region. Van de Hei had access to real time voting results in front of him. It was great. We were able to poke and prod updated numbers from every county simultaneously. A little before 10:45, with Van de Hei's help, I realized President Bush was going to be re-elected. I was euphoric. Our lead was too big, and there were too many outstanding votes for the President to be overcome by whatever was left of the Cleveland-area counties. I began calling friends and colleagues.

Fellow GOP lobbyist, and one of the Four Horseman, Mike William's email to our co-workers at the time stated simply, "Just spoke to Volz, he says Bush is up 200 thousand votes with 85 percent in."

Minutes later, another one of my lobbying colleagues responded, "Looks like Ohio will be the Florida of 04 unless we win or lose a state we don't expect."

I replied, "Florida + Ohio equals four more years."

Kevin Ring, also a lobbyist colleague and one of the Four Horseman, joined the chorus from Washington. "PLEASE let that be true. Just heard that Kerry is doing worse than Gore did in Cleveland. Great sign. PLEASE PLEASE PLEASE."

This was followed by another Republican lobbyist colleague's sarcastic comment, "Fl is in the bag. This is all on you."

"We win," I replied.

For a minute or two, Bob and I pondered whether he should go before the television cameras at his party and call the election. After the disputed 2000 results, people were shying away from bold predictions. He would have been the first public person to make such a call. We decided against it. Instead, our large group ordered several rounds of shots at the bar. It was time to celebrate.

By 11:00 PM, the public numbers in Florida suggested the race there was definitely over. Ring, my lobbying colleague, sent our group the following email: "Bush is up over 300K in FL with 91 percent reporting. Lead has grown. Neil, don't screw up OH."

Van de Hei and I talked again a little before 11:30 PM. "With Florida done, it is all coming down to Ohio," he said. Despite several television analysts who were finally predicting a Bush win in Ohio, Van de Hei said the *Post* was being very cautious about making official pronouncements. However, with their deadline fast approaching, they wanted to make a call if they could. I told him the paper should feel one hundred percent comfortable reporting a Bush victory on the front page, admitting along the way that I was just finishing my sixth or seventh drink. He seemed to agree. "Yeah, a Bush victory seems to be setting in around the newsroom. It was like Mardi Gras around here earlier in the afternoon when the exit polls were released," Van de Hei said. Jokingly, I told him "I can't believe it Jim, Rush Limbaugh is right. The main stream media wants Kerry to win don't they?" We both laughed as my old friend amusingly told me to "grow up." Any question I had about the final outcome ended with that conversation.

With Bob's official party winding down, we moved the ongoing celebration to a friend of the Chairman's house. An hour later, CNN officially called Florida for the President. With Florida being called, a media firestorm erupted about Ohio. Talk of a recount in the state became topic number one. Pressure built to count the outstanding provisional ballots in the state as part of a full recount. Since there were several of us who had written the new election laws in the same room, we knew about what the news media was trying to dissect. The provisional ballots in question were those ballots of voters who were not on a specific county's voter roll, but could prove that they were Ohio citizens and therefore eligible to vote. Having seen a lot of analysis about how provisional balloting worked, we all knew there weren't enough votes to change the outcome.

A friend of mine, who worked for the White House, was in Washington waiting for the official campaign party to begin. The recount story was gaining momentum, and he was wondering if there was anything to worry about.

"How are you looking?" he wrote.

"I look good, and the President looks great!" I replied.

"We are feeling great here," he continued. "Provisionals? We have heard there are two planes in Boston on the way full of lawyers to OH."

"Fuck 'em," I said in a heartfelt response.

"Right on, brother," he replied. "We hear Cheney is on his way to the Reagan Center." It looked like the celebration was officially beginning.

Around then, Ring, my lobbying colleague, sent me a nice email summing up what several of us had been saying. "Dude, you have to feel good, like you were part of a historical victory. OH was THE battleground."

He was right. I did feel good. My future options seemed pretty open.

Instead of working as a lobbyist or White House staffer, I began to wonder whether being a campaign consultant would be more lucrative and exciting than being a lobbyist. "I love politics," I told my partner in cards. "It is in my blood." Despite the sheer enjoyment and camaraderie of shooting pool and playing cards at the election party, I couldn't help but continue watching the news coverage. The shadow of Florida continued to hover over the entire situation. A little before 3:00 AM, Senator Edwards told a group of Kerry supporters, "We will fight for every vote." It was a shocking statement considering the numbers, I thought.

Almost instantly, a friend of mine sent an emotional message from campaign headquarters in Iowa.

"If you need me and some other very good people to go to Ohio tomorrow (people who were critical in winning today in Iowa), let me know. For me personally, I will fly on my own dime to be there in the trenches. Have a lot of experience from FL in 2000 – Broward County. I don't trust our lawyers to fight this battle. We need political soldiers. Lawyers f-ed everything up in FL."

I felt for him and definitely appreciated his earnestness. However, after some give and take, I tried my best to let him know I thought it was over. "They will concede tomorrow," I said. "We are 150K up this time, not a couple thousand. It's over, but if I am wrong, let's talk in the early AM."

And with that I called Alison for another of our always awkward election night conversations. She was very upset. I couldn't blame her. If it had gone the other way, she would have been consoling me. Instead, I comforted her.

When I woke up the next morning, on yet another couch, the sound of my Blackberry receiving a message only added to the atrociousness of my headache. It was my lobbying colleague Kevin Ring again. "Call me when you are sober....forget that, I can't wait that long....just call when you are awake."

Another great campaign had come and gone. Once again, the voters' decisions were creating a positive professional environment for me in Washington. *"Maybe I really can put all this scandal stuff behind me,"* I thought. If the Democrats had taken back the Congress or the White House, it could have been different. But we ran Washington. My opportunities seemed endless. The feeling wouldn't last long.

NOVEMBER 14, 2004
ATWOOD LAKE, OH

The Investigation

"NEIL: THE STAFF HAS ASKED to interview you in connection with the Abramoff investigation," the attorney representing my law firm wrote. "They have asked to do it before Wednesday's hearing. Please call me as soon as you get this. Thanks," he finished.

Until Sunday morning, it had been a beautiful fall weekend. My November trip home usually represented the end of a campaign cycle. It was like turning a page into a new two-year election story. The journey started out great. My family and I enjoyed long walks through the woods, relaxing meals, and some heated shuffleboard as we celebrated my dad's 65th birthday at Atwood Lake in Eastern Ohio. The interview my firm's attorney spoke of was with Senator McCain's investigative staff. His committee was conducting another hearing in their ongoing investigation of Team Abramoff. Since there was no mobile communication coverage at the lake, anyone who tried to contact me on Friday or Saturday couldn't get through. My two days of blissful ignorance kept the impending black clouds from ruining my dad's party. That was a blessing.

Within minutes of our early afternoon departure from the Eastern Ohio lake oasis, Alison and I were inundated by our backlog of email and phone messages. I could tell something was wrong right away. There were at least five "missed call" messages on my phone, all of which read, "Caller ID blocked." In my world, the Caller ID block meant the person calling was either Bob or his staff. No one else with blocked numbers called me. The fact that someone from Ney World called without leaving a message raised even more concerns. Bob had taught all of us who worked for him to leave messages every time we called someone. "Avoid the confusion," Bob would say. Yet now I was confused. Was it even Bob who called?

I fretfully started checking my email. *"Maybe the Congressman reached out on the Blackberry,"* I thought. That is when I found the message alerting me to the committee's interview request. I didn't need to see any more messages. It had to have been Bob calling. If the committee connected with me, they had definitely connected with him as well. The Chairman picked up the telephone on the first ring. We exchanged quick formalities before I asked the Congressman if he had called me. Cryptically, Bob said, "Yeah, I was just calling to see if everything was all right."

Even through the shoddy, mountain-impaired phone reception, his monotone response told me everything I needed to know. Bob had been contacted by the committee and did not want to talk with me about it at that time. Our conversation lasted less than a minute. We agreed to meet in his office the next day.

"Why didn't he want to talk," I thought right away. *"Maybe he was at a public function? Or didn't want to have the conversation on a mobile phone. Or maybe it was something else?"*

Whatever was going on, Bob sounded scared. That unnerved me. Instead of making me feel more comfortable, my conversation with the Chairman had only made things worse. Staring out the window, I fought to hide my fear. Something was dreadfully wrong. *"This is the beginning of the end,"* I told myself. "I can't believe McCain's people want to talk with me," I blurted out to Alison over and over again. "This is bullshit. This is about campaign finance reform." I refused to accept that the investigation had merit. Instead, I began picking up on the drumbeat Jack had been pushing about the hearings from day one. "They are just politics," he would say. In Jack's case, the hearings were the Arizona Senator's way of getting back at DeLay and conservatives for denying McCain the nomination during his 2000 presidential campaign. In Bob's case, "McCain is playing politics because we led the opposition to his campaign finance reform efforts," I continued to Alison. The argument made sense, from the perspective that it is nice to have someone to blame, especially since I was deeply involved, along with Bob.

No matter why the Senator was proceeding, the harsh reality of what was happening settled in while I drove my campaign-weary Accord through the hills of West Virginia. No matter how hard I hoped on top of hope, this storm wasn't blowing over. I felt like a scared teenager in a John Hughes movie. My life suddenly didn't seem like my own. *"Where is that guy from Finneytown who drove the same hills ten years earlier?"* I asked myself. The internal debate swirled. *"What kind of questions does the committee want to*

ask me? Was this about Abramoff and Scanlon? A client? Or Ney?" Judging by
my phone conversation, I knew it had something to do with Bob. And me.

"*It doesn't matter,*" I told myself, mid-sulk. Even if the committee staff
wanted to ask me my favorite color, the mere fact I had been contacted could
be devastating for business. I called the firm's attorney. He advised me to find
a lawyer and also suggested some specific names of good attorneys in town. I
quickly started the attorney search. Alison sat next me, shell shocked. Her
husband was being investigated by the United States Senate.

By the next day, I had met with an attorney and called several others.
I also met with Bob in his office. The meeting had been my idea. I knew
the possible scenarios were getting worse. The blackout on conversations
needed to end. It was time for Bob and me to talk. For the first time since
I had stepped down as the head of the Chairman's operation nearly three
years' earlier, Bob told the rest of his staff to leave when I popped my head
into his office. "*Is he making sure no one else is with us as a way to keep information from them?*" I wondered. "*Or to keep information from me?*" It was
just the two of us sitting across from each other, in front of his desk. We
were in uncharted territory.

"You want a beer?" the Congressman asked. It was almost noon, on
Monday.

"Sure," I replied. It wasn't the first time we drank alcohol together
during the work day. Not able to wait any longer, I jumped right into the
conversation. "I was contacted by the Indian Affairs Committee," I told
Bob. "They are investigating Jack and Scanlon." The Chairman cut me off.
He said he had been contacted by McCain's committee staff as well. They
had called him on Friday.

"Just between us," he said, after telling me the news, "I told McCain's
staff to come over here the minute they called so nothing looked suspicious."
He then walked me through the interview. Their discussion revolved around
the Tigua tribe and our efforts to help them on the Election Reform bill.
My heart sank. I got defensive. "I didn't get paid a cent by the tribe," I said,
in reference to the millions of dollars Jack and Scanlon made on the project.
Then I thought about the campaign contributions. And the trip. Explaining
our actions wasn't going to be easy.

"They asked about you," Bob said as he finished walking me through
his interview. "Don't worry. I told them we never discussed work, and that
we were just friends."

I couldn't believe what I was hearing. Unlike Bob, who had been beating back periodic questions about the Abramoff scandal by avoiding the

specifics, I had spent the last nine months contemplating our vulnerabilities, and patching them up where I could. Right away, I knew Bob's statement that the two of us never discussed work would not hold up. Even a cursory look at our emails would blow that lie out of the water. Not to mention the trip to Scotland. I told Bob that. He brushed it off. "You're worrying too much," he told me.

At about that time, my soon-to-be lawyer's words popped into my head. I couldn't even remember his name, but I remembered him telling me not to talk with anyone about the investigation. He had said it several times.

"I have a lawyer," I told Bob. "You should get one too." He brushed off that suggestion as well. The Congressman said he had called a campaign finance lawyer who worked for one of the Republican campaign committees.

"Don't worry. They were amateurs," Bob said, in reference to McCain's committee investigators. His words made me feel better - that is until he told me that the meeting had lasted more than an hour.

"More than an hour?" I asked, surprised and worried.

"Yes," Bob replied. He then said that he had to call the committee staff back after his interview. "I didn't know the name of the tribe," he laughed. "So when we checked my schedule and saw their name on there, I called the committee back."

"It lasted an hour?" I asked again. *"Does he not remember that I set that meeting up?"* I was frantic. Then it hit me. I did not attend the meeting Bob had with the Tigua tribe because of my one-year ban. We were covered, on the surface at least. Maybe Bob was right. I wasn't even there. Maybe I should stop worrying.

The next day I finalized an agreement with my attorney, Tim Broas. He would be my intermediary with the committee. I told McCain's staff that I had just hired counsel, and that we did not have enough time for me to fully prepare for a visit with them. At the same time, I did my best to appear helpful. I hoped that they didn't try to force me to appear. If I had to, I could just go talk my way around the issues, I assumed. But the more I looked into the matter, the more problematic it was for me to take part in any sort of official congressional investigation. Answering questions for the committee meant answering them under oath. That was serious business. I quickly hoped the call-them-and-tell-them-we-don't-have-time strategy would work. Much to my relief, the committee staff seemed fine with such an approach.

"Well, how about that?" I thought. *"Maybe Bob is right. I should stop worrying. Could it be that this thing is still going to blow over after all?"* My rationalization remained in high gear.

The McCain Hearing

"I JUST GOT RAPED!" SCREAMED BOB. Between drags of a cigarette and gulps of wine, I felt the Chairman's anger seep through the phone. The Senate Indian Affairs committee hearing on the Tigua did not go well. Midway through the public meeting, Bob and I were drop-kicked into the center of the Abramoff scandal. With a thud, we hit the ground. And right away, that ground started to shift underneath us.

In the days leading up to Senator McCain's Indian Affairs committee inquiry, most of the pre-hearing hype revolved around the clandestine working relationship among Jack, Scanlon and Ralph Reed. Their public relations effort to protect the gambling markets of the Coushatta and the Choctaw had preceded Bob's and my own involvement in the Tigua project. With the press eating up the trio's successful efforts to stoke Reed's conservative Christian constituency to shut down the Tigua's Speaking Rock casino in El Paso, and Scanlon and Jack's decision to approach the tribe about getting it re-opened, we weren't sure how much air play Bob and I would get at the hearing.

As had happened before the previous committee meetings, someone associated with the committee leaked the most explosive emails concerning the Tigua matter to the media in hopes of generating additional public interest. Like a movie trailer, they gave us a sneak peek of what we thought was to come. In a town where the press struggled to fill the news void after a year-long presidential election, the tawdry emails between Jack and Scanlon generated an enormous amount of attention. It was great theater for Senator McCain. And the fact that Scanlon was testifying only added gas to the fire.

In opening the meeting, Senator Nighthorse Campbell kicked off the hearing with a loud bang of the gavel. "Today's hearing will focus on the Tigua tribe of Texas," he said. "The story of Abramoff, Scanlon and the Tiguas looks to me like nothing short of a classic shake-down operation. While they were being paid tens of millions of dollars, Abramoff and Scanlon held their tribal clients in very low regard – often referring to them as monkeys, troglodytes, morons and worse. Our investigation has continued to uncover other distasteful and shocking details," the Senator continued.

With that, the committee voted to formally release documents uncovered in their investigation, many of which were enlarged and put on posters for the Senator's public presentation. I watched the hearing online with several colleagues in an office at Greenberg, and I couldn't believe what I was seeing. Nervously rocking back and forth in a leather chair, I stared ahead as the nightmare I had been avoiding for months started becoming a reality. I had hidden the fact that both Bob and I had been called by the committee from my lobbying colleagues. I quietly contemplated getting up and watching the looming train wreck alone in my office.

Obviously, Bob and I were going to be mentioned at the hearing. We both knew that. The question was, how bad would it be? Ever the optimist, I hoped our role in the scheme would somehow remain a sideshow to the larger Abramoff and Scanlon conspiracy. Bob did too. Both of us continued to cling to the belief that not knowing everything about Jack and Scanlon's work for the tribes excused our individual roles in the conspiracy. *"I mean come on,"* I told myself in full excuse-making mode. *"I didn't help shut down the casino or get paid a single cent for my Tigua work."* Of course, I had still done plenty. I had broken my one-year ban. I had exchanged money, the Scotland trip, and other entertainment with Bob to advance the tribe's interests. Having belittled my own actions for the past few years, I was just beginning to accept the fact that my decisions were both a big deal and fundamentally wrong.

Being contacted by the committee days earlier had stepped up that soul-searching process. Hiring legal counsel sped up my internal inquisition even more. Sitting down with my attorneys, without worry of my words being repeated or misinterpreted, was helpful and therapeutic. Before those meetings, it had been nearly impossible to have a real conversation about the Abramoff matter. After a decade in Ney World, talking with family or non-political friends about the inner workings of my professional life seemed out of the question. And nearly everyone else I turned to had a stake in how certain events and behavior were interpreted. I certainly did, too.

My lobbyist friends verified the point. For the most part, they compared what they were reading about in the paper with how they conducted their own business. The conversations were illustrative, as they tended to revolve around the assumption that I had not done anything wrong. My lobbyist friends were not trying to placate me, make me feel better, or be malicious. It is just that a person's perspective on whether a $100 dinner or a $5,000 donation is directly related to a public policy decision tends to be skewed by whether that person has taken or given $100 dinners and $5,000 contributions. In that respect, honestly talking with my lawyers represented a breath of fresh air. After just a few short meetings at my lawyers firm, I began to realize how important it was to talk through these many issues from the perspective of how they related to me personally, not how business was supposedly done in Washington.

The introspection began to show me that my own short-term survival instincts were in conflict with my long-term ability to understand why I was in this situation. In part, this was true because my initial instinct was to fully embrace the rationalization that any questionable behavior I had engaged in was nothing more than traditional lobbying. Or just a minor infraction of the law. This mindset helped me to keep my clients and my connections. But it blocked my ability to truthfully assess what I had been doing. Talking with legal counsel was my first step toward taking off the blinders. Looking at myself in the mirror, I didn't like what I was seeing. Granted, I didn't like what I was seeing in the Senate Indian Affairs hearing room, either.

Senator McCain picked up where Chairman Campbell left off. During the next few hours, the committee was going to examine what Jack and Scanlon did with the millions of dollars the Tigua tribe gave the two to influence Congress, he said. His words sent a shiver down my spine. Because of Bob's willingness to be the principal Congressional supporter of Jack's legislative plan, as well as his having been the leading cheerleader during several meetings with the tribe, if there was any doubt left where this circus was heading it ended right there. This wasn't going to be a question-and-answer session. It was going to be a hanging.

"They went to El Paso selling salvation and instead delivered snake oil," said McCain.

The first panel of witnesses included Marc Schwartz, a consultant for the Tigua, and the Honorable Carlos Hisa, the Lieutenant Governor of the tribe. Before getting to questions, however, the committee took a few moments to fully summarize the work Jack and Scanlon did to shut down

Speaking Rock. The Senators then added context by focusing on Scanlon and Jack's attempt to get the tribe to hire them to re-open the casino.

"I'm on the phone with Tigua!" wrote Abramoff in a February 6, 2002, email presented by the committee. "Fire up the jet baby, we're going to El Paso," he continued.

"I want all of their money," replied Scanlon to Jack's email.

Scanlon's comment knocked the wind out of me. "I wasn't even on the team yet," I wanted to scream. Instead I bit my lip.

A week later, Jack had emailed his old College Republican buddy, Ralph Reed, who was also working on the casino project, according to Senate documents. "I wish those moronic Tiguas were smarter in their political contributions," Jack said. "I'd love us to get our mitts on that moolah!! Oh well, stupid folks get wiped out." Knowing that Ralph would eventually join Bob, Jack and me in Scotland, I was intrigued by how the two men talked to each other in private. Such interest didn't last long. I was too focused on the Tigua to think about much else.

While Scanlon and Jack were celebrating, the tribe had remained in dire straits. In what ended up being my first full day at Greenberg, February 19, 2002, Scanlon sent Jack a private email with an attached *El Paso Times* news story. It was titled, "450 casino employees officially terminated."

"This is the front page of today's paper while they will be voting on our plan!" Scanlon wrote. "Is life great or what," replied Jack.

Scanlon had not even testified yet and my Blackberry was already buzzing continually with messages from both well-wishers and gossip hounds. I didn't reply. But the idea of people peering into my life like that alarmed me. Defensively, I tried to deflect the proceedings by reminding myself that the emails under scrutiny had occurred weeks before I had even heard the word *Tigua*. "*You are going to be OK, Neil, you are going to be OK,*" I chanted silently, as if saying it over and over would make it true. How could I have been so stupid?!

I wasn't the only one feeling overwhelmed. Some of my lobbying colleagues were, as well. "The Tigua were collateral damage!" one of them yelled at the screen. "Their casino was never supposed to be shut down," he continued, suggesting the story was more complex than portrayed by the committee. "This is bullshit."

I just sat back, confused and fuming along with the rest of the team. My mind raced.

The committee outlined how the tribe ultimately had signed up for the deal, agreeing to pay Scanlon $4.2 million in three large up-front installments for a massive public relations operation geared toward building public support for the measure. At the same time, Jack had promised the services of his lobbying team, for free, with a tacit agreement that the Tigua would start paying Greenberg around a $150,000 a month after their casino opened. Neither of the men told the tribe they were splitting Scanlon's take. Jack's secrets bothered me again.

"Thanks for cutting me in on the deal," I thought to myself. Somehow I felt jealous, greedy and ashamed all at the same time. Then I stopped mid-thought and played back what I just said to myself - several times. My comments shook me. Was I really ashamed of my role in the Abramoff scandal, or just upset at being caught? To be truthful, at that point, I wasn't sure. It was unnerving to look at myself that way.

Within what seemed like seconds of the tribal leader's opening testimony, the words *Scotland trip* began echoing through the computer's speakers. The committee began their Scotland discussion by showing the fact that Jack had hit the Tigua up for a contribution in late June to help pay for our trip to St. Andrews. Again, I wanted to scream to anyone who would listen that I hadn't known that at the time. In fact, I didn't know about it until I read about it in the papers before the hearing.

"Our friend asked if we could...cover a Scotland golf trip for him and some staff...and members in August," Jack had emailed the tribe.

In response to a question about the exchange, Schwartz testified that "our friend" in the emails referred to Bob, or as he was referenced in the hearing, "Congressman Ney." My heart sank when I watched that dialog on screen. I thought I had been ready for anything. That Bob had asked for money from the tribe to pay for the trip to Scotland, however, was not something I was ready to accept. Bob would never do that. *"That isn't possible,"* I said to myself. Still, that was what Jack had told the tribe.

Next, the senators dug into the efforts Bob and I made to insert the Tigua provision into the Election Reform bill. The committee showed the email traffic between Jack and Scanlon that occurred when the two learned that the provision for the tribe would not be included in the bill. Unlike the other topics, I knew all about this one. Seeing the email flashed my memory back to our meeting at Signatures Restaurant when Bob broke the Tigua news to Jack and me and when Jack had detailed Scanlon's actual involvement in the project as we drove to the office together in Abramoff's car.

"I just spoke with Ney who met with Dodd and raised our provision," Jack wrote to Scanlon on July 25, 2002, the committee outlined. "Dodd looked at him like a deer in headlights and said he never made such a commitment and that, with the problems of new casinos in Connecticut, it is a problem."

I thought about our later meetings with the tribe when promises of an open casino were made, but the people making them knew they weren't going to happen. I felt sick. I felt even sicker when I heard the next statement.

Schwartz testified that during Bob's post-Scotland meeting with the tribe, "We were told about the impending success of Mr. Abramoff's legislative plan and how much the Congressman wanted to help."

Those words fully implicated Bob and me in the Abramoff scandal. Instead of politicos toiling on behalf of the tribe, we now appeared to be nothing more than self-serving bagmen for Jack and his scheme. Seeming to defend one of his own, McCain meekly told those watching that Bob had denied any wrongdoing and in fact had barely remembered the get-together. Of course, the tribe described it differently. Their spokesman outlined how the Congressman met with them for almost two hours, discussed the golf trip, and sang Abramoff's praises.

"Bob Ney has got to be at the center of this," continued Schwartz. "There can't be the perpetuation of a fraud of the tribe unless Bob Ney has that meeting with us."

We were now center stage. I was dumbfounded. And angry. This time at myself.

All my talk of not knowing about the millions Jack and Scanlon were making or where the money for the trip to Scotland came from didn't matter. That may have separated Bob and me from Jack and Scanlon to a degree. And, sure, the tribe didn't seem to have all of its facts right, either. But, ultimately, I knowingly broke my one-year ban to lobby for the Tigua and didn't file the appropriate lobbying reports for my work on behalf of the tribe. I gave Bob tens of thousands of dollars in donations and entertainment in exchange for his willingness to help Jack's client and then helped mislead the Tigua when we knew their provision wasn't going to be included in the bill. Weeks later, the Election Reform bill passed without the tribe's fix, the Indian Affairs committee reported. I wanted to puke.

"Don't do anything rash," I said during my phone call Bob immediately after the hearing. "Let the dust settle."

The Chairman wanted nothing to do with that approach. He was furious. I felt horrible for him. After all, he was the headliner. Trying to console him was nearly impossible. He just kept yelling. And drinking. The call grew more and more one-sided as he talked about getting vengeance. I felt like I was his chief of staff all over again. Bob told me he was going to slam

Scanlon and Jack in the press. I urged him to reconsider. Demonizing political opponents had served him well throughout his career, but this was different, I said.

Not to him. He told me now was not the time to get antsy. "We have to be tough," Bob insisted.

"Mike and Jack are not stupid, nor the type to pick a fight with!" I argued, as he rambled on about how they would be punished. The alcohol added to his rage. The hearing seemed to symbolize how Bob and I dealt with the conflict of the scandal: avoid talking about it, drink alcohol, then go nuclear. "This isn't just a political story," I tried to tell him, to no avail. His drinking had taken over. Continuing to think whatever was good for Bob was good for me, I acquiesced to his preferences, as usual. All I asked was that he give me a call after he calmed down so we could discuss it further. After all, I had spent the last six months thoroughly thinking through the specifics of the scandal. My last words before hanging up echoed the sentiments of months worth of introspection, "Be careful; this is not a one-day or one-week story."

Bob didn't call back as I had asked.

A few hours later, a lobbying colleague forwarded me the Chairman's official reply to the hearing. It was a scathing rebuke of Jack and Scanlon. My colleague was amazed by his vehemence. So was I. Calling the two "nefarious individuals," Bob said he was "absolutely outraged by the dishonest and duplicitous words and actions of Jack Abramoff." He then added that he was "shocked, disgusted and appalled" by their behavior, before stating he had in fact been somehow "duped" by the two of them. His words not only defied reality, but they were also bound to lead to more questions. The last thing we needed was to drag this out longer.

Picking a public fight with two guys who regularly resided on page one of the *Washington Post* made no sense to me. It was the wrong strategy. As I stated several times to anyone who would listen, the best press strategy was to triage the Tigua hearing, ride out the storm, distract the media with some other story, and then just try to lie low until the storm passed. In retrospect, it, too, would have failed to stop the inevitable.

Furious, drunk and not remotely interested in talking with Bob, I wished the whole statement could be re-done. *"How could he say he had been duped?"* I asked myself. *"Hadn't he seen what had happened to Jack? It was one thing to say you were not aware of all the facts. Saying you were duped would suggest he wasn't that close to Abramoff. Anyone who had seen Bob at Signatures would know that wasn't true."*

After a few more drinks, I almost called the Chairman back to talk with him about a possible retraction. But I didn't. The cat was already out of the bag. Also, I assumed Ney, like me, was probably even more in the bag - alcohol-wise. And judging by his decision to keep me out of the loop, he was probably steaming mad at me. I was the one, after all, who worked for Jack. Nothing good could come from more conflict, I assumed.

The day after the hearing, the press ate us alive. As the *Post* reported, "Sen. John McCain, who is leading the investigation, vowed to pursue it wherever it leads – a path that increasingly is headed into the halls of Congress." The story snowballed from there. Before the end of the week, I found myself inundated with press inquiries about my role in the Tigua project. The attention made me begin to wonder if I would lose my job. The change in my professional prospects was dramatic.

On one day, I was implicated in both the *National Journal* and in the *Post's* lead opinion editorial. "Abramoff's Ney Contact" was the headline of the *Journal* article. It described me as Jack's "ace up his sleeve when he was trying to get House Administration Committee Chairman Bob Ney to help one of his Indian tribe clients." The piece then quoted an unnamed person as saying, "Volz was the contact guy with Ney's office."

"Sources told *National Journal* that Volz sent emails to Abramoff in mid-2002 providing updates on his contacts with Ney's office on the Tigua matter," it continued. From there the article went into the potential implications my work had in regard to the one-year ban: it outlined how federal law mandated that former Congressional staffers who earned six-figure salaries were not allowed to make lobbying contacts with their former bosses for one year after they leave the Hill. "Volz apparently fell under the lobbying ban," the article said. Reading the story reminded me how stupid I was to put my work with Bob, about the Tigua, in the numerous emails I sent to Jack. *"That was how he operated,"* I said to myself, in reference to Jack. *"You didn't have a choice."*

Initially, the facts in the article were less alarming to me than the fact that people supposedly close to me, "sources," were talking about my work to the press. What had I ever done to them? Then it hit me. In an effort to deflect attention from themselves, they were dishing dirt on me. *"I might have done the same thing,"* I thought. *"This is probably a sign of things to come."*

Bob's staff replied to the assertion that I was Abramoff's "Ney contact" by saying, "The Congressman has no recollection of Volz's playing any role in the matter whatsoever." Even though the statement couldn't have been further from the truth, I was comforted by it. The situation was confusing. On the one hand, I was thankful for the public cover and told Bob so. On the other, it was a lie - one that couldn't stand up to the least bit of scrutiny and was likely to get me into even deeper trouble.

Whatever the case, the Chairman's haphazard approach to the scandal was worrying me. "You need to hire an attorney," I kept telling him. "And not one that works for the party, but one who works for you. You're just going to have to spend the money." My pleas fell on deaf ears.

Our paths began to diverge further. As I was struggling to fully comprehend the seriousness of the situation, with help from my lawyers, Bob was in a daily public relations battle for his political survival. Since he was an elected official and I was a private citizen, the Chairman was in the position where he felt it was necessary to aggressively defend himself in the press at every turn, while I had the luxury of telling reporters who called, "No comment." With the press scrutiny intensifying by the day, differences in where we were heading grew starker. I became more serious about implementing my lawyers' advice not to talk about the investigation as best I could. In the meantime, the political impact of the investigation was all Bob wanted to discuss. Our conversations grew disjointed and less frequent.

When Bob did call, he wanted to talk about either his constituents' response to the scandal or what the news media was reporting. Calls involving his local constituency were enjoyable. In part, that was because the people who voted for Bob year after year wanted to believe him and seemed initially willing to give him the benefit of the doubt. Conversations about the press, in contrast, were just the opposite. Bob's volcanic rage against the media led to angry rants about what he called my "friends in the press." As if I liked the publicity. *The Post*, in particular, was relentless. They led the media feeding frenzy. Despite the fact that some members of Congress had failed to file travel disclosure forms for years, when Bob tried to correct his travel documents, he was crucified. When I suggested that "we had to expect that," the Chairman accused me of disloyalty. "I'll just keep my mouth shut," I told him, thinking that was probably best. Therefore, I kept quiet, while Bob continued to spar with the media.

To those who followed the story closely, Bob's "duped" argument fell apart with a *Roll Call* Newspaper article headlined, "Ney, Abramoff Have Long Ties." It was written by an old reporter friend of mine, who was close with Bob as well. Few journalists knew more about the inner workings of Ney World and Team Abramoff. His well-documented story thoroughly discredited Bob's assertion that he was misled by Jack, and somehow "shocked, disgusted and appalled" to learn about the true nature of Jack's work.

"Ney's ties to Abramoff are more extensive than the Ohio Republican has publicly acknowledged, and on at least two occasions, actions taken by Ney closely tracked campaign donations from Abramoff or his associates," the article read. "In addition, Ney's longtime Chief of Staff, Neil Volz, went to work for Abramoff at the law and lobbying firm Greenberg Traurig in February 2002 – shortly before Ney agreed to support a legislative provision benefiting the Tigua tribe of El Paso, Texas."

The article read like an indictment of Bob - and me. It listed deals on issues Bob and I made with Jack's team during my tenure on the Hill, issues Bob and his staff helped Jack's team with while I was a lobbyist, and worst of all, several issues that I worked on from both sides. I had spent years as a news source for the reporter, playing cards with him late into the evening at either Scanlon's house or Ney's office - and even going to ball games with him. His article stung. He knew too much. There was no getting around it. Friend or no friend, this reporter had a responsibility to write what he knew, not that it made it any easier for me to accept.

In a short period of time, both my professional and personal lives changed dramatically. I was tainted, with my dirty laundry hanging out there for all to see. More and more news stories followed. As the scandal erupted, I finally began talking with my family and non-Washington friends to see what they thought. Even if I couldn't share everything with them because my lawyer had advised against disclosing too much, I quickly learned that talking was healthy. I also began to realize just how far away from my moral upbringing I had flown. Such a realization was healthy, and shameful.

The contrast between the way Bob was dealing with the adversity and the way I was continued to astonish me. For survival purposes, he remained focused on the future and winning his next election, while I finally started to focus more on the past. Slowing down to look at old emails or notes helped remind me of what had actually happened over the past few years. The honest introspection allowed me to assess what was a complicated matter. Lots of different opinions about the scandal floated around, some of which made more sense than others.

Around this time, for instance, Bob began concocting storylines he would state as fact during a call or get-together. Whether knowingly or not, the practice was eerily similar to the catalyst for the term Ney World. That term - Ney World - represented the realities as Ney saw them and convinced us, his staff, to see them, even if they weren't exactly accurate representations of real world events or situations. During a political campaign or heated negotiations, it is important to stay on message with your candidate or employer. But playing with facts, like suggesting that we never really talked about Tigua, or that Bob didn't really spend time with Jack? That was asking for trouble.

One of my own conversation with Bob's chief of staff, Will Heaton, at Signatures Restaurant, helped keep me in line - and showed how I had once bought into all the spin. The conversation occurred when Heaton and I were discussing Bob's relationship with Jack, right before the trip to Scotland, and shortly after I gave Bob the Tigua donations. Heaton told me that he and Bob enjoyed all the free meals and drinks at Signatures. He also paraphrased Ney's comments that "to get ahead, sometimes you just have to cut a deal like the one Bob cut with Jack."

"I totally agree," I remember replying emphatically. Those comments stuck in my head for months. There was no getting around my own words. I said them. At the time, I thought they were a marker toward a better future. As I reflected on them, however, they were yet another reminder of how far off-course I had flown.

For the next several months, memories of those kinds of conversations haunted me. Wishing I could share them with my parents, my brother or the others closest to me, I instead imagined what they would say.

"You were raised better than that," is what they would have said.

And they would have been right.

The Prime Rib

A LITTLE BEFORE 10:00 P.M., I walked into the Prime Rib restaurant. Located on the corner of K and 20th, at the intersection of Washington's business district and Georgetown, the Prime Rib is a steak-lover's steak-house. The restaurant's decor is a throw-back to the Rat Pack era. Walking into it was like entering the kind of place where Sinatra would have hung out when he visited Washington. A piano played in the background. I was met by a tuxedo-wearing maitre d'. Bob and his staff were assembled in the corner of the restaurant's largest room. The five of them sat in sturdy black leather chairs. A chrome mirror wrapped around their table. The Chairman and his guys were finishing their meals when I arrived. The remnants of several Flintstone-sized steaks lined the table.

Something was going on. Bob had been frantically reaching out to me for the last few days. In the previous twenty four hours alone, he, as well as two members of his staff, called and emailed me several times to make sure I was still showing up at the Prime Rib. Getting together for late-night drinks didn't normally involve such pressure, nor did it occur very often after the McCain hearing. In the six months since the hearing, and during the press scrutiny that followed, my relationship with Bob continued to crater. Reports of a full-fledged criminal investigation into the Abramoff scandal engulfed Washington. Bob and I became gossip fodder. It was hard to get away from the scandal. Because neither of us liked all the insidious talk, the curious stares or our lives being controlled by the information-absorbing neuron that is the Washington political class, even walking into his office or going out for drinks became awkward.

The additional time apart also cultivated the growing divisions between us, something that was mainly determined by how we responded to the new dynamic in our lives. Both Bob and I were both dead-set on surviving the scandal. But, increasingly, the two of us defined survival differently. Bob defined it by staying in office. I defined it by being able to work in Washington. In part, that meant not angering the Chairman. He was under a lot of stress. Therefore, an underlying conflict that had not been there before the McCain hearing began to infect our conversations. Any action I took was scrutinized. I began to watch my words more closely around the Chairman and his team. Likewise, I also tried not to make any public moves that would put Bob in a bad light. That being the case, when Bob and I were able to hang out, we usually met at places that weren't part of the lobbying scene, places like the Prime Rib. Before I heard from Bob about getting together, the two of us had not seen each other in several weeks.

"Lets' blow off some steam," the Chairman said when he invited me to get-together. While the idea of having a good time might have been the reason he suggested we meet, I could also tell that Bob wanted to talk. I knew his tendencies. I also knew that the investigation was heating up. Because of that, I also knew that I wasn't supposed to be talking with anybody about the scandal, especially someone without a defense attorney - like Bob. All of this made me more nervous the closer I got to the restaurant.

A month or so before meeting at the Prime Rib, I had been contacted by the FBI. "This is Neil," I said that day, when the phone rang. "Hello, Mr. Volz, this is Agent X…with the FBI." The agent's words shook me. Sitting in my office, I had a sudden urge to yank the telephone out of the wall by its cord and throw it into the garbage can. It was like I wanted to erase everything that had happened up to that moment. I then wanted to run into the bathroom and vomit. My conversation with FBI didn't last long. The two of us agreed that it was best for the Justice Department to talk with my attorney. From that point forward, any official correspondence I had with law enforcement ran through my lawyer.

By that point, I wasn't really surprised to hear from the FBI. The process of dealing with the McCain hearings had given me much-needed insight into my potential legal liabilities. Unlike Bob, who impulsively met with McCain's investigators the day he was contacted, I didn't meet with the committee. In the meantime, I opened up to my attorney and his colleagues. Talking through the many aspects of the case helped me to better understand what my legal liabilities were, in relation to my political and professional liabilities.

After the Tigua hearing, I hoped McCain's committee wouldn't call back. And for weeks, they didn't. Then, after a new blitz of Abramoff-related news stories, they called and told me that they still wanted to talk. I stalled some more.

Unfortunately, the media maelstrom following Bob's public declaration of war against Jack continued to feed the Washington press corps' fascination with the scandal. The high-octane storyline was too good not to report. Here was one of Washington's most powerful members of Congress in a blood-curdling dispute with a man who, at one point, had been one of Washington's most powerful lobbyists. Making it more intriguing was the fact that only people on Bob's side of the dispute were talking publicly. Jack remained quiet, though behind the scenes, I was told, he relished watching Bob try to defend himself against incriminating documents that were continually being leaked to the press.

The ongoing controversy added fuel to McCain's interest in the scandal, I was told. This dynamic was obvious to anyone who followed the investigation. Since Bob and I had joined DeLay in leading the fight against McCain's campaign finance bill, and Jack had helped fund conservative opposition to McCain's presidential campaign, it wasn't surprising to be told that the Senator enjoyed raking us over the political coals. Investigating a lobbying scandal was perfect political theater for McCain, something that positioned him well for a future run for the presidency. Here was "Saint John" cleaning up Washington all over again.

As the call from the FBI showed, however, there was a lot more going on with the scandal than just political theater. Word quickly spread that Jack and Mike's silence meant a serious legal inquiry, with a large number of professional investigators perusing Team Abramoff-related emails. Increasingly, my former colleagues were hiring lawyers. Therefore, while Senator McCain clearly enjoyed taking advantage of a growing news story, it was hard to argue that his actions weren't also serving to expose real corruption in the political system. My corruption was a prime example of how that worked. Because of the concerns I had about the Scotland trip, decisions I made as a lobbyist, and my one-year ban, I had decided to join Jack in pleading the Fifth. For those involved in the investigation, the move put a bulls'-eye on my back. It screamed loudly that I had legal issues.

The decision to plead that way was a gamble. On the one hand, I wanted to defend my professional image. If news that I pleaded the Fifth were leaked to the press, my career could crater. Not cooperating with the Congress, the very organization I was supposed to lobby, would dramatically reduce my ability to keep my clients. Yet I had no other choice. Despite desperately wanting to put my side in a positive light, for the first time, I was forced to put my legal concerns ahead of my business concerns. And ahead of Bob. My fears aside, the committee held to their word that they would not leak the news of my plea to the press.

Contact from the FBI raised the stakes of the investigation even further. Frankly, it fundamentally changed my outlook on work, Washington and my life. I increasing became focused simply on surviving the scandal - no matter what. Any questions about where the inquisition was going ended with the phone call from the FBI. Not a day passed that I didn't shudder at the possibilities. The idea of prison began to enter my consciousness. Also, like my dealings with the McCain staff had shown, the Justice Department's investigation into Team Abramoff also showed me that my legal interests were not necessarily the same as Bob's interests. That reality strained our relationship even further.

Questions about the seriousness of the scandal were replaced by questions about who was the focus of the Justice Department's investigation. Was it Jack? Scanlon? The firm? Our clients? Other lobbyists? Members of Congress? Bob? Me? I wasn't sure. My impression was that they were focused on Jack and Scanlon's non-lobbying work for the tribes. *"That is where the big money had been spent,"* I told myself. Of course, that was also where I had the least legal vulnerability, a reality which led me to rationalize that the FBI was most interested in that aspect of the scandal. I wasn't alone in that kind of irrational hope. Since the *Post*-story had broken, more than a year earlier, those of us closest to the flame did our best to hope the scandal away. But it wasn't to be. Inch by inch, the fire that I lit long ago was growing closer.

Days before joining Bob and his staff at the Prime Rib, I went to the Department of Justice. It was my first time in their office. As a way for me to live with all the uncertainty, I decided it was in my best interest to show the government that I was willing to help in its investigation. My decision also reflected the fear I had about the hard-charging federal prosecutors and FBI agents investigating Team Abramoff. Since I had a lot to worry about, the calculated risk of going into the Justice Department was simply a way for me to protect myself. If the scandal grew as large as many people were beginning to suggest it could, showing the government a positive posture could help me down the unclear road ahead.

My visit to the New York Avenue offices of the Justice Department was short. I didn't go in for an interview, though that is what they wanted. I simply went in to read a statement. I told the prosecutors and FBI agents who were present that I was willing to be helpful, and could be helpful.

Other than that, I took no questions and had no official conversations. I viewed it as a buoy in uncharted waters. Those waters became clearer at the Prime Rib.

The tension of seeing Bob for the first time since my visit to the Justice Department gnawed at me as I approached the restaurant. I was met at the door by the maitre d'. "Ties are required," he said, while handing me a bland black tie. I quickly put it on. It didn't remotely match my khakis and blue sport coat, but that didn't matter. One of Bob's guys yelled to me from the back corner table. Before I could even sit down, the Chairman loudly joked that the recent weight I had lost must have been due to the stress of the scandal.

"That's probably right," I told them. Right away, I could see that Bob was drinking pretty heavily. Looking over at the waiter who followed me from the front of the restaurant, I said, "Can you bring me a glass of whiskey? It looks like I have some catching up to do."

After a little small talk, Bob proclaimed to the group at a high volume that I was probably wearing a wire, and that everyone should watch themselves. We all laughed. It wasn't the first time I had heard that joke. Bob then asked why it took me so long to get there. I told him I had had a business meeting earlier. While technically accurate, I actually had been out with one of Bob's former staffers before I headed to the Prime Rib. Ney and the staffer had become estranged. I could tell right away, especially in Bob's inebriated state, that telling him the full truth would have made him angry.

My instincts in the moment served me well. Better than I knew. While I wasn't aware of it at the time, the conflict between Bob and his former staffer stemmed in part from the investigation. Within Ney World, Bob was tightening up the official story of his relationships with Jack and with me. The pressure to get in line with his narrative didn't always go over real well, especially with the former staffer I met with earlier in the evening. Each situation was different. Whatever the case, it was clear that the stress of the scandal was causing upheaval throughout Bob's operation, not just between the Congressman and me.

A few of the guys had over-ordered. I picked off their plates while I worked my way into the conversation. The steak was awesome, and the wine was good, too. Scandal or no scandal, our evening appeared on the surface to be a typical Ney dinner in Washington. We slowly settled into our normal routine. We talked politics. We talked about the War in Iraq. We talked about the news. But mostly we laughed. Few conversations were more enjoyable than listening to Bob tell stories about his days in the State

Legislature, which is what he did that night. He loved talking about the wild, carefree days of Columbus politics in the 1980s and early 1990s. It was a time before there were lobbying laws and gift bans, when an elected official like Bob could party for free whenever he wanted.

As usual, I fed Bob lines during the conversation. He was Letterman. I was his sidekick Paul Schaffer. "Tell us about the deals cut, Bob," I would say. "Tell us about the rivalries. The parties. The secrets." His stories were always part Politicians Gone Wild and part Civics 101. They were a wonderful collection of the human condition, the allure of power, and the fragility of relationships. Over the years, his tales not only provided humor, but also taught me lessons. Some of the lessons were good. Some of them weren't. But they were always funny.

We didn't stop laughing until we got up as a group and went to the bar. After ordering more drinks, our little group split up. The Prime Rib's bar was set up around two large sets of chairs and tables. There were the chairs directly around the square bar, and there were the chairs and tables set up around that initial square. Three of the guys joined Bob in sitting around the bar. He was drinking Frangelico shots and continuing the laugh-a-thon with the guys. I was talking business with another member of the Ney team at a corner table away from the bar.

Several minutes later, Bob and I walked into the bathroom together. He started talking about the phone calls he made to me over the weekend. The Chairman had called me twice on Saturday, and then early Sunday. I did not get back to him until Sunday evening. Bob remained upset that it took me more than a day, on the weekend, to get back to him. When I worked for him, he trained me to always answer his calls, and to always return every important call within twenty-four hours, no matter what. Had I still been in Ney World, I would have broken a rule. If he needed you, and you worked for him, you called him back.

"But I don't work for you anymore," I told Bob.

His posture stiffened. I expected to see venom. Instead, he said, "It hurts my feelings when you don't call back."

That comment freaked me out. *Bob never talks like that,* I thought. *"What is he doing? Where is this coming from?"* We both knew our relationship was souring, and that a widening investigation hung over us collectively, and as individuals. For months, the fear of the scandal had planted doubts about each other in both of our minds. Several friends had mentioned to me that Bob was telling people I was to blame for his involvement in the scandal. One had even told me an illustrative story that took place on the

House floor. In that instance, a couple of members of Congress had tried to console Bob by telling him that they were sorry about how the press was going after him and "his guy."

"He's not my guy," I was told Bob replied. "He is the one in trouble, not me." When I heard the story, I wasn't sure what to believe, but I chose not to confront Bob about it. In fact, I understood his need to distance himself from me. "If that helps him, I am fine with it," I told the person relating the story. Of course, my unwillingness to address the growing conflict between us wasn't just about public relations. It was more serious than that.

Before I was contacted by the FBI, I had approached Bob about fixing some of the fundraising forms that we had not filled out correctly over the years. As he sat in his office, he listened as I told him how other members of Congress and Senators were with similar situations. I wasn't the only member of Team Abramoff scrambling to get my disclosure forms in-line, I told him. "The best way for you to get this paperwork right is to cut a check to the tribes who owned the suites," I said. It was a complicated situation since several entities contributed to Jack's sports and concert empire. "That is what other offices are doing," I continued. "The couple thousand dollar re-imbursement for the tribe's expenditures is a small price to pay for the peace of mind that comes with getting the paperwork in order."

Bob didn't agree, I found out later. While I was in the room, he told me that it was a good idea and that he would take care of the matter. After I left, he discussed the issue with his staff and had one of them tell me that I needed to cut the check to make up for the discrepancy. I told the staffer I'd pay it, but that it did not make the money trail clear. The staffer replied, "Off the record, Bob doesn't care about fixing that. He said that is your problem." Instead of wading into the conflict, I again meekly just did what I was told.

Nothing caused me more aggravation, though, than Bob's ongoing refusal to get a personal lawyer. Looking back, one of my biggest failures as a friend was my inability to make Bob see how badly he needed to get a good attorney. For months I begged and pleaded with him to make a move. But he refused. The Chairman would tell me that he was working with one of the Republican Party's election lawyers, and that everything was fine. I knew better, and told him so. "It is in our best interest to communicate through our lawyers," I said. Again, he disagreed. He felt that we could just talk about the scandal amongst ourselves. After hearing the government describe my emails as an "electronic wire," and learning that all of Team Abramoff was being thoroughly examined, I began to see Bob's assessment as yet another threat to my well being. And the vehemence of that view grew stronger by the moment.

Bob and I left the restroom together and went our separate ways. He went back to talking and laughing with the guys around the bar, and I went back to talking business in the corner. A few minutes later, he came by my table. Clearly drunk, Bob reached over and hugged me. He then patted the middle of my chest, and clumsily ran his hand down the front of me.

"Is he checking for a wire?" I wondered. *"Or is he just drunk?"* Either way, he was freaking me out even more. I contemplated leaving.

Then Bob began to commiserate with me about the Abramoff scandal. The topic made me nervous. Real nervous. "The Democrats on the Hill are even sickened by how partisan everything has gotten," he said. I nodded. As long as we stayed away from discussing the Scotland trip, the Tigua tribe and my one-year ban, I figured we would be fine.

Bob then leaned closer to me and said, "I want you to think about something." At that point, he looked me squarely in the eye. "I'm doing everything to look out for you all the time. Think about that." And with those words he was gone again. The night was getting weirder. Again, I contemplated leaving.

A few minutes later, Bob returned. This time he put his arm around me like we were long-lost cousins, and again brushed his hand over the middle of my chest. *"Two times is not a coincidence,"* I said to myself, fighting the urge to push him away. Every nerve ending in my system stood at attention. I couldn't believe how strange my life and my relationship with Bob were getting.

Almost on cue, the former Ney staffer I was talking to walked away and left Bob and me alone. The Congressman asked me to step further into the corner. His erratic behavior had to have something to do with the investigation, but what exactly I wasn't sure. My mind raced; *"Does he know I have gone in to the Justice Department? Has he gone in already? What is really going on? Why doesn't he get an attorney?"* There was a lot I didn't know. As I had told my wife before I left, "All I really know for sure is that this is the first time I've seen Bob since I talked to the Justice Department, and there is no way I am talking with him about the specifics of the scandal."

"I got a lawyer," Bob said. His words floored me. My brain activity went from fifth to first gear in less than a second.

"Really?" I replied, excited. Hearing about Bob's decision to hire counsel was like music to my ears. *"Maybe that is what has him on edge,"* I thought. *"His lawyer probably outlined how serious the situation is. Why hadn't he believed me?"*

Bob then told me that he and a prominent attorney from Columbus were going to sue Greenberg Traurig. "You can get in on it if you want," he continued. I was shocked by the ridiculous suggestion that suing a major law firm was a good next step.

"I have no interest in that," I said. He was taken aback by my response. I then asked him why that was a good idea. Bob said big law firms like Greenberg were afraid of bad publicity.

"We could easily get $1.5 million out of them because they couldn't control Jack," Bob continued. "You and I can split that," he said.

I wanted no part in such a suit, I told him.

Then, Bob said his attorney wanted to interview me.

"That sounds good," I replied. "I'm so glad you got counsel. Our first step should be to get our lawyers in contact with each other," I continued. "Let's set this up right."

The Chairman agreed. "*This is good,*" I thought to myself. But Bob kept talking. "We'll do that," he said. "But now we're just two friends here," he continued, setting up whatever conversation was about to come. My anger at the fact that Bob wanted to keep talking started before the next words even came out of his mouth. "You're the one who told me the Capitol Management Foundation was paying for the trip to Scotland, right?" he asked.

I couldn't believe what I was hearing. Bob wanted to jump right in to the heart of our legal issues. Not wanting a confrontation, I decided to answer his question in a way I felt didn't constitute discussing the investigation. "All you have to do is read the papers to know the Capitol Athletic Foundation paid for the trip," I said, using the correct name for the organization. Bob paused. For a second I thought my answer was going to be enough. But it wasn't.

"No, what I'm saying is YOU'RE the person who TOLD ME the Capitol Management Foundation was paying for the trip, RIGHT? You're the one who told me the trip was ethics approved, RIGHT?" he continued. I was horrified. Bob was no longer asking me what I remembered. He was telling me what to say. The fact was that I wasn't the one who had had the initial conversations about the trip with Bob. Rudy and Jack were the two who had approached and discussed the trip with the Congressman. They were the people who did or did not tell Bob those things, as I was sure their emails would presumably verify. "*I came into the picture later,*" I screamed silently. But I didn't want to say that to Bob.

Again, I tried to avoid the conflict. "It is in your best interest and my best interest to have our lawyers talk about this shit," I said. Because of the attorney-client privilege, our lawyers could share information in ways that did not put Bob and me in jeopardy of obstructing a criminal investigation. *"Doesn't he get it?"* I said to myself. *"They talk because we can't - and shouldn't."*

Unfortunately, Bob wasn't having any of it. He blew up. Bob pointed his finger at me and started screaming. It was a blistering attack.

"You're cut off, you are not allowed in my office anymore, you are *persona non grata!*" he yelled. The volume of his tirade grew by the second. The Chairman told me that he thought I was putting Jack ahead of him. "You're a whore!" he yelled.

I grabbed Bob and pushed him back to the corner where we were talking earlier. His yelling had not only attracted the attention of his suddenly frightened team, but also the entire bar.

"Not talking is in your and my best interest," I firmly told him. "I'm not choosing Jack over you. I haven't talked to Jack in a year," I said truthfully. "Let our lawyers talk. We should not be having this conversation."

"We're just two friends talking," he said. "Why the hell do we need lawyers?"

His words stopped me in my tracks. I stopped talking. It was a powerful question, one that bounced around my head like a racquetball. *"How have we gotten here?"* I thought. *"Why do we need lawyers to talk? Were we really just two friends talking? Or did the friendship leave along with the trust?"*

"You've changed!" Bob shouted, beginning another rant.

He was right. I had changed. I assumed his comments meant that I had become greedy and power hungry, someone who was willing to sell out my own political beliefs for money and influence. And while that was true, the change that really had Bob mad was the fact that he was no longer my top priority. As he could see, his interests were now secondary to my interests. While this process had taken many months, it was a transformational shift. For a decade, our shared interests meant never needing to fundamentally cross that threshold. But that threshold had now been publicly crossed. It was a big change, one Bob didn't like.

Out of habit, I walked over to the bartender and asked him for the bill. I was leaving. The Chairman and his crew scattered throughout the bar while I paid for our drinks. Without saying goodbye to anyone, I stormed out of the restaurant. *"Nothing good could come from any more of this,"* I said to myself. Then Bob followed me out the front door. Again, it was just the two of us, but now we were outside on the sidewalk.

Normally, it takes me a long time to get angry. But by the time we were on the sidewalk, I was fuming. Bob wasn't the only one who had been drinking. "Those are issues we can not be talking about," I said, digging my finger into Bob's chest. "I get that it's fucking awkward to be saying we should let our lawyers talk," I continued. "But we can't be talking about the trip in this way. Even just the two of us." My anger grew. What I really wanted to say was, "Stop pressuring me to lie, asshole." But I didn't.

Right about then, his guys all fell out of the front door, one after another - like circus clowns. Bob looked over before unleashing his venom on them. "Get back in there!" he yelled, pointing to the front door. His attention quickly returned to me.

"I will end your career," he said with fire in his eyes. "You're a whore just like Jack."

"I'll put you on your back, old man," I thought to myself, trying desperately to remain calm and get out of there. Not to mention, attacking a member of Congress was a federal crime. Biting my lip, I turned around and walked off.

Breathing through my nose like a bull in the ring, I paced down the street, and ripped off the black tie the restaurant had given me. My phone rang. It was Bob. I let his call go to voicemail. When the phone message registered, I retrieved it immediately. Midway through Bob's profanity-laced screaming tirade, I saw a call coming in from Alison.

"Did he call my wife?" I said out loud. "Now he brings Alison in to all of this? After years of demanding that I keep her out of Ney World, he's dragging Alison into this?"

Furious, I picked up the line. "Did he call you?" I asked. He did, she replied. He had yelled at her. She said that he kept calling me a "lobby whore" and "Jack's bitch." I was livid. I told her not to pick up the phone again, and that he was probably going to call back. She told me to do the same.

It was too late. Bob was calling on the other line. I punched the button to connect to him. "What the hell are you doing?" I said.

"What the hell am I doing? Do you know what you've done to me?" he shouted.

I cut him off. "What I've done to you?" I said. "How about what you've done to me? I've spent the last nine months protecting my interests, my family's interests and my friend Bob's interests. Now you've declared me an enemy. So fuck you," I said, and hung up. We didn't talk again.

Not that he didn't keep calling. He did. That night Bob left me numerous menacing messages, including one in which he threatened to call my law firm and tell them that my work with Jack was not appropriate and that he was not happy with me. Such a call would have been devastating. Losing my job was not something I wanted, but it was already something I was prepared for in order to survive the scandal. *"Bob screaming at me must have been some sight,"* I thought to myself. *"His staff probably heard it all."*

The next day, at a little after 8:00 A.M., I got an email from Ney.

"OK-out of control misunderstanding I believe-I hope we can have a civil non-business conversation," it read.

I didn't reply. Instead I went into my lawyer's office and told his team what happened. I then wrote down everything about the previous evening.

JUNE 14, 2005
WASHINGTON, DC

President's Dinner II

THE OPTIMISM OF LAST YEAR's President's Dinner was nowhere to be found. Back then, Washington's chattering class was whispering about Bob's political ascent, his speech at the dinner, and the possibility of him becoming the next Speaker of the House. Those thoughts seemed like remnants of a different life. Watching many of the people who helped build Bob up now discuss his political descent verified that new reality. Some openly suggested that he wouldn't survive the Abramoff scandal.

During last year's fundraiser, I joked backstage with Bob and President Bush, and even zinged the Chairman with emails before his big speech. This year, after the Prime Rib incident, we weren't speaking. Granted, no one outside of Bob's closest advisers, and my inner circle, fully knew what was happening.

Still, some parts of the event remained the same. Like the year before, I waited backstage to get my picture taken with President Bush. Similarly, the photography team struggled to push the line of big donors through the picture-taking process. Few people wanted to just snap a photo and move on. I was no exception. *"This could be the last time I talk with the President,"* I told myself. *"Better make the most of it."*

The Justice Department's interest in me had intensified after my initial meeting with them. Both the U.S. Attorney's office in Miami and the Public Integrity Section in the Washington office wanted to talk further. Whether their increased interest was the result of my initial visit or the activities of Scanlon and Jack, I didn't know. What I did know was that the prosecutors wanted to discuss the Scotland trip, the Mariana Islands trip, and my work with Scanlon and Ney. The increased attention was scary, and the stress of the scandal gnawed at me constantly. Add the run-in with Bob at the Prime

Rib, and I felt like my life was a runaway train. Barring a miracle, the Justice Department was either going to force me to talk, or bring me to trial. The emotional grip of the scandal tightened further.

Even worse, Alison and I were fighting. This evening was no different. We went back and forth several times on the phone. While I waited to meet with the President, she hung up on me, and soon afterwards I hung up on her. My wife was mad because she felt that I was more interested in fixing my crumbling professional career than in fixing our crumbling marriage. I was mad because I couldn't convince her otherwise. Mainly because she was right: I was spending more time worrying about work than our relationship. But I didn't want to see it that way.

As I closed in on the President, I pushed my worries aside. I heard him talking to a supporter about Social Security reform. His voice echoed through the hallway, and triggered a memory of our first meeting. It was 1999. He was Governor Bush at the time, and I was Bob's chief of staff.

The Governor was very talkative, brash and cocky, telling me several times that I looked far too young to be a chief of staff. I was 28. He then pulled over his chief of staff, Joe Allbaugh, and introduced us. We shook hands and exchanged business cards. "Don't you think he is too young to be a chief of staff?" Bush joked. They both laughed. My response wasn't as cheerful, something the future president noticed. "I'm just kidding," he said. "It isn't that you are too young, it is that you have too much hair to be a chief of staff," he continued, pointing to Allbaugh's buzz-cut-assisted receding hairline. We all laughed at that joke. The memory brought a smile to my face.

I was one of the last people in line. The President looked annoyed, as if he had tired of taking pictures for the last hour. When I reached him, I was fully engaged in a conversation with the people around me, on the topic of professional baseball returning to the Washington, DC, area. At the time, there were two investment teams battling to purchase the Washington area's new baseball club. One would bring a team and a new stadium into the District, while the other would bring a team to Virginia. Stepping into what looked like President Bush's portable photography studio, I asked the President if he had a preference for where the new team played. As a former owner of a baseball team, Bush was interested in the issue. He smirked. His eyes squinted. Then he responded. "I'm excited about baseball coming to Washington," the President said, dodging my question.

His answer was a letdown. I was hoping for some sort of personal insight. In the meantime, the two of us positioned ourselves for the photo.

With our hands locked in an iron grip, we smiled, and the photographer snapped our photo. "Thanks Mr. President," I told him, still hoping he would answer my question. But he didn't, and I didn't have the nerve to push the issue. Instead, I made a joke to the gentleman behind me. He was stepping in to take my place next to President Bush. "You know he has a preference," I said, pointing back with my thumb toward the president. Bush laughed along with us.

Then, President Bush leaned into the two of us and said, "If you want the team to be in the District, you're going to be happy." I smiled widely, glad to hear the news. I also immediately pictured myself retelling the story to my clients, colleagues and guests back at our table. "Now that is off the record," he said.

In order to get to the main room of the convention center, I had to walk through a makeshift wall of large blue curtains that separated the back section from the rest of the room. As I pushed my way through one of the curtains, a woman announced over the loud speaker that the president would be speaking in ten minutes. The clock was ticking. With a big smile on my face, I hurriedly looked for my table. My few minutes with the President had lifted my spirits. I forgot about my relationship problems, my legal problems and the scandal. I felt lighter than I had in quite a while. Then I heard someone yell my name.

"Neil," shouted David Safavian. I turned my head to see him jump out of his seat. He looked frightened and was headed my way. Right away, I knew it was bad news. Safavian had been part of the group that traveled to Scotland. He was also the top procurement official for the White House and remained a close friend of Jacks'. Our eyes met as we shook hands. I was confused. While, I could tell something was wrong, I was still riding the high of my recent conversation with the president.

"Just hung with the Prez," I told him, still upbeat. Safavian didn't reply. Instead, he pulled me by the sleeve of my suit, and motioned me back toward the curtain I had just walked through. He looked around before speaking. "The FBI came by for a visit the other day," Safavian said. "I called Will and told him about it," he continued. Safavian seemed to assume that Heaton or Ney had told me about the conversation. They had not. The disconnect among Bob, his office and me wasn't something I wanted my White House friend to know, so I just nodded along. "I called you a few times," he said, "but didn't want to leave a message." His words reminded me that I had seen his number on an incoming call a few days earlier, when I had been on the other line.

"They asked about Bob and the trip to Scotland," he said. "And they asked me about you." My heart dropped. *"Did they know about the Prime Rib?"* I wondered. *"Did they ask about my one-year ban? Did they have my emails? How could they not? What did David tell them?"*

"I gave Will the whole story," he said. "They wanted to know what you were doing in Scotland and how much you worked with Bob." I thanked him for telling me. Other than that, I did my best not to say a word. As if a small version of my attorney were sitting on my shoulder and advising me, I kept thinking, *"Say nothing, or tell the truth."* But telling Safavian the truth, that I, too, had been in to talk with the Justice Department, and that Bob and I were not speaking with each other, did not feel like the right thing to do, so I did my best to say nothing.

"We can talk later if you want. Now isn't a good time," Safavian said.

"No doubt," I replied. "The show is about to start. Thanks, man." The two of us shook hands, wished each other luck, and parted company.

I stumbled through the crowd toward my table. For a split second, I contemplated leaving the event. But then I thought better of it. *"Be cool,"* I reminded myself. *"Be cool."* As I approached the table, the official proceedings were getting under way. I quickly told our table of clients, colleagues and guests about meeting President Bush. After a few minutes of conversation, the lights dimmed and the speeches started.

Alone with my thoughts, I pondered what to do next. My mind raced. The more I thought about it, the more I was glad that I hadn't said anything to Safavian. For months, much of what had been Team Abramoff worried about Safavian's commitment to Jack. "He is still drinking the Jack Kool-Aid," one of my colleagues said about Safavian. By then, most of us had defected Camp Abramoff. While I respected his decision to be friends with Jack, I did not want any information I shared with Safavian to be repeated to my former boss. Likewise, while our lawyers spoke to each other, my turbulent relationship with Bob meant I should not tell him anything indirectly through Safavian either.

A few weeks later, I ran into Safavian again. The two of us were standing in front of his office, next to the White House.

"I'm running to lunch," I told him. He told me that he was busy as well, before jumping into a conversation about Jack and the investigation. I had not called Safavian after our conversation at the President's Dinner and the scandal was the last thing I wanted to talk about. But I felt obliged since he had given me the heads up about his FBI interview.

"I appreciate the information on the FBI," I said.

"We all have to stick together," he replied. Like my whole body shuddered, I contemplated what to say next. I didn't want to agree with him. *"Who is the we he is talking about?"* I wondered, before awkwardly telling him I had to go. It would be the last time the two of us spoke.

"Is he talking about Jack? Or Scanlon? Or who?" I wondered, while scrambling toward my lunch. *"That is not the kind of pact I am looking to join."* Conversations like the one with Safavian reminded me just how close to the edge I remained.

The roller coaster was climbing another hill. It seemed like my career could come to an end at any moment. The potential scenarios were numerous. Senator McCain's staff could leak to the press that I had pleaded the Fifth, a reporter could call with some devastating news, or the Justice Department could make a dramatic move. Anything seemed possible. So, I was careful with my words. I did whatever I could do to project an aura of assuredness without sharing too much information. Being on message was invaluable for my personal future. Rarely did I lose focus. But it did happen.

One such time occurred after a fundraiser I hosted for Congressman John Boehner. A fellow Ohioan, he was the Chairman of the House Education and the Workforce Committee. We were at the Washington restaurant, Sam and Harry's, with about 30 lobbyists in attendance. It was the same week as the incident at the Prime Rib. No one had any idea that I had made contact with the Justice Department about the Abramoff scandal, or that my relationship with Chairman Ney was melting down. We were simply meeting to raise money for Boehner, at a typical Washington fundraiser.

I was a bundle of nerves. My career seemed to be careening to a fiery end. Yet, as the host of the fundraiser, it was important that I keep my cool. I introduced Boehner to the group, even though he didn't need an introduction. As the food was delivered and we drank our drinks, Chairman Boehner answered questions and talked with the assembled group about current events - and legislation. A hot topic was pension reform. Boehner's committee was working on a bill with the Senate to modernize the way corporate pensions are regulated. I didn't have any clients with concerns about the legislation so I just sat back and watched the debate. Boehner was great. He listened to all sides, and had no problem telling his political suitors that he was opposed to what they wanted. It reminded me of how his staffer had proactively told me "no" years earlier, when I asked for help with the garment manufacturers of the CNMI.

"This is the way the system is supposed to work," I told myself, in full intro-spective mode. *"You buy access, not results. That means you have to say no."*

I was in a precarious place. My relationship with Bob was is dire straits. And the scandal was heating up. It was in my best interest to just continue saying the least amount possible about the scandal. I knew that any hint of uncertainty or scandal intrigue would become soap opera talk by the next morning. I also knew that I did not want to be in the business of sharing inside information about what was becoming a much more serious investi-gation. But I liked Boehner. We had known each other for years. He was a leader who cared about education, his district and the country. Additionally, I was close with several members of his staff.

The irony of the moment was not lost on me. For years, Boehner, a former House leader, had been a nemesis of Majority Leader DeLay. While both conservative, the two had different approaches about governing. Also, since there are only so many leadership positions, rivalries just develop. Boehner had been a Gingrich ally who was forced from his leadership position by DeLay after Newt's fall from power. During the next seven years, Boehner had slowly resuscitated his standing within the House. His re-emergence in the Congress was impressive. He had even floated the possibility of running against DeLay for a leadership post. As a chairman, Boehner had lots of influence over important matters. But the real power in the House remained in the hands of Majority Leader DeLay and Speaker Hastert. Of course, in the last few weeks and months, it had become in-creasingly clear to me that that was all about to change.

The fact is I didn't know much about Jack's actual relationship with DeLay. But I knew they were close at one point. I also knew that Scanlon and Rudy had been senior members of DeLay's team, which was going to be a problem for the Majority Leader. There were several reasons for that. One being that Rudy's wife had been paid by an Abramoff client while he was DeLay's deputy chief of staff. This news had become common knowl-edge among Team Abramoff members. But it wasn't public yet, though I knew it would be soon. The fact that Jack employed DeLay's wife made the situation even more dire.

"I'm involved in something much bigger than me," I had said to close associates at the time. How big was sometimes hard to see. DeLay remained the most influential Member of the House of Representatives. Yet, like Bob, the political damage was building. For the past year, Jack and DeLay's relationship had been under scrutiny. Of course, scrutiny was nothing new to the Majority Leader. His brashness and unapologetic conservatism had led to lawsuits and nonstop political attacks for more than a decade. Most people assumed he would beat back the Abramoff story like he had all the others. Most people didn't know what I knew. So I pulled Boehner aside as his fundraiser came to an end.

While lobbyists streamed out of the back room that we had used for the night, the two of us pulled up chairs around a small circular table at the end of the bar.

"DeLay isn't going to make it," I told Boehner over glasses of red wine. "He won't survive the Abramoff scandal. If you want to run for leadership again, you better get ready. It could happen fast." Boehner didn't say much in response. And I didn't go into specifics. One of his staffers had told me that Boehner had been contemplating a possible return to leadership, but the Chairman did not share anything like that with me. Boehner just nodded, listened and told me thanks. We then started talking about what was happening in our shared hometown, Cincinnati. Other lobbyists and staffers joined in the conversation. Before long, Boehner got up to leave.

"Thanks," he said while patting me on the back. I wasn't sure whether he was talking about my advice or the fact that I had hosted the event. Not that I cared.

"You bet," I replied as we shook hands.

"I try not to stay out past ten," Boehner told me. Looking at my watch, I saw that it was almost 10:00 P.M on the dot. "Nothing good happens in a bar after a certain time," he continued. Boehner knew what he was talking about. His family had run a bar in Cincinnati, and he had worked his way through school mopping the bar's floors. It was a good story, he had told it to me several times over the years. It was also a good exit. We didn't need to discuss anything further. I had told him enough.

FALL, 2005
WASHINGTON, DC

An Indictment, a Deal and
the End of a Relationship

IT WAS EARLY AFTERNOON ON September 19, 2005, when I received Bob's email alerting me that David Safavian had been indicted. In bold black capital letters, the subject line read, **"FW: FORMER GSA OFFICIAL CHARGED WITH MAKING FALSE STATEMENTS, OBSTRUCTING FEDERAL INVESTIGATION."** Before I even finished reading the headline, adrenaline began to surge through my body. *"Safavian?"* I asked myself incredulously. *"He is the first one they are going after? Really?"*

Included in Bob's message was a statement outlining the Justice Department's indictment. The government's announcement said Safavian was "arrested today based on a three-count criminal complaint filed at federal court in Washington, DC."

"Holy shit," I said, and got up to shut my office door. Seated again, I continued scrolling through the announcement. I couldn't believe it. Reading about Safavian's arrest and indictment was horrible. There was nothing good about the news. I worried about how the indictment could affect me, and then I worried about Safavian. I felt like someone had walked into the room and sucker-punched me in the back of the head. And it only got worse.

The government's document cited Safavian's position as the top staffer at the General Services Administration. "The affidavit filed in support of the criminal complaint alleges that from May 16, 2002, until January 10, 2004, Safavian served as Chief of Staff at the GSA. During that time he allegedly aided a Washington D.C. lobbyist in the lobbyist's attempts to acquire GSA-controlled property in and around Washington, D.C. In August 2002, this lobbyist allegedly took Safavian and others on a golf trip to Scotland."

Mention of the trip sent my growing panic into overdrive. *"Scotland and properties around Washington?* They were talking about the projects I worked on with Jack. I couldn't take my eyes off the screen in front of me.

"According to the affidavit, Safavian concealed the fact that the lobbyist had business before GSA prior to the August 2002 golf trip, and that Safavian was aiding the lobbyist in his attempts to do business with the GSA," the Justice Department's announcement continued. "The false statements and obstruction of the investigation charges relate to Safavian's statements to a GSA ethics officer and the GSA-OIG (inspector general) that the lobbyist had no business with GSA prior to the August 2002 golf trip."

I read and re-read the department's statement. It seemed the FBI was saying that Safavian had told a GSA ethics official that Jack had no work pending before his agency, and therefore it was no conflict for Safavian to take part in the Scotland trip. The FBI was also alleging that Safavian lied about his contacts with Jack three more times after this initial statement to the GSA ethics officer. The first was during a 2003 investigation by an internal inspector general who was looking into the trip after an anonymous caller to a government hotline had complained about Safavian. The second involved a letter Safavian had sent to Senator McCain's Committee on Indian Affairs, in response to the committee's questions. The third alleged that Safavian had obstructed justice during the FBI's interview with him in May 2005. That was that FBI interview Safavian had mentioned to me during the President's Dinner. I shuddered at the thought of being associated with such a conversation, and began to realize how bad the situation was.

The more I read, the more my mind returned to not only the conversations I had with Safavian at the President's Dinner, but also the conversations we had in Scotland, and the one we had a few weeks ago in front of the White House. I could see Safavian telling the FBI that Jack wasn't doing any business with GSA. Because of their friendship, I could even see Safavian convincing himself that such a claim was somehow true. But I knew that was wrong. My work with Safavian and Jack leading up to the Scotland trip was unquestionably business.

With a scrum of different thoughts running through my head, I tried to put what was happening to Safavian in context. His comments to the FBI and the work Jack and I did with GSA preceding the trip reminded me of those anxious moments when the *Washington Post* first reported on the Scotland trip. Bob's spokesman told the paper the trip to Scotland was a work trip. Safavian's spokesperson said it was a personal trip. I did my best to stay quiet, understanding the pull both men were feeling. Bob needed the trip to be official, and David needed it to be personal. And since they were both public officials, they each needed to justify their involvement publicly. Neither man liked the other's answer. Each had his own version of the truth, and being loyal meant agreeing with one or the other. Such blind loyalty was not something I was giving to anyone, anymore. Not that I didn't care about Safavian, Bob or Jack. I did. In part, that is why I was so sad.

"What hell was he doing?" I asked myself when I read about the charges. "David has kids. Why not just shut up? Don't tell me he is still covering for Jack. No wonder he wants us all to stick together."

My anger quickly subsided. "Who am I to say anything about him?" I thought. "I could be next. And then what?" My outlook shifted. "Why Safavian?" I wondered. "Is the government trying to send a message?" It looked to me like their message was loud and clear: Tell the truth or pay the price. Thinking about the price Safavian was already paying scared me even more, to the point that every sentence I read made me flinch further.

"A complaint is only a charge and is not evidence of guilt," the Justice Department's release continued. "A defendant is entitled to a fair trial in which it will be the government's burden to prove guilt beyond a reasonable doubt."

"A trial?" Until that point, I hadn't put it all together. But, of course, a trial was a possibility. Safavian had been indicted and arrested. "What am I going to tell my clients about this?" I wondered. "And my firm?"

Most of my clients had met Safavian over the years, or, at least knew of my work with him on their behalf. I had to tell them something. For months, my clients had hung in there with me. They had stuck with me through the McCain hearings and the unfavorable news articles. But would they stay through this? The news of Safavian's indictment could be the tipping point for my clients. An indictment was different from bad publicity or a hearing. Cops were making arrests. People could be going to jail.

I got in touch with my clients. Word of Safavian's situation would spread fast. It was better for them to hear the news from me than from someone else. But what would I say? I couldn't tell them the whole truth. All they had to do was read the indictment to see that Safavian's issues revolved around the Scotland trip, and his association with Team Abramoff. If they knew how close I was to the crux of the case against Safavian, they would probably fire me. But I had to do some kind of damage control. I started by telling my clients the basics, that Safavian had been indicted. I then said that I couldn't talk about the specifics of the investigation. That lack of forthrightness wasn't new; I had been telling them that for months. Still, my worried clients demanded more than the canned response they had heard before.

I shed the most favorable light on the story I could, based on what was in the public domain. Instead of telling my clients that a trial would be horrific for their business, I told them that I doubted Safavian would even go to trial. "He is probably going to help them in their case against Jack," I said. I also told them that while I was shocked that he was being arrested, it was important to remember that his arrest had to do with how he handled the investigation, not the underlying issues of the scandal. So they had no reason to worry. I found myself in survival mode, willing to say whatever I needed to in order to get through the day. If I could do that, I figured, I could get through to tomorrow. And then on to the next day. At some point, I figured, things would get better. My rationalization knew no bounds.

A half hour after Bob's initial email, he sent me another message. This one had a much different tone. "Let's establish a commune in Wyoming-do white water rafting trips for hire-play some poker-no tv's or radio-wives can make homemade ice cream and we can sing 'Colorado high, rocky mountain.'" Like me, Bob could see that Safavian's indictment had changed things. Our relationship had changed as well.

In the weeks following the incident at the Prime Rib, I had not replied to Bob's emails or phone calls. His staff became the bridge between us and told me that Bob missed his friend Neil. He wanted to talk again, they said. I replied with similar sentiments. But inside I was torn about what to believe. Based on what I was hearing from friends throughout Washington, Bob was pleading ignorance about all things Abramoff and squarely blaming me for what was happening. That made me think that Bob's effort to get back together was less about our friendship than about appearances. I stalled, as it turned out, for my own selfish reasons. .

The few weeks of navigating the scandal without having to worry about Bob's immediate interests made me realize it would be easier to just let the relationship go. I liked not worrying about how Bob would react to what I was doing or saying.

But I missed him. And the awkwardness of being estranged from Ney World was uncomfortable. Professionally, I felt like my clients were being short-changed by my unwillingness to engage the office I was presumably closest with. Such silence was bad for business. Legally, it also looked much better for the two of us to be seen together. There was no reason to encourage gossip. It just led to more questions. Eventually, after the President's Dinner, Bob and I reconnected.

Our breakthrough occurred at a memorial service for one of Bob's former staffers. The service took place in the House Administration Committee room. After the service, I hung out and drank beers with the Congressman. We talked as if nothing had happened between us. It was awkward not discussing our issues, but the approach was something we both chose. Neither of us wanted to start another fight. Getting together represented a step forward. However, my bond with Bob was never the same. The trust that had built up between us over the years was nearly gone. We both felt at ease with our public reunification. Neither of us had to worry about some sort of personal drama erupting out of the blue. Still, underneath our reconciliation was a harsh reality: Bob was looking out for himself, and so was I.

The awkward relationship I had with Bob symbolized the increasing awkwardness of the scandal overall. With each news story and legal announcement, I became closer to what we on the Hill called "radioactive," meaning someone nobody wanted to be associated with. The process was an evolution. For the first year of the scandal, in fact, I didn't even consider myself radioactive. I would call myself contagious. There was hope that things would get better. Slowly, though, I morphed from contagious to radioactive, which assumed a longer shelf-life for my pariah status. It took me a while to accept this new identity.

The change appeared in different places and in different times. Once, for instance, after an unusually nasty series of stories appeared about my role in the SunCruz Casino sale, I noticed several contacts on the Hill behaving differently. When one friend went out of his way to make sure I used his direct phone number, instead of a general office number, it didn't register as anything unusual. But by the end of the week, when several other contacts had also told me not to call the main lines of their offices, I could see that something was happening. They didn't want their colleagues to know I was talking with them. I was becoming radioactive.

Some of the changes were more pronounced. One incident occurred when I got onto the Washington subway system. As the doors closed behind me, I found myself standing next to a friend. It was about the same time as my direct vs. main phone line discussions. We shook hands and said hello to each other. My friend then spent the entire time between Metro stops looking around to see if there was anyone else we knew in the car. He was clearly nervous, and our conversation was incredibly uncomfortable. I felt bad for him. When the doors opened, he darted off, saying, "I'm going to walk off my lunch through the Mall. Have a good one." I told him the same, while laughing, since it was ten degrees outside, and he was more than a mile from his office - without a coat.

Making the situation more bearable was the fact that several of my lobbying colleagues were having similar experiences. We coped with the scandal together. Lobbyist Kevin Ring and I believed that we could either laugh or cry. Ring and I chose to laugh.

Ring's former boss, Congressman John Doolittle, was also being investigated for his relationship with Team Abramoff. Since Ring and I were both "lawyered" up, we did our best not to talk about the specifics of the investigation. But it wasn't always easy. Usually our "laugh or cry" conversations stemmed from the uneasiness of a breaking story in the media - like Safavian's indictment. Ring and I knew what it was like to talk in code about the scandal with our clients. In order to cope with the stress of not telling our closest professional allies what was really happening, we often engaged in a bit of role-play. The game went something like this:

"Is everything OK?" the "client" would ask.

"Sure, why wouldn't it be?" the "lobbyist" replied. The roles of lobbyist and client were easily exchanged between us, but the conversation remained pretty much the same no matter who played what role.

"Because you were mentioned in the paper," the client responded. "What is going on with all that?"

"Oh, you want to actually talk about the investigation.," the lobbyist chuckled. "Well, I can't talk about that right now. But everything is fine. I can have my attorney call you if you would like." Then Ring and I would laugh hysterically at the irony of it all. The very idea that a client's nerves could be settled by a chat with their closed-mouth lobbyist's lawyer was ludicrous. "Nothing breeds confidence about things being fine like telling someone to speak with your attorney," the two of us would joke.

We laughed for as long as we could keep the act going. "Here is the name of my attorney, but please keep the conversation short because this investigation is breaking my bank," the "lobbyist" would carry on. "But seriously, no worries." It was good material until the seriousness of our situation rose again to the front of our minds, and we stopped laughing.

While I was dealing with the discomfort of being an outcast, things were worse for Mike Scanlon. He was going to jail. Two months after

Safavian's indictment, Scanlon pleaded guilty to criminal public corruption charges. Scanlon's decision to admit that he bribed members of Congress was an explosive moment in the scandal. His guilty plea showed how serious the Abramoff investigation had become. If Safavian's indictment had verified that an investigation was under way, Scanlon's plea presented the public with a road map of where the scandal was headed. It didn't look good.

Scanlon's guilty plea was much more serious than Safavian's indictment, yet I felt less frantic. In part, that was because I was becoming numb to the scandal. I was also beginning to more clearly understand the investigation, due to my increased contact with the Justice Department. The department's ongoing inquiries helped to reframe my understanding of what was happening. This simultaneously scared me and soothed me. It scared me because I could see that the investigation was every bit as serious as some of us feared. The contact with the Justice Department soothed me, in contrast, because it provided some semblance of certainty - something that Scanlon's plea intensified.

For months, I had hoped that Jack was the investigation's top target. Such a theory meant that law enforcement's digging and questioning would primarily be geared toward charging Abramoff. The money he and Scanlon were paid by the tribes would have represented the crux of the case. But it wasn't the only possible scenario. The other theory was that the real targets of the Justice Department's case were public officials. This possibility was more problematic. It would mean that the government was looking at Bob, and also at me.

Safavian's indictment seemed to verify the theory that public officials were the real targets. This was also bolstered by the gossip that Jack, if he chose to cooperate, would probably turn on Bob first, in part because of Ney's unrelenting attacks on Abramoff following the McCain hearing. Most other elected officials mentioned in the scandal chose not to berate Jack in that manner. But there had remained a glimmer of hope that all that talk was wrong. With Scanlon's guilty plea, however, any idea that Jack was the final target of the investigation ended.

All it took was one look at Scanlon's plea to understand very clearly that the Justice Department's real target were members of Congress. Members of Congress like Bob. In fact, Scanlon's agreement with the Justice Department read like an indictment of Ney, or as the charging documents called him, "Representative One." Specific names of innocent people are not used in charging documents, even if the government believes they will eventually be found guilty. The plea outlined gifts, trips and donations that

Bob received from Scanlon and Jack, who was referred to as "Lobbyist A." It also outlined the alleged legislative favors and official actions given by Bob's office in return for the gifts, trips, meals and donations.

Scanlon's guilty plea was full of legal jargon, containing words that would soon become commonplace to those of us involved in the scandal. In addition to Bob and Jack's aliases, the tickets, trips, free meals and donations that built the foundation of our corrupt relationship were described as, "a stream of things of value." The assistance provided by Bob's office to Jack's clients was described as, "official actions." The conspiracy was therefore described simply as "official actions granted in exchange for a stream of things of value."

The specifics of Scanlon's plea painted a brutal picture of not only Bob, Jack and Scanlon, but also of me. "For Representative One and his staff," the agreement said, the stream of things of value included, "all-expense-paid trips, including a trip to the Commonwealth of the Northern Mariana Islands in 2000, a trip to the Super Bowl in Tampa, Fla., in 2001, and a golf trip to Scotland in 2002." Bob and his staff, including me, also took "numerous tickets for entertainment, including concerts and sporting events in the Washington, D.C., area," and were provided "box suites and food at various sport and concert venues and at a restaurant in the Washington, D.C., area," the plea continued. Reading such words made me cringe. Seeing it all on paper made my worst fears come alive.

Signatures was a prime example. The plea agreement benignly said that "Representative One" and his staff received "regular meals and drinks" at the restaurant. On the surface, it may not have seemed so bad. Lots of lobbyists take lots of public officials out for meals and drinks. Therefore, from the outside looking in, those words could have been as harmless as a few staff and elected officials getting a couple hundred dollars worth of meals over a few years. But the words meant more than that to me. I knew the facts, and they were much worse than it sounded. I hosted Bob and his senior staff at Signatures all the time. They also ate and drank for free at Jack's restaurant when I wasn't there, which was very often. As bad as the facts themselves was the reality that our arrangement was easily verifiable.

My email chatter with Bob and his staff had been almost non-stop. We had forwarded stupid jokes to each other, engaged in locker room banter and talked about current events, all of which tracked our actions. Our email conversations, even if they didn't relate to an official action, could easily verify that we were all at the restaurant together. From there, the credit card receipts I submitted to be repaid by my clients could be used to verify how much money was spent on any given night. During some nights, our partying went into the thousands of dollars. It didn't paint a pretty picture. Each line in Scanlon's plea agreement was laced with similarly haunting prose.

For me, the most alarming piece of Scanlon's plea deal involved how much his guilty behavior was being publicly associated with Ney. No other members of Congress were mentioned in his plea, a deal in which Scanlon was agreeing that he bribed elected officials. The basis for the charge he pleaded guilty to included numerous projects that Scanlon didn't even work on with Bob and me. One such example was the Foxcom Wireless project, in which Ney and I helped steer a wireless telephone contract to Jack's client - a client which I later managed as a member of Team Abramoff, and one that I don't ever remember associating with Scanlon, in any way. Yet there it was. It was like the Department of Justice was sending me a message through Scanlon's plea. As I would learn later, that is exactly what they were doing. The government wanted me to know that the investigation was coming my way, and it was time for me to think about whose side I was on.

Within minutes of the news breaking about Scanlon's guilty plea, Bob's office put out a statement. "Whenever Representative Ney took official action - actions similar to those taken by elected representatives every day as part of the normal, appropriate government process - he did so based on his best understanding of what was right and not based on any improper influence."

The words rung hollow. I understood the need for a statement and appreciated how he tried to lessen the blow of Scanlon's plea. But when I looked at the two documents and asked myself which one was more true, it wasn't Bob that I sided with. I was frightened by what it all meant, and continued to want it to just go away. Yet I also was beginning to accept the reality of the situation. Choices affecting my life and the lives of those around me were approaching. At home, Alison was hurting. The vision she had of our future was turned upside down. Everything from our financial security to the plans we had for a family were impacted by the high-profile legal proceedings. Our relationship suffered.

Then there was my relationship with Bob. The Justice Department's decision to "name" him in their official documents meant he was being targeted by their investigation, which meant I could no longer talk with him.

Our last conversation revolved around Scanlon's plea. Bob sounded scared. My heart broke for him. He stammered around for a bit before nervously telling me, "I'm Representative One," as if that needed to be said. The two of us wouldn't speak again for years. After Scanlon's plea, only our attorneys would communicate with each other. The boiling pot of the scandal was heating up further.

"Jack must be reeling," I thought to myself at that point. Not that I cared too much what he was feeling. Among reporters and lobbyists following the scandal, the general consensus was that Scanlon's decision to, "Flip," legal jargon for agreeing to cooperate with the government - was incredibly bad news for Jack. His business partner was now sharing information about him with the government. Even worse was the fact that it was now in Scanlon's best interest to do whatever he could to bring Abramoff down. None of us who knew him thought that Scanlon would do anything but ruthlessly help the Justice Department. As one colleague said, "That man will say anything to stay out of jail." The ground was shifting under me yet again.

JANUARY 3, 2006
WASHINGTON, DC

Jack Pleads Guilty

THE FIRST EMAIL ARRIVED AT 10:52 AM. It was from a reporter at the *Cleveland Plain Dealer*. "Subject: RE: feedback on Abramoff guilty plea.."

"Hi Neil. As you're probably aware, Jack Abramoff is pleading guilty to a bunch of things today and you appear to figure prominently in those charges. I am attaching a copy of Abramoff's plea. You seem to be identified as "Staffer B." I would like to get a comment from you on all of this, or at least get something from your attorney. Please email me back or call me."

I had worked with the reporter for years. She had followed the case closely, and was correct to surmise that I was aware of Jack's guilty plea. I replied immediately, referring her to my attorney Tim Broas.

Just as quickly, she replied back. "Thanks. And good luck."

Tim was already busy on my case. And about to get busier. Three minutes later another reporter contacted me. This one was from Bloomberg News. We did not know each other, but he had a similar message.

"Abramoff Criminal Information," read the subject line. This was followed by, "The criminal information filed against Jack Abramoff today in U.S. District Court mentions a "staffer B" who formerly worked as chief of staff to "Representative 1," which has already been identified as Representative Bob Ney. You are the only former associate of Jack Abramoff who meets the description. Are you "Staffer B," who has been accused of contacting his former employer within the one-year cooling-off period? Have you been contacted by Justice Department investigators or anyone else involved in the investigation?"

The media onslaught was just beginning. While Safavian's indictment and Scanlon's plea were big news, compared with the Abramoff plea agreement, they turned out to be small blips on the media Richter Scale. Jack's trip to the courthouse was like an earthquake. It took the scandal to an entirely different level.

The next morning I was awakened by a 6:00 AM phone call. It was a neighbor telling me that a camera crew had pulled up across the street. Days later, Jack would be on the cover of *Time* magazine, under the headline, *"The Man Who Bought Washington."* Being named in Jack's plea agreement ended my lobbying career. Within hours, the wings propelling my faltering flight melted, and with them, my struggle to stay afloat come to an abrupt end. It was a quick fall. In the blink of an eye, my career and political identity crashed into the sun. Life as I had known it was over.

Jack's guilty plea included a wide array of transgressions. None of them were necessarily news by that point. What was new, though, was Jack's decision to plead guilty, and how that impacted the ongoing scandal. As the front page Washington Post story said the next day, January 4, 2006:

"Jack Abramoff, the once-powerful lobbyist at the center of a wide-ranging public corruption investigation, pleaded guilty to fraud, tax evasion and conspiracy to bribe public officials in a deal that requires him to provide evidence about members of Congress," the story said.

"The plea deal could have enormous legal and political consequences for the lawmakers on whom Abramoff lavished luxury trips, skybox fundraisers, campaign contributions, jobs for their spouses, and meals at Signatures, the lobbyist's upscale restaurant," continued the Post piece.

Bob was the only Congressman mentioned in the official filings. But there were hints of the Abramoff-DeLay relationship mentioned between the lines. The press reported that Jack was providing information to the government about DeLay, and half a dozen other House and Senate members. The media also said he was providing insight into their investigation of Congressional staffers, lobbyists, Interior Department workers and other executive branch officials.

Under the terms of his plea agreement, Jack was looking at a prison sentence of between 9 and 11 years. Additionally, he owed tens of millions of dollars in restitution to the tribes. I was flabbergasted. *"Ten years,"* I said to myself. *"People die, get married and have children in that time period."* I spent the day in a daze.

In jargon similar to that in Safavian's and Scanlon's legal documents, the crux of Jack's public corruption charges were said to involve "the providing of a stream of things of value," to elected officials in exchange for "official actions." Within the area where Jack and I worked together, this included free meals, drinks and trips for Bob, a job offer to me, and payment of

$50,000 to Tony Rudy's wife. In exchange, the documents outlined, Bob, Rudy and I took corresponding official actions. There was also information pertaining to Jack's work with other officials throughout the government. Many of the facts were familiar to those of us in Washington who had been following the investigation. But among the people learning about it for the first time, the reaction was explosive.

Nearly a dozen prosecutors from the Bush administration's Justice Department marched out to a podium after Jack's courtroom appearance. One after another they gathered, in their suits and professional attire. To the gleeful prosecutors, civil servants and political appointees in attendance, it was the culmination of several years worth of work, and a point of pride they could point to for the rest of their career. Nabbing Jack Abramoff was a big deal. The news networks broke into their regular programming to cover the press conference.

Assistant Attorney General Alice Fisher spoke for the Bush administration, as well as for the non-partisan law enforcement professionals within the Justice Department. "Government officials and governmental action are not for sale," she said bluntly. It was a stock line, but one that struck me forcefully. Watching a leader of my own government talk about Jack and me in such harsh tones felt surreal. It also told me that the reports of a massive investigation had merit. The President's team was drawing a line in the sand. Fisher promised to follow the conspiracy wherever it led. "The corruption scheme with Mr. Abramoff is very extensive," she said, adding that the assembled group was committed to moving on wrongdoers as quickly as possible. Her words made me nervous. With the focus of the investigation no longer on Jack, that meant their attention was turning toward Bob. For the rest of Washington, though, the focus remained squarely on the man of the hour: Jack Abramoff.

At the White House, Bush spokesman Scott McClellan answered questions during his press briefing about the scandal and the President's reaction to news of Jack's guilty plea. McClellan immediately tried to distance President Bush from any wrong-doing. He called Jack's behavior "outrageous" and said that he "needs to be held to account, and he needs to be punished." The administration had made prosecuting political corruption a priority within their Justice Department. The 40 percent increase in the number of prosecutions since Bush's first election seemed to verify such a commitment. Yet, at the same time, the people involved in the Abramoff scandal were some of President Bush's top political allies. And they were now under siege. The White House press secretary found himself trying to explain that Jack, one of President Bush's biggest fundraisers, wasn't that close to the administration. It was a delicate balancing act.

Jack's plea led newscasts across the country. Since he was no longer the target of the investigation, the media's focus quickly pivoted to those elected officials who were potentially in trouble. Some of the early news reports pinned the number of those officials at more than a dozen. The narrative and facts were so damning they would soon cause Tom DeLay to resign from Congress, just as I had predicted to Congressman Boehner months earlier. Very quickly, the Abramoff scandal was no longer only a Washington story. It became a national one. News outlets and entertainment programs like *Inside Edition, People Magazine* and late-night comedians started reporting and commenting on the story. Actor George Clooney even mentioned Jack during his speech at the Academy Awards.

Trying to figure out who was in trouble turned into a Washington parlor game. This new dynamic increased people's knowledge of the scandal as well. In Ohio, that meant more calls and questions for my family. "Do you know Jack Abramoff?" people would ask my parents and those closest to me. "Is Neil going to be OK? Is he going to jail?" My anxiety rose every time I thought about the questions my family was now facing. It was horrible.

In contrast, the Democrats on Capitol Hill saw the Abramoff scandal as an opportunity. They smelled political blood. For them, Jack's guilty plea was a gift, one to be used on the campaign trail. If I had been in their shoes, I would have reacted the same way. The battle lines between the parties, which had been developing for months, solidified quickly. The Democrats began to attack the Republicans for operating within what they called "a culture of corruption." It was effective rhetoric. The charge stuck. Republicans with any connection to Team Abramoff were labeled corrupt and questioned by the media. In the process, I became the very symbol of corruption that had galvanized me against Washington 12 years earlier. After all, corruption has more to do with power than ideology. Instead of the corruption occurring mostly on the Democratic side, this time it was occurring on the Republican side.

Members of Congress who received campaign contributions from Jack, the team or our clients, became a target of the media's feeding frenzy. To distance themselves from the scandal, they started returning the money. President Bush was one of the first to take action. He told a press room full of reporters that he didn't remember Jack, and then donated the contributions he received from the lobbyist to a charity helping American Indian children. Hundreds of elected officials followed suit.

The increased attention made me uncomfortable. So did my new name,

"Staffer B." Over the years, like lots of people, I had collected my share of nicknames. Most of them I liked. I was called Volzie, Cornelius, Big Neil and Trucker Jr., the last being a remnant of one of my brother's high school nicknames. I was happy to wear these nicknames. Not so my newest one. The name Staffer B symbolized the shame I felt and the sadness that was all around me. From the minute I first heard the name I hated it, and knew I always would. It was like a bad tattoo, an indelible stain. I felt an urgent need to wash it away. But like the stupid decisions that name represented, undoing it wasn't possible. It was a feeling I presumed Jack knew all too well.

"I plead guilty, Your Honor," he had said in court. His words were unequivocal. He would have to live with them for the rest of his life. As I read the story of the proceedings online, I pictured my former boss standing before the judge. "*What is he really thinking?*" I wondered. "*Who else is in the courtroom? Does he ever think about how this scandal has impacted me? Has he regained all that weight he lost?*" My somewhat random questions suggested that I was still struggling to come to grips with the enormity of what was happening, of what I was involved with. I thought about Scotland, the CNMI and our work together. "*How quickly things change,*" I told myself, fighting any urge I had to feel sorry for Jack. I was still angry with him. "*You fueled my worst desires. I am not giving you any pity today. My life is falling apart, why should I give a shit about you?*" Then I read Jack's comments.

"All of my remaining days, I will feel tremendous sadness and regret for my conduct and for what I have done," he had said to Judge Ellen Huvelle. "I only hope that I can merit forgiveness from the Almighty and from those I have wronged or caused to suffer."

As over-the-top as it sounded, reading how Jack publicly wished to make amends with God made me take back my selfish promise not to feel for him. "*Jack wouldn't disrespect God at such an important moment,*" I thought. There were a lot of things he could have said, and probably did say, which I would have felt skeptical about, but I had no doubt that he took his religion seriously. He always had. Because I knew how Jack felt about his faith, his words took on new meaning to me. I felt like he was apologizing to the tribes, to his family, to our country and to me personally. Regardless, my moment of compassion didn't last long. The professional and personal wounds I was still trying to address remained very raw. "*Snap out of it, Neil,*" I said to myself. "*You don't know what is going on in his head.*"

As he always had been, to me, Jack was an enigma. A Rorschach test. Like others, I saw what I wanted to see. The years away from my former boss had not clarified my questions about who he really was. His ruthless business persona had been put on full display by all the leaked emails in the press and the Congressional hearings, yet somehow I was still able to sense real humility in him. That was how it had always been. He would run over our competition like they were sub-human, but be kind-hearted and great company to me and my family. I used to think his ruthlessness was just business and his commitment to free market principles. But I was no longer convinced that was the case. *"What ultimately made him do it?"* I wondered. *"Greed? Arrogance? Confusion?"* I didn't know.

The more I thought about it, however, the more I realized that my time away from Jack had clarified one thing. The work we did for most of our clients wasn't fundamentally about advancing our political ideology. We said it was, and even tried to convince ourselves that was the case. But at it's core, our work was about making money. Telling people that we were advancing our conservative revolution or operating like an extended wing of the Republican Party was a part of that process, but not our underlying motive. Most of the conservatives on Team Abramoff, myself included, believed that the tribes we represented would be better off if their members abandoned the overly socialistic culture of American reservations, one built around government assistance and victim hood. But the talk about conservatism was a secondary concern.

For instance, Jack would argue, and I would parrot, that paying politicians to give the tribes millions of dollars in federal money was a perfectly acceptable conservative practice. Even worse, we worked to deny other tribes access to the same gaming markets as our clients, in the name of encouraging the free market to work. But by using the government to block our clients' competition, we represented the antithesis of the free market. Our work was a collusion of big business and big government, the kind of much bigger government that is available to those who can pay to rig the rules in their favor.

The more I thought about my work with Jack, the more confused and angry I got. *"If he and Scanlon weren't so greedy, none of this would have happened,"* I said to myself. *"Or would it? I fueled Jack's selfish desires too. I could have said no. None of this would have happened to me if I had simply changed my behavior."*

"But they led the charge." I continued my internal debate. *"They knew everything, and made the money. I was just a bit player."* It felt good to cast blame at Jack and Scanlon. But it wasn't so simple. I was a Staff Director and a lobbyist with power, not a bit player. Accepting that truth wasn't easy. I had a lot of assistance. For instance, my law firm helped.

Like most major firms, my employer was full of former federal prosecutors. They knew all about plea agreements. And with a team at the firm in direct contact with my attorney, they also had an understanding of my specific situation. Like my clients and my colleagues, the firm had stood by me through some tough times. But being named in Jack's plea agreement was too much of a risk for anyone to take. The firm's view was pretty straightforward. Having been officially named in the Abramoff plea, it was likely that I would soon either be indicted and go to trial, or enter a plea agreement with the government. Neither option was acceptable to them, so I offered to resign. My lobbying career had lasted less than three years. I was now a 35-year-old man without a job.

The next morning, when I woke up, everything felt different. My career was gone, and my reputation was ruined. The high-profile news added even more stress to my marriage. At the same time, the investigation was still staring me in the face. While the public perception of the scandal was changing, for me, the fundamentals of the investigation itself had not altered one bit. Jack's plea had merely raised the public stakes of the decision I was already pondering.

After Scanlon's plea, my contact with the Justice Department had increased. Since his agreement read like an indictment of Bob and me, it would have been stupid not to engage them further. Within days of Scanlon's deal, the newspapers started suggesting that an Abramoff deal was possible, even imminent, according to unnamed sources familiar with the investigation. Part of what Jack was discussing, according to these sources, involved my negotiations with him about a job while I was still on Capitol Hill. Reading those reports were scary. I felt vulnerable to the charges that I had let Jack's job offer influence the help I gave him - because they were true. I *had* let the job offer influence the help I gave Team Abramoff. Since that was the case, I decided not to go in for interviews on that topic or other general topics that put me in harms way. It didn't make sense to go in to the Justice Department and admit something that could be so central in a potential case against me.

Eventually, however, just sitting there waiting for the government to indict me, or the Congressman and me, became unbearable. I began to contemplate cutting a deal with the government, as the Justice Department had suggested. I dug into the process of plea agreements and becoming a cooperating witness for the government. Specifically, I looked into the prospect of agreeing to some sort of charge related to my violation of the one-year ban. Based on email traffic alone, that seemed to be my most provable infraction. Also, there was precedent for such a deal.

Richard Holbrooke, President Clinton's Ambassador to the United Nations, had negotiated a deal with the Justice Department a few years earlier concerning a similar situation. According to the press, a State Department Inspector General had found that Holbrooke had met with at least one former colleague within months of his resignation from the State Department to discuss business involving his new employer, the investment firm Credit Suisse First Boston of New York. After some negotiations, according to media reports, Holbrooke agreed to pay a fine without any actual agreement that he had violated the ban.

Thinking I could get off so easy was naïve. My past bad choices had created a whole new set of bad choices to address. I consulted with Alison on what to do. She was supportive. After a lot of contemplation, we decided to make a move. My hope was that I could get a deal in which I agreed to a misdemeanor charge of breaking my one-year ban. In return, I would agree to help the government in its investigation.

Cooperating would mean an end to my career and many of my friendships, specifically with Bob and those people who were close to him. But it could also stave off an economically and emotionally expensive trial. The implications were confusing. I thought about it for months. Would cooperating make me a rat? Or a whistleblower? Was I willing to cooperate because I was guilty or because it was best for me? Or was it a little bit of both? On the other hand, if I decided to fight the charges, how would I pay for a trial without a job? What impact would the stress of a trial have on my Dad, whose troubled nervous system needed to avoid stress, and on all my family? No matter what path I chose, my marriage and many of my relationships had already suffered immeasurably.

After much contemplation, two things were clear. I was guilty, and getting a deal was in my best interest. So I decided to go for it. *"I can live with a misdemeanor,"* I told myself. *"Lay low for a year or two, and I'll be fine."* Within a year, I had gone from hoping the whole investigation would blow over, to hoping I could plead guilty to a career-ending public corruption charge.

Unfortunately, the Justice Department told me they couldn't support such a deal. My crimes were too serious to get off with an agreement like that, I was told. My heart broke. Hearing the news was one of the many low points of the scandal. Alison and I stared out the back window of our house, hoping for a miracle. I kept thinking. Could I accept a deal that included pleading to a felony?

By this point, Christmas was approaching. Alison and I were planning to be with my family in Ohio. A day or so before we left, I looked up the word *felon* in the *American Heritage Dictionary*. One definition read:

Fel*on (fel'en) n. 1. Law. One who has committed a felony. 2. Archaic. An evil person. -felon adj. Archaic. Evil, cruel (Middle English feloun, from Old French felon, wicked, a wicked person, from mideavil Latin fello, felon, possibly or Germanic origin)

"*An evil person?*" I asked myself. "*Is that what I am?*"

My family gathered in Cleveland, at my grandmother's house. It would be the last time I saw Gram. We all knew she was ailing and possibly near death. Nonetheless, it was a great trip. In the house my grandparents had built with their own hands in the 1940s, we played board games with my brother's three-year-old daughter, Lilly, and laughed into the wee hours of the evening. Gram had a wonderful time. During our last meal together, I brought out a plate of desserts from the kitchen. She struggled to decide whether she wanted the cake or the pie.

"Oh, I'll have both," Gram said with a laugh. "Why not, right?" she continued.

"Yeah, Gram, why not," I replied. We looked at each other, and laughed some more. In those few days, being at Gram's made me feel like everything was like it had always been. But it wasn't.

The next morning I told my parents, my brother, and his wife, Casey, that I would likely soon be pleading guilty to a felony conviction. It was a hard conversation. Tears dripped out of my eyes as I told my family the news. They were surprised by the rapid deterioration of my legal situation, and were nervous to second-guess my decision. Within minutes, they were the ones crying. I hated letting my family down. But they were supportive, and told me to do the right thing. "Just be honest," my parents said. "We love you."

A few minutes before leaving, as I scurried around packing the car, I overheard my brother and his wife talking to Lilly. I was in the hallway so they didn't see me. "Uncle Neil needs an extra long hug when he leaves, Lilly, so make sure to give him a real good hug and tell him that you love him, OK?"

I crouched down and put my hand on the wall to catch my breath. Hearing such a conversation almost broke me. I wasn't used to needing help. The last decade of my life had positioned me as a man who provided things for my family and weighed in on major decisions. For their most recent Washington visit, I had gotten my brother and his family into the White House to see President Bush's departure on Marine One. "*My role in the family is that of the guy who helps, not who needs help,"* I thought. Breathing slowly, I composed myself, and with the best fake smile I could muster, I bounded around the corner. "Hey guys," I said, with my arms open wide. Lilly jumped against my chest.

"Mom told me to give you an extra long hug," she said. We all laughed.

"Your mom's right," I replied, pulling Lilly tight so no one could see the tear trickling down the side of my face. I mouthed the words, "Thank you," to my brother and his wonderful wife. It wouldn't be the last time that I leaned on my family for help.

Keeping It Simple

I SAT WITH MY TWO LAWYERS in a small deli across the street from the Justice Department. From my seat, I could see the side door we would soon be walking through. A mammoth pile of fried mushrooms sat on my plate. I popped them in my mouth one by one. The restaurant's breakfast crowd walked around as we talked. For the first few minutes, we discussed my ongoing legal issues. Then our conversation turned personal. It was a moment of truth. Literally.

In a few minutes I would take a step toward becoming a cooperating witness for the government. There was as yet no concrete agreement, but that seemed to be where things were heading. It was a life changing decision, and a lot of history had led to that moment.

Riding the metro into town earlier, I was full of memories from my past eleven years in Washington. The excitement and idealism of the revolution. Standing up for steel, and running Bob's office. 9/11. The amazing experience that was Team Abramoff. While I rested my head on the subway seat in front of me and stared blindly at the ground, several specific moments in my journey worked their way into my consciousness.

One such memory was from when I was Bob's chief of staff, and a group of democracy activists from Iran came in to meet with us in the Congressman's office. Because Bob used to live in Iran and was the only Farsi-speaking member of Congress, he had become a leading international figure on Iranian-American issues. When the group walked into our office, they looked nervous. Bob put them at ease with some jokes in Farsi, and took them on a tour of the Capitol. The group wore looks of awe and wonder when they returned. Those looks would quickly change after we sat down in Bob's personal office.

Our new activist friends had smuggled a video out of Iran. It contained footage of several women being stoned to death in a Tehran soccer stadium. They wanted to show it to us, the leaders of America. While we watched man after man throw stones at a woman who had left her abusive husband, I noticed that one of the ladies in the visiting group appeared to be related to the victim. Others in the delegation kept consoling her. I reached over and touched the woman's hand, and said, "I'm sorry." She didn't know exactly what I was saying, but kindly showed her appreciation for my gesture by nodding at me and smiling. It felt good to be that Neil Volz.

As my train approached the Metro Center stop, I wanted to be him again. Unfortunately, that Neil Volz wasn't the one sitting with his attorneys, nervously eating fried mushrooms across the street from the Justice Department's massive New York Avenue office.

Melissa, the associate attorney on my case, started the personal conversation. "You look nervous," she said.

"I am," I replied. "I never thought I would be sitting here, getting ready to do this."

"I understand," she said. Melissa worked for Tim, who was the partner handling my matter for their firm. Over the past year, I had learned to appreciate the attorney-client relationship I had with my lawyers, and its unique position in our culture. There is an openness that comes from knowing that it is part of your attorney's job to hold your secrets. But there is also a fidelity to the truth that comes from working with someone who is a part of the judicial system. As a result, Tim's concept of "be honest or be quiet" became hard-wired into my brain quickly. While Tim's knowledge, calm demeanor and leadership was invaluable throughout the scandal, it was Melissa who helped to psychologically set me straight as we prepared to enter the Justice Department. Of course, I don't think that was how we planned it. She was just being nice.

Melissa's role in my case was to dig into the specifics of the Abramoff scandal, as well as to handle the administrative responsibilities of dealing with the numerous legal entities involved. Over time, she also became an emotional safe harbor for me and my wife. The fact that Melissa and her parents happened to be from Bob's congressional district in Ohio made that bond stronger. Her understanding of the relationship between the Congressman's constituents and the scandal helped her connect with us. During the past year, I had learned to appreciate Melissa because she was an uncompromisingly straight arrow. She believed in our legal system, not only the letter of the law, but the spirit of the law as well.

Melissa could tell what I was thinking as we prepared for my first un-fettered sit-down with the Justice Department prosecutors. My only other contact with the prosecutors had been very structured, in order to avoid certain topics. Melissa knew where the fault-lines of my decision-making resided, what I hoped for and what I worried about. She had seen my thought process develop over the past year, and been there when I met with the investigators under more controlled circumstances. But those days were now over. There would be no limits on this discussion.

Going in to talk, and potentially becoming what legal professionals call "a cooperator" was in my best interest. It was in my family's best interest. Intellectually, I had accepted the fact that becoming a cooperator was the best way to stay out of jail. But I was still struggling to emotionally come to grips with the impact of such a far-reaching decision. It wasn't just my life that would be affected. Telling the prosecutors the truth about what I had done would not only destroy any chance I had to defend myself in a trial, it would also be devastating for Bob - and all of Ney World. There was a lot I didn't know, and the uncertainty frightened me. There were also people beyond Bob whom I worried about hurting. I didn't take the decision to cooperate lightly.

Weeks earlier, a family friend had been willing to talk through the process with me. He was familiar with high-profile investigations like the one I was facing. And like my attorneys, he knew where I stood emotionally.

"There is no winning and losing here," he had said. "There is only survival. You know whether you are really innocent or not. If you go to trial, even if you win, you will put your family through a living hell and bankrupt yourself several times over. Not that I'm not saying don't fight it. Do that if you feel it is right. The people who really matter will be with you at the end of that fight. But get it out of your head that a win, as you've known it, is even possible."

Until the Abramoff scandal, the concept of not being able to work or think my way to a winning hand was foreign to me. Winning was what I did. It was who I was. All I had to do was work harder or be smarter than my competition, and everything would be fine. I didn't like what I was hearing. But as I was beginning to learn, he was right. Those winning days were over. It was during one of our conversations that I first used a phrase I would utter many times in later years. "I feel like my Rolodex has gone from 5,000 people to 5 in the matter of a few weeks, or months."

"That sounds like about 4,995 people who aren't worth going to jail for," my friend replied. Again, he was right. Of course, it wasn't his decision. It was mine.

Cooperating was not as simple as the government asking me to assist with the investigation, and me agreeing to do so. Before moving forward, the government prosecutors needed to interview me, and I needed to know that their intention was to use me as a cooperator - not as a witness in my own trial. Neither of us was willing to give firm commitments. Therefore, we agreed to take a step at a time. Becoming a witness for the Justice Department was a leap of faith, faith that the government officials were being honest in their intentions, and for them, faith that I was being honest in mine.

The closer we got to my first official interview, the more I worried about what it meant to be a cooperator. Was I rat? A tattletale? Or trying to undo some of what I had done? Was I being selfish? Or was this best for my family? I was confused. There were so many angles to think about. *"How will this impact my ability to get a job?"* I asked myself at one point. Discussing what powerful people would surely prefer I keep quiet didn't seem to have any up side for me, if I wanted to make a living in Washington. The gossip and ideological speculation seemed to verify this point.

After Tom DeLay stepped down, many of my conservative friends advanced the theory that investigations like the one I was involved with were nothing more than partisan witch hunts. They said the prosecutors were trying to "criminalize politics." To me, that meant accepting the fact that if I helped the government with their case, some of my colleagues would interpret the move as changing sides - and a betrayal of my party.

Then there were personal issues, like what cooperating meant to my friends. On the one hand, I worried that my decision to be a cooperator would put people who were guilty of nothing but being close to me in harms way. I also worried that those friends who had small issues, like taking a few tickets or meals, would somehow become bigger targets because I was cooperating. *"What if I get asked questions I don't want to answer?"* I wondered, *"and about people I don't want to discuss?"*

Deep down, I knew that helping the government was the right thing to do. But each time I took a step in that direction, I would second-guess myself about what it all meant, and how I was supposed to do the right thing in such circumstances. It became a non-stop circle of situational ethics. My thoughts about answering questions that impacted my friends led to more fundamental questions about the process. *"What do I do about questions for which there is no other evidence?"* I asked myself. *"I mean, sure, if the FBI puts an email of mine in front of me or an expense report to ask me a question, that is one thing. Right? But what about a conversation that took place between two people with no one else around?"*

In the movies, that kind of question seemed easy. You never sell out your friends, or you play the role of righteous whistleblower. It didn't seem so easy to me. When I first thought about it, I knew that becoming a co-operator would hurt both Bob and me. There was no getting around that. But since I didn't want to hurt those around me, I wasn't always sure what to do. I also wondered whether I really didn't want to hurt anyone else. It wasn't like all the people I worked with were angels. *"Don't you want to undo some of what happened by helping bring people to justice?"* I would ask myself. *"You bet, but if you start down that road, where does it stop?"* The debate went round and round.

"Being honest is the same thing as doing the right thing," my family friend said on the eve of my meeting with the Justice Department. "Put all that stuff out of your mind. Don't over-think this. There is a lot you don't know."

"I get that," I replied. "That is what my family says. They make it sound so simple. Just go in and tell the truth. Like it is that easy."

"What if it is that easy?" my friend asked.

"What if it isn't?" I replied. "What if I run into Bob in ten years, and he tells me that while I saved my ass at his expense, we both could have beaten the rap? Or what if I find out in ten years that there was some political game going on that I didn't know about? Or that I was just a pawn in the ambitions of a bunch of prosecutors and journalists who wanted to advance their own careers at the expense of some elected officials and lobbyists?"

My friend just paused, before telling me for what seemed like the hundredth time, "But that doesn't change the simple fact that you just have to be honest. For your own good. Everything else will take care of itself."

"Everything else will take care of itself," I thought. That was a funny concept to me. I was so used to living with the belief that I could shape the future - my future. All I had to do was set a goal and make it happen. Unfortunately, that mindset came with a price. Believing I was in charge of my fate made it easy for me to choose the version of the truth that would best help me achieve my goals. In politics, that meant choosing the Republican truth over the Democratic truth. Arguments concerning everything from how best to create jobs to what the people wanted from their government were filtered through the ultimate goal of winning and getting power. Like during my time at the House Administration Committee, I was able to choose whether to listen to the "yes lawyer" or the "no lawyer" - depending on what outcome I wanted. Working for Team Abramoff was no different. This mindset even impacted how I saw the scandal. I constantly second-

guessed whether I was on Jack's side or Bob's side. It took me a long time to stop seeing the truth as situational, a point of view that was sometimes prevalent in Washington.

A few days after Jack's guilty plea was announced, for instance, Senate Minority Whip Harry Reid was a guest on a Sunday morning political talk show. He was asked about his work for Team Abramoff and our clients. It was pointed out that he had received tens of thousands of dollars in contributions from the tribes and members of our firm. He was ready with an answer.

"Don't lump me in with them," he said. "This is a Republican scandal."

The Senator's words fit right into the Democratic narrative about the scandal. Since Jack donated his personal money only to Republicans, left-leaning office-holders quickly used that fact to shield themselves from media inquiries and attacks by Republicans. It was a Democratic truth, but not fully honest. Frankly, it reminded me of the kind of thinking I brought with me to Washington a decade earlier. Back then, I was convinced that Democrats were inherently more corrupt than Republicans. My time in Washington had proven that theory wrong. And the last few months solidified that belief even more. I now knew better. And presumed Harry Reid did as well. No matter what he said on television, the fact is corruption infects people, not political parties. Not that Neil in his glass house was interested in throwing any stones. I was still grappling with bigger issues. Nonetheless, the interview left a mark in my mind.

"What if it is as simple as just being completely honest?" I wondered again as my lawyers and I gathered our items together for the trip across the street. Obviously, that morning wasn't the first time I had had that thought. The fact is, not a day had passed in the last few months in which I wasn't actively engaged in some introspection about my role in the scandal. Additionally, since I met my lawyers, the commitment I had to being honest with investigators and law enforcement had been well established. Like any good lawyer, Tim and Melissa hammered that point home constantly. My family and friends did as well. But as I approached the Justice Department, something new happened. The words of my friends, family and attorney's resonated with me in a different way. Maybe it was my nerves or the idea that I was surrendering my spin, my lies and all the professional defense mechanisms I had used up to that point. Whatever it was, walking through those doors created an emotional response to the concept behind the words I had been hearing for so long. In some ways, it was even spiritual.

The grey in my life suddenly seemed gone. If just for a moment. In its place was the simplicity of a black and white world. Down one road was the unhealthy choice of a future built around rationalizing my decisions, second-guessing the motives of others, and doing everything possible to avoid the conflict associated with real accountability. Down the other road was the simple peace of mind associated with full disclosure. Instead of going in to the Justice Department to explain away my emails, my bills and my other correspondence, I could just go in and tell the unvarnished, bald truth. Maybe it *was* that simple.

As we got in the elevator, I focused on what was ahead.

"This won't be easy. But I will be able to look Bob or anybody else in the eye in ten years and live with the fact that I told the truth." My mind raced. *"Just answer their questions. Don't worry about all that other stuff. Everything else will take care of itself."*

The simplicity of the moment was a relief. I knew life would remain confusing and at times contradictory. But the principle of the moment was empowering. I would listen to my family, my friends, my lawyers, and my conscience - and just tell the truth. The moment harkened me back to some other simple words my dad had said on another occasion, "Neil, just remember, the guys with the badges are the good guys."

As I told him, "I sure hope so."

A Government Witness

DAVID SAFAVIAN'S CORRUPTION TRIAL HAD just started. I was secluded from the press and the activity in the courtroom, yet the trial hovered over me wherever I looked. Breakfast was no exception. While eating cereal at home, I opened the pages of the *Washington Post* and noticed that one article was cut out. It looked like a perfectly sliced letter "L" had been removed from the inside of the paper. Being a witness in the case, I was not allowed to read anything about the proceedings. Therefore, Alison had agreed to help me out by looking through the newspapers in the morning before she left for the office. If there were any pertinent stories, she would remove them. As I stared through the L-shaped hole in the paper, I couldn't help but feel like I was in an episode of *The Twilight Zone* - the episode where my life stopped being my own. *"So this is what it is like to be a cooperating witness for the government?"* I wondered.

Two weeks earlier, I had pleaded guilty to violating my one-year ban and to conspiracy charges associated with my corrupt activity as a Hill staffer and lobbyist. My plea meant agreeing to cooperate with the government in its investigation. That included testifying in the Safavian trial. It was a big change, going from the target of an investigation to a cooperator.

My brother and his daughter had flown in from Ohio to join me, Alison and some friends at the courthouse. I felt immense shame pleading guilty to crimes against my country. At the same time, I was grateful for the support of family and friends. Pictures of me fighting through hordes of reporters and cameramen led the nightly news. The story of my criminal activity was splashed across the front pages of the *Washington Post*, the *New York Times*, and *USA Today*, and was reported on by both National Public Radio and the *Rush Limbaugh Show*. My shame deepened as my friends and family,

340

across the country, increasingly found themselves in the awkward situation of having to listen to stories and answer questions about my wrongdoing.

Like Jack and Scanlon's plea agreements, my plea read like an indictment of Bob. By admitting that, as his top staffer, I had exchanged legislative favors for things of value, and then offered him things of value in exchange for legislative favors, I added water to Bob's rapidly sinking ship. My plea also played right into the culture of corruption message being pushed by the Democratic Party. Democrats sent out press releases attacking elected officials I had worked with over the years. The more guilty charges the Abramoff scandal generated, the more the issue of corruption became a priority for voters. I quickly became *persona non grata* to elected and non-elected Republicans alike.

Days after my circus-like plea hearings, I returned to Ohio for my grandmother's funeral. It was sad to think about life without Gram. She was a pillar of virtue and decency. I felt lucky to have enjoyed our last few days together at Christmas time. Yet a knot in my stomach developed whenever I recalled telling my family, during that trip, the devastating news about being a felon. While spiritual, celebratory and life-affirming, my grandmother's funeral was unfortunately filled with similar uneasy moments.

My initial hope had been to slip into the background so I didn't take anything away from Gram's service. But my family would have none of it. They engulfed me with their love and support. It was a nice feeling, but the attention made me feel like the black cloud of my scandal was tarnishing a sacred family ritual. Anytime one of my relatives tried to start talking about the upcoming trial, I told them that I wasn't allowed to discuss what was going on or hear anything that they were reading." Those were the easy conversations. The questions about my marriage, whether I would go to jail, if I blamed Bob for my problems, or how my parents were holding up, weren't so easy to deflect. Since Safavian's indictment eight months earlier, I had gone from being a powerful Washington lobbyist to a convicted felon, a felon who was unemployed and about to testify as a cooperating government witness against a former friend. It was mind-numbing to try to comprehend my new life. Therefore, I didn't really even try. I just focused on getting through each day.

When I returned to Washington from Gram's service, I immediately went to the Justice Department to begin preparing for Safavian's trial. That meant spending the next several days sitting in a conference room as federal prosecutors asked me questions. In some respects, preparing for the trial was like an extension of my cooperation. I sat across the table from note-taking FBI agents and answered questions posed to me by prosecutors. They would start with some general questions about a topic, and then begin to dig in deep when they realized I knew some pertinent information. The process was intimidating, yet I did my best to keep it simple. My job was to just be honest. And I took that responsibility very seriously. Being honest had quickly become my North Star, my way out of the scandal. When I was asked about my interactions with Safavian, I told the government what happened. I answered the questions fully. Nothing more, and nothing less.

My time preparing with the prosecution also included conversations about what I could expect at trial. Part of what the prosecutors were doing with my questioning involved teaching the jurors about lobbying and the political process. After that, I was going to answer questions about the work I was doing with Safavian and Abramoff before the trip to Scotland. From there, my job would be to walk the jury through the Scotland trip. At no point did the government tell me what to say or use a specific script. Instead, they tended to rotate their questions, and periodically examine certain lines of questioning more thoroughly. Sometimes I heard similar questions the next day, and sometimes I did not. Eventually, I got a feel for what the prosecutors kept calling my "direct," or opening examination, and the contours of my testimony came together.

Then there was the issue of my cross examination, or what the prosecutors and FBI agents called my "cross." The thought of Safavian's attorney being able to ask me anything, in an effort to discredit me as a witness, made me nervous. I was a felon who had admitted breaking the law, but that didn't mean I wanted to dig into every detail of my failures. It was embarrassing. But I knew my sole responsibility was to continue to answer questions truthfully. If Safavian's attorney could use my honest testimony to help her client and my former friend, that was fine with me. Of course, I didn't see that happening. The government would not have put me on the stand if they thought my answers would hurt their case.

Preparing for my cross examination meant sitting in front of Justice Department prosecutor after prosecutor as they played the role of Safavian's lawyer. Their job was to use their questioning to shake me up, to make me nervous or defensive, all in the hope of discrediting my testimony. Each attorney had a different style. One prosecutor sat down and calmly had a conversation with me. Another prosecutor screamed through his cross examination. "Mr. Volz, are you lying now, or were you lying then?" he asked, while holding some documents in his hand that contained contradictory statements I had made over the years. The process was horrible. Being pushed and pulled in every direction made me feel like a lab rat. Reliving the stupid decisions I had made over the years wasn't any fun either.

The prosecutors were good at their jobs. The questions they asked made me look like a liar, no matter how I answered. I hated every second of it. The only enjoyable part of my trial preparation was when I got to leave. Slipping my headphones on as I left the building was one of the few moments of relaxation I had had in the several weeks since the trial had begun. On many occasions, going home only added to the stress.

One night, for instance, I came home to find Alison sobbing uncontrollably in the living room. I could tell she had been reading something on her computer. Instead of talking through what was going on, she grabbed her laptop and ran downstairs. "We can't talk," she said. Her words meant that our inability to communicate that night had something to do with the trial. We barely spoke again for the rest of the evening. I didn't know what was going on. Had a bad email been approved as evidence, and therefore made public? Or had someone commented on the trial? There was no way of knowing. All I could do was watch as Alison went downstairs, upstairs and outside, anywhere that was out of earshot, to call friends and family. She was hurting. "I'm sorry," I told her, before going to bed. Things at home were getting worse.

After the trial I would learn what had upset my wife so badly. She was reading an article in the newspaper titled, "Safavian attorney seeks to discredit former Ney aide." In bold print, midway down one of the columns, Safavian's attorney was quoted as saying, "Neil Volz is trying to crawl out of jail on Mr. Safavian's back." It was the kind of sentiment counsel usually conjures up when dealing with cooperating witnesses like me. I would have said the same thing if I had been Safavian's attorney. The legal side of their argument wasn't a surprise. What ultimately shook me up about the argument was the underlying concept, namely what it said about me as a person. While I had seen much worse uttered about me, usually in the online comment section of the newspapers that ran stories about the scandal, these words suggested that I was still actively being a bad person. Something I desperately wanted to change.

"Cooperating represents a step forward, a new beginning," I had said to Alison many times. It was a belief both of us had pinned our hopes on. But we had to face the fact that the comments of Safavian's attorney were accurate. I was cooperating against my former friend in an effort to stay out of jail. On a certain level, that meant I was continuing to be selfish. I didn't like admitting that fact, especially in public. But then again, I wasn't going to lie about it, either.

The FBI coordinated my arrival at the courthouse. They wanted me to avoid the cameras and press camped out around the building. Since Safavian's trial was the first of the Abramoff scandal, the media was following it closely. I didn't know it at the time, but the press was referring to me as the "star witness" in the case. Therefore, reporters were awaiting my arrival. So I met the two FBI agents at the metro stop a few blocks away. In their business suits and with precision, the two escorted me to a side door, up the stairs, and toward a holding room on the side of Judge Paul L. Friedman's chambers. I blended in with the crowd milling outside the courtroom, so much so that as I walked past the front door, I overheard a reporter talking on his phone. "Volz is expected to arrive sometime soon," he said. I laughed as I walked in behind him.

The FBI agents escorted me to a windowless room where I quietly waited to be called into the court room. While I was sitting in the holding room, the general outline of the trial was developing in the judge's chambers. The prosecutors from the Department of Justice started by making their case. They told the jury that Safavian had concealed his relationship with Jack numerous times, including when Safavian and I had worked on projects together leading up to the Scotland trip. At that point, the prosecutors said, Safavian was helping Jack try to acquire government property for his school. They also said Safavian was using his position to help one of our tribal clients secure rights to the Old Post Office on Pennsylvania Avenue in order to build a hotel. Finally, the prosecution argued that Safavian covered up that assistance when he told the ethics office at the agency where he worked that Jack did not have any business before his agency. He covered the assistance up again, they continued, when he talked to investigators working for the Senate, as well when he spoke with the FBI.

Since much of the government's case was based on the email traffic between Safavian and Jack, several debates occurred over what could and could not be shown to the jury. Generally speaking, the judge sided with the government in letting the emails be used as evidence. This ruling was incredibly detrimental to Safavian's case. His correspondence with Jack leading up to the Scotland trip proved that he had been helping on our projects right before the trip. Therefore, the question became whether that work technically constituted "business" or not. It wasn't my job to wade into that debate. My responsibility was to just tell the jury what happened.

Safavian's attorney told the jury that Jack and Safavian were close friends. She encouraged the members of the jury not to believe everything they read. She added that she would prove that Jack had no business with

GSA, where Safavian worked as chief of staff, because he was not looking to actually conduct business with the government agency. She argued that Jack's intention was to conduct his business on Capitol Hill. Safavian's attorney worked to discredit the email traffic between the two men, and the perceived relationship between her client and Jack. This was especially important since Jack's status as a well-known criminal was part of the trial's narrative. "David Safavian was not in Jack Abramoff's pocket," she said. "In 2002, nobody knew that Jack Abramoff was a crook." With emails showing the two men bantering back and forth about golf, the trip and setting up meetings to help Jack's various causes, convincing the jury that Jack was guilty, but Safavian was somehow in the dark, represented a real challenge for the defense.

At the same time, since Jack wasn't testifying, and I was, she needed to discredit me, as well. "Neil Volz is crawling out of jail on Mr. Safavian's back," she said, arguing that I was trying to reduce my jail sentence by testifying against her client. She then questioned my credibility by telling the jury that I had pleaded guilty to crimes, including a violation of the one-year ban - also known as the "revolving-door law." "That door hit him," she said. "It did not revolve." Her premise to the jury was that I had been a liar, and was therefore going to lie again in order to get a better sentence. The premise offended me. Yet, again, I understood that Safavain's attorney was just doing her job.

After three days of waiting, one of the agents escorted me to the courtroom and opened the door. Walking through the two large wood doors was like walking into a 3D movie.

My heart raced. My legs felt wobbly I was nervous. Straight ahead, and behind the dais, sat Judge Friedman. Directly to my right sat Safavian's family, friends and supporters. They looked somber. I was sure they hated me. To my left, and through the rest of the seats, sat journalists and law enforcement agents.

There was a wooden swinging door that sat about three feet high separating those watching the courtroom from the judge, the jury, the prosecutors, and the defense. I walked toward the witness stand. To my right sat Safavian and his legal team. Across from them, on my left, sat the prosecutor's team. Their courtroom suits were in stark contrast to the more casual atmosphere of my prep sessions at their office.

As I approached the stand I passed the jury box. The jurors studied me as I maneuvered to my seat on the witness stand. Raising my right hand, I was sworn in by the court official, and told to sit down. In front of me was a computer monitor, several large black binders of documents and a water dispenser with a cup. The court stenographer sat ready to record my every word.

I looked over at Safavian. He was whispering quietly with the attorney sitting to his left. To his right, in a purple and grey jacket, sat his lead defense attorney, Barbara Van Gelder. *"She will be doing the cross examination,"* I thought to myself. Right away, I began to worry about what she might ask me. But I reminded myself that I was ready for this. *"Just answer the questions and tell the truth,"* I thought, as I poured myself a glass of water. *"Nothing bad can happen if you just answer the questions as they come. Keep it simple, stupid."*

Nathaniel "Nat" Edmonds rose to begin eliciting my testimony. Since I was the government's witness, it was the prosecution's responsibility to start the process. The defense would then cross-examine me. After that, the prosecution would be able to reply to the cross by asking me some further questions. I was told the first part of my testimony would probably last most of the day. I was looking at several days on the stand.

Nat stood up and approached the witness stand. His podium stood about ten feet from me.

"Hello, Mr. Volz," he said.

"Hello," I replied.

Nat asked me the basics.

"How are you doing? Do you know the defendant? What crimes did I commit? Who did I work for? Did I go on the trip to Scotland?"

The Scotland trip represented a turning point in my testimony. After the first mention of the trip, Nat began to ask me specific questions about the days preceding our golf trip, the golf trip itself, and the days following the trip. Standing behind the podium, Nat flipped through page after page in his binder. His questions followed.

"Is this a photo of you in Scotland?" he asked.

"Yes," I replied. There were lots of photos. And lots of questions.

"How much did you pay for drinks? Who paid for the golf? Where did you stay?"

Much of the questioning involved me reading my own emails, or someone else's emails. "Will you read email number..." Nat asked over and over again.

I never expected to be reading my own private emails in a court of law. It was unnerving. I looked over at Safavian a couple times to see his expression. Our eyes met. For a split second, I wondered what he was thinking. *"Is he mad at himself for telling the FBI that Jack didn't have business before the*

346

GSA? Or is he just focused on disputing whatever I say? Or anybody says?" I assumed the latter. His freedom was on the line.

The more I read, though, the more I could tell that disputing the facts was going to be tough for him. After all, the words on those emails had meaning. And the actions we took had occurred. Still, it wasn't my job to play attorney, and Safavian had the right to his day in court. All I could do was answer questions, something I would end up doing for several days.

During a recess between my direct examination and cross examination, I sat in the holding room and pondered what had just happened, and what was coming next. I could tell by watching the jury that my testimony had hurt Safavian's case. Many of them seemed to nod along as I walked through the work we were doing before the Scotland trip, and the extravagance of the trip itself. In contrast, they nodded disapprovingly when I explained how I had helped Bob's office fraudulently fill out their travel disclosure forms, and how Safavian had told me that "we all need to stick together," after being interviewed by the FBI.

"I'm sure he feels like I am a traitor," I thought. *"Neil the Narc."* But I reminded myself that I couldn't be responsible for what he did or said.

My anger was quickly replaced by pain. *"Maybe it isn't that easy,"* I thought. David had kids. He had a family. Why did I have to be on the other side? Was it as simple as me choosing to be on the other side? Or was there no choice at all? *"Of course there was,"* I reminded myself. *"David's interests came up against my interests, and I chose my interests."*

Van Gelder approached me for the beginning of what would be a four hour cross-examination. She was a former prosecutor. My heart rate quickened as the questioning began. I gulped down several cups of water. For days, I had tried to condition myself for the conflict. That meant accepting that I had no control over her questions. In the moment, therefore, I knew I had to set aside any other concern, and just answer her honestly.

Van Gelder's questions seemed to drift from topic to topic, like she was setting me up for something. She asked me about my conversation with her client in Scotland, where Safavian told me that he was paying Jack for his portion of the trip. She also asked me about the agreement Bob and I made to submit a statement in the *Congressional Record* for Scanlon. We battled over certain details, and I agreed with others. I told her what kind of golf clubs I owned. We discussed my handicap, and whether I enjoyed playing golf. I told her I did. She also asked me whether I considered Bob a good golfer. I told her I did not. It was a little bit of everything. My paranoid side kept telling me that she was setting me up for a surprise finish.

After our break, we returned for what would be the end of my cross examination. Van Gelder zeroed in on my cooperation with the government. Under my agreement with the Justice Department, it was possible for the government to recommend a lower sentence for me if I provided them "substantial assistance." Van Gelder wanted the jury to understand that there was an incentive for me to help the prosecution. Implied was the idea that my desire for a reduced sentence would somehow influence my testimony. I couldn't do anything to rebut the implication except to straightforwardly answer her questions.

After establishing the fact that my agreement created an incentive for me, Van Gelder began questioning whether my help was about something beyond my own self interest.

"Talking to the FBI was in your best interest?" she asked me.

I replied, "Yes."

"Have you ever thought about other people's best interests?" she continued. To which I again said yes. "Mr. Safavian's?" she asked. "Mr. Ney's?" Yes and yes, I said. She then went through a long list of other people associated with the case, people about whom I had testified. "Do you realize that your testimony will be used against all of these men?" she asked me.

I told her it was possible, and then simply agreed with the point she was trying to make. "There's no doubt I was looking out for my interests." And like that my turn was over. *Did she think I would say something else?* I wondered as her last question hung out in the air for a while.

After a few more questions from the prosecution, I walked out of the courtroom. As I pushed open the large double-doors, an FBI agent handed me my briefcase.

"We'll call you after the trial," he said. I put my headphones on and walked to the metro. Metallica and Eminem throbbed along the side of my head. The blaring music numbed the contradictory feelings I had. *"David is in trouble,"* I told myself. *"That sucks. I wish none of this had happened. But it isn't my fault."*

Within an hour, I was home, alone with my thoughts. For the last few months, weeks and days, I had sat down and answered every question thrown my way. Truthfully. A grin settled on my face. It shouldn't have made me feel so good to simply tell the truth. But it did. Not that I necessarily liked what I saw. It was clear that my selfish desire for money, power and prestige had played a large role in getting me in trouble. So had my willingness to say or do whatever was necessary to acquire that money and influence. Nonetheless, looking out at my tomato garden in the backyard, I began to see myself, in the slightest way, stepping forward. While I still felt like I was being selfish and focusing way too much on getting my professional life put back together, I was proud that I had let the process of simply being honest lead my way through the trial.

As painful as it was, I knew I could live with the long-term repercussions of my decision to cooperate, if I stayed on the path I was on. My heart broke for Safavian, but I knew I could look David in the eye and tell him that I didn't lie to save my own ass - I told the truth. And I knew that deep down he would know that. No matter where life took me in the future, embracing that simple premise meant I could look anyone in the eye in the years ahead and tell them I told the truth when it mattered. Even if it hurt someone, like Bob, whom I cared about quite a bit more than I cared about Safavian.

The news media had a feeding frenzy on some of my answers. Many liked all the golf talk at the trial. The fact that I told the court how bad Bob and I were on the course became fodder for the television pundit Keith Olbermann, then on MSNBC. Editorial writers joked about expecting a foursome of golfers to walk through the judge's chambers. When I was finally able to see the coverage, I was amazed at what they chose to dissect. Of course, their coverage wasn't all about golf. There were also several articles dissecting the importance of my testimony, as it related to a potential trial involving Bob. This dynamic was something I thought about several times while testifying, especially when I saw Bob's lawyers in the courtroom. Since I was the first government cooperator to testify in the Abramoff scandal, there was a lot of talk about how my credibility on trial could impact cases beyond just Bob. Many legal experts and pundits wondered how effective a former Team Abramoff member could be at trial. My effectiveness could either help or hurt future prosecutions, they argued. Such news was intriguing to read, but not very high on my priority list.

A few days after my testimony, I flew out to the West Coast to visit old friends. My life was in a shambles.

"You can cry if you want to," my unflinching good friend, John Cook, said upon my arrival.

"Screw you," I replied, before giving him a big ol' man hug. It was good to be around friends who didn't care about the scandal, but deeply cared about me. John, his pregnant wife Sheri and my friend Dale Warren then proceeded to take me on a day-long hike around beautiful Lake Tahoe. Their support was like putting down the foundation of the bridge I was hoping to build from the scandal toward a new life.

While I was out West with my friends, the jury found Safavian guilty of obstructing justice.

AUGUST 7, 2006
WASHINGTON, DC

═══════════════

Bob Steps Down

I REACHED DOWN TO HIT THE button on my answering machine. A loud beep preceded the news. "I am not sure if you have heard, but your former boss is stepping down. I wonder if you'd be willing to make a comment for the paper," the message said. It was from a reporter friend of mine. The rumors had been true. Bob was no longer running for re-election. I had imagined the Chairman's announcement a million times. While sad, I had hoped, even expected, that the end of Bob's congressional career would provide me some sort of clarity. Legal clarity. Emotional and psychological clarity. Something. But it didn't.

My first reaction to the news was actually one of astonishment. *"Is this happening?"* I asked myself. *"Is Ney World really coming to an end."* Expecting this day was one thing; actually watching it play out in real time was another.

"This is big news," I thought. *"But where does it go from here? Is this the first step toward a long, gut-wrenching trial in which I have to spend days on the stand, and years waiting for the process to play out? Or is Bob going to plead guilty?"*

I quickly fired up my computer to read the news. Besieged by the fact that there were a lot of good people who would soon be out looking for work, my mind began to run through the faces and places of those who remained a part of the Ney family. There was Bob's longtime staff in the district. There were the "new" young staffers in the Congressman's Washington office. Their names dripped through my head. I was partially responsible for the personal tragedy they were now facing. *"What will they do?"* I wondered. *"Where will they go? Getting jobs won't be easy. I want to help. But what can I do? Even if I could help,"* I continued to myself, *"would any of them take it, or for that matter, will any of them ever talk to me again?"*

The sadness I was feeling for my beleaguered former colleagues was overwhelming. So was my inability to do anything about, well, anything. The whole situation reminded me of just how trapped and out of control my life remained. *"Luckily, they have five months to look for work,"* I said, trying to bludgeon the guilt. Seeing Bob forced from office was awful, despite my sincere desire for clarity in the case. He had positively impacted thousands of lives during his decades of service in the Ohio Senate and Congress. Yet that would be forever overshadowed by the scandal. Remembering the good times and the positive things Bob had done for his district made me begin to think the situation was unfair. Then the bad times came to mind, and my shame and anger resurfaced.

The prospect of testifying against the Chairman continued to keep me up at night. It was the first thing that would pop in my head whenever his name or the scandal was mentioned. "A Ney trial would be a million times worse than the Safavian trial," I told a friend. "David and I shared a few days together in Scotland. Bob and I shared a life together."

My emotions swung from anger to sadness, and back again. Legally speaking, I wasn't really sure what to make of the news. I knew Bob would never give up his office, his base of power, unless there were no other choice. Either his polling said it was over, or he was getting ready to plead guilty. Or both. The more I thought about it, the more my gut told me Bob was about to cut a deal with the government. Nonetheless, I made sure not to get my hopes up.

With every day bringing a nonstop barrage of distressing news, the last few years had taught me not to get too optimistic. But for a brief second, I breathed a small sigh of relief. At a minimum, Bob's action symbolized movement, something I continued to crave. Even more important than what was happening was the fact that something was happening at all. After feeling stuck at every turn, both personally and professionally, I found the mere thought of reaching the bottom of my fall, or even better, seeing a real sense of personal momentum, an incredibly hopeful idea. But there was a long way to go. *"Am I even close to reaching the bottom?"* I wondered.

The initial wave of news came in the form of a statement on Bob's campaign website, as well as an exclusive interview the Congressman gave to the *Pittsburgh Tribune-Review*. "I am doing this for one reason: my family," Bob said in the *Tribune-Review* article. "My wife and children have been through enough. I really believe this is the best decision." The statement on the Congressman's website contained a similar sentiment. "After much consideration and thought, I have decided today to no longer seek re-election in Ohio's 18th Congressional District. Ultimately this decision came down to my family. I must think of them first, and I can no longer put them through this ordeal."

Envisioning Bob's wife, kids and parents was heartbreaking. Over the years, I had been lucky to have spent time with each of them. Like my family, I was sure the Ney clan had gone through immense changes in the previous few years. Watching a loved one go from a rising to falling star had to hurt. Their pain was undoubtedly real and I knew Bob felt it. At the same time, I knew that wasn't why he was stepping down. The Congressman loved his family, but the only reason Bob would ever step down was if he thought he would lose his re-election campaign. Weeks earlier, the Congressman had publicly sworn up and down that he would stand for election, even if under indictment. And nothing about Bob made me doubt his resolve. If it had been just about him, he would have battled through the scandal until Election Day. But there was the bigger picture to think about. With the deadline to put another person on the ballot rapidly approaching, the Congressman had to decide what his Congressional seat meant. He could give the seat to the Democrats by staying in the race. Or, by stepping down, he could give someone who shared his world view a chance to win. There was no doubt in my mind it was a tough choice for him to make. If he was stepping down, however, it meant he knew he couldn't win.

"Never give up your office," an animated Congressman Ney had told me almost ten years earlier. At the time, he was talking about Senate Majority Leader Bob Dole's decision to vacate his congressional perch during the 1996 presidential election. At the time, Dole had just stepped down from the Senate Majority Leader position to run for president. Bob's words struck a nerve in the moment, and would become even more pertinent later. I never forgot them. "Your power comes from the vote and the pin," he said, referencing the lapel pin members of Congress wear to identify themselves. "People treat you differently after you've stepped down." It was ironic that years later he would face a somewhat situation similar to former Senator Dole's. Do you give up your seat before you have to?

Bob's prescient comments colored my view of the Abramoff investigation from the minute speculation began about the potential for Bob to be forced from office. At no point did I get the impression that he viewed his Congressional office as anything but his core base of power. This made sense. Not a wealthy man, Bob knew his office provided him leverage to help raise money, acquire legal cover, keep his team employed, and, ultimately, give him the ability to take care of his family. I couldn't argue with the logic of staying in office for as long as possible. In fact, I was forced to share my views on the topic with Department of Justice prosecutors. Several months before Bob stepped down, I was asked during an interview session whether the Chairman would relinquish his seat due to his weakening legal position.

"No way," I replied. "The only reason he will step down is if public opinion swings against him in the district, and he realizes staying in office is no longer possible."

As usual, doing business was a one way street with the government. They asked questions, and I answered them. For nearly six months, I took part in a variety of meetings, interviews and phone calls with FBI agents and federal prosecutors. After agreeing to cooperate, the process almost became routine.

I would wake up early in the morning. It was a ten minute walk from my house to the DC metro system. After the twenty minute ride downtown, I would head to my new favorite diner across the street from the Justice Department. In addition to the bacon, sausage and ham breakfast extravaganza I ate religiously, several cups of coffee would usually provide me enough of a caffeine boost to help me muscle through the initial portion of the question and answer session. After a brief and healthier lunch break eating with the investigators, the far-ranging inquiry would continue late into the afternoon. Since there were numerous teams of FBI agents and prosecutors who worked on different components of the investigation, I occasionally met with several groups at once. Other times, we would stagger the meetings back to back.

I was usually exhausted by the end of the day. After leaving department headquarters, I slowly meandered toward the Metro for the ride home. Just as the diner across the street from the department became a part of my routine, so too did my final destination of the day - the back corner seat of the last Metro car. For those final twenty minutes of the routine, I liked to slouch into the cushion and try to imagine that I was somewhere else. My time in the Metro usually included a battle over whether to feel sorry for myself or not, as if my own actions had not caused the pain I saw all around me. Like some self-help guru, I took to the habit of saying over and over again, "*I am not a victim, and I will not be a victim.*"

Despite the fact that it helped to keep my head on straight, all the chanting in the world couldn't stop the feeling of sadness which enveloped me during those early evening commutes. From my parents to my wife, the pain and suffering I had caused to my loved ones was excruciatingly real.

As others happily piled in the train, I could not help but overhear them discuss the bar they were going to that night, what their kids were doing or how their jobs were proceeding. Staring through the window at the wall as it passed by, I turned my iPod up as loud as it would go. It was an effort to try to stop wishing that I hadn't taken so many things for granted, or hoping that I could get them back. The regret hurt.

As much as anything, I yearned to get back my pride. And my honor. Getting those back, of course, was easier said than done. As callously as I had thrown them away, I knew in theory that it was going to take me a long time to get my pride and honor back, if I ever really could. During those moments when it felt like I would never feel good about my public service again, I made sure to remind myself that I was restoring my lost sense of pride by helping the government prosecute their corruption cases. *"It may not always feel that way,"* I would say. *"But it is a step in the right direction."*

Such a step in the right direction seemed to make sense in the Metro. But when that assistance to the government's investigation included answering questions about friends I had known for years and did not want to hurt, however, the simplicity of getting my pride back wasn't so clear. The ride home, though, always seemed to restore enough faith in my decision to help me get up the next day to follow a similar script.

Neither the prosecutors nor the myriad of federal agents provided me much insight into what was going on in the investigation, but the questions and how they asked them gave me clues. In early summer, for instance, much of their inquiry revolved around the inner workings of the Ney operation - questions about which staff members handled what issue and who spent time with Bob. Also of particular interest to the government was the Congressman's 2003 trip to London with a foreign businessman. The businessman, who was trying to get some help from the Congressman on issues pertaining to Iran, had been represented by a former Ney staffer and close associate of Bob. Because we all liked to party together, I had some information on the trip. The more questions I was asked, the more clear it became that there was something fishy there. Like normal, I answered the government's questions honestly and fully. I simply told them what I knew.

At a certain point, I noticed a sudden hyper-interest surrounding who accompanied Bob on that trip, as well as questions about how the Chairman won the tens of thousands of dollars in gambling receipts he reported on his public financial disclosure forms. Around the time of the trip, Bob told me about his gambling success and what he did while he was overseas. But most of what I picked up in regard to the Chairman's second British adventure had come through random stories and jokes told over drinks with Bob's staff and former staff. The more I realized there was something serious associated with that trip, the more I wished I could forget all those stories and jokes. The way Bob described his winnings to me, for instance, did not match up with the public story his staff told the media when news of his gambling success broke. Something smelled. In that respect, it was no surprise that the questioning over that trip had an intensity to it that much of the other questioning did not.

The constant digging into that specific venture left me wondering what exactly was occurring. *"What are they after?"* I wondered. *"Who are they after? Is it Bob's staff? His former staff?"* Whatever or whomever it is, it seemed serious. *"The noose around him is tightening,"* I thought, shuddering.

Taking part in the investigation from my perspective was what I called thunder and lightning. Like the meteorological occurrence of the same name, the way it worked was simple. I would notice hours of high interest questions on a certain topic. That represented the thunder. The lightning would follow weeks or months later in the form of some legal activity or news story suggesting future legal action. In this instance, the lightning struck when the press began reporting about upheaval occurring in Bob's office. "Ney aide subpoenaed in lobbying investigation," shouted a headline in the *Cleveland Plain Dealer*. According to the story, Bob's campaign manager was being compelled by the court to turn over documents and testify before a grand jury in Washington. It was big news. But it wasn't the end of the lightning storm.

Three additional staffers were resigning from Bob's office, the media reported. Though I was expecting something, the grand jury activity and staff changes had me again nervously clamoring for more information. I could only guess what was going on for sure, but my initial thought was that all four of them had been subpoenaed to testify. Since congressional rules require Members of the House and their staff to announce when they have been subpoenaed, I assumed that three of the staffers decided to quit, rather than make such a public pronouncement. But I didn't know for sure. As expected, Bob released a statement saying the staff turnover in his office was nothing more than business as usual on Capitol Hill. Outlining how the three men had been with his office longer than the average congressional staffer, Ney spun his tale.

I devoured every possible angle of the story. By that point, I was fully skeptical of any public statement put out by Bob's office concerning the investigation. Therefore, I did my best to search for the full report behind the official words. With the help of unnamed sources, the press reported that Heaton and another senior staffer had basically gone underground, while Bob's spokesman had accepted a job in another office. The reporting on the three departing staffers was murky. But the facts were clear. Leaving a Hill job before securing someplace to land almost always represented a bigger story than that someone was merely moving on. It usually implied bad news, or, more likely, bad blood. In this case, the news suggested much more. It was anything but business as usual. It was "game over." The wheels had come off the Ney bus.

After working in Bob's office for so long, as well as going through what had happened at the Prime Rib, I knew his team was under enormous stress. With the Congressman expecting them to toe the party line at all costs, the daily pressure with which Heaton and the rest of the inner circle were dealing had to be a moral minefield, a minefield marked by a competition among each staffer's loyalty to Bob, what his own conscience was saying, and his need for survival. I knew the feeling. I also knew the anguish of being thrust into a position opposite Bob. It was scary. He was one of the most powerful men in Washington. And like all of us, he was in survival mode. I couldn't even imagine what that was like for Heaton and the rest of the staff.

It made me proud to think that they had stood up to Bob. It was the right thing to do. How or why they crossed that threshold, I wasn't sure, but I hoped that what appeared from the outside like a mutiny meant a better future for each of them. By putting their blind loyalty to Bob aside, they were, I presumed, doing the right thing for themselves and their families.

By mid-summer, Bob's legal situation began to mirror his political situation. He was in free fall. I had admitted taking part in a criminal conspiracy which involved the chairman. He had been named in Jack, Scanlon and Rudy's guilty pleas. According to public opinion polls released by the Congressman's Democrat opponent, Bob garnered a mere 35% of the vote in a hypothetical match-up. Since incumbent Members of Congress are well-known entities, once voters decide to change candidates it is hard to get them back. Therefore, a general rule of thumb in congressional elections is that an incumbent with under 50% preference in the polls is considered endangered. That meant the Congressman was doomed.

None of the bad news was a surprise to Bob. Months earlier, according to a staffer who was there, the Congressman's pollster had solemnly told him he could not win re-election. He should step down in order to give the party a chance to field a winning candidate, his pollster reportedly said.

Apparently, Bob took the idea seriously enough to begin preparing to step down before the Republican primary. Ultimately, he decided against it, however, and ran for re-election. His thinking was that he could gain some momentum with a win in the primary and then bloody up his Democrat opponent enough to convince the voters to stick with him. Bob won the primary, but lost a large percentage of Republican support.

From there, the situation only got worse. Several media accounts began reporting that the Congressman's colleagues had begun calling him a "Dead Man Walking" behind his back. They also reported that the various Republican campaign organizations had all agreed not to give any money to the Ney re-election efforts. Quarterly reports showed that his personal fundraising efforts continued to atrophy. Bob's expenditures on legal fees were exceeding what he was able to raise for the campaign. The writing was on the wall. It was time to go. So he stepped down.

Not only did Bob decide to end his congressional career, but he also decided to publicly name his successor, and then endorse her. It was as if the Congressman had turned off the keen political radar he had honed successfully for years, now that he was stepping down. Making the endorsement was a mistake.

Bob coyly told the Tribune-Review that he expected state Senator Joy Padgett to become his successor in the congressional race. "She is a person of passion and conviction," he crowed, talking about Padgett, before saying that she was the best candidate for the job.

In a sign of the times, the Democrats pounced.

"The first thing we know about Joy Padgett is that she is Ney's hand-picked candidate," said Bill Burton, the spokesman for the Democratic Congressional Campaign Committee. He then went on to say that Bob was "forced out of this race by the reality of an electorate demanding change from the culture of corruption in Washington and a Congress that compulsively puts special interests first at every opportunity."

For her part, Padgett, a twenty-plus year friend of Bob's, found herself on the defensive by the Congressman's ad-hoc announcement. In recounting the chain of events which led to her sudden position as candidate for Ohio's 18th Congressional District, Padgett was refreshingly honest. Her words stood in sharp contrast with the last year of legalisms and evasion by Bob and his team. With candor, she outlined how the Congressman had contacted her two days before to ask her to run in his place. I pictured every moment of her story.

"It's a very sad time," she said. "There is just so much he can take," before adding that he told her, "I have to do this." Padgett's description was heart wrenching. I could see Bob saying those words. It was hard not to feel his anguish. At the same time, recounting those kind of comments by the Congressman were not helpful to Padgett. Yet what was done was done. There were less than a hundred days to the election, and our new candidate was already scrambling to define herself to the voters in the wake of Bob's sudden endorsement. The next day, Padgett began singing another tune.

"Those are Bob Ney's problems, they are not my problems," she said boldly in her next round of interviews. "I do not know who Jack Abramoff is, I've never met him. I do not believe voters are going to hang that baggage on me." While I knew that distancing herself from Bob was probably not enjoyable, for either Padgett or Bob, I liked seeing it. *"If we lose this seat, I will feel totally responsible,"* I told myself, while closely following the campaign.

The Democrats pushed back. To most voters, Padgett was best known for her work as Governor Bob Taft's point person in the state's office of Appalachia, an economic development department for the southeastern region of the state. Like Ney, Taft was in ethical hot water, having pled no contest to corruption charges earlier in the year. It was a "twofer" for the opposition. "Bob Ney represented the culture of corruption in Washington, and Joy Padgett represents the culture of corruption in Columbus," said the campaign manager for Democrat candidate Zack Space. It was clear from the get-go that the drumbeat about a Republican culture of corruption was resonating with the voters.

The press and official Washington went into a full swoon over the impact Bob's decision would have on the upcoming congressional elections. While I read the various pundits' predictions, I began to feel like I was watching history leap forward. "Bob feels like this too, I'm sure," I mentioned to a neighbor. "I suddenly don't feel like I am making history anymore, but have become history." It was like the Smithsonian vans were going to pull up and take me to a show room somewhere, a relic to prepare for display.

Such feeling didn't last long. Bob's political career might have been over, but he still faced some major legal decisions. What he decided to do next would have a big impact on me. By early afternoon, several new stories had hit the wire. I dug through them thoroughly. Though Bob wasn't talking anymore, his lawyers were.

"Congressman Ney's decision was a political and practical one and not a legal one," said their statement. "In terms of the ongoing investigation, we have repeatedly made clear that Congressman Ney has done nothing wrong, and there is no credible basis to charge him with a violation of the law. If charges are brought, Congressman Ney will defend himself."

The words "if charges are brought" intrigued me. Combined with comments from the Pittsburgh paper stating "the Congressman said he would not step down from office until his term expires in December," any doubt I had about the political calendar driving this decision instead of some imminent indictment subsided. But that still didn't mean an indictment wasn't around the corner. Ultimately, Bob's decision to step down failed to help achieve the clarification I hoped for.

The next day, the *Washington Post* ran a front page story outlining how the new Majority Leader, John Boehner, had pressured Bob to resign. Two unnamed Boehner aides gave the *Post* reporter a blow-by-blow of the meeting between Ney and Boehner which had taken place the week before. I had no doubt that this type of orchestrated media offensive meant the new Majority Leader wanted to show his fellow colleagues that he was willing to make the tough choices necessary to protect the majority, even when it involved one of his old Ohio colleagues. *"That must have been some meeting,"* I thought.

The argument Boehner made was pretty straightforward. One, Bob was going to lose. Two, if he wanted a future career as a lobbyist or a job in which he needed to be on good terms with his fellow Members of Congress, Ney had to step down before the filing deadline. The fact they were talking about preserving Bob's ability to become a lobbyist was both disconcerting and amusing. It also told me the Congressman had not shared with Boehner the full extent of his legal woes. *"No one is going to hire a man on the precipice of a full-scale corruption trial,"* I thought to myself.

Then I began to think it through further. Maybe Bob didn't tell Boehner all the facts precisely because he was gearing up for a trial. If he were going to take on the Department of Justice, getting out there and lobbying for a bit was probably the second best way to raise money, outside of staying in office. I kept going round and round in an effort to grasp the various scenarios. *"Who is to say Bob couldn't get a high-paying job for a year or so as he worked to stonewall the investigation?"* I asked myself. Such an approach would allow him to stockpile cash for an eventual trial. I shuddered at the thought, and continued reading.

Whether it was because he had college-aged kids, staggeringly high legal bills or both, he was going to need to make money, Boehner argued to Bob, according to the article. In order to do that, it was crucial that he stay in the good graces of the House Republican team, the Majority Leader reportedly told him. And the window to take advantage of his colleagues' good will was closing, the article concluded. Bob's decision played out days later.

Boehner had known Bob for more than a decade, yet to protect the majority he went out of his way to publicly shame him. This meant the corruption issue was gaining even more traction in campaigns across the country. To think that Bob, Jack and I were part of a national dialog that threatened our majority was mind boggling. My heart broke every time I thought about it. A general feeling of depression took hold of me. I was desperate to get some kind of control back in my life. But it wasn't to be.

As much as my world was shaken by the news of Bob stepping down and its political ramifications, nothing I read or heard had helped me to settle the fundamental question I was dying to answer. Was Ney gearing up for a nasty, drawn-out trial down the road, or was this just another step toward an eventual plea agreement with the Justice Department? Until that was answered, I would continue to remain confused. And depressed. A trial could last for years. So could my jail sentence, if the investigation didn't play out like I hoped. More than anything, this uncertainty over my future, and my inability to plan ahead, was what had me feeling so lost.

SEPTEMBER 15, 2006
WASHINGTON, DC

Getting Right with the Facts

THE NEWS BROKE EARLY IN the morning. I was flipping from channel to channel on the television when Bob's face appeared on the screen. Like my thumb was suddenly glued to the remote, I stopped flipping. Fox News was reporting that Bob had agreed to plead guilty in the Abramoff case.

Like most mornings, I was on my exercise bike in the basement. Working out had become part of the new routine. With my feet tightly strapped into the bike's peddles, I almost pulled my shoes off trying to get free. I jumped up. *"Bob isn't going to trial,"* I thought. I couldn't believe it was over. *"Life is about to get better."* I called Alison. Unfortunately, she was in a meeting. So I called Tim, my attorney. We talked for a while. At the end of our conversation, Tim said he would contact the Justice Department to find out what was happening, and get copies of any paperwork they were filing with the court. After getting off the phone, I ran upstairs toward my computer to get more information.

I should have felt conflicted about Bob's decision to plead guilty. But I wasn't. His plea meant an end to the investigation. It meant I could move on with my life. I was ecstatic. Bob and I had been friends for years. We had lived together. I had been his top staffer. When I thought about what he was personally going through, I felt sad. It also hurt to know that so many of my closest friends now had to deal with the awkwardness of the dysfunctional relationship between Bob and me. Many didn't know how to navigate the new dynamic between the two of us. How could they? Even I didn't know how best to maneuver through our new reality. It was a tough environment for people to connect with each other generally, let alone understand what it meant for Bob and me individually.

For me, bringing my friends and family members into this new and changing situation was a challenge on many levels. The scandal was now more than two years old. During that time, I had tried not to make too many comments about the specifics of my work with Jack and Bob. The silence was awkward. Those around me had their own views of the scandal, and my role in it. Some of my friends and family thought I was just doing what everyone else was doing in Washington, while others thought I should go to jail. But few really had a feel for what I thought about it all.

That was mainly true because it was in my best interest to only talk about the specifics of the scandal when I had to, namely when I was being interviewed by the FBI, or when I was under oath at trial. Still, I yearned for an end to the silence. Bit by bit, I slowly began sharing my story with close friends and family. But for most of the outside world, it remained tough to know what was happening with me or anyone intertwined with the scandal.

Trying to interact with both Bob and me at the same time must have been an interesting experience. Before he pled guilty, the two of us were living in two very different worlds. It wasn't as simple as two people whose interests were no longer aligned, or who had grown apart, even though both of these elements were true. For people who knew Bob and me, our situation almost forced them to pick between different versions of the truth. Mine, the version where Bob was guilty, and his, the one where he was innocent. Of course, that was all changing. Quickly.

When I got upstairs, I turned on my computer. The news about Bob's guilty plea was spreading like wildfire. Reading the reports felt surreal. Since he was pleading guilty, that meant Bob was now admitting that his relationship with Jack and me was corrupt - and that we had exchanged free trips, meals, drinks, tickets and more for official action. Changing his public story was a big deal. But, according to a variety of news sources, actually hearing from Bob was going to take a while.

The media reported that Ney had checked himself into an alcohol rehabilitation center. The move represented the kind of change to Bob's story that I assumed the public would start to see more of. It was noted that checking himself into rehab would be helpful for Bob to get a lessened jail sentence. At the same time, those of us who worked for him knew how much he liked to drink. Many of us had been by his side at the bar when he was drinking. Therefore, we knew that his decision to go to rehab was more than just a ploy to reduce his punishment. But to many of Bob's constituents, the move was quite a surprise. Since he was in seclusion, Ney was not expected to personally visit the courthouse, the media reported. That would take place later. Instead, the Justice Department was expected to file Bob's signed plea agreement with the court.

I read every story I could. Each made sure to cover the basics. They outlined how Bob was the first member of Congress to plead guilty in the Abramoff scandal. They also reported that he was pleading guilty to one count of criminal conspiracy and one count of making a false statement. Under the sentencing guidelines for those crimes, Bob faced a maximum sentence of 10 years. But since the Justice Department and Ney's lawyers had agreed on a recommendation of 27 months in prison, he was assured of serving much less than ten years.

Bob released a written statement in which he apologized to his family, his constituents and his fellow members of Congress. "I know that this plea agreement will probably forever change the way people view my public service," the statement said. "I regret this very much because I hope and believe that I have helped people through my work, and I hope that some-day the good I have tried to do will be measured alongside the mistakes I have made."

My feet tapped wildly under the desk as I read Bob's statement. I felt mad, anxious and sad all at the same time. *"That must have been hard for him to send out,"* I thought. Most of the stories included some sort of background about how Bob had vociferously denied any wrongdoing for the past several years. They also mentioned my role in securing his guilty plea, and in the scandal generally.

For me, the most eye-opening part of Bob's plea involved his 2003 trip to London. I was not part of that trip, nor was I very familiar with the specifics. But I had provided information to the government about what I knew. According to the news reports, the false statement charge in Bob's guilty plea stemmed in part from financial disclosure statements he filed after his return from London. There was some sort of discrepancy about the $34,000 he said he won in a private casino during the trip. The articles didn't go into specifics. Whatever the facts, it was clear that those winnings had not passed the scrutiny of the Justice Department. According to various sources, the department had been alarmed by the winnings because the amount coincided almost exactly with the amount of debt that was outstanding on Bob's credit cards. I was astounded to see this piece of Bob's story play such a prominent role in his plea.

The host for that Ney trip to London had been a Cyprus-based aviation company. The company had been seeking Congressional support for the sale of airplane parts to Iran. While I didn't know a lot about the trip,

I did know that the owner of the company had approached Abramoff and me about representing them. Jack didn't want to have anything to do with a company that worked with Israel's sworn enemy, Iran. Therefore, after I talked with Jack, I gave the owner of the company the names of several lobbyists who could work with Bob on their Iranian concerns. At the time, I figured if I helped them, they would help me down the road.

Because of my cursory knowledge of this new angle to Bob's guilty plea, I very much wanted to hear the full story. My lawyer had said he would track down the paperwork and get it to me. I presumed that the information being filed in court by the government would help to answer my many questions. I waited to hear. Then I saw that many of the news sites contained links to the paperwork the Justice Department would soon be filing in court. *"That would have been be a much better way to get the information,"* I thought to myself. *"Sure would be a lot cheaper."*

My legal bills were piling up. Since the scandal started, I had racked up several hundred thousand dollars of legal bills. I paid for the first hundred thousand dollars or so by cashing out the mutual funds, stocks and savings that my wife and I had squirreled away over the years. Cashing out our investments was alarming. That money provided us economic security. It was also an emotionally gut-wrenching experience. My parents had filled out paperwork for my first mutual fund on my eighteenth birthday. I was raised to be a saver. Through school and a variety of retail and construction jobs, I contributed what I could. This continued during my first several years in Washington, before Alison and I continued the habit together. And then, within months, that money was gone.

Like my initial legal representation, working to transition into the role of government cooperator had also been time consuming and costly. It soon became a stark reality that I needed to cash out my retirement savings, as well. To do so, I went down to Capitol Hill to talk about my pension with the Congressional credit union. The representative of the credit union advised me that I should only close out my federal pension in the most dire of situations. Since there was a bill was being debated in the House to strip staffers and members who were felons from getting their accrued retirement money, I jokingly asked if that was a dire enough situation. The credit union representative laughed awkwardly, before closing out my pension plan.

Around the same time, I called the administrators of the Federal Thrift Savings plan, as well the administrators for my law firms' 401K plans. "Cash them out," I said to each one of them. Like my investments, my retirement scenario went from rosy to nonexistent in less than a week. It was disturbing on many levels. I was unsure of how my legal situation would play out going forward, and yet all I had left to pay for my legal costs was the house Alison and I owned. To keep my legal representation going, the two of us agreed to set up a home equity account on our home. The new financial situation added even more stress to our already strained relationship. It also required that we change our spending habits.

We began to dramatically cut back on our spending. Any extravagant or non-necessity had to be cut. Gone were the trips to Europe, the dog walker and the maid service. We cut everything from our *New York Times* subscription to our restaurant budget.

Few days passed that I didn't wish there was some sort of book on how best to handle a high profile political scandal. Each day seemed to present a new challenge. And since the ongoing investigation didn't allow for a lot of specific conversations with people I wasn't close to, it was hard to discern what to do next. So I focused on finding a job. It seemed simple enough to focus on.

Every week I made sure to send out at least 25 resumes and make at least ten follow up calls for the numerous potential jobs openings I found. Unfortunately, no one wanted to touch a radioactive former lobbyist who was currently working as a cooperating witness in the biggest congressional scandal of a generation. Most of the time I couldn't blame them. Then I would look at my bank account, realize how badly I needed to work, and re-assess my understanding. For months, I didn't even come close to finding a job. Finally, I decided to meet with a career counselor.

"I don't think this market is ready for your return," she said bluntly.

Her words were like a smack in the face. I didn't want to believe it. So I pushed back. "My situation is unique," I said. "Anything is possible."

She didn't bite. She told me I needed to start looking for work way outside of my field. She then told me a story from her own life. After leaving government work, the future employment counselor outlined how she started an antique business. For several years, that is what she did before deciding what to do with "the rest of her life."

"There is a lot out there besides government relations, consulting and campaigns," she continued. "It could be fun for you to try something new. It was for me. In fact, when I did return to working in the city, all my colleagues wanted to talk about was my antique business. They were great years of my life," she concluded.

Still, I persisted. I wanted to continue searching for public policy-related work. Eventually, the counselor agreed to try to find work for me there.

After sending her numerous resumes that got no results, I began to realize her assessment was probably right. Not that I was prepared to take the kind of step she was encouraging. But the fact was, my situation of spending way more money than I was taking in was untenable.

After weeks of internal debate and numerous discussions with Alison, I decided to file for unemployment insurance. At first, I did not want to accept the fact that I needed that kind of help. Then I worried about whether a regular check coming in the door would impede my efforts to get a job. The limited cash flow could take away the edge I felt was necessary to find a job. Also, the shame of being on government assistance was not something I would have wanted to share with my Washington friends.

With many friends off-limits, I had stopped hanging out at the places I used to go as a professional lobbyist and staffer. My lifestyle became slovenly and solitary. Walking my dog became the main activity of my day. *"Would filing for unemployment make me even more sloth-like?"* I wondered. Like all my decisions at the time, this one emerged from a depressed and uncertain place. Even simple decisions took on unwieldy emotional overtones. Supposedly simple decisions like whether or not to join a softball team were no exception.

Around the time of Bob's plea, a friend of mine sent an email out to a group of us to see if anyone wanted to join a softball team. Joining meant playing games on the Washington Mall with a team made up predominantly of people who worked for non-governmental organizations. It sounded perfect. Something new. Something to get me out of the house. Instantly, I said I would love to be a part of the team.

Within days, the coach of the team put my name on the email list. I started interacting with my new teammates. Then another Abramoff story hit the *Washington Post*, in which my name was prominently featured. It freaked me out. Not because I was in the story, I was used to that, but because I felt like my radioactivity could tarnish the friend who had set me up to play ball. If someone from the team connected my name in our email chatter to the story in the paper, it would make my friend look bad, I assumed. Therefore, I figured there was only one thing to do: quit the team to avoid any potential awkwardness.

"That is the silliest thing I have ever heard," my friend said in response. It was sweet. Really sweet. But it also made me think I was beginning to lose my mind. Why had I thought my association with the scandal would tarnish a softball team? My emotional rollercoaster seemed capable of swirling at any given moment. I desperately wanted to get a feel for where things were going. But I couldn't, even on a momentous day like the day that Bob agreed to plead guilty.

"Does this mean I have reached bottom yet?" I asked, when I finally was able to read through Ney's legal documents. *"Or will that occur in prison? Maybe it is best if I assume the worst is now over. Or will that just ruin me when I get sentenced to spend time in jail?"*

For a guy who used to have a sign on his desk that read "Patience is NOT a virtue," the lack of progress was beginning to immobilize me. Likewise, the lack of clarity over the meaning behind events had me questioning whether I could get on the right track anytime soon. When I agreed to become a cooperator, I was convinced that the scandal experience would help me become a better man, and help me right some of my wrongs. Yet most of the time it didn't feel like I was growing. In fact, it seemed as if I were aimlessly wandering. Like a bear chasing honey, I bounced from one post-scandal life idea to another. On any given week, I was either reading up on how best to be a house husband or what it meant to be a good friend. I started coaching soccer, set up an Ebay account to sell my belongings, and began to put together the contours of this book.

In a unique twist of fate, one of the people who helped to jolt me forward in a positive way was President Ronald Reagan's former Communications Director, Michael Deaver. He was one of my heroes. Deaver had been the ultimate press secretary.

When a friend of mine suggested I contact the 40th President's former advisor to see if we could meet to discuss my situation, I didn't know what to think. Deaver had been friends with Reagan. He was a giant. But in one way, the suggestion made sense. Like me, Deaver had violated the one-year ban. After leaving the Reagan White House in the mid-1980s, he inappropriately used the influence he had gained as a public official to make money as a private citizen. Getting caught changed Deaver's life. The guilty verdict cost him millions of dollars. It was easy to see why I should meet with him. *"But why would he want meet with me?"* I wondered.

For nearly a week, I contemplated calling him. Finally, figuring what the hell, I phoned his office. Deaver was now the president of a global communications firm in Washington. His assistant picked up. I started outlining the reason for my call. "You see, I got caught up in the Abramoff scandal and a friend of mine suggested I call to see if I could get some time with Mr. Deaver."

She didn't say a word. I could hear her scribbling notes. Something about the silence kicked my insecurity into gear. Within seconds I felt like a total idiot. *"She probably thinks I'm a raving lunatic."*

"You know, I am kind of embarrassed to be even calling now that I think about it," I told her. "Maybe I should go."

Like a good secretary, she put me at ease by laughing off my comments. Though she made no promises that my request would be honored, she did say she would get back to me. Nervously, I waited. A week later she called to tell me that Deaver's answer was yes. He wanted to meet with me. Having bought Deaver's book days before, I sat down and read it cover to cover. His road back had been tough. He, too, had felt confused. But over time he got back on his feet.

Pumped up, I walked into Deaver's posh downtown office. Just the thought of meeting with him had me feeling inspired. There was an extra bounce in my step. *"Finally, someone who will understand,"* I thought. While I waited for the elevator, my mind went into overdrive. There were so many things I wanted to discuss. Big things. I wanted to tell him why I broke the one-year ban, why I broke the law. I wanted him to know about my greed, my arrogance and my fear. I also wanted to know why he broke the law, and what had changed in him because of the scandal. Had he become more or less cynical about people? Or about politics? And what about his faith? My expectations of the man, and our meeting, were incredibly high.

Our meandering hour-long conversation flowed from the sacred to the profane, and then back again. Not knowing each other, we started small. He asked how I was doing. We talked about politics. The news. We discussed his life with President Reagan. And Nancy. Then we got down to business.

Over and over, Deaver emphatically told me, "You will get through this." It was obvious to me that he had thought through what he was going to say. "How you get through it is up to you," he would follow up each time, showing off the discipline that made him such an effective communicator. Repeat. Repeat. Repeat. If there was a singular message he wanted to get across to me that day, those two sentences summed it up. *Life will continue. How you lead it is up to you.*

Wise to what was ahead, he not only reminded me that I could change, but he also told me that I had to learn to accept those things I could not change: my past, and the way people would interpret what I did as I try to move forward. Way more than me, Deaver knew what it was like to go from high-profile power player to corrupt has-been in the public's mind. As I was learning, that process was a shock to the system. He could see that I was struggling with what I called, "it."

"You will never fully going to get it back," he said while looking me square in the eye. "It" wasn't just one thing. It was a combination of my view of myself, my place and my future. With my integrity in question at every turn, Deaver knew as well as I did that much of my time was going to be spent trying to get "it" back. My honor. My reputation. My pride. His words that I would never be the same cut deep. But they were important to hear, especially from him. It was a teachable moment. I wanted his advice.

"The first thing you need to do is get right with the facts," Deaver said sternly. "The rest will take care of itself," he continued. I loved the line "get right with the facts" the minute he said it. I burned those words into my memory. I hard-wired them into my brain like I was re-learning to breathe or eat.

Deaver's concept of being honest was not new. It was the practical application of his words that I appreciated - and needed. He was talking about a behavior, not a mindset. Asking myself if I was being "right with the facts" was a concept that would be easier to apply in my day-to-day life than the more legalistic, "Tell the truth." I felt like he was giving me a new starting point that I could monitor. That was big to me, especially when I thought about trying to re-connect with family and friends I had lost contact with over the years.

Deaver wasn't saying something ethereal like, "Neil, you need to keep it real and become a totally honest, loud and proud, straight-talkin' kind of guy." Not that those are bad things. Obviously. But I wasn't a character in a movie living a two-dimensional life. It was more complicated that that. Therefore, when he told me that moving forward in a healthy way meant first "getting right with the facts," it became simple for me. I liked the concept. To me, "getting right with the facts" didn't mean developing some sort of ideologically pure version of what had happened with the scandal, or creating a new politically correct set of historically revised "facts" that would better explain away my sins in public. It meant simply that the truth was out there. And my life would be better if I simply aligned myself with it the best I could. The rest would then take care of itself.

Deaver's "Get right with the facts" comment connected me to the "be honest" comments of my family, friends and attorneys. The phrases were two sides of the same coin. The comments of those closest to me reflected my need to put the complexities of the outside world to the side when I went in for my interviews with the FBI. In the Justice Department or on the stand, opinions, world view and the value of relationships don't matter. Deaver's comments, in contrast, reflected my need to navigate the complexity of the outside world, where those things do matter.

As I left his office, Deaver wished me luck. "You have a long road ahead of you," he said. "When things get confusing, try to picture your life years from now," he continued. "Imagine the gratification of knowing you have done everything possible from this moment forward to do the right thing."

"And get right with the facts," I replied. He smiled and we shook hands.

Getting right with the facts became words for me to live by. A prism to look through. I couldn't know everything or please everyone. But I could set a new foundation for moving forward. The concept provided me a real ray of hope. In fact, Deaver's comments made me start to see that I really could navigate what were sure to be choppy waters ahead. In that way, he was able to exceed the stupendously high expectations I set for our meeting in the first place. For that I was very grateful. Hope is a powerful force.

OCTOBER 13, 2006
WASHINGTON, DC

A Purpose

I WASN'T SURE HOW I WOULD react to Bob's appearance in court. In part, the actual event seemed anti-climactic. The news was now a month old and the die set. Then again, the thought of the Congressman standing before a judge and admitting his guilt gripped me with the force of an intense melodrama.

The myth of an infallible Bob Ney was gone, but remnants of my bygone world view remained. Because of those remnants, imagining the Congressman actually taking responsibility for his part in the scandal remained hard to envision. But the walls between our old mythic world and the reality of today were definitely coming down.

Ambling out the front door early in the morning, I bent down and picked up the newspaper resting in our front lawn. Throwing the *Post* toward the porch as my dog Winnie anxiously pulled on her leash, I muttered "Things will be different when we do this again tomorrow." It was a hint of optimism, an idea which had just started to creep back into my life.

The Congressman's official guilty plea was scheduled for that morning. Alison was out of town. It was just me, the dog and my haunted memories of life in Ney World. Returning from our walk, I quickly grabbed my laptop and plopped it down on the table in front of the television. They would be my portal into the day's events.

President Bush was the first to appear. Timed in part to blunt the news of Bob's court proceedings, the White House had scheduled a ceremony for the President to sign a piece of recently passed homeland security legislation. Playing the one card he had left to play with a public who had largely turned on him, Bush's speech was laden with talk of terrorism. But I knew

371

there was more to this bill than homeland security. It contained a provision to distance Congress from the scandal in which I found myself.

Included in the $400 million legislation to protect our ports was a provision titled the Unlawful Internet Gambling Act, a ban on internet gaming. It was an election-year attempt by the Republicans who ran Congress to turn the page on all things Abramoff. With the President's signature, the internet gaming industry became yet another piece of collateral damage in the scandal. For nearly a decade, Jack had represented that industry. Always a big player in the fight, Jack and our team's past lobbying efforts, as well as our well-known scandal, were now being used against our former clients. Proponents of the ban we fought for years started selling Members of Congress on the idea that a ban on online gaming represented some sort of antidote to the politically potent Abramoff scandal. Votes for the bill on Capitol Hill by scared elected officials appeared out of thin air.

Repercussions of the legislation were felt far and wide. I hated seeing my former clients punished by the politics of the scandal. The world's largest internet gaming company, PartyGaming, immediately suspended their business activity in the United States. Listed on the London Stock Exchange, PartyGaming's market value dropped by nearly sixty percent. For a company which had been valued at nearly $12 billion before it lost the U.S. market, that was a lot of money.

Despite being marketed as the remedy for a congressional lobbying scandal, the bill was shaped almost entirely by Washington lobbyists who worked overtime to cut their last-minute deals. Just because Jack was gone didn't mean the lobbying industry had stopped working. It never did. The irony of lobbyists using a lobbying scandal to advance their professional goals was not lost on me. Gaming lobbyists from Vegas to Indian Country lined up to influence the bill. Many succeeded. Loopholes in the law were written for everything from horse tracks to the NFL's popular fantasy football enterprise. The activity further ingrained in me the belief that the only way to reduce the influence of lobbyists was to reduce the influence of Washington decision makers.

After the president's story, word of Bob's arrival at the courthouse began to appear on the wire. Like the day of my plea, the preliminary series of news stories touched mainly on the fact that Bob was in the courthouse. In contrast to my public silence while in court, the Congressman had released a statement.

"While I have tried my best during my 12 years in Congress to serve the country in bipartisan ways, I have made mistakes of judgment and acted in ways I'm not proud of. I never intended my career in public service to end this way, and I am ashamed that it has. I never acted to enrich myself or to get things I shouldn't, but over time I allowed myself to get too comfortable with the way things have been done in Washington, D.C., for too long."

Having helped Bob write thousands of statements over the years, there was no doubt in my mind this was one he spent extra time putting together. It also verified what I continued to hear through the gossip mill, namely that the Congressman remained in deep denial. The thought of Bob going over his comments with a fine toothed comb and still ending up with such an appalling false and defensive statement infuriated me. His former staff and constituents deserved better.

"I never acted to enrich myself?" I asked incredulously. *"Come on, Bob."* I was suddenly fully aware that I was sitting in my own glass house throwing stones. Our decisions to travel, eat at fancy restaurants and drink for free epitomized what it meant to enrich ourselves. How could he say with a straight face that that wasn't the case?

Reading Bob's words made me wonder what kind of advice he was getting. Had he reached out to old friends and family for help? Or was he still being surrounded by young twenty-something yes-men? *"That can't be healthy,"* I thought. *"If you're not going to take a hard look at what really happened now, when will you?"* I demanded as if he was in the room.

Despite telling myself earlier to be careful about getting too emotional, I decided to open a bottle of wine. Bob's court appearance represented the perfect excuse to engage in some day-drinking. Like a young adult wanting to know what made his or her parents tick, understanding where Bob was at that moment became increasingly important to me. In that context, the Congressman's "blame Washington" defense was galling. *"He has a long way to go,"* I told myself hypocritically, as if I had all the answers.

At the same time, I could empathize with the struggle Bob was having. Since the scandal was so big, there was a whole lot Ney truly knew nothing about. Yet people had a propensity to demand that he take responsibility for everything, even those things he had nothing to do with. On top of that, there had been a large number of false stories and charges thrown Bob's way over the last two years. Stories had circulated about Bob and Jack rigging the 2004 Presidential election in Ohio, about Ney being involved in the Gus Boulis murder, and about the Congressman's purchase of a house boat somehow being a *quid pro quo*. Combined with rampant rumors of other people who seemed to have acted in similar ways, I could see why Bob was attracted to the "everyone was doing it" mentality. But at its core, that argument was bullshit. We may not have been the only ones acting the way we did, but that didn't mean everyone was doing it.

As angry as I was, my heart remained heavy as I watched him continue to struggle through his dramatic identity change. In less than a month, he had gone from high-profile declarations of innocence to admitting his guilt. And he had done so in a much more public manner than I ever went through. Having had what now seemed like the luxury of months and months of sitting quietly in a self-imposed exile while I plodded through my own inconsistent and emotional path, I tried to put myself in Bob's shoes.

It was the beginning of a maddening personal diatribe against the Congressman. A one man freak show. A conversation with no real beginning. And no real end. "I get it, Bob," I said out loud. "There is a simplicity to the culture of corruption argument. But you know better. Obviously power corrupts. We are the current poster children of that age-old truth. And yeah, it makes for great political fodder. Americans have been beating up on Congress for centuries. But the public doesn't know shit about the process. This is about us. Accepting the argument that the system is the problem means people like us have an out. If we aren't responsible for our own behavior, who is? If the government is nothing more than a selfish parade of power games and secret schemes, what do we have?"

The thought of our entire government acting like we had acted at our worst terrified me down to my soul.

"Bob, you, Jack and I may not have been the only corrupt bunch in town, but the truth is 'everyone' *wasn't* doing it either," I continued. "By simply making better choices, all of us could have stayed out of trouble. That is a base of understanding you and I should never waver from," I told the Congressman, as if he could hear me.

"The doesn't mean you didn't work your ass off for your constituents. You cared a great deal about your people. More than they will ever know. But I know. I saw it first hand. And yeah, it blows that all of that is going to be erased by the Abramoff shit. Big chunks of history gone."

In ways far more important to my own well-being than any continued judgment about Bob, the pretend conversation with the Congressman in my living room continued to pick up steam. Babbling like an idiot as I paced back and forth on our stained beige carpet, I asked him, "What does it hurt now to say you never really cared about the lobbying rules we were supposed to follow? Lets stop pretending. I didn't give a shit about them either. But at least we can get straight with the facts."

Fully venting by this point, I carried on, getting louder sentence by sentence.

"That doesn't mean other people haven't done worse," I continued. "Poor us, we got caught. Yeah, it sucks. Forever, we're the assholes. Even the assholes will call us assholes. But all that other stuff aside, the simple truth is it was a choice you made, we made, not the decisions of some fantasy Washingtonland secretly pulling all of our strings. If people start believing that, then we're all in trouble."

I stopped my rant in front of a mirror that hung on my wall.

"What the hell are you doing?" I asked the man in the mirror. "What do *you* know?"

Deep down, I believed that I was finally muddling forward. By getting right with the facts and refusing to be a victim, I truly believed I could get to the other side. *"But what if I'm wrong?"* I wondered. *"What if there is no other side?"*

I paced back and forth. I tapped my toes and cracked my knuckles. And then I got back in the ring with Bob.

"It was a simple statement you wrote," I said aloud. "Did I interpret it wrong? Behind the words, what are you really thinking? Are you looking for reasonable explanations as to why a guy who had done so many good things could also have made so many stupid decisions? Or are you taking the easy way out? It was Jack. It was Neil. It was my Washington puppet master."

Despite the rawness of my feelings about the Congressman, I worried for him. "You still have decades of life ahead," I said. "Don't be a victim."

And as quickly as it began, my diatribe ended.

I was exhausted by the debate and embarrassed by my outburst. Yet I was relieved at the same time. By saying my piece, in the moment, I once again felt like I was moving forward. The conflict was good. It wasn't like I saw myself getting to the "other side," but I could see that the "other side" existed. I could see myself actually talking with Bob sometime in the future. I could see myself fully accepting what I did, what we all did. Even though my diatribe was finished, my introspection continued. I once again began to focus on Bob's motives.

"Why did he do it?" I wondered.

Knowing why Bob broke the law would help me understand more fully why *I* broke the law. It was a question I got asked all the time - from friends and family, as well as the prosecutors and FBI agents at the Justice Department. "Why did Ney do it?" they all asked. Knowing that Bob was really the only one who could answer, I served up my opinion, nonetheless.

In the case of the Justice Department, I answered the question because I had to; in other cases, I did because I wanted to. However, the answer remained same.

First, I told whoever had asked that neither Bob nor I really cared about lobbying and good government rules. Secondly, our ambition took over. We had no business cutting some of the deals we cut, even if much was done in the name of service and moving up the ladder. Thirdly, Bob grew up in the pay-to-play Ohio legislature of the 1980s and early 1990s. At that time, rules against lobbyists paying for meals, trips and entertainment barely existed. Gifts were an institutional part of the process, according to Bob. Big decisions affecting the state were decided behind closed doors at the Speaker of the House's favorite restaurant, with lobbyists of the affected industries paying for everything. Similarly, some of those decisions would occur during high-end trips all over the country and the world, again, at lobbyists' expense.

Months or years later the voters had a choice as to whether they approved of the job an elected official was doing or whether or not they agreed with the outcome of such a pay-to-play system, Bob would tell me when I was a young staffer. He loved to talk about how much he admired the way things were done back in the day. Keeping the outside world insulated from the process meant do-gooder journalists and activists were kept at arm's length. As Bob told me on many occasions, governing that way allowed important issues to be addressed calmly by the state's leaders. The limelight of the media would only make solving the problems harder, he would say. At the time, it made sense to me. But that was then.

Adding to the complexity of the situation, Bob also grew up in a working class town in Appalachia. He wasn't like the several hundred other Members of Congress who were millionaires. They could easily afford a two-home lifestyle without the occasional free meal or drink. It was easy for them to say they didn't take special interest money. Bob would parody their self-righteous tone of voice.

Whether my analysis was right or not, it didn't change the rules we were supposed to follow. I tried my best not to suggest that any of that background was a reasonable excuse to break the law. But I did think it helped to tell a bigger story about Bob - a story that needed to be told since the scandal had turned a very complicated elected leader into a morbid caricature. "He is so much more than that," I tried to remind people.

Nervously strolling into the courthouse after nearly a month of treatment for alcohol abuse, the Congressman looked healthier than ever, friends told me. He was joined by his chief of staff, his legal team and radio personality Ellen Ratner. For most of the day, I couldn't help but continue to feel sorry for him. He had done a lot of good, much of which was about to be forever overshadowed by his time in the courtroom.

"That is accurate," the Congressman said again and again as Judge Huvelle peppered him with questions about what happened. The road ahead looked scary for Bob. He was going to jail, and we both knew that I helped put him there.

Much of the early afternoon reporting was conducted through the prism of the upcoming Congressional elections, elections which were increasingly becoming a referendum on Republican corruption. Much like the ambush following Jack and me after our guilty pleas, people continued distancing themselves from the Congressman. Since we were days away from the election and Bob remained a sitting Member of Congress, it was a hundred times worse for him than it ever had been for me. Like a herd of hard-charging bison, the stampede trampling the Congressman was powerful and unending. With our majority on the line and the Democrats smelling blood, the political battle lines required harsh action by people who used to consider themselves Bob's *friends*.

House Speaker Dennis Hastert, new Majority Leader John Boehner and the rest of the Republican leadership put out a scathing statement blasting the Congressman and threatening to expel him from the House if he didn't resign immediately.

"Bob Ney must be punished for the criminal actions he has acknowledged," they said. "He betrayed his oath of office and violated the trust of those he represented in the House. There is no place for him in this Congress. If he chooses not to resign his office, we will move to expel him immediately as our first order of business when Congress resumes its legislative work in November."

Ohio GOP Chairman Bob Bennett, with whom Ney and I partied with on many occasions, went even further. Bennett called on the state's delegation to begin removing Bob immediately.

"Bob Ney is a liar, a criminal and a disgrace to public service. He's a cancer in the Congress who needs to be removed," he said. "It is unfortunate that Mr. Ney continues to insult his constituency by refusing to surrender his arrogant grip on power."

Their anger reflected the fact that Bob's anointed candidate had failed to gain traction in the race to replace him. Barring a miracle, the seat and its valuable vote was gone, doomed by the Democrats' quick and effective campaign to tie State Senator Padgett to Bob.

As expected, instead of focusing on Ney, Democrat leader Nancy Pelosi focused her attacks squarely on the GOP leadership for allowing him to stay in Congress.

"House Republican leaders have a long pattern of protecting Republican members, even when it comes at great cost to the American people," she said. Pelosi referred to Ney's plea as a "tragedy" for the people of Ohio's 18th Congressional district and "further proof that the Republican culture of corruption has pervaded Congress."

By the time video footage of Bob at the courthouse appeared on the television news channels alongside the President's signing ceremony, my mind had turned to mush. The wine bottle was close to empty. I was drunk. After spending far too many hours looking backward and playing "what if" games, the sadness and insecurity I was feeling flavored my every thought. Bob looked out of sorts, like a deer in headlights. The president's seemingly robotic signing of legislation I had fought against for years only made the moment worse.

Getting a handle on the post-Ney plea situation was suddenly proving harder than expected. Here I was, a major behind-the-scenes player in the news of the day, yet all I wanted to do was hide in the confines of my safe little living room. Gone forever was the cocky kid with all the answers. In his place was a broken man searching for meaning, direction and a new career.

By late afternoon, the Ney-Bush stories started growing old. Then, out of nowhere, they were suddenly joined in the news loop by the rock star Bono. He and Kennedy family icon Bobby Shriver were promoting their anti-poverty campaign "ProjectRed." The U2 singer's sudden juxtaposition between footage of Bob and the President added a new strand to my introspection. Bono's mere appearance produced a refreshing rhythm to my day and a new path for my thoughts.

With emotions as tender as an open wound, I watched as this rock star tried to help save people's lives in Africa.

"3,000 kids a day die from preventable causes," Bono said.

To which I replied, "Look at him." And I did.

"*He isn't single-handedly focused on his career,*" I said to myself. "*He seems to live like his identity has to do with much more than just what he gets paid for. And yet what am I doing? Wallowing at home alone, mad at myself and the world, stuck in some subterfuge of an identity crisis in which my main goal sadly seems to be the restoration of my lost professional status.*"

I began to think that I hadn't learned a single lesson in the last two years. "Maybe you should stop yelling at Bob for a while and focus on what you can control," I told myself aloud.

The shame I felt was new. This shame had more to do with what I wasn't doing now than with what I had done in the past. I was intrigued by that idea, so I sat back down to do some thinking. And I continued watching Bono.

The personal connection I felt to Bono and his message was real. As the pop star encouraged watchers to engage in his mission, the tug I felt was resoundingly strong. That might have been because I had grown up with U2's music, or the fact that my mind was operating on a different plane. I grabbed the remote and turned up the television. Watching intently as the rock star and the Kennedy family icon outlined how their organization was working with the private sector to raise funds for the goal of reducing malaria-related deaths in Africa, I reflected on the day I had met Bono in the Capitol Building. At the time, I was still working for Bob.

While I was coming home from lunch, out of the blue, Congressman John Boehner's chief of staff, Barry Jackson, grabbed me. "Come on," he said. "You are going to love this."

Walking briskly, Barry and I hurried into the Capitol and into a small room filled with about twenty people. Without knowing such meetings even took place, I learned from Barry that we were at a weekly Bible study class for senior Congressional staffers. Looking around, I saw a couple of people I knew. Then Bono walked into the room. He was dressed all in black, right down to his singer's signature sun-glasses. A pending appropriations bill he wanted to discuss was the reason for his visit to the Capitol, Bono said. When he heard about the Bible-study group, he asked to join in. Our conversation began with the singer talking about his own Christian faith, as well as his recent visit with Pope John Paul II to discuss helping the poor in Africa. Bono quoted several pertinent passages from the Bible and encouraged the group to think big as a way to celebrate the new millennium.

"Our generation should be remembered for more than just the Internet," the rock star said. Bono tied that larger goal to the foreign aid appropriations bill funding debt relief in the globe's poorest countries. Playing temporary lobbyist, he asked us to support the measure and opened up the discussion to questions.

Jackson didn't realize what a huge role Bono and U2 had played in my earlier life. Their songs' messages regarding social justice and God's love moved me in ways no teacher's message could. I asked for (and received) their albums for Christmas and birthday gifts. I loved their concerts. And now I was watching Bono off-stage doing his philanthropic work that he sang about. Barry couldn't know at the time what a gift he had given me.

And now again, here was Bono on my television following his faith's call for service to the poor. *"He isn't working in government,"* I thought. *"Why should that be the only way to serve?"* It was a question my friends and family had been encouraging me to ask. After months of confusion and denial, it is sad to admit that it took a rock star to provide the catalyst for me to finally see what they were saying. Working in some Senate-confirmed government job or big law firm wasn't the only way to serve. In fact, that goal suddenly seemed very limiting. It was time to expand my search. I felt like I was being called to something bigger than myself. Grabbing the *Post* and jumping online, I started searching for a cause. My heart and mind were in sync. "If no one will hire me, why not volunteer? You've got to start somewhere," I said out loud.

One of the first places I called was an organization called the United States Veteran's Initiative.

OCTOBER 20, 2006
WASHINGTON, DC

An Unclear Road Ahead

LOCATED ON THE PROPERTY OF the Armed Forces Retirement Home, the Ignatia House rests at the bottom of a winding, hilly road, across from a golf course and next to several abandoned buildings. The space represents some of the last undeveloped land in the District. It is about a ten minute walk from the main entrance's security gate. In my car, I could get there in two minutes.

Isolated from many of the pressures and temptations of the city, the Ignatia House was home to the United States Veterans Initiative. Better known as U.S. Vets, the initiative runs a supportive housing program for thousands of formerly homeless veterans across the country. In Washington, the sixty or so former veterans who were part of the program lived on the grounds in Ignatia House. Not technically part of the armed forces retirement campus, the house's location remained ideal for the program's mission - helping veterans. It was a cause I was proud to join.

Leading the local U.S Vets' effort was a woman named Emily Button. She was the reason for my involvement with the organization. On the day of Bob's guilty plea, Emily had posted a "Volunteers Wanted" ad on Craiglist. I replied. While outlining to her that I was interested in helping the program, I also touched upon my involvement in the Abramoff scandal. Moments like that were when similar past conversations had turned a little weird. I was skeptical about how Emily would respond. My assumption was that she would either say she had to get back to me and then not take follow-up calls, or else tell me they weren't interested. The usual. Instead, Emily told me to meet her at the Fort Totten Metro stop the following Monday morning. Standing in the Metro, I waited for her pick me up and take me to Ignatia House. I wasn't sure what to expect. Intellectually, I was committed to the mission. It rekindled the fire that burned inside me for public service. Lighting that flame again made me nervous. But I was excited about the prospect of helping out what I hoped would be a new purpose and a new identity.

When Emily showed up, I liked her immediately. Her wit and easy-going manner eased my nerves as we approached the grounds. Walking into the homeless facility was heart-warming. The Ignatia House was part office and part home, and quite a bit more downtrodden than my posh Chevy Chase neighborhood. Still, it was well-kept. It had the feel of a medically-based living facility. Along the first floor corridor were handmade meeting notices, community news announcements and inspirational posters. Red, white and blue flags, paintings and memorabilia aligned the hallway wall.

From the outside, the building looked like a large, grey, cement tissue box. Inside, the ground floor housed the U.S. Vets office space, the veterans' kitchen, television room and employment center. All three floors contained housing for the men and women of Ignatia House. Most of the veterans stayed in single occupancy rooms. Some had their own bathrooms. Some didn't. To be a part of the program, each individual veteran needed to be self-sufficient. Or close to it.

The Ignatia House was a sober living facility. Inside were men and women who had donned the uniform for our country. Their service was a point of pride. At the same time, many had also lived other lives, lives of addiction, trauma and/or homelessness. Some had been called abusers, addicts, convicts or losers. Despite proudly serving their country, most had been told at one time or another that they didn't matter. Struggling to get back on their feet, the formerly homeless veterans of Ignatia House worked hard to battle the fear, anger and resentment they saw all around them. I could relate to their feeling and struggles.

I had experienced Washington as a winner for more than a decade. As a member of Washington's political class, I was one of the wheelers and dealers who thrived. All I had to do was look at my scrapbook of news clippings or my paycheck to verify my standing. My worth. Now many of those same people - the reporters, the lobbyists and the rest of professional Washington were telling me I was a loser. And sometimes I was calling myself one, too. Many of the veterans I would meet in upcoming weeks could relate to my story as well.

Because of that connection, I looked around the Ignatia House and felt like I was a part of a community, one built on the promise of second chances, on the belief that people can change. Without even thinking, I knew I was where I needed to be.

My Monday visits would soon become a regular occurrence. Arriving early in the morning, I spent the day assisting veterans who were looking for work. Whether it was helping to write a resume, fill out an application or find a specific employment opportunity, I enjoyed helping. And I very much liked the veterans.

The challenges these men and women faced were enormous. Adding a job search to what in many cases was a very fragile day-to-day existence took patience - more patience than most of us thought we had. The extra effort made each step of progress that much more of a reason to celebrate. For instance, I had the opportunity to help someone who had initially refused to use a computer for a job search find employment with the help of that same machine weeks later. The sense of jubilation over that was every bit comparable to the thrill of watching fireworks on the Mall during the fourth of July.

With the rest of my life so full of confusion, the time at Ignatia House helped to simplify my priorities. Instead of constant worries about my marriage, the scandal, money, and who in the hell I thought I was, sitting in front of a computer helping to find a formerly homeless veteran a job was as straightforward and positive an experience as I could get. There was no over-thinking. It wasn't some sort of escape from my past. I was simply serving others, and connecting with the part of my past that I wanted to continue feeling proud of. As bad as I felt sometimes, I needed to remind myself that everything I did in my past wasn't bad. Over time, helping my Monday morning vets soon became exactly the kind of purity in purpose I had been so desperate to find again.

Those first few visits to U.S. Vets were empowering. The veteran's strength in dealing with their own adversity inspired me. Talking with them or my fellow staffers was enlightening on a regular basis. One of the veterans regularly told me he was, "just happy to be on this side of the grass." It was a good line, one he once used during a particularly stressful time. I laughed. He then pulled up a chair next to me and sat down. "Seriously, when you have been through what I have been through, you really are happy to be on this side of the grass. Everything else is gravy," he said. I laughed again. This time, he did too.

The pretense of the power town side of Washington was nowhere in sight at Ignatia House. In its place was a commitment to the struggle: the daily struggle to eat, to connect with people, and find meaning. As much as I felt like I was making a difference, on most days I had to wonder who was really helping whom more, me or the veterans. Of course, that was part of what made U.S. Vets so special.

The introspection was needed, even if I regularly picked myself apart about what I was doing there. "*What made you come help the vets?*" I would ask myself on occasion. "*A Bono-inspired call to service, really? Or do you want people to think you are a good guy? Or maybe this is a way back into politics? Or just a public relations exercise?*" The questions persisted.

The last few years had shaken me up pretty good. The uncertainty of my feelings about my own identity proved this out. It also led to some scary introspection. On a daily basis, I feared going to jail, getting divorced, losing all my money and being shamed out of Washington. But my greatest fear of all was that, after much soul-searching, I would find out that I wasn't a good person who had done bad things, but that I was actually a bad guy at heart. What would I do then?

Such questions were painful, but healthy. Professional counselors say the use of questions like that is a classic self-help tool. It was a tool we used everyday at Ignatia House, and a tool that helped me immeasurably. I began to realize that the answers to my many questions weren't always consistent or necessarily going to appear in an easy-to-read self-help book. But honestly trying to get right with the facts was important, enough that it quickly became clear to me that the small amount of personal improvement I was beginning to feel had come about because of the questions I was asking, as much as the answers.

Figuring out "why" or "what" I was doing forced me to slow down and think. Instead of quickly trying to figure out the best "win" for my professional or personal situation, my slower, more introspective approach made me focus on the process behind my decision-making, not just the outcome. It was a breakthrough.

For nearly a decade, my outcome-based thinking had allowed me to soar to professional heights. Few could work through a public relations campaign or the complex battlefield of Capitol Hill politics as quickly as I could. This process allowed me to position myself on the winning side of many debates and then take part in the spoils of victory.

Unfortunately, step-by-step, my outcome-based focus had also clouded my moral compass. By focusing on *who* would win a legislative fight or *how* to win a political campaign, I sometimes lost track of *why* I had gotten involved in politics in the first place, or *what* it meant to actually serve the public. Like the veterans I talked to at length, such realizations made me feel both sad and happy: sad because it was upsetting to be reminded of how I had chosen to live my life, but happy because such realizations provided accountability and meant I could take a small step forward.

The more I dug in, the more I enjoyed my time with the veterans. The sheer enjoyment of helping someone else accomplish an important goal in his or her life made me feel good. It was that simple. I stopped worrying about how my help would be perceived. My one-on-one time with the vets was teaching me to just stay focused on the helping part. In doing so, I found myself being helped. Granted, I still had a long way to go.

Alison and I continued to struggle through our souring relationship. Her willingness to be so publicly supportive amazed me and I greatly appreciated it. Yet the tension between us continued to grow. The scandal didn't help, nor did it cause our problems. At the same time, we faced a family hardship that had nothing to do with the scandal. Our beautiful two-year-old niece was battling leukemia.

In a fight for her life, Chloe and her struggle impacted me in a deeper way than a Washington scandal ever could. When I returned from U.S. Vets after that first Monday of volunteering, Alison told me some dreadful news. The doctors said it was likely that we were going to lose Chloe. I was devastated.

Awash in grief, I headed downtown for my scheduled appointment with the FBI. Despite Bob's plea agreement, the government wanted to keep talking. I didn't have a choice. For this meeting, the FBI told me they wanted to discuss Nevada Senator Harry Reid. They wanted to dig into members of Team Abramoff's who were close with the Senator and his staff. I didn't want to go. I never did. But they kept calling.

My expectation had been that my cooperation would decrease with Bob's agreement. That wasn't how it played out. And since my cooperation agreement required that I make myself available to answer the department's questions, I did what I had to do. After all, I hadn't been sentenced yet, and providing assistance to the government was the best way for me to reduce my impending punishment.

The first question I got was about one of my old lobbying colleagues who had worked with Reid's office for years. The FBI wanted to know when the last time I had talked with him. "A few days ago," I replied. One of the agent's interest seemed to pique at the fact that I remained in contact with my old colleague. The agent asked about our conversation. I told him about it. In doing so, I let him know that my former Team Abramoff colleague was having a party at his house and had invited me. The agents looked at each other, and continued their questioning.

They then began asking me about the team's work with Senator Reid, and the Senator's assistance to the team. We talked about Reid's letter opposing the Jena tribe's casino pact, Jack's Russian client Alexander Koulakovsky, the Tigua tribe and the Senator's use of Appropriation Committee funding to help our clients. I didn't feel like I knew a whole lot on those topics, but I told them what I knew.

From there, I was asked about the trip Bob and I took to the Fiesta Bowl with my colleague and one of Senator Reid's top staffers. The trip had been a part of Bob's guilty plea, as well as mine. *"What had been such a good time didn't seem so fun in retrospect,"* I thought, as our conversation continued.

The FBI asked me about my firm's fundraiser for Senator Reid. I had been there so I told them what I knew. We then talked about a trip Senator Reid's chief of staff took to Malaysia that was paid for, in part, by one of Jack's clients. They even asked me about the Senator's numerous family members who were lobbyists. I answered all their questions as fully as I could.

After several hours, the interview concluded. At that point, one of the agents returned to the topic of my former lobbying colleagues upcoming party.

"Would you be comfortable wearing a wire at the party?" he asked.

I was floored by the request. Dumbfounded, I struggled to speak. Then simply told him the truth.

"That would break my heart," I replied, without saying yes or no.

"This isn't an official request," he said. "And it wouldn't work if you aren't comfortable."

Stammering, I told him I didn't know that kind of thing was a part of my plea agreement, and I wasn't sure I could get comfortable with it. Basically, I nervously filibustered his request before telling him that I wanted to talk with my attorney.

He replied by stressing again, "This isn't an official request. We are just talking about your comfort level. But think about it, like the voice mail recordings you gave us on Ney. That kind of thing is important. It is worth me asking you about," he continued.

I got out of there as fast as I could.

My heart raced as I hurried off to the Metro. Instead of being almost done with my cooperation, it seemed as if the investigation was just getting started. My mind went into overdrive. There was pain everywhere. At home. All around me. I tried to focus.

"Not an official request?" I wondered. *"What if I said yes? I bet it would be-come official right away."* The mere thought of wearing a wire freaked me out. I tried to calm down. The day had been such an emotional roller coaster. It had started with the optimism of my first day at U.S. Vets. It then came to

a crashing halt with my horrible family news. And now the FBI was asking me to wear a wire to a friend's party so I could tape our conversations about his work with Senator Reid, and Reid's staff. I felt like jumping off a cliff.

"*Since I am pretty much at rock bottom,*" I joked to myself, "*the fall shouldn't be too far.*"

Instead of doing anything so dramatic, I made my way to the back seat of the Metro car and headed home. With my eyes closed, I used both hands to maniacally rub the temples on the side of my head. My thumbs moved in a clockwise motion as I tried to get a handle on what I was feeling. It was soothing, so I didn't stop during the entire ride.

For whatever reason, I started thinking about a cultural analysis I had read about years before. The premise of the study was that much of the worst societal upheaval in history did not necessarily occur when times were at their worst or when people felt hopeless - but when a society was in a period of unrealistic expectations. Problems would happen, the study suggested, when a family, a community or a nation started to realize that their rising expectations would not be met.

"*Is that me?*" I asked myself. "*Am I living with unrealistic expectations?*"

My questions led to other questions. "*Should I really have expected to be done cooperating with the Justice Department after Bob pled guilty? Is it too early to be thinking that I can just find a new mission and move on? What about my former colleague? What do I owe him? Should I wear the wire? He is a friend. Right? What is a friend?*" The questions came fast and furious.

While there were no easy answers to my questions, the questioning itself slowed down my thinking. Franticness was eventually replaced with unease and confusion. That was good. I could deal with those emotions.

Ultimately, I was never officially asked to wear a wire. In the moment, however, that didn't matter. The mere fact that an FBI agent asked me to wear one sent me into an emotional tailspin.

When I got home, I quickly took the dog out for a walk, and continued to think. I walked poor Winnie for more than an hour.

"*Is Harry Reid next?*" I asked myself. "*Maybe I should I have seen this coming.*" Periodically, during the scandal, Reid's name had popped up in the papers. Also, I had been asked about the trip to the Fiesta Bowl during a previous interview. "*Was this a thunder and lightning situation?*" I didn't know. I didn't know Reid's office well enough to know what was really happening. Still, I knew the basic facts. And had been following every bit of the scandal with a microscope.

Months earlier there had been a flurry of news stories about Senator

Reid's decision to take some free tickets to a big boxing match in his home state of Nevada. His response had intrigued me, especially since I knew that I had already talked with the government about the Ohio State game in Arizona with his staff.

"I would be criticized if I didn't go," the Senator said, in reference to the fight. "It's just like going to an Ohio State football game, an Arizona State football game - in Nevada, boxing is it."

The quote jumped off the screen when I saw it. *"Is the investigation of Reid picking up steam?"* I wondered. *"If so, how would the public know?"* Unlike Bob, who had to raise money through his publicly filed defense fund, Senator Reid was worth tens of millions of dollars. He could discreetly pay for his own defense.

My questions didn't lead to many answers. I didn't know enough to know what was really going on with any sort of Reid-related investigation. All I knew was what I had seen and heard with my own eyes and ears. And that was enough to suggest that the Abramoff investigation was far from over. As much as I wanted to fully move forward, I was beginning to see that I would have to wait.

As Charles Dickens said in *A Tale of Two Cities*, it was the best of times, it was the worst of times."

The Naval Academy

I COULDN'T BELIEVE THE NAVAL ACADEMY was letting me, a felon, speak to the first-year midshipmen gathered at Alumni Hall. The students and I were cordoned off in a corner of the school's 6,500-person basketball auditorium. Seeing the cover slide of my Power Point presentation beaming out from a sixty-foot screen was a bit intimidating. I felt a long way from the safe confines of my second-floor home office. Giving speeches had never been an issue for me before, but I felt nervous. *"Is this really the best place for me to make my first public comments about the scandal?"* I asked myself. But it was too late to back out now.

The topic of my presentation was government and ethics. That meant leading a discussion on the nuts and bolts of modern congressional campaigns, as well as discussing my role in the ongoing Abramoff scandal. The talk was timely. Issues involving political corruption had become the top concern for voters going into the upcoming elections. That wasn't good for the Republicans in Congress.

For weeks I had been looking forward to talking with the nearly two hundred first-year students known as "plebes." After sitting by silently for years, I knew it was finally time to get out and try to use my cautionary tale for some good. Talking through my mistakes and learning my lesson in the moment was a concept my parents had instilled in me when I was young. It was a concept the introspection of the last few years had helped to reawaken.

As I drove into the complex earlier in the day, I passed a building that displayed the Academy's large seal. Consisting of a trident-wielding hand on top of a coat of arms, the seal's inscription read; Ex Scientia Trideas - From Knowledge, Sea Power. It impressed me. *"At some point, these plebes will* have the responsibility of wielding power on behalf of our country," I thought. "*Just like I did.*" The thought served as a good reminder of my goal for the day. I wanted the plebes to understand how the slippery slope of corruption works, and how it can corrode a persons' morals if they aren't careful - whether in politics, business or the military. After that, I wanted to emphasize to the plebes how important it is to listen to their conscience when the lines between right and wrong seemed blurry. I wanted them to learn from my mistakes.

With the elections a week away, I focused the beginning of my presentation on a specific campaign in northern Indiana, the state's 2nd congressional district. It was a heated battle between Republican incumbent Chris Chicola and his Democrat opponent, businessman and lawyer Tom Donnelly. I chose that race to discuss because it had no direct tie to me or the Abramoff investigation, as far as I knew. Additionally, it was a bellwether contest which could decide whether or not the Democrats took over the House of Representatives. Finally, the close contest also contained several hot button local issues. Having received several written questions from the students before my presentation, I knew many of them were focused on the impact of what was going on in Washington. I wanted to make sure they also saw first-hand the importance of district-specific issues in a congressional race.

The program director attached a microphone to my suit lapel and wished me luck. After turning to address the plebes, he gave them my background, with just a hint of the scandal, and introduced me. I rifled through my note cards. "*Time is going to be tight,*" I figured. The students ate their lunches from the small, sturdy, white lunch boxes sitting on their laps. Attentively listening in their dress uniforms, the plebes were amazingly well-behaved.

Entitled "The Election Process," part one proceeded as planned. Whether I was discussing the basic tenets of defining victory as simply "fifty percent plus one vote" in an election. or leading a detailed conversation about who votes and why, I could see the plebes were into it. I felt like a professor. It was empowering.

"The Chicola vs. Donnelly race is a good barometer of what is going on across the country," I told the plebes. "The trend lines and polling suggest a close race. The Republican candidate is being helped by the history of the district. The Democrat is being helped by the issues. Issues like corruption in Congress," I continued. Hearing those words come out of my mouth sent a shiver up my spine. I knew what was coming. Nonetheless, I swallowed hard and carried on.

To help them analyze the situation, I asked the plebes to picture themselves going door-to-door as a candidate. "Imagine raising money, meeting constituents and doing interviews," I continued. "As you can see, the campaign between these two guys is a big deal for them personally. At the same time, it is a big deal for their communities and for the country. Members of Congress are both people and representative of various causes important to their constituents."

That led me toward the Abramoff matter. It was the twelfth cue card of my presentation. In orange marker, along the top, I had scribbled "Just shoot straight." Only one of the several classes listening to my presentation had been pre-told about my Abramoff past. But word had spread among the plebes, according to the professors. The wide variety of student questions which had already been asked told me our conversation was going to go in directions for which I could not plan a response. Such a format was a good test of my commitment to focus less on the outcome, or how an answer would be perceived, and more on giving the interested young person a thoughtful answer to his or her question. It was like my discussion with the professor who had invited me to talk with the plebes. Days earlier, we contemplated whether the media should be told about my visit. For a headline-hound like me, it was hard to say I didn't care. A story about me talking at the Academy would have been the closest thing I had gotten to good press in years. But I demurred. "Whatever you want is cool," I said. And meant it.

I reached under the podium and grabbed a plastic cup of water. Gulping it down, I paused for a moment to look at my watch. We had about fifteen minutes. Since the plebes had heard me talk about my campaign experience, I asked them if they thought it was strange that someone like me was not out in the field. Several heads nodded.

In a quiet, shaky voice, I waded in. I told them I wasn't working on campaigns anymore. I told them that I had made terrible mistakes. "Because of those mistakes, I've lost my job," I said. "I'm deeply in debt and have become a felon. I am waiting for a judge to sentence me for my crimes," I continued. "I may end up going to jail."

The students sat quietly. It was what one of the Academy teachers would later call a "deafening silence." With the plebes sitting rapt, listening to the details of my criminal case, I urged them to learn from my mistakes.

"If you see an ethical or legal line up ahead, do not walk toward it," I implored them. "Walk away. If you feel the tug of your conscience, or as I call it, have a red flag moment, listen to it. The moment may seem small, but ignoring your conscience is always a big deal."

After my presentation, a handful of plebes and instructors stayed after to talk. Some wanted to talk politics. With those, I discussed specific campaigns they were studying or how the outcome could impact future public policy. It was awesome to talk shop with students who were interested in politics. I soaked up the enjoyment of their attention.

During our give and take, one of the instructors thanked me for coming. He did not hide the fact that he was very disappointed by my decision to break the law. But he did say my talk would provide his class a valuable teaching tool.

"That is why I came here," I replied.

It was the last plebe I spoke with, though, that left the most indelible mark. Out of the corner of my eye, I watched him as he waited in line to talk with me. He seemed cocky. And curious. Frankly, he reminded me of myself when I was his age.

Shaking my hand, he told me he was a Democrat. "We don't agree on our politics," he continued. "But I appreciate your willingness to talk with us." The young plebe then said, "Anyone who can accept responsibility for their actions gets my support." I smiled. His words made my trip. "Thanks," he concluded.

"Thank you," I said.

Gathering up my notes, I couldn't help but think that I had impacted that young man's life in a positive way. It made me feel great. It also reminded me how way off my expectations for the presentation had been.

Initially, I expected to feel like I had impacted lots of their lives when I was done. But that clearly wasn't the case. Many of the plebes were probably thinking about their other classes or something going on in their personal lives during my presentation, I assumed. And yet that didn't matter. Such expectations were remnants of my previous life, where I had the kind of influence to impact lots of peoples' lives on a regular basis. That wasn't the case anymore. It wasn't easy to accept, but with comments like those from the young plebe at the Naval Academy and my work with the formerly homeless veterans of Ignatia House, I could honestly say I was trying to move forward in a positive way. While I knew the road ahead remained uncertain, this understanding was a new normal I could rally behind.

NOVEMBER 7, 2006
KENSINGTON, MD

Election Day

DEPRESSED, I HEADED HOME EARLY. I had spent the last few hours at the house of my former Team Abramoff colleague, Kevin Ring, watching the election results. Republican candidates were getting trounced all across the country. It became too much to take.

As much as I wanted to keep riding the positive Naval Academy wave forward, it wasn't so easy. Keeping any sense of positive momentum was tough. My family was hurting. So was I. And yet the investigation plodded along. I continued to feel uneasy about my recent meeting with the FBI, the one in which I was asked to wear a wire. The meeting had been a harsh reminder of how serious the ongoing investigation was to the well-being of my former colleagues and me. Such a reality increased the feeling of angst I felt while hanging out with Kevin. He, too, was a target of the scandal. Therefore, the two of us tried to stay away from any specific conversations about the investigation.

That being said, Kevin and I spent much of the evening awkwardly laughing our way through the unfolding election. It was our way of coping with a campaign in which the Democrats had successfully labeled the Republicans as corrupt, in large part because of the Abramoff scandal. The circumstances were anything but funny. Kevin's former boss, California Congressman John Doolittle, faced a career-threatening election because of his relationship with Jack and the team. He was not alone. There were several other elected officials in a similar situation.

Gluttons for punishment, my former lobbying colleague and I watched campaign commercial after campaign commercial on Kevin's computer. Most of them were harsh, slash and burn negative advertisements which attacked our so-called "corrupt" friends. Some specifically mentioned me by name. It was depressing. Making matters worse was the fact that some of those ads had been put together by my wife's Democratic consulting firm. Elections were always tough for Alison and me. Needless to say, the fact that her firm was running advertisements about her corrupt husband's lobbying practice made our already uncomfortable Election Night ritual even more so. Unlike the past few election cycles, when I got to celebrate, Alison and her colleagues were celebrating this year.

I went home. Tail between my legs, I crawled into bed, but couldn't sleep. The results poured in throughout the night. Before long, our Republican majority evaporated. The political flood waters poured over many of the last minute levees constructed to withstand the storm. GOP offices I had hoped would survive failed to hold on. The night belonged to the Democrats. So did the future. At a minimum, they would be in charge of the House of Representatives for the next two years.

The following morning, a few Senate races remained too close to call. One was the race in Montana. Control of the upper chamber of Congress hung in the balance. In large part, the campaign in Montana between incumbent Republican Senator Conrad Burns and his Democrat challenger Joe Tester had been a referendum on Burns's relationship with Team Abramoff. The thought of that campaign resulting in a Senate majority for the Democrats infuriated me. Whether I actually woke up on the wrong side of the bed or not, that is where I quickly found myself.

I read through the paper as I drank my morning coffee. The political carnage was everywhere. The election was a bloodbath. In Ohio, Democrat Zach Space secured a landslide victory in Bob's old district. Space won by nearly fifty thousand votes more than the Ney replacement on the ballot, Joy Padgett. A handful of Abramoff associates in Arizona, California and Pennsylvania also lost. Likewise, the seats of former Majority Leader Tom DeLay and a Congressman from Florida who had also traveled with Jack to Scotland were picked up by Democrats. Even in Indiana's 2nd District, where Joe Donnelly beat Chris Chicola 54% to 46%, the Republican candidate lost. From sea to shining sea, the GOP brand was in freefall. The political pendulum was swinging to the other side.

I dissected the Election Day exit polling. More voters said corruption and ethics in government "was extremely important to their vote" than any other issue. Corruption placed ahead of terrorism, the economy and the Iraq War, in that order. I couldn't believe it. Shame shivered through my body. There were a lot of corruption-related stories that played into those exit polling numbers. But there was no escaping the fact that the Abramoff scandal was a big piece. *"How had I ended up playing a role in this catastrophe?"* I thought. It still seemed like a bad dream.

As if my own words were bubbled up in a comic strip, the question of my role in the election hung out there to examine. For the last twelve years, my politics had defined who I was. And yet, for almost two years now, my soul searching had been primarily a personal experience. Most of my time was focused squarely on my individual choices, my sins. It had been largely void of politics. That was until I sat in my dimly lit dining room running through page after page of election results.

"Surely some of this carnage is my fault," I thought. *"But how much?"* Thinking through the millions of individual choices that go into the public's electoral decision making, it became clear that it was going to be impossible for me to quantify the blame I felt I needed to accept for this massacre. Such a fact was tough to accept, though. *"How can I move on if I don't accept responsibility?"* I wondered. The questioning created a weird loop of over-analysis. *"If I'm not responsible, then who is? Jack Abramoff? Tom DeLay? Bob Ney? But if they are responsible, than surely I am too, right?"* I asked. *"Or am I? Outside of Bob's district, no one knows who Neil Volz is."* I was talking in circles. Even worse, it felt like I was trying to blame others for the corrupt role I played in the scandal. That screamed of victim hood, which was unacceptable to me. I was raised to never accept being a victim. Yet, at the same time, being honest meant accepting the fact that I didn't have enough control over events to impact all those races across the country. Therefore, how could I take responsibility? I didn't know what to do.

Incoming Speaker of the House Nancy Pelosi was all over the television. Making a compelling argument for change, the Democrats had run a stellar race. Their first piece of business in the new Congress, the future Speaker said, would be strong anti-corruption legislation meant to reduce the influence of lobbyists in Washington. She said such legislation was a way of verifying the support the people had placed in her party's hands. Whether Pelosi and her colleagues actually believed it or not behind closed doors, I did not know, but the Democrats were clearly listening to the public.

Like Gingrich in 1994, the incoming Speaker and her team effectively nationalized the congressional elections. As CNN reported, voters defied "the traditional political maxim that all politics is local, with 62 percent of voters saying national issues mattered more than local issues when deciding which House candidate to pick." It was eye-opening to read such a nugget of juicy political analysis. It was also a reminder that as much as I thought I needed a break from the political game, I still loved it. Then something weird happened. Re-reading the news about the nationalized elections sent my soul-searching back into high gear. Politics became personal again.

"If I had been honest with myself about the polling data leading up to the elections, I would not have been surprised by how nationalized the races became," I thought. Missing such a basic point irked me. It felt like I had decided to see what I wanted to see instead of getting right with the facts. I began to think that maybe I hadn't learned anything at all in the last few years. Having spent such a long time trying to get right with the facts, the mere suggestion that I may have had a blind spot in those efforts was incredibly worrisome. It took me several hours to get back on track.

When I did, my thoughts returned me to the heart of my failures: the slippery slope of American politics. In my cave of a home for the last few years, it seemed pretty easy to understand how a good guy had lost his way. Arrogance. Greed. A lack of accountability. And a willingness to see things as I wanted them to be, instead of as they were. But putting all that into the bigger context of competing world views, global interests and political agendas made the issues more confusing, and the goal of a simple answer more elusive. I renewed my commitment to move forward in the most honest way possible.

By the end of the day, a battle had already begun brewing amongst the GOP over who had caused our loss at the polls. The exit polling clearly showed the series of "national" contests had been decided by voters not affiliated with either party, known as political independents. Unlike during the last midterm races, where these independent voters split their vote somewhat evenly between congressional Republicans and Democrats, this time around independents favored Democrats by 18 points - 57 percent to 39 percent. It was hard not to see the impact of such a change in preference.

Other people chose to interpret the results differently. Former Majority Leader Tom DeLay suggested the GOP had been defeated because we weren't conservative enough. "The Democrats didn't win, the Republicans lost," he said. Outlining how an increased turnout by conservative voters in some races may have allowed certain Republicans to survive the Democrat wave, DeLay's analysis frustrated me. Yes, increasing the number of conservative voters is always good for Republicans. But fundamentally, his breakdown of the facts just wasn't true.

One of the things I had always admired about DeLay was his political intelligence. Another was his willingness to roll up his sleeves to get the job done. But that didn't mean I had to see things the way he did. Of course, DeLay wasn't speaking as the leader of our party anymore. He was playing inside baseball. His comments were more about his future than the party's future. In that context, his words began to make more sense, and showed again the differences between what a person like me needed to do to get back on track, and what a movement of people needed to do to get back on track, after being thrown out of the majority.

While DeLay was still perceived as a national leader of the party, what he was really angling for with his comments was to be the leader of the most conservative part of the party. There is a whole industry of right-leaning groups and organizations committed to pushing the agenda of the conservative movement DeLay had led for a decade. Being a leader in that community is different from being the leader of a governing coalition. In that respect, there was nothing at all wrong with what the former Majority Leader was doing. He could make a lot of money advocating for conservative causes. And having watched staffer after staffer leave his office to make millions as professional lobbyists and consultants, part of me hoped DeLay would be successful. People like Ralph Nader and Al Sharpton had been doing it for years on the left. But that didn't mean I had to agree with his facts.

The day, though, belonged to incoming Speaker Nancy Pelosi. At one point, she opined that the public had decided, "Maybe it takes a woman to clean house." Her words resonated with me in a way that I didn't expect. For nearly a decade, I had trained myself to immediately pick holes in whatever the political opposition said. I didn't do that this time. *"Maybe she is right,"* I thought. Not that I was thinking in the political way I presumed she meant. My assessment was more personal, namely that my corruption experience had really only involved men. *"How about **that** for getting right with the facts Mr. Deaver?"* I joked to myself. *"Agreeing with the new Democratic Speaker."*

After the dust settled, the only symbol of what now seemed like an age-old conservative movement was President Bush. He was our last hope, the only one left in office. His last two years would no longer be spent trying to implement our long-held goals of personalized Social Security accounts, streamlined government and pro-growth tax policies. They would be spent defending our previous accomplishments from Democratic Party attacks. As anyone involved in politics could see, elections again had consequences.

Out of sheer necessity, President Bush wasted no time adjusting to the new dynamic in Washington. "The message yesterday was clear," Bush said. "The American people want their leaders in Washington to set aside partisan differences, conduct ourselves in an ethical manner and work together to address the challenges facing our nation." Watching what had been my party struggle to accept the voters' verdict was brutal. It was like watching a professional sports team in transition. Our well-honed group of players had grown slow, lethargic, and over-the-hill. The rebuilding process was already underway. Within hours of the election, the President announced that controversial Secretary of Defense Donald Rumsfield was being replaced by incoming Secretary Robert Gates. It was a typical Bush decision. Instead of waiting for someone else to move, he chose to act. After such a resounding electoral defeat, Bush's aggressiveness was great to see.

With the White House on solid footing, I watched the Democrats celebrate their big victory. By mid-afternoon, I wasn't nearly as dejected as I had been in the morning. In a weird way, I was even soothed by the thought of thousands of idealistic progressive staffers and operatives packing their cars for a move to Washington, like I had done more than a decade before. *"New blood is good,"* I thought. *"Shake things up a little bit."*

On a personal level, the new majority on Capitol Hill meant my job search had just gotten much tougher. Many of my former GOP colleagues would soon be out looking for work. And they weren't felons. The prospect of so many good people with families out there clamoring for a new pay check saddened me greatly. It also eliminated whatever slim prospects I had for employment in the political arena.

I was no longer the only one wandering in the political wilderness. I now had company. My party and the movement which brought me to Washington were lost, too.

January 19, 2007
Washington, DC

Asking Questions and Getting Answers

J UDGE HUVELLE SENTENCED BOB TO thirty months in jail. Two-and-a-half-years. Huvelle increased Bob's sentence by three months over what the Department of Justice had recommended. With my own sentence looming, I paid close attention to how the Judge treated the Congressman. By increasing Bob's punishment, she seemed to be sending a message to the public, to Washington and to me.

"Both your constituents and the public trusted you to represent them honestly," Judge Huvelle said to Bob, before adding that, "As a member of Congress, you had the responsibility above all else to set an example and to uphold the law." It was harsh criticism. I felt for the Congressman as I pictured him standing before the Judge. Her words stung. But they felt appropriate. Someone needed to remind people like Bob and me that we had held positions of a sacred trust. That was especially true for the Congressman, who had been elected by tens of thousands of Ohio citizens.

Bob apologized to the Judge, his family, his friends and his constituents. Bob's attorney talked about the Congressman's exemplary public service and hard work on behalf of Ohio's 18th Congressional district. They both talked about his alcoholism, and the impact drinking had had on his judgment. As I read about the proceedings online, I remained flabbergasted by the numerous conversations about Bob's drinking. It wasn't like a discussion about his drinking was new. We staffers and former staffers used to talk about it behind his back all the time. But a public discussion about Bob's drinking, in a courtroom of all places, definitely took some getting used to. When Ney's plea agreement was announced before the election, it was reported that he had checked himself into an alcohol rehabilitation program. At the time, many of Bob's former staffers and friends didn't believe that

399

he was really serious about addressing his drinking problem. They thought he was just doing it to reduce his potential prison time.

I wasn't sure what to think. On the one hand, I had no doubt Bob was going through alcohol rehabilitation to lesson the time he would be spending in jail. And I had no problem with that. Having cut a deal with the government to reduce my own chances of going to prison, I understood his line of thinking completely. What I didn't understand, however, was whether reducing his punishment was the only reason he was talking about his alcoholism. That idea made me sad. In contrast, the idea that Bob was using his tough times to become a better person was inspiring. It provided me hope. I wanted to believe the sincere public servant I had travelled to Washington to follow was back. Unfortunately, there was no way for me to know for sure what he was thinking.

"I will continue to take full responsibility, accept the consequences and battle the demons of addiction that are within me," he told the court.

While reading his comments, I continued to have a hard time visualizing him addressing his alcoholism. For years, those of us on the top rungs of Ney World drunkenly lived our lives like we were at a big fraternity party. And Bob was our president and social director. This change was quite jarring. From afar, seeing the Congressman talk publicly about how much he drank suggested that he was getting right with the facts. Based on my work with the formerly homeless veterans of Ignatia House, I liked that idea. The corrosive impact of alcohol addiction can not be underestimated. But there was still no real way of knowing for sure. Not that I didn't do my best to comb every available public document for potential clues. .

Matt Parker was the former staffer I had been told remained closest with Bob. In a letter to Judge Huvelle, Parker wrote about the Congressman's appetite for alcohol. Since it was a key part of the Ney defense, and written by the guy most under the Congressman's influence, I was skeptical that the letter really represented Parker's own words. I figured a more likely scenario was that Bob told him exactly what to write. Whatever the case, I overanalyzed every aspect of the letter.

"*Unless someone partied with Bob, I never spoke about his drinking when I was in Parker's position,*" I thought, before waiting for a second. "*What am I talking about? Bob is going to jail,*" I continued. "*I've never been in a position like Parker's.*" Such a realization made me even more intrigued by what he was really trying to say with his letter.

When the scandal first broke in 2004, the Chairman began to drink more heavily, Parker wrote to the Judge. "Bob was a functioning alcoholic who could rarely make it through the day without drinking and would often begin drinking beers as early as 7:30 a.m.," he continued. I could feel the anguish of the scandal in his words, the words of yet another young Ney staffer. The image of Bob and Parker drinking brought back memories of my time with Ney, both good and bad. *"We did like to party,"* I thought, and smiled at the memory. That was unusual. A frown or sarcastic comment was now a more likely response to any thought of Ney World. The question at hand, though, was whether Bob's drinking was an acceptable reason for Judge Huvelle to give him leniency.

"Whether or not you've served your constituents well, on some level you have seriously betrayed the public's trust and abused your power as a congressman," Huvelle told Ney. "You have a long way to go to make amends for what's happened. An alcohol problem doesn't explain everything."

The judge was clearly not swayed by the argument. In fact, she told him that his lack of accountability was one of the reasons for his increased sentence. She even said that his comments in front of her suggested that he was continuing to avoid personal responsibility for his portion of the scandal. Huvelle's words resonated with me. I knew I would be standing in front of her at some point. Still, the judge did agree to Bob's request that he serve his term at the federal prison in Morgantown, West Virginia. He could receive alcohol rehabilitation there. She also ordered him to pay a $6,000 fine, take part in community service and remain on probation for two years after his release from jail.

"That will be me soon," I thought as I read and re-read the Judge's orders. My mind nervously raced. Motionless, I sat in front of my computer. *"But I'm not Bob. I'm not going to jail for two and a half years. At least, I hope I'm not going to jail for two and a half years."*

After I shut down my computer, I tried not to think about the Congressman's sentencing. It wasn't easy. "Bob wouldn't be going to jail if I hadn't cooperated with the Department of Justice," I whispered. My stomach heaved at the reality of the situation. No matter how mad I got at Bob, I hated the fact that the right decision for me meant he was going to jail. Just as sad was the fact that I knew I could have been a better friend to him. *"I doubt any of the fundamentals would have changed,"* I continued, contemplating all the things I could have done differently. *"I should have made him get a lawyer or told him how worried I was about the Tigua situation. I could have talked to him at the Prime Rib. I could have put my fears about him not having a lawyer aside and told him more about the investigation. I could have been a better friend."* That last one was especially hard to think about. I tried to repress the thought. "It is all over now," I said to myself. .

Whether I wanted to or not, the impact of my cooperation on others was something I constantly thought about. After being asked to wear a wire, the idea was kind of hard to get out of my head. But I tried. I also did my best not to get too emotional. *"He made his own bed,"* I said to myself, trying to put Bob's sentencing behind me. *"I just told the truth."*

Numb to the gravity of what the Congressman was going through, I remained emotionless through the morning. My updates to friends and family were clinical in nature. "Two and a half years behind bars," I calmly told a friend. He asked what was wrong.

"I want to feel bad for Bob," I said. "But I can't. I'm trying to move on."

The point was Judge Huvelle was right. Bob was avoiding personal accountability. I didn't want to be a part of that. At Ignatia House, personal accountability was vitally important. The veterans worked hard to get back on their feet, and holding each other accountable was an invaluable part of that process. Beating back past demons was almost impossible to do without acknowledging and owning up to past sins. Like the veterans I worked with, I had become a true believer in the power of personal accountability.

My Mondays at U.S. Vets were sacred time. It was time for me to learn about, cultivate and hopefully improve the human condition - mine as well as the veterans. Sympathizing with Bob's decision to avoid responsibility would have been an affront to my new friends at U.S. Vets. So I didn't do it.

Days after Bob's sentencing, I visited Ignatia House for a gathering of U.S. Vets volunteers and board members. Having spent at least one day a week for the last four months at the house, I felt a certain sense of ownership over the meeting. This was also true because a big part of our planned discussion revolved around my idea of putting together the first annual U.S. Vets golf tournament. Emily gave me free reign to make it happen. Despite the fact that the project involved golf, it was about as far away from Scotland as anyone could get. The tournament was simple and honest. We simply wanted people to play golf and help us raise money for a program that honestly assisted homeless veterans. I was excited. The therapeutic culture of the house was contagious. I quickly learned to embrace the life-affirming nature of my colleagues and the authenticity of the veterans.

People hugged and cried everyday at Ignatia House. In the name of being accountable, the veterans and the U.S. Vets staff also got into each other's business. If someone was lying, he got called out. If they didn't pass a drug test, they were told to leave. It was a process I waded into gingerly, since I wasn't sure how to engage the veterans about my past. After a long conversation with a couple of guys one Monday morning, I finally approached Emily about the topic.

"The guys are frustrated about the employment obstacles associated with their criminal records," I told her. "During my conversation with them, I wanted to talk about my legal situation. I know what it is like to look for work with a felony conviction," I continued. "But I wasn't sure what to say, so I held off."

Emily, an intelligent, compassionate and hard-working hippie chick from Louisiana, zinged me a quick response.

"I wouldn't worry about telling them that you are a felon," she said. "Many of the vets are, too. But I would be careful about telling them you are a Republican. You'll lose all your credibility if you tell them that," she snickered.

"So then, I suppose telling them I was a high-priced lobbyist probably isn't a good idea, either," I countered.

We laughed. And then laughed some more.

"Just follow your heart," she finally said after the laughter subsided. "You meet the veterans where they are as well as anyone who has ever worked here," she said. Her warm comments made me feel like I was having an impact. "Keep connecting with them and do what you think is right."

I loved the simplicity and empowerment of her response. Thanks in large part to Emily's supportive words, I started to open up with the veterans, with some more than others. As I quickly learned, opening up with the veterans had consequences.

"You would be in jail right now if you didn't have all that money," one resident told me. "Or if you weren't white."

"I can't disagree," I replied, before adding, "But let's not jinx things here. I haven't been sentenced yet. I could end up in jail. In the meantime, I'm going to focus on why I felt like I needed all that money in the first place."

He laughed. "I'm with you, man," he said.

While volunteering for the vets, I was able to secure a full-time job as an in-house salesman. My job was to spend several hours in a house with people I had never met, and then sell them thousands of dollars worth of products. If I succeeded, I received a commission on the deal. The culture of the new job was different than the culture of Ignatia House.

Somewhat like Team Abramoff, our team of salesmen thrived by having the right attitude. The all-male sales force fed off each others' encouragement. As I walked around the office re-supplying my materials before a potential sale, my colleagues would pump me up. And I would do the same.

"Yeah, baby, you're going to make a big sale today," we would say to each other. Similarly, as I left the office to get in my car, the team behind me would be on the second floor balcony chanting, "Neil! Neil! Neil!"

I enjoyed the work. In part, that was because getting a full-time job had been such a journey. It had taken me a year to secure a full-time position. The process was a rocky road. During that year, I had worked as a substitute teacher. I loved spending time with the kids and read numerous books about how best to do the job. But it was only part-time, and didn't pay too well. A little later, I joined several hundred applicants at a job fair. One of the companies, a health insurance firm, was interested in hiring me. For the next month, I trained with their local sales team and took my certification tests. By the end of my training, the local sales office was excited about me joining their team, scandal-baggage and all. Likewise, I was excited about the prospects. But the company's corporate headquarters decided to overrule the local branch's decision. My legal issues were too much for the company to take on, they said. It was a wasted month. So I had kept looking.

During my interview for the in-house sales position, I managed to avoid any discussion of my past with Abramoff and Ney. Since they didn't ask about a criminal background, I didn't offer up the information. The job began with a mandatory two-week training period. Get me in the house and I'll be fine, I figured. This was small potatoes compared to the big jobs I had previously. For several days I started to slack off a bit.

My new employer noticed my lax attitude. At that point, I was given twenty-four hours to get up to speed. If I did not have my two-hour long pitch down pat by the next day, it would be over, I was told. With a new-found sense of urgency, I practiced all night. The next day I nailed that pitch. I was in.

However, the idea of going into a house to sell the company's products without my bosses being aware of my criminal past raised all kinds of red flags. Before taking a single cent from the company, I wanted them to know about the scandal, and about who was working for them. I hadn't always been so upfront. Therefore, for no other reason than the fact that listening to my own conscience was important to me, I met with my superiors and laid it all out for them. They took it well and kept me on.

Then, a few weeks after securing my new post, I got a call from Emily's boss, an amazing woman named Stephanie. She offered me a job as a case manager at U.S Vets. We talked about the position. Aside from the money, which was less than what I was making as a salesman, it sounded great, I told her.

"Can I call you back in a few hours?" I asked. I was getting ready to go into a meeting at my sales job. It was a weekly meeting for the sales team. During our meetings, we would compare notes on what we were hearing from customers: what was working, what wasn't.

One of my colleagues outlined how he had been in a house making his pitch for two hours. Things looked pretty good, he said. "Until the guy tells me he has cancer," my colleague continued. He wasn't sure how his finances would be impacted by the treatment."

"So how did you get around that?" one of my other colleagues asked. The rest of us booed him, though, we recognized he was joking. But the comment stayed in the back of my head, nonetheless, and led me to question whether I was once again focusing too much on money.

"Haven't I learned my lesson?" I asked myself. *"Didn't greed play a huge role in my problems? Problems which could still send me to jail?"*

I took some time to think. Sitting outside my car in front of our office, after the meeting, I pondered the job offer from U.S. Vets. I wanted an easy answer, but like elsewhere in my life, none appeared.

"I enjoy selling," I told myself. *"And the services and products the company provide are top-notch."* It was honorable work, work that could help me dig out of the massive debt my wife and I were facing. But I couldn't get comfortable with the idea. My focus on the money already seemed to be growing at an alarming rate. And that seemed a little too close to what I had been doing in my previous life.

"This could take me way off the right path," I said aloud, in reference to the new job. Then the questions started. *"If this perfectly acceptable job was way off, then what was my previous life? Super way off?"*

Before long "way off" had turned into an acronym: W.A.Y.F.F. *"What are you fighting for?"* I liked it. If simple answers weren't going to easily appear to be my guide, maybe a simple question would do.

So I asked myself, in the context of suddenly having two employers wanting me to work for them, "Neil, *what are you fighting for?"* It was a telling moment.

Two weeks later, I started full-time at U.S. Vets.

MARCH 5, 2007
WASHINGTON, DC

Bob goes to Jail

Bob publicly denounced me the day before he reported to prison. In an interview with *The Hill*, he labeled me a bad person who was responsible for much of the scandal. The Congressman told the paper that I "instigated a ton of this," and that I did so for my "own paycheck." The public rebuke infuriated me. However, the dressing-down lessened the sadness I was feeling about Bob's impending prison term.

More than three years into the scandal, I continued to learn much of what was happening through the media, and yet I remained surprised whenever a news story that impacted me personally appeared in the paper. The news about Bob going to prison was no different. What was different, though, was the fact that the Congressman himself was the one finally doing the talking. After years of trying to glean insight into Bob's state of mind by interpreting statements made by his attorney, spokesman, or unnamed sources, hearing directly from my former boss was refreshing. It was sad, but refreshing.

"I feel like I am in a soap opera," I told a friend. "My life is playing out in the papers. And everything seems so dramatic. One day I'm optimistic, and one day I'm depressed. It is still hard to get a handle on everything. I mean, I shouldn't be upset at Bob's comments; I have said the same thing about myself. The fact is I did want the money, and was greedy. But I still feel like calling that reporter up and hitting Bob back. What an asshole."

My conflicting emotions about Bob's comments were what I had started calling "my new normal." The new normal tag was the result of several self-help books I was reading. Some of the books suggested that I needed to reframe my personal outlook to better embrace the life change I was experiencing. If I were going to channel my hurt feelings about the past into a better future, the books said, it meant first accepting what had happened. From there I could move forward into a new life. By working to get right with the facts and asking myself what I was fighting for, I felt like I was making a lot of progress when it came to accepting what I had done. As always, I yearned to move forward, even as I wasn't sure how best to embrace this concept of a new normal. Knowing that it had taken many little steps to walk down the slippery slope that had gotten me in trouble, I figured that the journey to a new normal would also require that I take it a step at a time.

I read through *The Hill* story very closely. It began by reporting that Bob did not plan on returning to Washington after his prison sentence. The article then touched on the Congressman's family and the personal impact of the scandal. Envisioning Bob's family dealing with his fall from grace was sobering. I couldn't help but compare what his family was going through with what my family was dealing with.

"Ney spoke about how his family, his staff and his outlook on life have been affected by his involvement in the Jack Abramoff lobbying scandal that led to his quick descent from power over the past six months," the story read. "The strain of the past year was audible in Ney's voice as he described the financial and emotional stress that hit him and his family."

The more I read, the more I shuddered at the thought of Bob's family dealing with their own new normal. In the story, he described how the scandal had impacted his daughter's school-life and his son's work-life. I knew both of his kids and couldn't imagine how much their lives had changed. Since he didn't have to work 17-hour days campaigning, Bob told the reporter he had more time to spend with his family. I was glad to hear the Congressman talking that way about his family. His busy schedule hadn't always allowed him to be home as much as I knew he wanted to be.

Bob then went on the attack.

"As he reflected on Will Heaton, his former chief of staff who pleaded guilty to one count of conspiracy on Feb. 26, Ney said that he believed that Heaton's predecessor, Neil Volz, pushed him to commit those crimes. Volz has also pleaded guilty but has not yet been sentenced. Said Ney: 'I wish the best for [Heaton]. He's a good person. Frankly, Neil Volz is not.' Ney said he thinks Volz 'pushed' Heaton and 'instigated a ton of this for his own paycheck.' Despite his belief that Volz was dishonest with him and Heaton, Ney acknowledged that the blame fell squarely on his own shoulders."

My sadness about Bob's plight quickly turned to rage. "Fuck you, Bob," I said as I read those words for the first time. "If I pushed Heaton, then did you push me? You still don't get it do you?" I continued, fully on the defensive. Then a question popped in my head.

"Do you get it?" I asked myself. The question slowed down my rant for a few moments. I knew I couldn't say yes. I *wanted* to "get it." But that was different from actually understanding how best to honorably move forward. This realization humbled me and tempered my anger.

Bob had said he was "determined to not let the next two years define him. To be a more positive person, I hope to use the experience I'm going to go through, to carry it through for the rest of my life."

With my anger now fully in check, Bob's comments struck me in a way I wasn't prepared for. His desire to become a more positive person was similar to what I was thinking. I, too, wanted to channel my experience in a way that would make me a better person.

The reporter went on to write that Bob "appeared to have come full circle since he defiantly denied any wrongdoing last May, when he vowed at a House GOP gathering to fight any federal indictment."

"Several months later," the article continued, "Ney admitted he accepted thousands of dollars of gifts from lobbyists in exchange for legislative favors, and he formally confessed his wrongdoings in November. On Jan. 19, he became the first lawmaker sentenced for involvement in the scandal surrounding Abramoff.

"I take responsibility, and I already said I apologized; [it's] time to move on with it," he said. "Incarceration is a traumatic thing."

My mind raced as I thought about Bob sitting in a jail cell. It was painful to envision. My family and friends, however, had little sympathy for him. Some of those closest to me lambasted Bob's decision to attack me in the media. A few told me to just get over it. Others said they thought his comments showed that he was in denial about how much he was to blame for my involvement in the scandal.

As usual, I thanked my friends and family for their support. But I couldn't accept what they were saying. Bob's comments were not something to ignore, nor were they something I felt comfortable using so I could blame my mistakes on him. As sad as they were, I knew his words had merit.

"Maybe he was right about Heaton," I began to conclude. The more I thought about it, the harder it was to argue with Bob's premise that I had pushed his young chief of staff. Heaton had become chief of staff at twenty-three, and the only real professional environment he knew was the Ney office. I felt more guilty by the moment when I thought about Heaton's time

with Bob. Unlike me, he had only had a few years to enjoy the positive side of Ney World. And then he was forced to help manage its collapse.

I remembered the night when Heaton became Bob's chief of staff. I was days away from officially joining Team Abramoff, and Bob, Heaton and I were at a restaurant called the Capital Grille. We were with some of Bob's constituents and another Member of Congress. After our meal, while the three of us continued drinking with the group, Heaton and I got an email from Bob. He wanted to ditch his constituents and colleague so we could go out and party.

Heaton emailed me. "What is this?" he asked.

I got up from the table and walked over to the bar. The Congressman's new top staffer joined me there. "Taking care of Bob is not my responsibility anymore," I told Heaton. He nodded. We then talked about how I could help him become a better staffer and how he could help me become a successful lobbyist. From the beginning, I corrupted Heaton. I told him that his personal success was based on taking care of my professional interests. Reflecting on that fact, I felt guilty and ashamed. It would have been easier to say that it was only Bob who corrupted his chief of staff, or that Heaton simply had to be responsible for his own actions. But if I didn't accept the truth that I played a role in corrupting someone I cared about, the new normal I was trying to create would be a fraud. And that was not acceptable.

As I thought more about Bob's remarks in the paper, I began to feel the urge to talk with him. I wanted to ask him some follow-up questions. There was only so much insight I could learn from his handful of comments. At that point, I wasn't sure what to do next. Part of me wanted to stop my introspection. Getting bogged down with Bob's melodrama was unhealthy, that part of me thought. *"Stop giving him so much control. It is time to move on."*

Or was it? Another part of me figured that stopping my internal conversation was unhealthy. Didn't I want to know Bob's thoughts? Couldn't I learn from what he was saying?

My internal debate continued for months. With Bob in jail, there was no way to talk with him or fully understand what he was thinking, so I did my best to slowly move on. Bob's comments in the paper had convinced me that he was going through some of the same type of soul-searching I was going through. Where he stood, I didn't know; and whether I cared or not depended on the day. But the mere fact that he was asking some of the same questions I was asking was important to me. It meant Bob and I were still on the same path. Whether those paths would ever cross again, time would only tell.

Being Judged, Part II

MY LONG-AWAITED SENTENCING DATE HAD finally arrived. Not a day had passed that I didn't contemplate the possibilities. Would Judge Huvelle put me in jail like Bob? Or would my punishment be something else? Time in a half-way house? A hefty fine? I would find out soon enough. Though prepared to go to prison, I desperately hoped for a lesser sentence.

In the preceding months, my wife and I had prepared for me to go to jail. The process brought us closer together, and yet, at the same time, it pushed us further apart. While Alison jumped into her work and the healthy support system of friends she had built up over the years, I began reinventing myself at U.S. Vets. The distance between us widened over time. Talking about how the bills were to be paid while I was in jail or discussing how we went broke didn't help to heal our troubled marriage. We leaned on our families, and did our best to move forward - both individually and together.

My feelings of detachment were not limited to my marriage. Many of the people I had been closest to over the years also remained at a distance. My friends who were most familiar with the scandal generally wanted or needed to stay away from me. I understood that this was usually for a legal or professional reason. But the emptiness remained. My hope was that getting sentenced would allow me to reconnect with the people in my life who had been pushed away by the scandal. While getting sentenced may not have meant the end of the investigation, I assumed it meant the end was close.

In contrast to the people I could not keep in contact with, those friends and family members I could talk to about the scandal provided me the support I needed to make it through the hard times, even though they

410

sometimes didn't understand how the intricacies of the scandal process impacted my life. This lack of understanding didn't lessen their value to me. I wouldn't have been able to make it through without them.

Many of them joined me in the courtroom. The tension surrounded us all. As my attorney, Tim Broas, wrapped up his speech to Judge Huvelle, I still wasn't sure what kind of punishment to expect.

"Mr. Volz has accepted responsibility," Tim told the Judge. "And in the face of ridicule, loss of employment, public humiliation, financial despair, and shame among those near and dear, he boldly stepped forward and chose to admit his errors and to pay his debt to society by helping the Department of Justice conduct this investigation and bring other wrongdoers to justice."

Even though these words were coming from a person getting paid hundreds of dollars an hour to say them, they were still reassuring to hear.

"Unlike many others, Mr. Volz did not publicly protest. He did not enter a joint defense agreement. He did not choose to be a victim. He came forward in April 2005, before anyone else had pleaded guilty, and began cooperating with the Department of Justice. And in the process, he led the Department of Justice to three major convictions, not including his own."

The more Tim spoke, the more I began to feel like my life itself was on trial. The shame, anger and confusion I felt bubbled to the surface. Tears welled up in my eyes, and I rubbed them away as they trickled down my cheek.

"Mr. Volz is a young man with potential to recover, and has a bright future," my attorney continued. "He has suffered immeasurably already. He is a convicted felon. His reputation is forever soiled and tarnished. His good name will always be associated with this scandal."

I looked back at my family. They were now the ones fighting back tears.

"His cooperation has been so valuable that the convictions he has helped DOJ obtain will undoubtedly deter public officials and lobbyists from committing similar crimes in the future," he said, making the argument that a lenient sentence for me could encourage other potential cooperating witnesses in the case to come forward.

"Can anyone doubt these convictions - and no doubt there are more to come - have put all of official Washington on notice?" Tim asked. "Putting Mr. Volz in jail will not advance the course of deterrence, Your Honor, nor would it advance the respect for the law. In fact, it would have just the opposite effect."

Judge Huvelle sat there, expressionless, listening to my defense with her arms crossed.

"Last and quickly, Your Honor, with respect to Mr. Volz's cooperation, he testified as the government's main witness in the Safavian trial. He was the first and only cooperator in this investigation to testify. He described Mr. Ney and Mr. Heaton and Mr. Safavian's conduct on the infamous Scotland golf trip, complete with photographs and bar receipts, all provided by Mr. Volz." He paused briefly.

"People took notice immediately," my attorney continued. "Mr. Heaton began cooperating shortly thereafter, in June 2006, and ultimately pleaded guilty to a felony. Mr. Ney began discussions with the Department of Justice, and he ultimately pleaded guilty and is now serving a 30-month sentence in jail. And it's not over, Your Honor. Mr. Volz has promised to continue to cooperate, and is doing so literally as we speak."

Like we planned, my attorney's presentation was short. As he had told me days before, "I am not the one the judge wants to hear from."

Looking over at me, as if to say, "It is go time," Tim motioned for me to get ready. Nervously pushing my chair away from the witness table, I stood up and told myself to breathe, talk slowly and be honest. Before beginning, I looked Judge Huvelle directly in the eye.

"I am here because I broke the law," I said as simply as I could. Despite the volcanic political ramifications of the still-erupting Abramoff scandal, its ongoing legal complexity, and the personal consequences of its eruption - those eight words hung out there as an embodiment of my belief in getting right with the facts. Before I could explain to Judge Huvelle why I did what I did and how I had learned from my mistakes, she needed to know that I was accepting responsibility for my part of what happened in the first place. "By putting my own interest ahead of the public interest, I defrauded the citizens of this country, and denied them the honest services they deserve."

Like a heated up boiler, pent up tension filled the courtroom. Not a movement could be heard.

"In some instances, I knew better and was too weak to stand up for what was right," I continued. "In others, I rationalized away the concerns of my conscience or convinced myself the ends somehow justified the means. No matter, they were my decisions, my crimes, and I am solely responsible for them."

Outlining in detail the many transgressions that had brought me to her courtroom, I persisted for several minutes while an unblinking Judge Huvelle took it all in.

"As Chief of Staff for Congressman Ney, I accepted things of value, including tickets, free meals and a new job with a nearly unlimited expense account. At first I thought the sports and concert tickets were acceptable. By the time I began negotiating for a job and helping Mr. Abramoff's clients at the same time, however, I had clearly crossed the line. There is no excuse whatsoever for my actions."

"Later," I continued "as a lobbyist, I delivered many things of value to the Congressman and his staff, including trips, tickets, free meals and drinks."

Seeing the judge listen so intently to my words, I began to assume things were going well. It was as if my speech were on cruise control. But then, in the blink of an eye, my emotions took over.

Glancing down at my statement to see the sentence stating, "My actions have resulted in an immeasurable amount of suffering by those I love the most," I froze. Terrified, I couldn't get my mouth to work. As if I had just stared at Medusa or was touched in a game of freeze tag, my entire speech came to a screeching halt. The tears in the corner of my eyes that I had fought off until that point started flooding down my face. Uncontrollably, my body began to shake. Rarely in 37 years had I faced such emotional paralysis. Battling periodic intervals of cavernous hyena-like breathing, I struggled to continue. My words slowly returned.

"Each and every family member, friend and colleague deserved better from me than what they got," I said before stopping again, this time for what felt like hours. My sobbing echoed off the courtroom's high ceilings in an endless loop of anguish. Rorschach-style tear drops soaked through the paper in my hand. Like a waterfall, they peppered the printed version of my speech.

As I took in the entirety of my courtroom drama, a bigger picture of what was really going on began to emerge in my mind. My time there wasn't just about how lobbyists influenced Members of Congress or the impact of big money on politics. Much more than the scientific analysis of a political scandal was being dissected. Standing in the cradle of a courtroom surrounded by family and friends, I saw that it was my personal failure and how I had chosen to live my life that was really on trial. It was a moment of clarity. A personal epiphany.

For much of my adult life, things had looked pretty rosy on the outside. I had a great job, a wonderful wife and made lots of money. On a first-name basis with Senators, Members of Congress and senior White House officials, I was a powerful man in a powerful town. Nonetheless, in many respects I had been rotting away on the inside. My unchained ambition for power and a selfish desire for money had crowded other priorities out of my life. Over the years, I lost touch with my friends, my wife, my family, and my country, as well as my faith in God. Very simply, the life I hoped to lead, one of real public service, had faded away.

Even worse, I had convinced myself it was exactly my family and friends that I was prioritizing. If I just missed one more family function, canceled one more event with friends or told my wife I won't be home one more time, things would get better. That time was the price we had to pay for a quality future, I would say. Likewise, I would tell myself, if I just cut one more backroom deal, suck up to one more influential person with power, or lobby for just one more year, ultimately I can return to a more pure form of public service. As I told Judge Huvelle, it was the ultimate rationalization: blind ambition masquerading as principle.

People far smarter than I have suggested we get but a few moments in life where it is possible to actually peel back the day-to-day layers of our existence and be presented with a real understanding of life and its meaning. For me, this courtroom time was undoubtedly one of those moments. In the starkest terms possible, I was reminded how it is those people we choose to include in our life who provide us meaning. Not our money. Not power. Not stuff. But people. It all suddenly seemed so clear.

Then, in another blink of an eye, I felt confused again.

Staring at my loving wife of seven years, I still couldn't tell her I had figured out how to make our life together work. Nor could I tell my family that I was truly on a path toward appreciating their honorable lives by living one of my own. As for my friends, many of them chose to step into the tornado of the last few years instead of watch from afar. Would I have done the same? That question alone helped me quickly reconnect with my previous line of thought, namely the importance of my personal relationships. It became clear to me that while my rights to liberty, due process and the rule of law all were on display in the courtroom, my purpose was sitting on the other side of the room.

"More than anything, it is my relationships that define me," I thought to myself. "It was my failure in the relationship department that led to the failures that have me standing here today." It was that simple. "Before I lied to my country, I lied to my friends. Before I defrauded my religious faith and my political ideals, I defrauded myself."

As I stood there awaiting a sentence for my admitted and serious crimes against the state, I realized that there was a lot more I needed to do than just get right with my legal facts. My crimes were serious, and my need

414

for a punishment was what Judge Huvelle was weighing, but the reasons I committed them in the first place needed to be addressed, too. My spiritual and emotional side needed honest introspection, as well. And I needed to repent for my wrongdoing in a way that would verify to those around me that something like this would never happen again. I knew I would never forget this moment - or this lesson - ever.

I wiped away the tears, cleared my throat, and carried on. Looking back at my family and friends I said aloud, "To you all, again, I am sorry."

Returning to face Judge Huvelle, I continued. "I'm sorry to this court for defrauding the citizens of the United States of the honest services expected and required by their government officials. Trust is needed for our government to operate properly. I violated that trust, and not a day goes by that I don't wish I could undo what I have done. My decision to live in a world of spin and fabrication corrupted me spiritually, just as my decisions to break the law were corrupting to our society. Therefore, I have the responsibility to myself and my family, as well as our country, to continue helping the government honestly pursue justice in this case, wherever it leads."

"Please know the lessons I have learned from this experience are real, and so is the change I have begun," I continued. "Cooperating with the government on their many investigations has helped me to repair some of the harm my behavior has created. It's also strengthened my inner resolve to live an honest life."

Convinced that Judge Huvelle knew what was going on in my head, I began to feel a growing connection with her. Like a parent who can understand a child's pain before it happens, she seemed to comprehend the full meaning behind my words.

"Thank you for allowing me to apologize in public today," I said earnestly, looking up to the Judge. I felt like I was growing up before her eyes.

"It's obviously important for me to do so now and continue doing so in the future," I continued. "I've become an example to others. I take that seriously and will honor that responsibility. Many others have written on my behalf. Their kindness is something I will always remember with great appreciation. Ultimately though, no matter what others may say, I am responsible, completely responsible, for my behavior and stand here ready for the consequences. Thank you, Your Honor."

I remained standing. Judge Huvelle and I looked at each other for a few moments before I pensively dropped my head and let my eyes fall. In a weird twist of fate, my angst surrounding the Judge's impending decision began to subside.

"*She is going to do what she is going to do,*" I thought to myself. "*There is nothing else I can do but wait.*"

It was now Judge Huvelle's turn. She began immediately.

"Mr. Volz, the court has read all the letters, the pleadings by both the government and your counsel, and finds your statement here today to be very helpful. You have obviously inflicted a lot of pain on a great number of family members and friends who think very highly of you, and I think there's reason to think very highly of you. And the fall is larger and longer because of what you've done here." She paused.

"You have let people down, Mr. Volz," the Judge said.

True as they were, her words still stung. Maybe it was the robe or Judge Huvelle's ability to fully encapsulate my crimes, but her comments had a much different feel than I anticipated. Her role seemed more that of a flesh and blood representative of our society than merely a top of the totem-pole law enforcement officer, doling out equation-driven punishments. As she outlined my failures, not only did Judge Huvelle see my shame, she made it stick. She also made sure to let me know that it was not acceptable for me to backtrack on the promises I made in her presence.

"I hope that you will continue to explain to others how serious your mistakes were," Judge Huvelle said. "I mean these are not just mistakes of judgment but violations of criminal laws and the public trust," she continued with a stare that could have shattered glass.

I listened intently to her words. My years of personal reflection began to catch up to the moment. With a searing intensity, Huvelle had branded me a criminal in ways I refused to fully acknowledge before hearing her speak. In part, that was because she also labeled me a changed man - words I additionally took to heart in a more profound manner.

As I quietly prayed, the Judge continued. Having suddenly accepted an identity I struggled for more than a year to accept, namely that of a reformed convicted felon, I focused on what I wanted my future to look like with renewed vigor and depth. It didn't involve big houses, expensive cars or the privilege of power. Frankly, it was much more simple than that. Going forward, I told myself, it was crucial to simply focus on honestly serving my family, my friends, my country and my faith - and letting the rest take care of itself.

Every signal I got from Judge Huvelle suggested that I was about to avoid a prison sentence. But I didn't know for sure. I was scared. Very scared. As the fear-induced endorphins continued to rush through my system, I saw that the next chapter of my life was about to begin. Jail or no jail, I waited for her verdict.

"I assume I won't see you back here again, Mr. Volz," Judge Huvelle said forcefully, and with meaning.

"No, your Honor," I replied. With unquestioned finality, she then sentenced me to probation, community service, and a $1,000 fine. My long-awaited sentencing was over. I wasn't going to jail. Judge Huvelle had given me a second chance. Then, as swiftly as she had entered, Judge Huvelle exited her courtroom. I breathed a deep sigh of relief, and hugged anyone I could get my hands on - even a couple of the reporters. Each hug was full of joy and relief.

"Your not going to jail, big guy," my brother-in-law told me. Never in my life did I expect to be so happy to hear those words. The party was starting.

I spent the next few hours filling out paperwork with my new court-ordered probation officer. When I returned home, my family, friends and neighbors were waiting. Focused so much on my actual sentencing, I had barely thought about what the rest of the day would look like. Visualizing "Good luck in jail" streamers and napkins never quite seemed appropriate. Yet, now that my sentencing was finished, a full-scale celebration had broken out at my house: a party to celebrate the fact that I wasn't going to jail.

As I opened the front door, standing there with my family, in the middle of the living room, was my old friend Channing Nuss. Until the Abramoff investigation forced us to stop talking for more than a year, we had been best of friends for a decade. Unlike many of my Washington friendships, ours had remained close through numerous professional transitions. Walking toward him in my living room was like walking into a movie. I almost didn't believe my own eyes. It was a total surprise. His decision to take part in the hysteria of hellos and hugs brought an immediate smile to my face. Channing's smile matched mine. We hugged like family.

The importance of our reconnection wasn't lost on those at the party. "I'm so glad you guys are able to hang out again," my brother told me. Like two high school buddies meeting at a reunion, we laughed about the old times and thrilled those who were interested with tales of our 9/11 heroics and work on the Capitol Hill anthrax evacuation. Though neither of us smoked anymore, we bought a pack and went out in the back yard to share a few cigarettes together. While we were in the backyard, the two of us scrolled through our phones contact lists and called long lost friends.

Channing's attendance was not only a wonderful surprise, it was also good for my understanding of what it meant to be a friend. Over the last few years, my comprehension of the concept of friendship had taken a beating, so much so that even the meaning of the word *friend* had become unclear to me. This lack of clarity wasn't just a result of my scandal. It also came from working in Washington, where professional friends come and go pretty easily. President Truman's famous quote has merit: "If you want a friend in Washington, get a dog."

The city's political culture seems to be set up to create disposable friendships. To be successful, people in Washington have to become comfortable with the fact that today's friend could become tomorrow's enemy. It is the nature of legislating and lobbying. Sometimes you have to tell your second most important ally, a friend, that you're opposed to their interests because you are helping out your best friend, or yourself. In Washington, rivals and hated enemies stand on the floor of the House or the Senate and call each other, "My friend." Likewise, lobbyists and reporters refer to colleagues they barely know as "one of my best friends" to secure potential clients or access to key decision makers. In such an environment, it is easy to become cynical about the business of friendship. The day I walked into my house after being sentenced, few people could have been as cynical as I was.

Nothing made me accept Truman's adage about friendship in Washington like going through the Abramoff scandal. Before the investigation, I never would have thought that I would soon seriously contemplate the question, "Whom would you go to jail for?" And the opposite: "Who would go to jail for you?" My relationship with Bob, a guy around whom I built so much of my life, exemplified the very real ramifications of answering those questions. He wasn't an answer to either of those questions. Nor were many people.

The process also worked the other way. Becoming "radioactive" because of my high-profile felonious behavior was an example. After my plea, Members of Congress whom I considered friends gave my campaign contributions away to charity, in order to avoid the negative publicity of being associated with a criminal like me. Fellow lobbyists, Congressional staffers and colleagues behaved in a similar way. Calls went unreturned, emails unnoticed. Losing contact with my hard-earned political network helped lead to my solitary existence in the cave. Yet I couldn't blame them for doing what they had to do. Politics, not friendship, was our business. That wasn't true for Channing and I.

Although Alison and I saw many of our closest friends rally around both of us, the friendship I had with Channing was more complicated. Like other former Ney staffers, Channing felt it was in his best interest to get a lawyer who told him to stay away from me and others involved in the scandal. I received similar advice. Aside from a random meeting in the beer line at a Washington Nationals baseball game, the two of us painstakingly followed our family and attorneys' advice.

During the height of the Abramoff probe, Channing was interrogated by the FBI. It was not an enjoyable experience for either of us. I felt horrible knowing my impropriety was costing him tens of thousands of dollars in lawyers' fees and forcing him into the treacherous waters of the Department of Justice's legal dragnet. The pain kept me up many nights. At the same time, Channing felt awful knowing his truthful testimony was being used to build a case against me. Either of us could have pulled up the stakes on our friendship. Yet several years later there we stood, hugging in my living room. Channing's presence in the courthouse, and then later at my house, was a testament to the strength of our friendship. And to the idea of friendship.

Like Dorothy awaking to the colorful world of Oz, I woke up refreshed the next morning. I took Winnie out for her morning walk. When I opened my front door, I was met by one of my neighbors, Charlie. He gave me a hug. He then gave me a book, a group of essays by the sixteenth century French philosopher, Michel de Montaigne.

Charlie and I hadn't known each other very long, a couple years at most. We met at the dog park. As the personal toil of the scandal grew, like many of my neighbors, Charlie's friendship became more important to me. He didn't know Jack or Bob and didn't express too much concern about how the scandal impacted his view of politics. Our relationship wasn't built on the game, it was built around our pets. But it was honest, and we accepted each other. He was simply a friend. Charlie signed the front cover and bookmarked an essay midway through the manuscript. It was titled, "Of Friendship." I was intrigued.

After dropping off my family at the airport later that day, I took out Charlie's book. I wasn't sure what to expect. I was skeptical that a four hundred year-old manuscript could connect with my modern day challenges. But the topic of friendship was top of mind, and I respected my friend's opinion, so I dug in. A few sentences immediately jumped out at me.

"Aristotle says that good lawgivers had more respect to friendship than justice," Montaigne wrote. "Now the supreme point of its perfection is this. For, speaking generally, all those amities that are created and nourished by pleasure or profit, public or private needs, are so much the less noble and beautiful, and so much the less friendship, than itself."

He was right. I had developed many friendships over the years. Some of those friendships were built on a foundation of securing money or glory.

I doubted many of those relationships would last. I could accept that. So I allowed myself to let most of them go. I figured life was too short to focus on what Montaigne called "the less noble and beautiful" relationships, especially when I was blessed with so many friendships that were, indeed, noble and beautiful. Channing had verified that for me. It was another lesson from an important day. Looking around, for the first time in years, I felt like I was falling upstairs again - just like when I moved to Washington in the first place.

======================

The Importance of
Healthy Relationships

I FIRST MET RICHARD, WHOM I initially knew as "Mr. Rogers," when I was his case manager. We met once a week to go over the basics. "Did you see your doctor at the VA today, Mr. Rogers? Are you attending your AA and NA meetings, Mr. Rogers? How about your finances? Your medicine?" It was one of the many U.S. Vets relationships that I learned to value greatly. After my sentencing, I purposely worked on becoming a better friend. That meant proactively befriending my colleagues and clients at Ignatia House, like Richard, whom I became friends with when he was one of my clients.

When Richard died, his sister and mother asked me to speak at his memorial service. Although I was still struggling from the unexpected loss of a new friend, I felt honored by their request. I looked around at the Igantia House's main room from behind the podium. Assembled were most of Richard's fellow veterans, much of the U.S. Vets staff, Richard's family, friends, and people he had met at the hospital. There were also professional grief counselors from the Veterans Administration on hand to help those veterans struggling to cope with their fellow resident's sudden death. He was only 58.

I kicked off the proceedings. "If we can all bow our heads for a moment of prayer," I started. It had only been four days, yet life around Ignatia House already seemed emptier without Richard.

"Anyone who knew Mr. Rogers will carry a part of him in their heart forever," I said. "Not a day passed that we didn't talk. We talked about his Redskins, we talked about my Buckeyes. He taught me about the Commodores, the Four Tops and the Supremes. I taught him about Kenny

Chesney, U2 and Kid Rock." The crowd laughed. Richard would have been happy to see so many smiling faces.

"When I started here at U.S. Vets, it was a time of a lot of pain in my life," I said. "Mr. Rogers and I bonded right away. He knew a lot about living with pain. And we both liked to make each other laugh."

Born in 1949, Richard grew up in segregated Washington. His sister told me his characteristic zest for life was present from birth. So was his love for music, fashion, sports and church, she said. He was a Cub Scout and a Boy Scout. As a teenager, he worked and saved to buy a car - mostly to go dancing and hang out with the young ladies, his sister said with that classic Rogers family smile.

Richard graduated from McKinley High School and studied at the University of the District of Columbia. From there, he became a member of the Metropolitan Washington Police Department and the U.S. Armed Services.

Years later, when I met him, Mr. Rogers was in recovery for alcohol and drug addiction. He also suffered from post traumatic stress syndrome, something which required regular medical care. For several years, Richard had lived on the streets of Washington, DC. Despite his many obstacles, he carried himself with honor and grace.

"Richard Rogers was a friend of mine." I paused so my listeners could let that sink in.

Over the years, there has been a lot of analysis about the root causes of homelessness, and there have been many studies conducted to discover why veterans make up such a high proportion of the country's homeless population. Most conclude that chronic homelessness is generally caused by one or more of the following: family problems, a mental or physical illness, trauma, lack of a healthy support system, financial troubles, addiction, and/or an inability to find affordable housing. Ultimately, the homeless population is like any other group of people. It is comprised of unique individuals with unique blessings and challenges. Richard, for instance, would suggest that we should add a loss of hope to any list about the root causes of homelessness. And a loss of faith.

As had happened in the courtroom, my emotions started to get the better of me the more I talked about my friend. With moist, reddened eyes, I battled through my notes. "Richard believed deeply in God," I said, slowly regaining my composure. Everyone in the room knew that about him. "And he showed us what faith can do."

Picking up on the theme of Richard's personal and spiritual renewal was the Pastor of the Victory Church of Jesus Christ. His congregation was just up the street. After the sermon, one of Richard's friends stood up at his chair and spoke. A Vietnam veteran, he, too, battled post traumatic stress syndrome. "I didn't laugh for eleven years until I met Richard Rogers," he said in utter seriousness. At which point he let his smile beam. "I love you, brother," he continued. "*What a gift it is to bring laughter into someone's life,*" I thought to myself.

The next person who popped up was a woman who had attended one of the addiction classes Richard led at the VA. She discussed what it was like to attend meetings with Richard. His upbeat nature. How he cared. "He saved my life," she said finally as tears streamed down her face. I melted while I watched her tell that story. Is there a better legacy than saving someone's life?

"*This probably isn't the picture Richard had of his own funeral,*" I thought, taking in the service. He was planning on moving out of Ignatia House and building a sober life with friends and family. At the same time, I knew that Richard would have been immensely proud to see the life change he had helped to bring about. Richard was good at helping people improve their lives. I know, because he changed mine.

Sitting in the office alone after the service, I reflected on the time I spent with Richard. The first two things I noticed when I met him was that he had dark black skin and centimeter-long fingernails. As we shook hands, he caught me looking at his long nails. With a skeptical stare, Richard smirked in my direction, his smile revealing a gap between his two front teeth. Around his neck perched the headphones he used to listen to music. I could hear a slight reverberation of sound emanating from them. The deep cavernous crevices that lived under his eyes made me think he was tired. But he wasn't. The crevices were just a part of Richard's appearance.

More than anything, the then Mr. Rogers was apprehensive about this strange new white guy entering his life. This was something he told me later. Our first few meetings were uneventful. He stayed quiet. Bit by bit, however, we got to know each other better. Richard started to open up. Sometimes too much. On more than one occasion, his rawness unnerved me and other staffers.

"My doctor said I am supposed to talk about what is on my mind," he would say during those moments. "Don't keep anything in." He was authentic to the core, and I learned to appreciate his bluntness. Before long, I was replying in kind. And the two of us grew closer. We didn't just talk during our meetings; we also talked around the Ignatia House's pool table, in the kitchen and during the house's social gatherings. Getting the veterans together was an invaluable part of the U.S. Vets program. Once or twice a month someone on staff was responsible for hosting a party at the house. The events were set up to encourage interaction among the residents, something that was especially important for those individuals who tended to isolate themselves in their rooms. The pool tournaments, barbecues and holiday gatherings were meant to help create what medical professionals call a therapeutic community, one in which people take care of each other.

Richard usually played a central role in our parties. In a room of shy and introverted veterans, he received great satisfaction from making his fellow residents laugh. Or at least making sure they had a good time. Richard was normally the honorary DJ. While heavy on old-school Motown, his music selection was always diverse enough to keep everyone happy. He danced the night away at our Thanksgiving dinner. During Christmas, Richard got up to play Pin the Tail on the Donkey with a politician's gift for the moment. On the one hand, he let all his buddies know that he was well aware that Pin the Tail on the Donkey was a juvenile exercise. On the other hand, he kept smiles on people's faces by playing along, blindfolded and all.

As much as I appreciated his gift for humor, it was Richard's embrace of the belief that a new life was always possible which left the most indelible impression on many of us who were close to him. My first real breakthrough with him as a friend occurred while he told me about his struggles with addiction. Like in a scene out of a *Scared Straight* video, Richard was very open about the pain associated with his life on the streets. He wanted people to know what could happen if they made the wrong choices. And he wasn't afraid to be brutally honest. Richard's commitment to use his own cautionary tale to help others was inspiring.

"The crack epidemic in America makes Hurricane Katrina look like a puddle," he would say to anyone who would listen. From there, Richard would outline what happened day in and day out during his years on the ruthless streets of Washington. "I was not the same person I am now when I was using," he told me. "All I was focused on was my own survival. When I was out there I was not a good man," he continued.

"Me, neither," I replied, surprised by own words. Richard saw my surprise, and like he had decided to hit the pause button on his own video, he stopped talking. Eyes wide open, Richard sat there, waiting for more. He wasn't going to let me stop with one small sentence of candor. So I kept going. I told him how guilty I felt about my crimes. "It was stupid and shameful to be so greedy," I said. He told me he understood. We then talked about what it was like to carry the weight of our bad decisions around every day. We talked about the importance of honesty. Getting better wasn't possible without getting right with the facts, we agreed. I felt better after talking about my failures with Richard. What made it feel even better was the fact that I was just talking honestly instead of worrying about what I was supposed to say, or what would advance my own short-term interests.

Over time, the two of us talked a lot about our sins. Richard stole so he could feed his addiction. I cheated to feed mine. By cheating my colleagues, my clients and my country, I fed an addiction for money and power that was similar to the desires that had hurt some of the veterans I was now serving. As it turned out, Richard and I weren't all that different. We both knew what it was like to be a social pariah. For me, that meant watching former colleagues cross the street rather than be seen with me, or living with the fact that elected officials would give away money I had given them rather than keep it. For Richard, being a pariah meant getting thrown off buses and being carelessly abused on the street. Neither of us would admit it at first, but the process had taken its toll on our self-esteem. It was nice to meet someone who understood. In that way, talking was good for both of us. So was our shared hope of redemption. Such fellowship was important, and helped to pick us up when we were down.

One day, after visiting Capitol Hill on my lunch break, I couldn't wait for Richard to plop down in the chair next to my desk so we could talk. My visit to the Hill had not gone well, even though I had gone there to simply do some business at the credit union. Outside the building, I spotted an old friend of mine, a lobbyist with whom I had traveled and worked for years. He had no affiliation with the Abramoff scandal. I was excited to see him. But he purposely crossed the street to avoid me. My stomach sank. This was far from the first time something like that had happened. When I got inside the building, I was spurned again, this time by a Hill staffer I had also known for years. He darted up the stairs rather than walk down the same hall with me. My stomach sank even deeper.

Feeling like I had a disease, I decided to just put my head down, avoid eye contact with anyone, and get my banking done. As I reached to open the glass door to the credit union, someone grabbed my shoulder. Surprised, I turned to see who was there. It was a friend of mine who was the top staffer for the Congressional Black Caucus, an organization of black members of Congress. We, too, had known each other for years.

"Hey man," I said, putting my hand out toward his.

Instead of grabbing my hand, however, he pulled me in for a hug. "I don't care what the papers say," my friend told me. "The Neil I know is a good guy, and someone I'm happy to call a friend." Without knowing it, my hill colleague had saved my day. A sense of relief came over me, knowing that some people were willing to treat me as the person they interacted with more than the one they read about.

When I returned to U.S. Vets, I shared the story with Richard. He laughed. "Sounds like a good brother to me."

Never fully comfortable with the always-present racial overtones of Ignatia House commentary, I nonetheless replied, "You bet."

"Hang your hat on the good, and try not to let the bad get you down," he concluded.

"Aren't I the one who is supposed to be telling you that kind of thing?" I asked. We laughed.

In many ways, Richard was like an angel to me. His belief in people and hope for the future was a reflection of his faith, and our relationship helped me to reconnect with my faith. It was a lesson I never saw coming. Raised Catholic from birth, I became a born-again Christian in high school. Then, over the next fifteen years, my faith receded. For most of the last decade, in fact, I had stopped going to church, reading the Bible, or seeking inspiration from fellow believers. Therefore, during the first few years of the scandal, I tended to think that God wouldn't want me back. So I focused mostly on getting a job, handling my finances and managing the slow-motion breakdown of important relationships in my life. Frankly, examining my conflicted feelings about God and religion scared me, so I avoided it. But then Richard and the veterans at Ignatia House rekindled my faith and changed the trajectory of my introspection - and my life. Unlike the emotionally driven moment in high school when I surrendered to Christ, this time the change evolved a step at a time.

"Jesus Christ saved my life," Richard told me proudly, over and over again. Unlike me, Richard's reconnection with God had occurred in an instant. His spiritual transformation happened one morning on the streets of Washington. It was raining, Richard said. He was soaked, and worried about getting sick.

"Don't you die out here on these streets as a bum," he had said to himself. It was then that he started to feel the touch of God. Richard, standing in front of a car wash, said he felt God telling him to change his life. "Jesus told me to stop worrying about the past, and that I could get right by letting him change my heart," he said. Richard then went on to tell me that he knew some people thought he was crazy when he discussed his car wash transformation, but he didn't care. That was the day he chose to visit a shelter and stop living in the streets. It was that encounter with Jesus Christ that allowed Richard to stop using drugs, and start using his experience to help other people struggling with addiction, disease and hopelessness. Some people see those kind of stories as delusional. And that is their right. But to Richard, and to me, his experience didn't just help to change his life, but it helped him to save other lives as well.

Not a week passed that I didn't get a spiritual update from Richard. Our talks helped me to feel my way through the increased spirituality I was feeling. I told Richard that my issues with Christianity didn't have anything to do with the inspiration of God, or the life of Jesus Christ. They revolved around man's use of organized religion and the Bible to control other people's lives. I didn't like the Bible, a book about relationships, being used to litigate history, I told him. People killing and hurting other people in the name of God defamed the life of Christ, I said. The manipulation was something I couldn't get over when I was younger, and I am not sure I can get over now. Richard would listen without much response. He didn't look at his faith that way. "God is my friend," Richard would say. "We have a personal relationship."

"When I was working so much, I was too busy to worry about God," I told Richard. "But now I am realizing that I was lost without the guidance the Bible provided me when I was younger. It was like my ambitions took over everything."

"Who knows, maybe I'm your angel?" Richard said one day during one of our discussions. Right away, his words resonated with me. I stopped talking. Instead of worrying about what that sounded like, I listened to my heart.

"Maybe you are," I replied with a big smile. He smiled back. That back-and-forth will stick with me for the rest of my life. Over the next few years, I would reestablish my relationship with Jesus Christ. More than any other relationship, reconnecting with my God helped me to grow out of the scandal. Of course, the progress took time.

My conversations with Richard continued until the day he died. We didn't always see things the same way. Sometimes we didn't even connect. But we kept talking. Step by step, I felt myself reconnecting with the values my parents instilled in me when I was young, values I lost during my ambition-fueled flight toward glory. With Richard's help, my time at U.S. Vets reminded me once again how important it was to focus on the purpose behind my decisions, rather than on what I thought the outcome would be. Discussing my beliefs with friends like Richard helped to reinforce the simple premise that our beliefs should determine our decisions, and then our decisions will determine our outcomes.

To some, abandoning such an outcome-based approach to decision-making may seem like a trivial matter. To me, it was huge. It was a reflection of my renewed faith. It was an invaluable lesson. Letting my values, instead of the potential outcomes, dictate my decisions quickly joined my previous insights: living life through my relationships, asking myself what I was fighting for, and getting right with the facts as a foundation for my new life.

The Man In The Mirror

My decision to leave Washington wasn't an easy one. "I am going to re-invent myself," I told friends and family. The move was bittersweet. On one hand, moving brought home my failures. It meant accepting the fact that I had failed as a husband and failed professionally. It also meant saying goodbye to lots of friends and to U.S. Vets. On the other hand, moving to Florida represented hope for a better future, away from the acrimony of my past. I also felt the guiding hand of God for the first time in years.

During a meeting a few days before my departure, I told the veterans at Ignatia House that I was moving to Fort Myers for "family reasons." I sounded like a politician. While I was very close with many of the residents, with others it was important to keep firm professional boundaries. "The 16th will be my last day as your Program Director," I said benignly. It was a sad moment, but the graciousness of the friends I had made at U.S. Vets made it easier.

"Moving on is part of the process here," said Phil Jones, one of the leaders of our veteran community. "You said that, Neil. Now its your turn to follow the advice." I wanted to joke to Phil that I didn't know what I was talking about, then or now. Instead of joking, however, the two of us hugged, Phil's big 6'6" frame wrapping around me like a teddy bear. He could feel my pain.

For the previous six months, my wife and I had lived in separate homes. Our temporary separation eventually become permanent - and expensive. With hundreds of thousands of dollars in new debt already hanging over our heads, adding an additional rent payment to an overly leveraged mortgage squeezed a tight budget even tighter. Since my U.S. Vets salary was minimal, and my savings gone, I quickly found myself living in a house

I couldn't afford. Honorable through the entire scandal, Alison did not want to push me out the door. Therefore, she did everything she could to make sure I was on a reasonable financial footing before we made any sort of move. Likewise, I did everything possible to make sure she could keep the house.

For a while, I thought about finding an apartment near Ignatia House. "The vets need me," I said. "Leaving them now would be selfish." In recent years, I had taken a certain amount of ownership over the program. But after conversations with my veteran friends and others, I decided to give myself permission to go ahead with the long-distance move.

"If there is an emergency on a plane, you have to put your mask on before you can help someone else," said on of my U.S Vets' colleagues. Her words resonated deep within me. I appreciated the honesty. It wasn't in her best interest for me to leave. My departure would mean more work and a bigger emotional burden for her. Helping the veterans was life-affirming, but not always easy.

I worried about what people would think. Just because I was leaving U.S. Vets didn't mean I was going to backtrack on my promises to make serving others a top priority. Some people would see the move that way. But I knew better, and that was what was important.

On the weekend before I left for Florida, I drove to Ohio to visit some of Bob's former staffers. I wanted to apologize to them. Through no fault of their own, the Congressman's district staff had seen their lives turned upside down because of the scandal. With Bob in jail, many were now pariahs in their home communities. Several remained unemployed. They were victims of other people's arrogance, greed and stupidity, including my own. I was told by a former colleague to expect some angry questions. The anger and skepticism was understandable, I replied. "If I can help them I will," I said. "But they deserve to hear me tell them honestly that I am sorry."

Our get-together took place in the home of one of Bob's former staffers. It wasn't the first meeting of their group. Since Ney's resignation, they had gotten together several times, partly in celebration and partly as therapy. It felt good to see my former staff. After everyone arrived, I apologized as simply as I could. "I'm sorry," I said.

Right away, one of Bob's former case managers summed up the sentiment in the room. "What happened?" she asked. Her question set the tone for our entire conversation, a conversation that was quite different from the discussions I had around the same time with Bob's former Washington staffers. To Ney's Ohio staff, the scandal remained a mystery. In part, that was because the culture of Bob's district office was fundamentally different from the culture of the DC office. The Washington office was built around the legislative process. The Ohio offices were built around interaction with the voters. These Buckeye-state office case managers diligently helped voters with services like Social Security claims, visa applications and veteran's benefits. They also attended local economic development, state planning and community meetings.

In doing their jobs, employees of the district offices were not allowed to accept free meals or free tickets. This policy was the result of a political decision. In most cases, they could have taken the free county fair or charity event ticket under the House rules. But the appearance of taking free tickets wasn't something Bob wanted his constituents to see or to gossip about. Therefore, while we Washington staffers cavorted with lobbyists and other professional politicos, the district staff focused on the voters. Because of this distinction, I spent much of my time explaining to the Congressman's former Ohio staffers how Bob and I behaved differently in Washington, and why.

In turn, they shared with me their perspective on the scandal. Members of the group had heard a lot of stories about the Congressman, some true and some not. The thoughts and feelings of Bob's constituents regarding the scandal varied wildly. Their words gave me insight into the district experience and helped me to better understand some of the pain I helped to cause. My disappointment in myself grew as I thought about letting down so many voters. They were supposed to have been able to trust me. I listened in horror as several of the Congressman's former staffers told me they heard about Bob deciding to plead guilty on the radio as they got ready for work. One of the women telling the story said she called a colleague to ask if they were still supposed to go into the office. "What are we supposed to do?" she asked. Eventually they confronted the Congressman. "Ney told us that people he thought were his friends had betrayed him," she said bluntly. I shuddered at her recollection of his words; they verified Bob's venomous comments about me in the paper. For several hours, we waded into the awkward, conflicting and emotional storyline of the scandal. Their candor was immensely helpful in my efforts to get right with the facts. As I drove home the next day, I prayed for the well-being of every single one of them. They truly were innocent victims of the scandal. I hoped in some small way that my willingness to honestly talk through what happened was as helpful to my former colleagues as theirs had been to me.

My trip to Ohio was the brainchild of Jim Forbes, the former

Communications Director for Chairman Ney. He had worked for Bob and me at the committee during the 9/11 attacks, the anthrax evacuation and passage of the election reform bill. After leaving Bob's office, he had returned to the Ohio Valley to take a job as a local television broadcaster. The two of us were good friends. We had an honest relationship.

Forbes and I first discussed the idea of my trip to Ohio to meet with the district staff during a trip Jim made to Washington. He stayed a few nights with me in what felt like an empty house. Like Channing's pilgrimage of friendship during my sentencing hearing, Jim's visit could not have come at a better time. I was confused and hurting pretty badly. I had let a lot of people down, and there were now some serious holes in my life because of those decisions.

When Jim arrived, he dropped his bags and the two of us immediately walked up the street to a local restaurant. Our primary goal was to talk. Our secondary goal was to eat as many chicken wings as we could. With sweat pouring down our brows and crumpled up wing-sauce-soaked napkins surrounding us, we quickly reconnected.

"I've been hearing some stories about you," Jim said.

"Yeah, me too," I joked.

"People are worried," he continued. "They don't think you are the same outgoing person you used to be. I can see it."

"What do you mean?" I asked.

"If we were at a restaurant like this a few years ago, you would have talked to everybody in here," Jim told me. "I don't see that now."

For a second I looked at my old friend. I thought about pretending that I didn't know what he was talking about. But, instead, I came clean. "My guard is up now, and probably always will be," I said plainly. "I don't want to be burned again by the people I choose to associate with."

Jim didn't reply directly. He instead shared with me some of his personal trials. An ordained minister, Jim told me that years earlier he had set up a ministry to help children afflicted with HIV. Unfortunately, some of his partners were not upfront with him about their finances. It put him in a bad spot, Jim said. "I fought off bankruptcy for years," he continued. His colleagues had let him down, too. He understood what I was going through. When I told him for the fourth or fifth time that I wasn't a victim of anything but my own mistakes, he asked me to stop talking for a second.

"Look man, life is complicated," he said. "Taking responsibility for what you did is one thing. It is healthy. But you can't keep beating yourself up for what other people did. That isn't good."

"But I can make sure I don't ever let another Mike Scanlon or Jack Abramoff into my life," I replied. "Or another Bob Ney." Such a stinging response surprised Jim, especially since I had just made some nice comments about our former boss. But it was also what he had expected, and what he had driven half-a-day to talk about.

"Or there is another way," he said. "You could also choose to live naively."

I stopped for a moment, intrigued by his comment. I trusted Jim. We weren't talking about my issues so he could gossip about it with others. He was serving God and his friend Neil.

"Just remember that however you want to move forward is your choice," he said. "You once told me that networking in Washington was great because all the people you met. Liberal or conservative, they cared about the country, and about important issues," Forbes continued. "You said that you could meet your next best friend at any time. That is how you met Channing. Do you really want to close that door?"

I considered the hard times I knew about Jim's past. I considered how they had helped him direct his life anew. And I shared my own epiphany on my sentencing date: how I saw that it was crucial for me to focus on building honest relationships as a way to live a healthy life.

"If you choose to keep your walls up, you won't let anybody in to build those relationships," he said. "I've been there. It is hard. But if you want, you can choose to live naively going forward. It made all the difference for me," he concluded.

There was that phrase again. "Live naively." The dictionary defines *naïve* as "simple and credulous as a child; and not subtle or learned." I liked the concept.

"What is the worst that can happen?" I said, joking my way back into the conversation. "I get burned again?"

"That is right," he said. "And then you'll get burned again, and again. But what is the best that can happen?"

"Today, tomorrow, next week or next year I can meet another best friend," I said. "One that I can trust, and one who will laugh at me for having even thought about putting my walls up."

"God doesn't want you to experience life alone," Forbes said.

My old friend was right. I could choose to live naively. I embraced the concept right away. In addition to infusing me with the hope of building positive, new relationships, it also had a wonderful subversive edge to it. *"Let the rest of the world get bitter,"* I thought. *"Let other people spend time judging and worrying. I am going to do life a different way."* Forbes's words re-invigorated me. More importantly, they made me start to feel proud again. The return of pride to my life was exciting. With the same vigor I had brought to the concept of getting right with the facts, I worked to begin living naively.

In part because of his words, my time at U.S. Vets took on a new tenor after Jim's visit, one built on my sentencing experience. Almost instantly, I felt my soul being enriched by the belief that there was a whole new world out there for me to experience - and my window into that world would be my relationships. New friendships throughout Ignatia House sprang to life. *"Some of these relationships will grow,"* I thought. *"Some will not. And I will be just fine."*

As I walked through the U.S. Vets offices for the last time, my heart was filled with the loving friendships that had developed during the nearly two years I had spent at Ignatia House. The honesty and youthful energy of these new relationships was a testament to the progress I was making. Leaving was painful, but I felt proud about how I had handled myself as the organization's Program Director. I was an honest leader and a real friend. At the same time, with my failed marriage and many failed professional relationships still reminding me of my past disappointments, I knew I had a long way to go.

Few showed me the power of living naively as clearly as Emily Button. Saying goodbye to Emily was tough. I walked into her office. She was sitting in front of her computer. Holding my arms open to hug the woman who was singularly responsible for my involvement with U.S Vets, I told her, "You gave me a shot when no one else would." With tears in our eyes, we hugged. Our time together had made memories for both of us.

We laughed about the challenges and successes of our golf tournament and talked about our colleagues. But mostly we talked about the veterans. Bringing homeless veterans from the street into the house, and then watching them work their way through the program was a shared experience Emily and I had celebrated on a regular basis. The process was proof that people could change.

"I learned so much here," I told her. "People really can change." Emily just smiled. Before working for the veterans of Ignatia House, I had believed that every homeless person could live an independent life if he just wanted to badly enough. I don't believe that anymore. It isn't a fact I can get right with. Most can change. But chronic homelessness is real, and we as a society should learn to accept that there are people who will need assistance from the government, a religious institution or a non-profit for the rest of their lives. And many of those people are veterans.

As we wrapped up our conversation, I thanked Emily again and again. "You showed me what it is like to lead with your heart," I told her. Wildly intelligent and incredibly hard working as she was, it was Emily's heart, though, that showed me how issues like homelessness are solved. They are solved more from the heart than the head. Her decision to embrace the concept of a second chance, to live naively, made the difference in so many of our veteran's lives. Every day, someone was hurting at Ignatia House, and every day, Emily helped. By creating a new program or fixing an old program, the process of administering an organization like U.S Vets, or any other organization, can obviously be made better. But putting our focus on the mechanics of the process misses the point - namely that the life change that occurred in the veterans of Ignatia House came more from the heartfelt decisions of people who cared about each other, more than an efficiently run program - as important as a well-run program is to the process.

After I left Emily's office, I went upstairs to visit with some of the veterans. More hugs and tears followed. "I'm not real good at keeping in touch, but know my heart will always be with you," one of the guys said. Another gave me a picture taken of him when he was in Vietnam. I was given a Miles Davis CD, a flag and even some food. The last guy I talked with was one of the veterans I had grown the closest to during my tenure.

"Stay on the right track," he said. "And don't forget to use the mirror." His words were followed by some scrambling through his disheveled desk. He pulled out a crumpled up piece of paper and gave it to me. "This is what I read when I need encouragement," he continued.

I didn't look at what he gave me until I got in the car. It was a poem entitled, "The Man in the Glass." I was familiar with the poem having discussed it with many of the veterans during sobriety meetings and talks about personal accountability. I read the poem again in my car. Right away, I assigned additional value to the words.

The Man in the Glass

When you get what you want in your struggle for self
And the world makes you king for a day,
Just go to the mirror and look at yourself
And see what that man has to say.

For it isn't your father or mother or wife
Whose judgment upon you must pass.
The fellow whose verdict counts most in your life
Is the one staring back from the glass.

You may be like Jack Horner and chisel a plum
And think you're a wonderful guy.
But the man in the glass says you're only a bum
If you can't look him straight in the eye.

He's the fellow to please-never mind all the rest,
For he's with you clear to the end.
And you've passed your most dangerous, difficult test
If the man in the glass is your friend.

You may fool the whole world down the pathway of years
And get pats on the back as you pass.
But your final reward will be heartache and tears
If you've cheated the man in the glass.

With the car running, I looked at myself in the rearview mirror. The poem was right. If I could learn to live with myself, then I could move forward in a positive way. It really was that simple. Whether moving forward in a positive way meant figuring out how to live with my scandalous past, re-establishing an honest relationship with God, staying right with the facts, asking questions, or cultivating healthy relationships in my life, using the mirror would be crucial. Considering I was moving to a place where I didn't know a single person, time for deep introspection wasn't going to be a problem.

Election Day

I RUSHED HOME TO CATCH PRESIDENT-ELECT Barack Obama's victory speech. The United States had just elected its first black president. The pendulum of history was swinging, and I didn't want to miss it. I hurriedly ran into my living room and turned on the television. A huge crowd was gathering in Grant Park to hear the Illinois Senator's address. The first thing I noticed was how cold the weather looked in Chicago. Kicking off my flip-flops, I sprawled out on the couch and called an old friend.

"Man, I'd love to be in Chicago right now," I told him. "That crowd just keeps getting bigger and bigger. It is going to be some kind of party."

He laughed. "They can take you out of politics, but they can't take the politics out of you," he told me. We both laughed some more. The two of us had followed the campaign together, a fact that probably had more to do with my need to talk to someone about it than his enjoyment of the election process.

After an epic primary campaign against New York Senator Hillary Clinton, President-elect Obama secured the 2008 Democrat Party's presidential nomination in early summer. His opponent for the general election was Arizona's Republican Senator John McCain. The Abramoff scandal continued to resonate with voters. Obama promised not to take money from federal lobbyists or allow them to work on issues associated with their lobbying in his White House. In response, McCain rarely missed a chance to exploit his role in exposing the Abramoff scandal.

During a debate in South Carolina, for instance, the Senator distanced himself from an unpopular GOP establishment by saying, "Ask Jack Abramoff if I'm an insider in Washington; you'd probably have to go during visiting hours in the prison." McCain didn't stop there. He mentioned the

Abramoff scandal during his convention speech and throughout the general election campaign.

Senator McCain's efforts to portray himself as the proverbial white knight, intent on cleaning up Washington, played out just like my lobbying colleagues and I had predicted when he began his hearings into Jack's lobbying practice years earlier. What I couldn't have predicted at that time, however, was that years later I would decide to volunteer for McCain's campaign when he finally did run for president. Unlike my campaign work for both Bob and President George W. Bush, my decision to assist McCain's team had little to do with actually impacting the outcome of the race. Nor did it have to do with advancing myself professionally.

When I arrived in Fort Myers, I didn't know anybody. My goal was simple. I wanted to use the second chance I had been given by Judge Huvelle to re-design my life. I wanted to not only continue to learn lessons from my past mistakes but live in a way that honored those lessons. Being alone gave me time to think in a way that I wished I had during the Washington chapter of my life. The financial, personal and professional challenges I faced meant that few days passed when I didn't reflect on my time in politics.

Getting a job was a prime example. I let my questions direct me. *"What kind of life do you want to lead? Should I try to find a non-profit job? Or should I focus on money so I can pay off my debt? What if I can't find work?"* As I thought through what steps to take, I was reminded of a conversation I had with one of the vets at Ignatia House before I left. Like I did now, my veteran client knew that he needed employment. His past, like mine, included holding several high-paying jobs in a specific field that he enjoyed. Unfortunately, after trouble followed for my veteran friend, he became homeless. His career opportunities disappeared. Nonetheless, his professional dreams remained. I knew the feeling.

At Ignatia House, he diligently worked to return to his old career. Yearning for professional opportunities that no longer existed, however, only made his efforts to find employment more difficult. "Sometimes you have to put your career on the back burner and just get a job," I told him, as I had learned during my training. When I got to Florida and had the time to honestly look at myself in the mirror, I could see that I was in a similar situation. My career as I knew it was over, so I gave myself the same advice. *"Neil, you need to just get a job."*

I pounded the pavement looking for work, and followed the exact advice U.S. Vets gave to its residents who were seeking employment. Every day I went out and talked to at least eight people who were hiring. My felony conviction was a hurdle. I could see it on the faces of those I talked to when they found out I was a criminal. The urge to hide my past grew stronger everyday. But I was committed to living with the facts and being honest.

Before long, I was offered two jobs. One was in the banquet department at a hotel, and the other was at a retail and jewelry shop on the beach. The application for the hotel had asked if I had a criminal background, while the application for the job on the beach did not. Being straightforward during both interviews, I still found myself with a dilemma. Did I want to work where my colleagues knew about my criminal background and the past scandal, or not?

I decided to take the job on the beach. From the store's entrance, I could see the Gulf of Mexico. It was a long way from the stuffy corridors of Washington's K Street corridor. No one knew about my Washington past. The anonymity was refreshing. The fear, intrigue and disappointment I usually felt when people learned about my involvement with the Abramoff scandal was replaced by the normal everyday struggles of working in a retail environment. I was just Neil, the guy from Ohio.

I did my best to naively meet people and labor honestly with my new colleagues. Though I remained lonely and the work was tedious, I started to enjoy the new experience. After searching around for a bit, I joined Next Level Church. This was also an important step. It helped me to continue growing spiritually and to connect with my community. Day by day, life got better.

Eventually, I started working behind the jewelry counter at the store. This meant greeting people as they entered the shop. I talked to so many people, I might as well have been a politician. I guess I gravitated to the job. In addition to selling traditional jewelry, I also sold the sunken treasure which was a part of the local lifestyle and lore. Never in my wildest dreams had I imagined that I would end up selling old gold and silver coins which had been found on sunken Spanish ships littering the Gulf of Mexico floor. But I did. Despite the fact I was getting paid in a week what I made in an hour as a lobbyist, learning about and selling the sunken treasure was genuinely enjoyable. It gave me a purpose.

The largest part of the store's collection was coins from a shipwreck called the *Nuestra Señora de Atocha*, or the *Atocha*. The ship was well known around the barrier islands of Southwest Florida, part of the area's seafaring history. On September 6, 1622, the *Atocha* encountered a hurricane and crashed onto the coral reefs near Key West. The ship had been loaded up with South American treasure and was heading back to Spain. Hundreds of people died in the wreck, and tons of gold, silver and other valuables were lost. For centuries, treasure hunters looked for the mythical *Atocha*.

It was finally found on July 20, 1985, more than 350 years later, by a local treasure hunter named Mel Fischer. Fischer, who bar-hopped through South Florida to find small-time investors willing to help him keep his salvage team operating, lost his son and daughter-in-law in the water during the sixteen-year hunt for the *Atocha*. When his crew finally found the mother lode, they said it was like walking into a room with walls of gold bars and Spanish artifacts. After the treasure was brought ashore, the singer Jimmy Buffet performed a concert along the top of an eight-foot wall of gold. The treasure was appraised at several hundred million dollars.

The federal government claimed ownership of the wreck after its discovery, and the State of Florida seized much of Fischer's treasure. An eight-year legal battle ended when the United States Supreme Court ruled in favor of Fischer. The shipwrecked treasure was his. To pay taxes on such a find, he and his team scattered throughout the area to sell what they could. That was how people throughout South Florida ended up with the coins, most of which were minted in the late 1590s and early 1600s, a time before Jamestown, America's first English-speaking colony, had even founded.

The process of selling the several hundred-year-old coins meant talking with lots of people. Every night, tourists, bikers, drifters, boaters, and other treasure hunters would come in to see the coins. Talking about Fisher's journey and his battle with the federal government inevitably led to conversations about politics. I couldn't help it. It was an election year. Before I knew it, and away from Washington, talking politics became fun again. I even began thinking about volunteering on a campaign.

Not that I was completely free of my past. Occasionally, remnants of the Abramoff scandal appeared. Sometimes they were expected, like when I was called by the Department of Justice to testify in yet another corruption-related trial in Washington. Other times, these remnants surprised me. One day, for example, a valuable coin from a different shipwreck called the *El Cazador* turned up missing from the store inventory. Management scoured the building to determine if it had been stolen. At first I didn't think too much of it. There were security cameras everywhere, I figured. "They'll find who did it," I said.

Then a more formal investigation began. When I showed up to work a few days later, one of my colleagues told me that management had started asking lots of questions. I got nervous. *"People could point their finger at me real easy,"* I thought to myself, despite the fact that only a few of the most senior people in the store even knew about my past. My heart raced and my thought became irrational. *"I'm an easy target. But I've never done anything but be honest to everyone in here."* The internal angst tormented me for several hours.

Finally, after getting myself all worked up, I stormed into the office of a senior person at the store. It was the first time I ever marched in like that. "Someone could put a gun to my head, and I wouldn't take a dollar from this place," I blurted out, surprising myself with my own vehemence.

Fortunately, the person I was talking to knew exactly where I was coming from. "I didn't think for a second that it was you, Neil," I was told.

Instantly, I felt relieved, and embarrassed. My shoulders dropped and I looked away. "I'm sorry," I replied.

"No worries," my colleague said.

It felt good to know that I was trusted. At the same time, I kicked myself for letting the opinion of someone else so define my happiness. It conflicted with my goal of just focusing on doing the right thing and letting the public perception of my actions take care of themselves.

Compared to the previous years of legal and political drama, that moment may not seem like a big deal to others. But to me, it mattered a lot. How I handled myself showed that I was relearning to treat the little things like they were big things, one of the values I learned growing up in small town Ohio. When it comes to your integrity, everything matters. On the one hand, I felt good about the progress I was making. On the other, it was yet another lesson I wished that I had taken to heart earlier. *"If I had just taken care of the little things in Washington, I never would have gotten in trouble,"* I told myself again and again. *"After all, my little problems turned into big problems, and my big problems turned into a felony."*

Another small decision I spent time contemplating was whether to volunteer for the McCain campaign or not. My decision-making process started by simply watching the presidential campaign develop from my new vantage point as a low-end wage-earner. No one I had met in Florida by that point had a professional connection to either campaign. While they knew the importance of the election, their livelihood would not be directly impacted in the same way my friends back in Washington faced, where political jobs and clients were directly on the line. More than any other issue, the one topic that got my new colleagues engaged in the campaign was the economy. They were worried about a looming recession and the plummeting local housing market. The declining real estate prices were hurting the regional economy, and like the rest of the world, a global credit freeze had led to a dramatic across-the-board reduction in business activity. In personal terms, that meant my colleagues were worried about losing their jobs. I was, too.

To the pundits on television, the economic unease was something to analyze. To the political class in Washington, it was something to debate. But to my new friends in Florida, the growing recession was a frightening reality. Several of my new friends had experienced home foreclosure. When I talked to them about their troubles, they told me how mad they were at themselves for getting in over their heads. They also said they were upset with the bankers and brokers who encouraged them to purchase beyond their means.

Some of my other friends, people who were still in their homes but also barely making ends meet, were just as mad, but for other reasons. They were mad at the prospect that President Bush and the Democrat-led Congress were thinking about using their hard-earned tax dollars to bail out the investors, mortgage professionals and failed homeowners who were at the heart of the housing market's collapse. It seemed unfair to them. These colleagues felt like they had worked hard for their money and played by the rules, yet now their own government was going to take that money to subsidize bad decisions made by other people. I couldn't blame them for being frustrated or cynical. People like the lobbyist I used to be were hard at work manipulating the levers of government to protect their financial service clients and bosses, I said. Still, in my opinion, the bailout was an evil necessity. The economy was on the brink of collapse.

It was the high point of the campaign. From afar, I knew Senator McCain and his people could feel the rapidly growing resentment against the Bush bailout. I also knew such a cauldron of political anger was creating a political dynamic that McCain could use to his political advantage. By opposing the bailout, he could not only generate votes among an anxious electorate, but also separate himself from Senator Obama and an unpopular Bush Presidency at the same time. With less than 30% of the public supporting the job President Bush was doing, his unpopularity was like a political noose around McCain's neck.

Cynically believing that Senator McCain had never seen a political opportunity that he didn't take advantage of, I waited for him to announce his opposition to the unpopular bailout. It was his best chance to win. But the announcement didn't happen. Despite the fact that the loudest cheers he and his running mate got on the campaign trail occurred when they criticized the potential bailout, McCain refused to fundamentally play politics with the economy. His opposition could have killed the bill. Instead, from my vantage point, he did what he thought was right and supported the bailout. It was as if he believed there was something more important than his election. While I didn't like the concept of losing an election, or, for that matter, support the bailout, I was enthralled with the concept of a person in Senator McCain's position potentially putting the country's interests ahead of his own. *"It was what I should have done,"* I thought. *"And should do going forward."* Whether that was how it actually played out inside the campaign, I don't know. But it changed my opinion of the man. The personal scars of watching McCain and his team use my mistakes for their gain years earlier faded away. I even began to see how the Senator's use of public shame and discourse had been healthy for the system, and for me. I decided to get involved.

Before working the evening shift, I spent election morning at McCain-Palin headquarters. In a perfectly square, first floor room that smelled of cellophane, I joined other volunteers working the phones, calling people to get out and vote. I was by far the youngest volunteer there. That fact alone suggested we were in trouble, I told myself. In President Bush's 2004 victory, we had lots of young volunteers.

"Hi, this is Neil, a volunteer for the Florida Republican Party," I said to whoever answered. After days of calling, I knew the script well. I also knew what I was doing was miniscule in the grand scheme of the campaign. But it was fun to listen to the people around me engage in the political process.

The woman sitting next to me said she was fasting for the day in the hopes of helping the McCain-Palin ticket. The guy next to her religiously quoted the latest polls to anyone he could reach. "Remember 2000," he said, in reference to the razor-thin election margin of the 2000 presidential election.

Occasionally, a random comment to a voter caught the attention of the room. "Ma'am, can I suggest you move to Cuba," one of the Cuban-American volunteers said in jest after hanging up with a caller who told him she was voting for Obama. We all laughed. It was a fun moment, one that made me feel even closer to my new community. I liked being part of the Senator's extended team. Win or lose, my decision to help the McCain campaign had been a positive move. It made me feel like I was serving something bigger than myself. For that I was thankful.

Now I watched as the soon-to-be President Obama arrived at the podium. My friend and I hung up with each other. "Hello, Chicago!" Obama said. The crowd went crazy. "This is your victory," he continued. With the election results scrolling along the bottom of the screen, the television cameras panned the crowd. Tears filled the eyes of everyday citizens. My mind wandered to a conversation I had days earlier with one of the veterans from Ignatia House. A black man, he joked to with me about how all of his family and friends in Southeast Washington were on their best behavior heading into the election. "One stupid move will tarnish all of us and cost him the White House," he joked. I could only imagine the very real emotions he was feeling as he watched the Illinois Senator's speech.

Obama hailed the millions of people who had voted for the first time. In many states, these new voters were the difference between winning and losing. He said their decision to get involved was "the answer that led those who've been told for so long by so many to be cynical and fearful and doubtful about what we can achieve, to put their hands on the arc of history and bend it toward the hope of a better day."

The idea of putting one's hand on the arc of history to make things better was mesmerizing and empowering. It reminded me how I felt during the 1994 campaign and helped me to discard some of the cynical, personal scar tissue that had built up in me since then. "That is the true genius of America," Obama said. "We can change." I sat on my South Florida couch in awe of the message of a man I had just spent a week working against. Though I was unsure of what the next four years would bring, I liked that his speech was not only inspiring the 100,000 people gathered in Grant Park, but also old, political-hack curmudgeons like me who were watching on television.

With his gift for oratory, the future President talked about a 106-year-old woman from Atlanta named Ann Nixon Cooper. "She was born just a generation past slavery; a time when there were no cars on the road or planes in the sky, when someone like her couldn't vote for two reasons — because she was a woman and because of the color of her skin," he said. "And tonight, I think about all that she's seen throughout her century in America — the heartache and the hope; the struggle and the progress; the times we were told that we can't, and the people who pressed on with that American creed: Yes, we can."

His words inspired me, not as a political professional, but as a citizen. My struggle was nothing like the one he was talking about, yet I connected with his belief that change was possible, and a good thing.

===================

Preparing to Meet Bob

THE CORNERS WERE ALWAYS THE hardest to clean. Despite my best effort, the grease-bristled broom never seemed able to pick up all the debris on the floor. Therefore, when it was finally time to mop, I had to bend down on one knee, place the end of the long yellow handle in my armpit, and methodically turn the mop's wet spaghetti-noodle head numerous times before I felt like things were clean enough to move forward. Bob would have been proud of my diligence. It was 4:30 in the morning.

Because of the unique angle and motion of my mop, the shadow dancing above me on the dark wood floor of the restaurant looked kind of like a cotton candy machine. *"Cue the carnival music,"* I joked to myself. *"Bring on the county fair. Or maybe my silhouette looks more like a steelworker,"* I thought, while continuing to scrub away.

"Either one would be better than mopping up this shit," I said aloud, with a sudden jolt of anger.

Stunned by my own outburst, I hurriedly regrouped, reminding myself that life is good. "In fact, it is great," I said calmly, meaning every word. Building myself up as quickly as I tore myself down, a smile returned to my face. "Focus on what you can do, not what you can't."

Normally I didn't slip up like that too much anymore. I'd moved on, in part on purpose and in part because I had no other choice. Either way, Southwest Florida was now my happy home. But there was a lot on my mind. Much more than just the janitorial job at hand.

There was the recent death of a friend and former Capitol Hill colleague. My heart broke when I heard the news. From afar, I prayed for those hurting the most as well as the cause and the country we both had served.

Also on my mind was the upcoming family trip with my new girlfriend.

445

Pam was an amazing gift. A wonderful addition to my life. But I was still a little nervous. To some, my divorce remained recent news. Fun as the trip would be, I hoped it wouldn't be too awkward for her or my family. And, of course, there was my impending meeting with Bob. After nearly five years, Bob and I were finally going to see each other. We hadn't communicated since before he went to prison. For two people who had talked almost every day, that was quite a change. And now we were just a few days away. The face-to-face gnawed at me constantly. My mind wandered as I mopped.

"What should I say? What will he say?"

"I wonder what he thinks. Who cares what he thinks. Maybe I should care what he thinks."

"Does he hate me? I would probably hate me."

"What is the healthy thing to do? What is the right thing to do? What is the wise thing to do?"

"If I don't care what Bob thinks, why do I keep thinking about it?"

Since life had slowed down, I started having a lot of conversations with myself, some funny, some sad. But they were all a big deal to me. The mirror was no longer something to avoid, to dress up. In fact, I now embraced it. After hitting rock bottom years ago, I found most of my internal discussions revolved around how best to get back on the right track. Or, if it was a good day, how to stay on the right track. My most important step forward involved putting Jesus Christ first in my life. From there, I tried to simply focus on doing the right thing for the right reason. It was easier said than done. On most days, in fact, I doubted my ability to meet such a lofty goal. Nonetheless, I felt content knowing that on a regular basis I was at least trying.

Much of my continued progress and introspection flowed from there.

Bob remained a big piece of my soul-searching puzzle. That is what made our get-together even more important. For so many years my life had revolved around him. Saying he was once the sun in my personal universe was not hyperbole or spin. I gave years to Bob. Time I can't get back. Of course, he also gave me his time. Because of Bob, I had the experience of a lifetime. I had loved working for the Congressman. My dreams had flowed through him. My world view had been shaped by him. On any given day, no one was more important. But that time was gone. *"You don't need to look at the mop in my hand to see that fact,"* I thought. *"The question is, what to do now?"*

When I heard that Bob and I would be meeting at the premiere of a documentary film about the Abramoff scandal, one we both were interviewed for, I did what I normally do. I put on a happy face, acted like our little get-together at the Sundance Film Festival wasn't a big deal - and then methodically called a handful of old colleagues who also used to work for the Congressman. We talked at length. We discussed the past. We discussed the future. The good times as well as the bad. We talked about him, and we talked about me. Like a bunch of gossipy moms discussing their kids at book club, we dug in deep.

These informal therapy sessions were helpful. Talking about the past made me feel good about the new foundation of my life; asking questions, getting right with the facts, having faith, using the mirror, serving others and not living on the edge. Working through that list helped me to keep the get-together with Bob in perspective. "*You've got this covered,*" I thought, as we got nearer to the meeting. "*Don't fly too high, and don't fly too low.*"

Re-creating my past with Bob, or, even worse, blocking it out entirely, was something I could have pulled off relatively easily if I had wanted to. But I didn't. Honest introspection required, well, being honest. Not that I didn't start down the road of whitewashing the past. I did. Initially, I wasn't really sure what to do with the emotional web that was our relationship.

"Just remember the positive things about Bob," one old friend of mine suggested in the name of moving forward.

"Fuck him," said another. "Don't live in the past." At any given moment, I found myself listening to both approaches, without digging too deep.

For a while, my lack of clarity seemed to serve a purpose. It bought me a little time to begin re-inventing myself. But, eventually, that approach fell apart when I realized the growth I was trying to achieve in other areas of my life kept being hampered by my unwillingness to truly reflect on my life in Ney World.

I dug in deep. Why did we get involved with the scandal? Was it greed? Corruption? Was it politics? What drove Bob? How about me? Was I blindly loyal or blindly ambitious? And Bob? Did he know what he was doing? What is he doing now? Is he a good guy? A guy like me who had made some stupid and selfish decisions, but wants to do the right thing? The conversations with my former colleagues helped me to sort through some of the issues. Many of them remained angry at the Congressman. Some at me. Others were sad, had become ambivalent or simply moved on. By the end of our conversations, however, it was clear to me that we weren't merely discussing two guys who hadn't seen each other in a while. It was bigger than that. There were lots of people still hurting. That insight helped me realize what I needed to do. The purpose of my impending conversation with Bob began to take shape.

Minutes after mopping the floor, I vigorously scrubbed the toilet stall walls. Scrubbing those black walls was a hard job. I never really knew when I was done. At one angle they looked clean. Then the light hit from another direction and I realized a few spots had been missed. So I was right back at it.

Before long, the smell of bleach infected the entire men's room. The inside of my nose burned. My eyes reddened. *"Who knew finger prints and smudge marks could build up so quickly? And in so many random places. I mean what the hell are people doing in here?"* I thought. *"This sure is a long way from Washington."*

Before long, my reminiscing led where it always did - to my lost integrity. The shame of the scandal. The pain and suffering of family and friends. My unfulfilled expectations. It turns out that depression never really leaves. Just when you think those feelings are gone, they come roaring right back. It was as if my depressing thoughts were saying, "Giddy up Neil; here we go again."

"But I've been here before," I remind them. *"And we're not going there tonight boys."* After all, I had a job to do. My colleague was down the hall and we didn't have much time. He normally cleans the kitchen. I clean the bar. We then share the bathrooms, the hallways, the eating areas and the outside of the building. Nameless and faceless, we are judged by nothing but our work. The two of us arrive at the restaurant after most people have left and leave before most people arrive. His English is about as good as my Spanish, which means not very good. But we both like to laugh and enjoy helping each other. Very simply, it is all good. It is *muy bueno*.

During the day, I work for a non-profit. At night, I clean restaurants and office buildings. Paying the always nagging debt of my legal bills requires keeping two jobs. My hope is that by September, on my 40th birthday, I can have all my Abramoff-related financial expenses paid off. It will be another important milestone.

When I'm not working, I'm usually writing. The thought of finishing my book provides me hope that I really will be able to undo some of what I have done, in a way that makes me feel proud. As Jack used to say, "It is what it is." Not that I am really sure what that means. But it does seem to describe my situation. *"I guess my meeting with Bob will be whatever my meeting with Bob will be,"* I think, before changing my mind. *"It doesn't have to be that way."*

At that point, I decided to break my routine. Instead of vacuuming the runners in the hallway after finishing the employee bathrooms, I went outside to sweep the porch. The cool breeze felt great. A slight semblance of orange and pink sunlight broke through the spiral-like cumulous clouds hovering above the horizon. It was tourist season and the view looked like one on a postcard. Golf carts zipped around the Fort Myers Country Club. Anticipation of a new day permeated the crisp morning air as I sat down on the carpet-covered steps leading down from the porch. The palm trees swayed in the wind.

"*How lucky am I?*" I asked myself rhetorically, already knowing the answer. "*I never would have experienced this if I hadn't been involved in the Abramoff scandal,*" I told myself with a laugh. I chuckled every time I said those words. They were words that, years before, wouldn't have seemed possible.

Even then, they somehow seemed wrong. How could I be happy about anything that resulted from the shame of the scandal? Yet, they were words I had found myself saying quite a bit in recent months. They were powerful words, which served as a reminder that people can change, lessons can be learned, life is a blessing, and God has a plan.

The first time I uttered those miraculous, almost mind blowing words was during a day trip to the Everglades with Pam. Midway through a fun little wildlife walk, the two of us stumbled upon several massive alligators in a shallow pond. It was the dry season, so water was scarce and hiding places were few. Channeling my inner paparazzo, I moved quietly behind some bushes and began to snap some photos.

Suddenly, a battle broke out between the two largest gators. Pam and I were less than six feet from the action - far too close for comfort for this city boy. Nonetheless, I put on my macho bravado and kept taking pictures.

My bravado deserted me when the largest of the scaly beasts let out a deafening roar - a deep, guttural roar that shook everything around. Our bodies vibrated with the intensity of the sound. It was like nothing we had ever heard before, not on television, not at the zoo, nowhere. In fact, to this day I'm not even sure I actually "heard" anything. It was nature at its rawest, and we did not want to become part of the drama.

Slowly, silently, Pam and I backed away, hand-in-hand and keeping our eyes glued on the two massive beasts. At first, neither of us said a word. A sense of frenzy continued to surround the pond. When we were finally at what we deemed to be a safe distance, we laughed in relief. As we reviewed the photos I had just taken, the enormity of the experience made itself felt.

"Wow," I said, grinning in amazement. "How lucky was THAT?" I shook my head, still smiling. "That is not something you'd see in DC!" I paused. "I guess I never would have experienced this if I hadn't been involved in the Abramoff scandal."

There it was, that phrase, ordinary and seemingly insignificant. Our conversation that day rolled like it always did, free and easy, and I didn't think of those words until later. But eventually, I began to see those words as a marker of my personal progress, one which told me that I had moved beyond the fray and was able to see that life still held good things for me - simpler things, certainly, but positive, all brought to me in the wake of my shame-filled exit from Washington.

The fact such a change in mindset sneaked up on me like it did made the experience more important. More real. Additionally, it gained in significance because the moment stood out in such stark contrast to how I thought my lessons from this scandal would develop. In all the self-help books I read and with all the people I talked to, no one had mentioned anything about alligators.

Not that people hadn't told me that eventually, if I was on the right track, there would be a moment where I would learn to be happy because the scandal had led me in a more positive direction. They did. In fact, they said it would be important for me to learn how to be thankful for something that caused me and others so much pain. And they were right. Part of me had assumed those kinds of words would end up presenting themselves while I was assisting a homeless veteran, delivering Meals on Wheels or playing football with one of the kids in the neighborhood our church had adopted. It was like I expected a big sign to light up and say, "You're on the right track; you're not being selfish anymore." Ultimately, my gator experience was helped along by the growing love Pam and I felt for each other, more than anything else. That made the experience that much better.

The change in perspective was good. I felt like I was finally beginning to break my old habit of putting the outcome first in my decision-making process. During the infancy of the scandal, things could not have been more different. Not a day passed back then when I wasn't working tirelessly to get myself to the "other side." I wanted so badly to just pull the band-aid off, speed up the healing process and get to that place where my stupidity, my arrogance and my mistakes were are all in the rear view mirror. Eventually, I realized that line of thinking was holding me back. I had wanted to use the same formula for solving my problems that had gotten me into trouble in the first place.

After years of outcome-based thinking, I started to change my decision-making process. Instead of focusing on how I could "win" in a particular situation, I learned to let my beliefs, intentions and purpose determine what I did. Sometimes this kind of thinking seemed counterintuitive. Outcomes are important, after all. But they are less important than choosing behavior I can live with no matter the outcome. Clearly understanding how I wanted to behave during the upcoming moments with Bob - based on my beliefs about the man, myself and our relationship - was vital.

I believed that Bob and I were capable of interacting in a positive way. A lot of people disagreed with that analysis. Some suggested I just stay away from my former boss at the film premiere. I appreciated their fears about the potential for conflict with Bob. But avoidance did not seem like a good idea to me. Nonetheless, I told those people I would use my best judgment in the moment.

In terms of the purpose of my potential meeting with Bob, I didn't want any conversation to be just about us. There were thousands of friends, family and constituents who had been impacted by the scandal. I needed to think about them, too. Still, the conversation would come down to Bob and me. Whether our meeting turned into a life-affirming moment or a bad Jerry Springer episode, I couldn't know for sure. But I could honestly go to Sundance with the naïve intention of re-establishing my friendship with Bob. We both deserved the effort.

With morning marching toward the restaurant, I jumped to my feet and began to get back to the daily grind. I vacuumed under the chairs on the porch and emptied all the ashtray containers. Having put seven hours in already, I could have easily slowed down and glided to a perfectly acceptable end to my shift. But all the harkening back to the Ney days had me hustling with the type of intensity I was known for when I was a Capitol Hill staffer. Tired or not, I was going to finish strong. *"Intentions matter,"* I thought. *"Whether anyone is watching or not."*

MAY 7, 2010
WASHINGTON, DC

An Apology

T HE E STREET CINEMA SITS on the corner of E and 11th Street in downtown Washington. Reporters, lobbyists, Hill staffers and other political professionals squeezed into the hallway leading toward the theater. It was opening night for *Casino Jack and the United States of Money*, a documentary about the Abramoff scandal. The entrance was packed. Movie posters lined the walls. Jack's picture was everywhere. After getting some popcorn and a beer, I reminisced with former lobbying colleagues, talked to a few reporters and chatted with Department of Justice prosecutors and FBI agents, many of whom continued working on the investigation. They were all there to see the movie. It was like an Abramoff-scandal family reunion.

Watching myself on the big screen was a new experience. I had never been in a movie before. Seeing my image jump off the wall made me feel relevant again, like my appearance was somehow having an impact on the people in the theater. It was cool. Hearing my words boom through the surround-sound speaker system reminded me that I used to be a powerful person. Everyone was listening. The thought brought back more good memories than bad, which was a bit of a surprise.

Being in a movie was also a bit awkward. Several people pointed in my direction. Some even made comments. "We know who you are," said one of the two ladies sitting directly behind me. I turned around. The two well-dressed women appeared to be in their seventies or eighties. The lady doing the talking leaned forward while pulling my seat back. "Thanks for talking," she whispered in my ear. Smiling, I nodded along in response. The three of us spoke at length after the film ended.

When the investigation started, I could not have imagined such a moment. The idea of happily talking about some of my most shameful mistakes with a retired teacher and her friend would have seemed impossible. Yet the woman's comments in the theater were exactly what I had hoped to hear when I agreed to be interviewed for *Casino Jack*.

Engaging in the film-making process represented yet another unexpected step in my journey. For many reasons, it was an important step. The decision to openly discuss the scandal meant taking my private thoughts public. Though nerve-wracking, this new perspective pushed me out of my comfort zone. It was like injecting my introspection with steroids.

Theoretically, I understood that the process of making my thoughts public could be healthy. While the give and take of public debate meant acknowledging my failures, it also meant engaging in conversations like those I had at the premier. Hearing people I didn't even know thank me for being willing to share my story was life-affirming. They made me feel like I was serving the public again. I liked that a lot.

It was in the area of my relationships, however, where the movie had its biggest impact. Academy Award-winning director Alex Gibney interviewed both Bob and me for *Casino Jack*. It was because of Alex's film that Ney and I reconnected. As with my individual soul searching, the movie process forced me out of my relationship comfort zone. The friction of talking publicly about my shattered friendship with Bob gave me the opportunity to fully address, and then embrace, the emotional conflict that existed between my old boss and me. The two of us first spoke in January, when the film debuted at the Sundance Film Festival. Three months later, we reunited again in Washington, this time for the documentary's national premier. Reconnecting with Bob allowed me to finish my final chapter of the Abramoff scandal.

Unlike in most cities, people in Washington were familiar with the specifics of the Abramoff scandal. To those at the E Street Cinema, therefore, *Casino Jack* was an insiders' view of a drama that occurred during their time in the nation's capital. People wondered what Alex had included in his version of the story. For me, however, the time in the E Street Theater was different. I had seen the movie several times by that point. Because of that, my mind wandered when the theater lights went dark.

The memories blurred together. Before long, I felt like I was in a time machine. *Casino Jack* had spanned an important part of my life. When I was first contacted about taking part in the documentary, I was living in Washington and working for U.S. Vets. It was right after my sentencing. My marriage was unraveling. My faith was still dormant. It was a depressing time. Bob and I had not spoken to each other for years. In contrast, by the time the Abramoff documentary played the E Street Cinema, I was living in Florida, working as a janitor, and I had recently set up a nonprofit to work with the local homeless community. My relationship with Pam was getting more serious. My faith was reborn. And I was in regular contact with Bob. It was an optimistic time. As a *Washington Post* article about the movie said, "One thing is clear: Neil Volz is a changed man."

Similar to becoming a cooperating witness for the government or moving to Capitol Hill, sitting down to be interviewed for *Casino Jack* was a leap of faith. The process started a few days after my sentencing when I was contacted by one of Alex's producers, Zena Barakat, who asked if I would do an interview. I was apprehensive. Opening myself up to several hours' worth of questions in front of a camera seemed like a radical step from the last several years. It was one thing to write my thoughts down in a controlled environment with the hope of publishing them in the future. It was quite another to voluntarily sit down and answer a series of unplanned questions, especially knowing my comments could be shown to the public or be used to cross-examine me in future court cases. I asked Zena to give me a little more time to think.

In theory, the decision about the interview shouldn't have been that big a deal. I had made bigger choices in my life. But the more I thought about the movie, the more I decided to make it a big deal. *Small decisions are big decisions*, I kept telling myself after talking with Zena. *Isn't that one of the lessons of the scandal?*

My question stuck with me. I dug in a little further. It was undoubtedly a fact that I made some bad choices because I did not take the process of making certain decisions seriously enough. So I looked myself in the mirror. *Are you going to continue that kind of behavior? Or change?* The answer was obvious. I was going to analyze every question I had about the movie before making a decision. What wasn't so obvious, though, was how my commitment to treating the interview decision more seriously would impact my perspective on the movie. But it did.

As if a light bulb went off in my head, from the moment I added personal value to my decision I began to view the potential involvement in *Casino Jack* as an opportunity to embrace the lessons I was learning from the scandal. The prospect of taking part in the movie quickly became a vehicle for me to test-drive the changes I wanted to make in my life. Or, as I found out, to scrutinize the changes I was already making in my life. The shift in emphasis meant the movie became much bigger than just an interview. It became about the future. My future. My excitement grew.

Zena set up a time for me to meet Alex. Our planned get-together intensified my internal debate. *What kind of movie is he making? What impact will it have? If you do this, who are you fighting for?* The questions helped me focus on what was important. I talked to my family and friends. Most of them liked the idea of taking part in the movie. In a family full of teachers and lifetime-learners, the prospect of a public analysis of the scandal seemed appropriate. "You could help make it a teachable moment," my brother said.

Some of my Washington friends saw it differently. They suggested that I should avoid the interview. "There is no professional up side for you," one of my buddies told me. "You need to move on to whatever is next. No one who can help you professionally wants to hear anything Abramoff-related. It isn't in your best interest." My friend's analysis was right, and it was important for me to hear. If my priority was to get back in the political game, the best thing I could do was shut my mouth. I appreciated the honesty. Getting right with the facts was important.

Alex and I met at the Westin Hotel, located in Washington's Embassy Row neighborhood. He gave me a copy of one of his previous films. I told him about my family, and how they hoped he was going to tell the Abramoff story in a way that could resonate in the classroom. He said that was his intention. We then dug into the scandal. Despite different political leanings, it was surprising how much we agreed upon.

It was late-2007, and the stale public narrative surrounding the scandal had become shallow. We both saw it. The Democrats in power stopped having any interest in discussing political corruption. Likewise, the Republicans didn't want to even mention the word *Abramoff*. Therefore, instead of a real conversation occurring about the relationship between lobbyists, money and elected officials, both parties seemed to agree that the best method to deal with the still simmering scandal was to scapegoat Jack, and, to an extent, Bob. The strategy was simple. Blame Abramoff and Ney for everything. Then pleaded the fifth. The bipartisan consensus was built on the misleading notion that corruption in Washington had been eliminated now that my two former bosses had gone to prison. Both Alex and I thought the notion was ludicrous. We dug in further.

In the last year, the momentum of the Abramoff investigation had slowed. Capitol Hill had begun to push back on the Justice Department. Their view was that the constitutional separation of powers between the legislative and executive branches meant that Members of Congress had special protections from certain investigations. While legitimate, this slowed up the inquiry. It also played into the growing reticence by both sides to talk about the specifics of the scandal. But such Constitutional uncertainty wasn't the main reason for the silence. The more Alex and I talked, the more I could see that he was serious about understanding the history of the scandal.

"It isn't like lobbying, as a profession, is necessarily bad," I told him at one point. "I mean, no substantive action by the government is taken without some sort of lobbyist playing a role. You know?" I continued.

"I do know," Alex replied. "The question is whether that is good or bad."

"Or, whether it is good *and* bad," I said.

"Maybe so," he continued. "What I would like to look into is whether there is too much money in politics, and if there is, how that corrupts the system."

"I'm not sure there is too much money in politics," I said. "We spend more money advertising potato chips in this country than we do advertising political campaigns."

"I get that argument. But don't you think Members of Congress feel too much of their time is spent raising money? And that those interests with money get more influence because of that desire for campaign cash?"

It had been a while since I had had a good political give and take like the one Alex and I were having at the Westin bar that day. There was an intellectual purity to the way the conversation flowed. Neither of us knew what we would be talking about next. I was honest with Alex. And he made me think.

"There is no doubt Congressmen and Senators feel the need to raise money," I said. "Of course they do. Our business model was based on that simple truth. They want money to pay for advertisements so they can get re-elected, and we gave them money. But why is that always the focus? Why not talk about the influence of the revolving door between high-paying jobs and public servants? Or the influence of gifts and travel on staffers and elected officials? There is a culture of the lobbying game that gets lost in the simple talk of campaign contributions." I gave him the abridged version of how lobbying had affected me and my life.

"Talk to me about that," Alex replied, with a smile across his face.

Our meeting went well. In addition to the scandal, we also discussed the potential on-camera interview.

"I'll honestly answer whatever question you ask me, but there are certain people I do not want to talk about," I told him. "I'm not trying to hide anything substantial," I explained. "If there is something relevant to the scandal, I'd be happy talk with you about it. There are just certain friends of mine who have been through enough."

Alex told me he understood. Not that he really had a choice. "We'll take what we can get," he joked. "But we obviously would like as much as possible." After that, Alex told me that Zena had worked for the news program, *Nightline*. For years, that had been one of my favorite shows. He picked up on my excitement. "Yeah, she is a truth-teller," he said casually. Like Michael Deaver's "get right with the facts," I liked the sound of the "truth-teller" label the minute I heard it. The comment stuck with me for the entire *Casino Jack* endeavor.

I thought about my conversation with Alex during the Metro ride home. It had been a positive experience. Unfortunately, sitting in the back corner-car of the train was eerily similar to my Justice Department routine. My mood began to change. I got nervous. At one point, I envisioned what people would say about my decision to be in the movie. *Look at him, he is acting like none of the scandal was his fault. Who is he to preach to us? If Neil didn't get caught, he would still be lobbying. What a hypocrite.* The imaginary comments had merit. It was hard not to assume the worst. Why wouldn't a movie about the scandal follow the same script of the last few years?

Maybe it would, or maybe it wouldn't, I thought, trying to end a downward spiral of depression before it got too out-of-control. *The worst case scenario doesn't always happen,* I reminded myself. At one point in my life, in fact, it seemed like the best-case scenario always played out. *Hadn't that been a lesson too?* I couldn't always know or control the outcome of my actions. Nor could I fall in the trap of letting my fears or my environment determine what I did. *Focus on the process, and the rest will take care of itself. On some level, I will get out of the movie what I put into it,* I told myself. *People can think whatever they want.* After a small detour, the internal debate over the movie ended.

I naively befriended both Alex and Zena. We set up a time for an interview. The filming took place at the Russia House Restaurant and Lounge, in the Dupont Circle neighborhood of Washington. I fought through some last-minute jitters as the crew set their lighting and arranged the cameras. Alex asked me what I was thinking.

"Several of my friends told me not to take part in your film," I said. "They said your a liberal filmmaker. And they think your interview will be used to make conservatives look bad."

"Then why are you here?" Alex replied.

"I think talking is better than staying quiet," I said simply.

"Look, Neil, I'm not sure how the movie will come out," Alex continued. "It depends on what we find out and who we talk with. I can't make any promises." His comment made me smile.

"I'm not looking for promises," I replied. Whether Alex was just giving me a good line or not, I couldn't know for sure. But I liked what I heard. Like me, he seemed to be letting the process, not the outcome, lead the way. "I can't control what you do with my interview," I continued. "All I can control is what I say. I'm in uncharted territory here, Alex. It is one thing to be forced by the government to talk about what happened. It is completely different to proactively talk with you about the specifics of the scandal. Some people will get mad. But I've thought this through. I know I can go home after this interview, look myself in the mirror, and be confident that I did the right thing - at least until I see the movie," I joked nervously. Alex and I both laughed. It would be more than two years before I saw *Casino Jack*.

Started in 1981 by the actor Robert Redford, the Sundance Film Festival is a tribute to independent filmmaking. Based in and around Park City, Utah, the moviemaking extravaganza is one of the most prominent festivals of its kind in the world. Sundance has introduced the public to such highly regarded films as *Reservoir Dogs, American Splendor, Little Miss Sunshine* and *The Cove*. It is held every January.

Pam and I weren't sure what to expect when we arrived in Utah. I still had not seen the movie. Nor had I talked with Bob, who hadn't seen the film, either. Alex had told both Bob and I that he would be tweaking *Casino Jack* until just before the festival. His decision not to give either of us a sneak-peak added to the Sundance drama. While I was anxious to see what was in the film, I was much more anxious about the prospect of seeing Bob. I wanted to talk with him.

There was no consensus among my friends and family regarding my desired meeting with Bob. In the lead-up to the festival, I had prayed about and talked to dozens of people about getting together with him. Several people cautioned me that to do so would be foolish. One of my former Ney World colleagues told me how he had seen Bob a few weeks earlier at a funeral.

"Bob spent half an hour telling a group of us how the whole thing was your fault," my friend told me. "The man is still angry. You would be smart to just stay away. There is nothing to gain there. He is too bitter. Seriously, don't cause a scene," he concluded.

Another friend of mine who had remained in contact with Bob had similar advice. "Dude, don't go near him," he said. "Neither of you guys want a physical confrontation."

"There is not going to be a physical confrontation," I replied, somewhat offended.

"You never know," he said. "Just be ready."

"I'm sure the director and the company producing the film would love the publicity, but it takes two to fight, and I'm not going there," I replied. The conversation frustrated me. *How did we get to this point?* I asked myself. *This isn't my life. I want nothing but the best for Bob. My faith has changed me, saved me.*

Getting in a fight with Bob was the farthest thing from my mind. But it did reflect the hurt that kept circulating through Ney World. During my pre-festival conversations with former colleagues and friends, I tried my best not to fan those painful flames. I didn't always succeed. Picking at our shared scabs was painful. Deep down, though, I was looking for reconciliation. Or, at minimum, something that would allow the people around Bob and me to move past the pain of our shared experiences. Lots of us had made bad decisions and hurt other people in the process. It was time for our past to stop controlling our present. Helping Ney World move forward was important to me, and I knew that I was in a position to help bring about that kind of catharsis. The emotional crescendo gained steam as Sundance approached. It felt like I was gearing up to put my wings on for another flight.

Snow fell as we approached the Temple Theater. The show was about to start. Pam and I clasped hands. The lights dimmed. "This should be interesting," I said. We were sitting twenty rows from the front, on the left-hand side of the theater. Bob was several rows closer to the screen, on the right side of the audience. I had tried to make eye contact with him when he entered the theater. But we never connected. His seat was near the doors people had to use in order to enter or exit. I looked at the large crowd and began to realize that it would be hard to reach him if he was dead-set on avoiding a get-together. That had me worried. *Maybe we aren't going to talk after all,* I thought. The reality of that possibility settled in as the movie began.

Casino Jack begins with a visual representation of an email exchange that occurred between Alex and Jack. The two men are talking about Alex's film. Via rolling text on the screen, Abramoff asks Alex, "Why would you want to make a documentary?" Jack then says that no one watches documentaries. "You should make an action film!" he exclaims.

The crowd laughed. "That's funny," I whispered to Pam.

From there, footage of the light-hearted email conversation morphs into a re-creation of the deadly serious mob-hit in Miami that took the life of Jack's SunCruz Casino business partner, Gus Boulis. It was an emotional jolt. With the opening credits rolling across the screen, the shame of my past began to resurface. Alex used local television coverage and grainy photos from the murder scene to grab the audience's attention. *I wonder what Pam is thinking*, I asked myself, feeling depressed. The moment didn't last long.

Within seconds, Alex was taking the emotional momentum of Jack's story to introduce us to the characters in his movie. He started by outlining the explosive growth of Jack's career. "He was the number one lobbyist in Washington, who could get you in touch with the best and most influential members of Congress," said the head of a respected political institute.

At that point, my image appeared on the screen. "It is amazing how many members of Congress wanted in with Jack," my screen-self said. *So, those are my first words, huh*, I thought. On the screen, I was dressed in a blue, button down shirt with brown dress pants. Sitting next to a couple of small oak tables, I spoke to the audience from a chair that sat in front of some nearly closed maroon curtains. *You're looking a little pudgy in the face there, buddy*, I said to myself, feeling both self-conscience about the way I looked, and proud of the weight I had lost since the interview. *Good thing they can't see the belly*, I continued.

My segment was followed by footage of President Bush. He was at a news conference discussing the Abramoff scandal. As he leans into the podium, the President tells the assembled members of the media that he didn't remember meeting Jack. That is when Bob appeared. While his hair was gray, instead of brownish blond, he looked years younger than I remembered him. Sobriety had clearly been good for his health. He, too, had lost a lot of weight in the past few years.

"All of a sudden, nobody remembered Jack," Bob joked to the camera. His comment merged with another clip of President Bush saying, "I didn't know him," to which Bob said, "Of course Bush knew him."

The next two hours were an emotional rollercoaster. The audience could feel the tension between Bob and me throughout the movie. While the movie's official storyline was built around Jack, a large portion of the film revolved around my relationship with Bob. I did my best to glean information from every word uttered by my old boss and former friend. Many of his comments included the words, "Neil," or "Neil Volz." Pam squeezed my hand every time he said my name. It was almost like Bob didn't mention the word "Jack" without mentioning "Neil." *Man, he is even more defensive than everyone says*, I thought. *Maybe we shouldn't talk tonight.*

A couple of points drove me crazy. Bob discounted the tens of thousands of dollars spent at Signatures as a "place that Neil Volz hung out." But one line stuck out above the rest. "Neil Volz introduced me to Jack Abramoff," Bob said midway through the movie.

His words sent me through the roof. "What the fuck is he talking about?" I muttered under my breath, using the kind of harsh language I had been trying to stop saying so much. "*Scanlon introduced us, Bob. What are you talking about? You wanted to meet Jack. Seriously, maybe it IS best that we don't meet - you asshole.*"

Of course, I wasn't the only one with a reason to be mad. Bob was probably stewing in his seat, as well. I had given Alex whatever he wanted, as long as it dealt with Bob, Jack, Scanlon, Rudy, myself, or some other major player in the scandal. That included photos, business cards and old newspapers. It also included the threatening voicemails Bob left for me after our confrontation at the Prime Rib Restaurant. The Justice Department had them, and days after my trip to Ohio to apologize to my former staff, so did Alex. I wanted him to have everything. Not that I enjoyed watching the exchange on the big screen. I'm sure Bob didn't enjoy them either.

Alex did a good job walking through our relationship. He included footage of Bob outlining how I had morphed from his idealistic press secretary to vaunted member of "the Abramoff family." In a scene that Ney would later describe to me as an "ah-ha!" moment, I talked about how it had hurt to see the Chairman turn into a public caricature of corruption and greed. "He had given me my chance," my screen self said. "There was another side to him. He was a good public servant."

As I watched that scene play out in the theater, I thought back to my interview with Alex and Zena. We were in Washington, a lifetime ago. I specifically remembered Alex asking me how I felt when Bob went to jail. It was one of the few times he directly asked me how I felt about Ney. I answered him honestly. As mad as I sometimes felt at Bob, it was important for me personally, and for my future relationship with him, to get right with the facts.

For years, I had accepted the fact that Bob and I might never speak again. That changed with *Casino Jack*. Going into Sundance, I felt like I had a good plan to deal with our potential meeting. My goal was to tell him three things. One, I wanted him to know that no matter what had happened in our past, I wished him well going forward. Secondly, I wanted to let him know that I knew how many good things he had done for his constituents over the years, and how hard it was to deal with the fact that the Abramoff scandal now overshadowed all that work. I also wanted him to know that I could have been a better friend. I wasn't sure exactly how to get into the last one with him, but it seemed like an acknowledgement that Bob would appreciate. Unfortunately, after watching the movie, I wasn't sure what to make of my plan.

Bob's defensiveness had rattled me. It hurt my feeling to watch him suggest that I was to blame for decisions that were not mine. At the same time, I felt bad for Bob. The many stories I had heard over the years came to life in my mind. *I hope he isn't as bitter as it appears,* I thought. At the same time, I realized that the movie had not changed anything. The facts were still the same. I knew what Bob was saying in public before I got to Sundance. What I didn't know was what he would say to me in private, or what he really thought deep down. *I gotta talk to him,* I figured. *It is now or never.*

The theater lights came on to thundering applause. As my eyes adjusted to the light, I could see Alex making his way the front of the theater. He had a microphone in his hand. "I bet that feels good," I told Pam. "He made a great movie." For the next couple of minutes, Alex spoke to the audience about *Casino Jack*. He then introduced Bob, who was there to take part in a question and answer session.

It was a surreal moment. Before the questions started, I couldn't believe I was looking at Bob.

His complexion, hair and weight all looked different. The last time I saw Bob his hair was colored blond, his skin was reddened from alcohol and he was overweight. Now he looked healthy. It was quite a change. When Bob started answering questions, however, I felt like I was back on Capitol Hill with him. For ten years, I had watched him answer questions. His mannerisms, grammar and timing hadn't changed.

"Neil is here," Bob said midway through one of his first questions. He pointed in my direction. I waved my hand aimlessly in the air, not sure whether I was waving in his direction or acknowledging the crowd. "He did a great job working for the people of Ohio," Ney continued. At first, I thought his comment was just a ploy to make sure I didn't say anything bad to the reporters standing outside in the hall. But that made me feel like I was paranoid. *"He does seem genuine,"* I thought, still not sure what to think - except that the two of us actually needed to talk. Reading between the lines was too confusing.

"We only have time for a couple more questions," Alex told the audience. His words created a sense of urgency. The time Bob and I had in the same room was coming to an end. If Ney and I were going to connect, I needed to make a decision. Was I going to make a meeting happen, or not? My mind went into overdrive.

"*Why change your mind now?*" I asked myself. "*Because of what was said in the movie? Please. Because you don't want to give him a second chance? You want him to hate you for the rest of his life? You want people to give the homeless second and third chances, but some guy who was a friend doesn't deserve one? Really?*"

Alex thanked the audience for attending the premiere. He also asked the audience to vote for his film if they saw fit. Sundance gave some of their awards based on viewer response.

"Bob and I could gin up some votes for the movie, I'm sure," I joked to Pam. "Everything comes back to politics." She smiled.

I looked up and saw Bob on the move. He was walking in front of the screen. Twenty rows up, I remained stuck near my aisle seat. "*Are you going or not?*" I asked myself. "*The clock is ticking. Does every barrier need to be settled before we talk? That just means doing nothing. Is there really a line that needs to be crossed between understanding your past friendship, and actually being a friend in the moment?*"

The thought of doing nothing scared me. It wasn't the first time that I worried that the last few years might cause me to become a more passive person. But it was the last time I worried about it seriously. Looking at Bob walk through the doorway of the theater cleared my head. "*The goal is not to fly too high or too low,*" I said. "*It isn't to stop flying.*"

I grabbed Pam's hand, and started pushing my way through the theater. "Excuse me," I said. "Can I get through there? Thanks." "*The crowd already thinks I'm an asshole,*" I joked to myself. "*Why not verify it?*" Our pace quickened as we got closer to the bottom of the steps.

The hallway leading outside was packed. A reporter asked me a question. I told her I would have to talk with her later. Bob was nowhere to be found. Suddenly, I spotted him. We darted through the crowd in his direction. When we got there, I grabbed Bob's shoulder.

"Neil?" he asked, as he spun around. I think he knew I was on my way.

"Hi, Bob," I said quickly. A few flashbulbs started flashing, and a guy with a video camera appeared on my left.

"I just wanted to say hello," I continued. The conflict of the last five years surrounded us, along with the pandemonium of the movie. "I figured this may be the only time we see each other, and I wanted to wish you the best of luck."

"Thanks," Bob said. He seemed to be genuinely listening to my words.

"Some kind of situation, huh," I said, pointing to the crowd around us after introducing him to Pam.

"Yeah," Ney continued. He looked somewhat stunned by the outreach, or maybe everything else that was happening. I felt bad. It was unfair of me to bombard him in such a public setting. He didn't have the luxury of thinking about the moment for weeks, like I had, and it showed. While I was prepared to keep talking, it was clear that Bob was not.

"Thanks for saying hello," he said, shaking my hand.

"You bet," I replied. And with that, Bob turned toward the front door and made his way out.

I was disappointed. I didn't want to be, but I was. The exchange ran through my mind. While it was nice to make contact with Bob, the lack of depth to our conversation was frustrating. *"We lived together for four years and that is the conversation we have?"* I asked myself. I tried to calm down by reminding myself that I couldn't control the outcome of a get-together like that. I had done what I thought was right. But it was still disappointing.

Alex called me the next morning. He wanted to discuss the movie and Bob.

"What did you think about the film?" Alex asked.

"I liked it," I told him.

"Did you see any problems?"

"Not really."

Our wide-ranging hour-long discussion included everything from my view of the movie to a heated debate about a recent Supreme Court case concerning the funding of political campaigns. In fact, by the time we got to the topic of my relationship with Bob, I was on an outing with Pam and some cousins who lived in the area.

"You seemed hesitant when I asked you whether there were problems in the film," Alex said. "I will be making changes before it is distributed nationwide. Therefore, I really would like to know if there are problems."

After punting the first time he asked me, I decided to jump into the fray a little bit more the second time around. "Look, Alex, all I will say is that my answers to you will stand the test of time. But I'm not sure Bob's will. When you asked me a question, I listened and tried to tell you how it was straight up, even if it made me look bad. And I don't think he did that."

"And you think that is reflected in the movie?" he replied.

"I don't know. All my comments are fine, Alex. I made them," I continued, wary to even be talking about how Bob seemed to be blaming me for his role in the scandal, fearing that doing so would make me sound like I was blaming Bob for my role in the scandal. Which I was not.

"But what?" Alex prodded.

"Bob's comments didn't seem entirely accurate," I continued. "I mean, when he dismissed Signatures as just a restaurant where I hung out, I wanted to laugh. If he had gone to trial, the prosecution would have marched bartenders, hosts and waiters out to say they personally knew Bob. Then they would have taken my emails with Bob to show that we were at Signatures together all the time. From there, they would have plopped down my credit card expense reports and shown night after night after night of hundred and thousand dollar expenses. It wasn't just a place I hung out. Look, I'm not comfortable going into all this blame Bob stuff."

"No worries," Alex said. "I know what you are saying." He then asked me to keep talking. He even went so far as to say that the relationship I had with Bob was at the heart of what his movie was about. "The rise and fall of yours and Bob's friendship shows the audience the personal side of corruption. When they hear those tapes, the audience gets to feel what all that power and corruption has done to two guys who had gone to Washington to try and do good stuff. And that is why I appreciate your willingness to talk it through with me." His words made me feel like my story was being used for a higher purpose, and not for some sort of soap opera or self-aggrandizement. That made me feel good.

"I thought a lot about the movie last night, Alex," I continued. "So much so that I couldn't sleep. But ultimately there was really only one comment that got to me. It was when Bob said that I had introduced Jack to him. And then you know what? Honestly, I realized that I couldn't truly complain to you about that comment. After digging into it, I began to see that his comment was technically true. That statement is a fact. I have to live with it. At the same time, when I heard him say that, I took it to mean that somehow I had introduced Jack's team to Bob's team. And that isn't true at all. Bob and some of his staff were the guys who brought Scanlon into the office. Bob was the one pushing me to help him gain power. But, you know what Alex? None of that really matters."

"What do you mean?" he asked.

"I have lots of great people who are happy to say that Bob is the reason for my involvement in the scandal. I was just a college student, they say. Or whatever. But, you know, this isn't a political campaign. I don't get to be right by saying it was Bob's fault or Jack's fault. And he doesn't get to be right by saying someone else was wrong. I was wrong, and he was wrong, too. And yet I don't know how I am supposed to express all that, let alone how Bob is supposed to express all that. If I point out the faults I see in Bob's comments, I look like a public hypocrite who is trying to say he is wrong, and I am right. On the other hand, If I don't point out the faults in his or other people's comments, I feel like an internal hypocrite for not shooting straight. And yet none of those words can stop it from pissing me off every time he blames me for what he did. You know? I mean, I walked up to him after the movie and he basically just walked off."

"I know," Alex said. "That is partially why I am calling," he continued. "*Alex is calling about my conversation with Bob?*" I wondered. His words stopped any urge I had to continue talking. My guard went up. "*I wish I knew that before I just spilled my guts to him. I would have thought through my comments more thoroughly. How close are those two?*"

Alex picked up on the awkwardness. "I like both you guys," he said. "I don't like what you did. But I like that both of you are willing to talk. My job is to take all the stories I am told and try to make sense of them. That means taking Bob's story and taking your story, and then taking my own path that is somewhere in between."

"And you did a good job on that, man," I interjected. "There is just so much more there between Bob and me than what was on the screen. And it involves so many other people. That is why it is such a struggle to answer your question."

"I can tell that there is a lot of baggage between you guys." he said. "Why wouldn't there be after all you have been through? But I can also tell how close you used to be, and that you both still care about each other. I also know that you both have changed because of everything that happened."

"Is that right?" I asked Alex, somewhat skeptically. "I want to believe you, but how do I know that Bob has really changed?"

"Neil," Alex said, raising the volume and seriousness in his voice. "The man spent seventeen months in jail."

Our conversation went quiet. Alex's words hit me hard, so hard I almost dropped the phone. With Utah's picturesque mountains zooming by, I stared out the car window. The phone remained on my ear. But I didn't talk. I was too busy taking in his words. As much as I wanted to act like I had let things go with Bob, it was clear that I had not. For the first time in a while, Alex's comments made me look in the mirror to see what I was really thinking about Bob.

"*The man spent seventeen months in jail,*" I said to myself. "*How does that fit into the slights, bad memories and rumors that I keep letting block my forward momentum?"* A lot had happened. Yet I suddenly felt small. I thought through the many recent conversations I had with old Ney colleagues and friends. One snide comment or the reminder of a decision of Bob's that hurt me could ignite the very anger I was trying to eliminate. *"That is unacceptable,"* I said to myself, looking back.

It was in that moment that Bob's time in prison began to take on a new meaning. Much like the movie had become a personal challenge for me to live the lessons I was trying to learn from the scandal, beginning at that moment, I chose to view Bob's time in jail from a more personal perspective. While he had been sentenced for crimes against the state, my new perspective meant accepting that Bob's time in jail was also punishment for the personal hurt that many in Ney World continued to feel. This new outlook was a big deal. The pressure I felt to address every facet of the frayed relationships Bob had with others reduced dramatically. If someone was mad with Bob because their relationship soured when the FBI started asking questions, for instance, I decided I was no longer going to make that my fight. *"The man spent seventeen months in jail."*

"That is a good point, Alex," I said, finally continuing our conversation. "It really isn't fair for me to impose on you all the different personal stories involved in my portion of the scandal. You are trying to tell a bigger story than just what happened to me."

"I appreciate that Neil, and appreciate what you are trying to do with Bob," he said. "And I know that Bob appreciates it, too."

"Really?" I asked.

"I do. His team told me he was really touched by the fact that you tracked him down, and were so nice to him."

"That is cool," I told Alex. "I wish it wasn't the case, but there clearly is still a lot of tension between us. Maybe it will always be like that."

"I'm not sure," he replied. "I think Bob was taken a little off-guard by some of your comments in the movie, and your willingness to embrace him afterwards," Alex continued. "But I know he is hoping to talk again."

"Is that right?" I asked.

"I don't want to screw this up because I can't really speak for him, obviously, and I'm not a hundred percent sure, but I think he is planning on attending the event tonight in Park City. Are you going?" Alex asked.

The event he referred to was a sit-down discussion with Alex and some other directors, including Davis Guggenheim, the director of *Waiting for Superman* and Lucy Walker, the director of *Countdown to Zero*. It was being hosted by the magazine *Entertainment Weekly*, and Pam and I had sent in our RSVPs. But that was before we had plans with my family. Since my cousin and his wife had expressed interest in going to the sit-down the night before, I told Alex we would probably go. But that we weren't a hundred percent sure either.

"Great," he replied. "I hope to see you tonight." The two of us said goodbye.

"Sorry about that," I told Pam and my cousins, in reference to the long phone call.

"No worries," my cousin Joe said.

"Looks like I'm going to see Bob again," I replied. "Maybe we'll actually get to talk this time."

After a day in the mountains, Pam, Joe and I walked into the Park City gallery hosting Alex and the other directors. The event was fun. The three of us enjoyed seeing clips and listening to the directors talk about their movies. It wasn't until the end of the event that I ran into Bob. He was there with a friend from the Ohio Valley.

"Hey man," I said, as the two of us shook hands.

"We are a lot more casual this time." Bob replied.

"No doubt," I answered back. Instead of the suits we both were wearing when we met after the premiere, the two of us sported collared shirts and jeans.

"Yeah, I was laughing as I got dressed this morning," Bob said. "I couldn't help but think about you in Miami at that fundraiser," he continued. I knew exactly what he was talking about. Bob and I had attended several fundraisers in Miami over the years. He looked over at Pam and Joe. "So Neil and I go to this fundraiser, and we are staying at some high-end Miami hotel. As our group prepares for dinner, Neil comes out of the elevator. He is laughing. But he is also shaking his head back and forth," Bob said.

"Neil then tells us that he had tried on like three different outfits in his room, before deciding to wear a suit that he wore to work all the time."

"I can't pull it off, Neil said," Bob continued with a laugh. "I'm just not cool."

Pam, Joe and I all smiled at my old boss. I was happy to see his change in tone.

"I'm still not cool," I joked back.

"Me neither," Bob replied. "I don't know that I have ever been cool."

"I think I had about ten minutes of cool when I was nineteen," I said. "But that was it."

"Hanging out here in Sundance might not be Miami, but it was enough to remind me of that story," Bob continued.

"That is funny," I replied. Ney's comments were a good ice-breaker. "I was thinking about that a few weeks ago. It was our first Mark Foley golf trip. Long before the scandal. Man, things sure are different now, huh?" I asked.

"Big time," Bob replied. "I bought this shirt and these pants at Wal-Mart."

"Oh, big-spender," I joked. "I'm more of a Goodwill guy myself." Our banter lasted for a few minutes, before turning more serious.

"Alex and I had a great conversation this morning," I told Bob. "We discussed your time in jail. What was that like?"

"It was hard," he said. "I was glad that I talked with people who had gone through it before. People like Webb Hubbell." Hubbell had worked for the Justice Department during the Clinton Administration. "He told me that jail could either tear you down, or be a spiritual experience," Bob continued. "And I didn't want it to tear me down."

I wasn't sure what to say, so I just listened as he told story after story. My heart felt for him. "That sounds horrible," I said. "I'm glad you are out."

"Me too," he said. "Trust me. I did meet some good people in there," Bob continued. "And made real friends."

"That is cool," I replied. "Turns out you can meet friends anywhere."

Our conversation meandered from topic to topic.

"I think it is cool that you worked with the homeless veterans. How did you get into that?" Bob asked. I told him about U.S. Vets, and shared some stories with him about my time at Ignatia House. Talking about the vets meant discussing my spiritual growth and the positive impact of alcohol rehabilitation programs.

"You look really healthy," I told him. "Sobriety is doing you well."

"I feel better," he replied. "I just take it one day at a time."

"So I wanted to tell you a couple things yesterday," I continued. "I'm not sure how to transition into it, so I'll just say it." Bob looked at me with a curious look. He seemed intrigued. Or annoyed. I wasn't sure. But I plowed ahead.

"You did so much for your constituents," I said. "Way more than the average Congressman. I know a lot of people will forget because of the Abramoff stuff. And it may not mean anything to you, Bob, but I want you to know that, at a minimum, I know how much you did, and how much you cared for your people. And how hard all this shit is to accept."

"Thanks, Neil," he said. "I know it hasn't been easy for you either."

"I try not to complain," I replied, beginning my deflection routine - one I usually used to divert from any discussion about the pain of the last few years. But in that moment I decided to keep talking. "I know you know how it is," I told Bob. "Being broke sucks. So does being a pariah. And being a felon is no picnic either. On the bright side, Alison and I had a relatively easy divorce," I joked, trying to bring the conversation to a close. Bob smiled.

Feeling guilty for going on despite his discomfort, I told Bob, "I would definitely have done a lot of things different."

He laughed. "Me too."

There were few people who really got how the many layers of the scandal fit together. Bob was definitely one of them. It felt good to talk to him this way.

"Look," I said. "I hear from people who think they have to pick between two competing sides. Your side and my side, as if one of us is completely right and one of us is completely wrong. Or that Jack did everything. Or whatever. I don't look at it that way. My view is that we all have blame, and we all could come up with reasons to be mad at each other. I mean, you have a right to be mad at me. The fact is, I helped put you in jail." I didn't see Bob's reaction, but Pam and Joe told me later that Bob's eyes almost popped out of his head after my comment.

"I don't look at it that way," Bob replied. "You did what you had to do for your family. Seeing the movie and seeing you talk about what happened on the screen was like an "ah-ha!" moment for me," he continued. "A lot happened. But I want to move forward."

It was a moment of raw honesty. Both of us knew that we could cast stones at each other for years. We also knew how destructive that was for us personally, and for those around us. It felt like Bob and I had turned a corner. Where we were going, I wasn't sure. But I liked the road we were on.

Our conversation got easier. We talked about the movie, our families, and what we wanted to do in the future. We even talked about the concept of living with the concept of "forced" humility. It was an idea we both understood.

"Sometimes, you can't win," I said. "And shouldn't even try."

"I know what you mean," he replied.

"I'm sorry for all the pain I caused people," I told Bob. "I think about it all the time. But some people won't ever believe that. Some won't let me move on because of the mere fact that I didn't choose to get out of lobbying, or choose to live a new life. They think I would still be lobbying, if not for the scandal. And you know what? They may be right. That is what is weird. If Jack and Mike didn't get in trouble, and we didn't get in trouble, what would have happened? Would I be working for the homeless? I doubt it. But that doesn't change the commitment I feel to my new cause. You know?"

"Definitely," he said. Granted, Bob's focus seemed to be more on how our new "forced" expectations impacted friendships, and former friendships. "It is what it is now," he continued. "That is what I don't get. If people were only friends with me because I was a chairman, fine. But if you said we were friends for other reasons, why stay away now?" he asked, before sharing the names of several guys he had hoped to stay connected with but who didn't talk to him anymore. Bob's point served as a reminder that repairing our relationship was not going to be easy. Several of the individuals he mentioned were people I talked to regularly. I kept that fact to myself.

"A friend gave me some good advice on that one, Bob," I told him. "I'm not sure if it will help you the way it helped me. But a year or so ago, I started calling all kinds of people to apologize for any pain I had caused them. It was important to me that I reach out. I called Members and staffers who got mentioned in the paper because they knew me. I called colleagues who had to spend money on lawyers because of their association with me. Like I said, I called all kinds of people."

Bob listened intently to my comments.

"It felt good to say I was sorry," I continued. "And it felt horrible to not get a call back, especially since all I wanted to do was apologize, and hopefully help someone I was once close to release any pain they were feeling about the situation. It was heart-breaking. That is when a friend used a great phrase that I will never forgot. In the context of reminding me that I couldn't control what other people did, my buddy said, 'Some will, some won't; move on.' It was great advice. His simple words helped me to deal with everyone from potential employers to old friends. I can't control whether they want to hire me or reconnect. Nor can I control whether someone thinks I have integrity. But I can control whether I live my life with integrity. Some will, some won't; move on. Frankly, it is the perspective I used to figure out what to say to you."

Bob liked that. Our conversation continued. We talked about the inner workings of the American prison system and legal system. Before long, it was time to leave. The two of us shook hands and said goodbye. Thirty seconds later, Bob walked back in the door. He hugged me.

"I'm sorry," Bob said, mid-embrace.

"I'm sorry too," I told him.

We looked at each other with smiles on our faces.

471

"Thanks," I said.

"Thank you," he replied. Then, as quickly as Bob had returned, he took off.

In the next weeks and months, Bob and I talked periodically. The importance of his apology grew on me over time. Mainly because I knew he meant it. Also, because I could tell that he was committed to paying the penance required for his wrongdoing, the penance needed for those around him to know that he had learned his lesson. The process was invigorating. Taking off my cynical glasses had a big impact. Instead of primarily focusing on the bad memories I had of Bob, I let the good memories slowly return. Then the flood gates opened. The people of Ohio benefited greatly from Bob's hard work and political skills. They may not have seen those late nights when he called hospitals and embassies to help individual families struggling with a problem. And they might have forgotten about those early mornings when he met with nearly every school group who visited Washington and took time to personally answer his constituent letters. But I remember, and it is good to have those memories back.

Bob and I met again in Washington to promote *Casino Jack*. Midway through the publicity tour, I spent some time in my hotel's business center, reading online what people were saying about the movie – and about me. *Roll Call's* headline was, "Ney, Volz go from power brokers to ex-cons." *The Hill* said, "Bob Ney, Neil Volz reunite for Casino Jack and the United States of Money." The headline of the *Huffington Post's* link read, "Neil Volz, Abramoff Lobbyist, Now a Janitor." These were pretty much what I had expected. What I hadn't expected was the venom in the readers' comments which followed each article.

I had forgotten what those kinds of comments felt like. For the most part over the years, people had been far nicer to me than I deserved. Now, however, I was again seeing calls for me to spend my life behind bars, even some calls for my death. I tried to remind myself, "Some will, some won't, move on," but the magic behind those words got lost in the ugliness of the others. Luckily, a few friends came through with comments that lifted my spirits. One was the lead FBI investigator in my case. Few people know more about me and my life in Washington than he does.

"I was kind of annoyed at some of the comments linked to the articles," he said. "You are a good man, Neil Volz. The people who know, know that." His kind and beautiful words mean as much to me today as they did when I first heard them. On most days, I even believe them!

That brings me to you, the reader. I have some words of my own just for you. I have learned a lot of lessons from the scandal, one of which is to speak the truth honestly and from my heart. In that spirit, what I want to say to you is this: I am sorry. I am sorry for hurting all the people who were so terribly affected by my actions, and I am sorry for letting down the country I meant to serve wisely and well. I wish I could go back and do things differently, but I cannot. What I can do is continue to learn from my mistakes, and through those lessons, become a better citizen and a better man. I promise you, with God guiding my way, that's what I'll be doing in the years ahead.

A Note About The Manuscript

TWENTY ONE SENIOR GOVERNMENT OFFICIALS and lobbyists pleaded guilty or were convicted by a jury in the criminal investigation surrounding the Abramoff scandal. People guilty of corruption charges included lobbyists, Congressional staffers and Executive Branch officials.

I was a witness for the government in four different federal trials. That is more than any other person in the scandal. The government didn't compel me to answer questions in front of a jury because I was the central figure of the investigation. They did so because the Department of Justice viewed me as a credible witness. I have tried to bring that same spirit of openness and candor to my writing. That said, there are obviously differences between writing a memoir and testifying under oath.

I wrote *Into the Sun* the way a friend would share a story with another friend, not from the perspective of a witness on the stand. That means the book is accurate. It will stand up to the test of time. But that does not mean it is "in the courtroom" accurate. This book is not the equivalent of testimony.

Direct quotes, for instance, illustrate this point. In some cases, the quotes used in the book are the exact the words I said, or heard someone else say. In other cases, the quote simply reflects what was said in the moment. To a skilled attorney and a jury, the difference between those two types of recollection can be a big deal. A quote that can't be remembered directly is easily minimized in a courtroom - as it should be. To a reader or a friend, though, telling the story through conversations can better describe the specifics, as well as the context, of my cautionary tale.

The Abramoff scandal lasted for years. It has been litigated and fully examined. Seeing the investigation from the perspective of both a target and a cooperating witness showed me the many points of view people had on the same series of events. While some may try to suggest that this book is a critique of other people's views and experiences, that isn't the case. *Into the Sun* is simply my story, my perspective of these events. It is a factual re-telling of what I saw, what I heard and what I thought.

What I can't say, however, is what someone else was thinking, or why they might have behaved in a certain way. None of what I wrote is meant to draw a legal conclusion about another person's behavior. Decisions about whether someone broke the law or not are not mine to make. Those type of conclusions occur within the legal system. As an example, if I mentioned that an elected official or staff person was investigated by the Department of Justice, it does not mean they did anything wrong. People are innocent until proven guilty.

While my goal was to simply tell my story, writing in such a highly-charged legal environment meant being mindful of how I discussed certain topics. This included my attorneys, Tim Broas and Melissa O'Boyle. Tim and Melissa were incredibly skillful in helping me navigate the many sides of the multi-pronged investigation. While I included public comments Tim made, and personal conversations the three of us had, I avoided certain substantive conversations. As such, none of what I wrote was meant to waive my attorney-client privilege.

Unfortunately, because of my own actions, this kind of note is needed. Once again, I would like to thank you, the reader, for taking the time to read through my story.

List of Characters
(In Order of Appearance)

Honoria Jackett, Grandmother.

Jack Abramoff, Lobbyist, Conservative Activist.

Bob Ney, Member of Congress.

Gay Volz, Mother.

Joseph Volz, Father.

Ellen Segal Huvelle, Federal Judge.

John McCain, Senator.

William Heaton, Senior Congressional Staffer.

Kendall Day, Prosecutor, United States Department of Justice.

Tim Broas, Attorney

Lynn Volz, Brother.

Dave Bean, High School Teacher.

Steve Elliott, High School Teacher.

Bill Clinton, President of the United States.

Rush Limbaugh, Radio Personality.

Newt Gingrich, Speaker, House of Representatives.

Richard Gephardt, Majority Leader, House of Representatives.

George Will, Author, Political Pundit.

Tom DeLay, Majority Leader, House of Representatives.

Ronald Reagan, President of the United States.

Paul Bucha, CEO, Wheeling-Pittsburgh Steel, Corporation.

Mark Glyptis, President, International Steelworkers Union.

Robert Rubin, Secretary, United States Treasury Department.

Monica Lewinsky, White House Intern.

Mike Scanlon, Senior Congressional Staffer, Political Consultant.

Franklin Roosevelt, President of the United States.

Kenneth McKellar, Senator.

Albert Einstein, Scientist.

George W. Bush, President of the United States.

Shelly Moore Capito, Member of Congress.

Dick Cheney, Vice President of the United States.

Alison Betty, Ex-Wife, Friend.

Dennis Hastert, Speaker, House of Representatives.

Tony Rudy, Lobbyist, Senior Congressional Staffer.

Osama bin Laden, Terrorist.

Tom Daschle, Majority Leader, United States Senate.

Harry Reid, Majority Leader, United States Senate.

Trent Lott, Majority Leader, United States Senate.

Cal Ripken, Baseball Player.

Ariel Sharon, Prime Minister, Israel.

Channing Nuss, Senior Congressional Staffer.

Reynold Schweichart, Senior Congressional Staffer.

Steny Hoyer, Majority Leader, House of Representatives.

Chet Khalis, Senior Congressional Staffer.

Tom Brokaw, Reporter.

Pierre C. L'Enfant, City planner.

Lesley J. McNair, Army General.

Jack Nicholson, Actor.

Tom Cruise, Actor.

Demi Moore, Actress.

Jay Eagen, Chief Administrative Officer, House of Representatives.

Jeff Trandahl, Clerk, House of Representatives.

Bill Livingood, Sergeant at Arms, House of Representatives.

Tim Hutchison, Senator.

Dolph Lundgren, Actor.

Sylvester Stallone, Actor.

John Boehner, Member of Congress.

Tom Reynolds, Member of Congress.

Paul Vinovich, Senior Congressional Staffer.

Joe Reeder, Undersecretary of the Army, Attorney.

Andrew Jackson, President of the United States.

Kevin Ring, Lobbyist.

Todd Boulanger, Lobbyist.

Phillip Martin, Chief, Mississippi Band of Choctaw Indians.

John Doolittle, Member of Congress.

John Breaux, Senator.

John Ensign, Senator.

William Worfel, Council Member, Louisiana Band of Coushatta Indians.

Ralph Reed, Political Consultant.

Grover Norquist, Conservative Activist.

George Miller, Member of Congress.

Benigno Fitial, Governor, Northern Mariana Islands.

Juan Babauta, Governor, Northern Mariana Islands.

Christopher Dodd, Senator.

Ed Buckham, Senior Congressional Staffer.

Mike Williams, Lobbyist.

David Safavian, Senior Congressional and White House Official.

Willie Tan, Businessman.

Michael Jordan, Professional Athlete.

Max Cleland, Senator.

Saxby Chambliss, Senator.

Zell Miller, Senator.

Gale Norton, Secretary of the Interior.

Roy Blunt, Majority Whip, House of Representatives.

Eric Cantor, Member of Congress.

John Cook, Friend.

Susan Schmidt, Reporter.

Mike Smith, Lobbyist.

Duane Gibson, Lobbyist.

David Pingree, Lobbyist.

Bob Paduchik, Political Consultant.

Ken Mehlman, Senior White House Staffer, Chairman, Republican National Committee.

Jim Van de Hei, Reporter.

John Edwards, Senator, Vice Presidential Candidate.

Kevin Downey, Attorney.

Ben Nighthorse Campbell, Senator.

Marc Schwartz, Political Consultant.

Carlos Hisa, Sub-Chief, Tigua Indian Tribe.

John Bresnahan, Reporter.

David Letterman, Television Personality.

Paul Schaffer, Television Personality.

Joe Allbaugh, Senior White House Staffer.

Alice Fisher, Senior Department of Justice Staffer.

Scott McClellan, Senior White House Staffer.

George Clooney, Actor.

Nancy Pelosi, Speaker, House of Representatives.

Rahm Emmanuel, Member of Congress.
Richard Holbrooke, Ambassador, United Nations.
Lilly Volz, Niece.
Casey Volz, Sister-in-Law.
Melissa O'Boyle, Attorney.
Paul L. Friedman, Federal Judge.
Barbara Van Gelder, Attorney.
Nathaniel Edmonds, Prosecutor, Department of Justice.
Keith Olbermann, Television Personality.
Sheri Cook, Friend.
Dale Warren, Friend.
Bob Dole, Majority Leader, United States Senate.
Joy Padgett, State Official.
Bill Burton, Campaign Professional.
Bob Taft, Governor of Ohio.
Zack Space, Member of Congress.
Michael Deaver, Senior White House Official, Political Consultant.
Nancy Reagan, First Lady of the United States.
Ellen Ratner, Television Personality.
Bob Bennett, Chairman, Ohio Republican Party.
Bono, Rock Star.
Bobby Shriver, Philanthropist.
Barry Jackson, Capitol Hill and White House Staffer.
Emily Button, Friend, Nonprofit Professional.
Charles Dickens, Author.
Chris Chicola, Member of Congress.
Tom Donnelly, Member of Congress.
Conrad Burns, Senator.
Joe Tester, Senator.
Richard Rogers, Friend.
Paul Braithwaite, Senior Congressional Staffer.
Phil Jones, Friend.
Jim Forbes, Friend.
Sarah Palin, Governor, Vice Presidential Candidate.
Pam Newton, Girlfriend.
Alex Gibney, Movie Director.
Zena Barakat, Movie Producer.
Joe Mullen, Cousin
Lara Mullen, Cousin

CPSIA information can be obtained at www.ICGtesting.com
Printed in the USA
BVOW012346150112

280524BV00004B/5/P